UNDERSTANDING THE OLD TESTAMENT

UNDERSTANDING

Prentice-Hall, Inc., Englewood Cliffs, N.J.

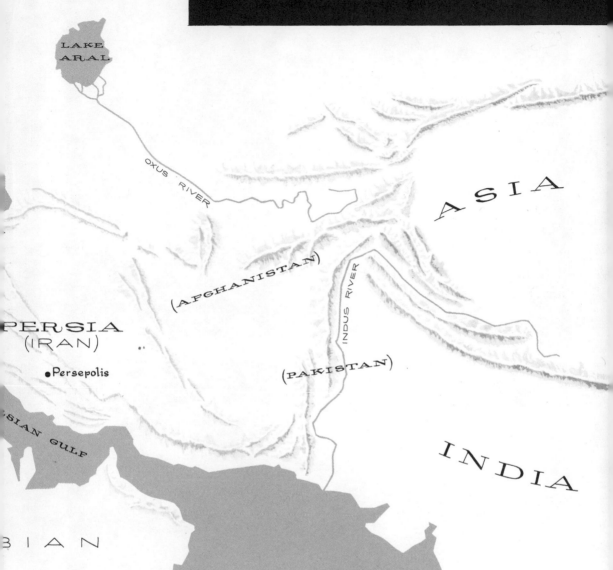

LAKE
ARAL

OXUS RIVER

ASIA

(AFGHANISTAN)

INDUS RIVER

PERSIA
(IRAN)

•Persepolis

(PAKISTAN)

'SIAN GULF

INDIA

BIAN

ESERT

INDIAN OCEAN

Second Edition

THE OLD TESTAMENT

BERNHARD W. ANDERSON

Professor of Biblical Theology, The Theological School, Drew University

PRENTICE-HALL INTERNATIONAL, INC., *London*
PRENTICE-HALL OF AUSTRALIA, PTY., LTD., *Sydney*
PRENTICE-HALL OF CANADA, LTD., *Toronto*
PRENTICE-HALL OF INDIA PVT. LTD., *New Delhi*
PRENTICE-HALL OF JAPAN, INC., *Tokyo*

Current printing (last digit):

11   10   9   8   7   6   5   4   3

Understanding the Old Testament

Second Edition

Bernhard W. Anderson

The Bible text in this publication is from the Revised Standard Version of the Bible, copyrighted 1946 and 1952 by the Division of Christian Education, National Council of Churches, and used by permission.

Quotations from ancient, extra-biblical texts, as indicated in footnotes, are made from J. B. Pritchard, *Ancient Near Eastern Texts*, 2nd ed., 1955, with the permission of the Princeton University Press.

Maps by Alan Young

Design by John J. Dunleavy

93612-C

TO MY FAMILY

Joyce

Carol

Joan

Ronald

Ruth Anne

and the new generation

PREFACE

To open the Bible is to enter a world that is strange to the modern mind. This ancient literature, written thousands of years ago in a far-away place, may seem obsolete in a streamlined age when men demand to have the latest in everything. Its idioms of speech, reflecting the life and thought of the ancient Near East, are so different from the West's scientific and philosophical ways of thinking that, so it may seem, "never the twain shall meet." Moreover, this sacred literature is peculiarly enigmatic in a time when traditional religious words and symbols have lost their meaning for many. The Bible speaks boldly of "the Living God" whose presence is inescapable in history even when men flee in guilt or hide in the shadow of despair; but modern men often search for God in vain and dare to face the possibility that he is dead. Because of the tension between the biblical outlook and the modern world view, the interpreter is constantly pushed toward the realm of apologetics—the intellectual defense of the validity of biblical truth. This book is written with an awareness of that tension, and with the conviction that the biblical message about life's meaning makes a claim upon us in the twentieth century. But before we can face such questions squarely, we must understand the Bible on its own terms, insofar as we can.

This book, written at the request of the Society for Religion in Higher Education, appeared in its first edition in 1957.

Like its companion, *Understanding the New Testament* (the second edition, by Howard C. Kee, Franklin W. Young, and Karlfried Froehlich, was published by Prentice-Hall in 1965), it attempted a fresh approach by interweaving the oft-separated elements of historical study, literary criticism, and biblical theology. The gratifying response has persuaded me that this is a helpful way to approach the Old Testament, and therefore the fundamental structure of the book in its new edition remains the same.

The purpose of this book—to echo what was said in the original preface—is not so much to forge into new areas of biblical studies as to bring the reader up to the advancing frontier. During the past decade the field of Old Testament research has been in great ferment. Not only has our knowledge of the biblical period continued to expand through the contributions of archaeology and Near Eastern studies but, in addition, the methods of biblical research known as form-criticism and tradition-history have made important contributions. The basic and—as yet—unresolved problem, however, is that of historical methodology. On one side of the debate stand a number of American scholars who maintain that archaeology has provided external sources which enable us to check early biblical traditions and to understand the positive connection between these traditions and the events which occurred in the ancient Near East during the second millennium B.C. On the other side stand a group of German scholars whose exercises in form-criticism and tradition-history have led them to sceptical historical conclusions regarding Israel's early history. These scholars allege that, just as criticism has destroyed the framework of the Synoptic Gospels, so it has shown that the historical outline found in the Pentateuch is only a construction based on the community's confession of faith.

There can be no doubt about the position taken in this book. The presentation accents the kerygma of the believing community and especially the crucial significance of the Exodus for Israel's faith, but avoids deriving from these confessional materials a historical scepticism. Admittedly, the issues are complex, and the scholarly discussion will undoubtedly take new turns in the future. Therefore, I have expanded the footnotes throughout the book so that the reader may be aware of the ongoing discussion. Moreover, I have updated and completely reworked the bibliography in the effort to make it a helpful tool for further study.

After considerable hesitation I have decided against expanding the treatment of Pentateuchal criticism, whether in the text or in a special appendix. From the first it has been my intention not to highlight literary criticism but to present it as an aid to understanding. Moreover, there is no substitute for the creative teacher. Although the bibliography draws attention to collateral readings which may prove helpful, in the last analysis the teacher is the only one who can decide how best to present this difficult subject in his own situation. There has been one major addition, however. In the original edition the psalms of Israel were treated at various points along the way; but in the new edition, in response to the urging of many readers, I have included a chapter on (and so titled) "The Praises of Israel," which deals briefly with the major types of psalms in the Psalter and their setting in Israel's worship.

One of the most promising developments of our time is the revival of biblical studies within the Roman Catholic Church. This movement, which has reached its full tide during the past decade, has influenced the present edition not only in the bibliography but in the more careful attention to the canon. In this connection, I should like to express appreciation to Catholic scholars who, through correspondence, conversation, and critical reviews, have contributed to the revision of the book; and especially to Raymond E. Brown, S.S., who has helped on matters of bibliography and canon.

Biblical quotations are from the Revised Standard Version, with the kind permission of the National Council of Churches. Since this Version, following ancient synagogue practice, uses "the Lord" as a substitute for the Hebrew personal name for the deity, I have felt free to reintroduce into the text the word *Yahweh*, which is generally recognized to have been the original sacred name. Now and then during the discussion, other Hebrew words are transliterated into English for the purpose of clarifying nuances of meaning. In these instances, as scholars will recognize, I have not been bound by any rigid system of transliteration, but rather have considered what is most intelligible to the reader who is not familiar with Hebrew.

One of the most difficult problems in the Old Testament is the dating of events. For the sake of consistency, I have adopted the chronology of W. F. Albright and, with his permission, have arranged dates in my chronological charts accordingly. This chronological scheme is given in full at the back of John Bright's *A History of Israel*.

A book of this kind is possible only because of the creative work of many scholars—some of whom are mentioned in footnotes or bibliography, and many others of whom are unnamed. To all these scholars who have influenced me directly or indirectly, I acknowledge indebtedness and express appreciation. A special word of thanks goes to my wife, whose patient encouragement supported me through the long days and nights of both the original writing and this subsequent revision of the book and who, in addition, assumed major responsibility for the selection of pictures. Also, I owe thanks to my graduate assistant, the Rev. David A. Lutz, who has carefully and helpfully worked through the manuscript and bibliography. And finally, my thanks to the staff of the Project Planning Department of Prentice-Hall, Inc.—to the editor, George A. Rowland, to the production manager, Nancy Hall, and to the designer, John J. Dunleavy—for their excellent and friendly assistance in bringing this book into final shape.

This book is not intended as an "introduction" to the Old Testament in the technical sense which that word has acquired in scholarly circles. Rather, it aims to introduce the general reader to the range and depth of the scriptural heritage from ancient Israel which has profoundly influenced Western civilization. In a time when world events urge us to face seriously the question of what life is all about, it is hoped that this book will help the reader to understand what the Bible has to say.

Bernhard W. Anderson

March 25, 1966

CONTENTS

    xi

MAPS

A major source used in the preparation of maps has been *The Westminster Historical Atlas to the Bible*, Revised Edition, Copyright 1956 by W. L. Jenkins, The Westminster Press.

ILLUSTRATIONS

COLOR PLATES

All color plates were made from 35 mm color slides
taken by the author.

CHRONOLOGICAL CHARTS

KEY CHARTS AND TABLES

ISRAEL'S

SACRED HISTORY

INTRODUCTION   Memory is one of man's supreme endowments. Each of us acts today and hopes for tomorrow in the light of past experiences that have been woven into his life-story. When we want to know another person, we ask him to tell us something of the story of his life, for in this way he discloses who he really is. To be a self is to have a personal history. This history is what defines one's uniqueness.

In a larger sense this is true of human communities, especially those in which people are bound together primarily

Biblical readings: A good introduction to the historical character of Israel's faith is to read some of the hymns of worship, such as Psalms 78, 98, 105, 106, 135, 136.

by shared experiences rather than natural factors like blood and soil. National self-consciousness finds expression in the remembrance of events that people have lived through and that have given them a sense of identity and destiny. If, for instance, a visitor from outer space were to drop down on American soil and ask why this country is a *United* States rather than a mixed multitude, we would probably try to explain what it means to be an American by narrating our history: the dramatic epic of the migration of the Pilgrim fathers to the New World, the Revolutionary War and the Declaration of Independence, the Civil War, the recent events that have thrust this nation into the center of the world arena. To be an American is to share a particular history, whose events are retold and relived from generation to generation.

THE LIFE-STORY OF ISRAEL

The most distinctive feature of the Jewish people is their sense of history. In many respects, the Jews have always been diverse—in theology, in culture, and even in racial characteristics. But Judaism is the religion of a people who have a unique memory that reaches back through the centuries to the stirring events of their Bible, events that formed them as a people with a sense of identity and vocation. Whenever the Passover is celebrated, whenever the Law is read in the synagogue, whenever a parent instructs his child in the tradition, this memory is kept alive. Indeed, if historical memory were destroyed, the Jewish community would soon dissolve.

Christians, too, have this historical sense. The Christian church is diverse culturally, socially, and to some extent theologically; but it is also a distinctive community with a long memory that reaches back through the Christian ages to the crucial events of which the Bible is the record and witness. To be sure, Christian remembrance focuses especially on the coming of Jesus, the Christ—his life, death, and resurrection. But in the Christian community this event is viewed as the fulfillment of the historical drama of Israel set forth in the Jewish Bible, which in Christian circles is known as the "Old Testament." [1] The Christian faith may be expressed in many forms, but in the last analysis there is no substitute for retelling what Christians call "the story of our life"—that is, the history to which the Old and New Testaments bear witness.[2]

---

[1] It should be emphasized that the distinction between scriptures of the "Old Testament" and the "New Testament" is a Christian one, though based on a passage from the prophet Jeremiah (31:31-34). For the Jews there is only one Testament or "Covenant." Today the Jewish people refer to their scriptures as Tanak—a word made up of the initial consonants of the three major divisions of the Hebrew Bible: Law (Torah), Prophets (Nebi'im), Writings (Kethubim). See Samuel Sandmel, *The Hebrew Scriptures* [20], especially pp. 1-22.

Note: To keep footnote material as brief as possible, we have adopted the device of using numbers in brackets which refer to the bibliography at the end of the book, where full information is given.

[2] See H. Richard Niebuhr, *The Meaning of Revelation* [86], chap. 2.

Within the Christian community there is some disagreement, as can be seen from the chart on pages 4-5, over the number of books making up the Old Testament. The "canon" or standard list of books accepted by most Protestants is essentially the same as the twenty-four books of the Jewish Bible, though the arrangement differs.[3] Sometimes a few other books, commonly called "Apocrypha," are printed in a separate section of the Protestant Bible, with an explanatory note that they deserve to be read but should not be put on the same level as canonical books. Most of these extra books, according to the official verdict of the Roman Catholic Church, deserve full canonical recognition, even though there was a long period of uncertainty about their status.[4] Thus the Roman Catholic canon, when compared with the Protestant (and Jewish) canon, is seven books longer. Eastern Orthodox churches also recognize almost all the extra books. But these differences should not be overestimated. Despite the problem of fixing the outer boundary of the "Old Testament," it is clear that Jews, Protestants, and Catholics hold in common a body of sacred literature which is substantially the same.

This sacred library is in many respects very diverse. The Greek words *ta biblia,* "the books," from which our word "Bible" comes, aptly suggest the diversity of the literature. But the Old Testament is more than a mere collection of books under one cover. The various writings bear witness to the unique historical experiences of a particular people, Israel, from the time of its beginning shortly after 2000 B.C. down to the period of the Maccabean Revolution which broke out slightly more than a century and a half before the Christian era. The Old Testament is the life-story of Israel, the people of God. Judaism and Christianity may differ in their understanding of the outcome of this historical drama, but they agree on the unique character of the history with which the Old Testament deals.

THE THEATER OF GOD'S ACTIVITY

Leaving aside the prologue to this historical drama, which is given in the first eleven chapters of Genesis, the biblical history—reduced to its barest skeleton —may be summarized as follows: Shortly after the turn of the second millen-

---

[3] The number twenty-four is reached by counting as one book each of the following: I and II Samuel, I and II Kings, I and II Chronicles, the Twelve (minor prophets), and Ezra-Nehemiah. The order of books in Christian lists has been influenced by the Septuagint, or Greek translation of the Old Testament, which was begun in Alexandria, Egypt, in the third century B.C. For further discussion of the canon, see pp. 554 ff.

[4] In Catholic usage "protocanonical" refers to the books whose place in the canon was never challenged, and "deuterocanonical" refers to those which were recognized only after a period of hesitation and debate. The criterion of canonicity which the Council of Trent (A.D. 1545-63) used was that of long use in the church as evidenced by the presence of the books in the Latin Vulgate. See A *Catholic Commentary on Holy Scripture* [8], pp. 15-18.

	ROMAN CATHOLIC [a] AND ORTHODOX [b]	PROTESTANT	JEWISH BIBLE [c]
Pentateuch	1. Genesis	1. Genesis	1. Bereshith ("In the beginning")
	2. Exodus	2. Exodus	2. Shemoth ("Names")
	3. Leviticus	3. Leviticus	3. Wayiqra ("And he called")
	4. Numbers	4. Numbers	4. Bemidbar ("In the wilderness")
	5. Deuteronomy	5. Deuteronomy	5. Debarim ("Words")
Historical Books	6. Josue	6. Joshua	6. Yehoshua
	7. Judges	7. Judges	7. Shofetim ("Judges")
	8. Ruth	8. Ruth	17. Ruth
	9–10. I and II Kings	9–10. I and II Samuel	8. Shemuel
	11–12. III and IV Kings	11–12. I and II Kings	9. Melakim ("Kings")
	13–14. I and II Paralipomenon	13–14. I and II Chronicles	24. Dibre Hayamim ("Chronicles")
	15–16. I and II Esdras [d]	15–16. Ezra and Nehemiah	23. Ezra-Nehemyah
	17. Tobias	Apocryphal(Tobit)	Noncanonical
	18. Judith	Apocryphal	Noncanonical
	19. Esther [e]	17. Esther	21. Ester
Poetry and Wisdom	20. Job	18. Job	15. Iyyob
	21. Psalms	19. Psalms	14. Tehillim ("Praises")
	22. Proverbs	20. Proverbs	16. Mishle ("Proverbs of")
	23. Ecclesiastes	21. Ecclesiastes	19. Qoheleth ("Preacher")
	24. Canticle of Canticles	22. Song of Solomon	18. Shir Hashirim ("Song of songs")
	25. Wisdom of Solomon	Apocryphal	Noncanonical
	26. Ecclesiasticus (Wisdom of Ben Sira)	Apocryphal	Noncanonical

Prophetic Writings

Douay (Roman Catholic):
27. Isaias
28. Jeremias
29. Lamentations
30. *Baruch* including "The Epistle of Jeremiah" (R.C. only)
31. Ezechiel
32. Daniel ᵉ
33. Osee
34. Joel
35. Amos
36. Abdias
37. Jonas
38. Micheas
39. Nahum
40. Habucuc
41. Sophonias
42. Aggeus
43. Zacharias
44. Malachias

45. *I Maccabees*
46. *II Maccabees*

Protestant:
23. Isaiah
24. Jeremiah
25. Lamentations
    Apocryphal
26. Ezekiel
27. Daniel
28. Hosea
29. Joel
30. Amos
31. Obadiah
32. Jonah
33. Micah
34. Nahum
35. Habakkuk
36. Zephaniah
37. Haggai
38. Zechariah
39. Malachi

Apocryphal
Apocryphal

Hebrew:
10. Yeshayahu
11. Yirmeyahu
20. Ekah ("How")
    Noncanonical
21. Yehezqel
22. Daniel
13. Tere Asar ("Twelve")
    "
    "
    "
    "
    "
    "
    "
    "
    "
    "
    "

Noncanonical
Noncanonical

ᵃ In this column deuterocanonical books are italicized. The spelling is that of the Douay-Rheims Bible. However, in the final edition of the new, officially sponsored American Confraternity Translation, Catholic scholars will adopt the standard spelling currently in use in Protestant Bibles. In the future, the names of biblical books will have one spelling in English Bibles.

ᵇ Note that item 30 was not included in the Old Testament canon established for Orthodox churches at the Synod of Jerusalem in A.D. 1672.

ᶜ In this column, numbers indicate the order of books in the Hebrew Bible. In Hebrew, books are often titled by opening or key words. A table of the order of books in the Hebrew Bible is found on pp. 556-557.

ᵈ I and II Esdras (= Ezra and Nehemiah) of the Roman Catholic canon must not be confused with I and II Esdras of the Protestant Apocrypha. The latter appear in the Vulgate as appendices to the New Testament, where they are labeled III and IV Esdras.

ᵉ Two books of the Roman Catholic canon, Esther and Daniel, are larger than their counterparts in the Protestant and Jewish canons. This surplus material is included in the Protestant Apocrypha as Additions to Esther and Additions to Daniel (The Story of Susanna, The Song of the Three Children, and The Story of Bel and the Dragon). The Prayer of Manasseh, also found in the Apocrypha, is not included in the Roman Catholic canon.

nium B.C., Israel's ancestor, Abraham, migrated from Mesopotamia into the land of Canaan, otherwise known as Palestine. The patriarchs, or founding fathers of Israel, moved about in the hill country of Canaan, with Abraham, Isaac, and Jacob succeeding one another. Eventually, during a time of famine, Jacob's family migrated to Egypt. There, after enjoying initial favor, they were subjected to forced labor by the Egyptian pharaoh. Under the leadership of Moses (about 1300 B.C.), however, and favored by an extraordinary series of events, they escaped into the desert, where they were forged into a community with a single religious allegiance. Later, under the leadership of Joshua, they successfully attacked Canaan and claimed the land as their own. During this time, they had to wage ceaseless wars of defense. Enemy pressure became so intense that a monarchy was established under Saul, and in the time of kings David and Solomon (1000-922 B.C.) Canaan was an Israelite empire.

On the death of Solomon, the United Kingdom split into the two kingdoms of north and south, Israel (Ephraim) and Judah. These kingdoms, by virtue of their strategic location in a buffer zone between Mesopotamia and Egypt,

THE SCROLL OF THE PROPHET ISAIAH *was found in Cave I at Qumran (see pp. 552 ff.). In the left-hand column, over to the left of the black blot, the text (reading right to left) says: "A voice cries: 'In the wilderness prepare the way of the Lord'" (Is. 40:3; cf. Mark 1:3). From such a scroll Jesus read in the Nazareth synagogue (Luke 4:16-30). Notice the scribal corrections of the text, the sewing together of the parchment sheets, and the soiled outer side of the scroll caused by handling.*

were drawn into the power struggle of the Near East. The Northern Kingdom fell under the aggression of Assyria (721 B.C.); and the Southern Kingdom, after more than a century of vassalage to Assyria, fell victim to the Babylonians, who wrested world rule from Assyria. Jerusalem fell to the Babylonians in 587 B.C. and the people were carried away into Babylonian captivity. But under the benevolent rule of the next empire, Persia, the exiles were permitted to return to their homeland, where they rebuilt Jerusalem and resumed their way of life. The restoration took place chiefly under the leadership of Nehemiah and Ezra (about 450-400 B.C.).

After more than two centuries of Persian rule, Palestine came within the orbit of Greek control, as a result of the world conquest of Alexander the Great (332 B.C.). Alexander's policy of imposing Hellenistic cultural uniformity upon the world was continued by those who inherited his divided empire, especially by the Seleucid rulers of Syria. When this policy was forced upon the Jewish community by one Seleucid king, open revolution broke out under the leadership of the house of the Maccabees (168 B.C.). Literature of the Jewish Bible suddenly breaks off at this point. The sequel was the achievement of a period of Jewish independence, which was finally eclipsed by the next world empire— Rome. The events heralded in the Christian collection of writings known as the New Testament transpired within the vast arena of the Roman Empire.

From a secular viewpoint, this history is no more unusual than the courageous story of other small nations that have been caught in the whirlpool of power politics. In this sense, Israel's history is a minor sideshow in the larger history of the ancient Near East, and her culture is overshadowed by the more brilliant cultures of antiquity. *But the Old Testament does not purport to be simply a book of secular history or culture.* It is sacred history, to both Jews and Christians, because in these historical experiences, as interpreted by faith, the ultimate meaning of human life is disclosed. From Israel's standpoint, this history is not just the ordinary story of wars, population movement, and cultural advance or decline. Rather, the unique dimension of these historical experiences is the disclosure of God's activity in events, the working out of his purpose in the career of Israel. It is this faith that transfigures Israel's history and gives to the Bible its peculiar claim to be sacred scripture. To put it in a nutshell, the Old Testament is Israel's witness to its encounter with God.

For this reason, we cannot begin to understand the Old Testament so long as we regard it as merely great literature, interesting history, or the development of lofty ideas. The Old Testament is the narration of God's action: what he has done, is doing, and will do. All human history is the theater of his self-disclosure, and nature too is his handiwork; but he acts particularly within the career of a comparatively obscure people in order to initiate a historical drama that has changed human perspectives and has altered the course of human affairs.

The Crucial Event

When an individual seeks to understand the meaning of his life-story, he does not actually begin with his birth or infancy, even though his written autobiography may start at that point. Rather, he views or re-views his early childhood in the light of later experiences that are impressed deeply on his memory. Analogously, Israel's life-story did not really begin with the time of Abraham or even the Creation, although the Old Testament in its present form starts there. Rather, Israel's history had its true beginning in a crucial historical experience that made her a self-conscious historical community—an event so decisive that earlier happenings and subsequent experiences were seen in its light.

This decisive event—the great watershed of Israel's history—was the Exodus from Egypt. Even today the Jewish people understand their vocation and destiny in the light of this revealing event which made them a people and became their undying memory. Just as the Christian remembers and relives the sacrifice of Jesus Christ in the celebration of the Lord's Supper, so the Jew recalls and makes contemporary the Exodus as he celebrates the Passover. This act of worship is not just a form of "archaism," a retreat from the present into the unrecoverable once-upon-a-time. Rather, the believing Jew sees himself as a participant in that experience; this event of the past enters into the present with deep meaning. According to the traditional interpretation of the Passover: [5]

> In every generation one must look upon himself as if he personally had come forth from Egypt, in keeping with the Biblical command, "And thou shalt tell thy son in that day, saying, it is because of that which the Lord did to *me* when I went forth from Egypt." For it was not alone our fathers whom the Holy One, blessed be He, redeemed, but also us whom He redeemed with them, as it is said, "And *us* He brought out thence that He might lead *us* to, and give *us*, the land which He swore to our fathers."

Down through the ages Israelites have re-enacted this historic moment when God marvelously brought his people out of bondage. And when we turn to the Old Testament itself we find that the Exodus is the central event in Israel's memory. It is particularly important in the prophetic literature that comes from the period before the fall of the nation in 587 B.C., the so-called pre-exilic period. It is interesting to notice that the prophets of this period do not even mention the migration of Abraham, as related in Genesis 12. Instead, they trace Israel's historical beginning to the time of the Exodus and the sojourn in the wilderness.

---

[5] David and Tamar de Sola Pool, eds., *The Haggadah of the Passover* (Bloch, 1953), p. 51. This is cited and discussed by James Muilenburg in his *The Way of Israel* [68], chap. 3. See also Will Herberg, "Beyond Time and Eternity: Reflections on Passover and Easter," in *Christianity and Crisis*, IX, 6 (April 18, 1949), pp. 41-43.

In the eighth century B.C., Amos reminded his hearers that Israel was bound together as a "whole family" by God's act of deliverance from Egypt (Amos 3:1-2), and he rebuked the people for forgetting the great events in which their God had made himself known (Amos 2:9-11). Hosea, his contemporary, traced Israel's "call" to that same event:

> When Israel was a child, I loved him,
> and out of Egypt I called my son.
> —HOSEA 11:1

About the time of the nation's fall, Ezekiel put the matter emphatically:

> Thus says the Lord God: On the day when I chose Israel, I swore to the seed of the house of Jacob, making myself known to them in the land of Egypt, I swore to them, saying, I am the Lord your God. On that day I swore to them that I would bring them out of the land of Egypt into a land that I had searched out for them, a land flowing with milk and honey, the most glorious of all lands.
> —EZEKIEL 20:5-6

Other passages in the literature of the prophets and the Psalms stress the pivotal significance of the Exodus.[6]

The Heart of the Pentateuch

The same accent is found, though not so obviously, in the section of the Old Testament that is regarded as most authoritative by Jewish tradition: the books of Genesis, Exodus, Leviticus, Numbers, and Deuteronomy. The Hebrew word for these five books is *Torah*, meaning "Law" or, better, "Teaching." Scholars also refer to them as the Pentateuch, a word based on a Greek compound meaning "five scrolls"; and frequently the first six books of the Old Testament (Pentateuch plus Joshua) are considered as a unit called the Hexateuch.

As it now stands, the Pentateuch begins with an extended prologue to the story of the Exodus: the account of primeval beginnings (Gen. 1-11) and the stories of the Israelite "fathers" or patriarchs (Gen. 12-50). Actually, when we begin with Genesis and read to Exodus we are reading the story backward, as it were, for the period before Moses was remembered and interpreted in the light of the events that brought Israel into existence in the Mosaic period, just as Americans view Columbus' voyage and the landing of the Pilgrim Fathers in the light of the decisive historical events of the Revolutionary War. In a later time of theological reflection, Israel could trace the beginning of her history back beyond the Exodus to the first Hebrew, Abraham, and could portray

---

[6] See Amos 9:7; Hosea 2:14-15; 13:4; Micah 6:4; Jeremiah 2:2-7; Psalm 66:6; 78:18-53; 136:10-11.

her "call" (election) in the story of Abraham's migration into the Land of Promise. Historically, however, Israel's call was made known in the event of the Exodus. Properly, the book of Genesis must be regarded as a prologue to the time when the curtain rises on the scene of the oppression of Hebrews in Egypt.

The heart of the Pentateuch or the Hexateuch is found in a little liturgy, now embedded in the book of Deuteronomy. It is a confession of faith which the worshiper is to make when he presents the first fruits of the harvest at the sanctuary:

> A wandering Aramean was my father; and he went down into Egypt and sojourned there, few in number; and there he became a nation, great, mighty, and populous. And the Egyptians treated us harshly, and afflicted us, and laid upon us hard bondage. Then we cried to the Lord the God of our fathers, and the Lord heard our voice, and saw our affliction, our toil, and our oppression; and the Lord brought us out of Egypt with a mighty hand and an outstretched arm, with great terror, with signs and wonders; and he brought us into this place and gave us this land, a land flowing with milk and honey. And behold, now I bring the first of the fruit of the ground, which thou, O Lord, hast given me.
>
> —DEUTERONOMY 26:5-10

This liturgy sounds very much like a quotation from a much older source, just as the ancient language of the Apostles' Creed is preserved in the liturgical use of the Christian church today. It is highly probable that this archaic ritual antedates the establishment of the monarchy under David, and may well reach back to the time of Joshua, the immediate successor of Moses. This was the creative period of the "judges" when—as we shall come to realize more clearly —Israel existed as a worshiping community, bound together by a common confession of faith and by common obligations to the central sanctuary.

This little confession of faith makes only a brief reference to the patriarchal period, when it alludes to Jacob as a "wandering Aramean." It dwells primarily on the events of the time of the Exodus and concludes with a grateful acknowledgment that the God who delivered Israel from bondage also led his people into "a land flowing with milk and honey." Since themes of this liturgy are elaborated at much greater length in the Pentateuch and the book of Joshua, we can think of this passage as "the Hexateuch in miniature." [7] It is significant that the central content of Israel's faith, reaffirmed annually in the harvest ritual, was the Lord's "mighty act" of deliverance from Egyptian bondage.

Blaise Pascal, a famous French writer of the seventeenth century, observed that the God of the Bible is "the God of Abraham, Isaac, and Jacob," not the

---

[7] This is the position of the German scholar Gerhard von Rad in his study of the form-critical problem of the Hexateuch [100].

God of the philosophers and the sages. This is true in the sense that biblical faith, to the bewilderment of many philosophers, is fundamentally historical in character. Its doctrines are events and historical realities, not abstract values and ideas existing in a timeless realm. The God of Israel is known in history— a particular history—through his relations with Abraham, Isaac, and Jacob. The attempt to reason away the essential historical content of biblical faith, says a modern Jewish interpreter, is like paraphrasing poetry: "Something called an 'idea content' remains, but everything that gave power and significance to the original is gone." [8]

But it is important to realize that the history of God's dealings with the patriarchs—Abraham, Isaac, and Jacob—is understood in the light of his revelation to Moses. As a psalmist testified:

> He made known his ways to Moses,
> his acts to the people of Israel.
> —PSALM 103:7

Throughout the generations, Israel's God was known and worshiped as the Lord who brought his people out of the land of Egypt (Ex. 20:1). The Exodus, therefore, is the central moment in Israel's history. Here was her true beginning, the time of her creation as a people. Here began the purposive movement of events that made it possible later to see all history and nature embraced within the divine design. So deeply was the Exodus etched upon Israel's memory that her maturing faith was essentially a reliving and reinterpretation of this historic event.

A Look Ahead

Accordingly, we shall begin our investigation of the Old Testament with the Exodus. This event, however, must be viewed in relation to the preparatory events of the patriarchal period. Therefore, in the next chapter we shall consider the prologue to the Exodus: the story of Israel's descent into Egypt and her oppression under the pharaohs. Then in successive chapters we shall take up the deliverance from Egypt and the making of the covenant, the conquest of Canaan, the rise of the monarchy, and the nation's involvement in the vortex of the world struggle. In other words, the outline of our book is based on Israel's historical career. No other approach, we believe, does justice to the historical character of Israel's faith.

This approach demands that in each chapter we must keep before us several things at once. Literary criticism is necessary, for the traditions dealing with a certain episode of biblical history often come from later times or have been reworked by editors. Also, we must consider Israel's relation to the political

---

[8] Will Herberg, "Biblical Faith as Heilsgeschichte: The Meaning of Redemptive History in Human Existence" [84], p. 25.

and cultural situation in the ancient world. This will make it necessary to look beyond the biblical text to other historical sources and to heed the important contributions of archaeology. And, of course, we must never lose sight of our central task: the exposition of Israel's faith. Usually books on the Old Testament treat these three elements—literary development, historical study, and theology—separately. We shall attempt to weave them together in a fugue-like fashion as the story of God's dealings with Israel unfolds chapter by chapter.

Our attention will focus on the community of Israel, known as "the people of God." Individualism, in the modern sense of the word, has no place in the mainstream of Israel's faith. To study isolated personalities like Moses, or to deal with abstract ideas like "the idea of God," is to miss the point of the Old Testament. Personalities and ideas must be considered in relation to the corporate experiences of Israel in the drama of her history.

Our task, then, is to try to understand the biblical message in its dynamic context of culture, politics, and geography. We shall seek to enter into the concrete life-situations out of which the various writings have come, and to understand what the writers were saying to their times. Toward this end, a series of maps has been provided to help the reader familiarize himself with the biblical setting. Pictures and chronological charts have been included to show how Israel's sacred history is bound up with the international affairs of the ancient Near East.

One final word: If we are really to enter sympathetically and imaginatively into this community and to relive its sacred history, there is no substitute for reading the Bible itself. The purpose of the present book is to aid in the understanding of the Bible—not to urge the mastery of another book about the Bible. The literal meaning of "understand" is "stand under." Through the reading of selected Bible passages, which are listed at the beginning of each chapter, it is hoped that the reader will "stand under the Bible," so that the light it sheds upon the meaning of human life may fall directly upon him.

If you will obey my voice and keep my covenant, you shall be my own possession among all peoples; for all the earth is mine.

—EXODUS 19:5

PART ONE

THE
COVENANT COMMUNITY
IS FORMED

THE BEGINNINGS
OF ISRAEL

CHAPTER ONE   A stirring historical drama unfolds in the book of Exodus. The protagonist is Israel's God, who intervenes on behalf of a helpless band of slaves. The plot, developed through a succession of suspense-filled episodes, is God's contest against the Egyptian pharaoh, the mightiest emperor of the day. The denouement comes when, in the nick of time, Israel's pursuers are swallowed up in the waters of the Red Sea. The leading theme of the drama is the action and triumph of Israel's God.

Biblical readings: For this chapter and the next the most essential reading is the story of the Exodus and Sinai Covenant, found in Exodus 1-24 and 32-34. The reader should also familiarize himself with the prologue to these events as related in Genesis 12-50.

Viewing the Exodus story as a historical drama, rather than as a colorless, factual report, will help us enter more imaginatively and sympathetically into its spirit. Drama emphasizes involvement; it pictures life in contemporaneous terms; it purports to tell *our* story in the actions that unfold. It was in these terms that the Israelites retold and relived the Exodus story through generations. Exodus 1-15 may be based on an old Passover narrative that was recited annually in connection with the feast celebrating the deliverance of Israel from Egypt.[1] In other words, these narratives are written in the confessional language of worship, not in the language of scientific prose. The purpose of the story is to communicate the meaning of the events in which the worshiping community participates.

THE NATURE OF THE TRADITION

Just as there is a place for the literary criticism of Shakespearean drama, so there are literary questions that must be faced if we are to understand the Exodus narrative. This need becomes evident when we consider the whole book of Exodus, for we find irregularities, inconsistencies, and repetitions that must be accounted for. For instance, in some passages the sacred mountain is called Horeb, in others Sinai (compare 3:1 and 19:1). In Exodus 2:18, Moses' future father-in-law is named Reuel, and in 18:1-27 the same man is called Jethro. Moreover, the narratives differ on the respective roles of Moses and his brother Aaron. According to one view, Moses is the principal figure: God calls him to go before the pharaoh and, when Moses protests that he is a poor speaker, Aaron is delegated to help him persuade the Israelites (4:14-17). Both men are to go to the pharaoh, but Moses is to make the request of him and to work wonders with his rod (4:21). Elsewhere, however, Aaron is the spokesman and with his rod performs wonders (6:28–7:13). And to take just one more example, the Pentateuch has two versions of the Ten Commandments, one in Exodus 20 and the other in Deuteronomy 5. How are we to account for these, and other, irregularities?

Among biblical scholars, the dominant view is that the Pentateuch is a composite work in which several major traditions have been blended together. According to this hypothesis, which rests on the critical labors of more than two centuries of intensive study, there are four main literary strands, to which are assigned the symbols, J, E, D, and P. J, the earliest source, comes from the time of the early monarchy, perhaps about 950 B.C.; E, a closely related source, comes from the Northern Kingdom and is usually dated about 750 B.C.; D, which is best represented in the book of Deuteronomy, comes from the Southern Kingdom about 650 B.C. or later; and P, so designated because of its priestly

---

[1] This is the view of Johannes Pedersen, *Israel* [69], III-IV, pp. 728-737.

interests, comes from the period after the fall of the nation in 587 B.C. These strands were woven together in various stages until the Pentateuch assumed its final form in about 400 B.C.

We shall not try at this point to go into these hypothetical sources in great detail, or describe the editorial process by which they were conflated.[2] Suffice it to say that this view points up the enduring importance of the Exodus event in the life of the Israelite community. The various inconsistencies, repetitions, and stylistic differences reflect the ways in which the story was relived, reworked, and reinterpreted in different historical periods. In this literary "mosaic," the original meaning of the Mosaic faith has been preserved and blended with the overtones of meaning experienced by the community down through the years.

Moreover, behind the earliest written stage of the Exodus story there was a long period—certainly more than three centuries—of oral transmission. Even before the writing of J or E, the main outlines of the later Pentateuch were beginning to take shape, especially in connection with the religious festivals at which Israel's traditions were rehearsed. The great themes of Israel's faith, handed down through the chain of tradition, were:

1. The promise to the patriarchs.
2. The divine deliverance of Israel from Egypt.
3. The guidance in the wilderness wanderings.
4. The giving of the Law at Sinai.
5. The inheritance of the Promised Land.

In the early period, these themes were already being blended together into a great historical epic, the prototype of the J, E, and P material found in the book of Exodus.[3] Very often these literary sources cannot be disentangled, not only because the editing was so skillful, but also because each of the writers drew from a common fund of oral tradition.

The Narrator's Point of View

We have already mentioned two problems that arise in our study of the Exodus drama: (1) there are irregularities in the narrative that suggest composite literary sources; (2) the literary sources are several centuries removed from the event of the Exodus, and this period is bridged by oral transmission of the story.

But there is a third problem: the Exodus story, either in its original oral form or its written version, does not pretend to be "objective history." It is obviously

---

[2] See further Chapter 6 for J, Chapter 8 (pp. 230-232) for E, Chapter 10 for D, Chapter 12 (pp. 380-393) for P. For brief introductions to Pentateuchal criticism, see Walter J. Harrelson, *Interpreting the Old Testament* [15], pp. 28-40; R. De Vaux, O.P., *La Genèse*, 2nd ed., Jerusalem Bible (Paris: Éditions du Cerf, 1962), pp. 9-24.

[3] These themes are analyzed in Noth's study of the history of Israel's traditions [99].

an interpretive account of events which, viewed from another standpoint, could very well be presented in quite a different manner. Israel's account happens to be an interpretation of faith. But the fact that the account is interpretive does not necessarily discredit it, even though at some points it may seem fanciful to the modern mind.

It will be helpful at this stage to clarify the meaning of some of our terms: What is "history"? What is an "event"? What do we mean when we say that something "happened"? Much of the difficulty in interpreting the biblical account arises from our confused situation in which words like "history" or "historical" have several different meanings in English usage.[4]

Today historians usually recognize that there is no uninterpreted history. History is not a series of naked facts arranged in chronological order like beads on a string. It is absurd to suppose that an event is a kind of "thing in itself" which can be recovered after all interpretation is stripped away. An event is a meaningful happening in the life of a people. And history is the narration of these experienced events—events so memorable that they are preserved in the oral memory and eventually written down in records. Obviously the historian does not report everything, as though he had a movie camera which objectively recorded all that was done or a tape recorder that took down all that was said. His narration is selective. He recounts only the events that to him, or to the community he represents, are meaningful or history-making.

Now, some events have a public meaning which can be discerned by anyone in the vicinity of the occurrence. Let us take an illustration from American history. The Civil War was a political struggle to preserve the unity of the nation at a time when the slavery issue threatened to make a division. Of course, historians differ somewhat in their assessment of the historical data and the place of the event in the whole context of American history. But as a political event the war has a public meaning. It can be appreciated by any people who struggle to preserve national unity or to overcome the cleavages of race or class.

In his Second Inaugural Address, however, Abraham Lincoln perceived another dimension of meaning in the conflict: the judgment of God upon the involvement of both North and South in the inhumanity of slavery. To him the war was not just a political event with a public meaning, but a divine event whose meaning was apprehended only in a circle of faith. His famous address raises important questions that ought to be faced by the historical interpreter: Did God's judgment really *happen* in the tragedy of the Civil War? Is the historian's view too narrow if he fails to see God at work in political events? Is history not just the narration of human deeds, but of the acts of God as well?

When we deal with the Exodus, the question of the meaning of "history" is

---

[4] For a perceptive treatment of this language problem, see Will Herberg, "Five Meanings of the Word 'Historical,' " in *The Christian Scholar*, XLVII, 4 (1964), pp. 327-330.

put in the sharpest form. From one standpoint, the Exodus was just a political event: the liberation of a band of slaves from the pharaoh's yoke. This was its public meaning. So viewed, it can be described externally or objectively and compared with similar political events in the lives of other peoples. But to the biblical narrators, who spoke out of the community of faith, the Exodus was a .divine event. What *happened* was God's redemption of his people, not just their liberation from political servitude. The Exodus was an act of God. It was the sign of his revelation and of his presence. Therefore the Exodus story deals with history on a different plane from that on which "history" is usually written today. For Israel, to write history was to narrate the "mighty acts" of the Lord.

But to speak of history "on a different plane" may be misleading. It may suggest that biblical history belongs in some Olympian realm far removed from the ordinary affairs of human life, or that the story may be treated merely as the poetry of faith that has no direct connection with prosaic facts. This would be a grave misunderstanding of biblical history. To be sure, the central testimony of the biblical account concerns the revelation of God—but *it is in the concrete affairs and relationships of people that God makes himself known.* No external historical study can demonstrate that the Exodus was an act of God; but to Israel this "political" event was the medium through which God's presence and purpose were disclosed. God's revelation did not come like a bolt out of the blue; it came *through* the crises and affairs of human life and *to persons* who perceived in the events a divine dimension of meaning of which the general public was unaware.

Thus Israel's sacred history does not belong to a completely different sphere from that with which the historian can deal. There is a concreteness and factuality with which the reader of the Old Testament must reckon if he is to do justice to the narrative of God's dealings with men. So before examining the Exodus more closely, we shall first look into the historical and cultural background of the event. Modern archaeology and historical research have helped us to understand this event in a credible historical context.

THE PROLOGUE TO THE EXODUS

The account found in the opening chapters of the book of Exodus is linked closely with the history and religion of the patriarchal period—that is, the period covered by chapters 12 through 50 of the book of Genesis. This continuity is indicated by a reference to events that transpired after the death of Joseph, one of the twelve sons of Jacob (Ex. 1:8), and by the vivid story of the theophany, or manifestation of God, in the episode of the "burning bush." There we read that Moses is addressed in these words: "I am the God of your father, the God of Abraham, the God of Isaac, and the God of Jacob" (3:6). These narratives, at least in their present form, presuppose that the speaker is the same God who appeared to the "fathers," and that the patriarchal period is the prologue to the divine deliverance from Egypt.

What can we say about the historical antecedents of the Exodus? This is not an easy question for, as we have just seen, the story of the beginnings of Israel has come to us through a long process of oral tradition and has been shaped to confess faith in God.[5] This is clearly the case with the narratives about the prehistory of Israel in Genesis 12-50. Not only is the sovereignty of the God of the Exodus traced back into the whole course of previous history but the conception of the unity of *Israel* as God's people is pushed back into the times of Abraham, Isaac, and Jacob. Strictly speaking, this results in an oversimplified picture, something like a historian tracing the conception of a *United* States back into the period before the Revolutionary War. Nevertheless, the tradition has undoubtedly preserved the memory of historical events and relationships which later were understood as a preparation for the decisive event of the Exodus and the formation of the people Israel.

To consider the prologue to the Exodus we must turn our attention to the area known as the Fertile Crescent. As the accompanying map shows, this title is applied to the fertile arc of land that skirts the Arabian desert, reaching from the Persian Gulf up through the alluvial plain of the Tigris and Euphrates, curving around through Syria and Palestine, and continuing toward the Nile in Egypt. As the cradle of ancient civilization, the Fertile Crescent had been the scene of human activity for centuries before the appearance of the first Hebrews.

The patriarchal history began in "Ur of the Chaldeans," if we may trust the text of Genesis 11:31, rather than that of the Greek translation of the third century b.c. which makes no reference to Ur. Terah, the father of Abraham (Abram),[6] moved his family from that city near the Persian Gulf to the city of Haran in northwestern Mesopotamia about 600 miles away. From there, Abraham migrated into Canaan, the earlier name of Palestine. Stopping first at Shechem, he moved down through the central hill country and eventually settled in southern Canaan. Abraham was succeeded by his son Isaac, and Isaac by his son Jacob, whose twelve sons carried the names of the twelve tribes of Israel.

These patriarchs are described as living peacefully among the native Canaanites, although they maintained contact with relatives in Haran and secured wives from that source rather than mixing freely with the Canaanites (Gen. 24

---

[5] Some students of "tradition history" are skeptical about the historical reliability of the biblical tradition concerning the pre-Mosaic period or even the whole period before Israel's settlement in Canaan; so Martin Noth who begins his *History of Israel* [44] with the Israelite settlement (c. 1200). On the other hand, John Bright, in his *History of Israel* [40], defends the substantial historicity of the biblical tradition. The issue has been debated by G. Ernest Wright and Gerhard von Rad in articles on "History and the Patriarchs," in *Expository Times*, 71 (1960), pp. 292-296, and 72 (1961), pp. 213-216. See further George Mendenhall, "Biblical History in Transition," in *The Bible and the Ancient Near East* [43], pp. 32-53, for a reappraisal of the reliability of the traditions.

[6] The name Abraham is a dialectical variant of Abram. See Gen. 17:1-8 for a harmonizing explanation of the survival of the two names in the tradition.

THE FERTILE CRESCENT

LIMIT OF FERTILE CRESCENT

and 29). Various family troubles developed, such as the quarrel between Isaac's twin sons, Jacob and Esau, and the rivalry between Jacob and his father-in-law, Laban. These troubles came to a climax in a dissension that broke out in the circle of Jacob's twelve sons. Jealous of Joseph, his brothers conspired to send him off to Egypt. There Joseph rose to the position of prime minister of Egypt, the most influential post next to that of the pharaoh himself. Then in a time of famine, the family of Jacob migrated to Egypt, where they settled in the Delta area near the pharaoh's capital and received the bounty of Joseph's wise administration. The book of Exodus takes up the story at this point, stating that Hebrew fortunes changed when a new Egyptian king arose who did not know Joseph.

THE VICTORY STELE *of Naram-Sin (twenty-third century B.C.), the grandson of Sargon I. With his soldiers, the Akkadian king triumphantly ascends a mountain whose peak almost touches the stars, while his victims, the mountain-dwelling Lullubians, fall beneath his feet or plunge headlong from the cliffs.*

The Coming of the Amorites

A great deal of light has been thrown on this biblical period by the study of international developments in the Fertile Crescent. Ur, Abraham's ancestral city at the southern end of the Euphrates River, has been excavated by archaeologists, and its remains bear eloquent witness to its ancient glory. Other archaeological discoveries, especially in northern Mesopotamia around Haran, have helped us to become better acquainted with the early patriarchal period. Let us take a brief look at the situation in Mesopotamia.

During the third millennium B.C. (3000-2000) the alluvial plain of the Tigris and Euphrates had been the scene of a struggle between two centers of power, Sumer in the south and Akkad in the north. The Sumerians established a brilliant civilization, whose richness spread through all Mesopotamia during the first part of the third millennium (c. 2800-2360 B.C.). But in the twenty-fourth century B.C. this cultural treasure was seized by the Semitic Akkadians, under the leadership of Sargon I of Akkad, who has been called the first empire-builder of history. Then the political pendulum swung again, and the Sumerians came to power at the end of the millennium under the so-called Third Dynasty of Ur (c. 2060-1950 B.C.). But their return to power was brief. The Ur regime was brought to an end by a devastating attack of Elamites who stormed down from their mountainous homeland (modern Iran) into the coveted Mesopotamian plain.

In the resulting political confusion, a semi-nomadic people known as Amorites flooded the country. These Semites came from the Arabian desert, the cradle of all Semitic peoples. With amazing political energy, they took control of Mesopotamia and finally established the First Babylonian Dynasty, whose last and greatest king was Hammurabi (c. 1728-1686 B.C.).

By the year 1750 B.C., the Amorites had extended their influence throughout all Mesopotamia and down through Syria into Palestine where they came to be the dominant element of the Canaanite population. A vivid picture of the time was provided by the discovery, in 1935-1939, of about twenty thousand tablets at Mari (near the border between modern Syria and Iraq) dating from the latter half of the eighteenth century B.C. Many of these documents represent diplomatic correspondence between the Amorite king of Mari, Zimri-Lim, and officials in surrounding states, some of them with Hammurabi himself. Since Mari was conquered by Hammurabi in about 1700 B.C., the Mari tablets illumine the cultural backgrounds of the early patriarchal period. They are of extraordinary interest to the reader of the Bible, for they contain biblical names like Benjamin and David, and mention 'Apiru—a term that in the judgment of many scholars is almost equivalent to "Hebrew."

It is probable that Abraham's migration into Canaan was connected in some way with the Amoritic invasion into Mesopotamia and Syria. This would mean that he lived during the eighteenth century B.C. and that he may have been a contemporary of the Amorite king Hammurabi. Haran, Abraham's home town, was an Amorite settlement in this period. It is striking that towns in the area had names that in the biblical tradition are credited to Abraham's relatives: Peleg, Serug, Nahor, Terah, Haran. The Amorite personal names, such as Benjamin, Jacob-el, and Abram (*Abamram*), may not refer to the biblical characters themselves, but they certainly point to a common Semitic background.[7]

---

[7] The Amorite background of Abraham is stressed by E. A. Speiser in his commentary [134], pp. xxxvii-lii. It is doubtful, however, whether the tradition permits us "to attempt to read his [Abraham's] mind at a critical juncture in his life" (p. xlv)—that is, to divine his own thoughts on leaving Mesopotamia.

Probably the patriarchs brought with them from their Amoritic homeland some of the traditions that were later transformed and incorporated into the religious epic now found in the first eleven chapters of Genesis: stories of the Creation, the Garden of Eden, the Flood, and the Tower of Babel. From the First Dynasty of Babylonia comes the creation story known as *Enuma elish,* as well as the flood story preserved in the Gilgamesh Epic.[8] Both stories show formal similarities to the biblical accounts, although—as we shall see in Chapter 6—there is a world of religious difference between them. Furthermore, the prototype of the biblical "Tower of Babel" (Gen. 11:1-9) is the ziggurat or tiered temple-tower of the city of Babylon, one of the famed wonders of the age of Hammurabi (compare the Ur ziggurat, p. 178). This tower was known as Etemenanki, "the House of the Terrace-platform of Heaven and Earth." Finally, the Hebrews may have come to know Mesopotamian law in their Amoritic homeland, although it is more likely that they were later influenced by the famous Code of Hammurabi through the Canaanites among whom they settled. A copy of the code can be seen today in the Louvre Museum, inscribed on a huge black stele beneath a relief of Hammurabi standing before the sun god Shamash, god of law and justice. The code, which influenced jurisprudence in the Fertile Crescent for

[8] See J. B. Pritchard, *Ancient Near Eastern Texts* [2], pp. 60-99.

THE STELE OF HAMMURABI *is a monolith, nearly eight feet tall, inscribed with a code of laws. The relief at the top depicts Hammurabi, King of Babylon, standing before the sun god Shamash, who extends a rod and ring, symbols of royal authority, to the worshiping king.*

centuries afterward, was unquestionably one of the most brilliant achievements conceived by the foreward-looking Hammurabi regime.

The Hurrian Movement

Into the political vacuum created by the downfall of the Sumerian dynasty of Ur came another wave of population known as Hurrians (the Old Testament calls them Horites). Even before the turn of the second millennium, they started to push down from the Caucasian mountains of Armenia into the plain of the Tigris and Euphrates. Unlike the Amorites, they came not as military conquerors, but in a steady, ever-increasing stream of infiltration. At first they settled in northern Mesopotamia, around Mari and Haran, but by the time of Hammurabi they had spread through the entire country. By the fifteenth century, their political power had become so great that they constituted the majority of the population of a new Mesopotamian state, Mitanni. Hurrians migrated into Palestine in such numbers that Egyptians, from the time of the Eighteenth Dynasty, referred to the area as Hurru—that is, Hurrian country.

Before 1919, almost nothing was known of the Hurrians. But the discovery of thousands of clay tablets at the Hurrian city of Nuzi, dating from the time of the Mitannian kingdom (about 1500-1370 B.C.), has thrown a great deal of light on the patriarchal period. For instance, we can now understand better the story about Rachel's theft of the household gods (teraphim), as related in Genesis 31:19, 30-35. According to Hurrian custom, a man's possession of the household idols insured his leadership of the family and his claim on the family inheritance. With some justification, Laban protested against what he construed to be Jacob's shrewd attempt to despoil his family of everything—his daughters, the best of his livestock, and even the household gods! Moreover, according to Nuzi law a sterile wife could give her maid to her husband for the purpose of obtaining an offspring, precisely as Sarah proposed to do (Gen. 16:2). And the sale of a birthright and the deathbed blessing were attested at Nuzi. In these and other ways the Nuzi tablets have helped us to understand how faithfully the book of Genesis reflects the customs and conditions of the times.

The Hittites

Even before the rise of the Hurrian kingdom of Mitanni, another political power encroached upon the Fertile Crescent. Beyond the western mountains, in the region of present-day Turkey, a people known as Hittites established a vigorous nation.[9] From time to time, they ventured from their

---

[9] Although the Hittite state was formed in the seventeenth century B.C., the real expansion came later. The first Hittite empire was created in the sixteenth century (1600-1500 B.C.). Their power was temporarily eclipsed by the rise of the state of Mitanni (1500-1370 B.C.).

A ROCK SANCTUARY *built by the Hittites at Yazilikaya ("Inscribed Rock"), about two miles east of the great mountain fortress of Hattushash, the former Hittite capital (see Plates 3 and 4). The sanctuary, a monument to Hittite state religion of the thirteenth century* B.C., *lies in a natural circle of rocks which is entered through a narrow gorge.*

A PROCESSION OF HITTITE GODS *carved in bas-relief on the walls of the rock sanctuary at Yazilikaya. It was thought that the whole Hittite pantheon—"the thousand gods of Hatti"—were present in the holy place. Hittite treaties (covenants) were placed under the protection of the gods.*

mountain-locked homeland in Anatolia or Asia Minor (see Plate 4 *) to expand into Mesopotamia, Syria, and Palestine, and eventually they vied with Egypt for the control of the Fertile Crescent. In the heart of their rugged land, atop an impressive height, they built their lofty capital of Hattushash, and not far away they carved upon the walls of a rock-sanctuary scenes of their major deities and of lesser gods marching in procession. Not too long ago the Hittites were little more than a name. But the excavation in 1907 of the Hittite capital, now called Boghaz-köy, has uncovered the evidence of the former glory of the Hittite empire, manifest not only in massive fortifications and impressive struc-tures (see Plate 3) but also in a whole library of literature, including a code of laws and treaties with other peoples. The biblical tradition that Abraham pur-chased his burial cave from some Hittites (Gen. 23) suggests that their influence extended south as far as Canaan.

The Habiru

We see, then, that the patriarchal period was a time of unrest, a time when many peoples were mingling together in the Fertile Crescent. Canaan was, indeed, "the land of the Canaanites, the Hittites, the Amorites, the Periz-zites, the Hivites, and the Jebusites" (Ex. 3:17).

Particularly interesting are the numerous references in the documents of the second millennium to Habiru, or 'Apiru, a comparatively inconspicuous people scattered throughout Asia Minor, Mesopotamia, Syria, Canaan, and Egypt.[10] The term does not refer primarily to a racial or ethnic group, although appar-ently many of the Habiru were Semites. Rather, it refers to a social class of people in relation to the established nations of the Near East. The Habiru were "wanderers" or "outsiders" who lived a rootless existence on the fringes of society. Like modern gypsies, many of them moved from place to place with their flocks and families. Sometimes they formed themselves into guerrilla bands, attacking caravans or making nuisance raids on villages. Sometimes they hired themselves out as mercenary soldiers, or were forced into slave labor on public projects. It was not unheard of for one of them to rise to a position of leadership in an established nation. As we have said, the word "Habiru" is probably equivalent to the biblical word "Hebrew." This does not mean, how-ever, that the mention of Habiru in Mesopotamian and Egyptian texts refers to the Hebrews who were relatives of Abraham. Rather, the biblical Hebrews belonged to the larger floating class of semi-nomads to whom more established groups applied the descriptive term "Habiru."

This picture agrees with the description of Abraham, the traditional ancestor of the Hebrews according to the Old Testament (Gen. 14:13). He is described

---

* Plate numbers refer to pictures in the series of color pages.

[10] For a discussion of the Habiru in relation to the patriarchs, see John Holt, *The Patriarchs of Israel* [91], pp. 44-68.

as being a "sojourner" (ger) in the midst of the established peoples of Canaan. With his flocks and his family he moved through the sparsely settled hill country, wandering from place to place until he settled down in Mamre, near the place where Hebron was later established. The same picture is given of his son and grandson, Isaac and Jacob. Indeed, so shallow were the roots of these Hebrews in Canaan that, during a time of great famine, Jacob migrated with his family into Egypt.

The God of the Fathers

It is hard to tell just what the religion of the patriarchs was, because, as we have already pointed out, the traditions of Genesis have been revised in the light of the Exodus and the Sinai covenant. Still, many statements of the book of Genesis, when considered against the background of the culture of the Fertile Crescent, help us to understand the probable character of religious beliefs before Moses.

When the Hebrews left Mesopotamia, they brought with them a religion which in many respects was like the nature religion of the Fertile Crescent (to be discussed in Chapter 4). Apparently their chief god was known as Shaddai (or El Shaddai), which means "the One of the Mountains"—a mountain-deity or storm-deity usually known by the title Baal ("lord") among the Canaanites. As elsewhere in the Fertile Crescent, the father of the gods was known as El. In addition, other divine titles appear, such as El Elyon (Gen. 14:18-20), El Olam (Gen. 21:33), and El Bethel (Gen. 35:7). Later, in the time of Joshua, the Hebrews were reminded that their fathers who once dwelt beyond the river (Euphrates) had served "other gods" (Josh. 24:2), and Joshua exhorted them to put away the remnants of their ancestral polytheism. But in spite of the general similarity of patriarchal religion to the religion of the Fertile Crescent [11] there were certain major differences which in the course of time took on profound significance.

In Genesis 15:7-21 a curious incident is described. Abraham cut some animals in two, placing half of the carcasses over against the other half. Then after the sun had set and an eerie darkness had fallen over the place, "a smoking fire pot and a flaming torch"—representing the presence of the deity—passed between the pieces. The account, though overlaid with later theological interpretation, seems to preserve a very ancient ritual of covenant-making in which the deity binds himself under the power of the curse to fulfill his promise.[12] The story points up one of the main characteristics of patriarchal religion: the practice of

---

[11] See Roland de Vaux, *Ancient Israel* [62], pp. 289-294, for discussion of the veneration of the supreme God, El, at the patriarchal sanctuaries: Shechem, Bethel, Mamre, and Beersheba.

[12] Apparently the covenant partner, by passing through the bloody corridor, invoked upon himself the curse of becoming like the divided animals if he violated the covenant obligation. Compare Jer. 34:18.

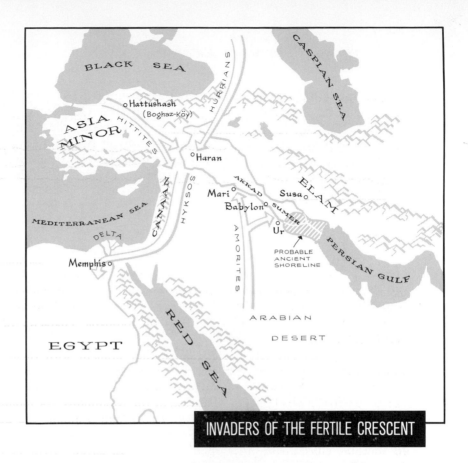

INVADERS OF THE FERTILE CRESCENT

entering into a personal relationship or "covenant" with the deity. So we are told that Abraham entered into relationship with the God who was known as the "Shield" of Abraham (Gen. 15:1). Isaac was covenanted with "the Fear [possibly, "the Kinsman"] of Isaac" (Gen. 31:42, 53). And Jacob was bound in covenant with "the Mighty One of Jacob" (Gen. 49:24). In each case, the family God manifested himself personally to the patriarch and gave demands and promises. Therefore, the deity was known by the name of the patriarch who received the revelation: the God of Abraham, the God of Isaac, and the God of Jacob.[13]

Further, patriarchal religion was infused with a historical sense that is characteristically Semitic or Hebraic. Unlike the sedentary Canaanites, who were more concerned with adjusting to the cycles of nature and preserving the social equilibrium, the unsettled Hebrews were more prone to express their faith in the dynamic language of history. They were wanderers and adventurers who,

---

[13] This view is set forth in the classic study of patriarchal religion: Albrecht Alt, "Der Gott der Väter," in *Kleine Schriften zur Geschichte des Volkes Israel*, I (Munich, 1953), pp. 1-78. See now the reconsideration of this view by Frank M. Cross, Jr., "Yahweh and the God of the patriarchs," in *Harvard Theological Review*, LV (1962), pp. 225-259.

in response to a divine summons, left their homeland and went into the unknown and the uncertain—toward a land that their God would give them in due time. They lived by a venture of faith, trusting that the future was in the hand of their personal God. To be sure, the story of Abraham's migration from Mesopotamia, in response to God's call, is colored by later theological reflection. Yet some dim apprehension of divine guidance of a people's historical destiny must have provided the background of the account in the book of Exodus which relates that Moses was addressed by the God of the fathers.

THE DESCENT INTO EGYPT

In the latter part of the book of Genesis, we find the story of Joseph's rise to power in Egypt and the friendly reception of the family of Jacob into the Delta area during a time of famine. Since Habiru sometimes rose to prominence in other governments during this period, there is nothing particularly incredible about Joseph's elevation to political leadership.

Admittedly, the biblical story about Jacob and Joseph contains elements of folklore. It was intended to be an interesting and edifying story, rather than a straight biographical account. The Joseph story has been colored by popular imagination and embellished with themes drawn from the oral tradition of the time. It displays the kind of creative literary artistry that captures the interest of modern novelists like Thomas Mann. (On the theological purpose of the story, see pp. 185-186.) Nevertheless, the biblical account is more than fiction. In its broad outline, as well as in many of its details, it agrees with the historical setting of the second millennium B.C.

The Hyksos Invasion

Earlier, we considered two great waves—the Amorite invasion and the Hurrian movement—which surged into the Fertile Crescent shortly after the turn of the second millennium B.C. In the wake of these and other political disturbances came another tidal wave, known as the Hyksos movement, which swept down through Syria and Palestine into Egypt. The Hyksos—or "rulers of foreign countries," as the Egyptian word means—were a motley array of peoples. Many of them seem to have been Semites, but some were Hittites and Hurrians. Unlike the earlier Hurrian movement from the Caucasian highlands, this wave of Asiatics was bent on conquest. Aided by a new military weapon, the horse-drawn chariot, they invaded Egypt at a time of political weakness and over-threw the native rulers. The date of their invasion of Egypt is placed at about 1720 B.C. The Egyptian historian Manetho (about 275 B.C.) recalled with horror the Hyksos invasion in the reign of Tutimaeus, probably a pharaoh of the Thirteenth Dynasty:

> In his reign, for what cause I know not, a blast of God smote us; and unexpectedly, from the regions of the East, invaders of obscure race marched in confidence of victory against our land. By main force they easily seized it without striking a blow; and having overpowered the rulers of the land, they then burned our cities ruthlessly, razed to the ground the temples of the gods, and treated all the natives with a cruel hostility.[14]

Manetho also reports that one of the Hyksos was made king in Memphis and that he rebuilt the powerful stronghold of Avaris (Tanis) in the Delta area.

For a century and a half, the Hyksos dominated Egypt. The rulers of the Fifteenth and Sixteenth Dynasties, who were all Hyksos, established a powerful empire that included Palestine and Syria. For instance, excavations have shown that during this period Shechem was a Hyksos fortress, equipped with the characteristic ramparts which the Hyksos introduced to protect a city from attack by horse-drawn chariots.[15] Shortly after 1600 B.C., however, an Egyptian revolution broke out. At about 1550 B.C., Ahmose I, the founder of the brilliant Eighteenth Dynasty, overthrew the hated foreign regime. The city Avaris was captured, the routed Hyksos were pursued into Palestine, and cities like Shechem were overthrown. Thus began an Egyptian revival which, especially under the Napoleon-like pharaoh Thutmose III (c. 1490-1435 B.C.), resulted in the extension of Egypt's sway throughout Palestine and Syria.

The account of the Hebrew descent into Egypt accords well with circumstances in Egypt. It is quite credible that the pressure of famine forced Jacob's family to settle in "the land of Goshen," the fertile area in the eastern part of the Nile Delta. Semi-nomads in Palestine, a land that depended on seasonal rainfall, would naturally turn their eyes in time of drought toward Egypt, where the periodic overflow of the Nile irrigated the land. We know from Egyptian records that it was the practice for Egyptian officials to allow hunger-stricken people from Palestine and the Sinaitic peninsula to enter the Delta frontier. One Egyptian frontier official in about 1350 B.C. sent word to the pharaoh that some nomads "who knew not how they should live, have come begging a home in the domain of Pharaoh . . . after the manner of your father's fathers since the beginning." [16]

Since the biblical account depicts a peaceful migration into Egypt, the Hebrew settlement in Egypt could not have been a part of the Hyksos movement, for the Hyksos came as conquerors. But there is probably some connection between the two events; the patriarchal migration may well have occurred on the fringe of the Hyksos population movement. As we have said, many of the Hyksos were Semites, a fact that is strikingly demonstrated by the appearance of Hebrew

---

[14] *Manetho*, tr. by Helen Waddell, pp. 79-81; see Josephus, *Against Apion*, I, 14 (75-76).
[15] Consult G. Ernest Wright, *Shechem* [58], chap. 5.
[16] See *The Westminster Historical Atlas* [5], p. 29; also J. B. Pritchard, *The Ancient Near East in Pictures* [4], pp. 14-20.

names like Jacob and Hur in Hyksos lists of nobles. In the Hyksos period, when Egypt was under Semitic rule, the conditions were right for the friendly welcome of Jacob's family and for Joseph's rise to a position of leadership in the royal court.

Furthermore, according to the biblical narratives the Hebrew settlement in the Goshen area (called "the land of Rameses" in Gen. 47:11) was near the pharaoh's court (Gen. 46:28 ff.). Before the Hyksos period the Egyptian capital had been at Thebes, but the Hyksos built their capital, Avaris, in the Delta or Goshen area. When Ahmose expelled the Hyksos, Avaris was destroyed and the capital was moved back to Thebes. Thus the location of the pharaoh's capital, as presupposed by the Joseph story, suggests that the Hebrew settlement in Egypt took place during the Hyksos period.[17]

THE OPPRESSION IN EGYPT

Now we are ready to return to the first chapter of the book of Exodus. There we are told that after Joseph's death the family of Jacob lost favor in Egypt, owing to a change of administration. "Now there arose a new king over Egypt, who did not know Joseph" (Ex. 1:8). As a result, the Hebrews were reduced to the status of state slaves and were put to work building the store cities of Pithom and Rameses in the Delta.

The Date of the Exodus

This account points to the political change that took place at the beginning of the Eighteenth Dynasty when Ahmose I expelled the Hyksos. Not all the Semites were driven out, however. The Hyksos leaders were ousted and a number of their subjects may have fled with them into Palestine. But many Semites—and particularly the relatives of Jacob—survived Ahmose's purge and remained in the Delta region. There they fell victim to the oppressive policies that accompanied the Egyptian revival during the Eighteenth and Nineteenth Dynasties. During this period—the sixteenth through the thirteenth centuries—

---

[17] This view is defended by G. Ernest Wright in *Biblical Archaeology* [57], pp. 54-58. There are, of course, other possibilities for reconstructing the historical background of the patriarchs. Some historians place the patriarchs in the period after the expulsion of the Hyksos (i.e., after 1500 B.C.), specifically during the disturbances of the Amarna Age (see later, pp. 80-81) and the establishment of such small states as Aram, Edom, Moab, and Ammon. This would account for the absence of reference to the Egyptian domination of Canaan in the book of Genesis; but the view hardly does justice to the clear Amorite connections of Abraham. Other historians modify this view by connecting Abraham with the period of Hammurabi and associating Jacob with the Amarna period of the fifteenth-fourteenth centuries. So, for instance, H. H. Rowley, *From Joseph to Joshua* [95], chap. 3, who specifically connects Joseph with the time of the Amarna king Akhnaton (1370-1353 B.C.). But, as Rowley admits, this requires a radical separation of Abraham (and Isaac) from Jacob and Joseph.

the pharaohs needed cheap labor for their ambitious projects. According to Egyptian documents, they conscripted the service of 'Apiru (Habiru)—a term which, as we have seen, is not necessarily limited to the particular Hebrews with whom we are concerned.

If Ahmose I was the "king who did not know Joseph," then there is probably quite a gap of time between Exodus 1:8 and the narrative in Exodus 1:9 and following. In this sequel we find that once again the pharaoh's court is in the Delta area, as shown by the story of the Egyptian princess who went down to the river to bathe and found herself near the Hebrew colony (2:5-10). Evidently some time had passed since Ahmose destroyed Avaris and moved his capital to Thebes. The account seems to presuppose a time in the Nineteenth Dynasty, which began about the last quarter of the fourteenth century B.C. At that time, the Egyptian court was moved once again from Thebes to the Delta frontier in order that the pharaohs might be in a better position to control their Asiatic empire. Seti I (c. 1309-1290 B.C.), the first strong king of the Nineteenth Dynasty, began the reconstruction of the old Hyksos capital Avaris (later called Tanis). The project was continued by his son, Rameses II (c. 1290-1224 B.C.), who renamed the capital "House of Rameses." This city is specifically mentioned in Exodus 1:11, where we are told that the Hebrew slaves built Rameses. And according to Egyptian documents, Rameses II was one of the pharaohs who used 'Apiru (Habiru) in his public projects. The next pharaoh, Merneptah (c. 1224-1216 B.C.), bragged about victory over Israel in Canaan about 1220 B.C. and this report indicates that at that time the people were already firmly entrenched in the land (see pp. 81-83).

In view of the complexity of the picture, it is not surprising that historians differ in assessing the evidence presented by archaeology and the biblical account. And yet it seems more and more evident that the background of the narratives of the first chapters of Exodus is the situation in Egypt under the Nineteenth Dynasty, and that the Exodus took place about the beginning of the reign of Rameses II—that is, shortly after 1290 B.C.[18] In this case, Rameses II —the pharaoh who immortalized himself in colossal statues throughout Egypt (see Plate 1)—was the pharaoh of whom Moses demanded: "Let my people go." According to Exodus 12:40, "the time that the people of Israel dwelt in Egypt was four hundred and thirty years." If this statement refers to the total time the Hebrews lived in the Delta area and not just to the years of oppression,[19] it

---

[18] This is the position of the American scholar, W. F. Albright, which has been followed in this discussion. See his historical summary, *The Biblical Period* [38], pp. 6-13.

[19] However, Exodus 12:40 can be interpreted to refer only to the years of oppression, as in Genesis 15:13. The Greek Version of the Old Testament (Septuagint) complicates the matter by saying, in Exodus 12:40, that the Israelites lived in Egypt *and in the land of Canaan* 430 years. In other words, the figure covers the whole period from the call of Abraham to the Exodus (cf. Gal. 3:17). None of these figures can be taken with mathematical exactness, but must be weighed against archaeological and biblical evidence. On the figure given in I Kings 6:1, see G. E. Wright, *Biblical Archaeology* [57], pp. 83-84.

brings us back approximately to the time of the Hyksos invasion (1290 + 430 = 1720 B.C.). The situation in Egypt may have been something like this:

Period of favor: 1720-1550 B.C.	HYKSOS RULE *XV to XVII Dynasties*	Capital at Avaris
Period of disfavor: 1550-1309 B.C.	EGYPTIAN REVIVAL *XVIII Dynasty*	Capital moved to Thebes
Period of the Exodus: Seti I (c. 1309-1290 B.C.) Rameses II (c. 1290-1224 B.C.) (pharaoh of the Exodus)	EGYPTIAN REVIVAL *XIX Dynasty*	Capital at Avaris
Period of the Conquest: Merneptah (c. 1224-1216 B.C.)		

From all that has been said, it is clear that the biblical narratives reflect the sober realities of the political situation. But these realities were interpreted through the eyes of Israelite faith. Many other peoples, and many other Habiru, were involved in the disturbed political situation of the Fertile Crescent during the latter half of the second millennium B.C. But only the Hebrews who stood in the circle of Moses experienced the depth of historical meaning that led to the remembering and eventually the writing down of these historical traditions. Historical investigation can help us to understand that the biblical story was intimately tied up with the political development of the time. But it takes religious imagination to go beyond the externals to the inner meaning of the events that Israel proclaimed in the exalted language of worship. In the last analysis, the significance of the Exodus is not determined by its date but by its place in the unfolding of the divine purpose in human affairs.

THE ROLE OF MOSES

Earlier, we said that divine revelation comes *through* events which externally are part of ordinary political and social affairs, and *to* persons who perceive in these events a dimension of sacred meaning. In the preceding pages we have confined our attention to the first half of that statement; now we must consider the second half, for the Exodus cannot be separated from Moses, the prophetic interpreter of the event. Moses' role, as described in the biblical narratives, is not merely that of a political hero who leads his people to freedom. It is that of a mediator between God and the enslaved Hebrews. And this role involved his declaration to them of the meaning of the crisis and the marvelous deliverance from it. While brooding over the fate of his people, Moses' understanding was illumined by an experience that took place in a lonely mountain spot. On the basis of this experience, he returned to Egypt to rally his countrymen and to announce the meaning of the events that were taking place. Let us, then, turn our attention to the narrative dealing with Moses in Exodus 2-4.

CHRONOLOGICAL CHART I

B.C.	EGYPT	PALESTINE AND SYRIA	MESOPOTAMIA (AND ASIA MINOR)
(Middle Bronze Age) 2000 to 1900	XII Dynasty	Egyptian Control	Third Dynasty of Ur (c. 2060-1950) Hurrian Movement Amorite Invasion
1900 to 1800	XII Dynasty		First Babylonian Dynasty (c. 1830-1530)
1800 to 1700	Hyksos Invasion (c. 1710)	Abraham (c. 1750?)	The Mari Age Hammurabi (c. 1728-1686)
1700 to 1600	Hyksos Rule (XV to XVII Dynasties)	Hyksos Control Descent of Jacob family into Egypt	Decline of Babylonia
(Late Bronze Age) 1600 to 1500	XVIII Dynasty: Ahmose (c. 1570-1546) Expulsion of Hyksos	Egyptian Control	Old Hittite Empire (c. 1600-1500)
1500 to 1400	Thutmose III (c. 1490-1435)		Kingdom of Mitanni (c. 1500-1370)
1400 to 1300	Amenhotep III (c. 1406-1370) Amenhotep IV or Akhnaton (c. 1370-1353)	Amarna Age (1400-1350) Egyptian Weakness	New Hittite Empire (c. 1375-1200) Rise of Assyria (c. 1354-1197)
1300 to 1200	XIX Dynasty: Seti I (c. 1309-1290) Rameses II (c. 1290-1224) Merneptah (c. 1224-1216)	Egyptian Revival (The Exodus, c. 1290) Israelite Conquest (c. 1250-1200) Merneptah's Victory (c. 1220)	Assyrian Dominance

Note: The date of Hammurabi is still uncertain. Some scholars put him in the nineteenth century—that is, the early Amorite period. Others argue for a date in the seventeenth century—the period of Babylonian decline. The former suggestion would not affect our basic outline.

Moses' Background

All that we know about Moses is contained in the biblical narratives. Even this knowledge is limited by the fact that the narrators were not interested in Moses' biography. Although the narrative portrays a historical figure of heroic stature, it focuses not so much on Moses' personality as on the God who prepares and summons him to be the agent in the accomplishment of the divine purpose.[20]

The tradition of Exodus 2 that Moses was brought up and trained in Egyptian circles is probably authentic, although it is colored with elements of folklore. The story of the baby in the basket of bulrushes (Ex. 2:1-10), for example, is reminiscent of a similar account from Sargon of Akkad (c. 2300 B.C.). In an inscription, Sargon says that his mother gave birth to him in secret, placed him in a basket of rushes sealed with bitumen, and cast the basket adrift on the river. Akki, the drawer of water, lifted him out of the water and reared him as his son. So from humble beginnings Sargon rose to be the mighty king of the city of Agade, from which the Akkadians took their name.[21] The theme of Moses' humble birth and his upbringing in the pharaoh's court is the sort of thing that delights popular imagination. Yet Moses' name is an authentic indication of his Egyptian nurture, which is after all one of the main points of the story. To be sure, the Hebrew storyteller, by a play on words, tries to derive the name Moses (Hebrew: *Mosheh*) from a Hebrew verb meaning "to draw out" (*mashah*), and even says the Egyptian princess knew enough Hebrew to explain the name in this manner (2:10). But this is an example of the popular explanation of names on the basis of assonance, or the similarity of sound, as though we were to explain the name Abel by the English verb "to be able." *Mosheh* really comes from an Egyptian verb, "to beget a child." Perhaps originally it was joined with the name of an Egyptian deity, as in the names Thut-*mose* or Ra-*meses*. Other members of Moses' tribe, the tribe of Levi (Ex. 2:1), also had Egyptian names, such as Phinehas, Hophni, and Merari.

Despite his nurture in the pharaoh's court, Moses continued to have a strong feeling of identification with his Hebrew kinsmen, as is shown vividly by his impulsive action on seeing an Egyptian taskmaster beating a Hebrew slave (Ex. 2:11-15). Fearing that the news of this act of murder would reach the ear of the king (probably Seti I),[22] Moses fled into the land of Midian, an area of the

---

[20] In this connection Gerhard von Rad's little study *Moses* [112] is illuminating.

[21] See Pritchard, *Ancient Near Eastern Texts*, p. 119.

[22] Apparently Moses fled from Egypt during the reign of Seti I, who began the imperial projects in the Delta, and returned when there was a change of administration—that is, at the beginning of the reign of Rameses II (see Ex. 4:18-20).

Sinaitic Peninsula controlled by certain Midianite shepherds.[23] There, after a "romance" that started at a well, he married the daughter of Jethro (Reuel, Hobab), the priest of Midian (2:15-22). Moses' connection with the Midianites, and especially with a Midianite clan known as the Kenites, is undoubtedly authentic.

The Burning Bush

The story of Moses' encounter with "the God of the fathers" and of the mighty struggle that this strange meeting precipitated within him is one of the masterpieces of the Old Testament (Ex. 3 and 4). It should be read with religious imagination and empathy, as one would read a piece of poetry, for it communicates a dimension of meaning that cannot be cramped into the limits of precise prose. It would be foolish, for instance, to rationalize the burning bush, as though this vision were something that could have been seen with the objective eye of a camera. In the Old Testament, fire is frequently a symbol for the manifestation of God. Whatever Moses saw with his naked eye was transformed into a religious "sign" of the divine presence. Moses' vision awakened the realization that he was truly standing on holy ground, for at that mountain rendezvous he was met by God.

At first Moses, like most of us, wondered how a bush could burn without being consumed. But in the story attention quickly shifts from seeing the bush to hearing the God who speaks. The way God is described as speaking is clear evidence that the problem of the Hebrew slaves in Egypt lay deeply upon Moses' heart. It must be remembered that Moses had run away from Egypt after an indignant outburst of anger against a slavedriver. So when God speaks to Moses, he speaks in the accents of history. His speech is a declaration of what he plans to do. Notice how several verbs are employed to describe the divine intention: "I *have seen* the affliction of my people . . . and *have heard* their cry . . . I *know* their sufferings, and *have come down to deliver* them . . . (3:7-8). According to the Mosaic faith, God is not aloof from the human scene of travail and oppression. He takes part in human affairs to work out his purpose. He makes himself known by his deeds, which are historical events. In this narrative we come to the very heart of Israel's historical faith.

According to some religions, man's highest aspiration is to be lifted above sense experience into immediate union with God. In such an ineffable experience individuality fades away and the self, like a drop of water in a great ocean, is absorbed into the Divine. This is not the kind of mysticism with which the

---

[23] Properly "the land of Midian" lay farther east on the other side of the Gulf of Aqabah (see map, p. 53). However, because of their roving way of life and their special interests in copper resources, the Midianites apparently extended their power into the southern part of the Sinaitic Peninsula; see *Westminster Historical Atlas* [5], p. 38.

Old Testament deals. Moses' encounter with God sharpened his sense of *individuality* and made him more acutely conscious of the demands of the historical situation. In the "I and thou" dialogue, Moses was given a task and was summoned to take his part in the historical drama: "Come, I will send you to Pharaoh . . ." (3:10). With profound religious insight, the narrative describes his uneasiness about the call and the various protests he offered in an attempt to stay on the comfortable sidelines of history. The "voice of God" did not come literally out of a burning bush, but out of a historical situation that was illumined with new meaning and depth as Moses reflected on it. In that historical crisis the God of the fathers made known his purpose, his demand, and his promise. And the divine call to decision and responsibility is one of the characteristic notes of Israel's faith.

The Name of God

One of Moses' protests was that if he were to go to the Hebrews in Egypt and tell them about his experience at Sinai, he would have to know God's name (4:13). In antiquity this was a vital question not just because it was popularly believed that there were many gods, but because the character or identity of a god (or person) was expressed in his name. We use names as convenient labels to distinguish one thing from another, one person from another. So we are apt to say with Shakespeare's Juliet, "What's in a name?" (*Romeo and Juliet*, Act II, scene ii). In Hebraic thought, however, the name is filled with mysterious power and significance, for the name represents the innermost self or identity of a person.[24] Consequently, when a person went through an experience that changed and reoriented his life, he was given a new name (as in Gen. 32:27-28). Moses' question, then, represented an attempt to know the mystery of the divine nature—that is, the name of God.

At this point we come to one of the most cryptic passages in the Old Testament. According to the narrative, God answered Moses: "I am who I am" or "I will be what I will be." Moses was then instructed to tell the people: "I AM has sent me to you" (3:14). In the next verse (15), the instructions are more specific. Moses was to tell the people that YHWH (Revised Standard Version: "the Lord"), the God of Abraham, Isaac, and Jacob had sent him. Apparently the narrator intends to connect the words I AM with the four consonants YHWH, the special name for the God of Israel in the Old Testament. In Hebrew, I AM is the first person singular of the verb h-w-h (to be, or to happen); YHWH is the third person singular of the same verb—that is "He will be," or better "He causes to be."

The name YHWH has had an interesting history. In the Old Testament period the Hebrew language was written only with consonants; vowels were

---

[24] See the discussion of "Name" by Johannes Pedersen in *Israel* [69], I-II, pp. 245-259.

not added until the early Christian era, when Hebrew was no longer a living language. On the basis of Greek texts it is now believed that the original pronunciation of the name was *Yahweh*. But because of its holy character, the name was withdrawn from ordinary speech during the period after the Exile, and the substitute Hebrew word Adonai, or "Lord," was used (as is still the practice in synagogues). The word Jehovah is an artificial form that arose from the erroneous combination of the consonants YHWH with the vowels of Adonai by a Christian during the late thirteenth century A.D. In English versions, the name is usually rendered "the Lord."

Only in this passage (Ex. 3:13-14) is there any attempt to explain the name on the basis of the verb "to be, to happen." It is tempting, at first glance, to suppose that the narrator refers to God's changeless being—that is, he is the God who eternally is, who is not affected by the flux and flow of time. The ancient Greeks, who struggled philosophically with the problem of the changing and the changeless, would have favored such a view. But in Israel's faith the emphasis is upon *divine activity*, not passive, eternal being. Just as a person discloses himself to another through his words and deeds, so God reveals himself by what he does. The Hebrew verb has a dynamic meaning that cannot adequately be rendered by our verb "to be"; in fact, often it is best translated as "it came to pass" or "it will come to pass." The late Jewish philosopher, Martin Buber, maintained that in the present instance the verb has the dynamic meaning, "I will be present"—that is, God is the one who is actively present with his people, even as he had promised Moses "I will be with you" (3:12).[25] Other scholars construe the enigmatic expression in 3:14 to mean, "I cause to be what is [or, what happens]"—that is, natural phenomena and historical events have their origin in the will of the God who is Creator and Lord.[26] This is a good explanation of the Hebrew. But perhaps the words originally were intended to be more cryptic and evasive. Moses had asked for information about the mystery of the divine nature (the name), but this information was withheld, lest by having the name men would hold God himself in their possession and keep him under their (magical) control (see Gen. 32:29 and Judg. 13:17-18).[27] Instead, God made known his demand of lordship, summoned Moses to obey his will, and assured him that he would know who God is by what he brings to pass. In other words, the question "Who is God?" would be answered in events that would take place in the future.

---

[25] Martin Buber, *Moses* [105], pp. 18-19. See further the discussion of "God, Names of" (Bernhard W. Anderson), in the *Interpreter's Dictionary of the Bible*, II, pp. 409-411.

[26] This view is championed by W. F. Albright, *From the Stone Age to Christianity* [59], pp. 258-261. It is given a new twist by Frank M. Cross, Jr., *op. cit.*, pp. 250-257, where Yahweh is regarded as a cult name of the high God, El.

[27] This view has been restated in a fresh way by Gerhard von Rad in his *Moses* [112], pp. 18-28.

The Origin of the Yahweh Cult

Moses was to say to the Egyptian pharaoh: "Yahweh, the God of the Hebrews, has met with us" (3:18). Even though it is difficult to explain the word Yahweh on the basis of verses 13 and 14, we can at least ask this question: Where did this name come from? How does it happen that Yahweh, rather than some other name, is the personal name of "the God of Israel"?

Careful reading of the narrative in Exodus 3 discloses that two terms for deity are used alternately. At times the general term translated "God" (Hebrew: *'Elohim*) is used (3:1; 4, 11, 12, 13); sometimes the special Hebrew word Yahweh is found (3:2, 4, 7, 15). This is one of the evidences that have led many scholars to conclude that the narrative represents a blending of sources, J and E, so closely that they can hardly be separated.[28] As a matter of fact, study of the Pentateuch received a great impetus from the discovery, in the eighteenth century, of this alternation in the use of divine names in the book of Genesis. The narrative of Creation (Gen. 1:1-2:4a), for instance, consistently uses the name Elohim; and the story of the Garden of Eden (Gen. 2:4b-3:24) uses Yahweh in combination with Elohim. The same alternation is found in the rest of Genesis. This criterion, along with the evidence of differences in style, theological idiom, and the presence of repetitions and inconsistencies, led to the hypothesis that various sources are woven together in the Pentateuch.

The alternation in the usage of divine names seems to be based on two views of the time when the name Yahweh was introduced. According to J, the worship of Yahweh reached back into the period before the Flood, to the generation of Enosh, the grandson of Adam:

> At that time men began to call upon the name of Yahweh.
> —GENESIS 4:26b

On the other hand, the E and P sources refrain from using the name Yahweh in the period covered by the book of Genesis, agreeing that the name is associated with the special revelation to Moses. One passage (P) puts the matter emphatically:

> And God ['*Elohim*] said to Moses, "I am Yahweh. I appeared to Abraham, to Isaac, and to Jacob, as God Almighty ['*El Shaddai*], but by my name Yahweh I did not make myself known to them."
> —EXODUS 6:2-3; *cf.* GENESIS 17:1

Apparently the presupposition of the E passage in Exodus 3:13-14, in which

---

[28] On the basis of source analysis 3:1-8 belongs essentially to J, with the exception of the second half of verse 4, which suddenly introduces the word "God" ('*Elohim*). The section 3:9-15, which begins with a duplication of the statement that '*Elohim* has heard the people's cry (compare verse 7 [J]) belongs to E.

Moses asks for the name of the God of the fathers, is that the name had not been introduced before that time.

Here, then, we have two traditions. According to one, God was known and worshiped as Yahweh from the earliest times; according to the other, the name was introduced only in the time of Moses. Which of these is right?

There is a sense in which the writer of J is theologically right (as we shall see in Chapter 6). He wants to affirm that Yahweh, the God of Israel, is actually the Lord of all history and creation; hence, he traces the worship of Yahweh back to the remote beginnings. But the writers of E and P are truer to the actual situation when they suggest that the name became commonly accepted during the time of Moses. It is worth noticing that parents began to give their children names compounded with an abbreviated form of the name Yahweh (such as Joshua, which means "Yahweh is salvation") during and after the time of Moses, whereas in the pre-Mosaic period names of this type are lacking. This evidence suggests that the name Yahweh was introduced at the time of the Exodus.

Today there is no complete agreement on the source from which Moses derived this name. According to one very attractive hypothesis, Yahweh was formerly the mountain god of the Kenites, a clan of the Midianites, and Moses was initiated into the Yahweh cult through his marriage to the daughter of Jethro, "the priest of Midian." While Moses was tending Jethro's flocks in Midianite territory, he received a revelation from Yahweh at Sinai (Ex. 3:5). The implication is that Yahweh was worshiped by the Kenites and that the mountain was a Midianite holy place. Moses went back to Egypt and acquainted his countrymen with the new deity, whom they had not known previously, and rallied them to return with him to Sinai and worship him there. The advocates of this hypothesis point out that it was Jethro, not Moses, who offered the sacrifice to Yahweh on the occasion of a desert rendezvous (Ex. 18:9-12), and that the Kenites were allies of Israel or zealous champions of Yahweh in later periods.[29]

The honest truth is that we do not know for sure the source from which Moses received the name Yahweh. It may have come from Midian, Arabia, or elsewhere. But the significant point here is not where the name came from, or even what its literal meaning was. Rather, the important point is what the name stood for in the worship of Israel, from the time of Moses on. Even supposing that Moses borrowed the name from the Kenites, we must recognize that Yahweh meant something radically different in the experience of the Hebrews who followed Moses out of Egypt. And granting that the name literally meant something that we can no longer recover with certainty, still it was filled with a new meaning in the time of the Exodus. The Israelites knew and

---

[29] The Kenite hypothesis is usually associated with the name of Karl Budde; see his *The Religion of Israel to the Exile* (New York, 1899), ch. 1. For a recent defense of the hypothesis, see H. H. Rowley. *From Joseph to Joshua* [95], pp. 149-160; for a vigorous criticism, see T. J. Meek, *Hebrew Origins* [94], ch. 3; also Martin Buber, *The Prophetic Faith* [118], pp. 24-30.

worshiped God as the One who had heard their cry of oppression, who had graciously intervened on their behalf, who had led them toward a future full of promise. In itself, the word Yahweh can be only a name, either empty of meaning or symbolic of many meanings. But in Israel's experience, as interpreted by Moses, it had just one meaning: "I am Yahweh who brought you up out of the land of Egypt." To worship Yahweh was to remember that revealing event, to accept its demand, and to live in its promise.

EVENT AND INTERPRETATION

In this chapter we have considered two inseparable facets of Israel's faith: the historical event and the historical interpreter. The Exodus event did not happen in a vacuum, but was part of the political situation of the Fertile Crescent during the second millennium B.C. Against this background of political developments, we can understand better than ever before—thanks to our greater knowledge of the period—the biblical story of the migration of Abraham, the descent of Jacob's family into Egypt, and the oppression of the Hebrews under the pharaoh. But in the midst of the historical event stands the historical interpreter, Moses. Without his historical vision, the experience of the Exodus and the memory of preceding events of the patriarchal period would never have been understood as they are presented in the biblical narratives. As we have said, God's revelation comes through events to inspired persons whose eyes are opened to perceive in a historical crisis a depth of meaning that is not obvious to everyone. Not only were the Hebrews liberated from Egyptian servitude, but God raised up a man to lead the people and to declare to them the meaning of their deliverance. In the next chapter we shall consider further God's revelation and the people's response.

REVELATION

AND RESPONSE

CHAPTER TWO   In her ancient confession of faith (Deut.
26:5-9), Israel affirmed that "Yahweh heard our voice, and
saw our affliction, our toil, and our oppression; and Yahweh
brought us out of Egypt with a mighty hand and an outstretched arm, with great terror, with signs and wonders."
Israel understood her history as originating in divine initiative and grace. She would not have become a people at all
had not Yahweh acted on her behalf in the time of her
oblivion and oppression. He heard, he saw, he rescued.

Biblical readings: The sections of the biblical narrative treated in this
chapter are Exodus 5-15 (the triumph over the pharaoh), 16-18 (the
journey toward Sinai), and 19-24 (the making of the covenant).

43

In this chapter we continue the discussion of the dramatic narratives of the book of Exodus where the themes of Israel's confession are elaborated. Let us turn first to the story that is recounted in Exodus 5-15. Before raising critical questions about this material, it would be well to read through the chapters as you would read a drama. In a series of episodes the narrator builds up intense dramatic suspense. Each visit to the pharaoh accentuates the crisis. Each plague increases the gravity of the situation. Finally the pharaoh's stubborn hold on the Hebrew slaves breaks. In a moment of weakness, he permits them to leave, only to change his mind and send his warriors in hot pursuit. The denouement is reached when the Israelites are marvelously delivered from their pursuers as the waters of the Red Sea close in. Here is a story filled with powerful dramatic qualities that have stirred men's imaginations down through the centuries.

THE CONTEST WITH THE PHARAOH

Consider the "plot" of this drama. We have here a contest between two opposing powers: on the one side stand the stubborn pharaoh and his crafty magicians; on the other is Yahweh, "the God of the Hebrews," who is represented by Moses and Aaron. Yahweh's conflict is not with the gods of Egypt (they are mentioned only in 12:12), but with an arrogant pharaoh who presumptuously supposed that he was running history. This was not the boast of an ordinary

SLAVES MAKING BRICKS *for the Egyptian pharaoh are shown in a tomb painting from the period of the Eighteenth Dynasty. The clay is moistened by water drawn from the pool (left), kneaded with the aid of small hoes, and carried in baskets to the brickmakers, who shape it in rectangular moulds. After the bricks are laid out to dry in the sun (just right of the pool), they are carried away. Notice the two dark-skinned taskmasters who oversee the work. These scenes illumine the story of how the Hebrews made "bricks without straw" during their oppression in Egypt.*

mortal, however, for according to Egyptian religion the pharaoh was the em-
bodiment of deity and therefore he was believed to possess superhuman wisdom
and power.[1] Remember that at this time Rameses II had shifted his political
center to the Delta in order to be in a better position to control Egypt's Asiatic
empire. The building of the cities of Pithom and Rameses, both of which have
been excavated by archaeologists, was part of his grand political ambition.

The narrative presupposes that Yahweh was in complete control of the situation, for the whole earth belongs to him (Ex. 9:29). In the trial of strength,
Yahweh was so completely sovereign that the pharaoh is represented as wholly
under his power. Again and again it is said that Yahweh "hardened" the pharaoh's heart (e.g., 7:3). This statement must be balanced with others in which
it is asserted that the pharaoh hardened his own heart—that is, his obstinacy
was the result of his decision (8:15, 32; 9:34). The narrator's central purpose
was to tell the story in such a way as to glorify the God of Israel. Pharaoh was
given a lot of rope, as we would say, but he could not run beyond the bounds
of Yahweh's sovereign control (cf. Romans 9:17). The various "signs and wonders" were performed in order that men might know who really runs history:
"that you may know that I am Yahweh" (Ex. 10:2).

The Plagues against Egypt

The modern reader has many difficulties with the story of the plagues.
One question always comes to mind: How could all this have happened? And
his credulity is further strained by the repeated claim that none of the plagues
touched Israel in the land of Goshen, that Yahweh "made a distinction" between the Hebrews and the Egyptians (8:23; 11:7). We cannot go very deeply
into the question of miracles at this point, but we can suggest a few avenues
of approach.

Remember what has already been said about the motive for remembering

---

[1] Egyptian kings were regarded as the divine sons of the supreme god of Egypt, the sun-god
Re or Amon. A typical letter to a pharaoh begins: "To my king, my lord, my sun-god"
(see, for instance, Amarna Letter No. 288, in Pritchard, *Ancient Near Eastern Texts*, p. 488).

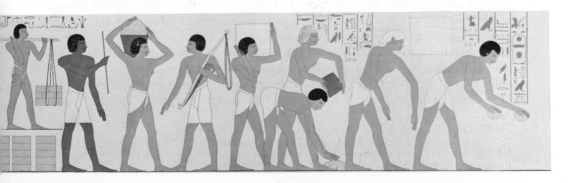

and writing down these traditions. The Israelites did not have our kind of historical curiosity. These narratives do not purport to be an objective photographic report of exactly what took place, devoid of all bias and interpretation. Rather, they testify to events as Israel experienced them, as they were interpreted within the community of faith. The supreme event to which the narratives bear witness, the redemptive action of God on behalf of slaves in bondage, belongs to a dimension of history with which modern men often are unwilling or unable to deal. The happenings could have been interpreted differently by others who stood outside the community of faith and who viewed them from a different stance or perspective. But for Israel the events were interpreted as the acts of Yahweh.

But having said all this, we need not jump to the conclusion that the whole account belongs to the realm of pure fancy or fiction. The action of God takes place within concrete situations and actual crises. Therefore, the biblical account must be taken seriously, although critically. The wisest course lies between a naive, unquestioning acceptance of the record just as it stands, and an equally dogmatic, wholesale rejection of the tradition as having no credibility. One scholar asserts that "none of these plagues, except the last, contains anything strange or abnormal; all are events which may naturally take place at the end of the inundation of the Nile." [2] This may be going too far, however, and it still leaves a major question unanswered: How do the events "which naturally take place at the end of the inundation of the Nile" come to signify the redemptive action of God?

The Nature of the Miracle Tradition

In dealing with the individual plague stories, there are several points that should be kept in mind. First, the narratives were written down several centuries after the time of Israel's sojourn in Egypt. Granting that Orientals have very retentive memories, and that the oral tradition of Israel is in many respects highly accurate, we still have to take into account the irregularities, inconsistencies, and folk elements that now appear in the narratives. The plague stories reflect an Egyptian locale and display a recollection of Egyptian life and manners, but they also show an interest in matters that properly belong in the category of folklore. An illustration is the rod of Moses, or the rod of Aaron. According to one passage (4:2-5), Moses cast his rod on the ground and it became a serpent. In another passage (7:8-13), Aaron did the same thing and with the same result. But neither action is treated as extraordinary, for the magicians of Egypt are said to have accomplished as much by their secret arts. "For every man cast down his rods and they become serpents" (7:12). These

---

[2] W. O. E. Oesterley and T. H. Robinson, *History of Israel* (Oxford, 1932), Vol. I, p. 85. See also J. L. Mihelic and G. E. Wright, "Plagues in Exodus" (*Interpreter's Dictionary* [11], III, pp. 822-824), who maintain that there is a natural basis for the first nine plagues, even though the tradition has been heightened in liturgical usage.

and similar features of the account have a meaningful place in the whole Exodus story, but taken by themselves they undoubtedly have their source in the reservoir of popular beliefs of the ancient Near East.

In the second place, there was a tendency to heighten the miraculous element as the tradition was retold through the generations to glorify Yahweh for his mighty acts. The account of the plagues (chaps. 7-12) received its final form in the circle of Jersualem priests (P) who edited the older tradition (J and E) and supplemented it with material of their own, as indicated in the following analysis.[3] In the older tradition of J, seven scourges are recounted; in the com-

THE PLAGUES AGAINST EGYPT

PLAGUES	OLDER TRADITION		P SUPPLEMENTS
	BASIC J ACCOUNT	E TOUCHES	
Introduction to the Account of the Plagues against Egypt 6:28-7:13			
1. Water to blood	7:14-18, 20 (from "in the sight of")-21 (to "from the Nile"), 23-25.	E elements in vss. 15, 17, 20 stress Moses' rod	7:19-20 (to "the Lord commanded"), 21 (from "and there was blood")-22.
2. Frogs	8:1-4, 8-15		8:5-7
3. Gnats			8:16-19
4. Flies	8:20-32		
5. Cattle plague	9:1-7		
6. Boils			9:8-12
7. Hail	9:13-35	E elements in vss. 22, 23, 24, 25, 35 stress Moses' rod	
8. Locusts	10:1-20, 24-26, 28-29	E elements in vss. 12, 13, 14, 15, 20	
9. Darkness (probably sandstorm)		10:21-23, 27	
10. Death of the firstborn	11:1-8	(11:1-3)	11:9-10
	12:21-23 (24-27) 12:29-39	Passover Legislation	12:1-20, 28 12:40-51

[3] This analysis represents a broad consensus of scholarship, although admittedly the E material is so fragmentary that doubts may be raised as to whether three sources are blended in the plague narratives. Martin Noth (*Exodus* [110], pp. 67-84) insists that only two literary strata, J and P, are present here.

pleted tradition of P the number is expanded to ten.[4] It is noteworthy too that in the older tradition Moses is the chief actor in the pharaoh's presence while Aaron, if he is mentioned at all, stands by silently. In the final priestly version of the story, however, Aaron—the great ancestor of the Jerusalem priests—always goes along and Moses negotiates with the pharaoh through this priestly spokesman. This view of the relation between Moses and Aaron is set forth in the P introduction to the plague stories (6:28-7:13).

The plagues in the J tradition are described with more restraint than in E and especially in P. For instance, the J account of the locust plague affirms that an east wind brought a cloud of locusts and, with a shift of wind, they were driven into the Red Sea. Farmers in Egypt and other parts of the world have often witnessed such a plague. Here the miracle is not the natural event itself but the fact that Moses predicted it and that it came at a particular time and with a particular meaning. The E and P traditions, however, show a tendency to heighten the miracles. In E there is greater stress on the wonder-working power of Moses' rod. In P, Moses is overshadowed by the priestly Aaron. Yahweh commands Moses: "Say to Aaron, 'Stretch out your rod. . . .'"; and Aaron wields the rod with the most marvelous results. (See, for instance, 8:16-19.)

Signs and Wonders

3

Third, in the Bible, miracle is something different from our conception of miracle as a disruption of natural law. As a matter of fact, the biblical writers had no conception of "nature" as a realm for which God has ordained laws. Rather, God himself sustains his creation, and his will is expressed in natural events, whether it be the coming of the spring rains or the birth of a child. Not that they believed the world to be capricious, however. There are regularities on which men may count—"seedtime and harvest, cold and heat, summer and winter, day and night" (Gen. 8:22)—but these are the expressions of God's faithfulness to his covenant. God is constantly active. His will is discernible in every event. There is a biblical truth behind Gilbert Chesterton's whimsical remark that the sun does not rise by natural law, but because God says: "Get up and do it again."

In the Exodus narratives the plagues are described as "signs and wonders." A sign may be defined as a visible evidence of the presence and purpose of God. The use of the word conflicts with our distinction between "natural" and "supernatural." In Exodus, everything that happens is a potential sign. It might be an ordinary event such as the coming of a plague of locusts, or some phenomenon connected with the overflow of the Nile. (Elsewhere the word "sign" is applied

---

[4] J. L. Mihelic and G. E. Wright (op. cit.) demonstrate that Psalm 78 in its rehearsal of the Exodus events follows the seven-plague tradition of J, and that Psalm 105 is apparently based on the completed P account of ten plagues.

to the rainbow, the heavenly bodies, the birth of a child, or a seeming coincidence in the day's affairs.) Or it may be an extraordinary event, a sensational wonder like the death of the firstborn in Egypt. (Other examples of this type are the restoring to health of a leprous hand, the turning of water into blood, the retreat of the sun's shadow on a dial.) This approach to the subject by no means answers all our questions, but it may lead us to ask the questions in a new way. Basic to Israel's faith is the conviction that God is not aloof from the world of daily affairs, or bound by an iron chain of cause-and-effect sequences. The Israelites had a sense of the immediacy of God's presence. They believed that any event—ordinary or extraordinary—could be a sign of his will and activity. To them an event was *wonder*-ful, or *sign*-ificant, not because it abrogated a natural law, but because it testified to God's presence and activity in their midst.

These signs were not proofs given to convince men once and for all that God is sovereign, however. The narratives of the Exodus show that their meaning was not self-evident to those who witnessed them. Whom did they really convince? We are told that the first two plagues (water to blood, the scourge of frogs) left the pharaoh unmoved because his magicians were able to perform the same feats (7:22; 8:7). Beyond that point, the Egyptian sorcerers could not go. Nevertheless, although the pharaoh was impressed by subsequent miracles, he was not so completely convinced that he was unwilling to change his mind. Furthermore, the Israelites, though they had witnessed the signs performed by Moses, did not believe him, "because of their broken spirit and cruel bondage" (6:9). Even after their successful escape across the Red Sea they murmured in disbelief and longed for the fleshpots of Egypt. So a miracle, in the biblical sense, is an indication of God's purposive activity, but never a final proof. God gives evidence of his presence and redemptive purpose, but in an ambiguous way that demands faith and trust.

Every reader of the Bible has to make up his mind about the historical nucleus which lies at the heart of the tradition that has been elaborated and colored by Israel's faith over a period of generations. Some miracles are more central to the Exodus story, more native to the Mosaic period, than others. Other aspects of the story are an artistic and imaginative expression of the conviction that Yahweh was active in history, delivering his people from servitude and calling them to serve his purpose. Since the whole account is interpretative, it is very difficult to separate sharply the central elements of the tradition from later accretions. Nevertheless, Israel's ancient faith undoubtedly was based on the experience of actual events which facilitated the escape of slaves from Egypt, events in which they perceived in moments of faith the work of God. The clearest historical evidence for this is found in the account of the crossing of the Red Sea. No event was fixed more firmly in Israel's memory.

THE VICTORY AT THE RED SEA

In the narrative of the book of Exodus, the crossing of the Red Sea is the climactic moment in a series of events springing from the last plague, the death of the firstborn of the Egyptians. Right in the midst of this tense crisis—between the announcement of Yahweh's intention (11:1-10) and the falling of the plague (12:29-32)—the narrator pauses to introduce the ancient feast of the Passover (see the table on p. 47 for the J and P versions).[5] Even before the period of Moses this rite was observed in the springtime at the first full moon by shepherds, perhaps just before setting out for spring pastures. The original purpose, still echoed faintly in the biblical account, was to secure the welfare and fertility of the flocks when the baby lambs and goats were being born, and to drive away evil spirits that were especially active at such a time. Accordingly, the blood of the sacrificed lamb was smeared on doorposts to keep away the Destroyer (specifically mentioned by J in 12:23!) and the meat was eaten during the nocturnal family festival. This primitive meaning, however, was superseded by a radically new understanding of the significance of the Passover. As a result of Moses' prophetic interpretation of the Exodus it became a time to remember that in the darkest hour Yahweh broke the pharaoh's yoke and graciously delivered his people.

> When your children say to you, "What do you mean by this service?" you shall say, "It is the sacrifice of Yahweh's passover, for he passed over the houses of the people of Israel in Egypt, when he slew the Egyptians but spared our houses."
>
> —EXODUS 12:26-27

The Route of the Exodus

So the people set out from Egypt in haste. According to the statement in Exodus 12:37, there were six hundred thousand men, in addition to women and children. This is obviously an exaggeration, for it does not square with the information in Exodus 1:15-20 that two midwives served the whole Hebrew colony. Needless to say, the Delta area could not have accommodated that many Hebrews, and the wilderness of southern Canaan could not have supported them. Undoubtedly the band of slaves was comparatively small. The record is correct, however, in stating that they were a motley group; not only the family of Joseph but "a mixed multitude" (12:38) representing Habiru of other origins. Indeed, it is historically inaccurate to speak of these people as "Israelites" at

---

[5] In Exodus 12 the Passover is now associated with the Feast of Unleavened Bread, an agricultural festival connected with the barley harvest. On the origin and significance of both feasts, see R. De Vaux, *Ancient Israel* [62], pp. 484-493.

was the pharaoh of the Exodus. This granite statue shows him wearing the distinctive royal helmet and holding the symbolic scepter. The little lady at his side is his wife.

this stage, although the narrative does so repeatedly. Only later, as they shared the experiences of the desert and remembered a common history, were they forged into a *community*, the people Israel.

The narrative expresses the belief that God himself was guiding their journey, taking an active part in the course of events. As their leader, he "went before" them. One tradition (J) expresses this conviction by saying that "Yahweh went before them by day in a pillar of cloud to lead them along the way, and by night in a pillar of fire to give them light" (13:21). Some scholars, in an attempt to rationalize this language, have conjectured that Sinai, toward which the people moved, was at that time an active volcano, whose eruptions produced a cloud in the daytime and a fiery glow at night. But this explanation hardly does justice to the description of the way the pillar of fire and of cloud moved about (see 14:19-20); so it is best to understand the fire and cloud as symbols of the divine presence.

One passage declares that the very route of escape was providential, for "when Pharaoh let the people go, God did not lead them by way of the land of the Philistines, although that was near" (13:17). The route referred to here is the main coastal highway leading up into Canaan through the coastland which, shortly after 1200 B.C., was invaded by the Philistines.[6] Since this was the main caravan and military highway, and was strongly fortified with Egyptian outposts, the Hebrews would not have had a chance on that road. Before they could face such hazards, the people needed to be unified and bound together through the experiences of the desert. So instead of a short cut, God's strategy called for a roundabout journey. "God led the people round about by the way of the wilderness toward the Red Sea" (13:18). In other words, they left the city of Rameses and struck out into the wilderness that today borders the Suez Canal.

The map opposite clearly shows that this route did not take them toward the Red Sea, which is a long way off. It has been suggested that they headed toward Lake Sirbonis, a lagoon which lies on the Mediterranean side of the coastal highway, but this view is difficult to square with the biblical narratives.[7] Rather, the route probably took them in the direction of the marshy area around Lake Timsah, a shallow extension of the Gulf of Suez. The Hebrew words that are usually translated "Red Sea" are *yam suph*. *Yam* means "sea"; *suph* means "reed, papyrus." Hence the words should be translated "Reed Sea," or 'Sea of Reeds," or "Papyrus Lake." The reference is to the reeds that grow around the body of water. A great deal of confusion was caused by the Greek translation of the Old Testament (Septuagint), which rendered the words "Red Sea," thus making the story of the crossing of the water much more of a problem than it actually is. For on the basis of the Hebrew text there is no need to suppose that the Hebrews crossed that large body of water, which has no reeds.

A Path Through the Waters

Realizing that the fugitives had escaped across the frontier, and that they would be "entangled in the land" and "shut in" by the wilderness (14:3), the pharaoh's charioteers raced to take their easy prey. The ensuing account

---

[6] Thus, strictly speaking, the expression "the way of the land of the Philistines" is anachronistic, since the Philistines did not occupy that area until almost a century after the time of Moses. This is evidence that the story, in its *literary* form, comes from a later period.

[7] For a discussion of the various possibilities for the crossing, see J. L. Mihelic's article "Red Sea" in *Interpreter's Dictionary* [11], IV, pp. 19-21.

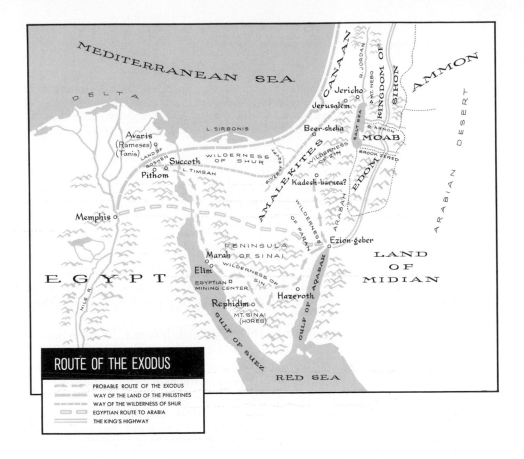

ROUTE OF THE EXODUS

- PROBABLE ROUTE OF THE EXODUS
- WAY OF THE LAND OF THE PHILISTINES
- WAY OF THE WILDERNESS OF SHUR
- EGYPTIAN ROUTE TO ARABIA
- THE KING'S HIGHWAY

of the cataclysm at the Reed Sea represents a blending of traditions and shows the same tendency to heighten the miracle that we have already noticed in the accounts of the plagues. The earliest tradition is approximately as follows:

Moses said to the people, "Fear not, stand firm, and see the salvation of Yahweh, which he will work for you today; for the Egyptians whom you see today, you shall never see again. Yahweh will fight for you, and you have only to be still" (14:13-14).

The pillar of cloud moved from before them and stood behind them, coming between the host of Egypt and the host of Israel. And there was the cloud and the darkness; and the night passed without one coming near the other all night (14:19b-20).

And Yahweh drove the sea back by a strong east wind all night, and made the sea dry land. [And the people of Israel went into the midst of the sea on dry ground.] And in the morning watch Yahweh in the pillar of fire and of cloud looked down upon the host of the Egyptians, and discomfited the host of the Egyptians, clogging their chariot wheels so that they drove heavily; and the Egyptians said, "Let us flee from before Israel; for Yahweh fights for them against the Egyptians" (14:21b to "dry land," 24-25).

And the Egyptians fled into it [the sea], and Yahweh routed the Egyptians in the midst of the sea. Thus Yahweh saved Israel that day from the hand of the Egyptians; and Israel saw the Egyptians dead upon the seashore. And Israel saw the great work which Yahweh did against the Egyptians, and the people feared Yahweh; and they believed in Yahweh and in his servant Moses (14:27b, 30-31).

This account is substantially that of J, the oldest literary tradition. One of the characteristics of this source is that Yahweh's action is represented in human terms (anthropomorphism). For instance, he "fights" for Israel, he "clogs" Egyptian chariot wheels. Notice that in this account the crossing of the Reed Sea, probably at the eastern shore of Lake Timsah, occurred when an east wind drove the waters back. This happening is not impossible in this marshy area where the waters are shallow; in fact, it has been witnessed at other times. The miracle was that it happened at a particular time and with a particular meaning. To Israel it was not a freak of nature, but a sign of the active presence of Yahweh in their midst, who summoned a power of the ordinary world (the wind) to serve his purpose.

The account has been considerably magnified, however, by other elements of tradition, E and P, which are closely blended with it. According to E, the waters were divided by the miraculous power of Moses' rod (14:16; see also verses 21a, 26, 27a); in the later P version the rod divided the waters so that they stood up like walls on both sides of the passage-way (14:22b)! These embellishments of the account show how the story was reworked by later generations as this memorable event was retold and rehearsed, especially during the celebration of the Passover (see, for instance, Ps. 78:13; 136:13-14).

A Holy Event

The narrative comes to a climax when it tells how Miriam, the sister of Moses and Aaron, took a tambourine and, while all the Israelite women followed her with music and dancing, sang an ecstatic hymn of praise to Yahweh:

Sing to Yahweh, for he has triumphed gloriously;
the horse and his rider he has thrown into the sea!
—EXODUS 15:21

This couplet is one of the oldest pieces of poetry in the Old Testament, and in all probability it originated during the very event it celebrates.[8] It is an eyewitness testimony to the meaning of the event that was experienced at the time. Israel experienced the occurrence as a "wonder"—an event that signified the redemptive activity of God on behalf of his people.

---

[8] The Song of Moses (15:1-18), which is a poetic elaboration of the theme of the Song of Miriam, arose in a later period, as shown by the reference to Israel's pilgrimage toward Canaan (verses 13-16) and the establishment of a central sanctuary (verse 17). It may date basically from the period of Joshua and the Judges or from the early monarchy (tenth century B.C.).

In view of the overwhelming significance of the Exodus in the biblical narratives, it may seem strange, at first glance, that the Egyptian records, so far as they are known, make no reference to Moses and the escape of the Hebrew fugitives from the pharaoh's power. We are reminded again that archaeology and the study of ancient history give, at best, only circumstantial evidence to support the credibility of the Israelite record. But the Egyptian silence is not really so strange. We would hardly expect the escape of a band of slaves to be mentioned in Egyptian records, when far more important things were happening. This border incident, which caused scarcely a ripple in Egyptian affairs, was not a memorable, history-making event in the experience of the Egyptians. Hence it was not recorded in their monuments. From their viewpoint, the decisive events were the wars and cultural achievements of the pharaohs of the Nineteenth Dynasty. But to the Israelites who participated in this event, and who passed on the story to their children, this was the most important news of the time. It was in the light of the meaning of this event that they described what was going on in Egypt. And in its light they understood the subsequent events of their history, as well as their prehistory in the patriarchal period.

THE COVENANT OF SINAI

So the Hebrews turned their backs on the land of Egypt and plunged into the trackless wilderness. According to the present arrangement of the narratives found in Exodus 15:22-19:2, they set out for the Wilderness of Sinai (see Plate 3) for Moses had been sent to bring the people out of Egypt so that they might serve God on the sacred mountain (see 3:12). The journey was difficult. Freedom in the desert was, to many of the pilgrims, a poor substitute for slavery in Egypt. Water was scarce; there was no food; existence was precarious. It is a tribute to the realism of the narrators that, instead of idealizing the past, they present life as it surely must have been. It was a time of murmuring, discontent, internal strife, rebellion against Moses, and, above all, lack of faith. Despite all that had happened, the people cried out: "Is Yahweh among us or not?" (17:7).

Divine Guidance in the Wilderness

In two ways the narratives emphasize the theme of God's guidance in the wilderness, a motif that recurs throughout the Old Testament. First, daily sustenance was providentially provided. Here, again, we encounter the question of miracle. Two illustrations are the stories about the manna and the quail (see 16:1-36). Both are familiar phenomena of the area. Manna probably refers to a sweet, sticky substance produced by a number of insects that suck the tender twigs of tamarisk bushes in the desert region of Sinai. This "honeydew excretion" falls to the ground where, in the hot desert air, the drops quickly evaporate, leaving a solid residue. During the day the sweet grains are carried off by ants, but overnight they accumulate, and thus early-risers can gather the substance for food. In the Arabic world *man* is still the name for these plant insects, and their honeydew, which is regarded as a great delicacy, is called "man essimma" or "manna from heaven." [9] As for the quails (16:13; compare Num. 11:31-34), flocks of them migrate over this region in the spring, and, when exhausted, are easily caught. Some modern readers might say that these occurrences showed how "lucky" the Hebrews were. In Israel's faith, however, these were signs of Yahweh's daily guidance, although they were never proofs that removed the possibility of doubt and murmuring.

In the second place, divine guidance was made known in the Hebrews' fierce struggle for survival against hostile desert tribes. Chief among these were the Amalekites, who claimed the desert oases in the Negeb, the southern wilderness of Canaan. The battle against the Amalekites (17:8-16) made a deep impression on the memory of the Hebrews and was the beginning of a long and bitter feud (see I Sam. 15). The story, which comes from the old tradition and which gives us our first glimpse of Joshua, shows fanciful features like the magic power of Moses' rod. But the fierce battle undoubtedly rests on an actual experience and was another event that sharpened the historical emphasis of Israel's faith. Out of this conception of holy war came the later prophetic demand for faith in Yahweh who alone gives the victory—a demand that found expression preeminently in the prophet Isaiah (see Is. 7:7-9).

Despite enemy attack, lack of food and water, and the murmurings of the people, the indomitable Moses led the pilgrims on until at last they staggered into the oasis of Sinai. Here they had an opportunity to reflect upon the experiences that had brought them together. Here they came to understand in a deeper way the nature of the community into which they had been called. The peculiar nature of this community is expressed in the covenant relationship between Yahweh and his people, and the laws and institutions by which this relationship was to be expressed. In Israel's faith, Sinai is pre-eminently the scene of the establishment of the covenant. True, the location of Sinai eventually was forgotten. But Israel's historians were interested not in geography, but in the covenant scene that was enacted in the wilderness after the exodus from Egypt.[10] For through the generations it became increasingly clear that the covenant was the basis of Israel's historical existence.

---

[9] F. S. Bodenheimer, "The Manna of Sinai," in *The Biblical Archaeologist*, X, No. 1 (Feb. 1947), pp. 2-6. Reprinted in *The Biblical Archaeologist Reader*, I [47], pp. 76-80.

[10] The traditional site of Sinai is Jebel Musa (Arabic for "Mount of Moses") on the Sinaitic Peninsula (see Plate 3)—a view defended in *Westminster Historical Atlas* [5], pp. 38-39. Other scholars theorize that the mountain was in a volcanic region of Arabia, east of the Gulf of Aqabah, or in the vicinity of Kadesh-barnea, the desert oasis where the Israelites encamped.

The Sinai Narratives

Before we turn to the covenant itself, let us look for a moment at the material which, in the present form of the Pentateuch, clusters around the revelation at Sinai. In the sequence of the narrative, the Israelites arrive at Sinai in Exodus 19:1; they do not break camp until Numbers 10:11. All the intervening material has Sinai as its locale. In other words, the last half of the book of Exodus, all the book of Leviticus, and the first ten chapters of the book of Numbers purport to set forth incidents and laws dealing with this period.

Much of the material in this long section belongs to the late P source, as evidenced by the priestly interest in the tabernacle, sacrifice, and various cultic regulations. All the book of Leviticus is priestly material, as are the first ten chapters of Numbers except 10:29-36 (JE). Of the Sinai material in Exodus, a good proportion belongs to P: chapters 25 through 31, and chapters 35 through 40. So by a process of reduction, most of the rest belongs to the older J and E sources (D is not found in the Pentateuch until Deuteronomy). After taking away P, the JE residue is chapters 19 through 24, and 32 through 34, speaking in general terms.

In isolating the P material we do not mean to imply that it has no historical value. Although this material was finally written down only in the period after the fall of the nation in 587 B.C., actually it preserves many ancient recollections. In dealing with biblical literature, the date of a writing is no sure index of the age of the traditions it records. This principle also holds for the J and E narratives. Though written down in the period of the monarchy, they not only reflect the interests of their day but also preserve material from earlier periods. Some of the JE material in the book of Exodus goes back to the time of Moses; some of it reflects Israel's life in the agricultural situation of Canaan—that is, the time of Joshua and later. Hence we shall refer to some of the Sinai material— for instance, some of the JE laws and the P material—later on when it is appropriate.

The Making of the Covenant

The story related in Exodus 1-24 deals with two series of episodes. The first is the deliverance from Egypt and its sequel, the guidance through the wilderness; the second is Yahweh's revelation at Sinai, his giving of the Law, and the making of the covenant. In the story as it has come down to us, these two series are inseparably related. The first is the preparation for the second (cf. 3:12); and the second is based theologically on the first. Hence in chapter 19, which begins with the notice that finally the people arrived at Sinai, we read that Yahweh had been carrying his people, just as an eagle lifts its young on its wings, toward this spot for a particular purpose. His people were not intended to be a crowd but a _community, bound to him_ and to one another by a covenant bond. Accordingly, Moses was commissioned to announce the nature of the covenant that Yahweh proposed to make:

> Thus you shall say to the house of Jacob, and tell the people of Israel: You have seen what I did to the Egyptians, and how I bore you on eagles' wings and brought you to myself. Now therefore, if you will obey my voice and keep my covenant, you shall be my own possession among all peoples; for all the earth is mine, and you shall be to me a kingdom of priests and a holy nation. These are the words which you shall speak to the children of Israel.
>
> —EXODUS 19:3-6 (_probably_ E)

This passage, which was probably shaped by catechetical usage, represents a mature theological reflection on the meaning of Israel's special calling (election). This calling is grounded on the event of the Exodus, which manifested God's action in delivering Israel from Egyptian bondage ("you have seen what I did"). But Yahweh's initiative evoked a response from the people. It placed them in a situation of decision, summoned them to a task within the divine purpose. What Moses had experienced earlier at Sinai—the call to take his part in Yahweh's historical plan—was experienced by all the people at the same sacred mountain, and with far-reaching implications for the future. Whether in fact these people would be the people of Yahweh depended upon a condition: "if you will obey my voice and keep my covenant." Then they would be Yahweh's personal "possession" (the Hebrew word means "private property"), the community that belongs to him in a special sense and whose vocation was to order its entire life according to his sovereign demands. Here we find a characteristic of Israel's faith that will engage our attention later on: the strange combination of the universal and the particular. Yahweh's sovereignty knows no boundaries, for "all the earth" is his. But from his many peoples he singles out one people, not for privilege but for a task. They are to be "a kingdom of priests"—that is, a community separated from the world and consecrated to the service of God (cf. I Peter 2:5, 9).[11]

After this theological introduction, the narrative describes the divine appearance (theophany) on Sinai, which was accompanied by the giving of the laws that were to be binding upon the covenant people (19:9-20:20). Some scholars

---

[11] The expression translated "kingdom of priests" is not altogether clear. It may express Israel's uniqueness—that is, her separation from the profane and her peculiar belonging to God; so William L. Moran, S.J., in _The Bible in Current Catholic Thought_, ed. by J. L. McKenzie S.J. (Herder and Herder, 1962), pp. 7-20. Or it may mean that Israel is "a kingdom set apart like a priesthood" for a special service; so R. B. Y. Scott in _Oudtestamentische Studien_ VIII, ed. by P. A. H. de Boer (Leiden: Brill, 1950), pp. 213-219. The verse seems to affirm that Israel's priestly role is to minister on behalf of the nations before Yahweh (cf. Gen. 12:3).

argue, on the basis of this passage, that Sinai was once a volcanic mountain or that the theophany was accompanied by a violent thunderstorm (see verses 16-19). It is more likely, however, that the traditional storm imagery of "earthquake, wind, and fire" (cf. I Kings 19:11-13) is used to describe the awesome holiness of God and the majesty of his coming to visit his people. It is significant that Israel adopted religious metaphors not from the quiet rhythms and beauties of nature, but from the violent storm that shakes the earth, overwhelming man with an awareness of the transcendence and holiness of God and a sense of the frailty and precariousness of human life (see Is. 2:12-22; Ps. 29).

The ceremony of the making of the covenant is described in the important twenty-fourth chapter of Exodus, in which elements of two traditions are blended together. According to one version (24:1-2, 9-11; probably J), the covenant is made effective in a sacred meal on top of the mountain. The participants in this summit ceremony are the representatives or "chief men" of Israel who, in addition to Moses, include the priestly Aaron and his two eldest sons (Ex. 6:23), and seventy elders. The statement "they beheld God, and ate and drank" suggests that during the covenant meal God was so vividly present that he could be seen in his heavenly majesty without his holiness causing harm (see Ex. 33:20; Is. 6:5).

According to the other tradition (verses 3-8; E), the whole assembly of Israel takes part in a covenant ceremony at the foot of the mountain. In this case the covenant is made effective by a sacrifice. Moses builds an altar and sets up twelve pillars to represent the people according to the twelve tribes. Animals are sacrificed, and half the blood is dashed against the altar, as a symbol of Yahweh's participation in the rite. The other half is put in basins, and Moses, acting as covenant mediator, reads to the people "the book of the covenant." When they pledge themselves to accept and obey Yahweh's demands, Moses dashes the blood upon the people, saying, "Behold the blood of the covenant which Yahweh has made with you in accordance with all these words."

As we see, these two traditions differ in regard to the ceremonial means of concluding the covenant. Sharing a common meal was one way to seal a covenant between men, as we know from the contract which Jacob and Laban made (see Gen. 31:46 and especially verse 54!). Moreover, the practice of making a covenant by a sacrifice was well known in ancient society. In the Mari tablets (see p. 23), a treaty or covenant alliance was consummated in the sacred rite of "killing the ass" (compare Gen. 15:7-21 and especially Jer. 34:18-19). Not exactly the same practice is described in the E tradition in Exodus 24, but we do find there the ancient belief that sacrificial blood has the sacramental power to bring together two parties in covenant. The belief in the efficacy of blood figures prominently in the theology of sacrifice in the Old Testament, and is further refined in the covenant theology of the New Testament, as can be seen from such a passage as I Corinthians 11:25.

However, even more important than the different views of the covenant ceremony are the divergent understandings of the covenant itself which each tradition presupposes. In one, the people are involved only through their representatives; in the other, the people take part directly. In one no stipulations seem to be imposed as part of the covenant-making ceremony;[12] in the other the covenant rite includes the reading of requirements in which the big "If" of Ex. 19:5 reverberates: "If you will obey my voice and keep my covenant. . . ." Both of these covenant conceptions were deeply rooted in Israel's history.[13] And since both were important for a full understanding of Yahweh's relationship with his people Israel, they are dovetailed together in Exodus 24.

COVENANT AND LAW

The covenant was made on the basis of "the words of Yahweh." In the present context, this phrase seems to refer to the whole body of law found in chapters 20-23—that is, it embraces the Ten Commandments (Ex. 20:1-17) and the Covenant Code (20:23-23:19). This section, however, includes laws of later ages that were added to the original covenant ceremony. The Pentateuch in its present form, with its great diversity, shows how successive generations continued to respond to Yahweh's covenant demand in the changing circumstances of their history. The priestly legislation found in Exodus 25-31, as we have said, bears the stamp of later times. The Covenant Code, for the most part, betrays the interests of an agricultural rather than a wilderness environment, as we shall see in the next chapter. And the group of ritual laws in Exodus 34:10-28 reflects a Canaanite background. So, by a process of reduction, not much is left that may have come from the time of Moses.

Does all this mean that no laws were transmitted from the Mosaic period, but only a sense of absolute responsibility to the will of God that had to be spelled out in detail later on? Some scholars have answered this question with an affirmative. But on the basis of recent studies of the form and content of laws in the Pentateuch, we can affirm with a high degree of probability that the Jewish tradition which traces the law back to Moses has a solid basis in historical fact.

Two general types of law are found in the Pentateuch: conditional (or case) law, and absolute (or apodictic) law.[14] Conditional law has a characteristic formula: if *this* happens, then *that* will be the legal consequence. Each case includes numerous conditions. Conditional law was found throughout the an-

---

[12] In the present sequence of the narratives the J covenant law is introduced in 34:10-28.

[13] See Murray L. Newman, Jr., *The People of the Covenant* [109], who traces the two covenant traditions back into the period of Israel's sojourn in the wilderness at Kadesh-barnea.

[14] This distinction was made by Albrecht Alt in his important study of the form and history of Israelite law: *Die Ursprünge des israelitischen Rechts* (1934); reprinted in his *Kleine Schriften zur Geschichte des Volkes Israel*, I (Munich: C. H. Beck, 1959), pp. 278-332. (See the announced translation, *Essays on Old Testament History and Religion.*)

cient world, and is best represented in the Code of Hammurabi. Absolute law, on the other hand, has no "ifs" or "buts" about it. It is unconditional; it is stated in sharp, terse language. The difference between the two types of law may be seen at a glance by comparing the casuistry of the law about buying a Hebrew slave (Ex. 21:2-6) with the staccato command: "Whoever curses his father or his mother shall be put to death" (Ex. 21:17). Absolute law seems to be more characteristically Israelite, and expresses the unconditional demands of the covenant. In all probability, law of this type goes back to the wilderness period.

In the light of this analysis, there is good reason to believe that the Ten Commandments in Exodus 20:1-17 come from Moses. In Hebrew they are called "the Ten Words." Several of the commandments are expressed in two or three words, and others, though they are much longer in their present form, undoubtedly have been expanded in the process of being handed on. It is probable that originally all Ten Commandments were terse, absolute demands of the apodictic type mentioned above. Here is one possible reconstruction of the original Decalogue: [15]

> God spoke all these words: I am Yahweh your God, who brought you forth out of the land of Egypt, out of the house of slaves.
>
> 1. You shall have no other gods before me.
> 2. You shall not make for me any graven images or any likeness.
> 3. You shall not invoke the Name of Yahweh your God in vain.
> 4. Remember the Sabbath day to keep it holy.
> 5. Honor your father and your mother.
> 6. You shall not commit murder.
> 7. You shall not commit adultery.
> 8. You shall not steal.
> 9. You shall not bear false witness against your neighbor.
> 10. You shall not covet your neighbor's house.

The Motive of Obligation

The Law, then, was the form that was used for expressing the covenant bond. New light has been thrown on the relationship between covenant and law by a study of international treaties of the late second millennium B.C., found chiefly in Hittite archives.[16] On the basis of an analysis of the form and content of these treaties, scholars distinguish two types of covenants: parity and suze-

---

[15] See James Muilenburg, "The History of the Religion of Israel," *Interpreter's Bible*, Vol. 1, p. 303.

[16] George E. Mendenhall, *Law and Covenant in Israel and the Ancient Near East* [108]. See also his more recent article on "Covenant" in the *Interpreter's Dictionary* [11]. Other important studies on the treaty or covenant form are: Klaus Baltzer, *Das Bundesformular* [103], and Dennis J. McCarthy, S.J., *Treaty and Covenant* [107].

rainty. A parity covenant is reciprocal—that is, both parties bind themselves to each other by bilateral obligations. The suzerainty covenant, on the other hand, is more unilateral, for it is made between a king and his vassal. To his vassal, the suzerain "gives" a covenant, and within the covenant the vassal finds protection and security. As the inferior party, the vassal is under obligation to obey the commands issued by the suzerain, for the suzerain's words are spoken with the majesty and authority of the covenant author. To make a covenant in no way infringes upon the sovereignty of the great king. And yet the covenant is not just an assertion of power over his inferior, as though the vassal were forced into obedience. The most striking aspect of the suzerainty covenant is the great attention given to the king's deeds of benevolence on behalf of the vassal. The vassal's motive for obligation is that of gratitude for what has been done for him. Appropriately, the covenant form begins with a preamble in which the author of the covenant identifies himself, "thus saith the great king so-and-so." Then comes a historical prologue which recounts the king's past gracious acts on behalf of the vassal.

This political form, familiar no doubt in the time of Moses, provided an analogy in terms of which Israel expressed her covenant faith. The Sinai covenant was in no sense a parity contract in which both parties were equal and mutually dependent. It was a relationship between unequals, between God and man; and the holiness and majesty of God are portrayed in the account of the awesome thunder and lightning before which the people stood back in fear. The covenant was *given* by God; the relationship was conferred upon the people by their sovereign. Yahweh was not legally bound to Israel, for his sovereignty was not limited by the covenant. He had freely initiated the relationship and, as later prophets said, he was free to terminate it. But the Exodus story (Ex. 1-15) puts the emphasis on what Yahweh had done on Israel's behalf, upon his "mighty acts" of deliverance. Therefore Israel's pledge of obedience, as expressed in the covenant ceremony, was based on gratitude for Yahweh's marvelous goodness, on the realization that her whole life was dependent upon his sovereign grace and promise. This gratitude and trust found expression in every celebration of the Passover Feast. Israel was beholden to Yahweh. Such was the character of the relationship between Lord and servant expressed in the Sinai covenant. It is significant that the unconditional obligations of the Ten Commandments are prefaced with a brief historical prologue: "I am Yahweh your God, who brought you out of the land of Egypt, out of the house of bondage" (20:2). Thus the Law was preceded by Israel's gospel—the "good news" of what God had done.

These form-critical studies have helped us to understand the Mosaic covenant more clearly. Sometimes the question is raised as to whether the sequence of "gospel and law" resulted from *editorial arrangement* of the traditions, perhaps under the influence of the suzerainty treaty form, or whether the connection was rooted in *the people's historical memory* that Sinai really did come after the Exodus. Admittedly, there is some reason for supposing that the former is the case: the connection seems purely formal. Surprisingly, in Israel's early confessions of faith (e.g., Deut. 26:5-9), mention of the Sinai covenant is conspicuously absent. These epitomes of the sacred history concentrate on the beginnings of the patriarchal history, the deliverance from Egyptian oppression, and the entrance into the promised land. Hence some scholars interpret the silence regarding Sinai to mean that originally the Exodus story and the Sinai story were separate traditions, based on events experienced by different groups. When these groups came together into the larger Israelite community they pooled their traditions and eventually, through the creative artistry of the author known as J (the Yahwist), the Sinai covenant material was neatly inserted into the heart of the expanded sacred history.[17] But arguments from silence are notoriously fragile. Probably the Sinai covenant is missing from early confessional summaries for the simple reason that it was not one of Yahweh's mighty acts but rather Israel's *response* to that action,[18] just as the Eucharist (Lord's Supper) is not included in the Christian confession because it is the occasion for responding in gratitude to God's gracious action in Christ.[19] Despite the problems which the biblical traditions present, there is good ground for affirming that the sequence of gospel and law is historically correct: the Sinai covenant actually took place *after* the Exodus in the experience of a single group of people. In the light of Moses' prophetic interpretation, the people accepted the obligations of the covenant in gratitude for what Yahweh had already done on their behalf.

SUMMARY: THE MOSAIC FAITH

Beyond this point, our story in Exodus tells of the people's continuing lack of faith, as illustrated in the dramatic story of the making of the Golden Calf (Ex. 32).[20] For a time it seemed that all hope for the future was lost; for how could Yahweh accompany such a sinful people without his holiness becoming a consuming fire? Yet Moses, the covenant mediator, interceded for the people and received the assurance that Yahweh's name (nature) means that he is gracious to whom he will be gracious (33:19). In this context there appears for the first time a great confession of faith which is echoed in various parts of the Old Testament:

---

[17] This view has been set forth by Gerhard von Rad in his essay on the form-critical problem of the Hexateuch [100]; see also his commentary on *Genesis* [133], pp. 13-23. The view is accepted with modifications by Martin Noth; see his *History of Israel* [44], pp. 126-137.

[18] This point has been emphasized by Artur Weiser, *The Old Testament* [30], pp. 83-99, and has been further strengthened by Herbert H. Huffmon in "The Exodus, Sinai and the Credo" [106]. Walter Beyerlin also gives strong arguments for the common origin of the Sinai and Exodus traditions in his study of the Sinaitic traditions [104].

[19] This comparison is made by John Bright, *Early Israel* [41], p. 105.

[20] After chap. 24 of Exodus the old JE traditions are found only in chaps. 32-34. The rest (chaps. 25-31 and 35-40) is P material dealing with the tabernacle and various cultic arrangements. See the later discussion in Chapter 12 (pp. 380-393).

> Yahweh, Yahweh, a God merciful and gracious, slow to anger, and abounding in steadfast love and faithfulness, keeping steadfast love for thousands, forgiving iniquity and transgression and sin, but who will by no means clear the guilty, visiting the iniquity of the fathers upon the children and the children's children, to the third and the fourth generation.
>
> —EXODUS 34:6-7

These narratives in Exodus 32-34 are marked by a sober realism. They show that Israel could not claim to be *better* than other nations, either morally or religiously, for the people displayed the same weakness and strength that are found in the life of any people. If there was any difference, it lay in the extraordinary experience that had formed them into a community and the destiny to which they were called in the service of God. Moses is represented as saying: "Is it not in thy going with us, so that we are distinct, I and thy people, from all other people that are upon the face of the earth?" (Ex. 33:16). It was with the conviction that Yahweh, their Leader, was going before them that the people faced the future.

Let us summarize briefly the main aspects of the Mosaic faith. First, as the preface to the Ten Commandments states, Yahweh is pre-eminently the God of history. This conviction represented a radical break from the polytheism of the surrounding world. In the religions of the Fertile Crescent, the gods were primarily personifications of nature, and the purpose of religion was to establish a proper relationship with nature gods through various forms of ritual and myth (of which more later). Israel, however, believed that the depth of life's meaning was laid bare in a decisive event, the Exodus, and the series of events that it initiated. To be sure, Yahweh was Lord of nature. His theophany could be described in the thunder and lightning bursting over Sinai; he could command the wind to drive back the waters of the Reed Sea; he could bring plagues to remind men that "all the earth is mine." But Yahweh himself was no natural power. Rather, Israel affirmed that Yahweh could use the powers of nature to accomplish his purpose in history: to humiliate the pharaoh, to help his people escape from Egypt, to guide and sustain them in the wilderness. History is the theater of his revelation and activity.

Secondly, Israel believed that in these extraordinary events Yahweh had taken the initiative in establishing a close relationship between himself and his people. The narratives never suggest that the distance between God and man is removed. Even Moses, through whose mediation Yahweh spoke to the people, was warned that he could not see Yahweh's face ("for man shall not see me and live") and therefore was allowed only to see his "back"—a human figure of speech which emphasizes that God himself remains hidden from sight even though he makes enough of himself known to confirm the reality of his active presence (33:17-23). But Israel believed firmly that God was also near and that he had invited them into a covenant relationship. The relation of Israel to

Yahweh was not that of a slave but that of a "first-born son" (4:22-23) who had been graciously redeemed by Yahweh. Gratitude for this deliverance was the primary motive for Israel's response of faith. And that faith took the form of obedience to Yahweh's Law and of living by the promise that he would go with them into the future. The covenant relationship was the basis of the Israelite community.

Finally, for Israel there was to be only one God—Yahweh. The first command of the Mosaic Decalogue says categorically: "You shall have no other gods before [or besides] me"; and the second command asserts that Yahweh is not to be worshiped in the form of any image or likeness. If the First Commandment implies that other gods exist, they were not to claim Israel's allegiance and they paled into insignificance before the glory of Yahweh. As we have seen, the contrast in the Exodus drama is between Yahweh and the pharaoh—not between Yahweh and the gods of Egypt. Yahweh alone controls the events of history and the powers of nature. Moreover, in Israel's faith Yahweh is not part of a pantheon, he has no female consort, and no image could be made of him. All this stands in contrast to the polytheism and idol worship of the ancient world.

The question is often raised as to whether Mosaic religion was monotheistic —that is, whether it affirmed belief in only one God. It is doubtful whether the question should be put in this way, since it assumes a degree of intellectual sophistication which is alien to Israel's ancient faith. Instead of raising the abstract question as to whether other gods existed, Israel heard the command that it was forbidden for other gods to lay claim on her allegiance. The commandment does not say, "There are no other gods," but "You shall have no other gods." [21] The covenant ceremony itself was an invitation to decision: to serve Yahweh or not. There is not the slightest hint that the people were generously allowed to straddle the fence: to serve Yahweh *and* some other god of their preference. It was either-or. Yahweh made a complete, absolute claim upon Israel's devotion. Hence the earliest way of expressing Israel's sense of divine sovereignty was in terms of Yahweh's "jealousy." Yahweh's name is Jealous, we are told (Ex. 34:14). This is a figurative expression of the truth of the First Commandment: Yahweh makes an unconditional demand upon the loyalty of his people. As we shall see in subsequent chapters, this religious demand was put to the test when the Israelites settled down in Canaan and faced the temptation of serving other loyalties (see 34:11-16).

A stream, we say, never rises higher than its source. This proverb may be applied to the source of Israel's faith in the Mosaic period. In subsequent periods the stream widened, its channel was deepened, its flow was interrupted by many cataracts. But Israel's greatest moments of worship and prophetic insight were regarded as a return to the source: the Exodus and the covenant of Sinai.

---

[21] See Martin Buber, *The Prophetic Faith* [118], pp. 19-23.

THE

PROMISED

LAND

CHAPTER THREE   The struggle for land has always been

one of the most powerful drives in national history. This is

obviously true, for instance, in the case of the United States.

In story and song, Americans rehearse the stirring epic of

immigrants who landed on the Atlantic seaboard and, at the

cost of great hardship and often fierce warfare, pushed the

frontier to the shores of the Pacific. Jokingly we say that

the early settlers first fell on their knees, then on the abo-

Biblical readings: The reader should turn to the account of Israel's
sojourn in the wilderness and the march through Transjordan, found in
Numbers 11 through 14, and 18 through 24 (JE narratives in the
main). Also the narrative of the conquest in Joshua 1-12 and the account of the Shechem assembly in Joshua 24.

rigines. But in more serious moments Americans affirm that, despite the sordid aspects of injustice and violence, the hand of God was guiding the destiny of the new nation.

From earliest times the Fertile Crescent was the scene of a fierce struggle for land. As we have seen, this coveted area periodically was invaded by peoples from Arabia, Asia Minor, the Caucasian highlands, or Egypt—peoples who sought a strip of the good earth to call their own or who fought to expand their territory, at the expense of others. Palestine was, by virtue of its geographical location, inevitably drawn into the incessant conflict. This little country was the place where small nations rudely and brutally fought for *Lebensraum*, or "living space," and where big nations fought their wars of empire.

Into this dynamic arena came the Hebrews. Like other Habiru in the ancient world, they were at first a landless people. They belonged to the floating population, the unsettled elements of society. But these wanderers were seeking a land, in order that they might participate fully in society and fulfill their historical destiny. Their struggle to obtain land entailed much suffering and bloodshed, and the slaughter of many Canaanite natives. But it was their firm conviction that Yahweh, their God, was with them in the rough-and-tumble of the conflict, leading them victoriously into the land.

A LAND FLOWING WITH MILK AND HONEY

According to the ancient liturgy preserved in Deuteronomy 26:5-10 (see above, p. 10), the worshiper offers the first fruits of the harvest in grateful acknowledgment that Yahweh had given Israel the land. Confessing that Yahweh delivered Israel from slavery in Egypt, the worshiper affirms that "he [Yahweh] brought us to this place, and gave us this land, a land flowing with milk and honey." Anyone who has been in Palestine, and has been impressed with the abundance of rocks on every hand, may wonder at the extravagant description of the "land flowing with milk and honey." According to the ancient view, milk and honey in abundance were blessings of Paradise. To wanderers who were used to life in the barren wilderness, Canaan was a veritable paradise (see Deut. 8:7-10). It was therefore with deep gratitude that they affirmed: "Yahweh brought us to this place."

Since the liturgy was connected with a harvest festival, it is clear that it dates from a time after Israel had settled in Canaan and had made the transition to agriculture. Some scholars believe that the promise of land had been an aspect of "the faith of the fathers"—that is, religion of the patriarchs (see above, pp. 28-30). It is quite clear that the Hexateuch in its present form gives great emphasis to this theme in the stories of the patriarchs. According to Genesis 12:7, Yahweh said to Abram, "To your descendants I will give this land." This promise was reaffirmed to Isaac and Jacob, and was renewed in the time of Moses.

Hence Canaan is known as "the Promised Land." We must keep in mind, however, that the traditions of the patriarchal period were written down after the conquest of Canaan was an accomplished fact. Whatever the promise of the land meant in the patriarchal period, it was understood more clearly later on, when the traditions were recast in the light of Yahweh's revelation in the event of the Exodus.

It is significant that this liturgy—which we have described previously as "the Hexateuch in miniature"—comes to a climax with the affirmation about Yahweh's gift of the land. This is understood to be the high point in the rehearsal of Israel's sacred history. As such, it is given great prominence in the whole Hexateuch, especially Joshua, which deals with the conquest of Canaan. True, this theme is colored by Israelite nationalism, which accounts in part for its important place in the Hexateuch. But it is noteworthy that even the great prophets, who vigorously attacked Israel's proud nationalism, did not surrender the conviction that the gift of the land was the supreme sign of Yahweh's benevolence and grace toward his people. Amos (2:10), Hosea (chapter 2), and Jeremiah (3:19) all emphasized the gift of the land. And the book of Deuteronomy, which is a sermon about life in the Promised Land, describes the land of Canaan as Israel's "inheritance," received from Yahweh.

Considering the terrible suffering involved in the conquest of Canaan, especially for the defeated people, it is difficult for most of us to understand the Israelite conviction that God was actually taking part in the struggle. Yahweh is seemingly portrayed as a God of holy war who ruthlessly demands the *hérem* —the wholesale destruction of Israel's enemies as a sacrifice to him. The book of Joshua bristles with theological difficulties, many of which were removed or refined by Israel's prophetic movement, as we shall see. On the other hand, Israel's faith is not founded upon a conception of a God who is aloof from the human struggle. Rather it rests upon a response to the God who is active within the human struggle, guiding and shaping the course of human affairs according to his sovereign purpose. In Israel's experience the conquest of Canaan did not happen by accident of circumstance or by the assertion of superior human power. It occurred within the providence of God. Therefore, the land was not a possession to boast about, but a gift to be received with humility and gratitude (Josh. 24:13).

With this preparation, let us turn our attention to the narratives that deal with Israel's sojourn in the wilderness, her designs to invade Canaan, and the long circuit around through the countries of Transjordan. In general terms, this period of Israel's history is covered by the books of Numbers (from 10:11 on), Deuteronomy, and Joshua. Fortunately, it is not necessary to read through all this material at this stage of our study. A great deal of priestly material (P) is found in the latter half of the book of Numbers, and possibly the book of Joshua, and we shall defer treatment of it to a later chapter (see Chapter 12).

Moreover, the book of Deuteronomy, which purports to be a sermon given by Moses on the eve of the invasion of Canaan, belongs to the D tradition, which was written down in the period just before and after the fall of the nation in 587 B.C., and will be considered later on (Chapter 10). We are left, then, with the JE tradition of the book of Numbers (found mainly in chaps. 11-14 and 21-24), and the story of the conquest in the book of Joshua.

FORTY YEARS OF WANDERING

According to the tradition, Israel spent forty years wandering in the wilderness south of Beer-sheba. But we must not take this figure as being mathematically exact. The number forty is often a stylized expression for a full generation and sometimes it means only "a long time," as in the statement that Elijah journeyed into the wilderness forty days and forty nights (I Kings 19:8), or the tradition that Jesus fasted in the wilderness for the same period of time (Mk. 1:13). Nevertheless, the statement is probably approximately right here. We are told that none of the adults who left Egypt were permitted to enter into Canaan; all of them died during the sojourn in the wilderness (Num. 14:26-35; 26:63-65). It was a new generation, under the leadership of Joshua, that was privileged to set eyes on Canaan.

The Sojourn at Kadesh

The narratives of the Pentateuch in their present form concentrate on the sojourn at Mount Sinai. As we have seen, the Israelites arrive at Sinai in Exodus 19:1 and break camp in Numbers 10:11. All the intervening material deals with the laws and institutions—given at Sinai—by which the covenant people are to live. But the Israelites undoubtedly spent the greater part of their wilderness sojourn at a desert oasis known as Kadesh-barnea, located in the barren Negeb about fifty miles south of Beer-sheba (Num. 13:26; cf. 12:16 "Wilderness of Paran"). Many of the traditions concerning the wilderness sojourn have their original setting at Kadesh, which presumably was not far from Sinai. This is especially true of the material found in Numbers 11-20, much of which comes from the JE tradition (with the exception of chapters 15, 17, 18, 19, which come entirely from P).

In these chapters we find a renewal of the theme that, in spite of the providence of Yahweh, the people continued to murmur and, on occasion, to rebel against the leadership of Moses. The desert fare of manna was not good enough for them, for they remembered too well "the fish we ate in Egypt for nothing, the cucumbers, the melons, the leeks, the onions, and the garlic" (Num. 11:4-6). Dissension broke out in Moses' own tribe, the tribe of Levi, over his leadership.

The revolt was instigated by his own brother and sister, Aaron and Miriam (Num. 12). It was renewed on a larger scale by a certain Korah, who stirred up factional strife among the Levites, and also by Dathan and Abiram, who aroused other tribesmen against Moses (Num. 16). Not too much is known about the years of Israel's sojourn at Kadesh and vicinity, but the tradition affords vivid glimpses of how the people were forged together into greater unity and solidarity through bitter struggle and suffering.[1]

It is apparent, then, that the "rabble" (Num. 11:4) under Moses' leadership did not become a stable, unified community overnight. A powerful centripetal force, the redemptive action of Yahweh, had pulled them toward the center of a common covenant allegiance. But there were also powerful centrifugal forces that pulled away from that center: human factors such as tribal rivalry, power struggles for leadership, hunger and thirst, and the human incapacity for faith. At the oasis of Kadesh-barnea these two forces came into sharp conflict. Humanly speaking, there is every reason to expect that the covenant bond would have dissolved in the disruptive tensions of the wilderness. But as Israel looked back on the desert experience in the perspective of the covenant faith, it became clear—much clearer, no doubt, than in the wilderness days—that through these trials Yahweh was uniting and disciplining his people for the historical task that lay ahead of them. A later discourse forcefully affirms this truth:

---

[1] On "controversy at Kadesh" see Murray L. Newman, *The People of the Covenant* [109], chap. 3.

THE OASIS OF 'AIN EL-QUDEIRAT *which, in the judgment of some scholars, is the location of Kadesh-barnea, where the Israelites settled for a long time during their wilderness sojourn. The spring pictured here is one of three in the area, all of which the Israelites may have used.*

You shall remember all the way which Yahweh your God has led you these forty years in the wilderness, that he might humble you, testing you to know what was in your heart, whether you would keep his commandments, or not. And he humbled you and let you hunger and fed you with manna, which you did not know, nor did your fathers know; that he might make you know that man does not live by bread alone, but that man lives by everything that proceeds out of the mouth of Yahweh.

–DEUTERONOMY 8:2-3

The Holy One in the Midst of Israel

According to ancient tradition, Yahweh's presence in the midst of Israel was evidenced by two sacred objects. One was the Tent of Meeting, first mentioned in connection with the sojourn at Sinai (Ex. 33:7-11) and later in connection with Kadesh and the wilderness (Num. 11:16-17, 24-26; 12:14; cf. Deut. 31:14-15). The P tradition also gives an elaborate description of this tent or "tabernacle" in Exodus 26-27 and 35-38. Not all of P's description fits the ancient wilderness situation; a great deal of it reflects later theological and cultic development. However, the P account undoubtedly preserves authentic reminiscences of the ancient desert sanctuary, which must have been something like the red leather tent-shrines known among ancient Semites.[2] We are told that Moses pitched the Tent outside the camp and that he used to go there to encounter Yahweh, who would descend from heaven in a pillar of cloud to the door of the tent and speak with him "face to face, as a man speaks to his friend" (Ex. 33:11). The Tent was the place of "meeting" with Yahweh, where an oracle could be sought or where Yahweh's word could be proclaimed to assembled Israel. Those who had difficult problems would go out to the Tent and Moses would bring their petitions before Yahweh. In this way, we may imagine, the covenant law was expounded and expanded.

The other sacred object was the Ark of the Covenant, which P describes in Exodus 25:10-22 and 37:1-9, probably in dependence upon ancient tradition. Originally, the Ark seems to have been a portable throne on which, Israel believed, Yahweh was invisibly enthroned. As we said in the previous chapter, Mosaic religion strictly vetoed the worship of Yahweh in the form of a visible image. In this respect, the religion of Israel differed radically from the religions of other ancient peoples, who represented the deity's presence by setting up his image in a temple or bearing his statue in festival processions. Nevertheless, it was firmly believed that the holy God of Israel was invisibly present in the midst of his people. In times of wandering or of battle he went before them in person as their leader, enthroned upon the Ark. One of the oldest fragments of the Pentateuch is the "Song of the Ark":

[2] See Frank M. Cross, Jr., "The Tabernacle," in *The Biblical Archaeologist*, X, No. 3 (Sept., 1947). Reprinted in *The Biblical Archaeologist Reader*, I [47], pp. 201-228.

> Whenever the ark set out, Moses said, "Arise, O Yahweh, and let
> thy enemies be scattered; and let them that hate thee flee before
> thee." And when it rested, he said, "Return, O Yahweh, to the ten
> thousand thousands of Israel."
>
> —NUMBERS 10:35-36

Undoubtedly, at Kadesh Israel borrowed patterns of worship and legal admin-
istrations from others—for instance, the Midianites (see Ex. 18:13-27). Sacred
objects like the Tent and the Ark were found among other peoples of antiquity.
Under Moses' interpretation, however, they came to express the distinctive faith
of Israel. Yahweh was worshiped as the transcendent God who dwells in heaven
and who also, without any limitation upon his sovereignty, is present in the
midst of his people as their leader. It is likely that very early these two cultic
objects were separated from one another, each becoming the focal point of a
particular understanding of Yahweh's relation to his people. The Tent seems
to have represented a theology of "manifestation" (the transcendent God manifests himself to Israel); the Ark apparently was associated with a theology of
"presence" (Yahweh is present with his people).[3] Moreover, the Tent apparently became the shrine of a southern group (especially the tribe of Judah),
whereas the Ark came to be identified with a northern group, particularly the
Joseph tribes that Joshua led into Canaan.[4] Later on, probably during David's
time, these two objects were reunited; hence priestly tradition, which reflects
the new situation under David and Solomon, could affirm that the Ark rested
inside the tabernacle at Sinai (Ex. 40:2-3).

A Foolhardy Attack on Canaan

Eventually, the hardships of the desert and the lack of living space
compelled the Israelites to look elsewhere for a home. So a group of spies was
sent out from the Kadesh base to survey the hill country of Canaan in the
vicinity of Hebron, which lay directly north (Num. 13 and 14). This recon-
naissance force brought back the report that the land was fertile, indeed that
it was "a land flowing with milk and honey." However, the scouts also reported
that the land was strongly fortified and that the inhabitants were men of such
great stature that "we seemed to ourselves like grasshoppers, and so we seemed
to them" (Num. 13:32-33). A sharp division of opinion arose over whether the
Israelites should try to enter Canaan from the south. Two of the spies, Joshua
and Caleb, were in favor of making the attack in spite of the odds against them,
but the majority of the people were so discouraged that they proposed finding
a leader to guide them back to Egypt. Finally, believing that an adventurous

---

[3] This is the interpretation of Gerhard von Rad, *Old Testament Theology* [80], pp. 234-241.
[4] Murray Newman associates two different covenant theologies with the Tent and the Ark
respectively and traces the separation of these cultic shrines to a major controversy at Kadesh
(*op. cit.*, especially pp. 55-71).

attack was preferable to wandering for a lifetime in the wilderness, they decided to make the attempt. The foolhardy move lacked divine sanction, for the Ark of the Covenant and Moses remained at Kadesh. The result was what might be expected. The Israelites were decisively repulsed by the Amalekites of the Negeb and by the Canaanites of the hill country (Num. 14:39-45).

Since Israel was too weak to break past the fortress guarding the southern approach to Canaan, she had to seek another way to escape from the wilderness. There was only one other route: a long circuit through the country of Transjordan.

DETOUR VIA TRANSJORDAN

The rest of the book of Numbers deals with Israel's advance through Transjordan in order to make an attack on Canaan from the east. This route, too, was beset with many hazards, for Transjordan was occupied by several small kingdoms which resented the appearance of a band of armed intruders. A glance at the map (p. 85) will reveal the tactical problems Israel had to face. Just south of the Dead Sea, and directly opposite Kadesh-barnea, was the kingdom of Edom, traditionally related to Israel through Esau, the twin brother of Jacob (Gen. 36). Just above Edom lay the kingdom of Moab, with the river Arnon as its northern frontier and the brook Zered as its southern frontier. Above Moab was the Amorite kingdom of Sihon, bounded by the river Jabbok to the north and the river Arnon to the south. And to the east of this kingdom lay the kingdom of Ammon. According to tradition, Moab and Ammon were distant relatives of the Israelites through Lot, the nephew of Abraham (Gen. 19:30-38). In other words, other Habiru groups had already made the transition from semi-nomadic life to sedentary culture and had succeeded in establishing themselves in this area some time before the Hebrews under Moses' leadership had found a homeland.

Disputes over Thoroughfare

Modern archaeology has thrown light on the date of the Israelites' passage through Transjordan. During 1932-1943, archaeological surveys suggested that the petty kingdoms of this area were founded in the thirteenth century B.C.[5] For about 500 years before that time, if this archaeological inference is right, there were only nomadic groups there. Had the Israelites tried to make a circuit through Transjordan before the thirteenth century, they would not have encountered resistance from the organized states of Edom, Moab, and Ammon. If, on the other hand, the Exodus took place around the turn of the thirteenth century, as we have suggested, and if the Israelites spent at least a

[5] See Nelson Glueck, *The Other Side of the Jordan* (New Haven, Conn.: American School of Oriental Research, 1940), ch. 5.

THE KING'S HIGHWAY *seen from the air as it runs north to cross the Brook Zered. This ancient caravan road the Israelites attempted to use during their detour via Transjordan (Num. 20:17). Paved by the Romans, the road has remained visible in its outline through the centuries. The rectangular structure beside it is the ruin of an ancient guardpost.*

generation ("forty years") in the wilderness, they would have encountered the well-organized resistance of these newly established agricultural kingdoms against nomadic incursions from the desert. Hence archaeology helps us to fix the period after which the Exodus and the wandering in the wilderness must have taken place.

According to Numbers 20:14-21, Moses sent messengers from Kadesh to the king of Edom, asking for permission to travel on the King's Highway. This ancient route, which is still followed by the modern road in that area, was the highway link between Syria and Ezion-geber, the seaport town which was located on the Gulf of Aqabah. From Ezion-geber, the road ran north through Moab, then through the Amorite land of King Sihon, touching at one point the kingdom of Ammon, and on up through the kingdom of Og (Bashan) to Damascus, the capital of Aram or Syria. In spite of Moses' promise that the Israelites would stay on the highway, turning neither to the right nor to the left, the suspicious Edomite king refused to grant them passage. So they traveled along the western border of Edom, turning east at the boundary brook Zered in order to circle Moab.

As the Israelites approached the territory of the Amorite kingdom of Sihon, Moses again sent messengers asking for permission to use the King's Highway. The king not only refused but sent an army to crush Israel (Num. 21:33-35). The result was the first major military victory that Israel ever achieved. So decisively did the Israelites defeat the Amorites that they took possession of the whole kingdom. The taste of victory spurred them to move farther north, where they met and defeated the king of Bashan, a gigantic man named Og, whose main claim to fame was his unusually large and sturdy bed (Num. 21:22-25; Deut. 3:1-11). Thus Israel came into possession of a large strip of land in Transjordan, including the lands of Sihon and Og. Israel was now encamped in Transjordan just across the Jordan near Jericho, and the stage was set for a bold thrust into Canaan from the east.

The Oracles of Balaam

At this point the narrator has placed the story of Balaam, a Babylonian diviner who was summoned by the king of Moab to pronounce a potent curse against the victorious Israelites (Num. 22-24). The story has elements of popular humor and fancy—as in the incident of Balaam's ass, which is described as speaking up in protest because of his master's irate treatment of a "dumb" beast. The "talking ass" is not the main feature of the story, however. Rather, it is what Balaam said as a prophetic spokesman of God. In ancient times it was believed that words spoken as a curse or as a blessing had power to achieve the desired result. A familiar illustration is the case of Jacob, who, to the great distress of his brother Esau, stole the deathbed blessing of their father, Isaac (Gen. 27). Because of this belief in the power of the spoken word, Balaam was invited to stand on a hilltop where Israel could be seen, and say, with a force greater than any show of military power, "Let them be damned." But the tradition affirms that a foreign diviner like Balaam had to obey the dictate of Israel's God, even though King Balak promised him a good fee and great honor:

> How can I curse whom God has not cursed?
> How can I denounce whom Yahweh has not denounced?
> For from the top of the mountains I see him,
>   from the hills I behold him;
> lo, a people dwelling alone,
>   and not reckoning itself among the nations!
> Who can count the dust of Jacob,
>   or number the fourth part of Israel?
>   —NUMBERS 23:8-10

According to this ancient view, Israel was not a nation, but a unique people set apart by Yahweh, who had delivered them from Egypt. Hence no magic or divination could avert the blessing that Yahweh chose to bestow upon them. The oracles of Balaam, which in their original form may date back to the thirteenth or twelfth century B.C., affirm the lusty faith of the victorious Israelites.

A more refined expression of Israel's covenant faith is given in Deuteronomy, the last book of the Pentateuch, which we notice now only in passing (see Chapter 10).[6] The book is cast in the form of a farewell address given by Moses in

---

[6] The rest of the book of Numbers, with few exceptions, comes from the P tradition, and deals largely with ritual matters.

the plains of Moab just before the Israelites crossed over the Jordan to storm the land of Canaan. Moses is rehearsing the stirring events of Israel's history—the Exodus, the making of the covenant, the wandering in the wilderness, the victories in Transjordan—in order to exhort Israel to remember gratefully all that Yahweh has done for her and to be faithful to the covenant obligations amid the temptations of Canaan. In its present form, the address comes from a time centuries later than Moses. But it shows how this "sacred history" was kept alive in Israel's memory through the generations and was reflected upon with deepening insight.

THE INVASION OF CANAAN

The book of Deuteronomy ends with an account of the death of Moses and the elevation of Joshua to be his successor (Deut. 34). In this abrupt manner the Torah or Pentateuch breaks off. It is quite obvious, however, that the story is not intended to end at this point, for the climax, toward which the narratives of the Pentateuch point, lies in the future: the fulfillment of the promise that Israel will be given an inheritance in the land of Canaan. Moses' death on Mount Nebo, in full sight of the Promised Land, occurs just when the Israelites are poised for the attack.

The story is resumed in the book of Joshua. This is the first book in the second major division of the Hebrew Bible, known as the Prophets. As can be seen from the accompanying chart, the canon of the Prophets is subdivided into two sections, each of which has four scrolls. The first is known as the Former Prophets; the second is known as the Latter Prophets. In the rest of this chapter we shall consider the first book of the Former Prophets, Joshua.

THE LAW AND THE PROPHETS*

TORAH	NEBI'IM
Genesis	Former Prophets:
Exodus	Joshua
Leviticus	Judges
Numbers	I-II Samuel
Deuteronomy	I-II Kings
	Latter Prophets:
	Isaiah
	Jeremiah
	Ezekiel
	The Twelve:
	Hosea, Joel, Amos, Obadiah,
	Jonah, Micah, Nahum, Habakkuk,
	Zephaniah, Haggai, Zechariah, Malachi

* For a complete table of the arrangement of books in the Hebrew Bible see the chart on pp. 556-557.

At first glance it may seem strange that this book, which is largely historical narrative, should be considered as "prophecy." The major reason is that all the books of the Former Prophets are governed by a prophetic interpretation of Israel's history which was profoundly influenced by the great prophets of the eighth and seventh centuries. This theology of history was championed by a Deuteronomic historian who reworked Israel's traditions in the period just after the fall of the nation in 587 B.C. The characteristic style and viewpoint of the Deuteronomic historian, which are well illustrated in the sermonic material in the opening chapters of Deuteronomy, pervade the books of the Former Prophets. Since D material is not found in the first four books of the Old Testament, Genesis through Numbers, it is proper to regard all the material found in Deuteronomy through I-II Kings as a comprehensive Deuteronomic History which begins with the Mosaic period and interprets the events of Israel's history to the time of the fall of the nation.[7]

The Land of Canaan

The first verses of the book of Joshua (1:1-9) are written in the style and from the theological perspective of the Deuteronomic writer. Yahweh is represented as summoning Joshua to lead Israel across the Jordan into the Promised Land, a land extending from the southern wilderness to the high Lebanon ranges to the north—and even beyond to the river Euphrates (see Gen. 15:18). Joshua is told that this segment of the Fertile Crescent will be Israel's on one condition: that the "book of the law" (the Deuteronomic Law) must be obeyed and studied diligently (Josh. 1:7-9). This is the key to success. Here we find the Deuteronomic formula for success and failure: obedience to Yahweh's commands will be rewarded with victory and prosperity; disobedience will bring the divine judgment of suffering and failure. This rather neat doctrine of reward and punishment, which probably arose out of ceremonies of covenant renewal when the formulas of divine blessings and curses were solemnly recited (see pp. 95-97), runs through the whole Deuteronomic History.

It stands to reason that whatever success Israel had in the invasion of Canaan depended upon other factors besides her faithful obedience to the covenant law, important though that was. Israel's success was facilitated by the historical situation in the whole Fertile Crescent: the lay of the land, the culture of Canaan, the political relation of this strategic corridor to the foci of political power in Egypt and Mesopotamia. It may be that in another time and under different circumstances the invasion under Joshua would have been no more successful than had been the earlier attempt to storm Canaan from the south. But now the time was right for a bold venture, and Israel had been prepared

---

[7] This view has been advanced by Martin Noth in his *Ueberlieferungsgeschichtliche Studien*, I [117] and is now widely accepted.

and disciplined for it by years of desert experience. This is not to deny Israel's doctrine of providence, the conviction that "Yahweh your God is with you wherever you go" (Josh. 1:9). Rather, we must view the doctrine of God's providential guidance of Israel in a wider perspective, such as archaeology and ancient history provide, if we are fully to appreciate its significance. So, before considering the narrative of the conquest in Joshua 2-12 let us look for a moment at the situation in Canaan.

The Lay of the Land

First, we need a general idea of the geography of Canaan.[8] The most striking topographical feature, as can be seen by looking at the map in the back of this book, is the central backbone of hill country lying between the deep cleft of the Jordan and the coastland of the Mediterranean. The hill country is cut, in the area of Mount Carmel, by a valley known as Jezreel (or Esdraelon),[9] which gives access to the Jordan Valley. In ancient times, the main military and commercial highway from Egypt to Mesopotamia ran along the coast, then turned into the Valley of Jezreel, and veered northward to Damascus. Important fortified cities were located along this route—notably Megiddo, which guarded the pass leading from the southern coastal plain into the Valley of Jezreel. Many decisive battles, ancient and modern, have been fought for the control of this strategic pass (see picture, p. 112) and for the fertile valley.

The broken terrain of Canaan was not well suited for the establishment of a strong, centralized government, such as was achieved in the plain of Mesopotamia or the valley of the Nile. In the period of the Israelite conquest, Canaan was divided into a number of autonomous city-states—that is, political centers that embraced a fortified city and a number of satellite cities or villages. Since the best farming land was located on the coastal plain and in the valleys of Jezreel and the Jordan, most of the major Canaanite cities were concentrated in these areas. In addition, cities located on the plains could be defended by chariots and other heavy military equipment. The central hill country was more suited to a pastoral economy and was vulnerable to attack by guerrilla bands.

The political importance of Canaan lay in the fact that it was a strategic corridor between Egypt and Mesopotamia. The possession of this corridor was indispensable for any nation that sought to extend its control through the Fertile Crescent. Ever since about 2000 b.c., Canaan had been either nominally or actually under Egyptian suzerainty. But Egyptian control of Canaan fluctuated with the changing fortunes of Egypt's internal political affairs. We saw

---

[8] See the brief treatment in the *Westminster Historical Atlas* [5], pp. 17-20, or H. L. Grollenberg, *Atlas of the Bible* [6], pp. 11-16.

[9] In Greek the name Jezreel was corrupted to Esdraelon—a term used to designate the western part of the valley.

PHARAOH AKHNATON *and his wife,
Nefertiti, offering a libation to
the sun god Aton, represented
by the solar disc. Each of the
rays streaming from the sun ends
in a hand opened caressingly,
and the two hands just above
the faces of the royal pair hold
a hieroglyph meaning "life."*

earlier (Chapter 1) that in the latter part of the eighteenth century a flood of
Hyksos swept into Egypt and seized control. The expulsion of the Hyksos by
Ahmose I, however, renewed Egypt's determination to regain control of her
Asiatic empire. The pharaohs of the early Eighteenth Dynasty (1570-1310 B.C.)
carried out extensive military campaigns in Canaan and Syria. Egyptian outposts
in Canaan were strengthened, such as the one at Beth-shan in the upper Jordan
Valley (see Plate 4). Egyptian inspectors saw that local Canaanite rulers paid
tribute and supplied laborers to work on Egyptian projects. Troops supported
the Egyptian officials as they policed and exploited the country under the
authority of the pharaoh.

The Amarna Age

Toward the end of the Eighteenth Dynasty, however, Egyptian control over Canaan weakened considerably, especially during the reign of Pharaoh Amenhotep IV, otherwise called Akhnaton (c. 1370-1353 B.C.). Archaeologists have excavated the library of his Egyptian capital, modern Tell el-Amarna, and have found many documents that shed light on Egyptian foreign affairs in Canaan during the fourteenth century, the so-called Amarna Age.[10] Unlike his predecessors of the Eighteenth Dynasty, Akhnaton was far less interested in pursuing an aggressive foreign policy than in effecting a religious revolution in Egypt with the introduction of a kind of monotheism based on the worship of the sun god, Aton. Consequently, the situation in Canaan got completely out of hand. In Akhnaton's archives was found the correspondence from a number of Canaanite kings, which gives a vivid picture of the disorder.[11] Apparently these city-state rulers were taking advantage of Egyptian weakness to advance their own political purposes, though they protested their loyalty to the Egyptian crown. The Egyptian officials were so corrupt that they only contributed further to the confusion and intrigue.

The correspondence from a certain 'Abdu-Heba, Egyptian ruler of Jerusalem, mentions 'Apiru raids that were having a devastating effect on Egyptian control in Canaan.[12] He complains that he is not to blame for the loss of Egyptian land, for "like a ship in the midst of the sea" he is surrounded by opposition on every hand. The situation, he says, is one of anarchy, and "now the 'Apiru capture the cities of the king." In desperation, he begs: "Let the king take care of his land!" Even a garrison of fifty men to guard the land would help considerably!

Some have thought that the Amarna letters refer to the events described in the book of Joshua, but this is hardly the case. As we have seen (p. 27), the term 'Apiru refers to a semi-nomadic class which included far more than the particular Hebrews who followed Moses and Joshua. So there is no need to equate these Habiru raids with the Israelite conquest. It is quite likely, however, that some of the Habiru who entrenched themselves in the hill country during the Amarna Age were relatives of the followers of Joshua who entered the country more than a century later. The Amarna letters refer to a certain Lab'ayu, Canaanite ruler of Shechem, who is bitterly accused of turning over his land to the Habiru.[13] As we shall see later, it was precisely in the Shechem area that Joshua met with no resistance and where he seems to have made a covenant alliance with Hebrew relatives and others who had not been in Egypt.

---

[10] The Amarna Age covers the reigns of Amenhotep III (c. 1406-1370 B.C.) and Amenhotep IV (c. 1370-1353 B.C.). See the chronological chart on p. 35.

[11] See Pritchard, *Ancient Near Eastern Texts*, pp. 483-490.

[12] See Pritchard, letters 286-290, pp. 487-489.

[13] Pritchard, letter 289.

SETI I *returning on his chariot from a campaign against the Hittites: a scene from the north wall of the Temple of Karnak (near Luxor). The wings of the falcon sun god are outspread protectingly over his head. To the left are prisoners taken by the pharaoh.*

The Amarna Age of Egyptian weakness in Canaan soon came to an end. After the death of Akhnaton, all traces of his monotheistic "heresy" were removed, and Egypt began to restore order and prosperity within her borders. Under the pharaohs of the Nineteenth Dynasty, especially Seti I and Rameses II, whom we have already met in connection with the Exodus, there was an enormous revival of Egyptian power. By this time the major obstacle to Egypt's recovery of her Asiatic empire was expansion of Hittite imperialism throughout the Fertile Crescent (see Plates 3 and 4). Owing to the disruptive attacks of the Habiru and the intrigue of Canaanite rulers, Hittite influence had extended into Canaan itself. Both Seti I and Rameses II carried out military expeditions against this foe. Rameses, though unable to crush the Hittites, fought them to a stalemate in Syria. Throughout the rest of Rameses' long rule (c. 1290-1224 B.C.) the Hittite boundary remained north of Mount Lebanon, and Canaan was under the hegemony of Egypt.

At the death of Rameses, weakness set in once again—and this time it was chronic. Rameses' son Merneptah (c. 1224-1216 B.C.) lacked both the youth and the ability to control the Egyptian empire, which was being menaced by a threat far more serious than the Hittites. A great population upheaval was being created in the Aegean [14] world by the movement of tribes from southern Europe. Some of these people swept into Greece and Asia Minor, where they brought the old Hittite empire to an end. Another wave moved upon Egypt, some coming by sea and others taking the land route from Libya. These "Peoples of the Sea," as the Egyptians called them, included an assortment of names, one of which was the "Philistines"—the people from whom Canaan later received the name "Palestine." Merneptah was able to hold back the flood during his brief reign,

---

[14] "Aegean" refers to the islands of the Aegean Sea, off the mainland of Greece.

81

THE STELE OF MERNEPTAH *contains the earliest mention of "Israel" outside the Bible. Under the winged sun disc stands the god Amon in double representation. The king is also shown twice, standing before the god with a sickle-sword in one hand and a scepter in the other. Behind him stands the goddess Mut (extreme left) and the hawk-headed god Horus (extreme right).*

but in the years after his death the invasions were renewed. Rameses III (c. 1175-1144 B.C.) managed to push the Philistines up into their beachhead on the coast of Canaan. But this effort exhausted Egyptian power, and in the succeeding centuries Egypt never regained the glory that was once hers.

It is against this historical and political background that we must understand the biblical account of the invasion under Joshua, which began in approximately 1250 B.C. Rameses II was on the throne (see Plate 1), but already his hold on Canaan was beginning to slip as a result of his preoccupation with the Hittite power to the north. Egypt seemed unconcerned about, or was unable to cope with, this latest invasion of Hebrews from Transjordan. The invaders moved into the central hill country, avoiding contact with Canaanite strongholds and Egyptian outposts on the plains. After the Hebrews had established a firm foothold in Canaan, the Egyptians decided it was time to act. In about 1220 B.C., Merneptah set up a stele which contains our earliest extra-biblical reference to "Israel." Celebrating Merneptah's alleged triumph over Asiatic peoples, the hymn contains these poetic lines:

> Israel is laid waste, his seed is not.
> Hurru is become a widow for Egypt.[15]

Obviously the military claim is exaggerated. The Israelites may have suffered a reverse in battle, but if they did the Old Testament passes over the incident in discreet silence. In any event, Merneptah was in no position to follow up whatever victory he achieved, for his energies were soon diverted by the greater problem of resisting other invaders who came to his country in great numbers from the Aegean region. Thus the stage was providentially set for Israel to inherit the Promised Land.

THE ISRAELITE CONQUEST

The first section of the book of Joshua (Josh. 1-12) sets forth the dramatic story of the Israelite conquest of Canaan. The reader is told how the whole land fell into the hand of Joshua as the result of three swift campaigns. The first campaign gave the Israelites a firm foothold on the other side of the Jordan, which was dammed back at Adam (modern ed-Damiyeh), presumably by one of the landslides that frequently occur in the geological fault followed by the river. After fording the Jordan with the Ark in the lead (see map, Plate 2) they encamped at Gilgal (Josh. 3-5). From this base they laid siege to Jericho, which fell at the sound of their trumpets, and then moved up a few miles into the hill country where they captured the city of Ai (probably confused with Bethel) by means of a tactical ambush. Apparently finding no resistance in central Canaan, the Israelites went as far as Shechem, where Joshua built an altar on a mountain overlooking the city (Josh. 6-8).

During a second campaign the victorious Israelites moved into the southern hill country. Near the fortress of Jerusalem, which they carefully avoided, they were tricked into making a treaty with four federated cities, chief of which was Gibeon (chap. 9). When the Gibeonites were threatened with reprisals from a coalition of Canaanite kings because of their alliance with Israel, the Israelites moved swiftly to their defense. According to a quotation from a lost book of

---

[15] See Pritchard, *Ancient Near Eastern Texts*, pp. 376-378. The Egyptians referred to Palestine as Hurru—i.e., the land of the Hurrians (see above, p. 25).

Israelite poetry, the Book of Jashar, Joshua prayed for the sun to stand still over Gibeon and the moon over the Valley of Aijalon in order to give his soldiers enough time to finish off the Canaanites (Josh. 10:12-13a). The original poetry perhaps expressed "the desire that the sun should not rise high in the east [over Gibeon], nor the moon set in the west [in the valley of Aijalon] so that, hidden by the morning mist, the Israelites might steal upon their foes unawares." [16] The writer who quoted from the old poetic collection took the poetry literally (10:13b)—as have many modern prosaic readers of the Scripture—and commented that the sun actually stopped in its course (or in our terms, that the earth ceased to rotate for almost a whole day).

From this victory the Israelites moved on to further conquests that included the city-states of Libnah, Lachish (see Plate 5), Eglon, Debir, and Hebron (see map opposite), apparently bypassing some heavily fortified towns like Gezer and Beth-shemesh (Josh. 10:16-43).[17]

Finally, they carried out a successful campaign in the northern hill country, above the Valley of Jezreel in the area known especially in New Testament times as Galilee (cf. Is. 9:1). Here Joshua won a decisive victory at the city of Hazor (Josh. 11).

The Deuteronomic View

According to this account, Joshua, the leader of united Israel, masterminded an effective strategy and, in three lightning thrusts into the center, the south, and the north, took complete possession of Canaan. Cities were burned to the ground; the native Canaanite population was almost exterminated; all obstacles were swept away in the inexorable advance of Israel's hosts. "The whole land" was given to them "because Yahweh, God of Israel, fought for Israel." The thoroughness of the conquest is indicated in the summary found in Joshua 11:16-23.

This is the view of the Deuteronomic historian, whose characteristic style dominates Joshua 1-12 and the farewell address found in Joshua 23. Undoubtedly he was using older traditions: tribal stories, cultic legends, and perhaps the J and E tradition found in Genesis, Exodus, and Numbers of the Pentateuch. He picks up the theme of the promise made to the patriarchs that Israel would inherit Canaan, and then shows how it was brought to marvelous fulfillment in the time of Joshua. But apparently he was carried away with religious enthusiasm. As a result, the historical realities of the conquest are made to appear much simpler than they actually were. Even this historian realized that Joshua did not make a clean sweep of the land, for he has Joshua remind the

---

[16] John Bright, *Interpreter's Bible*, II, p. 605.

[17] The text of 10:33 does not state that the city of Gezer was conquered (which would go against archaeological evidence), but only that forces from this city attempted to intercept the Israelites and were defeated.

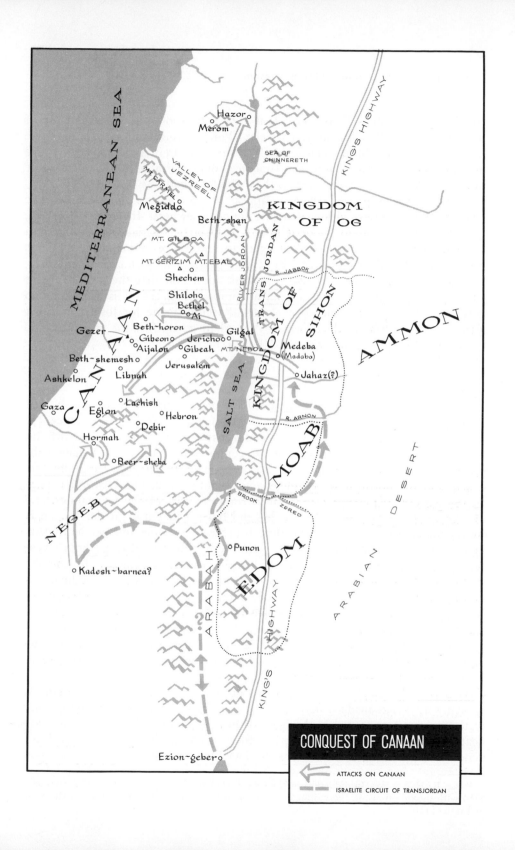

MEDITERRANEAN SEA

Hazor
Merom

SEA OF
CHINNERETH

KING'S HIGHWAY

VALLEY OF
JEZREEL

MT. CARMEL

Megiddo

Beth~shan

KINGDOM
OF OG

MT. GILBOA

MT. GERIZIM MT. EBAL

Shechem

R. JABBOK

Shiloho
Bethel
Ai

Beth~horon
Gibeono
Aijalon

Gezer

Jericho
Gibeah

Gilgal

MT. NEBO

Medeba
(Madaba)

AMMON

Beth~shemesh

Libnah

Jerusalem

Ashkelon

Gaza

Eglon

Lachish

Hebron

Debir

Hormah

Beer~sheba

NEGEB

Kadesh~barnea?

Jahaz(?)

R. ARNON

BROOK ZERED

Punon

ARABIAN DESERT

EDOM

ARABAH

KING'S HIGHWAY

Ezion~gebero

CANAAN

SALT SEA

RIVER JORDAN

TRANS JORDAN

KINGDOM OF SIHON

MOAB

CONQUEST OF CANAAN

ATTACKS ON CANAAN

ISRAELITE CIRCUIT OF TRANSJORDAN

Israelites in his farewell discourse that they must not join "the remnant of these nations left here among you" or else "Yahweh your God will not continue to drive out these nations before you" (Josh. 23:12-13). Apparently there was much work to be done before the Israelites could claim, as the Deuteronomic historian does in one place (11:23), that "the land had rest from war."

A more complex picture begins to appear as we compare the Deuteronomic view of the conquest with statements found elsewhere. In Joshua 10:38-39, Joshua is reported to have taken the city of Debir (or Kiriath-sepher [modern Tell Beit Mirsim]), but in Joshua 15:13-19 and Judges 1:11-15 the credit is given to a man named Othniel. In several passages in Joshua (15:63; 16:10; 17:12, 18) and in Judges 1 there is a frank admission that the Israelites were unable to expel the Canaanites from a number of places. It is interesting to note that, despite the tremendous claims of victory made for Joshua, the first question asked after his death was: "Who shall go up first for us against the Canaanites, to fight against them?" (Judg. 1:1).

The Nature of the Conquest

In the past, critical historians have agreed almost unanimously that these scattered statements are fragments of an older, more reliable source (J) which the Deuteronomic writer ignored because it did not accord with his theological interests.[18] Their view of the conquest has been almost exactly the opposite of that given Joshua 1-12. According to this scholarly view, the conquest was not a decisive assault but a gradual infiltration, in which initial guerrilla warfare was followed by settlement in the midst of the Canaanites, and by intermarriage with them. The tribes did not act in unison under the single command of Joshua; rather, individual tribes won victories independently during the lifetime of Joshua and later. Joshua was only a local tribal hero whose fame grew as his people, "the house of Joseph," gained prominence. In time the story was embellished and exaggerated until at last Joshua became the hero of a united Israel. It has been questioned whether Joshua was the successor of Moses, and, indeed, whether he existed at all. So viewed, the conquest of Canaan was a gradual process that took place over many generations and that was not completed until the time of David. Scholars who accept this picture of the conquest have virtually scrapped the account given in Joshua 1-12 as having little historical reliability.

√ Modern archaeology, which has revolutionized our understanding of the Bible in many ways, has made it necessary for us to look more carefully at the story of the conquest presented in the book of Joshua. Admittedly the picture is too neat, too simplified, too idealized; but there is considerable archaeological evidence to support the tradition that the Israelites made a decisive assault upon

---

[18] See R. H. Pfeiffer, *Introduction to the Old Testament* [28], pp. 296-301. This view persists, with modifications, in the writings of Martin Noth, such as his commentary on the book of Joshua [116].

the Canaanite hill country in the latter part of the thirteenth century. Excavations have demonstrated that some of the cities allegedly attacked by Joshua actually did suffer violent destruction in this period. Lachish, mentioned in Joshua 10:31-33, is known to have fallen in about 1220 B.C. Excavations at Hazor, the city said to have been captured by Joshua during his northern campaign, have shown that the city was destroyed in the thirteenth century. Other cities—Bethel, Debir, Eglon—suffered violent destruction in the same period. Presumably, cities taken by Joshua in the thirteenth century had to be retaken later, which may account for some of the fragmentary materials in Judges 1. Contrary to the common assumption, Judges 1 is not a single document, a remnant of "the lost J account of the conquest," but an anthology of material from differing dates and circumstances." [19]

✓ On second thought, then, there is an element of truth in both views: the view of the "sudden conquest," based on Joshua 1-12, and the view of the "gradual conquest," supposedly based on Judges 1. Both views must be taken into account if we are to do justice to the complexity of the situation. There was a decisive campaign by Joshua in the thirteenth century which smashed into the hill country and dealt the Canaanites a shattering blow. The Israelites at this time were successful only in the hill country, where they could use their fairly simple methods of warfare and could take full advantage of the broken terrain. Even in the rather one-sided picture given by the Deuteronomic historian there is no claim that the Israelites attacked the major Canaanite strongholds and Egyptian outposts located along the coastal plain and in the Valley of Jezreel. The reason for his honest silence on this matter is undoubtedly given in the following statement:

> And Yahweh was with Judah, and he took possession of the hill country, but he could not drive out the inhabitants of the plain, because they had chariots of iron.
>
> —JUDGES 1:19

Against the weapons of the Iron Age, Israel was about as effective as Indians with bows and arrows facing the white men's guns. Consequently, this major assault upon the hill country in the thirteenth century had to be followed up by continued struggle for possession of the land after Joshua's death. As we have seen, in more restrained moments the Deuteronomic historian recognized that there was much to be done in the way of mopping up remaining centers of Canaanite resistance and culture (Josh. 13), although this side of the picture is not presented as fully as it should be. After the initial assault, continued military action was necessary, sometimes carried out by individual tribes in local areas. Moreover, the conquest of the Canaanites was facilitated by treaty,

---

[19] See G. Ernest Wright, "The Literary and Historical Problem of Joshua 10 and Judges 1," *Journal of Near Eastern Studies*, V (1946), pp. 105-114. See also his *Biblical Archaeology* [57], for further discussion of the archaeological evidence.

intermarriage, and the absorption of city-states into the Israelite confederacy, about which we shall have more to say presently.

A Glorified Account

The Deuteronomic account of Joshua's achievement, then, is exaggerated. The purpose of the writer was not to give a colorless, factual report, but to proclaim to the Israelite community the dramatic story of Yahweh's

THE MOUND OF JERICHO *shows this deep cut made by archaeologists at the site of the oldest city of Palestine. The upper edge of an excavated stone tower runs across the base of the photo. Dating back to about 7000 B.C., this circular structure was part of the city's defense system in the Stone Age. One level of occupation was built upon another through the centuries until the city came into the possession of Israel, though the story of Joshua's conquest is archaeologically enigmatic. In the background is the traditional Mount of Temptation.*

victory through his servant Joshua. Hence the writer telescoped the account of the invasion by attributing feats to a great military commander which were actually carried out by others, or he glorified the story by magnifying modest gains into whopping victories, as is sometimes done in modern war summaries. An illustration, perhaps, is the account of the fall of Jericho. A British excavation, conducted during 1930-36, set the date of the violent destruction of the city—apparently by earthquake—at about 1385 B.C., which suggested a tempting connection with the activity of the Habiru invaders described in the Amarna letters. Recent exploration of the site, however, has resulted in a complete reassessment of the evidence. Scientific study has shown that the wall which supposedly "came tumbling down" in Joshua's time actually dates back to the third millennium B.C. The mound suffered such heavy erosion that virtually nothing from the thirteenth century remains. If "the Jericho of Joshua's day may have been little more than a fort," [20] the military feat of the Israelites was far less dramatic than the cultic account in Joshua 6 portrays it.

Another illustration is the account of the conquest of Ai (literally, in Hebrew, "the ruin"). Excavations at Ai have shown that this ancient Canaanite city was destroyed about 2200 B.C. and was still a heap of ruins in Joshua's time. On the other hand, excavations conducted at Bethel, just a short distance away, have demonstrated that this city was destroyed during the thirteenth century B.C. It may be that the story about "the ruin" has been combined with the account of Joshua's capture of the city of Bethel, which had been built nearby to take its place (see Josh. 12:16; Judg. 1:22-26).

In spite of signs of telescoping and exaggeration, there is good evidence for the central claim of the book of Joshua, that in the thirteenth century the warlike Israelites—probably spearheaded by the Joseph tribes and the tribe of Benjamin [21]—were victorious in wresting a good part of the central hill country from the Canaanites. Moreover, deeply imbedded in Israel's memory was the conviction that these victories were not achieved by mere military power or strategy. In those stirring events the Israelites recognized the active presence and guidance of Yahweh, who had delivered them from Egyptian bondage and in a marvelous way had led them into a land where they could fulfill the historic role for which they had been called. It was their faith in the God who actively took part in the historical struggle that unified them and inspired them with tremendous zeal. Against these invaders from the desert, the Canaanites, split up into city-states, divided by the hills and valleys, and lacking a dynamic religious faith, were unable to stand.

---

[20] G. E. Wright, *Biblical Archaeology* [57], p. 79. For the excavator's account see Kathleen Kenyon, *Archaeology in the Holy Land* [54], pp. 209-212.

[21] Notice that the Joseph tribes (Manasseh and Ephraim) and the tribe of Benjamin are linked closely together in tradition, for Joseph and Benjamin were Jacob's two sons by his favorite wife, Rachel (Gen. 30:22-24; 35:16-20). Joshua himself was an Ephraimite.

THE SHECHEM PASS *is the strategic gateway to the heart of Canaan. Located at the caravan crossroads between Mount Gerizim (left) and Mount Ebal (right), Shechem was the first center of the Israelite confederacy.*

THE FORMATION OF THE TRIBAL CONFEDERACY

We turn now to the important incident related in the last chapter of Joshua. We have noticed that the Deuteronomic book of Joshua is confined to chapters 1-12 and the concluding address found in chapter 23. The intervening material (Josh. 13-22) consists for the most part of ancient lists of tribal borders and towns, which need not concern us here. Chapter 24, however, is one of the most important chapters in the Old Testament. After Joshua's farewell address in chapter 23, this chapter seems to stand by itself and may well relate an incident that happened earlier in Joshua's career, perhaps after his first campaign. Much of the narrative is probably based on an old source of the Pentateuch (E), but in substance it seems to date back to an early period when the tradition circulated orally.

The Assembly at Shechem

The subject of Joshua 24 is a great convocation at Shechem, a city located near Joseph's grave (Josh. 24:32) and Jacob's well (John 4:6). From at least the turn of the second millennium B.C., it was a great Canaanite city-state, strategically located in the narrow pass between Mount Gerizim and Mount Ebal. From this vantage point it commanded the major highways that necessarily had to run between the two mountains. Excavations at the site (the modern village of Balatah, near Nablus), in earlier years by a German team and subsequently by Drew University and McCormick Theological Seminary, have uncovered the impressive remains of the ancient city.[22] The discovery of a type of rampart, known to be typical of the Hyksos, indicates that for a while it was a strong fortress of the Hyksos empire. Evidence of violent destruction in the middle of the second millennium B.C. suggests that the city was retaken by the Egyptians when Ahmose I expelled the Hyksos from Egypt and carried his conquests into Palestine. In the fourteenth century, as we know from the Amarna letters, it was lost to Egypt as a result of Lab'ayu's treaty with 'Apiru. So the city was the scene of decisive political struggles long before Joshua arrived.

Not only was Shechem an important fortress, but it was also a religious center. In the acropolis was built a large temple, called the temple of Baal Berith ("Lord of the Covenant"; see Judg. 9:4). Today the visitor to the ruins

[22] The Drew-McCormick archaeological expedition, which had its first campaign in the summer of 1956, was under the archaeological direction of G. Ernest Wright. See his book, *Shechem* [58]).

THE TEMPLE OF BAAL-BERITH (*or El-berith*), *first built by Canaanites during the Hyksos period (c. 1650 B.C.) and, in a later phase, standing when the city peacefully passed into the control of Israel and became the first center of the Tribal Confederacy. During excavations by the Drew-McCormick Expedition in 1960 and 1962, the sacred pillar was restored to its original position in front of the temple, and a retaining wall was built around the reconstructed temple courtyard.*

can see the foundations of this ancient temple—the largest pre-Roman temple that archaeologists have ever discovered in Palestine—and can visualize how impressive the shrine must have been in ancient times. According to the story, Joshua gathered the people "before God" at the city of Shechem (Josh. 24:1).

In the presence of the assembled Israelite tribes and their leaders, Joshua rehearsed Israel's "sacred history," beginning with the patriarchal period and dwelling especially on the events of the Exodus and the conquests in Transjordan and the Canaanite hill country. On the basis of this confessional summary, Joshua then challenged the people to decide either to serve Yahweh in sincerity and faithfulness, or to serve the gods their fathers served beyond the River (Euphrates) and the gods of the Amorites (Canaanites). With the warning ringing in their ears that Yahweh is a jealous God, a holy God who would not tolerate the worship of "strange gods," the people affirmed their decision to serve Yahweh, who had brought them out of Egypt and guided them into Canaan. So Joshua demanded that they put away the foreign gods. The ceremony concluded with the making of a covenant, the giving of law, and the erection of a memorial stone beneath a sacred tree.

It is quite clear that Joshua was not officiating at a covenant ceremony that brought Yahweh and Israel together for the first time. Israel did not become in *this* moment "the people of Yahweh," nor did Yahweh become "the God of Israel." This was not the initiation of the covenant relationship, but a reaffirmation of the sacred covenant that was made at Sinai. To be sure, Joshua's rehearsal of the events of Israel's past makes no reference to the Sinai covenant, but this was hardly appropriate since, as we have seen previously (pp. 62-63), the Sinai covenant was not one of Yahweh's mighty acts but rather the response to his deeds. It was appropriate that this covenant renewal took place in the new land of Canaan where the people, in the flush of victory, were tempted to violate their covenant obligation and adopt the religious practices of Canaan. Joshua's challenge was put with the urgency that was later voiced by the prophets: *Today* you must decide. Yahweh demands exclusive devotion from his people. In the answer of the people, "We will serve Yahweh, for he is our God," we find a reaffirmation of the Mosaic belief that for Israel there can be only one God.

New Converts to the Mosaic Faith

But there was probably more to this ceremony than a renewal of the covenant allegiance by those who had taken part in the wilderness warnings. It is noteworthy that the ceremony took place at Shechem. One of the strange things about the story of the conquest of the hill country is the complete silence about any activity in the area around Shechem. The fact that Shechem was not attacked and, moreover, that it was the scene of the tribal convocation, suggests that the people of this vicinity were friendly to the invaders, either through kinship or alliance. We have already seen (pp. 80-81) that in the Amarna Age Habiru were active in the vicinity of Shechem and entered into a treaty with the Canaanite ruler of the city. It has been suggested that before Joshua's time there existed at Shechem an alliance of six tribes, based on a covenant allegiance and the common worship of El (the name of the chief Canaanite deity). Old traditions relate that Jacob purchased land near Shechem where he erected an altar to "El, the God of Israel" (Gen. 33:18-20) and that Hebrew tribes very early attempted to enter into cordial relations with this Canaanite city-state (Gen. 34).

There are faint recollections, then, that some of Israel's ancestors—broadly speaking, the Leah tribes [23]—settled in Canaan at a comparatively early date and did not take part in the Exodus or the experiences of the wilderness. If the invaders under Joshua—that is, the Rachel tribes of Joseph and Benjamin—found friends or relatives already settled in central Canaan, we can understand why it was unnecessary for them to conquer this region. Supposing all this to be true, then Joshua 24 describes not just the renewal of the Mosaic covenant but its extension to embrace other tribesmen who had not been involved in it before. To them, Joshua's words would have had special force: "Choose ye this day." And if they were to choose the service of Yahweh, they had to put away all foreign gods, whether retained from the patriarchal period or adopted from the Canaanites in whose midst they had been living.

But why did Joshua rehearse to these new converts to the covenant community the stirring events of the Exodus and the wilderness sojourn—events in which neither they nor their immediate ancestors had participated? How could they say, "This is *our* life-story too?" This is not so strange after all, for the only way outsiders can be initiated into a historical community is to share its memories and to participate fully in its life. In the United States, for instance, the stirring story of the Revolutionary War does not belong merely to the Thirteen Colonies or the descendants of the first colonists. Other states, joining the Union, appropriated those memories as their own. Moreover, many of us are children of immigrants who arrived on the American scene fairly late, but we too thrill to the rehearsal of the epic of early American history and affirm that this is *our* story. Similarly, to become an Israelite was to appropriate the whole sacred past. It was not just a matter of blood relation, for even Canaanites were absorbed into Israel in the early period—as were the Gibeonites, for example. Fundamentally, it was a matter of being identified with the whole drama of Israel's history, and of being willing to acknowledge the God of the covenant and to accept the obligations of membership in the covenant community.

---

[23] For Jacob's six sons by Leah, see Gen. 29:31-35; 30:14-20. The duality of the Leah tribes and the Rachel tribes undoubtedly reflects the historical relationships of the tribes in the early period.

The name for this covenant community was Israel. We have already seen that the term Habiru had a broad meaning during the second millennium. Not all Hebrews were Israelites. The Israelites included only those Hebrews, whether they went down into Egypt or settled in Palestine before Joshua's time, who were bound into a covenant alliance. In other words, Israel is basically a religious term—not just an ethnic or national one. The Old Testament shows how the word Hebrew was eventually superseded by Israel to designate the particular people whose life-story we have been following. The term Israel gained currency especially during the period of the conquest and the era of the judges.

The Twelve-Tribe Confederacy

One of the striking features of "Israel" was its organization into twelve tribes. In recent years, scholarly studies have shown that the twelve-fold tribal pattern originated in the time of the early settlement in Canaan.[24] The fragmentary biblical evidence is interpreted to mean that Israel was organized into a tribal confederacy somewhat like the tribal federations found in ancient Greece and elsewhere under the term "amphictyony" (e.g., the league of Delphi). In the amphictyony, a number of tribes, sometimes six and sometimes twelve, were loosely bound together on the basis of a common religious obligation. There was a central sanctuary which the tribes cared for in turn. At this religious center regular festivals were held, and the basic laws that were binding upon all the tribes were administered. The bond that held these tribes together was primarily religious, in contrast to the political basis of a city-state or a nation. In times of military emergency, however, the tribes united to face the common foe, and the federation brought about some degree of unity in language, customs, and political interests.

This seems to be the kind of tribal organization that Joshua instituted at Shechem, and that prevailed in the period of the judges, as we shall see. The tribes of Israel were bound together into a covenant alliance that allowed for considerable autonomy on the part of the twelve participants. Primarily it was a theocratic community, as indicated by the word Israel, which perhaps should be translated: "may God rule." Shechem seems to have been the center of the confederacy for a while, but later on the central sanctuary was located at Shiloh, where the Ark was kept and where the tribes assembled for religious festivals, especially to renew the covenant. Above all, the tribal covenant was based on a rehearsal of the great events in which Yahweh had acted on behalf of his people. In this respect it rested on the same basis as the Mosaic covenant.[25]

---

[24] This study has been made by the German scholar, Martin Noth, in his book, *Das System der zwölf Stämme Israels* (Stuttgart: Kohlhammer, 1930). See also his *History of Israel* [44], pp. 85-108. De Vaux (*Ancient Israel* [62], pp. 3-15) prefers to find analogies to the twelve-tribe federation among the Arabs.

[25] See the discussion of the suzerainty type of covenant, above, pp. 61-63.

The Covenant Law

We are told that when Joshua made a covenant with the people at Shechem he also "made statutes [Hebrew: *ḥoq*] and ordinances [*mishpaṭ*] for them" (Josh. 24:25). Another version of Joshua promulgating the Mosaic Law is found in Joshua 8:30-35, where it is said that in a religious ceremony he read before assembled Israel "all the words of the law, the blessing and the curse." This latter refers to the absolute or apodictic law (*ḥoq*, or statute) which, as we saw in the last chapter, was associated with the Mosaic covenant. This type of law is illustrated in the twelve curses found in Deuteronomy 27:11-26. Here are some examples:

> Cursed be the man who makes a graven or molten image.
> Cursed be he who dishonors his father or his mother.
> Cursed be he who removes his neighbor's landmark.
> Cursed be he who slays his neighbor in secret.

These laws are formulated in the short, categorical manner that we have noticed in the Ten Commandments. The law is made absolutely binding by being put in the form of a curse that expresses Yahweh's unqualified disapproval of a particular act. The twelve curses are very old. They go back at least to the time of the Israelite tribal confederacy. According to the above passage in Deuteronomy, they were recited in connection with a ritual ceremony that took place at Shechem, when the tribes arranged themselves half on Mount Gerizim and half on Mount Ebal.

There is good reason to believe, then, that Joshua did promulgate law at the convocation described in Joshua 24. It is tempting to conclude that the curses found in Deuteronomy 27 were read at the Shechem assembly. In any event, we may assume that from this time on covenant law was recited to the tribal assembly, probably each Fall when the feast of Tabernacles was held at the central sanctuary.[26] There the tribes gathered from year to year to hear again the great story of Yahweh's redemptive deeds, to pledge themselves anew to his covenant, and to listen to the solemn recitation of the regulations and obligations that were binding upon them. Only fragments of the covenant service have survived in the Old Testament. Here is a plausible reconstruction of "the drama of covenant reaffirmation":[27]

---

[26] According to Deut. 31:9-13, the gathering for public reading of the law is to take place every seventh year. This sabbatical scheme, however, was probably a later modification of the practice of holding a covenant renewal ceremony annually at the time of the Fall festival or New Year (see Ex. 34:22).

[27] The following eight items are excerpted from the book by Walter Harrelson, *Interpreting the Old Testament* [15], p. 122, with the permission of the publisher, Holt, Rinehart and Winston, Inc. Harrelson also suggests (p. 124) that on regular occasions of covenant renewal villages, tribes, and families may have had the opportunity to join the covenant community.

1. The call to assembly, Josh. 24:1
2. Historical prologue—confessional statement of Yahweh's past acts of mercy and deliverance, 24:2-13
3. Call to decision for or against Yahweh, 24:14-22
4. Removal of foreign gods, 24:23-24 (see Gen. 35:1-4)
5. The covenant ceremony itself, 24:25 (see Ex. 24:4-8)
6. The reading of the covenant law, 24:25-26
7. A ceremony of blessings and cursings (see Deut. 27; 11:26-32; and Josh. 8:30-35)
8. The dismissal of the tribal representatives, 24:28

Israel's law was covenant law. It was not "secular" law, or even civil law in a narrow sense. Indeed, Israel did not recognize any separation between the secular and religious realms. The whole of life was to be lived under Yahweh's demand, within his covenant. This sense of total accountability before God led to an expansion of law as new situations were faced, such as the new adjustment to the agricultural life of Canaan. Israel borrowed laws from the culture of the Fertile Crescent and transformed them according to her needs and religious concerns. Undoubtedly this legal development was accelerated during the period of the Tribal Confederacy. It has been suggested that covenant renewal festivals provided the occasion for arbitrating disputes between, or even within, the tribes.

Many of the "ordinances" (i.e., the *mishpaṭ* case laws) in the so-called Covenant Code (Ex. 20:23-23:19) are similar in form, and to a great degree in content, to the law codes of the Babylonians, Hurrians, and Assyrians. The same is true of the code of Deuteronomy (12-26). Here is one example of the affinity between Old Testament legislation and the Code of Hammurabi:

Code of Hammurabi [28]	*Covenant Code*
Par. 120	Ex. 22:7-9
If a seignior deposited his grain in a(nother) seignior's house for storage and a loss has then occurred at the granary or the owner of the house opened the storage-room and took grain or he has denied completely (the receipt of) the grain which was stored in his house, the owner of the grain shall set forth the particulars in the presence of God and the owner of the house shall give to the owner of the grain double the grain that he took.	If a man delivers to his neighbor money or goods to keep, and it is stolen out of the man's house, then, if the thief is found, he shall pay double. If the thief is not found, the owner of the house shall come near to God, to show whether or not he has put his hand to his neighbor's goods. For every breach of trust, whether it is for ox, for ass, for sheep, for clothing, or for any kind of lost thing, of which one says, "This is it," the case of both parties shall come before God; he whom God shall condemn shall pay double to his neighbor.

[28] Pritchard, *Ancient Near Eastern Texts*, p. 171.

Not that the Old Testament law was copied from the Code of Hammurabi; the latter code presupposes an aristocratic class system that did not prevail in Israel. Moreover, Israel never could accept the view that the state is the custodian of law; according to Israel's covenant faith, even kings were subject to the law, which had its ultimate source at Sinai. But the similarity of form and even of some of the details indicates that Israel has borrowed from a fund of legal tradition that was known throughout the Fertile Crescent. Both laws are casuistic—that is, they begin with "if" and precisely define the case that is to be adjudicated. This conditional law contrasts with the unconditional law that was peculiar to the Israelite covenant.

Nevertheless, there are vast differences between Israelite law and other Near Eastern codes even when there is evidence of borrowing.[29] Israel's law is characterized by a humane spirit, a high ethical emphasis, and a pervading religious fervor which make it unique. This is because all the law of Israel, regardless of its source, is set within the "I" and "thou" of the covenant relation. As the tribes gathered at their common sanctuary to rehearse the stirring events of their past and to hear the absolute requirements of Yahweh, the covenant was reaffirmed again and again. A passage in Deuteronomy says, "Yahweh made not this covenant with our fathers, but with us who are here alive this day" (Deut. 5:3). This is not exaggerated language. In each great covenant-renewal ceremony, like the one described in Joshua 24, the covenant was made contemporaneous. The Deuteronomic passage preserves an echo of the spirit that animated the Tribal Confederacy and infused the expanding laws of the community.

---

[29] See the excellent study of the nature of Israelite law by Martin Noth, "The Laws of the Pentateuch" [111].

THE STRUGGLE
BETWEEN FAITH
AND CULTURE

CHAPTER FOUR   The turbulent scenes portrayed in the book of Judges show that life within the Israelite confederacy was a continuing struggle during the period between the death of Joshua and the rise of the monarchy under Saul. Those were "the days when the judges ruled" (Ruth 1:1)— the twelfth and eleventh centuries B.C. Having won a foothold on the soil of Canaan, Israel faced the problem of adjusting to the agricultural ways of the land and taking her place among the nations. In the days of the judges the

Biblical readings: The book of Judges, at least 2:6–16:31, and the narratives in I Samuel 1-12. The theological commentary on the meaning of the settlement in Canaan, found in the book of Deuteronomy, is relevant here, but will be treated at length in Chapter 10.

Tribal Confederacy, straining under conflict with forces both without and within, found itself put to the severest test.

In part, the struggle was for Israel's physical survival. Although the decisive phase of the conquest took place in the thirteenth century, the contest for Canaan went on relentlessly for many years afterward. The Israelite offensive was continued by means of war, treaty, and the gradual absorption of the Canaanites into the Israelite alliance. But at a deeper level an even more important conflict was being fought on the soil of Canaan: a conflict of religious loyalties. In modern language, an ideological struggle was being waged, not just a military one. And it was as true then as it is now that final victory goes to the side that wins the allegiance of men's hearts.

THE TEMPTATIONS OF CANAANITE CULTURE

In the long course of the centuries, many victorious nations have been moulded by the superior cultures that they vanquished. In ancient Mesopotamia, for example, the brilliant Sumerian culture was overcome by the aggressive Semitic Akkadians, who, under the leadership of Sargon, established the first empire in history. But the Akkadians were profoundly influenced by Sumerian culture. Centuries later, Rome vanquished the Greeks and established a political order, the famous Pax Romana, which probably has not been surpassed by any world empire. But Rome also was dependent upon the glorious legacy of Greek culture. During the Israelite conquest of Canaan, the stage was set for a similar development. Archaeological excavation in Palestine has shown that Israelite life was crude in comparison to the highly sophisticated, aristocratic culture of Canaan. Would the victor again be overcome by the vanquished?

Coming out of a desert background, Israel reacted strongly against the culture of the Fertile Crescent. Echoes of the antipathy of seminomads for this culture are found in some of the traditions preserved in Genesis 2-11 (J). In its earliest form, the story of the Tower of Babel expressed scorn for the proud culture of the Fertile Crescent, which was symbolized by the famed temple-tower (ziggurat) of Babylon (Gen. 11:1-9). According to another narrative, the first city was built by a murderer, Cain, who was incensed that his agricultural offering of the "fruit of the ground" was not as acceptable to Yahweh as his brother's nomadic gift of the firstlings of the flock (Gen. 4:1-17). Noah, we are told, was the first man to till the soil and plant a vineyard—the characteristic agriculture of Canaan; but his activity led to a revolting spectacle of drunkenness and nakedness, and Canaan, the son of Ham, was cursed with a threefold curse (Gen. 9:18-27). This nomadic reaction against Canaanite culture persisted in some Israelite circles long after the time of the conquest (see Jer. 35).

But this negative attitude toward Canaanite culture was offset by the opposite extreme, which became increasingly popular in the period of the settlement in Canaan—namely, the wholesale adoption of Canaanite ways. This was a great temptation because, contrary to some of the exaggerated claims of the book of Joshua, the Canaanites were not exterminated or even reduced to insignificance by Israelite military victories. Although the Canaanite population must have been diminished significantly, the Israelites nevertheless had to settle down in their midst. Moreover, we must remember that the Tribal Confederacy had been formed at Shechem in the very heart of Canaanite culture, and it embraced new converts who previously had been worshiping the "strange gods" of the pre-Mosaic period. The very diversity of the Israelite confederacy undoubtedly made a relapse from the stern demands of the Mosaic faith unavoidable.

Hence the sermonic warnings of Moses in the book of Deuteronomy, though they were actually written many years later, appropriately emphasize the great dangers and temptations of life in Canaan. Israel's transition from the status of seminomadic Hebrews to the sedentary existence of farmers in the Fertile Crescent had fateful and far-reaching implications. Previously, Yahweh had been the God of the wanderers, but now Israel's relationship was to the soil, which had to be tilled. The human problem increasingly came to center around man's relation to nature: the need of rainfall for crops, the dependence upon the rotation of the seasons, and the concern for fertility which pervaded the whole Fertile Crescent. In the past, Yahweh had shown his power to control history; the new question was whether he could win out in the rivalry with the gods who controlled the cycles of nature.

The Deuteronomic Interpretation

Our major source for studying the transitional twelfth and eleventh centuries is the book of Judges, the second book in the Deuteronomic History. Not all the present book of Judges belongs to the Deuteronomic edition. The preface (Judg. 1-2:5), which has been mentioned in connection with the Conquest (see pp. 86-87), and the appendix (Judg. 17-21), contain extremely valuable information for the period. These passages, however, stand outside the Deuteronomic framework which embraces the material found in Judges 2:6-16:31.

The Deuteronomic "theology of history" is found in capsule form in the introduction to the Deuteronomic section (Judg. 2:6-3:6). After a recapitulation of the conclusion of the book of Joshua (compare Josh. 24:28-31 and Judg. 2:6-9), the narrative describes the new situation that prevailed after the death of Joshua. During Joshua's lifetime, we are told, the people remained faithful to Yahweh, for they had lived through the great events in which his saving power had been made known. But "there arose another generation after them, who did not know Yahweh or the work which he had done for Israel"

(Judg. 2:10). Faith in Yahweh was not belief in a body of knowledge that could be transferred, like a bank account, from father to son. To *know* Yahweh was to acknowledge him personally, to be in covenant relation with him. The faith of the fathers does not necessarily become the faith of the sons, as we well know. Each generation must either renew or repudiate the covenant in its own way.

According to the Deuteronomic view, the history of the period followed a neat pattern. Israel's ups and downs illustrated the basic theological conviction of the Deuteronomic historian: obedience to Yahweh leads to welfare and peace; disobedience leads to hardship and defeat. This lesson of history is illustrated graphically in the rhythm of events:

> 1. The people of Israel did what was evil by forsaking Yahweh, who brought them out of Egypt, and by turning to serve the gods of the surrounding peoples.
> 2. Therefore Yahweh's anger was kindled against them, and he delivered them into the power of their enemies, who oppressed them.
> 3. In their affliction, the people cried out in penitence. So Yahweh, moved to pity, raised up a judge who delivered them from their enemies. Throughout the lifetime of the judge, the land enjoyed rest.
> 4. However, when the judge died the people fell back into idolatry. Therefore the anger of Yahweh was kindled against Israel and he sold them again into the hands of their plunderers.

This is the scheme that is outlined in Judges 2:6-3:6. Usually the Deuteronomic summary is found at the beginning and end of the stories of the major judges, as in the cases of Othniel, Ehud, Deborah (and Barak), Gideon (also called Jerubbaal), Jephthah, and Samson. The account of Othniel (Judg. 3:7-11) is an excellent illustration. These stories, which were drawn from ancient tribal traditions, have been incorporated loosely into the Deuteronomic framework, somewhat as an old picture is put into a new frame. As a result, the events of the period are interpreted as following a rhythm of rebellion and return.

This Deuteronomic pattern is too neat and schematic to do justice to the complexity of events in the period of the judges. But it does contain much truth. As we well know, the downfall of a people often begins not with external military pressure, but with internal moral and spiritual degeneration. The Deuteronomic historian attempted to emphasize the central truth that Israel's vitality and solidarity lay in a united, exclusive loyalty to Yahweh. When this covenant faith was strong, Israel was in a better position to cope with the inrush of foreign ideas and armies. But when this faith was weakened by the morally decadent nature religion of the Fertile Crescent, Israel was an easy prey to her enemies. In that ancient period, the most divisive and destructive threat that Israel faced was the Canaanite religion. Undoubtedly Israel would have been lost in the cultural melting pot of the Fertile Crescent had it not been for the military crises which providently rallied the Israelites to the standard of the Mosaic faith and renewed their loyalty to the God of history.

Religion and Agriculture

To appreciate the nature of the struggle of the period of the judges, we must know something about the religion of Canaan, which in the Old Testament is described as the worship of the Baals and Ashtarts (Judg. 2:13; 10:6; I Sam. 7:4; 12:10). The title "Baal" means "lord" or "owner," and designates the male deity who owns the land and controls its fertility. His female partner is known as "Baalath," "lady," although in the cases cited above her personal name is Ashtart. It was believed that these fertility powers were connected with particular localities or towns, in which case one could speak of many Baals and Ashtarts, as numerous as the cities of the land (see Jer. 2:28). But it was also possible to regard these local powers as manifestations of the great "lord" and "lady" who dwell in the heavens, in which case worshipers could address Baal and Ashtart in the singular as cosmic deities.

A modern farmer, despite his training in the science of agriculture, sometimes marvels at the strange powers of fertility that work in the soil (even yet called "Mother Earth") to bring about a fruitful harvest. In those moments he is linked with his ancient predecessors—men of the soil who from time immemorial have marveled at the astonishing mystery of nature without which there could be no agriculture. In the Fertile Crescent,

THE "BAAL OF THE LIGHTNING" *was found in a sanctuary at Ras Shamra, Syria. Apparently treading upon mountains, the god—lord of storm and fertility—wields a club in his right hand and with his left hand holds a lance, the upper part of which may symbolize lightning. On his helmet are the horns of the bull, the cult animal which represents the power of fertility. Notice the poetic use of this imagery in Micah 1:3 and Numbers 24:8.*

THE MOTHER—GODDESS
*known as "the queen of
wild beasts": this ivory
representation (from the
fourteenth century* B.C.)
*was found in a tomb near
Ras Shamra. Two goats
stand on their hind legs,
apparently reaching for
the stalks of grain she
holds in her hands.*

where the whole culture was dependent upon the fruitfulness of the soil, this mystery was viewed in a religious way. The ground, it was said, is the sphere of divine powers. The Baal of a region is the "lord" or "owner" of the ground; its fertility is dependent upon sexual relations between him and his consort. When the rains came and the earth and water mingled, the mysterious powers of fertility stirred again. New life was resurrected after the barrenness of winter. This astonishing revival of nature, men believed, was due to sexual intercourse between Baal and his partner, Baalath.

Furthermore, man was not a mere spectator of the sacred marriage. It was believed that by ritually enacting the drama of Baal it was possible to assist—through magical power—the fertility powers to reach their consummation, and thereby to insure the welfare and prosperity of the land. The cooperation with the powers of fertility involved the dramatization in the temples of the story of Baal's loves and wars. Besides the rehearsal of this mythology, a prominent feature of the Canaanite cult was sacred prostitution (see Deut. 23:18). In the act of temple prostitution the man identified himself with Baal, the woman with Ashtart. It was believed that human pairs, by imitating the action of Baal and his partner, could bring the divine pair together in fertilizing union.

Enough has been said to indicate that Canaanite religion was highly erotic. But this eroticism was not just the expression of a desire for pleasure through sex (as it so often is in modern culture). Rather, it was believed that the whole natural sphere, to which the existence of the farmer was intimately bound, was governed by the vitalities of sex—the powers of the masculine and the feminine. Through sexual ceremonies farmers could swing into the rhythms of the agricultural world, and even keep those rhythms going through the techniques of religious magic. The kind of magic in question is often called sympathetic or imitative magic. It rests on the assumption that when men imitate the action of the gods, a power is released to bring that action about. (For example: the "rainmaker" who, by pouring water from a tree and thereby imitating rain, induces the gods to end a drought.)

The Ras Shamra Epic

The pattern of nature religion found in Canaan was of one piece with the myth and ritual which, in varying forms, was spread throughout the whole Fertile Crescent.[1] In Babylonia, for example, the Tammuz cult dramatized the relations between the god Tammuz and the goddess Ishtar. In Egypt the Isis cult was based on the worship of the god Osiris (Horus) and his female counterpart Isis (Hathor). And, as we have seen, in Canaan the Baal cult dramatized the relations between the storm god Baal and his consort, known as Anath or Ashtart (the Canaanite equivalent of Ishtar). The basic similarity of these religions encouraged a great deal of borrowing back and forth, for they appealed to a common concern about man's relation to nature.

We can get a clear picture of Canaanite religion from the Ras Shamra tablets, first discovered in 1929 at Ras Shamra on the coast of northern Syria, the site of the ancient Canaanite city of Ugarit.[2] These mythological texts date from about 1400 B.C.—that is, from the Amarna Age. Just as the Amarna letters (see above, pp. 80-81) give a picture of the political conditions in Canaan before the conquest, so the Ras Shamra texts give firsthand information about the religious situation. In many respects, this was a highly developed, sophisticated religion, far ahead of the belief in local fertility spirits which scholars once thought the religion of the Baals and the Ashtarts to have been. At the head of the Canaanite pantheon was the high god, El, "the King, Father of Years," whose consort was Asherah. Next in rank was the great storm-god, Baal, who was celebrated as lord of the gods and creator of mankind. In the ritual poems the chief role is played by Baal, the god of rain and fertility, who, like his father, takes the form of a bull, the animal of strength and fertility. His consort-sister is the warrior goddess Anath, known for violent sexual passion and sadistic brutality.

---

[1] See especially H. and H. A. Frankfort, et al., The Intellectual Adventure [123].

[2] See Pritchard, Ancient Near Eastern Texts, pp. 129-155. A brief summary is given by W. F. Albright, "The Old Testament World" [39]. See also G. R. Driver, Canaanite Myths and Legends [120]; John Gray, The Legacy of Canaan [124].

It is difficult to piece together the fragments of the Baal epic into their original dramatic sequence. Apparently the drama opens with an account of Baal's rise to pre-eminence as a result of his victorious conflict with the primordial water dragon, who was known as Prince Sea and Judge River. We next hear of Baal's preparations to build a temple, with the assistance of his sister, the maiden Anath. Evidently these plans are interrupted by the action of Mot, the god of summer drought, who kills Baal and carries him down to the underworld. When the gods hear that "the lord of the earth" has perished, they mourn deeply; but Anath is seized by a great passion for Baal and searches for him. When she finally finds him in the possession of Mot, a furious struggle ensues. Mot is killed, Baal is resurrected and put on his throne, and the lovers are reunited. There is great rejoicing in heaven.

> In a dream, O Kindly One, God of Mercy (?),
> In a vision, Creator of Creatures,
> The heavens rained oil,
> The dry valleys flowed with honey;
> So I know
> That Triumphant Baal lives,
> That the Prince, Lord of Earth, is alive! [3]

These lines show the connection between Baal's resurrection and the revival of fertility. Indeed, the myth of Baal's death and resurrection represents the conflict waged in nature as the seasons come and go. Baal personifies the fertilizing powers of springtime; Mot personifies the destructive powers that bring death to vegetation and life. There is a rhythm in nature: springtime and summer, fertility and drought, life and death. According to the ancient view, the farmer's life is caught up in this alternation. Existence is a precarious dependence upon the powers of nature. It was believed that religion gave man a way to control nature and thereby to insure the fruitfulness of the soil. By re-enacting the mythological drama of Baal's death and resurrection in the temple, so it was believed, a magical power was released that would guarantee fertility and well-being. And through myth and ritual the worshiper related himself to what was believed to be divine.

Attempts at Compromise

Here, then, was a practical religion for farmers. In Canaan, Baal was recognized as the lord of the earth: the owner of the land, the giver of rain, the source of the grain, wine, and oil. People believed that the agricultural harvest would not be plentiful unless the fertility powers were worshiped according to the ways of Canaan. To have ignored the Baal rites in those days

---

[3] Translated by W. F. Albright, *Interpreter's Bible*, I, p. 261.

would have seemed as impractical as for a modern farmer to ignore science in the cultivation of the land.

It is not surprising, then, that the Israelites, unaccustomed to the ways of agriculture, turned to the gods of the land. They did not mean to turn away from Yahweh, the God of the Exodus and the Sinai covenant. To Yahweh they would look in times of military crisis; and to Baal they would turn for success in agriculture. Thus they would serve Yahweh and Baal side by side. Like many modern people who keep religion and science in separate compartments, they would acknowledge that each was lord in his own sphere. Perhaps it was believed that one faith was the official public religion, and the other was a religion for home and farm life. In any case, it was not felt that the two religions were contradictory or mutually exclusive.

There was a strong tendency for the two faiths to coalesce in popular worship. As we know from archaeology, in the outlying regions of Israel people had in their possession figurines, small statuettes of the goddess of fertility, Ashtart. Elements of ritual and mythology were taken over from Canaanite religion and incorporated into the worship of Yahweh. Former Canaanite sanctuaries, like Bethel, Shechem, and perhaps Gilgal, were rededicated to Yahweh, and the Canaanite agricultural calendar was adopted for the timing of the pilgrimage festivals (Ex. 34:22-23). Parents began naming their children after Baal, apparently with no thought of abandoning Yahweh. One of the judges, Gideon, was also named Jerub-baal, which means "let Baal contend," or perhaps "may Baal multiply." Saul and David, both ardent devotees of Yahweh, gave Baal names to their children.[4] As late as the eighth century B.C., Israelites—according to the prophet Hosea—actually addressed Yahweh as "Baal," and by worshiping him according to the rituals of Baal sought the blessings of fertility (Hos. 2). At the popular level this syncretism—that is, the fusion of different religious forms and views—went on to some degree from the time Israel first set foot on Canaanite soil.[5]

As we have noticed, this syncretism was going on constantly in the commingling cultures of the Fertile Crescent, for the religions of the area had a great deal in common. But Israel's faith was based on the novel belief in a *jealous* God who would tolerate no rivals. According to the terms of the covenant, Israel was to have "no other gods before Yahweh." Yahweh's lordship over his people was absolute, extending into every sphere of life. Therefore, to believe that Yahweh was lord in one sphere (history) and Baal in another

---

[4] Two of Saul's children were called Mephi*baal* (Mephibosheth) and Ish*baal*. Jonathan had a son named Meri*baal* (Meribosheth). The word *bosheth* (Hebrew: "shame") was later substituted by someone horrified at the presence of "baal" in the name. See II Sam. 21:8; 4:4; 9:6; I Chron. 8:34. One of David's daughters was named Beeliada (I Chron. 14:7).

[5] This "crisis due to the conquest" is discussed by Gerhard von Rad, *Theology*, I [80], pp. 15-35, who points out that in the course of the struggle between Yahweh and Baal the Israelite faith adopted new forms of expression and "came more than ever before into its own."

(fertilization of the soil) was a fundamental violation of the meaning of the covenant. Later, prophets saw clearly the basic conflict between the two faiths and threw down the challenge: Yahweh versus Baal. Joshua's appeal, voiced at Shechem, echoed through the years. "Choose this day whom you will serve." There could be no compromise, for Yahweh willed to be the lord of the whole of life and to receive the devotion of man's whole heart.

Religion and Sex

It has been well said that "only as a religion has to meet the challenge of its opposite does it discover its own nature and potential strength." [6] Despite popular attempts to blend Canaanite religion and the Mosaic faith, the two were basically incompatible, like oil and water. Since both understood man's relation to the deity in radically different terms, they found expression in diametrically different world outlooks.[7] The opposition expressed in the phrase "Yahweh versus Baal" comes to focus in the meaning of sex.

In Canaanite religion, sex was elevated to the realm of the divine. The divine powers, it was believed, were disclosed in the sphere of nature—that is, in the mystery of fertility. The gods were sexual in nature, and were worshiped in sexual rites. The erotic relations of god and goddess were hidden within the ever-recurring cycle of the death and renewal of fertility, represented mythologically by the annual death and resurrection of Baal. But this cycle of fertility, according to the ancient view, did not take place by itself through natural law. Rather, the purpose of religion was to preserve and enhance the fertility upon which man was dependent for his existence. It sought to control the gods in the interest of human well-being. And since this religion aimed to maintain the harmony and rhythm of the natural order, it was a serviceable tool for the aristocracy who wished to maintain the social *status quo* against disruptive changes.[8] Baalism catered to man's desire for security in the precarious environment of the Fertile Crescent.

According to Israel's faith, on the other hand, the power of the divine was disclosed in the sphere of history—that is, in the wonder of a *non-recurring event* (the Exodus) which was at once the sign of God's deliverance of his people from servitude and the call to obey his will within a covenant com-

---

[6] H. Wheeler Robinson in *A Companion to the Bible*, ed. by T. W. Manson (Edinburgh: T. & T. Clark, 1939), p. 293.

[7] An excellent analysis of the religion of 'archaic' man is found in the writings of Mircea Eliade, especially *Cosmos and History* [121], and *The Sacred and the Profane* [122]. In the preface to the former he writes (p. vii): "The chief difference between the man of the archaic and traditional societies and the man of the modern societies with their strong imprint of Judaeo-Christianity lies in the fact that the former feels himself indissolubly connected with the Cosmos and the cosmic rhythms, whereas the latter insists that he is connected only with History."

[8] See G. Ernest Wright, *The Old Testament Against Its Environment* [125], pp. 42-46, for a contrast with the social dynamic of Israel's faith.

munity. Unlike Baal, Yahweh has no consort at his side.[9] He is neither sexual in nature, nor is he to be worshiped by sexual rites. To be sure, Israel's faith does not take a negative view toward sex, for sex belongs to the divine creation and as such is hallowed (see Gen. 1:27-28). But although Yahweh is Lord of fertility, he is not a fertility god subject to the death and resurrection of the natural world. He is "the Living God" who reveals himself in the arena of men's history—where human life touches life, where injustices oppress and hopes for deliverance are felt, where men are called to make decisions that alter the course of the future. While Baal religion taught men to *control* the gods, Israel's faith stressed *serving* God in gratitude for his benevolence and in response to the task which he lays upon his people. Yahweh could not be coerced by magic. He could only be trusted or betrayed, obeyed or disobeyed, but in all things his will was sovereign.

With their desert background, Israel's more discerning leaders sensed the fundamental opposition between the stern demands of Yahweh and the erotic religion of Canaan. Was the meaning of man's life in Canaan disclosed in his relation to divine powers within nature, or in his relation to the Lord of history? This fundamental question was not answered overnight. In Canaanite religion, Israel's faith met the challenge of its opposite, but it took many generations for the true strength and uniqueness of the Mosaic faith to be seen. The victory, when it finally was won, shook the religious foundations of agriculture in Canaan and gave to farmers a new understanding of their vocation.[10]

The first phase of the conflict was waged during the period of the judges. Israel's initial response to the new environment of Canaan was to turn to the Baal cult for agricultural success. But, though obsessed with the problems of fertility, Israel could not forget the demands of history, for her existence was threatened by enemies on all sides. As the Deuteronomic historian points out, in times of crisis, when Israel was oppressed by foes, the people turned with renewed zeal to the worship of Yahweh, the God of history. Let us examine briefly the history of Israel during this period.

LEADERS IN CRISIS

Israel's invasion of Canaan and her expansion in the hill country were made possible, as we have seen, by the lack of political interference by any strong power from Egypt or Mesopotamia. There is, significantly, no reference in the

---

[9] In the fifth century B.C. a Jewish colony in Elephantine, Egypt, apparently believed that Yahweh had a partner, Anath. This interpretation, however, is challenged by W. F. Albright, *From the Stone Age* [59], pp. 286-287.

[10] This point is made forcefully by Martin Buber, *The Prophetic Faith* [118], pp. 70-76. It will become clearer in our later discussion of prophets such as Elijah and Hosea in Chapters 7 and 8.

book of Judges to Egyptian intervention. After the death of Pharaoh Merneptah in about 1216 B.C., Egypt lost control of her Asiatic empire and, with the exception of a brief revival under Rameses III (c. 1175-1144 B.C.), lapsed into confusion and political impotence. The Hittites, who had been fought to a standstill by the Egyptians, soon disappeared as a world power as a result of population disturbances in the Aegean at the beginning of the twelfth century. In Mesopotamia, Assyria was beginning to rise to power (about 1250), but as yet she posed no threat to Canaan. Thus Israel's political rivals were confined to Canaan and its immediate vicinity: the new nations in Transjordan, raiders from the Arabian desert, the Canaanite city-states, and the new arrivals known as the Philistines.

The stories in the book of Judges that picture the local conflicts and tribal jealousies of the period are unquestionably derived from very old sources. The Deuteronomic editors have touched up some of the narratives by adding introductory and concluding formulas. But for some reason the narrative of Abimelech and the accounts of the so-called minor judges (Judg. 10:1-5 and 12:8-15) were not altered at all. Similarly, chapters 17-21 show no traces of Deuteronomic editing, and were evidently added to the Deuteronomic edition of Judges (2:6-16:31) by someone else. Thus when the Deuteronomic "framework" is removed, we have at our disposal ancient and reliable traditions concerning the period which began with the death of Joshua (c. 1200 B.C.).

When we read these stories by themselves, we gain a clear impression of how loosely organized the Israelite tribes were. The present book of Judges relates how twelve judges, in successive reigns amounting to 410 years, held sway over all Israel. But this is an oversimplification. Actually, tribal leaders arose from time to time in certain trouble-spots in order to relieve the pressure on a specific area. For instance, Ehud was a member of the tribe of Benjamin. Sometimes these leaders were able to appeal to other tribes for support, but by and large their leadership was local in character and was confined to emergency situations.

Nevertheless, there was a sense of participating in a community that transcended the boundaries of any particular tribe. The twelve-tribe confederacy, whose beginnings we have already considered (see above, pp. 90-97), provided a common basis of worship and social responsibility. Not only did the tribes gather at the common confederate sanctuary of Shiloh for annual religious festivals, as we learn from Judges 21:19 (see also I Sam. 1:3; 2:19),[11] but in times of emergency they were summoned to concerted action in the name of the God

---

[11] After the central sanctuary was moved from Shechem, apparently Bethel was the confederate center for a time (Judg. 20:26-27) and then Shiloh was selected. During this period Gilgal, near Jericho, was probably visited by pilgrims who celebrated there the crossing of the Jordan and the entrance into the Promised Land. This suggestion has been advanced by H. J. Kraus, "Gilgal: Ein Betrag zur Kultusgeschichte Israels," in Vetus Testamentum, I (1951), pp. 181-199. See also his Gottesdienst in Israel [206], pp. 179-193.

of the covenant. A vivid example of such action is given in the story of the Gibeah outrage, related in Judges 19-21. There we read that a Levite, incensed at the rape-murder of his concubine by some Benjaminites, cut up her corpse into twelve pieces and sent the parts throughout "all the territory of Israel." The act of dividing the body into twelve parts (see also I Sam. 11:7) indicates, of course, the twelve-part structure of the Israelite confederacy. The tribal response to this symbolic act was quick and decisive, indicating that the tribes were bound together by a common sense of law and decency, even when one of the tribes was an offender:

> And all who saw it said, "Such a thing has never happened or been seen from the day that the people of Israel came up out of the land of Egypt until this day; consider it, take counsel, and speak."
>
> —JUDGES 19:30

So, we are told, all the men of Israel gathered together in the "assembly of the people of God" and resolved to take punitive action, "united as one man."

The Role Of The Judge

Within this framework of the Tribal Confederacy we must understand the role of Israel's judges. The Hebrew word *shofeṭ* is not an exact equivalent of our word "judge," which is restricted to legal functions. In ancient Semitic thought, the role of leadership meant procuring the right of the people either by taking military action or by judging legal disputes. The word *shofeṭ* is close in meaning to "ruler," as we see in this passage from the Ras Shamra tablets:

> Our king is Triumphant Baal,
> Our judge, above whom there is no one! [12]

Hence the statement that so-and-so "judged Israel" must be taken in a wider sense than the English translation implies. Primarily, the judge was a military champion or "deliverer" (Judg. 2:16), although he did play a part in internal arbitration, as in the cases of the judge Deborah (Judg. 4:4-5) and the last judge, Samuel (I Sam. 7:15-17). The authority of a judge extended beyond the locale of his tribe, and was recognized in the territory of the Tribal Confederacy. It is possible that when the tribes convened at the central sanctuary for covenant-renewal festivals the judge presided as "covenant mediator." [13]

---

[12] See Amos 2:3 and Isaiah 40:23, to cite just two passages in which *shofeṭ* means "ruler." In ancient Carthage, the heir of Phoenician (that is, Canaanite) culture, magistrates were known as *sufetes*.

[13] Martin Noth, in "Das Amt des 'Richters Israels'" (*Festschrift A. Bertholet* [Tübingen: J. C. B. Mohr, 1950], pp. 404-417), maintains that the so-called "minor judges" mentioned in 10:1-5 and 12:7-15 were actually legal administrators selected by the Confederacy. But this theory presupposes the dubious view that the book of Judges tells about two different kinds of leaders, whereas the tradition indicates that the two functions—legal and military—were combined in one person.

Unlike the dynastic office of the king, which was passed on from father to son, the office of the judge was non-hereditary and rested upon a special endowment of Yahweh's spirit. For this reason, the judges have been called "charismatic leaders"—that is, leaders qualified to head the Tribal Confederacy by virtue of the divine *charisma*, or spiritual power, which possessed them. So we read, for instance, that "the spirit of Yahweh took possession of Gideon" or literally "clothed itself with Gideon," empowering him with an authority that was recognized not only in his own clan but in surrounding tribes (Judg. 6:34-35). More vivid examples are found in the legendary Samson stories, where we read that "the spirit of Yahweh came upon him mightily," empowering him to accomplish superhuman feats (see Judg. 14:6). Deborah, too, was a charismatic leader who summoned the tribes of Israel to military action against the Canaanites in the name of Yahweh (Judg. 4-5). Presumably, a judge's success in battle or his extraordinary physical prowess encouraged people from the various tribes to consult him also in cases of legal dispute. In this way, Israel's covenant law (see above, pp. 95-97) was applied to specific cases and was expanded.

Since the judges did not follow one another in chronological succession, contrary to the impression created by the Deuteronomic historian, it is difficult to outline the sequence of events between the death of Joshua and the time of Saul, the first king of Israel. However, we do have in these stories vivid vignettes of conditions and crises during the twelfth and eleventh centuries B.C. We deal with them in terms of areas of pressure upon the Israelite confederacy.

The Battle of Megiddo

The Israelites, as we have seen, had managed to entrench themselves in the central hill country, but could not dispossess the Canaanites on the plains. The most strategic area under Canaanite control was the Valley of Jezreel, through which the main commercial route ran from Egypt to Mesopotamia. Guarding the pass into the valley was the Canaanite fortress of Megiddo, the scene of many decisive battles and, according to religious imagination, the scene of the final battle of Armageddon.[14] So long as the Canaanites were in control of this commercial lifeline, they could throttle Israel's economic life. This was the situation, we are told, during the days of the judge, Shamgar (Judg. 3:31):

> In the days of Shamgar, son of Anath,
> in the days of Jael, caravans ceased
> and travellers kept to the byways.
> —JUDGES 5:6

Spurred into action by Deborah and under the command of Barak, the Israelite forces met General Sisera's Canaanite army in the vicinity of the fortified city

---

[14] Ar-mageddon, referred to in Revelation 16:16, literally means "hill of Megiddo."

THE PASS OF MEGIDDO *as viewed looking to the southwest. Through this pass ran the main coastal highway from the plain of Jezreel to Gaza and the Egyptian frontier. Many battles, ancient and modern, have been fought in this strategic area which in antiquity was guarded by the heavily fortified city of Megiddo.*

of Taanach (Judg. 5:19), which provides a commanding view of Megiddo and the whole plain.[15] Apparently only half of the tribes of the Israelite confederacy responded to the summons of Deborah, a charismatic leader. Victory was theirs that day, thanks to a terrific rainstorm that caused the river Kishon, which flows through the plain of Jezreel, to overflow its banks, with the result that the Canaanite charioteers were helplessly trapped in miry clay.

The account of this battle is given in two versions: a poetic version, the Song of Deborah, in Judges 5; and a prose version in Judges 4, which differs somewhat in details. By general agreement, the Song of Deborah is a first-hand, authentic historical witness. It is one of the oldest passages of poetry in the Old Testament, written by one who stood very near the event, perhaps by a participant. Archaeological work at Megiddo has produced evidence for dating the battle and the song that celebrates the event in the latter part of the twelfth century B.C., approximately 1125 B.C.[16]

The meaning of the victory is far more effectively communicated in the poem than in the later prose version. Even in English translation the reader is made

---

[15] Recently Taanach has been excavated under the archaeological direction of Paul Lapp; see *The Biblical Archaeologist*, XXVI, 4 (1963), pp. 130-132.

[16] W. F. Albright, who argues for this date, points out that the poetry of the Song of Deborah has striking affinities with Canaanite style known from the Ras Shamra literature. See his article "The Song of Deborah in the Light of Archaeology," *Bulletin of the American School of Oriental Research*, LXII (1936), pp. 26-31.

vividly aware of the spirit of the battle. He senses the quickened pulse beat that responds to the summons to participate in the historic crisis. He is carried along with the "galloping rhythm" toward the climax of victory. He feels the fiercely victorious passion of Jael the Kenite (cf. 4:11; see above, p. 41) and by contrast the bitter pathos of Sisera's mother looking for a son who would never return. The poem deals with history as it was lived, not with history as reported by a detached observer.

To the author of the poem, the event was overwhelming because of its religious meaning. The storm that defeated the Canaanites is seen to be the sign of Yahweh's active presence as the leader and champion of his people. According to the poet's passionate faith, no array of human forces can stand against Yahweh. He is Lord of the heaven and the earth, the Sovereign of history who makes the elements of nature serve his purpose. Even the stars—conceived as Yahweh's heavenly host—join in the battle:

> From heaven fought the stars,
> from their courses they fought against Sisera.
> —JUDGES 5:20

Hence his song begins and ends with an exclamation of praise. In the experience of the poet, it was Yahweh's participation in the battle that made the event historic and momentous.

The poem forcefully expresses the cardinal conviction of the Mosaic faith: Yahweh is the "God of Israel" (verses 3, 5) and Israel is "the people of Yahweh" (verses 11, 13). Although there is no reference to the covenant, this close relationship between God and people is the basis of the whole poem. Yahweh is praised as the Leader of his people, who comes in a storm from Sinai through the region of Edom (verses 4-5). The people are exhorted to rehearse his "triumphs," his mighty acts (verse 11: literally, "his righteous deeds"). And since Yahweh goes forth at the head of his people, the tribes are summoned to decision—to come to his side in holy war.[17] Those tribes who did not answer the summons, who "came not to the help of Yahweh against the mighty" (verse 23), are denounced in the strongest terms, for they were not acting as "the people of Yahweh." Here we see that the basis of Israel was not just political or family ties, but voluntary dedication to Yahweh, the exclusive Lord of the Tribal Confederacy. To the true Israel belong only those tribes who choose to serve Yahweh with their full measure of devotion. They are his "friends," those who love him (verse 31). There is no clearer witness in the Old Testament to the historical character of Israel's faith than the Song of Deborah.

---

[17] On holy war see especially De Vaux, *Ancient Israel* [62], pp. 258-267. An important work in German is Gerhard von Rad, *Der heilige Krieg im alten Israel* (Zurich: Zwingli Verlag, 1951).

Foes from Other Directions

Israel's decisive victory over Sisera's host marked the end of any united Canaanite resistance against Israel. However, troubles came to Israel from other directions. The newly established kingdoms of Transjordan looked with jealous eyes on Israel's holdings both in Transjordan itself and in Canaan. Moab, under

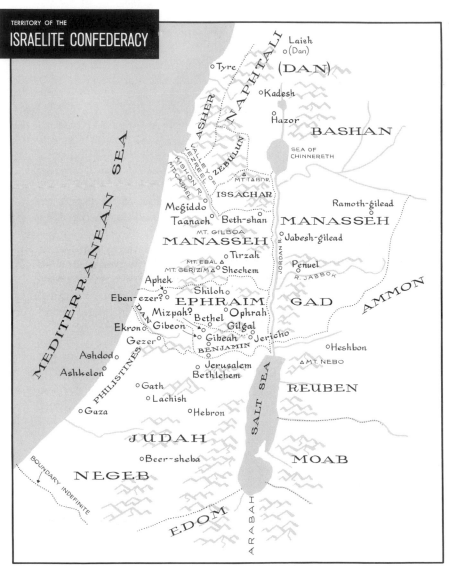

TERRITORY OF THE

ISRAELITE CONFEDERACY

the leadership of a king named Eglon, invaded Israelite territory and took "the city of palms," Jericho (see the mosaic map on Plate 2). The tide was turned by a deliverer named Ehud, who delivered "a message from God" to Eglon in a left-handed manner with a dagger (Judg. 3:12-30). Later, Israel suffered a series of attacks from the Ammonites, both in Transjordan and in the Canaanite hill country. This threat was met effectively by Jephthah (Judg. 10:6-12:7).

Even more serious, however, was a series of devastating attacks by Midianite raiders who came in from the Arabian desert on camels. The use of the camel was something new in military tactics. The wild tribesmen of Arabia had learned how to use fleets of camels for traveling long distances to make surprise attacks on settled villages. So effective were the raids of these camel-riding nomads that the Israelites had to leave their villages and take to mountain caves:

> For they [the Midianites] would come up with their cattle and their
> tents, coming like locusts for number; both they and their camels could
> not be counted; so that they wasted the land as they came in.
> —JUDGES 6:5

In the face of these raids, the Israelites could not carry on their farming, and were in danger of losing everything they had gained by the conquest. In this dire emergency the day was saved by a judge named Gideon, otherwise known as Jerubbaal (Judg. 6-8). Gideon's military leadership was based on his charismatic zeal for Yahweh—zeal directed against those, even of his own family, who had turned to Baal. Although Gideon's father, Joash, had a Yahweh name (including the element *Yah* [Yo]), he erected a Baal altar with a fertility tree, an Asherah, beside it. Gideon destroyed the Baal cult objects and built an altar to Yahweh instead, much to the displeasure of the men of the city of Ophrah (Judg. 6:25-32). This story is important because it shows how deeply Canaanite rites and conceptions had infiltrated, and because it shows how Israel's strength in time of crisis was connected with a revival of a vigorous faith in Yahweh, the God of the Tribal Confederacy. To the surprise of Gideon, and perhaps to the dismay of any man who wants to stand on his own feet, the narrator insists that the victory belongs to Yahweh *alone*, who needs a task force of only 300 men for the huge offensive.[18]

Throughout the twelfth and eleventh centuries, the threat to Israel was increased by the pressure of newcomers known as Philistines. As we have seen, the Philistines were one of a number of "sea peoples" who poured out of the Aegean onto the eastern shores of the Mediterranean (see above, pp. 81-82). Shortly after 1200 B.C., they swarmed into Canaan by sea and by land, and established a beach-head on the coastal plain. They came during a great transi-

---

[18] It is interesting to compare the biblical story with a modern interpretation: *Gideon, A New Play* (New York: Random House, 1962), by Paddy Chayefsky.

tional epoch which in archaeological terms marked the beginning of the Iron Age (1200-600 B.C.). Their natural aggressiveness was augmented by their skill in making instruments and weapons of iron, a trade in which they achieved a virtual monopoly. From their restricted base on the coast, the Philistines began to move inland, sweeping away Canaanite resistance and coming into contact with the already entrenched and victorious Israelites. In fact, the Philistines came close to making Canaan a Philistine empire. One of the great ironies of history is that the name later given to Israel's land, Palestine, is derived from the name of Israel's archenemies, the Philistines!

Early in the book of Judges we read briefly of the exploits of a certain Shamgar, who slew six hundred Philistines with an oxgoad (3:31). This must have occurred fairly early in the Philistine occupation, for Shamgar is referred to in the Song of Deborah (5:6). Elsewhere we hear of the Philistines only in passing, until we come to the Samson cycle at the very end of the Deuteronomic edition of Judges (chapters 13-16). It is unnecessary to go into the details of these lusty stories, which have as their theme the discomfiture of the Philistines by an Israelite Tarzan whose fatal weakness was women. The Samson stories are more legendary than any other material preserved in the book of Judges. Although Samson is regarded as a judge, he is unlike the other judges in that he was not a military leader. These stories deal with the marvelous exploits of an individual and are more designed to tickle the fancy than to record history. Viewed theologically, the story of Samson's tragic demise portrays what happens to a man filled with the *charisma* when he disregards the guidance of Yahweh in a time of crisis to pursue his own passions.

CHRONOLOGICAL CHART 2

B.C.	EGYPT	PALESTINE (AND SYRIA)	MESOPOTAMIA
(Iron Age) 1200 to 1100	XX Dynasty (c. 1180-1065) Sea Peoples defeated by Rameses III (c. 1175) Egyptian decline	Period of the Judges (c. 1200-1020) Philistines settle in Canaan Battle of Megiddo (c. 1125)	Collapse of Hittite Empire Assyrian decline
1100 to 1000	XXI Dynasty (c. 1065-935) Egyptian decline	Philistine ascendancy Fall of Shiloh (c. 1050) Samuel and Saul (c. 1020-1000)	Brief Assyrian revival Tiglath-pileser I (c. 1118-1076)

But the Samson tales do give us a valuable picture of the relations between Israelites and Philistines, probably at the beginning of the eleventh century. We see that the Philistines had consolidated their position on the coast and were strong enough to worry the Israelites up in the hill country into spinning yarns that poked fun at their uncircumcised neighbors. But there were no pitched battles, and we find no expressions of despair over Philistine ascendancy. At the most, these stories reflect border incidents that were not sufficiently grievous to disrupt commercial relations between the two peoples. But by the end of the eleventh century, all this was to change, for the Philistines soon were to be in control of all the arteries leading into the Israelite hill country. As things turned out, this was the first stage in an all-out Philistine offensive that had only one objective: the total destruction, once and for all, of the Israelite confederacy.

PRISONERS OF RAMESES III *are shown bound and tied together by a rope around the neck in this relief carved on the wall of a temple at Medinet Habu, near Thebes (Luxor). The structure was erected to celebrate Rameses' victory in repelling the Sea Peoples, one of whom was the Philistines. The figure wearing the feathered helmet (fourth from the left) is one of the Sea Peoples, perhaps a Philistine. The others are Libyan (with pointed beard and side-lock), Syrian (wearing a kilt), Hittite (beardless and wearing a long garment), and on the far right another unfortunate captive from Syria.*

THE DECLINE OF THE CONFEDERACY

As political pressure mounted, it became increasingly apparent that the Israelite confederacy was an ineffective organization for coping with the troubled situation in Canaan. Even in a time of great peril, as we have already noticed, only half the tribes responded to Deborah's charismatic summons and helped to hurl back Canaanite aggression under Sisera. The twelve tribes were bound together, not by a centralized government, but only by a common devotion to Yahweh, the God of the covenant, and by common religious and legal responsibilities. The Confederacy by its very nature encouraged a high degree of tribal independence. God alone was the ruler of the Israelite tribes. His rule was made known through charismatic judges and through the High Priest who attended the central sanctuary, like Eli at the shrine of Shiloh (I Sam. 1-4). Only when religious festivals were held at the confederate shrine, or when dire emergency arose—such as the Gibeah outrage—did the tribes come together in concert "as one man." This form of organization, at least for a time, spared Israel from the political despotism of the Near East. Moreover, in times of political crisis it threw the people back upon Yahweh, the Lord of history, with the consequent renewal of Israel's distinctive historical faith. For all its merit, however, the Tribal Confederacy was vulnerable to the political forces of the time, as the Philistine menace made clear.

The Shechem Experiment

The first abortive experiment to establish a centralized government was carried out at Shechem, the very place where the Tribal Confederacy had been established in the time of Joshua. Although the name of Abimelech is connected with this incident, some precedent had been established for it previously in the city of Ophrah. Gideon (Jerubbaal) had been successful in his charismatic leadership against the nomadic raids that had all but ruined Israel. In view of his success in the engagement with Midian, and doubtless in view also of the increasing political tension caused by the Philistine menace, the men of Israel offered to crown him king. "Rule over us," they said, "you and your son and your grandson also" (Judg. 8:22). In other words, they proposed to change the basis of his authority from that of nonhereditary, charismatic judgeship to that of a hereditary monarchy modeled after the kingdoms of Transjordan, notably Moab and Ammon.[19] Gideon firmly replied: "I will not rule over you, and my son will not rule over you; Yahweh will rule over you." His answer was con-

---

[19] According to the list in Gen. 36:31-39, the kingship of Edom was dynastic; apparently the petty kings of the Canaanite city-states did not establish a hereditary line.

sistent with the foundations of the Israelite theocracy. Yahweh alone was Israel's king, and it was presumptuous for any man to usurp his throne.

Now, besides the many wives of his harem, Gideon also had a concubine in the city of Shechem who bore him a son named Abimelech. Abimelech's career is recounted in Judges 9. After Gideon's death, so we are told, Abimelech went to his mother's kinsmen in Shechem. Pointing out that he was a kinsman of the Shechemites, he persuaded them that he was entitled to rule over them as king. With money furnished him from the treasury of the Baal-berith ("Lord of the Covenant") temple, he hired rascals as his followers and forthwith liquidated his seventy brothers, with the exception of the youngest, Jotham. With these rivals out of the way, the citizens of Shechem crowned him king, possibly near a sacred pillar that can be seen even today in the ruins of the acropolis known as Beth-millo (9:6). (See the picture on p. 91).

But this incident did not go without rebuke. Standing on Mount Gerizim, Jotham told the famous fable of the trees which, seeking for a king to rule over them, asked the olive, the fig, and the vine in turn, and finally had to settle for the bramble, which still grows abundantly in the area (9:7-15). The implication was that Abimelech's rule, like the inflammable bramble, would be a tinderbox for the fires of revolution. In this pointed attack upon Abimelech's kingdom, Jotham was expressing the attitude toward monarchy that prevailed in the conservative circles of the Israelite confederacy. Abimelech's main support, right from the first, had come from the priesthood of the Baal-berith temple who advocated a kind of government that ran counter to the Israelite theocratic ideal.

For three years (9:22), Abimelech was able to impose his rule over a considerable territory, with Shechem as the chief city of his kingdom. True to Jotham's prediction, however, revolution broke out in Shechem. By means of a strategem of ambush, Abimelech successfully stormed the city and destroyed it, probably about 1100 B.C. (9:45). The revolution must have spread into other parts of his kingdom, for we learn that he met death while attacking the city of Thebez, on the road from Shechem to Beth-shan. Although the Shechem experiment in monarchy failed, it was a fateful shadow of things to come. The days of the Tribal Confederacy were coming to an end. A stronger form of government was needed.

The Fall of Shiloh

At this point we must turn from the book of Judges to the first twelve chapters of the book of I Samuel. In I Samuel 12, Samuel, the last judge of Israel, is giving his farewell address to Israel. Here the Deuteronomic historian concludes his survey of the period of the judges. We shall not attempt to survey all the material in these twelve chapters, but shall refer only to those matters that bear on the collapse of the Tribal Confederacy during the period of Philistine aggression.

Chapters 1 to 3 of I Samuel deal with events at Shiloh, the central sanctuary of the Confederacy, to which it was customary for Israelites to make a pilgrimage each year (1:3, 7, 21) for the purpose of making a sacrifice to Yahweh. There Eli, the High Priest, was "ministering to Yahweh," and the boy Samuel was ministering under Eli. In this troubled period, it was hoped, apparently, that the tribes would be united around the priestly rule of Eli and his sons, who were custodians of the Ark and the sacred oracle. Thus an alternative to monarchy was a hierocracy—that is, the hereditary rule of priests at the confederate sanctuary.

The next section (4:1-7:2) deals with the fortunes of the Ark of the Covenant, which was kept at Shiloh. The Philistines and the Israelites were at war, and the battle was going against Israel. After a serious reversal, the elders of Israel suggested that the Ark be brought out to the battlefield, as had often been done in the past, in order that Yahweh "may come among us and save us from the power of our enemies" (4:3). So the Ark was taken from Shiloh, accompanied by Eli's two sons. Its presence in the Israelite camp caused the raising of a mighty shout "so that the earth resounded." The Philistines were almost panic-stricken when they realized that—in their pagan language—"the gods have come into the camp." Nevertheless, they braced themselves to face the worst. Doubtless to their surprise, they decisively defeated Israel and the Ark was then taken into Palestine territory as a trophy of war.

From this point on, there is no more reference to Shiloh, the Israelite sanctuary. Why this strange silence? Centuries later, when the people of the Southern Kingdom were putting great confidence in the Temple of Jerusalem, Jeremiah reminded them of what had happened to Shiloh:

> Go now to my place that was in Shiloh, where I [Yahweh] made my name dwell at first, and see what I did to it for the wickedness of my people Israel.
>
> —JEREMIAH 7:12-14; see 26:6, 9

Evidently Shiloh was destroyed in some great catastrophe. We now suspect, on the basis of archaeological excavations, that Shiloh was destroyed by the Philistines when they invaded the hill country of Palestine. This occurred at the battle of Ebenezer, when the Ark was taken into captivity. Excavations also show that at the same time the Philistines destroyed a number of other Israelite towns in the highlands.

Quite obviously, Israel was in a desperate plight. A devastating blow had been struck at the very foundation of the Israelite confederacy. The central sanctuary of Shiloh had been burned to the ground. The Ark of the Covenant, the ancient symbol of Yahweh's protecting and guiding presence in the midst of his people, had been seized by uncircumcised pagans. The Philistines were well on their way toward making Canaan a Philistine empire. The shock and despair that these events created among devout Israelites find expression in the stories that cluster around the fate of the Ark. When the High Priest Eli heard the shocking report of the outcome of the battle of Ebenezer, he keeled over, broke his neck, and died. His daughter-in-law, who gave birth to a son in the fateful hour of Israel's defeat, named the child Ichabod, an unhappy name which testified that "the glory has departed from Israel" (I Sam. 4:12-22)—that is, the Ark, the seat of Yahweh's presence, had gone into exile.

Why the Philistines failed to take full advantage of their military opportunity, when the mastery of Palestine was almost in their grasp, is something of a mystery. There may have been internal weaknesses in the Philistine alliance of city-states. But the one factor with which they could not reckon was the Yahweh faith, which, as we have seen in the case of previous disasters, showed an amazing resilience and vitality in time of political crisis. Yahweh's control of history was not bound up with any form of political organization, not even the Israelite confederacy. Therefore political defeat was not Yahweh's defeat, even though in times of despair this may have been the popular sentiment. Yahweh had the power to discipline his people with political disaster, as well as to bless them with victory. In terms of Israel's prophetic faith, political crisis was an occasion for the people to search their hearts penitently and to renew their allegiance to the God of the covenant. Such a religious renewal took place in the dark hour of the Philistine ascendancy.

THE LAST JUDGE OF ISRAEL

The person who was instrumental in this religious renewal was the prophet-judge Samuel, unquestionably the greatest spiritual leader of Israel since the time of Moses. His career marked the transition from the old type of charismatic leadership to the new prophetic leadership which, from this time on, played an outstanding role in Israel's life. Under his spiritual guidance, Israel made the shift from the politically inadequate Tribal Confederacy to the more stable government of the monarchy.

Samuel's leadership is portrayed in two types of tradition, which can be traced rather easily in I Samuel 1-12. In both, Samuel is described as playing an important role in Israel's fateful decision to establish a monarchy. One tradition, which was unquestionably the first to be written down, is found in I Samuel 9:1-10:16 and in I Samuel 11. Here we find the engaging story of how Saul, "a handsome young man" who "stood head and shoulders above any of the people," set out to search for his father's lost asses and found a kingdom. The story goes that Saul was on the verge of giving up the search for his father's livestock when, at the suggestion of his servant, he decided to obtain some clairvoyant advice from the seer, Samuel—in return, of course, for the necessary fee. It turned out that Samuel was more than a local seer. He was also the recognized priestly authority in the city who officiated at a sacrificial rite on a "high place," that is, a shrine; and, more than that, he was a prophet who, in the name of the God of Israel, could appoint a king. Seeing in Saul the man who could save Israel from the power of the Philistines and other enemies, Samuel took the initiative and secretly anointed Saul as "prince" over the people.

According to this tradition—let us, for convenience, call it the Saul Source— Saul was not publicly acclaimed king until after he had shown his victorious leadership in the battle described in I Samuel 11. This conflict was not with the Philistines, but with the Ammonites, who were expanding in Transjordan and were taking advantage of Israel's preoccupation with the Philistine menace. The men of Jabesh-gilead, finding themselves overwhelmed by Ammonite forces, asked for a treaty, only to receive the arrogant reply from the Ammonite king that he would make a treaty only if the right eye of every Israelite were gouged out. The men of Jabesh sent an appeal for help throughout all the territory of Israel. Saul happened to be coming from the field behind some oxen when he heard the report about the Ammonite ultimatum. Suddenly the divine charisma, "the spirit of God," came mightily upon him in a manner reminiscent of the ancient judges. What the spirit impelled him to do is exceedingly significant:

> He took a yoke of oxen, and cut them in pieces and sent them throughout all the territory of Israel by the hand of messengers, saying, "Whoever does not come out after Saul and Samuel, so shall it be done to his oxen!" Then the dread of Yahweh fell upon the people, and they came out as one man.
>
> —I SAMUEL 11:7

Like the severing of a corpse into twelve pieces (see above, p. 110), this was a symbolic summons to the whole Israelite confederacy to engage in concerted action in the name of Yahweh. Inspired by Saul's charismatic leadership, the Confederacy brought about the decisive defeat of the Ammonites. As a result, the Israelite militia offered the crown to Saul. Unlike Gideon, he accepted, and was crowned in Gilgal "before Yahweh." [20]

The Request for a King

The other tradition—which for the sake of convenience we shall call the Samuel Source—is found in I Samuel 7:3-8:22, also 10:17-27, and chapter 12. Here the picture of Samuel is somewhat different. Samuel is not called a seer, but a judge—the last and the greatest judge of Israel. Undoubtedly his

---

[20] Verses 12-14, which speak of a "renewing" of the kingdom, are an editorial addition to harmonize the story with the account in 10:17-27, which comes from the second source. Similarly, the words "and Samuel" in 11:7 are an attempt to harmonize the two accounts.

judgeship involved settling legal disputes, for which purpose he made an annual circuit of the shrines of Bethel, Gilgal, and Mizpah (7:15-17). But his judgeship also led to triumph against the Philistines, although he is said to have accomplished this not by military leadership but by prayer and sacrificial rite (7:5-14). Even more noteworthy, however, is the different way in which this source deals with the establishment of the monarchy. In the Saul Source, we find nothing about divine disapproval of the anointing of a king; indeed, Samuel, as Yahweh's prophetic spokesman, took the initiative in selecting Saul. But in the Samuel Source, the idea of the monarchy was displeasing to Samuel and, by the same token, to Yahweh. Samuel had tried to adapt judgeship to the political situation by changing it from a charismatic office to a hereditary one; hence he appointed his own sons as judges. But they did not have the same stature as their father. So we read:

> Then all the elders of Israel gathered together and came to Samuel at Ramah, and said to him, "Behold you are old and your sons do not walk in your ways; now appoint for us a king to govern us [literally: "to judge us"] like all the nations."
>
> —I SAMUEL 8:4-5

The Israelites were trying to set up a stable political government by imitating the nations around them. This attempt, however, was interpreted to be a rejection of Yahweh himself:

> Yahweh said to Samuel, "Hearken to the voice of the people in all that they say to you; for they have not rejected you, but *they have rejected me from being king over them.*"
>
> —I SAMUEL 8:7

So Samuel sought to dissuade the people from their plan by warning them of what would happen if they had a king: by centralizing power, he would limit their freedom and subject them to despotic tyranny. But the people insisted, and Samuel grudgingly consented to go along with them. I Samuel 10:17-27 reports Samuel's selection of Saul by lot from all the tribes of Israel. According to the Samuel Source, Saul was acclaimed king at the city of Mizpah (not Gilgal, as in the other source). Chapter 12 gives Samuel's valedictory speech as the last judge of Israel.

The Samuel Source was written at a later date than the Saul Source. It bears the marks of Deuteronomic revision, as can be seen from a passage like 7:3-4, which reminds one of Deuteronomic language found in the book of Judges. It has fanciful features, like the notion that the Philistines were subdued by a thunder storm which came in answer to Samuel's prayer. Quite obviously, the portrayal of Samuel and the attitude toward the monarchy found in the two sources cannot be readily harmonized. However, we must not jump to the conclusion that the Saul Source, just because it is earlier and more restrained, is the only one that has historical value. Again we must underline this important axiom of biblical study: *The date at which a tradition is written down does not necessarily indicate the date at which the tradition originated.* Certainly the Samuel Source was not created by the Deuteronomic historian, even though it was revised to fit into the Deuteronomic History. The Deuteronomist was working with an older tradition that goes back at many points to the time of Samuel. We do not know exactly what Samuel's role was. The view that he was only a "local seer," which is usually based on the Saul Source, has been grossly exaggerated. There is no absolute reason why he could not have been the last in the succession of Israel's judges, as the Samuel Source portrays him.

Moreover, what we know about the Israelite confederacy makes the attitude toward the monarchy expressed in the Samuel Source seem authentic. Gideon had refused the crown for precisely the same reason Samuel opposed the kingship—namely, that Yahweh alone was Israel's king. Jotham's parable of the trees also expressed the distaste for centralized power that was felt by the Israelite confederacy. Not everyone in Israel felt this strongly, however, as we saw in Abimelech's experiment with monarchy at Shechem. The Saul Source comes from the modernistic wing, and probably emerged from Saul's tribe, Benjamin, where he was glorified as a tribal and national hero. The Samuel Source, on the other hand, shows the persistence of the more conservative belief of the Israelite confederacy.

Israel and the State

In the early part of this chapter, we saw that the struggle between Israel's faith and Canaanite culture found expression in the temptation to compromise with Canaanite naturalism, the worship of the fertility gods of the farmer's world. Now we see that the struggle was waged on a second front, that of nationalism. At the time, the cultural situation seemed to demand that Israel should become "like the nations," if she were to be saved from destruction. Yet this step, although expedient, threatened to undermine the distinctive character of the Israelite community. From the earliest times Israel was bound together, not by human factors such as race, economics, or politics, but by her relationship to Yahweh, the Lord of the covenant community. Israel was not a nation, but a *people*—distinguished from the nations. The Tribal Confederacy, as we have seen, allowed for some political solidarity, especially in times of emergency, but fundamentally the basis of the organization was a religious covenant. In view of this history, the elders' request for a king was a shocking thing, for it threatened to destroy the true identity of Israel as the "people of God." In becoming like the nations, Israel would be "secularized" and thus no different from any other nation.

So in I Samuel the establishment of the Israelite monarchy is viewed in an ambivalent light. The Samuel Source is not just a reflection of the later unhappy experiences of the monarchy, but represents the early criticism made by representatives of the Tribal Confederacy. According to them, the Israelite state was not founded with divine blessing. Rather, it was allowed as a grudging concession, just as a parent lets a child have his way in order that he may learn his folly from experience. And even in the Saul Source, where the monarchy is welcomed, it is not regarded as a divine kingdom descended from heaven to earth, like a Babylonian dynasty, but as a providential development in history occasioned by the Philistine menace.

In one sense, the creation of the monarchy *was* providential, as the Saul Source emphasizes. In retrospect, one can say that events which brought about the collapse of the Confederacy and the rise of the Israelite state were not completely devoid of divine purpose. God's revelation is relevant to the whole of human life—to economics, politics, and every sphere of human activity. If God would speak to the nations through Israel, then Israel must undergo the experience of being a nation in order that she might both appreciate the wealth of nationhood and attack the domestic power of nationalism.[21]

Nevertheless, Israel could not, with an easy conscience, become a nation like the surrounding nations, for the religious faith of the Confederacy survived its collapse and found new expression in Israel's prophetic movement. Israel was not allowed to identify a human kingdom with the Kingdom of God, for Yahweh alone was king. Sometimes great Israelite kings like David and Solomon, in their consuming ambition to make Israel great in the eyes of the world, forgot this truth, with the result that prophets arose to remind the people in the spirit of Samuel that Israel's calling was not to be "like the nations" but to be the people of the covenant. This conviction was underscored, as we shall see, by the prophetic criticism of the state and the announcement that the Israelite nation must fall in order that Israel might be reborn. And the conviction has found expression in modern forms of political thought which stress that the state cannot be given absolute devotion, as in totalitarianism, for God alone is king. He is the judge of every social order and the champion of minorities whose rights are crushed by men who arrogate to themselves absolute power.

It must be admitted, however, that the ambivalent attitude toward the monarchy, which finds expression in the combined "Saul" and "Samuel" traditions, was rooted in Israel's actual historical experiences. The early account was written before Israel had succumbed to the dangers and temptations of becoming a kingdom after the model of neighbors roundabout. It reflects the vigor and vitality of a new beginning, unspoiled by mistakes of the past or the corruptions of political power. Therefore, the monarchy is portrayed as a new possibility, received from the gracious hand of God in response to the people's petition, just as Moses was sent—according to the Exodus tradition (Ex. 3)—in answer to the

---

[21] This discussion is indebted to an essay by the German scholar Walter Eichrodt, *Israel in the Prophecy of the Old Testament* (1951), to give an English translation of the German title.

people's cry of affliction. So the early tradition regards the anointing of Saul as Yahweh's saving action to send a deliverer.

> "He shall save my people from the hand of the Philistines; for I have seen the affliction of my people, because their cry has come to me."
> —I SAMUEL 9:16b

On the other hand, the late source looks back to the anointing of Saul through the disillusioning experiences which Israel had during the period of the monarchy. Like a "prophecy after the event," this account portrays the dire consequences which follow from Israel's decision to have a king like other nations. And these unhappy experiences added up to the conclusion, at least in the judgment of some prophetic interpreters, that this was a step taken in defiance of Yahweh's will. Just before the fall of the Northern Kingdom in 721 B.C., the prophet Hosea condemned the institution of the monarchy, seeing in it a rejection of Yahweh as king (Hos. 8:4; 9:15; 10:3, 9). When the Southern Kingdom fell almost a century and a half later (587 B.C.), it was clear to discerning interpreters that Israel's history as a kingdom had ended in failure. Because the traditions about the founding of the monarchy were shaped near the end of the monarchy, the negative judgment upon Israel's attempt to be a kingdom "like the nations" almost drowns out the other, more positive view.[22] Thus Israel's eventual failure as a nation, which we shall study in Part II, casts its lengthening shadow back across the pages of her history.

---

[22] This point is brought out effectively by Gerhard von Rad, *Theology*, I [80], pp. 324-327.

A star shall come forth out of Jacob,
and a scepter shall rise out of Israel.

—NUMBERS 24:17

PART TWO

ISRAEL BECOMES

LIKE THE NATIONS

THE THRONE

OF DAVID

CHAPTER FIVE   In the twelfth century B.C., forces were

set in motion that profoundly affected the whole Fertile

Crescent and that inevitably left a deep impression upon

the life and faith of Israel. In archaeological terms, this was

the beginning of the Iron Age. This shift from the use of

bronze to iron had important economic and political reper-

cussions, somewhat like the changes brought about by the

harnessing of nuclear energy in our own time.

Biblical readings: This chapter covers the narratives found in I Samuel 13-31, all of II Samuel, I Kings 1-11. The account is paralleled in
the Chronicler's History (I Chron. 10–II Chron. 9), which will be
discussed more fully in Chapter 14.

The Philistines, who came into Canaan around the beginning of the Iron Age, capitalized on the new mode of life. They held the secrets of smelting the new metal and guarded their monopoly so effectively that they were able to keep other small nations, like Israel, at their political mercy. A picture of their stranglehold is given in I Samuel 13:19-22, where we learn that the Hebrews had no smiths who could make swords and spears, and that farmers had to go down to Philistine country to sharpen their agricultural implements. So long as the Philistines were powerful enough to throttle Israel's economic and political life, Israel had no future. The destruction of Shiloh and the ignominious capture of the Ark were vivid reminders of that fact.

Philistine aggression, as we have seen in the preceding chapter, gave the final blow to the old Tribal Confederacy. But this blow served as a stimulus for Israel to rally under a new form of political-religious unity: *the monarchy*. This happened under the leadership of the first kings of Israel: Saul, David, and Solomon. Under these kings, especially David, the long story of the conquest of Canaan came to an end. Israel established a miniature empire that extended from Mesopotamia to Egypt. Once the Philistine stranglehold had been broken, the way was opened for a period of economic boom and political fortune that enabled Israel to take her place proudly among the nations of the Fertile Crescent. For Israel, the Iron Age proved to be a Golden Age.

A TIME OF INTERNATIONAL FAVOR

As with Israel's earlier invasion of Canaan, so now her expansion was favored by the political situation in the Fertile Crescent. There was no nation to the north strong enough to interfere. The Babylonians had fallen into political weakness after the demise of the Hammurabi regime and did not interfere in Canaan for more than a thousand years. The Hurrians, who founded the great kingdom of Mitanni (1500-1370 B.C.) in northern Mesopotamia, were conquered in the fourteenth century by the Assyrians—a nation whose star was destined to rise later on the political horizon. The Hittites, who sought to expand from their base in Asia Minor throughout the Fertile Crescent, were finally overwhelmed by the population upheaval in the Aegean world at about 1200 B.C. With the Hurrians and the Hittites out of the way, Assyria was free to expand, but after the reign of Tiglath-pileser I (c. 1114-1076 B.C.) she sank into obscurity until the ninth century, the time of Elijah.

Israel, then, was safe from the north, and the situation in Egypt was just as favorable. Although Canaan nominally was under the political control of Egypt during the Late Bronze Age (1500-1200 B.C.), Egypt's control vanished during the Twentieth Dynasty, especially after about 1150 B.C. During the reign of Solomon there was a brief revival under Shishak I (935-915 B.C.), but after this Egypt was to remain politically impotent for more than three centuries.

It is against this favorable international background that we must read the account of how Israel attained national unity and extended her political control throughout Palestine and Syria. The account is stirringly presented in the books of Samuel and the first eleven chapters of I Kings. This material, it will be recalled, belongs to the great Deuteronomic History. Within the Deuteronomic framework, the historian has included materials that represent different circles of tradition and that show varying degrees of historical reliability. In discussing the account of the establishment of the kingdom (I Sam. 1-12), we have already noticed two types of narrative: a pro-monarchic tradition, and a theocratic tradition (see pp. 121-126). Attempts have been made to trace these two types of tradition throughout the rest of the books of Samuel, but after the conclusion of the Samuel story, the division becomes much less clear-cut. Some material is undoubtedly legendary (for instance, the story of David and Goliath in I Sam. 17), and some shows a political or theological bias (as the story of Nathan forbidding David to build a temple, II Sam. 7). Allowing for legendary and theological embellishments, however, the narratives on the whole are so vivid and unimpeachable in their historical authenticity that they must have come from a time close to the events described. This trustworthiness is especially evident in the account of David's court life in II Samuel 9-20 and I Kings 1-2 —an account that is generally regarded as one of the finest examples of historical writing in antiquity. By contrast, the history found in Chronicles is so thoroughly dominated by theological bias that the historical picture is blurred, even though some of the traditions preserved in this late work are valuable.[1]

ISRAEL'S RUSTIC KING

The account of Saul's reign in I Samuel 13-31 is the tragic story of a heroic leader who lived in the transitional period between the collapse of the old Tribal Confederacy and the birth of a new order. The psychic weaknesses that marked Saul's personality were only aggravated by the fateful historical situation in which he was destined to be Israel's first king. The tragedy of his career revolves around his alienation from two persons: Samuel, who represented the old order, and David, who represented the new. Samuel, as we have seen, is portrayed as the last representative of the old Confederacy, which gradually collapsed under the pressure of political necessity. David represents the youth and vigor of the new national order within which Israel was to find a new unity and was to search for a new formulation of her historic faith. Saul himself belonged more to the old period than to the new age that was coming with historical inevitability. But Saul's rejection by Samuel put him outside the sanc-

---

[1] The Chronicler's History, comprising Ezra, Nehemiah, and I-II Chronicles, was composed in the post-exilic period and reflects the priestly theological interests of Judaism. See later, Chapter 14.

tions and supports of the old regime; and David's popularity was a constant reminder that Saul could not enter the new. Caught between these two worlds, Saul's life became the arena on which was waged an intense psychic conflict—a conflict that eventually destroyed him.

It would be interesting if we had a historical narrative written in a circle sympathetic to Saul—for instance, an account written by a member of Saul's own tribe of Benjamin. But the narratives of I Samuel are now dominated by the bias of historians of the southern kingdom of Judah, and Saul is put in an unfavorable light in order to enhance the prestige of David, who founded the dynasty of Judah. We must remember that all the traditions of the monarchy were preserved in and edited by Jerusalem circles, which were sympathetic toward David. From a different point of view, perhaps Saul would emerge as a heroic figure who, like Hamlet, was the victim of baffling, uncontrollable circumstances and the dark depths of his own sensitive and passionate nature. The narratives testify that Saul was capable of inspiring great devotion from his followers, even after Samuel deserted him. And Saul's military successes, though limited and finally eclipsed by the dismal defeat at Mount Gilboa, must have had considerable effect, especially in wresting from the Philistines their monopoly of iron-smelting and thereby paving the way for the economic developments in the reigns of David and Solomon. His victories over Israel's enemies were impressive (I Sam. 14:48), and under his rule unity and harmony came to the tribes of Israel. Much can be said to Saul's credit!

Saul's Charismatic Leadership

One of the clearest points of contact between Saul and the old Tribal Confederacy was his possession of the divine charisma, the "spirit of Yahweh," which, as we have seen, endowed the judges with the authority of leadership. Throughout the territory of the Confederacy, Saul was acknowledged as leader not because of his heredity or a *coup d'état*, but because the spirit of Yahweh had rushed upon him and had enabled him to act as a deliverer in the Ammonite crisis (I Sam. 11:6-7). Recognizing that he was charismatic, the people of Israel made him king after this military success in the hope that he would deliver them from the Philistine oppression. Saul was more like one of the ancient judges than were the kings who succeeded him. In fact, the oldest source (I Sam. 9:16; 10-1) carefully avoids calling him a king (*melek*), but describes him instead as a "prince" or "leader" (*nagid*). In contrast to David and Solomon, Saul made no attempt to transform the tribal structure of Israel into a centralized state. He levied no taxes, made no military conscription, had no hierarchy of court officials and no harem. His only army was a band of volunteers whom he recruited from his supporters (I Sam. 13:2; 14:52). Excavations at Saul's fortress of Gibeah have confirmed the biblical picture of the "rustic simplicity" of his court.[2] No oriental despot, he perpetuated the tribal democracy of the earlier period, and claimed authority among the tribes only because of the charisma. Since his authority was charismatic, it is understandable that he became very melancholy when it seemed that the "spirit" had departed from him, owing to the rejection by Samuel and the popular acclaim that attended David's military exploits.

Reading the vivid story of Saul's reign at Gibeah, we sense that, for all his weakness, he was a man of sincere, passionate faith in Yahweh. According to one interpretation, in his early career Saul broke with the orthodox Mosaic faith and leaned toward the worship of Baal, the nature god of Canaan. The evidence for this interpretation is that while Saul's first son was given a Yahweh name, Jonathan (meaning "Yahweh [Yo] gave"), his later children were given Baal names—for instance, Ishbaal (meaning "man of Baal"). Moreover, Saul ruthlessly slaughtered the priests of the Eli family who had been the guardians of the central sanctuary at Shiloh (I Sam. 22). This interpretation, of course, would help to explain why Samuel came to repudiate the leader he had anointed. But it is doubtful whether the acts mentioned above give solid support to the view that Saul was a modernist or a heretic. Despite his impulsive actions, he evidently intended to serve Yahweh with his whole heart.

In contrast to Samuel, Saul was not gifted with profound insight into the meaning of Israel's faith. The chapters of Saul's tumultuous life portray life-situations in which men were called to act in faith, to trust when the odds were desperate, and to decide and accept the consequences. Here is a story that belongs in Israel's scripture not because of its edifying ideas, but because of its clear, uncensored description of the human situation. Later prophets understood the covenant faith more profoundly. But Saul was no prophet, even though he came under prophetic influence on occasion—to the great surprise of those who knew him (I Sam. 10:10-11; 19:18-24). He was a soldier who had to face a state of military emergency throughout his reign, for "there was hard fighting against the Philistines all the days of Saul." His task was to "fight Yahweh's battles," which, to the popular mind, were the same as the battles of Israel.

Through the narratives breathes an intensity that springs from the conviction that Yahweh himself was actively engaged in the conflict. Believing this, Saul was not deterred by Israel's pitiful lack of armor, by the number of discouraged Israelites who deserted when the going was rough, or by the handful of recruits who constituted his army. What mattered that the odds were against him when, as Jonathan put it just before setting out on a daring exploit at Michmash,

---

[2] Gibeah was excavated in 1922-23 under the direction of W. F. Albright; see his references in *The Biblical Period* [38], p. 24. Re-excavation of the site in 1964 under the direction of Paul Lapp largely confirmed Albright's results; see his report in *The Biblical Archaeologist*, XXVIII, No. 1 (1965), pp. 2-10.

"Nothing can hinder Yahweh from saving by many or by few" (I Sam. 14:6)! And when the tide of battle turned against Israel, Saul was humble enough to suspect that something had been done to incur Yahweh's displeasure. As a military strategist, he had a very limited view of the divine purpose in history, but he must be given credit for coming to realize through bitter experience that it was Yahweh who was in supreme command, shaping the course of events according to his sovereign will and demanding the zealous devotion of his people.

A Holy War

Saul's devotion to Yahweh was put to the test in an incident related in I Samuel 15, the battle with the Amalekites. In the judgment of many scholars, this chapter comes from a literary tradition related to the one we have earlier designated as the Samuel Source (see pp. 121-126). But although it may have arisen in circles different from the sources of some of the other narratives found in the Saul story, it is surely based on an authentic historical memory. The Amalekites, who lived in the Negeb to the south of Beer-sheba, were ancient enemies of Israel (Ex. 17:8-16). Their all-out effort to destroy Israel during the wilderness march still rankled in Israel's memory (see p. 56). Possibly the old animosity was reawakened by some immediate provocation, such as recent Amalekite raids upon southern settlements at a time when Israel was preoccupied with the Philistine problem. In any event, through the prophet Samuel, Saul was given the divine command to utterly destroy them—man, woman, child, cattle, and goods.

According to modern ethical standards, this act of total extermination was a barbarous thing (though it was scarcely less refined than modern warfare!). But instead of making a value judgment from our standpoint, let us try to understand the act within the religious ideology of ancient Israel. According to the story, the initiative was taken by Yahweh, who commanded Israel to punish Amalek for its ancient atrocity. In other words, this was not to be an ordinary "secular" war, but a holy war. It was to be a religious action.

To understand the holy war, we must recall the period of the Tribal Confederacy. As we have seen in preceding chapters, the covenant bond imposed certain obligations upon the participating tribes, one of which was to respond to Yahweh's summons given through a charismatic leader in time of battle.[3] The response to the call was a test of loyalty to the God of the covenant, of response in faith to Yahweh's "going before" his people. The people would "offer themselves willingly" (Judg. 5:2, 9), and would consecrate themselves by submitting to certain disciplines such as abstinence from sexual intercourse (I Sam. 21:4-5; II Sam. 11:11). In such times they engaged in holy activity, for, it was believed, Yahweh himself was in their midst as their military Leader.

---

[3] See the previous treatment of holy war in connection with the Song of Deborah (above, pp. 111-113 and footnote 17).

The method of holy war was not so much to fight pitched battles as to frighten the enemy with the "terror of God" so that they would flee in panic and confusion.

In a holy war, the spoil was to be *hérem*—that is, devoted to Yahweh as a holocaust or sacrifice. Since the spoil belonged exclusively to Yahweh, it was regarded as a great sin for anyone to take anything, regardless of his personal motive. The story of Achan, who stole some precious things from the spoil of Jericho with disastrous results for himself and his family, is an excellent illustration (Josh. 7). To take anything from Yahweh's sacrifice was regarded as "breaking faith" (Josh. 7:1); it was an offense against Yahweh's holiness.

With the collapse of the Tribal Confederacy, the old conception of holy war soon disappeared.[4] When the Israelite state emerged, charismatic leaders were superseded by hereditary kings who, after the manner of surrounding nations, fought wars for political gain and without qualm took all the booty they could. But in Saul's day the old standard was still in effect. Saul was a charismatic leader who was commanded to destroy the Amalekites completely—that is, to put them under the sacrificial ban (*hérem*). So decisively did he defeat them that they vanished from the historical scene shortly afterwards.[5]

In terms of this old-fashioned standard we must understand Saul's action in taking part of the spoil. According to the ancient view, his sin was that he used his own judgment in deciding how far to go in obeying the divine command. To us, the sparing of Agag appears humane, and the taking of the best of the livestock seems practical wisdom; but in the ancient view these all belonged to Yahweh—they were holy. Saul's defect was his refusal to give complete obedience to Yahweh, as obedience was understood in holy war. It was an act of disloyalty that polluted the whole Israelite community. Not even Saul's explanation that Agag and the spoil were brought back to be sacrificed to Yahweh would satisfy Samuel, the spokesman of the old Confederacy, who is represented as saying:

> Behold, to obey is better than sacrifice,
> And to hearken than the fat of rams.
> —I SAMUEL 15:22

Because Saul had "rejected the word of Yahweh," said the prophet, Yahweh had rejected him as king over Israel. With fierce devotion to Yahweh, the enraged Samuel finished performing the sacrificial ban; he "hewed Agag in pieces before Yahweh in Gilgal."

---

[4] The conception, however, was revived later by the writer of Deuteronomy (for instance, Deut. 7:1-2; 20:1-21:14). See Gerhard von Rad, *Studies in Deuteronomy* [163], pp. 45-59. The Deuteronomic prescription of rules for conducting a holy war were followed in the Maccabean Revolt and accepted by the Essene sect of Jews at Qumran (see pp. 536, 552).

[5] The last reference to action by the Amalekites is their raid on a Philistine outpost, which was avenged by David (I Sam. 30).

A Rejected Man

This story marks the turning point in the cycle of stories dealing with Saul, although quite clearly it is colored by a bias in favor of David, the "neighbor" who was better than he (I Sam. 15:28). Not even Saul's confession of sin and plea for pardon could deliver him from the consequence of his deed, which, like a nemesis, pursued him in the days ahead. Just because he was so passionate in his devotion to Yahweh, the prophetic word of rejection preyed upon his mind and drove him to the edge of insanity. Outwardly he enjoyed some measure of popularity and success for a while, but inwardly his life was distracted and maddened by his consciousness of being rejected. To him there were two developments that pointed clearly to his estrangement from Yahweh.

One was the decisive break with Samuel, the last representative of the Tribal Confederacy. A more sympathetic view of Saul would portray his impulsive acts, which led to the final rupture with Samuel, in a better light. Saul was a man of action who did not consider the religious implications of his acts, especially in times of emergency. He summoned the priest Ahijah to obtain a divine oracle, but evidently he abruptly terminated the investigation when the military situation indicated that there was no time to wait for Yahweh to give an answer (I Sam. 14:18-23). When his hungry soldiers slaughtered cattle and began to eat meat with the blood—that is, without the proper ritual procedure —Saul himself built an altar for sacrifice (I Sam. 14:31-35). These actions may show only Saul's impulsiveness, rather than his determination to take things into his own hands. But, together with the Amalekite episode, they were convincing evidence to Samuel that Saul was out to defy the Israelite theocracy, the "Rule of God." Thus the break between prophet and king occurred, "and Samuel did not see Saul again until the day of his death" (I Sam. 15:25). To Saul, the absence of Yahweh's prophet was the absence of Yahweh. He was a man cast off by God, shut up within the loneliness of his own tumultuous being.

The other development that pointed to Saul's estrangement from Yahweh was the rise of David's star on the horizon. From Saul's point of view, David must have appeared as a threat to his very existence, even a greater threat than the Philistine menace. Denied the security of Yahweh's acceptance, Saul's instability was only aggravated by David's personal charm, gallantry, and success. It must have seemed that David had only one aim from the very first: to gain the throne for himself (see I Sam. 18:8). How else could one explain David's ability to ingratiate himself with the people, his cunning attempt to marry into the royal family, his friendship with Jonathan, and his support from the priests of Nob? The more Saul brooded over David's actions, the surer he was that David was a pretender to the throne. Haunted by his dark moods and inflamed by insane jealousy and rage, he suspected the loyalty of his best friends (I Sam. 22:6-8) and was obsessed by one determination: to hunt David down and kill him.

This was more than a personal rift between two men of heroic stature. What really happened was that the divine charisma, the spirit that endowed the old Israelite leaders with authority and strength, had departed from Saul. This is the judgment given by the narrator in I Samuel 16:14, and this sorry fact must have tortured Saul's mind more than anything else. Everywhere, David met with success. Saul's plots to humiliate him were all turned to David's advantage. When Saul returned from his battles, the women met him with music and song; but his armor-bearer, David, received the greater praise:

> Saul has slain his thousands,
> And David his ten thousands!
> —I SAMUEL 18:7

This was more than Saul could stand. More and more it became apparent that David was the man of charisma. Indeed, one passage states that when Samuel anointed David, "the Spirit of Yahweh came mightily upon David from that day forward" (I Sam. 16:13). His actions were evidence that Yahweh's favor was upon him. Ironically, Saul was still a man of charisma, but it was "an evil spirit from Yahweh" that tormented him until he was beside himself. Today, Saul would be regarded as a fit subject for a study in abnormal psychology. In antiquity, however, it was believed that unusual psychic behavior, such as David's feigned insanity in the Philistine court (I Sam. 21:12-15), was a sign that the divine spirit had invaded the center of one's being and had taken control. According to this view, the line separating the spiritual leader from the disordered mind is a very fine one indeed.[6]

Saul's desperate efforts to find himself again and to recover his kingly prestige proved futile. Frustrated in his efforts to track down the fugitive David, he at last found himself confronted with a concerted Philistine drive into the plain of Jezreel. The Israelite armies were gathered by Mount Gilboa, on the south flank of the pass that led to the Philistine fort, Beth-shan. Panic-stricken at the sight of the large army concentrated in the valley below, Saul made one last effort to inquire of Yahweh; but no answer came by any of the usual channels —either through the sacred lot (Urim and Thummim), dreams, or prophetic oracles (I Sam. 28:5-6). Even though he had banned mediums from the land, Saul made a clandestine visit to a necromancer at En-dor, hoping to hear a word from Yahweh through Samuel's ghost, which was summoned from the underworld. This story (I Sam. 28:8-25), one of the most vivid in the Bible,

---

[6] It is interesting to note that prophets were sometimes called "madmen" (II Kings 9:11). Moreover, the Hebrew word used in I Samuel 18:10 to describe one of Saul's fits literally means to prophesy under the influence of the divine spirit (the Revised Standard Version translates "rave").

gives a moving portrayal of the tragedy of Saul's last hours. Having heard from Samuel the crushing prophecy of doom, he went out into the dismal night— and to the defeat and suicide of Mount Gilboa. We can hardly read the story without being moved by its pathos and by the greatness of its tragic hero. In his magnificent elegy, once contained in an old collection of Israelite poetry called the Book of Jashar, David paid immortal tribute to Saul, the fallen leader of Israel, and to Jonathan, whose love surpassed the love of man for woman (II Sam. 1:19-27):

> How are the mighty fallen,
>   and the weapons of war perished!
>   —II SAMUEL 1:27

THE ARCHITECT OF THE ISRAELITE STATE

The Philistine victory at the battle of Mount Gilboa was decisive. The Israelite armies were dispersed in leaderless rout and Saul's decapitated body was impaled on the walls of the Philistine fortress of Beth-shan (see Plate 4). The victors now controlled the valley route leading from the Mediterranean Sea to the Jordan Valley, and the complete conquest of Israelite territory was within easy reach. Why the Philistines did not follow up their victory by wiping out all pockets of resistance immediately is not altogether clear. One reason, certainly, was the rise of David, one of the greatest military commanders and statesmen of history. With amazing swiftness he reorganized the Israelite army, dealt a death blow to Philistine power, and established a dynasty that was destined to last for more than four hundred years.

The story of David's early career is interwoven with the fateful events of Saul's reign (I Sam. 13-31). Here we can only allude to the fascinating course of events: David's rise from the obscurity of a shepherd's life, his appearance as a harp player in the king's court, his victory over the giant Goliath, his gallant exploits among the Philistines, his adventures as the "Robin Hood" leader of a band of outlaws, and his elevation to the rank of king of Israel. The story, as we have already mentioned, was written to glorify the man whose personal charm and charismatic success had made him a great popular idol. It has captured the imagination of people in every generation, including our own. Indeed, posterity hailed David as the greatest of Israel's rulers—"a man after God's own heart." He was both the architect of the nation and the royal champion of Israel's faith.

This high estimation is all the more remarkable when we consider the true-to-life picture of David that is presented in the narratives. To be sure, the book of Chronicles, written some centuries later, touches up the portrait in order to make David's better traits stand out (I Chron. 11-29); but the account

PLATE 1

Rameses II's rock temple at Abu Simbel as seen shortly before being cut into huge blocks and reassembled on higher ground above the lake formed by the dam south of Aswan. Above: Two of the four colossi of the pharaoh which guard the entrance. Below: A view from the smaller queen's temple to the king's temple, which—from entrance pylon to the innermost holy of holies—was hewn from solid rock.

PLATE 2

This famous mosaic map from the sixth century A.D., inlaid on the floor of a church at Madaba (biblical Medeba) near Mount Nebo, depicts the ford of the Jordan near Jericho (the area marked by date palms). A church incorporating twelve stones (Josh. 4:8, 20) stands at Gilgal. Fish swim past the ford, here spanned by a small bridge, but turn back in terror when they taste salty Dead Sea water.

Top: Craggy Jebel Serbal, linked with Sinai by some scholars, looms above the oasis of Feiran. Middle: Jebel Musa, traditional "Mount of Moses," is a few miles east of Feiran in the mountainous tip of the Sinaitic Peninsula. Bottom: The Lion Gate at Hattushash stands in the Hittite capital's ruins.

PLATE 3

Above: The imposing mound of Beth-shan, on the edge of
the Plain of Jezreel where it opens into the Jordan Valley.
This strategic outpost, in turn Egyptian, Philistine, and
Israelite, guarded the route inland from the coast to
Damascus. Below: The Hittite capital of Hattushash lay
on the ridge (right) that slopes down to the modern city
of Boghaz-köy; the rugged terrain enhanced its defenses.

PLATE 4

in the books of Samuel and Kings, especially the Court History in II Samuel 9-20 and I Kings 1-2, presents a series of candid snapshots of David in real life. He stands before us not as an idealized saint in a stained-glass window, but as a flesh-and-blood figure of extraordinary winsomeness and charm.

There are, of course, notable inconsistencies in the account. For instance, there are two accounts of how David was introduced into Saul's court. According to one (I Sam. 16:14-23), he was brought in as a musician to cheer the depressed king; according to the other (I Sam. 17:1-18:5), he first won the king's attention when he vanquished Goliath.[7] Moreover, in II Samuel 21:19 the slaying of Goliath is attributed to a certain Elhanan from Bethlehem, a detail that casts doubt on the story of David the giant-killer.[8] But taking into account these legendary stories that gathered around a great national hero (compare the stories about George Washington), we are given on the whole an authentic, if somewhat romanticized, account of David's rise from the sheepfolds to the royal throne.

The death of Samuel and Saul marked the passing of an era. With David, a new way of life began that was revolutionary when compared with the simplicities of the old Tribal Confederacy. Under Saul's charismatic rule the tribes were held together in the loose union of the Confederacy, and it is a tribute to his leadership that there were no signs of tribal rebellion during his lifetime. Despite military reverses and his preoccupation with David's maneuvers, Saul was able to preserve the unity of Israel and the affection of his countrymen. But with David we see the transition from charismatic leadership to a centralization of power in the crown. From a tribal league, Israel was transformed into a miniature empire modeled after the surrounding nations. David's problem was to maintain the tribal unity of the old Confederacy under the new nation-state.

David's Rise to Power

The methods used by David show that he was a shrewd politician who stopped at nothing to achieve his political ambitions. At the time of Saul's death, David was an exile in Philistia. His first task was to put himself in a strategic position from which his political scheme—to set himself up as ruler over the tribes of Israel—could be achieved. Fortunately, he had already prepared the way for readmission to his native tribe of Judah, from one of whose cities (Bethlehem) he had come. During his outlaw period, both in the Wilderness of Judah and in the service of Philistia, he had ingratiated himself with the Judeans by protecting landholders from robbers and by dividing with the

---

[7] Notice that in I Samuel 17:55-58 Saul questions David about his identity, which apparently indicates that he had not known of him before. Compare 16:17-22.

[8] This discrepancy is smoothed over in I Chron. 20:5 where it is stated that Elhanan killed the brother of Goliath, Lahmi, and not Goliath himself.

elders of Judah the spoil taken from raids on their enemies (I Sam. 23:1-5; 25:2 ff.; 27:8-12; 30:26-31). It is not too surprising, then, that shortly after Saul's death David was anointed king at Hebron, where he reigned for over seven years, evidently as a kind of Philistine vassal.

During this period, however, David had his eye on the whole territory of Israel. The northern tribes still owed allegiance to Saul's weak son, Ishbaal,[9] who was only a stooge of his army general, Abner. David's Judean forces were under the command of his able general, Joab. Apparently the conflict between the house of David and the house of Saul was touched off by a curious incident that occurred by the pool of Gibeon, uncovered by archaeologists in 1956-57.[10] The two army commanders, facing each other from opposite sides of the pool, agreed to a test of strength. Twelve young men would represent each side in a kind of gladiatorial contest. But the ordeal settled nothing, for the champions

---

[9] In the biblical text he is called Ishbosheth. Editors have substituted *bosheth* (Hebrew, "shame") for Baal, the despised name of the Canaanite deity.

[10] See James B. Pritchard, *Gibeon: Where the Sun Stood Still* (Princeton, N.J.: Princeton University Press, 1962), pp. 64-72.

THE POOL OF GIBEON *was the scene of a gladiatorial contest, according to II Sam. 2:13. First excavated in the summer of 1956, Gibeon was one of four federated cities that entered into alliance with Joshua during his invasion of southern Canaan, and came to be an important Israelite city by the time of the early monarchy.*

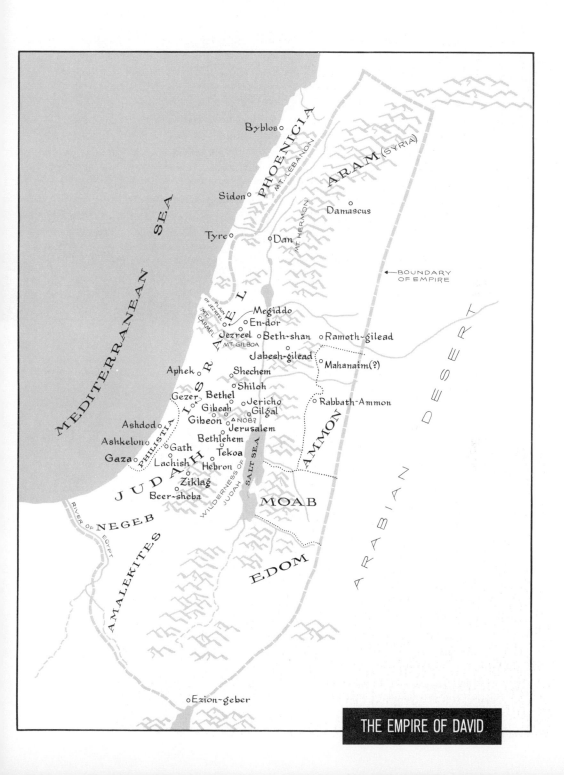

THE EMPIRE OF DAVID

JERUSALEM FROM THE SOUTH *with the hill called Ophel,*
the site of David's city, highlighted in the center fore-
ground. Behind the walls can be seen the Dome of the
Rock, a mosque built over the site of Solomon's Temple.
Ophel slopes off to the deep Valley of Kidron, on the right
of which is the modern village of Silwan.
    As the relief map on the opposite page shows, the Val-
ley of Hinnom (Gehenna) branches off to the left from
Kidron. The Tyropoeon Valley, now almost filled in, is on
the left side of Ophel.

only killed each other off, with the result that general fighting broke out between the armies (II Sam. 2:12-17). From this time on there was fighting off
and on, with David's power growing stronger and stronger. The political struggle between David and the house of Saul came to an end when Abner, stinging
under a deserved rebuke from Ishbaal, offered to deliver the remnant of Saul's
kingdom to David. Part of the deal was for David to receive Michal, Saul's
daughter and David's first wife. Michal's tearful parting from her own husband
is described with great pathos (II Sam. 3:12-15). Governed chiefly by cold
political calculation, David sought to establish a claim upon Saul's throne by
taking Michal into his harem. Saul's male descendants were either liquidated
in typical oriental style or put under careful custody (II Sam. 21:1-14). At the
age of thirty-seven, David had become the unchallenged ruler of all Israel.

During David's reign at Hebron, the Philistines had not interfered with him.
Probably they regarded him as their vassal and were content for Israel to be

divided by civil war between the house of Saul and the house of David. But when David's power increased with the union of all the Israelite tribes, the Philistines felt that it was time to act (II Sam. 5:17). Not much is said about the Philistine wars, but one of David's greatest accomplishments was breaking the Philistines' control over Canaan once and for all and shutting them up in the coastal plain (see II Sam. 5:17-25; 21:15-22). Moreover, he waged successful wars against Moab, Ammon, Edom, Amalek, and Aram (Syria), and he concluded a treaty with the Phoenician king, Hiram of Tyre. So he became recognized as the ruler of an empire that stretched from the Lebanon mountains to the very borders of Egypt, from the Mediterranean Sea to the Desert of Arabia. The narrator, seeing the hand of God in these dazzling achievements, comments: "David became greater and greater, for Yahweh, the God of hosts,

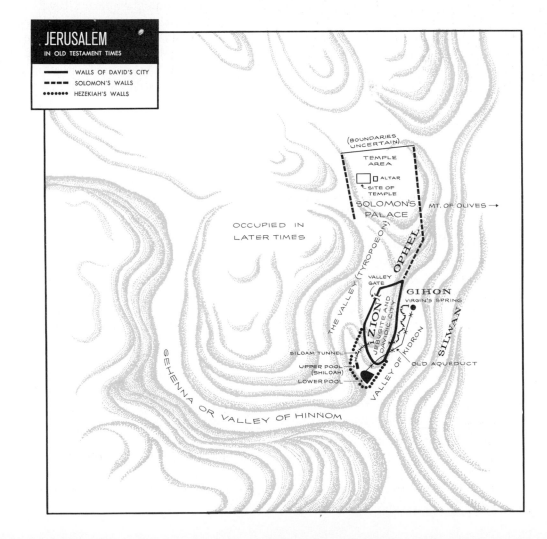

was with him." (II Sam. 5:10). Never before or after the time of David did Israel exceed this zenith of political power.

Consolidating the Nation

But David was more than a brilliant military commander. Desiring a greater centralization of power in the throne, he took several important and fateful steps to limit the independence of the confederate tribes. One of his most brilliant maneuvers was the capture of the old fortress of Jerusalem despite the boast of its occupants, the Jebusites, that it was an impregnable stronghold.[11] Consider what David's feat must have meant at a time when northern tribes had gathered around the house of Saul and southern tribes had sworn allegiance to David in Hebron. Bypassed by the invading armies of Israel at the time of the conquest, Jerusalem had never been incorporated into the tribal territory of Israel. David made his bid for power by capitalizing on the sectional feeling of the southern tribes; but since his political ambitions also included the northern tribes, he wisely sought a place for his capital that was neither "northern" nor "southern." By selecting the neutral site of Jerusalem, right on the boundary of the northern and southern tribes, he revealed his intention of elevating his throne above all tribal claims and jealousies. His action has been compared with the selection of Washington, D.C., as the federal capital on territory independent of the states.

Jerusalem was known as "the city of David" (I Sam. 5:9). In his capital David gathered around him a group of courtiers who derived their support and authority from the crown. This organization represented a great change from the days of the Confederacy when leadership was based on a person's status in his tribe or on the divine charisma. The administration of law, which previously had been vested in the tribal "elders" who sat at the gate, or in the judges of the Confederacy, was taken over by the king himself, although we may infer that he delegated much of this responsibility to judges whom he appointed to office (see II Sam. 14:4-17; 15:1-6). Other royal officials are mentioned (II Sam. 8:15-18). In the cases of two of these officials—the Recorder and the Secretary—scholars have detected the influence of the governmental organization of Egypt. Thus Israel was rapidly becoming "like the nations," with a special class of men known as "servants of the king" who exercised power over Israel's social life.

It was not enough, however, to supervise the kingdom in this manner. If he was to capture the allegiance of all Israel, David also needed to establish his throne on the religious sanctions and Mosaic traditions of the Tribal Confederacy. He had to demonstrate that his political innovations would not sweep away Israel's sacred heritage, but bring it to glorious fulfillment. So one of his

---

[11] Apparently David's men penetrated the stronghold by ascending a water shaft (II Sam. 5:8) that had been cut through rock, from the Gihon spring outside the walls to the interior of the old city (Ophel). (See map on previous page.)

shrewdest acts was to rescue the Ark of the Covenant from the place of oblivion in which it had rested since the fall of the confederate sanctuary of Shiloh and to bring it to Jerusalem with great pomp and ceremony (II Sam. 6). With the Ark stationed in a "tent" in Jerusalem, the city of David also became "Zion, City of God," for Yahweh's presence once again "tabernacled" in the midst of Israel. Moreover, the priests of the house of Eli (of whom Abiathar was the chief) who had survived Saul's bloody purge at Nob were brought to Jerusalem and attached to the royal court. In this way too David sought to encircle his crown with the religious halo of the past. Thus the religious center of Israel was shifted from the confederate sanctuary of Shiloh to the royal shrine in Jerusalem. Here was the beginning of a "royal theology" which suppressed the anti-monarchic conservatism represented by men like Samuel and insisted that Yahweh had made a special covenant with David, promising to establish David's throne securely through all generations (II Sam. 7). It came to be believed that Yahweh would certainly be in favor of any king who was a son of David.

David's ambitions soared ever higher. Already, it seems, he had placed the Ark of the Covenant within the Tent of Meeting (see II Sam. 7:2), thus joining together the two major cultic objects which had become separated since Mosaic times (see above, pp. 71-72). And, according to a tradition preserved in II Sam. 24:18-25, he purchased from a citizen named Araunah a threshing floor upon which to build an altar to Yahweh. But to David these were only beginnings. He wanted to replace the old Tent with a splendid royal temple patterned after the temples of other nations. However, the conservative religious tradition of the Confederacy was voiced by the prophet Nathan, who argued that Yahweh had not dwelt in a house since the time of the Exodus.[12] So David wisely conceded to the prophet that this was going too far—for the time being at least. He contented himself with reorganizing Israel's religion in other spheres, especially temple music. According to the Chronicler (I Chron. 25), David organized the temple musicians into guilds. And, since David was a reputed musician (see Amos 6:5), this is not impossible.

David took other measures to control and modify the independence of the Tribal Confederacy. Against the advice of his counselors, he insisted on taking a census of all Israel, an ambitious project that took over nine months to complete. The census findings evidently were used as a basis for military conscription, taxation, or forced labor. By this action every man was reminded that he owed his primary allegiance not to his tribal unit, but to the king. The bitter popular resentment against numbering Israel's fighting forces is expressed in the story of the plague, which was interpreted as a sign of Yahweh's wrath against the king (II Sam. 24).[13] Moreover, it is probable that David first con-

---

[12] Nathan's words, as reported in II Sam. 7:5-7, are exaggerated, for the confederate sanctuary of Shiloh had a temple or "a house of Yahweh," according to I Sam. 1:7, 9.

[13] Note that the Chronicler attributes the temptation to number Israel to Satan rather than to David's imperial ambitions (I Chron. 21:1).

ceived the idea of reorganizing the territory of Israel into administrative districts which, for the most part, did not coincide with the old tribal boundaries (see p. 157). He also inaugurated the policy of forcing his subjects into work camps (II Sam. 20:24), a despotic practice which, under Solomon, eventually became a hated symbol of tyranny.

David's Troubles

It is not surprising, then, that David's initial popularity began to wane. The people became more and more restive under the yoke of centralized power, and longed for the independence they had enjoyed before Israel became a state. Outwardly, the Israelite state was brilliant in its achievements, the envy of the nations round about, as we learn later from the story of the Queen of Sheba's visit to Solomon (I Kings 10:1-10). Throughout the Fertile Crescent, David's name was renowned. The city of Jerusalem, whose royal buildings were designed and constructed by the best artisans of Phoenicia, was a monument to the skill and diplomacy of David. Into David's kingdom poured the commercial wealth of the Near East. As a result, social life underwent profound changes and Israel's faith was exposed to a more cosmopolitan atmosphere. New conceptions of property were introduced as commercial entrepreneurs, protected by the military power of the king, exploited the opportunities of trade. But all was not well. Even in David's reign were heard the volcanic rumblings that eventually, at the death of Solomon, broke forth with pent-up fury. Absalom, David's son, instigated a revolution in Judah that almost cost David his crown. And among the northern tribes a certain Sheba sounded the call to revolution:

> We have no portion in David,
> and we have no inheritance in the son of Jesse;
> every man to his tents, O Israel!
> —II SAMUEL 20:1-2

David proved equal to these crises, but they foreshadowed future trouble.

The story of David's domestic troubles is recorded in the Court History found in II Samuel 9-20 and I Kings 1-2.[14] Scholars generally regard this narrative as first-hand historical writing, so vivid and reliable that it must have come from one who was a contemporary of David and probably a member of his court. Here we are given a glimpse into the intrigues of David's own family. Only from this biographical angle do we learn about the character of David's administration. Unlike the Chronicler's portrait of David, the Court History portrays the king in his strength and his weakness. No attempt is made to depict

---

[14] The basic study of the Court History (or Succession Document) is Leonhard Rost, *Die Überlieferung von der Thronnachfolge Davids* [129]. Gerhard von Rad builds upon this study in his excellent discussion of "Israel's Anointed" in his *Theology*, I [80], especially pp. 306-318.

him either better or worse than he actually was, or to suppress or distort the facts in the interests of theological bias.

Nevertheless, the Court History is dominated by a religious theme that makes the David story one of the greatest biographical tragedies ever written. The key to the story is the encounter betwen David and the prophet Nathan, as recorded in II Samuel 12. The background of the incident is the Bathsheba affair, which understandably has captured the interest of the Hollywood movie industry. David desired Bathsheba. What was to prevent him, the most powerful man in the land, from satisfying his lust? Accordingly he took her, only to find out later that she had become pregnant. David then brought Bathsheba's husband, Uriah the Hittite, home from battle so that it would appear to everyone that Uriah was the father of the child who was conceived. But Uriah was a faithful warrior who refused to break the rules of purity that applied to a sanctified soldier during a holy war (II Sam. 11:11). David entertained Uriah until he was drunk, hoping to weaken his will. When this attempt failed, he contrived Uriah's murder in a manner that would put himself beyond suspicion. It seemed to be a perfect crime; "but," says the record, "the thing that David had done displeased Yahweh." Then follows one of the most dramatic encounters recorded in Scripture. The prophet Nathan appeared before David as the spokesman of Yahweh, and got the king to condemn himself by his infuriated reaction to the parable of the poor man's pet ewe lamb that was stolen to provide meat for a rich man's table. Nathan's exclamation, "You are the man," struck home like a dagger to David's guilty heart. With true remorse and penitence, he confessed, "I have sinned against Yahweh"; but not even his penitence could free him from the fateful consequences of his actions.

In the rest of the Court History we see how this incident set off a chain reaction of troubles as David's lust and murder, like a demonic spirit, corrupted his own sons. One episode followed swiftly upon another. Amnon forced his virgin half-sister, and Absalom in revenge assassinated Amnon. Estranged from his father, Absalom fomented a revolution and to the great sorrow of David was murdered by Joab as he dangled from a tree with his hair caught in its limbs. There is no more poignant passage in the whole Old Testament than the description of the king's anguished response to the news about his rebellious son:

> And the king was deeply moved, and went up to the chamber over the gate, and wept; and as he went, he said, "O my son Absalom, my son, my son Absalom! Would I had died instead of you, O Absalom, my son, my son."
>
> —II SAMUEL 18:33

And at the very end of David's days his sons were engaged in intrigue and treachery over the succession to the throne. So Yahweh's word through Nathan came to dreadful fulfillment: "Behold, I will raise up evil against you out of your own house." Though still surrounded by the glories and wealth of the state he had created, the old man David described in I Kings 1-2 was a pathetic, broken-hearted, effete figure who, in vain, sought to warm himself at the dead embers of his former lusts (I Kings 1:1-4). In Solomon, born of the fateful marriage with Bathsheba, the nemesis continued until the United Kingdom was split in two.

It is a testimony to the realism of the Israelite faith that tragedy like this could be written. Because the David story ascends the heights of human aspiration and plumbs the depths of human anguish it has outlived the practical circumstances from which it came. In one sense, David was a victim of his own greatness, of an indomitable will that urged him to scale the tempting heights of power. Yet, in spite of his drive for success and national glory, he was never lacking in the magnanimity and winsomeness that endeared him to friend and enemy alike. But in a deeper sense David was involved in the conflict with the God he sought to serve, the God with whose will he had to reckon in the practical affairs of daily life. This, at any rate, is the testimony of the narrator who tells David's life story. It is significant that tradition has ascribed to David the authorship of the great penitential psalm, Psalm 51, which is described as "a psalm of David, when Nathan the prophet came to him after he had gone to Bathsheba." [15] If David was serious in his conviction that Yahweh, enthroned on the Ark, had taken up his dwelling in the capital of the kingdom, he had to be ready to hear the word of Yahweh spoken by a prophet, the word that brought David's power under judgment. Faith in Yahweh's kingly rule prevented Israel from following the oriental practice of making the royal power absolute and—as in Egypt—of deifying the king.

The Ideal King

In time, David's weaknesses were forgotten and his greatness was extolled, just as tradition has idealized such figures of American history as Washington, Lincoln, and Lee. Israel's historians believed that David, more than any other king, typified the ideal combination of power and goodness. He was remembered as "Yahweh's servant," the God-fearing king who "executed justice and righteousness unto all his people" (II Sam. 8:15).

According to an important passage which we have touched on previously (II Sam. 7), the special relationship between Yahweh and David was extended to the whole dynasty of David. David asked the prophet Nathan for divine approval of his plan to build Yahweh a house of cedar, a temple comparable in glory to his own palace. But Yahweh refused David's request, promising

---

[15] Some psalms may have been composed by David, but it is generally agreed that he was not the author of the whole Psalter. (See further Chapter 15.)

instead that *he* would make David a "house" (that is, a dynasty) and that the throne of his kingdom would be established *forever* (verses 11-13). The Davidic king, it is said, would have a special relationship to God: "I will be his father, and he shall be my son" (verse 14). Moreover, Yahweh promised that, although the chastening of divine judgment might fall upon individual kings for their weaknesses, his mercy would not be withdrawn from David's house, as it was from Saul, for he had made with David an "everlasting covenant." Thus later generations believed that David's dynasty had a unique place in the unfolding of the divine purpose in history. Although II Samuel 7 is colored by the later theological reflection of Jerusalem circles, the chapter undoubtedly is based on an understanding of the Davidic throne which goes back to the Davidic court itself. This view is brought out in II Samuel 23:1-7, the so-called "Last Words of David" (cf. Ps. 132:11)—a passage which is so old in both style and content that it was either composed by David himself, or by one of his court circle.[16] David says:

> Yea, does not my house stand so with God?
>   For he has made with me an everlasting covenant,
>   ordered in all things and secure.
> For will he not cause to prosper
>   all my help and my desire?
>
>   —II SAMUEL 23:5

We shall have occasion to notice repeatedly that this belief in a special covenant between Yahweh and the house of David had far-reaching implications for the future of Israel.

The bitter political experiences of Israel after David's death gave rise to the hope that a Messiah ("Anointed One") would come, who would be of David's lineage, who would reunite the tribes of Israel, and who would restore Jerusalem to a position of prestige among the nations (see Is. 9 and 11). In times of national calamity people prayed ardently to God to remember the covenant he had made with David (see Is. 55:3) and to restore the kingdom to Israel. Psalm 89, for instance, is a poignant petition to God to look upon the distress of his people and, in his mercy and power, to fulfill the promise once made to David by the prophet Nathan. When everything seemed lost, men looked back to the glorious rule of David as the foreshadowing pattern of God's future kingdom on earth. Indeed, the whole conception of the kingdom of God, which plays such a large part in the Old and New Testaments, is profoundly influenced by the new impetus given to theological reflection by Israel's having become

---

[16] So, for instance, Gerhard von Rad, *Theology*, I [80], pp. 310-314, who points out that the motif of the "everlasting covenant" found in the "Last Words of David" is actually very ancient and prepares the way for II Sam. 7. Murray Newman, in *The People of the Covenant* [109], has traced the theology of the "everlasting covenant" back to a J covenant tradition, with which David became acquainted during his reign at Hebron.

a nation under David. Just as Israel's covenant faith found new expression within the Tribal Confederacy, so it found new expression again within the radically different conditions of the monarchy. Hence the theological importance of the kingdom, the city of David, the Davidic dynasty, the Temple, and the covenant with David increased.

We must emphasize, however, that this fateful step in Israel's pilgrimage was resisted by the conservatives, who feared that the transition from confederacy to monarchy would corrupt the people of Yahweh by making Israel "like the nations." This prophetic reaction is voiced by Nathan in II Samuel 7, and is probably an authentic tradition even though the chapter, in its present form, comes from a late literary source which is concerned primarily with the continuance of the Judean, Davidic dynasty. David succeeded in transferring the traditions of the Confederacy to Jerusalem: the Ark, the Tabernacle, the priesthood. But in this change something happened to the character of "Israel," to the structure of the community. No longer was Israel, the people of God, bound together on the basis of *covenant allegiance* to Yahweh at the central sanctuary; Israel was now bound together *politically*, on the basis of a covenant between king and people (II Sam. 5:3). As citizens of the state, the men of Israel owed allegiance to a king who could take a census, exact forced labor, and require submission to his power. Throughout the history of the monarchy there was a deep-seated conflict between these two conceptions of "Israel." As Israel became a state modeled after other oriental monarchies, more and more she lost her distinctive character and faced the danger of being swallowed up in the power-struggle and cultural stream of the Near East.

SOLOMON IN HIS GLORY

The familiar words of Jesus, "Even Solomon in all his glory was not arrayed like one of these," referring to the natural beauty of the lilies of the field, show how the name of Solomon came to be the symbol of the wealth and glory of empire. No other king of Israel, not even David himself, ascended a higher pinnacle of worldly splendor. Solomon's vast building program, his fabulous wealth and large harem, his far-flung commercial enterprises, his up-to-date military program, his patronage of wisdom and the arts, all were admired with open-eyed wonder by his subjects and by visitors from afar like the Queen of Sheba.

An octogenarian of the time who had spent his early life amid the rustic simplicities of the last days of the judges must have marveled at the swift changes that had taken place during his lifetime. In the brief span of fifty or sixty years, Israel had risen from political obscurity to the rank of a small empire that could command the political attention and economic envy of nations roundabout. Much of the credit was due, as we have seen, to the leadership of David. Although Solomon, unlike his father, was not a military man, by political shrewdness and international diplomacy he was able to execute and stabilize the policies that David had initiated. To be sure, before his death the empire established by David had begun to slip out of control as a result of the revolt of Edom and Syria (I Kings 11:15-25); but during most of his reign peace prevailed.

Solomon's achievements were favored by the political situation of his day. Egypt continued to be politically feeble; Assyria was not to be a threat for almost a century; and other small nations were either kept in military subjugation or bound to Israel by commercial treaty. The outstanding figure on the political horizon was Hiram I, King of Tyre, under whose leadership the Phoenicians (one of the Canaanite peoples) established a vast colonial empire throughout the Mediterranean world. David had entered into alliance with Hiram; and Solomon, since he had military control of the land highways, could easily continue the policy of cooperation. Thus the stage was set for a period of dazzling material prosperity.

The Historian's Slant

The court history of David concludes in I Kings 1-2 with an account of the intrigues that brought Solomon to power, rather than Adonijah, his half-brother, who was first in the line of succession. Solomon's claim to leadership was not based on the charisma, as had been the case with Saul and even with David, but solely on his birth and the political influence of his supporters. By removing from the picture any possible contender to the throne, "the kingdom was established in the hand of Solomon" (I Kings 2:46). This was the royal road to power that kings of the ancient world frequently traveled, and in this respect Israel had indeed become "like the nations." Henceforth Israel's charismatic leadership was to be vested in a special class of men known as prophets (see Chapter 7). Later on, men wistfully looked to the messianic age of the future when the "spirit of Yahweh" would rest once again upon the king, as it had upon David (see Is. 11:1-2).

The Davidic Court History ends abruptly at the conclusion of I Kings 2, and we must depend upon the material in chapters 3-11 for our knowledge of Solomon's reign. Evidently this historical information was extracted from a royal document no longer extant, one which is referred to in I Kings 11:41 as "the book of the acts of Solomon." In its present form, however, the account betrays the hand of the Deuteronomic historian. The language is often in the same style and shows the same thought as the Deuteronomic sections of Joshua, Judges, and Samuel, especially II Samuel 7 (for instance, I Kings 3:3-14; 6:11-13; 8:14-61; 9:1-10; 11:1-13). Since the Deuteronomic historian wanted to emphasize his central theological teachings, he extracted from the royal annals whatever served his purpose and added interpretive passages.

The Deuteronomic convictions stand out rather clearly. For one thing, the historian adhered to the view that the true worship of Yahweh must be centralized in the Temple of Jerusalem, not in the outlying "high places." As a result, he glossed over or neglected many of Solomon's acts, and gave most of his attention to the building of the Temple. Moreover, he wrote with the conviction that the Davidic line was the only legitimate one, for Yahweh had promised David that he would build him a "house" (II Sam. 7). So the writer did not hesitate to touch up the portrait of Solomon, the famous temple-builder. He apologized for Solomon by saying that at first he had to worship in "high places" because no temple had yet been built (I Kings 3:1 ff.). But in the same breath he stated that "Solomon loved Yahweh, walking in the statutes of David, his father," although this judgment is later qualified (I Kings 11:4-6). In later narratives of the books of Kings the historian affirmed that Yahweh was gracious to the kings of the Davidic dynasty "for David's sake." And finally, the writer looked back wistfully to the time before the sinful secession of the northern tribes when the people were united and strong. With a nostalgia for the glorious past, he remembered the time when Solomon ruled over all the kingdoms from the Euphrates River to the very border of Egypt, doubtless comparing that ideal situation with the unhappy state of affairs at the time of his writing. Right in the midst of a passage that describes an oppressive policy of Solomon, he exclaims: "Judah and Israel were as many as the sand by the sea; they ate and drank and were happy" (I Kings 4:20-21)! With some exaggeration, he boasts that "Solomon excelled all the kings of the earth in riches and wisdom."

But this is a view of Solomon's reign seen through rose-colored glasses. As a matter of fact, the portraits of David and Solomon—father and son—present a study in contrasts. David came to the throne the hard way—up from the shepherd's field and the warrior's rough life. His greatness was that he never rose so high as to be cut off from the common soil that had nourished him in his youth. Solomon, on the other hand, was "born to the purple," and never knew anything but the sheltered, extravagant life of a king's palace. The legendary story in I Kings 3:3-15 describes him at the outset of his career as choosing God's gift of an understanding heart to judge (that is, to rule) his people, rather than riches and honor. But the actual facts of his administration show that he lacked the common touch that would have turned this pious dream into reality. Ambitious and selfish by nature, his lavish court in Jerusalem was a hall of mirrors that reflected the glory and reputation of the great king of Israel. The law in Deuteronomy 27:14-20 must have been composed with Solomon in mind.

A Program of Building and Expansion

Thanks to the favorable international situation, Solomon was able to concentrate on an ambitious twenty-year building program. Since the historian regarded the building of the Temple as the most important enterprise in this program, he gave a proportionately large amount of space to a description of its erection, design, and furnishings (I Kings 5-7). It was located on a ridge above (north of) the site of the old city (Ophel; see map, p. 143), on ground which David had purchased for an altar (II Sam. 24:18-25)—probably the very spot marked by the sacred rock which today is enclosed by the Mosque of Omar, otherwise known as the Dome of the Rock.[17] Compared with a modern cathedral, it was modest in size (about 90 x 30 x 45 feet), but for its time it was a great architectural achievement. It was appropriately consecrated as Yahweh's home in the midst of his people by bringing the Ark of the Covenant from Zion, David's old city, and by an elaborate ceremony in which Solomon himself officiated, even to the offering of a magnificent prayer which is cast in the Deuteronomic language of a much later time (I Kings 8:22-53)![18] The Ark, however, was one of the few points of contact with Israel's Mosaic heritage. By contrast, the Temple—designed by Phoenician (that is, Canaanite) architects—represented the invasion of Canaanite culture right into the center of Israel's life and worship.[19] Any conservative Israelite who cherished the faith of his fathers must have been shocked by Solomon's bold imitation of foreign ways. It took some years for the Temple, which was essentially a state sanctuary, to become the focus of Israelite affection.

Actually, the building of the Temple was overshadowed by other phases of Solomon's building program. Seven years were spent building the Temple, but thirteen years were devoted to the construction of his palace complex, consisting of government buildings, the king's house (about 150 x 75 x 45 feet), and the house of his Egyptian queen. Moreover, outside Jerusalem Solomon built "chariot cities" and other fortifications at Gezer, Megiddo, Hazor, and elsewhere (I Kings 9:15-19). A large fleet of horse-drawn chariots enabled him to protect his land and to control the trade routes over which wealth poured into his kingdom from Phoenicia, Egypt, Arabia, and other parts of the world (I Kings 4:26; 9:10; 10:26). At one of these chariot cities, Megiddo, which guards the pass through which the main commercial and military highway from Egypt to Syria ran, archaeologists have found evidence of about 450 stalls for horses. Solomon's traders purchased chariots from Egypt and ranged far up into Cilicia (Kue), located in old Hittite country, to import horses. Solomon was, indeed, such a clever "horse dealer" that his agents exported horses and chariots to other nations at a handsome profit (I Kings 10:28-29).

---

[17] For a discussion of the location, see R. De Vaux, *Ancient Israel* [62], pp. 318-319.

[18] To the Deuteronomic theologians, the older idea of Yahweh dwelling in a temple seemed to limit him (I Kings 8:27). They overcame this difficulty by saying that Yahweh is transcendent, for not even the highest heaven could contain him, but he causes his "name" (his *alter ego*) to dwell in the Temple (vss. 28 ff.).

[19] On the Canaanite architecture of the Temple see G. E. Wright, "Solomon's Temple Resurrected," *The Biblical Archaeologist*, IV (1941), pp. 17-31; W. F. Albright, *Archaeology and the Religion of Israel* [50], pp. 142-155. De Vaux (*ibid.*, pp. 312-330) discusses fully the structure, furnishings, history, and theology of the Jerusalem Temple.

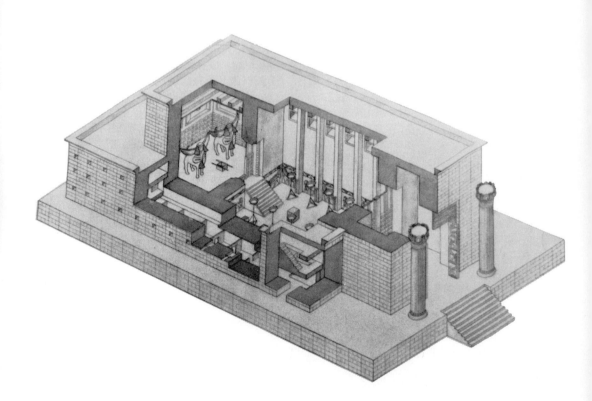

SOLOMON'S TEMPLE (*upper left*): *a reconstruction showing the two massive, free-standing pillars flanking the ornamental east door. The Temple was originally built according to Phoenician architectural patterns. In front of the Temple was a courtyard, within which was placed the altar of burnt offering.*

The interior of the Temple (lower left): a cutaway drawing by Edward S. Winters. (Since the drawing is isometric, the perspective is slightly distorted.)

The congregation worshiped in the court outside, near the high altar of sacrifice. Like other temples of the Syro-Phoenician region, this one was divided into three parts: the Ulam (vestibule), the Hekal (sanctuary), and the Debir (cella or inner shrine).

The priest first ascended the ten steps of the Temple, passed through the huge cypress doors guarded by two elaborately adorned bronze pillars, known as Jachin and Boaz, and entered the vestibule. He then passed through another pair of cypress doors into the main sanctuary, which contained the sacred furniture: the seven-branched golden candlesticks, the table of showbread, and a small altar. This huge room, 45 feet high, was paneled with cedar and floored with cypress. Its flat roof was supported by huge cedar beams, and the room itself was dimly lit by latticed windows on either side, just below the ceiling. On the wall-panels were carvings of palm trees, flowers, chain work, and cherubim.

Just beyond the small cedar altar, which was situated in the center of the main sanctuary and decorated with gold leaf, another series of stairs led up to a raised room, a perfect cube, access to which was gained through a small double door. This was the Holy of Holies. It was lined with cedar and, having no windows, was pitch dark. In it were the two large cherubim, made of olive wood decorated with gold leaf, standing about 15 feet high. Beneath their outstretched wings stood the Ark of the Covenant, which was regarded as Yahweh's throne. (The above description is based on an article by G. E. Wright, "Solomon's Temple Resurrected," in The Biblical Archaeologist, IV, No. 2 [May, 1941]. *See also Roland de Vaux,* Ancient Israel [62], *Part IV, chap. 3.)*

An excellent example of Solomon's far-flung commercial enterprises was his construction of a "fleet of ships" at Ezion-geber on the Gulf of Aqabah, an arm of water extending northward from the Red Sea (I Kings 9:26-28; 10:22). In cooperation with Hiram, King of Tyre, these ships were navigated to distant ports, thus giving Solomon what Palestine lacked most of all: a seaport. The Phoenicians, a seafaring people who were ancestors of the later Carthaginians, had already been exploiting the commercial opportunities of the Mediterranean world. Solomon's league with Hiram brought wealth into Palestine through Phoenician ports (see I Kings 10:22) and enabled him to take advantage of Phoenician maritime skill in exploiting the area of the Red Sea and Indian Ocean.

The building of the seaport at Ezion-geber was in itself a major political achievement.[20] It may be that the real purpose of the Queen of Sheba's long trip from southern Arabia to visit Solomon (I Kings 10:1-13) was to negotiate a

---

[20] Ezion-geber (Tell el-Kheleifeh) was excavated under the direction of Nelson Glueck in 1938-40. See his book, *The Other Side of the Jordan* (New Haven: American Schools of Oriental Research, 1940), chaps. 3 and 4. Recently he has retracted his interpretation of the ruins as a copper refinery. See his discussion in *The Biblical Archaeologist*, XXVIII, No. 3 (Sept. 1965), pp. 70-87.

THE STABLES AT MEGIDDO *apparently date back to the time of Solomon. The top picture shows a reconstruction based on available data. Between the hitching posts, which functioned also as supports for the roof, were mangers. Each unit stabled about 24 horses, and it is estimated that about 450 horses could be accommodated in this "chariot city," which is mentioned in I Kings 9:15, 19.*

commercial treaty with the king, who was cutting into the prosperous camel-caravan trade of Arabia. If that was her aim, when she "told him all that was on her mind" the conversation must have come around to economic relations between the two countries. Evidently her diplomacy was not in vain, for "King Solomon gave to the queen of Sheba all that she desired" (I Kings 10:1-13).

Rumblings of Discontent

Had anyone withdrawn from this brilliant spectacle, however, he would have heard the rumblings of an approaching storm. Like the great pharaohs of Egypt, Solomon carried out his program of expansion by means of harsh measures of exploitation. To pay for his tremendous overhead, he divided his kingdom into twelve tax districts, each with an officer in charge (I Kings 4:7-19). One of the duties of these governors was to see that the royal larder was amply provided (I Kings 4:22-28). Scholars have argued convincingly that the real purpose behind this administrative reorganization was to centralize power in the crown by replacing the old tribal system with twelve districts, under the supervision of royal appointees—two of them sons-in-law of Solomon.[21] The boundaries of about half the tribal territories were deliberately changed. No move could have been better designed to destroy the last remnants of tribal independence. In this respect, Solomon was only implementing a policy that had been initiated by David.

Equally oppressive was Solomon's program of forced labor. Although much of the slave labor for his building projects was drawn from conquered peoples, Solomon also brought the lash down heavily upon his own people. We are told that some 30,000 Israelites were conscripted and sent off to the labor camps in Lebanon one month out of every three (I Kings 5:13-18). It has been estimated that this number would be comparable to a draft of 5,000,000 Americans during the mid-40's! They felled the great cedars of Lebanon, floated them down the Phoenician coast to Joppa, and thence hauled them over the hills to Jerusalem. Eighty thousand Israelites were reported to have been put to work in the stone quarries, and 70,000 toiled as burden-bearers. Thus the great Temple was completed at a cost far greater than the financial outlay—the cost of the life and liberty of exploited people. The ominous warning of Samuel had a ring of reality: if the people wanted a king like the oriental monarchs to rule over them, they must reckon with the danger that his power would drastically limit their liberties, secularize their outlook, and undermine the very foundations of the covenant community.

It is no wonder, then, that the pent-up resentment of the people eventually exploded into revolution. The leader of the revolt was a man whom Solomon had appointed as an officer over one of the work gangs: a certain Jeroboam, son of Nebat from Ephraim, one of the northern tribes. We have seen that even during David's reign the northern tribes, formerly under the crown of Saul, had attempted to secede from the united monarchy. Solomon's oppressive policies did nothing to eliminate this restiveness, and his death provided the

---

[21] See De Vaux [62], pp. 133-135, who points out that Judah, the tribal area from which David had become king, was not incorporated into this system but had an administration of its own.

spark that touched off the powder keg. (See Chronological Chart 3, p. 198.) Moreover, just as it was a prophet, Nathan, who had led the court intrigue that placed Solomon on the throne, so it was a prophet, Ahijah, from the former confederate center of Shiloh, who announced that Yahweh would "rend the kingdom out of the hand of Solomon," leaving only the tribe of Judah under the rule of a Davidic descendant (I Kings 11:29-39). Israel was to re-learn under prophetic teaching the lesson that had been impressed upon her memory in the period of Moses and Joshua: that Yahweh participates in the historical struggle. The God who had rescued his people from the bondage of Egypt was able to deliver his people from the tyranny of a king whose pretensions to absolute power were hidden behind the glorious façade of a state religion. For Israel's faith, unlike other religions of antiquity, did not promote and sanction the harmony of the existing order; rather, it promoted social change by emphasizing the conflict between God's will and men's ambitions, between the kingdom of God and the kingdom of Israel. The God of Israel made himself known in political events that shook the very foundations of the kingdom that men sought to build.

Solomon's Broadmindedness

"Yahweh was angry with Solomon" (I Kings 11:9; cf. 9:1-9). This is the testimony of the Deuteronomic historian who pondered the meaning of Solomon's reign. Solomon's kingdom was weighed in the balance of God and found wanting. To be sure, the historian has been quite lenient in evaluating Solomon's reign. He attributed his defects to his dotage, for "when Solomon was old, his wives turned away his heart after other gods; and his heart was not perfect with Yahweh his God, as was the heart of David, his father" (I Kings 11:4). To this writer, Solomon's weakness was an excessive broadmindedness, most evident with respect to his harem. It should be said that Solomon's possession of "seven hundred wives and three hundred concubines" was not evidence of mere sensuality. True, Solomon was a "lover of women"—and doubtless his harem displayed the greatest feminine beauty. But many of his marriages were for the purpose of establishing close political and cultural ties with surrounding peoples. Thus his marriage with the pharaoh's daughter was a diplomatic marriage that linked Israel and Egypt together as allies and brought to Solomon the city of Gezer as a wedding dowry (I Kings 3:1; 9:16). Since marriages of this type were motivated primarily by political considerations, Solomon was quite willing for his foreign wives to practice their native religion, and he went so far as to build them special shrines in his capital city. To the Deuteronomic historian this was carrying tolerance too far, for Israel's king was giving sanction to an idolatrous policy that diluted and perverted Israel's faith.

This judgment need not have been limited to Solomon's old age, for the record indicates that his entire reign tended toward religious syncretism—that is, the amalgamation of alien elements with Israel's native tradition. These foreign influences brought radical changes in the character of Israel's life. The former simplicities of Israel's agricultural society were swept away in the wave of Solomonic prosperity, bringing to some people sudden riches and royal favor and to others abject poverty and royal slavery. Jerusalem, the capital of the kingdom, became a cosmopolitan city into which caravans came from all parts of the world bringing new ideas and practices along with coveted wealth. The Temple itself, designed by foreign artisans, was the chief symbol of "the new look." Although Solomon probably regarded himself as a loyal worshiper of Yahweh, his broadminded hospitality led him to appropriate elements of the Baal religion along with his Mosaic heritage. For instance, the "sea" (symbolic of the primeval ocean), which was supported by twelve bulls (I Kings 7:23-26), reflects fertility and mythological motifs of the Fertile Crescent. Apparently the Temple was intended to be a replica of Yahweh's heavenly abode, a microcosm of the macrocosm, in line with the ancient pagan view that there is correspondence between the earthly and heavenly spheres.[22]

Thus the age of Solomon is another chapter in the conflict between faith and culture, between Yahweh and the gods—a conflict that can be traced throughout Israel's history as a nation in Canaan. It was not Yahweh's intention that Israel should become a great nation, as other nations measured greatness; rather —as affirmed in Solomon's "Deuteronomic" prayer (I Kings 8:51, 53)—Israel was to be separated from other nations by her covenant calling. From the very first, Israel's covenant accented Yahweh's uncompromising, "jealous" demand for absolute allegiance. But it was difficult to maintain faithfulness to the Mosaic tradition in the cultural cross currents of Canaan, where the gods of the Fertile Crescent made an irresistible claim upon men's lives. Incited by political aspirations and commercial expansion, the tendency of popular religion was toward tolerance and compromise—the very attitudes that were encouraged during the reign of Solomon. Had not this pursuit of the devices and desires of men's hearts been rebuked and arrested by the prophets, Israel's distinctive faith would have fallen into oblivion along with the religions of the Fertile Crescent. Influenced by the convictions of Israel's prophets, the Deuteronomic historian insisted that the regime of Solomon stood under divine judgment. Yahweh himself acted to stir up the revolutionary ferment, even to raising up adversaries against Solomon (I Kings 11:14, 23).

---

[22] See R. E. Clements, *God and Temple* [201], chap. 5; also M. Eliade, *Cosmos and History* [121], pp. 6-20.

ISRAEL'S

NATIONAL EPIC

CHAPTER SIX   Before we go on with Israel's life story
during the time of the divided monarchy, we shall pause
for a bit to consider the literary awakening that occurred
during the reigns of David and Solomon. For the first time
in her history, Israel had attained political and economic
leadership. From a dozen semi-nomadic tribes loosely bound
together in a covenant confederacy, she had been forged
into a powerful state, able to hold her head proudly among
the other nations of the ancient world. Although political

Biblical readings: The Yahwist (J) narratives of the book of Genesis,
as outlined on pp. 170-171.

greatness brought with it great temptations, as we have seen in the preceding chapter, it also stimulated a literary activity that produced a more important and lasting heritage than all the architectural monuments of the age. As in the case of the period of Queen Elizabeth I of England, the political achievement of the age of David and Solomon furnished the impulse for the creation of a classical literature.

The view that nationalism produced a national literature has been challenged by an important group of Scandinavian scholars. The flowering of literature, they say, occurred much later, some time after the fall of the nation in the sixth century B.C. Before that time, Israel's traditions were transmitted mostly through oral memory, and writing was employed only for practical matters like letters, contracts, official lists, inscriptions, and so on. Literature began to appear, they believe, when the memory—the oral tradition—lost its vitality. And this occurred not in a time of national vigor like that of David and Solomon, but in a time of cultural degeneracy and national decline. Thus literary activity really began *after* the fall of the state, when the people were uprooted from their homeland and dispersed into exile.[1]

One merit of this extreme position is that it warns us against regarding the Old Testament from the point of view of Westerners. Today we rely on books, libraries, newspapers, and lecture notes, and assume that the people of antiquity must have done the same. Our slavery to the written word contrasts with the ancient Oriental, whose power of memory was not debilitated by the literary crutches used by Westerners to educate themselves in forgetfulness. The oral tradition was exceedingly important in ancient Israel, not only in the time before David but in the whole period covered by the Old Testament. But this does not justify our jumping to the conclusion that Israel's traditions were transmitted *only* in oral form during the period of the monarchy, and that the appearance of literature was a sign of national decline. The impulse to write must have been furnished—as it has been in so many nations, ancient and modern—by the stirring events that brought the people upon the stage of history with a sense of national destiny.

It is hardly accidental that the Court History of David found in II Samuel 9-20 and I Kings 1-2, regarded by scholars as one of the best examples of Hebraic prose in the Old Testament, evidently was composed during the reign of David. One authority praises the "early source of Samuel," especially the Court History, as "the outstanding prose writing and historical masterpiece of the Old Testament." Convinced that its account is so vivid and accurate that it must have been written by an eyewitness, he looks for the author among the persons associated with David's court. He acclaims this author as "the 'father of history' in a much truer sense than Herodotus half a millennium later," and points to

---

[1] A representative statement of the Scandinavian school is found in Eduard Nielsen's little book, *Oral Tradition* [102].

the national renaissance under David as providing the conditions for this literary achievement.[2]

In all probability, an even greater work was composed during the period of the United Kingdom: the masterful "J" epic from the pen of the "Yahwist." [3] We have already referred to this source, as well as to the later literary sources, E, D, and P, in our survey of Israel's history before the rise of the monarchy. Although J is an invaluable source for the study of early traditions, it is primarily a monumental *literary* and *theological* creation of the time of Solomon. In this epic Israel's faith, stimulated by the stirring events of the period of David and Solomon, found one of its profoundest expressions in the Old Testament. At the very time when Solomon's policies introduced influences that corroded the Mosaic tradition, the Yahwist emerged as the champion of Israel's covenant faith and the precursor of the great prophets.

In order to appreciate the Yahwist's literary achievement, we must consider again the far-reaching changes brought about by the decline of the old Tribal Confederacy and the rise of the monarchy.

FROM TRADITION TO LITERATURE

The period from Moses to David was the period *par excellence* of the oral tradition. To say this does not mean that, beginning with David, the oral tradition was superseded by a literary period, for unfortunately the matter is not that simple. Even after David's time, many of Israel's religious traditions—stories, hymns, and prophetic oracles—were handed down orally, with the result that there was a fruitful interplay between the written and the remembered word.

The art of writing, of course, was known in Israel quite early. From the second millennium B.C. have come a number of literary works, among them the Canaanite Ras Shamra literature of the fourteenth century (see pp. 104-105). And future archaeological discoveries may show that writing was employed more widely in ancient Israel than the few allusions in the Old Testament seem to indicate (see Ex. 17:14; 24:4 Josh. 24:25 f.). In any case, there are references to written sources that are no longer extant, and quotations are made from them. One of these is "The Book of the Wars of Yahweh," mentioned in Numbers 21:14. Another is "The Book of Jashar," from which quotations are made in Joshua 10:13 (the command for the sun to stand still), II Samuel 1:18 (David's

---

[2] R. H. Pfeiffer, *Introduction to the Old Testament* [28], pp. 356-359. Gerhard von Rad reaffirms this view by saying that the "realism" and "secularity" of the Succession Document represent a new kind of historiography, "without parallel in the ancient East" (*Theology*, I [80], pp. 312-317).

[3] This anonymous author is so designated because his writing employs the divine name Yahweh (spelled by German scholars with an initial "J": Jahweh) in the time before Moses, while the "Elohist" who wrote the E epic preferred Elohim. See above, pp. 40-42.

dirge over Saul and Jonathan), and possibly I Kings 8:13 (Solomon's ritual of dedication).[4]

But in general the period before the monarchy was a preliterary one, in the sense that the poems, proverbs, and stories were inscribed primarily on the human memory. Writing played a fairly insignificant role, and was confined for the most part to business and practical affairs.

Yet we are not left in the dark about this early period just because we have no written documents. Our bias in favor of the greater reliability of writing contrasts with the practice of ancient people who "learned by heart" the traditions that were meaningful to them and trained the human memory to be extraordinarily retentive. The Homeric poems were transmitted orally for generations; Jewish rabbis committed to memory the traditions of the Mishnah centuries before any of them were written down; the materials of the Christian Gospels circulated orally before taking the form of written literature; and today there are Arabs who can recite the whole Koran without faltering, and Brahmins who know the whole Rig Veda by heart. Similarly, in the period before David the great religious traditions of Israel were preserved and shaped in the human memory, and no doubt were recited publicly by poets and singers at the great religious festivals or at other social gatherings.

Forms of the Oral Tradition

In recent years, a great advance has been made in the study of the history of the oral tradition. On the basis of this study, we can isolate the small "memory units" and understand their characteristic type or form. In each case, the unit of tradition came out of a living situation—that is, it was associated with some act or event, just as Americans remember the story of Paul Revere's midnight ride in connection with the Revolutionary War. An excellent example is the Song of Miriam (see p. 54), which was a spontaneous outcry of praise after a great victory.

Here we can give only a brief summary of the preliterary tradition, although it is discussed in detail in various introductions to the Old Testament. There were various kinds of poetic units: songs to accompany work (the "Song of the Well," Num. 21:17-18), songs of taunting victory (the "Song of Deborah," Judg. 5), hymns of praise (Song of Miriam, Ex. 15:21), songs of lament (David's dirge over Saul and Jonathan, II Sam. 1:19-27). There were poetic sayings (aphorisms) of various kinds: the saying that was used when the Ark was carried (Num. 10:35-36), the saying about the shedding of human blood (Gen. 9:6), Lamech's saying about blood-revenge (Gen. 4:23-24), the proverb about Saul among the prophets (I Sam. 10:12), and Samson's riddle (Judg.

---

[4] In the Septuagint, the Greek translation of the Old Testament, this ancient ritual is said to have come from "The Book of Songs," which by a slight misreading of the Hebrew could have been "The Book of Jashar."

14:14, 18). There were all kinds of narratives: stories about creation and primeval history, about a place, a custom, a tribal hero, a cultic practice, or about the idiosyncrasy of a people. Sometimes stories were told to explain the origin of something (etiologies), sometimes for the purpose of entertainment, sometimes to express the moods and feelings evoked by daily affairs. So the oral tradition was marked by a diversity as rich as life itself.

These popular forms are very important in undersanding the historical life of Israel during the age of song and legend. Often it is assumed that when something is "legendary," like, say, the legends of King Arthur, it has virtually no historical authenticity. What is legendary is opposed to what is historical—that is, according to our view, exact sober history. Now it is quite true that legend (saga) lacks the precise accuracy demanded by a twentieth-century historian. In our sophisticated age no historian would think of writing history in the form of the narrative of the Flood, or the story of Jacob's dream at Bethel, or the Joseph cycle. But in a deeper sense these ancient popular forms tell us something about history that is sometimes ignored by the modern historian who is concerned only with giving a dispassionate report of wars, daily events, relations between nations, and so on. Saga is able to communicate to us out of the past *history as experienced*, the internal meaning of events and happenings. And if the deepest meaning of man's life is his relation to God, saga and poetry are exceedingly important ways of telling history.[5]

The Formation of an Israelite Epic

Many of the units of the oral tradition were appropriated by Israel from other people during the occupation of Canaan. This is also true of many of the sagas in Genesis that purport to deal with the ordinary course of history. Undoubtedly many of these stories were non-Israelite in origin and probably were associated with Canaanite shrines that the Israelites took over. For instance, it is widely held that the story of Abraham's sacrifice of Isaac (Gen. 22) and the story of Jacob's dream at Bethel (Gen. 28) were pre-Israelitic, Canaanite cult legends that had a completely different meaning in their original version. But these independent units of tradition were not just borrowed. Rather, they were *appropriated*, for Israel made them her own by baptizing them into the Yahweh faith.

The oral tradition did not take shape overnight. It was a gradual process that took place over many years. Undoubtedly the major catalyst was the Yahweh

---

[5] In this connection the fundamental study is *The Legends of Genesis* [131], by Hermann Gunkel, which is the preface to his monumental commentary on the book of Genesis. Since the English word "legend" has come to mean a fanciful story, it is perhaps better—as W. F. Albright points out in his introduction to this reprinted work—to use the old Norse word "saga," which refers to "a prose or more rarely a poetic narrative of historical origin or coloring." For a helpful discussion of the relation of saga to history, see Martin Buber's essay, "Saga and History" [130].

faith itself as confessed within the old Tribal Confederacy. In Chapter 3, we noticed that the Confederacy was established at Shechem, in the heart of territory that had long been under the domination of Canaanite culture. There it would have been natural for Israel to inherit from Canaanites various types of tradition: agricultural laws, cult legends, stories about primeval history, etiologies, tribal tales, and so on. But what Israel borrowed she transformed and made the vehicle for expressing her covenant faith. For Israel came into Canaan with her own native tradition, with the memory of the incidents in which Yahweh had delivered his people from Egyptian bondage and had graciously led them through the barren wilderness. Faith in Yahweh demanded that the popular traditions be changed to give expression to the deep experiences of Israel's history. Even the slightest change in an old story, one as minor as the addition of "Yahweh," was enough to bring about a complete change in its meaning.

Thus in the period before the monarchy the oral tradition was not just a formless mass, haphazardly thrown together. The story of Yahweh's dealings with Israel, later to assume elaborate form in the great historical narratives of our Old Testament, was beginning to take shape. The tribes were weaving the units of tradition into cycles of stories, stamped with their peculiar interests and experiences. Moreover, it is probable that the annual ceremony of covenant-renewal initiated at Shechem, and then performed at the confederate sanctuary of Shiloh, was an occasion for the recitation of laws and narratives that were binding upon all Israel. The early credal confession, found in Deuteronomy 26:5-10, was being expanded into a great Israelite epic that included the career of the "fathers," the deliverance from Egypt, the wandering in the wilderness, the giving of the Law at Sinai, and the conquest of Canaan. Israel's traditions, shaped by liturgical usage at the central sanctuary, had reached a fairly unified *oral* form even before the rise of the monarchy.[6]

It is against this background that we must understand the flowering of literature in the period of David and Solomon. The Yahwist's composition of an epic in *literary* form was a completely new thing in Israel. What was the historical situation during the period of the United Kingdom that occasioned this literary achievement?

THE YAHWIST'S EPIC

In the preceding chapter we noticed that the establishment of the monarchy brought about a radical change in the structure of Israelite society. Up to that

---

[6] The formation of the tradition during the period of the tribal confederacy is stressed by Martin Noth in his *Ueberlieferungsgeschichte* [99]. Gerhard von Rad tends to place more emphasis on the creative work of the Yahwist during the period of Solomon; see his study of the form-critical problem of the Hexateuch [100].

time, the social matrix of Israel's life had been the twelve-tribe confederacy, which had provided Israel's only unity and social solidarity for at least a century and a half. We have traced the decline of the tribal league under the political pressures of the early Iron Age, and have seen how David and especially Solomon sought to organize Israel around a new center: the royal city of Jerusalem. Toward this end the old confederate Ark was brought to Jerusalem and the land was re-divided into twelve administrative districts subject to the crown.

This radical change, which met with the protest of conservative religious circles, must have had far-reaching implications for Israel's oral traditions. For generations these traditions had been taking form at the various tribal shrines, especially at the confederate sanctuary at Shiloh. They came to express the faith and worship of the covenant community, no less than the legends of King Arthur mirror the age of chivalry. But just as the age of chivalry came to an end in the social changes that brought about the decline of feudalism, so Israel's age of song and legend was superseded by the new way of life in the monarchy. Shiloh was no more—Shiloh the common sanctuary to which the tribes came annually to renew their covenant with Yahweh and to hear a recital of the stirring stories of Israel's history. With the rise of the monarchy the cultic basis of Israel's life—in the tribal shrines and in the confederate sanctuary— was changed. Israel became a nation with a centralized government and a state sanctuary at Jerusalem. Were the Israelite traditions to go out of date in this new situation? Or could they be adapted to the new way of life?

The Yahwist's Accomplishment

This crisis was met by the Yahwist, one of the most creative literary artists of Israel.[7] Stimulated by the national renaissance of the Davidic era, the Yahwist reworked the traditions of Israel to make the old relevant to the new. Out of the reservoir of the oral tradition he took the materials that had been circulating more or less independently and combined them into a literary structure for the first time. The result was a comprehensive epic extending from the creation of the world to the entrance into the land of Canaan.

We must remember, however, that the Yahwist was not an independent author, acting with the freedom of a modern writer. He did not create the content of Israel's faith; rather, it was given to him in the tradition itself. The core of this faith is expressed in the cultic recitation found in Deuteronomy 26:5-10 (cf. Deut. 6:20-24; Josh. 24:2-13), to which we have alluded before. This was the story of Yahweh's saving acts: the deliverance from Egypt, the guidance through the wilderness, and the conquest of Canaan. Moreover, these elementary themes were being expanded into a unified saga during the period

---

[7] The interpretation followed here is that of Gerhard von Rad; see his commentary on Genesis [133], pp. 13-30. See also the author's little book, *The Beginning of History* (New York: Abingdon, 1963).

of the Tribal Confederacy. So the Yahwist did not start from scratch. Like Paul in the New Testament, he might have said: "I delivered to you as of first importance what I also received" (I Cor. 15:3). In his re-interpretation of the past, the Yahwist, like Paul, was bound by the central themes that constituted the faith of the community.

Let us see how the Yahwist wrote his epic. In his time a great many traditions were circulating: separate stories and cycles of stories. Some of these stories had already been naturalized within the Israelite community; others still bore the marks of their pre-Israelite origin. On the basis of the great convictions of Israel's faith (summarized in the cultic credo), the Yahwist gave these traditional materials a new literary and theological setting, changing what he received only in minor ways. He had no intention of rewriting all the traditions to make them fit into a smoothly consistent theological system. In fact, he permitted theological archaisms to stand. Individual stories taken by themselves—say, the story of the marriage of the Sons of God (Gen. 6:1-4), or the Tower of Babel (Gen. 11:1-9)—often betray a less refined theological belief than that of the Yahwist himself. Instead of trying to censor the legacy of the past, he sought to conserve it faithfully, but in a new literary and theological context. If we are to appreciate the Yahwist's creative artistry and theological profundity, we must look at the total context within which he set the individual stories.

A More Comprehensive View of History

The Yahwist also did something else that was quite new. So far as we know, he was the first to combine the Mosaic tradition with stories concerning primeval history (Gen. 2-11) in such a way as to present an unfolding drama of God's dealings with men from the Creation to the conquest of Canaan (the material now covered in the Hexateuch). The basic confession of faith found in Deuteronomy 26:5-10 is a simple recital of events, beginning with the Exodus and coming to a climax with the inheritance of the land of Canaan. Only a passing reference is made here to the patriarchal period covered by Genesis 12-50, in the sentence: "A wandering Aramean was my father"—an allusion to Jacob's ties with Aram or Syria. Nothing is said about the sojourn at Mount Sinai-Horeb (Ex. 19 ff.). There is no allusion to the Creation, Garden of Eden, the Flood, or the Tower of Babel (Gen. 2-11).[8] As we have said, quite probably Israel's epic was expanded during the period of the Tribal Confederacy to include some of these materials, especially the traditions of Sinai. Nevertheless, there is a striking contrast between the short recital of Israel's life story in this simple confession of faith and the comprehensive elaboration of these themes

---

[8] Reference to the first chapter of Genesis is omitted here because, by general agreement, the story found in Gen. 1:1-2:4 comes from the Priestly writer, whose work will be considered in Chapter 12.

in the present Hexateuch. It is safe to say that the symphonic expansion of the themes of Israel's faith was largely the accomplishment of the Yahwist.

The following diagram indicates how the Yahwist expanded Israel's view of history:

C	B	A
GEN. 2-11	GEN. 12-50	EX. 1 TO JOSHUA
Creation, Garden of Eden, other narratives of primeval history which include all mankind.	The patriarchal period. Israel's early history as represented by Abraham, Isaac, Jacob, and Joseph.	Israel's life story from the Exodus to the Conquest. The Mosaic tradition.

The Yahwist wrote his epic backward, as it were, looking through the historical experiences that had brought the community of Israel into being. Accordingly, the first step (A) was the expansion of the themes of the Mosaic tradition. This involved a full narration of the Exodus story, the wandering in the wilderness and the people's murmuring and rebellion, and the march toward Canaan.[9] The next step (B), reading the story backward, was the unification of the traditions of the patriarchal period, with the result that the stories concerning Abraham, Isaac, and Jacob are now governed by the theme of the promise given to Abraham (Gen. 12:1-4). In the Yahwist's account, the patriarchal period is one of anticipation—a movement toward the inheritance of the Promised Land and Israel's full participation in the divine plan that embraces all nations. The final extension (C) was the prefixing of the stories of primeval history—stories that deal not with Israel alone, but with the potential glory and the actual tragedy of human history.

We see, then, that the Yahwist accomplished an extraordinary feat of literary creativity. In the very period when the Mosaic tradition was threatened by the collapse of the old Confederacy and the syncretistic tendencies of Solomon's reign, he gave new expression to the faith of his fathers. In his epic the Mosaic period is decisive. The events of the deliverance from Egypt, the guidance through the wilderness, and the conquest of Canaan were proclaimed as the great acts of Yahweh, by which he had called Israel to be his people and had summoned them to fulfill a task in his plan. From this perspective, the Yahwist re-viewed the whole range of history before the monarchy: the struggles of Israel to become a nation, the dim memories of the patriarchal period, and ultimately the whole sweep of history from the Creation. All this he saw in a new light as he reworked Israel's traditions and cast them into dramatic literary

---

[9] Von Rad believes that the theme of the giving of the Law at Sinai was not part of the earliest tradition, but was first introduced into the Israelite epic by the Yahwist. However, in spite of the silence of Deuteronomy 26:5-10 on the Sinai covenant, we believe that this was an authentic part of the Mosaic tradition and had already been elaborated during the period of the Confederacy. See above, pp. 62-63.

form. Moreover, his work was undoubtedly influenced by the nationalism that awakened his literary genius. Thanks to the brilliant political achievements of David, the "promised land" was at last in Israelite possession. The conquest was complete. When the Yahwist represents Yahweh as saying to Abraham, "I will make of you a great nation" (Gen. 12:2), he must have believed that the promise was far along the way toward fulfillment in the time of David and Solomon. Even though the Tribal Confederacy had declined, and with it the simplicities of a previous day, the Yahwist wrote with the conviction that Yahweh had set before his people a glorious future into which they were about to enter.

The Yahwist's epic proved to be a controlling factor in the formation of subsequent literature. In later periods, other historians took up anew the task of reinterpreting the past in such a way that it could speak to their own situation. Later on, another literary work, that of the Elohist (E), was produced, reflecting the interests of the Northern Kingdom (see pp. 230-232). Although it lacks the universal perspective found in J, this source is closely dependent on the J epic, so much so that in many places the two sources are fused indistinguishably together (JE). Still later, about the time of the fall of the nation, the Deuteronomic historian (D) wrote a great historical work in which attention focused on Yahweh's deliverance of his people from Egypt and the making of the covenant at Sinai. Later yet, after the fall of the nation, priestly writers (P) wrote a history of God's dealings with Israel, beginning—as had the Yahwist—with the Creation (Gen. 1). Each of these sources, now blended with J in the Pentateuch, shows important theological variations. But none of them departs from the main outline laid down in the Yahwist epic, an outline based ultimately upon the central religious themes that constituted the core of Israel's tradition in the preliterary period. Therefore, the theological influence of the Yahwist has been stamped on the whole literary development that finally resulted in the Pentateuch as we now have it.

THE YAHWIST'S THEOLOGY OF HISTORY

Let us turn directly to the Yahwist epic, confining our study to the part found in the book of Genesis. In Chapter 1, we covered some of this ground briefly because of our interest in the historical background of the Exodus. The Yahwist, however, was not interested primarily in writing about the antecedents of the Exodus in a way that would satisfy modern historians and archaeologists. His purpose was to confess Israel's faith in Yahweh, whose saving deeds had been manifested in Israel's history. With the Exodus as the fulcrum of his historical interpretation, he reworked the traditions now found in the book of Genesis. To the Yahwist the meaning of the Exodus was the meaning of all history, right back to the Creation. And to substantiate his conviction that

THE YAHWIST'S EPIC IN GENESIS

I. Primeval History
The Garden of Eden — Genesis 2:4 (from "In the day . . .")-3:24

Cain and Abel — 4:1-16
Cain and his descendants — 4:17-26
The marriage of the sons of God — 6:1-4
The Flood (J and P blended in 6:5-8:22)
Noah's favor with Yahweh — 5:29; 6:5-8
Into the Ark — 7:1-5, 7, 16 (from "and the Lord . . ."), 8-10

The Flood comes — 7:12, 17 (from "and the waters . . ."), 22-23

The Flood abates — 8:2 (from "the rain . . .")-3 (to ". . . continually"), 6-12, 13 (from "and Noah . . .")

Conclusion — 8:20-22
Noah's culture of the vine — 9:18-27
Noah's descendants — 10:8-19, 21, 24-30
The Tower of Babel — 11:1-9

II. History of the Patriarchs
The ancestry of Abram (Abraham) — 11:28-30
The promise to Abraham — 12:1-4 (to ". . . with him"), 6-9

Abraham's visit to Egypt — 12:10-13:2
Abraham and Lot separate — 13:3-5, 7-10, 13-18
Yahweh's covenant with Abraham — Chapter 15 (with E elements in verses 1, 2, 5, 13-16 and elsewhere)

The birth of Ishmael — 16:1-14 (except verse 3)

Yahweh's appearance at Mamre — 18:1-16
Abraham's intercession for Sodom — 18:17-33
The destruction of Sodom — 19:1-28
The birth of Moab and Ammon — 19:30-38
Isaac's birth (J is fragmentary; the story of Isaac's circumcision is P) — 2:1-2 (to ". . . his old age"), 7, 33
The line of Nahor — 22:20-24 [10]

---

[10] E. A. Speiser, in his commentary on Genesis [134], p. 166, suggests that the story of the testing of Abraham (Gen. 22:1-19) may come from J. This is very doubtful, however. The passage beginning with Yahweh's angel calling from heaven "a second time" (vss. 15-18) sounds like an additional comment from a Yahwist editor and suggests that an old E story has been reworked.

II. History of the Patriarchs (*Continued*)

Finding a wife for Isaac	Genesis Chapter 24
The sons of Abraham's concubine	25:1-6
The birth of Esau and Jacob	25:21-26 (to "... called Jacob")
Jacob steals the birthright	25:27-34
Isaac's travels	26:1-33
Jacob steals the blessing	27:1-45
Jacob's dream at Bethel	28:10-22 (E elements in verses 12, 17-18, 20-22)

The Jacob and Laban cycle

Jacob's meeting with Rachel	29:1-14
Jacob weds Leah and Rachel	29:15-30
The birth of Jacob's children	29:31-30:24 (with E elements)
Jacob outwits Laban	30:25-43
Jacob's flight from Haran	31:1-55 (JE, except for P in verse 18 [from "he had acquired ..."])
Jacob prepares to meet Esau	32:3-12 (verses 13-21 probably E)
Jacob's wrestle with an angel	32:22-32
The reunion with Esau	33:1-17
The attack on Shechem	Chapter 34
Reuben's incest	35:21-22 (to "... heard of it")

The Joseph short story

Joseph is sold into Egypt	37:3-36 (E elements in verses 21-24, 28-36)
Judah and Tamar interlude	Chapter 38
Joseph's temptation	Chapter 39
Joseph's rise to power	(Chapter 41 is basically E, with some J elements)
The brothers' first visit	(Chapter 42 is basically E, with some J elements)
The brothers' second visit	Chapter 43
Joseph tests his brothers	Chapter 44
The brothers recognize Joseph	Chapter 45 (JE)
Jacob's family settles in Egypt	46:1-5 (JE), 28-34
Jacob's family is a blessing to Egypt	47:1-5 (to "... to Joseph"), 6 (from "let them dwell ..."), 13-26
Jacob approaches death	47:29-31
Jacob's death-bed blessing	48:1-2, 8-22 (JE)
Jacob's burial	50:1-11, 14

Yahweh is Lord of all history, he insisted that men began to worship Yahweh in the earliest times (the grandson of Adam, Gen. 4:26). He holds this to be true even though the divine name was introduced to Israel with a new meaning only in the time of Moses, as both E and P testify (see pp. 40-41).

Since the theology of the Yahwist can be discerned in the way he joined the units of tradition together into a comprehensive story, it is important to read the episodes of the epic in sequence. Although scholars differ somewhat on the material in Genesis that should be assigned to J, the outline on pp. 170-171 is adequate for our purpose.[11]

Notice that in some instances J and E materials are blended together so closely that they cannot be disentangled. These passages are designated as JE, indicating that later editors have supplemented and enriched the J narrative with excerpts from another ancient epic, that of the Elohist. But J is definitely the basic literary source to which the other narratives have been subordinated.

So the Yahwist's epic stands out sharply enough from the surrounding material for us to read it as a continuous narrative. Let us consider some of the main episodes in this dramatic account.

PRIMEVAL HISTORY

The most original contribution of the Yahwist is shown in the way he has prefaced the traditions concerning primeval history to the stories of the patriarchs, with the result that the call of Israel is viewed in the perspective of Yahweh's purpose for all mankind. The other ancient epic, that of the Elohist, is not found in Genesis 1-11, but begins with Abraham. Thus it lacks the breadth and depth of the J narrative. The Yahwist, however, affirms that Yahweh, who brought Israel out of Egypt, is the Lord of all mankind. With epic scope and grandeur, he portrays the story of God's dealings with Israel within the larger context of general human history from the very beginning of things.

To do this, the Yahwist appropriated a number of traditions that can be paralleled in the folklore of antiquity. The motifs of creation, paradise, the flood, and the deliverance of mankind from total destruction were expressed in various forms in the myths and legends of the ancient Near East. Most striking of all is the famous Gilgamesh Epic, which relates how Gilgamesh, a legendary king who once ruled in Sumerian times, tried to find out the secret of immortality from the hero of the flood, Utnapishtim. In Tablet XI, Utnapishtim vividly relates the story of how the gods capriciously decided to destroy mankind in a great flood. However, Ea, the god of wisdom, took it upon himself to advise Utnapishtim to build a large boat and take aboard the seed of

---

[11] A good literary analysis, which covers the whole Pentateuch, is found in the Appendix of Walter J. Harrelson's introduction [15].

all living things. Then the flood came with such destructive fury that "the gods cowered like dogs" and crouched against the walls of heaven, weeping about their decision to destroy mankind. The storm finally subsided on the seventh day, with the boat grounded on the top of Mount Nisir. Seven days later Utnapishtim sent forth a dove, a swallow, and—since these birds found no resting place—a raven. Then he offered a sacrifice of such sweet savor on the mountain top that "the gods crowded like flies" around it.[12] The similarity of this ancient story to the biblical account shows that the Yahwist borrowed freely from the fund of popular tradition, though he transformed the material in accordance with his theological perspective.

The stories concerning primeval history, then, cannot be regarded as exact, factual accounts of the sort that the modern historian or scientist demands. These stories are "historical" only in the sense that, as used by the Yahwist, they communicate the *meaning* of history.[13] The manner of presentation is pictorial, for the writer is dealing with a subject that eludes the modern historian's investigation—namely, the ultimate source of the human drama in the purpose and activity of God.

The Paradise Story

This is evident in the story of Paradise (Gen. 2:4b-3:24). Taken by itself, the story is filled with images—like the Tree of Life and the cunning serpent—which are found in ancient folklore. Indeed, the story evidently once circulated as the storyteller's answer to several questions: Why are man and woman attracted to each other? Why does social propriety demand the wearing of clothes? Why must there be the pain of childbirth and the misery of hard work? Why is the serpent hated by men? These, and other questions, were answered in the story that bears even yet the marks of an ancient popular tradition. But in the Yahwist's scheme the story deals with the deeper question of why man, God's creature, refuses to acknowledge the sovereignty of his Creator, with the result that history is a tragic story of man's banishment from the life for which he was intended.

The Yahwist's interpretation was based on the faith of the covenant community. In the covenant faith, Yahweh is the sovereign Lord upon whose grace and goodness, manifested in the great events of the past, Israel was utterly dependent. But the Yahwist knew too from tradition that Israel was bent upon flouting the authority of Yahweh in a spirit of murmuring and rebellion, wildly and heedlessly betraying her Lord in order that she might follow the

---

[12] See Pritchard, *Ancient Near Eastern Texts*, pp. 93-97.

[13] "The description of this age," writes Bruce Vawter, "is done by conviction [based on Israel's encounter with Yahweh in the time of Moses and the Exodus] rather than remembrance." See his discussion of the "historical sense" in the book of Genesis, in "Understanding Genesis," *Studies in Salvation History* [135], pp. 57-68.

devices and desires of her own heart. And he knew the "jealousy" of Yahweh, summed up in the First Commandment of the Decalogue—a divine holiness that would not tolerate man's pride and false allegiance. This was the meaning of God's dealings with Israel in her history. And in the Paradise story the Yahwist affirms that it is a true portrayal of the life of all mankind. For these chapters do not focus attention on the Hebrews (Abraham is regarded as the first Hebrew), but on "man," which is the meaning of the Hebrew word *'adam*. The existence of man is personalized in the story of "Adam." (Notice that in most instances the Revised Standard Version translates "man" or "the man" instead of the proper name, Adam.)

The Yahwist was not concerned primarily with the creation of heaven and earth, or with man's relation to the cosmic scene, but rather with man's *earthly* environment.[14] In a profound way he portrays the character of human existence. Man is made from the ground (*'adamah*, which is a play on the word *'adam*, man). The good earth is the stage of his life. He is a tiller of the ground and to the ground he must return at death. But man is not just a product of nature; he is a creature of Yahweh God, whose breath ("spirit") animates the dust, making it become a "living being." [15] He exists in relation to God, in dependence upon him—and, as the episode of the creation of "the woman" shows, in relation to another human self, his counterpart (2:18). This is man's freedom. To this free being God can speak, giving him a task ("to till and keep the garden") and placing him in a situation where he must decide to obey or disobey. According to this picture, life is a dialogue between God and man, "I and Thou." [16]

We cannot trace here all the nuances of thought in the Paradise story.[17] Suffice it to say that the story goes on to portray man's rebellion against the divine authority and his determination to assert his freedom in his own way, by grasping for the fruit of the forbidden tree. Sin, according to this story, is an act of the will in revolt against God. It is occasioned by man's ambition to overstep his status as a creature, to become "like God" or perhaps "like the gods," the divine beings in Yahweh's heavenly court (3:5; note the "us" in 3:22). Man's defiant act brings in its train a sense of guilt ("they knew that they were naked," 3:7; cf. 2:25), the futile effort to hide from the presence of

---

[14] Creation in the broader sense is the concern of the priestly narrative of Genesis 1:1-2:4a. The two stories, P and J, supplement one another in interest, even though they differ from each other in many respects.

[15] It is proper that the Revised Standard Version translates *néfesh* as "being" ("self" is another possibility). The passage implies psychosomatic unity, not a dualism of perishable body and deathless soul.

[16] See the work of the Jewish philosopher, Martin Buber, entitled *I and Thou* (Edinburgh: T. & T. Clark, 1937).

[17] See especially the treatment of Gen. 2-3 in Gerhard von Rad's commentary on Genesis [133]. An illuminating Christian commentary is also given by Dietrich Bonhoeffer, *Creation and Fall* (London: SCM Press, 1959).

Yahweh God, the attempt to rationalize the act by shifting the blame to the woman or the serpent,[18] the misery of woman's travail at birth and man's travail on the soil, and finally the banishment from the primeval peace of the garden.

Here we find a theme similar to that of the Greek tragedies: man's pride (*hybris*) prompts him in Promethean fashion to assert himself against Fate (*moira*), with the result that retribution (*nemesis*) comes upon him for his deed. However, in the Hebraic view there is a profound difference. Man does not revolt against a blind, impersonal fate but against the will of the sovereign God, whose personal relation with man is portrayed in the anthropomorphic language in which the Yahwist delights. (Notice the vivid portrayal of Yahweh "walking in the garden in the cool of the day.") Man is a creature, related to the ground and responsible before Yahweh. This is his God-given lot. Therefore, revolt against Yahweh is none other than a revolt against man's humanity —a revolt that evokes the judgment of God. Man's punishment is that henceforth he must live in suffering and anxiety, with the threat of death hanging over his head like a Sword of Damocles.

The Story of Cain and Abel

In the Yahwist's epic, banishment from the garden is the beginning of the course of history in which man is an agriculturalist, a "tiller of the ground." Although the background of the story of Eden is evidently agricultural, this background is not quite so clear in the next episode: the story of Cain and Abel. In its earliest form, the tradition probably reflected the animosity between the farmer and the nomad. The divine preference was given to the nomadic Abel, who sacrificed to Yahweh the firstlings of his flock, rather than to the agricultural offering of Cain, a tiller of the ground (*'adamah*). But the Yahwist does not attempt to smooth out inconsistencies;[19] rather, he uses this story as a vehicle for expressing his central purpose: to show how things went wrong as a result of Adam's revolt against his Creator. Just as in David's court history the father's sin lives on in his sons (see pp. 146-148), so in this case family life was spoiled by the father's act. Cain too was susceptible to an evil impulse—to sin, which couched at the door like a predatory animal, waiting for an opportunity to spring upon its prey (4:6-7). The break-up of the community for which Yahweh intended man is evident in Cain's question: "Am I my brother's keeper?" Again we hear that the ground (*'adamah*) is accursed, for

---

[18] In the religion and mythology of the ancient Near East the serpent-god was worshiped as a representation of the power of fertility and death. In the biblical story, however, the serpent has been stripped of mythological associations and is merely one of the animals made by Yahweh, distinguished by its uncanny wisdom and craft.

[19] For instance, the modern logician insists that Cain would have had difficulty finding a wife if he was actually the son of the first man!

from it Abel's blood cries out to Yahweh for retribution (4:11; cf. 3:17-19).

It is ironical that, according to the Yahwist epic, the first city was built by Cain—a murderer (4:17). Human culture got off to a bad start! The Yahwist knew, of course, about progress in technology and the arts. One of Cain's descendants was Jubal, the father of musicians; and another was Tubal-cain, a forger of metals—the metals that played such an important part in the cultural advance of the second millennium (4:21-22). But cultural advance was accompanied by violence, lust, and unbridled passions—a chain reaction of evil running from bad to worse. The last straw, according to the Yahwist, was the strange affair of the union of the sons of God (the heavenly beings) with the beautiful human maidens (6:1-4). This archaic story, which taken by itself defies understanding, was held up as proof that "the wickedness of man was great in the earth and that every imagination of the thoughts of his heart was only evil continually" (6:5). Yahweh, who in the Yahwist's view experienced human feelings, was "sorry," "grieved to the heart" that he had ever created man.

The Flood

In the Yahwist's scheme, the Great Flood was not just a natural event. He used the ancient popular tradition as a vehicle to express a fundamental theme of Israelite faith: God's judgment in the affairs of history. When we compare the biblical account with the Gilgamesh Epic, or with other ancient versions of the legendary deluge, we cannot help noticing the profound differences. There are, to be sure, naive anthropomorphic touches, like the statement that Yahweh shut the door of the Ark (7:16b), or that he smelled the pleasing fragrance of Noah's sacrifice (9:21). But these details—inherited from the popular tradition that the Yahwist used—do not obscure the central view that Yahweh, the one God (in contrast to Babylon's many gods), acts on the stage of human history to accomplish his righteous purpose (in contrast to the caprice of the Babylonian gods).

Moreover, Yahweh's judgment is also mixed with solicitous concern for man. This has already been evident in the story of Eden, where Yahweh's curse is followed by his clothing Adam and Eve in skin garments (3:21), and in the story of Cain, where Yahweh's judgment is mitigated by putting a protecting mark on Cain's forehead (3:15). Similarly, in the Flood Story, Noah finds favor with Yahweh. The boat into which he takes his family and the pairs of animals was a sign of Yahweh's intention to deliver a remnant with which to make a new beginning in history. The story concludes with the statement that even though "the imagination of man's heart is evil from his youth" Yahweh would never again curse the ground with such severe judgment. The regularities of nature— "seedtime and harvest, cold and heat, summer and winter, day and night"— would be signs of his covenant faithfulness (8:20-22).

The Temptations of Culture

But the divine judgment did not check the evil impulses of the human heart. In fact, culture itself—especially the culture of the Fertile Crescent—was infected by evil. This is the point of the two episodes that followed the Flood: the story of Noah's drunkenness (9:18-27) and the story of the construction of the Tower of Babel (11:1-9).

Noah, we are told, was the first successful tiller of the soil. He planted a vineyard—the chief symbol of Canaanite agriculture; and from the fruit of the vine he made a potent wine. Drinking the wine put him into a drunken, debauched condition, which led to what was regarded as a sexual abomination on the part of one of his sons, Ham, the father of Canaan. The point of Noah's indignation —contrary to people who try to find support here for racial prejudice—is not that Noah placed a curse on Ham, the father of black-skinned peoples, thereby degrading them to a position of inferiority. Rather, the passage is a pointed attack on agricultural *Canaan* (represented as a person), with its wine-drinking and sexual license. As we have seen (pp. 102-108), this culture, unlike the wilderness from which Israel came, was obsessed with the problem of controlling the fertility of the soil. In the time of Noah, so the story implies, the curse on the ground was removed (see 5:29; cf. 3:17-19) and Noah himself was successful as a farmer.[20] But Noah was unprepared for this potent taste of Canaanite agriculture. When he saw that he was overcome by the new powers of culture available to him, he pronounced a terrible curse on Canaan.

After the Flood, we are told, the earth was peopled by the descendants of Noah's three sons, Shem, Ham, and Japheth, who are regarded as the ancestors of the nations and social groups (see the J fragmentary table of the nations in Gen. 10). So we come to the conclusion of the Yahwist's sketch of primeval history: the story of the Tower of Babel. Before this tradition was incorporated into the Yahwist's epic, it had circulated independently as an explanatory story of the origin of diverse peoples and languages. We can detect the independence of this unit by comparing it with the J table of nations, in which the diversity of mankind is already presupposed. But the Yahwist appropriates the story, in spite of this inconsistency, to set forth his theological perspective on the primeval history of mankind.

The scene is laid in Babylonia (Shinar), where nomads, wandering in the east, found a plain and decided to establish a settled way of life—the culture for which Babylon was to become famous. Urged by the ambition to achieve unity—even a unity against God—they decided to build a city and a tower. The tower is a reference to the ziggurat, or terraced temple tower, the most

---

[20] The statement, "Noah was the first tiller of the soil" (9:20), apparently means that Noah was the first to try farming successfully, in contrast to Cain, who, when tilling the soil, was unsuccessful owing to the curse upon the ground (4:11-12).

THE ANCIENT ZIGGURAT OF UR *as it may be seen today in reconstructed form. The upper terraces of this temple tower, which resembled the structure at Babylon (Gen. 11:1-9), have been destroyed. The Akkadian word "ziggurat" means "pinnacle" or "mountain top." Believing that deities revealed themselves on mountains, dwellers in the plain constructed an artificial mountain with a sanctuary at the top.*

famous of which was the one known as Etemenanki in Babylon.[21] In the Yahwist's epic, however, the episode is the climatic evidence of the self-assertion which prompted men to revolt against Yahweh, to take things into their own hands in their desire for greatness and power. In the Yahwist's view, the culture of the Fertile Crescent, symbolized by the cult of Babylon, was corrupted by the rebellious will of man, who sought to "make a name" for himself. As in the case of the Flood, Yahweh again visited the earth with judgment and brought the building project to an end by imposing a language barrier. By means of a Hebrew pun, the word Babel is understood to mean "confusion" (compare English "babble"), for Yahweh confused their languages so that they could not understand one another, and dispersed them in various language groups over the face of the earth.

Primeval history, then, had a sad outcome, for man had failed to find the fullness of life—life in communion with God and in community with his neighbor. From Adam to the Tower of Babel the human tragedy increased, despite advances in the arts and sciences. History was urged on by an evil impulse that

---

[21] The Greek historian, Herodotus, gives some interesting comments on the ziggurat (*Persian Wars*, I, 181-182). See the discussion by R. De Vaux, *Ancient Israel* [62], pp. 281-282. The ziggurat, as he points out, was actually an artificial mountain with a huge stairway so that, ascending and descending, worshipers and the god could meet.

spoiled God's creation, leaving man estranged from his Creator and at odds with his fellow men. Taken by itself, the story would be extremely pessimistic. But the primeval history is part of the larger epic of the Yahwist. It is a prologue to what follows: the call of Abraham.

THE HISTORY OF THE PATRIARCHS

As we pass from Genesis 11 to Genesis 12, we leave the realm of primeval history and enter the historical arena of the second millennium B.C. The form of historical narration in Genesis 12-50 is saga, just as in Genesis 2-11. There is an important difference, however. The sagas of the patriarchal period, as we saw in Chapter 1, are clearly related to what was going on in the Fertile Crescent at that time. They present a kind of historical evidence with which the historian and archaeologist must reckon. But none of the primeval stories is anchored to anything with which a modern historian could deal. They are "historical" only in the broad sense that they portray concretely the meaning of man's historical existence in all its glory and tragedy, and give an interpretation of history as the drama of God's dealings with man.

But in stating the matter this way, we are influenced by a twentieth-century concept of history quite different from that of the Yahwist, who undoubtedly would have described the transition from Genesis 11 to Genesis 12 in a completely different way. In his epic, the stories of primeval history set forth the human predicament in universal terms, the predicament of men who are estranged from God and scattered over the face of the earth in confusion and strife. These stories provide the *prologue* to what is central in the Yahwist's epic: the special place of Israel in Yahweh's history-long and world-embracing plan.

God's Promise to Abraham

Thus the turning point in the Yahwist's literary drama is found at the very beginning of Genesis 12 (verses 1-4a). Out of the descendants of those who were dispersed from the abortive enterprise at Babel, Yahweh chose one man, Abraham, and summoned him to leave his country for a new homeland that would be shown to him. To Abraham was given the promise:

> I will make of you a great nation,
>   and I will bless you, and make your name great,
>   so that you will be a blessing.
> I will bless those who bless you,
>   and him who curses you I will curse;
>   and by you all the families of the earth will
>   bless themselves.
>
> —GENESIS 12:2-3

To possess a land, to become a great nation, to be a blessing to the peoples of the earth—this three-fold divine promise runs like a golden thread through the woven tapestry of the J epic, from Abraham to the Conquest. In the Yahwist's view, the story of Abraham's call initiated a new kind of history—*the history of Yahweh's action through Israel* to bring blessing upon all mankind. So from the story of Paradise his vision constantly narrows down until it concentrates upon the solitary figure of Abraham, the father of the people whom Yahweh chose for a special task in his historical plan.[22] Coming almost immediately after the story of the Tower of Babel, which presents a dark picture of divine judgment upon mankind, the story of Abraham's call is like a burst of light that illumines the whole landscape. In contrast to the ambitious builders at Babel who aspired to make a name for themselves, it was promised that Yahweh would make Abraham's name great (12:2; cf. 11:4). Israel's greatness would lie, not in herself, but in the God who was active in her history to overcome the confusion, disharmony, and sin sketched in lurid colors in the primeval history.

In working out the theme of the promise, the Yahwist—and this fact warrants repetition—wove together stories that once had a completely different meaning. What Abraham, Isaac, and Jacob were like in their oldest dress is difficult to say, in view of the complete reworking of the traditions over a period of many years. The evidence suggests that Abraham was connected with the sanctuary near Hebron; Isaac, with the shrine at Beer-sheba; and Jacob, with the "house of God" (*beth 'El*) at Bethel. Each of these places was an old Canaanite shrine that had been taken over by the Hebrews, and some of the stories about these three figures were probably Canaanite in origin. In any case, we are not dealing with biographies, but with stories in which Israel personified her history. The personification is clear in the case of Jacob and Esau, who represent Israel and Edom, respectively (25:22-26). But it is also true with respect to Abraham. He too is more than an individual; he is a representative of the people whom Yahweh has called and covenanted.

By the time of the Yahwist, these miscellaneous traditions had already been fairly well adapted into the story of a single family bound together by the relation of father and son: Abraham, Isaac, Jacob, Joseph. The Yahwist, however, was primarily responsible for giving to the patriarchal period a unity that did not actually exist until the time of the Tribal Confederacy or the United Monarchy. This is what we would have if some modern historian were to project the concept of a United States, personified in "Uncle Sam," back to the heterogeneous peoples who settled in this country before 1776.[23] No longer are the

---

[22] In the P scheme, the writer displays through genealogies the same movement from the universal to the particular: Creation—Adam—Noah—Shem (father of the Semites)—Terah and Abraham. See pp. 391-392.

[23] The retrospective view of these stories is clearly indicated in Genesis 15:13-16, where we find references to the duration of the oppression in Egypt and to the Exodus.

patriarchal stories mere cult legends or tales of tribal heroes: they now pertain
to the whole of Israel. For from Abraham's seed, in direct succession through
Isaac and Jacob, sprang the twelve tribes of Israel. Moreover, the religion of
the patriarchs is no longer the worship of Canaanite gods in Canaanite shrines
—El Olam at Beersheba (21:33), Baal Berith or El Berith at Shechem (see
Judg. 8:33; 9:4, 46), or El Bethel at Bethel (Gen. 35:7, an E passage). It is
now the worship of Yahweh, the God of Abraham, Isaac, and Jacob. And it is
Yahweh who appears to each of the patriarchs and renews the promise given
to Abraham. (Refer back to the discussion on pp. 28-30.)

The Trials of Faith

For the Yahwist, then, the patriarchs were wanderers toward a goal
that Yahweh had set before them. Their history was a nomadic movement from
promise toward fulfillment, not an aimless quest for pastureland for their flocks.
Yet it was not easy for them to live by the promise, for again and again they
found themselves in situations that made the promise seem incredible. At such
times their trust in Yahweh was put to a severe test, and they were moved to
the verge of despair. In episode after episode the Yahwist builds up a sense of
dramatic suspense, only to resolve it by showing how Yahweh intervened at
the critical moment, just when everything seemed lost, and renewed the promise.
Let us see how this theme is worked out in the narratives.[24]

ABRAHAM. We read that Abraham, after migrating from Mesopotamia,
came to Shechem, the very heart of Canaanite country. There, at a sacred oak,
Yahweh appeared to him and reaffirmed his promise to give the land to his
descendants (12:6-7). But after a while Abraham was driven by famine to
Egypt, where, to save his life, he ingratiated himself with the pharaoh by an
act of deceit involving his wife Sarah. True, his hunger was severe, and it seemed
expedient to take things into his own hands rather than to trust Yahweh's providence. But Abraham's act was tantamount to surrendering the promise, even
though it brought him great material advantage, for with Sarah (the ancestress
of Israel) in the pharaoh's harem the Israel of the future could not come into
being. Then, just in the nick of time, Yahweh saved the day, and Abraham,
despite his rash deed, was sent away from Egypt a rich man (12:10-13:2). He
returned to Bethel and "called upon the name of Yahweh," as he had done
there before his Egyptian adventure.

The next moment of suspense came when strife between the herdsmen of
Abraham and those of Lot made it necessary for the two relatives to part and
go their respective ways. Lot, the ancestor of Moab and Ammon (see 19:30-38),

---

[24] An excellent treatment of the Yahwist's use of dramatic suspense is found in R. H.
Pfeiffer, *Introduction* [28], pp. 142-147.

was given the freedom to choose where to go, and the future of Israel hung in the balance of his decision. Providentially, Lot chose, not the Land of Promise, but the area of the Jordan Valley, whose wicked cities—Sodom and Gomorrah —Yahweh later destroyed by volcanic fire and brimstone (13:3-13). Once again, Yahweh renewed his promise to Abraham (13:14-18).

But there was still a major obstacle barring the door to the future: Abraham had no son. It was incredible that the promise could be fulfilled when Abraham's sole heir was Eliezer, his household slave. Again Yahweh renewed his promise that Abraham would have a great progeny and that he (through his family) would inherit the land. This time the promise was sealed with a covenant (Gen. 15). The covenant ceremony is very archaic—an indication of the antiquity of the legend material used by the narrator (see pp. 28-29). In its present context, however, Yahweh's covenant with Abraham is an anticipation of the covenant of Sinai.

ISAAC. Yet it was still incredible that the promise could be fulfilled, for Sarah was barren. Faith needed more evidence. So this time Sarah took things in her hands, urging Abraham to have a child by her Egyptian maid, Hagar, only to regret her nagging and later to force the maid out of the house. Suspense is heightened when Hagar, at a well in the wilderness, received from Yahweh the promise that she would bear a son to Abraham and that Ishmael (regarded by Muslims as the ancestor of the Arabs) would grow to be a formidable bedouin—"a wild ass of a man." But Ishmael, who was conceived in a moment of failure of faith in Yahweh, could not be the child of the promise, even though Yahweh was deeply concerned for Hagar and her non-Israelite child (Gen. 16). Later, Yahweh appeared to Abraham at the sanctuary near Hebron (by the sacred oak of Mamre; cf. 13:18) and announced that a son would be born to his wife. Sarah, who was eavesdropping on the conversation, laughed heartily to herself, knowing that she had reached the age when this was physically impossible. She failed to believe that with Yahweh all things are possible (18:1-16). The incident of Sarah's laughter is one example of the many puns in the J narrative, for in Hebrew "she laughs" is *titzhaq*, and "Isaac" is *yitzhaq*.

The birth of Isaac, the son of Abraham's and Sarah's old age, is reported in 21:1-2, after the stories about Sodom and Gomorrah (18:17-19:38). In the preface to the latter story, we find again the theme that "Abraham shall become a great and mighty nation, and all the nations of the earth shall bless themselves by him" (18:18). Because of Abraham's role in the divine plan, Yahweh confided in him what he was about to do, and even listened to his intercession

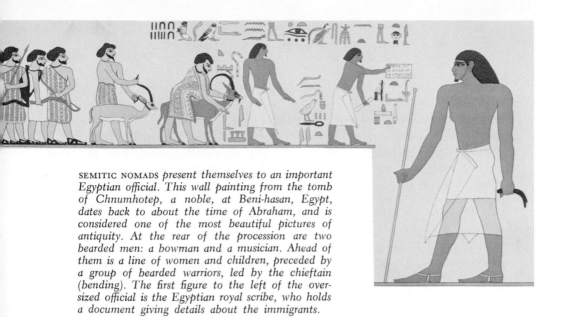

SEMITIC NOMADS *present themselves to an important Egyptian official. This wall painting from the tomb of Chnumhotep, a noble, at Beni-hasan, Egypt, dates back to about the time of Abraham, and is considered one of the most beautiful pictures of antiquity. At the rear of the procession are two bearded men: a bowman and a musician. Ahead of them is a line of women and children, preceded by a group of bearded warriors, led by the chieftain (bending). The first figure to the left of the over-sized official is the Egyptian royal scribe, who holds a document giving details about the immigrants.*

on behalf of Sodom. The divine judgment upon Sodom, where Yahweh could not find even ten righteous men, throws into sharp relief Israel's calling to be the agent of universal blessing.

In the story of the selection of a wife for Isaac (Gen. 24), the author again has created dramatic suspense. Isaac could not marry a local Canaanite girl, for that would contaminate the line of Abraham and bring the promise to naught. So Abraham's servant was sent to the ancestral homeland in Mesopotamia (Haran) with express instructions to have the prospective wife brought back to the Land of the Promise. Would Abraham's servant find the right maiden? Would Rebekah decide to come to Isaac's country? The story leaves no doubt that Yahweh was guiding the servant's journey, despite the uncertainty in the servant's mind. Nothing happened by chance: Yahweh meant it to turn out just as it did.

JACOB. Then the drama is acted out all over again, this time with the spotlight on Jacob. (Not much is said about Isaac, who seems to be little more than a replica of his father; see Genesis 26.) Rebekah, like Sarah, was barren, and would not have presented Isaac with a son had it not been for Yahweh's intervention. But a new complication arose that almost abolished the promise. Rebekah conceived two sons: Esau, the father of the Edomites, and Jacob, the ancestor of Israel. Already in the womb they were struggling together, as these nations did in real life. Esau won the first round, since he was born first, and therefore had a right to be his father's heir (25:21-26). But Jacob shrewdly tricked his twin brother out of his birthright (25:27-34), and later tricked him out of their father's final blessing (Gen. 27). To appreciate the point of the latter story, it should be remembered that, according to the ancient belief, words

183

spoken in blessing (or curse) were efficacious. They had the power to produce the intended result.[25] And, like an arrow in flight, they could not be retracted. So Jacob, having received his father's blessing, was destined to gain pre-eminence over Esau (Edom), as Israel later did, especially in the time of David.

But in spite of Jacob's victory, everything seemed hopelessly lost. For what good was the blessing to him if, because of Esau's hostility, he had to flee to Haran, an exile from the land on which the promise was to be fulfilled? Jacob's flight to Haran gives the Yahwist a chance to introduce a cycle of legends that had originally circulated independently—legends dealing with the entertaining adventures of Jacob in the territory of Laban, the ancestor of Syria (Aram). The Yahwist, however, has built this cycle into his literary architecture, suspending it "like a bridge supported from within by two pillars." [26] Over on one

---

[25] See the discussion of Balaam's oracles, p. 75.
[26] The figure of speech comes from von Rad's commentary on Genesis [133], p. 38, whose interpretation we are following here.

THE MOUND OF PENUEL *is located in the deep gorge of the Jabbok River and is almost surrounded by the bend of the river. Favored by natural defenses, the city atop the mound commanded access to the Jordan Valley via this river route from the hills of Transjordan. Here, according to Gen. 32:24-32, a nocturnal Stranger attacked Jacob on his way back to the Promised Land. In the time of the Israelite confederacy, Penuel was a strong city (Judges 8:8-9, 17). Later, under Jeroboam I of North Israel, it was refortified because of its religious and strategic importance (I Kings 12:25).*

side, the bridge is secured to the story of Jacob's dream at Bethel (28:10-19); on the other, it is anchored to the story of his wrestle with an Assailant at the river Jabbok (32:22-32). In the first story, Yahweh meets Jacob in the time of his despair, appearing in a dream and renewing the three-fold promise given to Abraham: that he will give to Israel the land; that he will make Israel a great and numerous people; and that through Israel all the families of the earth will bless themselves (28:13-15). So, assured that Yahweh was going with him and would bring him back to the Promised Land, Jacob journeyed to his kinsmen in Haran. There, through the providence of Yahweh, not to mention his own shady dealings, Jacob came into the possession of great wealth: two wives (Leah and Rachel), two concubines, eleven sons, numerous servants, and the best portion of Laban's flocks (Gen. 29:31). With this wealth he managed to escape from the clutches of his wily Aramean relative and prepared to win over Esau by a lavish display of gifts (32:1-21).

Then we come to the other main pillar of the Yahwist's bridge spanning the Jacob-Laban stories. Formerly, Yahweh had appeared to Jacob in a nocturnal dream in the time of his despair; now he comes in the form of a nocturnal visitor in the time of his prosperity, when it seemed that all he had to do was buy his way into the Promised Land by winning Esau's favor. With this angel (which, in the earliest form of the story, was perhaps a night demon) Jacob wrestled until daybreak. Jacob finally received the angel's blessing, but he went away limping from the wound of the combat. Soon he was reunited with Esau and thus gained access to the Promised Land (Gen. 33).

JOSEPH. From this point the Yahwist moves quickly to the Joseph cycle (Gen. 37-50). We have already noticed (see pp. 30-32) that the Joseph story reflects the historical conditions of the second millennium B.C., when it was not unheard of for a Semite to rise to power in the Egyptian court. Moreover, this story so faithfully mirrors customs, laws, and language which prevailed in Egyptian society in the times before Moses that it must have been handed down from those who knew the historical situation in the Delta very well.[27] In its present form, however, the Joseph story is embellished with various popular motifs. It has been suggested, for instance, that the incident of Potiphar's wife attempting to seduce Joseph (39:7-20) has been influenced by the Egyptian "Story of Two Brothers," in which the same motif appears.[28] Whatever the source of the motifs, they have been blended into a short story in which scene follows scene in the artistic development of a single plot. The Israelite short story emphasizes the theme of the hidden realization of God's purpose in

---

[27] This has been demonstrated by Joseph Vergote in his book, *Joseph en Egypte* [97].

[28] See Pritchard, *Ancient Near Eastern Texts*, pp. 23-25. The Egyptian seduction-story tells of a man's refusal to lie with the wife of his older brother, the wife's false accusation to her husband, and the husband's attempt to destroy his brother for the alleged deed.

human affairs. This view is magnificently expressed in Joseph's magnanimous words to his brothers in the E narrative:

> As for you, you meant evil against me; but God meant it for good, to bring it about that many people should be kept alive, as they are today.
>
> —GENESIS 50:20, cf. 45:5-7

The story affirms that affairs were not governed by the evil designs of men, or by the economic stresses that led to Jacob's migration to Egypt, but by the overruling providence of God, who makes all things serve his purpose. As a psalmist exclaimed, even the wrath of men shall praise him (Ps. 76:10).

The Yahwist has incorporated the Israelite story, one that circulated independently, into his continuous epic, and has made it serve as the conclusion to the history of the patriarchs and the prelude to the Exodus. It seems a little strange that in the J version of the Joseph story there are no explicit references to the promise made to Abraham—the thread by which the Yahwist bound the patriarchal stories together.[29] Perhaps it was felt that it was unnecessary to touch up the story with a restatement of the promise, for by being put in its present position—between the stories of Abraham, Issac, and Jacob on the one hand, and the story of the Exodus on the other—the Joseph cycle is embraced within the theme. In any case, the story now serves the Yahwist's central theological purpose. Indeed, in its present dramatic context the Joseph story seems to hint that the promise made to Abraham, the promise that through Israel the nations would bless themselves, was moving toward fulfillment. For Joseph, elevated to the position of prime minister of Egypt, saved the land from famine and brought security and prosperity to Egypt.

NEW HORIZONS OF FAITH

From the Joseph story the J epic moves on through the books of Exodus, Numbers, and perhaps Joshua—the story of Israel's life that we have surveyed in earlier chapters—toward the fulfillment of the divine promise announced at the opening of Genesis 12. At the outset of the book of Exodus the promise seemed eclipsed, for Israel was reduced to the utter despair of slaves who had no future except that of pawns in the pharaoh's hand. But once again Yahweh, "the God of Abraham, the God of Isaac, and the God of Jacob," intervened, appearing to Moses with the assurance that he was on the verge of bringing his people to a land flowing with milk and honey (Ex. 3:7-8). And so the drama moves on to the climax: the inheritance of the Promised Land and Israel's rise to

---

[29] J and E traditions are blended together in the present biblical story of Joseph. The theme of the promise is mentioned only at the very end of the E narratives: Genesis 48:3-4; 50:24.

the status of a great nation. This part of the story has already been dealt with in preceding chapters.

We have observed that the Yahwist—even when dealing with the patriarchal period, which is open to modern historical investigation—is concerned primarily with a deeper dimension of history than the events that we usually think of as historical. He portrays the "shared history" of a people. And for Israel this was a history with Yahweh—a history that was set in movement toward the future by his promise, a history of his deeds of judgment and grace in the midst of the daily affairs of his people, a history of God in action. Hence, the sagas of Genesis are mirrors turned inward to reflect the interior struggles of the community of faith: despair about the hiddenness of God's ways, the temptation to trust more in man's devices than in God's providence, and the alternation of faith and disbelief. Yet through these ups and downs of experience is the unshakable confidence, which dominates the Yahwist's epic like a symphonic theme, that Yahweh's promise does not fail. He is Lord of history. Events are linked together in his purpose; history presses toward the goal he has in view.

Most extraordinary is the new horizon which, according to this epic, surrounds the history of Israel. The conviction that Israel is Yahweh's people and Yahweh the God of Israel was not new with the Yahwist. He had inherited it from the Israelite tradition, in which it had been expressed in song and story (as, for instance, in the Song of Deborah, Judg. 5). But the Yahwist understands Israel's special relationship to Yahweh in the context of an unfolding plan that embraces all nations. Israel's task is to be the agent by which Yahweh will bring blessing upon all the families of the earth—a task that is thrown into the foreground of attention by the stories of primeval history that precede the call of Abraham. Israel, therefore, is chosen for a purpose. Yahweh's promise to Abraham includes all mankind.

We can understand the circumstances that prompted this historical vision during the Yahwist's time. In the era of David and Solomon, Israel was breaking out of her parochial ways of thinking, and was welcoming influences from the farthest parts of the world. In the very time when Israel's distinctive faith was in danger of being drowned by the new cosmopolitanism, advocated especially by Solomon, an unknown writer re-interpreted the Mosaic tradition in such a way as to make it profoundly relevant to the larger world in which Israel was to fulfill her special task in the unfolding drama of history. The breadth of the Yahwist's historical vision was not surpassed until centuries later, when a prophetic poet of the Exile, echoing the Yahwist's epic, proclaimed that in Yahweh's providential plan Israel was to be a light to the nations (Is. 40-55).

PROPHETIC

TROUBLERS

OF ISRAEL

CHAPTER   SEVEN   Today the term "prophecy" suggests a

variety of meanings. We speak of prophets of the weather,

prophets of the news, prophets who champion a social cause.

Even when there is some interest in "biblical prophecy,"

popular understanding is distorted by preachers who some-

times give the impression that the biblical prophet gazed

into God's crystal ball and predicted the shape of things to

come. All this is evidence that many of us are woefully

ignorant of the role of the Old Testament prophets and fail

Biblical readings: I Kings 12 through II Kings 8, with special attention to the Elijah stories. The account is paralleled in II Chronicles
10-21.

to understand properly and appreciate fully the remarkable spiritual legacy that we have received from them.

In this chapter we shall take up Israel's life story where we left it at the end of Chapter 5, and consider the rise of the prophetic movement against the background of the stormy events that followed the death of Solomon. But first let us raise a basic question: What is a prophet? Our English word comes to us from the Greek word (*prophētēs*), which literally means one who *speaks for* another, especially for the gods. And this Greek word, in turn, is a fairly accurate way to render the Hebrew *nabi'*, which refers to one who communicates the divine will.[1]

We can get an idea of how the prophet's role was understood in ancient Israel by glancing at a couple of passages which deal with the relationship between Moses and Aaron (Ex. 4:14-16; 7:1-2). Here the language is used figuratively. Moses was to be, as it were, "God" to Aaron, and Aaron was to be Moses' *nabi'*. That is, Moses was to tell Aaron what to say, and Aaron was to speak on behalf of Moses to the pharaoh. On the basis of this analogy, it is clear that the prophet was regarded as a person through whom God speaks to the people. Called to be God's spokesman, he received the promise that God's "words" would be put in his mouth (see Jer. 1:9).

Studies of the forms of prophetic speech have shown that the prophets often employed a "messenger style," which was well-known in the ancient world.[2] For instance, when Jacob was returning to his homeland he bridged the distance between himself and his brother Esau by dispatching messengers.

> And Jacob sent messengers before him . . . instructing them,
> "Thus you shall say to my lord Esau:
> Thus says your servant Jacob, 'I have sojourned. . . .' "
> —GENESIS 32:3-4

It is striking that almost the same language is used in prophetic oracles. The prophets understood themselves to be *sent*. They had received Yahweh's commission, "Go and say to my people." Moreover, a prophetic message often begins with the formula "Thus says Yahweh" and concludes with "the oracle of Yahweh" or "says Yahweh" (e.g., Amos 1:3-5; Jer. 2:1-3; Is. 45:11-13). All of this indicates that the prophets thought of themselves as *messengers* sent to communicate "the word of Yahweh" to the people.[3] Their authority lay not

---

[1] Apparently the Hebrew word *nabi'* is related to the Akkadian *nabu*, which means "to call, announce." There is some uncertainty, however, as to whether the Hebrew has an active meaning ("caller, announcer") or a passive meaning ("one who is called"). In either case, the word points to the prophet's role as the messenger of God.

[2] This is discussed by Claus Westermann in his analysis of the basic forms of prophetic speech [147], pp. 70-91. See also James F. Ross, "The Prophet as Yahweh's Messenger," in *Israel's Prophetic Heritage* [136], pp. 98-107.

[3] Martin Noth has found a striking parallel to the messenger-speech in a Mari text. In a dream, the god Dagan says to a man: "Now go! I send you to Zimri-lim [the king of Mari]; [to him] you yourself shall say: 'Send me thy messenger. . . .' " Cited by Ross, *op. cit.*, p. 100.

in themselves—in their religious experience or in their opinions—but in the One who had sent them. Accordingly their message rang with an authority which could shake nations: "Thus says the Lord."

The purpose of God's speaking through his prophet was not to communicate information about a timetable of events for the distant future. To be sure, the prophets often made predictions, in the conviction that Yahweh was shaping the course of events according to his purpose. But these predictions, some of which came true and some of which did not, had reference to the immediate future, which impinged on the present. Just as a doctor's prediction that a patient has only a short time to live makes the patient's present moments more precious and serious, so the prophet's announcement of what God was about to do accented the urgency of the present. The prophet was primarily concerned with the present. His task was to communicate God's message for *now*, and to summon the people to respond *today*.

In the course of Israel's history there arose great prophets whose perception of God's "word" was deeper and more refined than that of many prophets whose names and oracles have not survived. Let us consider first, however, the humble origins of prophecy. In a broad sense, prophecy arose in connection with God's revelation in the Exodus; for, as we have seen (pp. 34-42), God not only delivered his people from servitude but raised up a leader to proclaim the meaning of that historical experience. Moses, then, can be properly called a prophet (see Deut. 18:18; Hos. 12:13). This holds true also for the Yahwist, whose epic gives grand expression to the prophetic interpretation of Israel's history. But in the time of Samuel, the word *nabi'* was applied to a special class of men in Israelite society. The prophets of that day were the immediate forerunners of the great prophets, of whom Elijah came to be regarded as the representative *par excellence*.

THE BACKGROUND OF PROPHECY

We first hear of this company of prophets in connection with the Philistines' attempt to overrun the territory of Israel (I Sam. 10:5-13). It was a time of great crisis, when the very existence of Israel hung in the balance. Shiloh, the confederate sanctuary, had been destroyed and the people were in despair. Samuel, the last judge of the Tribal Confederacy, attempted to rally the people to a militant devotion to Yahweh, as Deborah had done at the Battle of Megiddo. He was supported by a band of prophets who evidently had been carrying on their prophetic activities for some time, for their presence in Israel seems to be taken for granted. After Samuel anointed Saul as leader over Israel, he enumerated the various "signs" that would show Yahweh's confirmation of his choice. One of them was that Saul would come to the "hill of God" (that is, a religious "high place") near to a Philistine outpost.

And there, as you come to the city, you will meet a band of prophets coming down from the high place with harp, tambourine, flute, and lyre before them, prophesying. Then the spirit of Yahweh will come mightily upon you [literally, "fall upon you"], and you shall prophesy with them and be turned into another man.

—I SAMUEL 10:5-6

Ecstatic Prophecy

The Hebrew word that is here translated as "prophesy" has a stronger meaning than we give to that word. It means "to prophesy ecstatically." Usually we use the word "ecstasy" to describe an experience of being overcome with an emotion so powerful that self-control or reason may be suspended.[4] In this case, however, the ecstasy arises not from mere emotional rapture but from the spirit (*rúah*) of Yahweh which falls upon a person, takes control of the center of the self, and makes him an instrument of the divine will. No wonder Samuel promised that Saul would be turned into "another man": no longer would he be just Saul the son of Kish, but Saul *possessed* by Yahweh's spirit! In such a prophetic state unusual things happened, as we learn in another story which tells how Saul, again seized by prophetic ecstasy, stripped off his clothes and lay naked in a stunned condition all day and all night (I Sam. 19:19-24). These stories remind us of those Christians who on the Day of Pentecost were "drunk with the spirit" (Acts 2:1-13) or, better yet, of the charismatic warriors of the Israelite Tribal Confederacy.

Since the stories from I Samuel presuppose that the ecstatic prophecy was already in full swing in Israel during the days of the early monarchy, we must look further back to find the origins of this movement. In Numbers 11:24-29 there is a curious story about the spirit of Moses which was transferred to the elders of Israel, and caused them to prophesy ecstatically (the same verb as above is used). It it doubtful, however, whether this is an authentic episode from the Mosaic period.[5] Most likely, Israel first became acquainted with ecstatic prophecy in Canaan, where it was connected with Baal religion. The Egyptian story of Wen Amon (from the eleventh century B.C.) tells of a religious festival in the Phoenician port of Byblos where "the god seized one of [the] youths and made him possessed"—that is, he fell into an ecstatic state.[6] Centuries later, prophets of Baal, imported from Phoenicia, worked themselves into an ecstatic frenzy on the top of Mount Carmel as they danced around the altar, cut themselves with knives, and raised their cultic shouts (I Kings 18:20-29). This type of orgiastic prophecy was also known in Asia Minor, from which it spread into

---

[4] The word comes from a Greek compound "to set or stand out," thus, "to put out of place, derange, to be beside oneself."

[5] In the judgment of many scholars this is another anachronism—that is, description of the Mosaic period in terms of the language and experience of a later time.

[6] See Pritchard, *Ancient Near Eastern Texts*, pp. 25-29.

the Mediterranean world and later took the form of the orgies of the cult of Dionysus.

Probably, then, Israel borrowed ecstatic prophecy from the Canaanite environment, as she did so much else. But in this case, too, what was borrowed was transformed. To be sure, there are certain external similarities between the Baal prophets, like those on Mount Carmel (I Kings 18), and the Israelite prophets of the early monarchy. Israel's prophets also went around in companies, delivering oracles when some inquirer sought a decision from God. Stimulated by the rhythm of music and bodily movements, the contagion of the prophetic ecstasy could carry away a man who fell in among them.[7] Under the influence of the divine spirit, the body was sometimes stimulated to hyperactivity, as in the case of Elijah, who ran before the king's chariot with superhuman energy (I Kings 18:46). But these are superficial similarities. The real difference between Israel's prophets and the prophets of Canaanite society was that the former were spokesmen of Yahweh who interpreted the promises and demands of the covenant.

Many of these early prophets belonged to guilds or schools, which were known as "the sons of the prophets." They lived together in communities, where they were under the leadership of a chief prophet who was apparently known as their "father." We catch brief glimpses of Elijah and Elisha, for instance, as leaders of prophetic communities at Bethel, Jericho, and Gilgal (II Kings 2:3, 4; 4:38). These guilds were not tied permanently to any one place but were free to travel around and deliver oracles as the occasion demanded.

Cultic Prophets

In addition to these roving bands of ecstatics there were other prophets who were more closely tied to the great sanctuaries of Israel. Recent studies have emphasized that sanctuaries like those at Bethel or Jerusalem had on their staff priests and prophets who served side by side in a joint ministry.[8] The "cultic prophets," as they have been called, had a special part in the services of worship. Regarded as experts in prayer, particularly intercessory prayer, they were called upon to bring the people's petitions before Yahweh. Moreover, as Yahweh's spokesmen, they communicated the divine answer to a particular petition, or indicated whether or not an offering was acceptable to the deity. On the occasion of the great religious festivals, such as the covenant-renewal

---

[7] According to an interesting passage in II Kings 3:15, Elisha, when asked for a word from Yahweh, first summoned a musician, "and when the minstrel played, the spirit of Yahweh came upon him."

[8] See especially A. R. Johnson, *The Cultic Prophet in Ancient Israel* [141]; also R. E. Clements, *Prophecy and Covenant* [137], pp. 11-34. A good discussion of various types of "primitive prophets in ancient Israel" is given in J. Lindblom, *Prophecy in Ancient Israel* [142], chap. 2.

festival, they may have had an important part in announcing the demands and promises of the covenant.

Increasingly we are coming to realize that these anonymous prophets had a great influence upon Israelite tradition. Even the forms of oracular speech which the great prophets used effectively may have been received, in some instances, from these prophetic ancestors. Oracles of cultic prophets, composed originally for use in situations of worship, may lie embedded in the body of prophetic literature which has been transmitted under the names of the classical prophets. And some of the psalms now found in the book of Psalms seem to reflect their role in Israel's worship. In difficult times, when Israel was exposed to dangers from without and within, many of these unknown prophets must have been sincere and passionate interpreters of the covenant between Yahweh and Israel.

Prophets and Politics

As we have seen in the passage discussed above (I Sam. 10:5-13), prophecy was intimately associated with politics from the very first moment it appeared in Israel. The prophetic band was stationed right next to a Philistine garrison. Their purpose was to incite Israelites to engage in holy war against the Philistine foe, and to do this they must have sung, with the fervor of their ecstasy, war songs which aroused the people to action. (The writer has witnessed this kind of dervish activity in modern Arab circles, where the purpose of singing and group dancing was to awaken patriotic feeling.) Like the charismatic judges of an earlier day, they were intoxicated with "enthusiasm"—a word that means literally to be inspired of God (Greek *entheos*). Elijah and Elisha were such vigorous champions of Israel's faith that they were called "the chariots of Israel and its horsemen" (II Kings 2:12; 13:14).

The early prophets, however, were more than zealous champions of holy war. Primarily they were called to deliver Yahweh's word for a specific situation. In that time there were three accepted channels for ascertaining the divine will (I Sam. 28:6,15): dreams (particularly those experienced in a holy place), the sacred dice (Urim and Thummin) which were handled by the priests, and prophecy. Saul, it will be recalled, had tried all three of these channels in the hour of desperation and had received no answer. Of the two types of religious leaders—prophet and priest—the prophet was more suited to be the spokesman for Yahweh in a time of political crisis. A priest could officiate at sacred rites, teach the people the traditions of the past, and manipulate the sacred lot in answer to yes-or-no questions. But the prophet, speaking under the influence of Yahweh's spirit, was able to interpret the meaning of events and to proclaim the will of God in concrete terms. This, of course, was not possible so long as the prophetic group was acting or singing in unison. So more and more we see individuals standing out from the prophetic band, even breaking from it, in order to proclaim the word of God for a particular crisis. Already in the time of David, as we have seen, the single prophet Nathan achieved a position of great influence in the royal court. His oracle concerning Yahweh's covenant with David had a lasting effect upon Israel's life and thought (see above, pp. 148-150). At the same time, he did not hesitate to summon the king before the highest tribunal to hear the word of divine judgment against the misuse of power.

In the time of Saul, devotion to Yahweh, fired by the energy of prophetic ecstasy, was Israel's bond of unity and strength. But although prophecy performed a real service in that national crisis, it also had its dangers. Losing its original fire and spontaneity, it could easily degenerate into a professional trade. Moreover, the kings of Israel and Judah, who felt increasingly that politics was their exclusive field, wanted to bring "the sons of the prophets" under their control, just as they attached the priesthood to the state shrine. When this happened, prophecy became the servant of nationalism—a shrill crying out of what men wanted to hear rather than the proclamation of the word of God. The great prophets were often at odds with these professional prophets, and Amos in particular did not want to be identified with them (Amos 7:14). But despite the attempt of kings to silence the prophetic voice, it was heard more and more plainly in the period after the death of Solomon.

A HISTORIAN'S VERSION OF THE TIMES

In view of what has been said about the prophets' activity in the sphere of politics, it is necessary to consider the events that took place after Solomon's death. Specifically, we are interested in the period that extends from the split of the United Kingdom to the revolution of Jehu—that is, from about 922 to 842 B.C. From this period we have no literature that purports to have been written by prophets. Instead, the tradition about the prophets is interwoven with the historical narrative of the book of Kings, which carries the story of Israel from the end of David's reign to the time just after the tragic fall of the nation in 587 B.C.

This book, it will be recalled, forms the conclusion of the Deuteronomic History which begins with Deuteronomy.[9] As in the case of other periods covered by this work, the history of the monarchy is interpreted in terms of the fundamental theological conviction of the covenant faith: Yahweh acts to bring blessing to those who are obedient to him (as prescribed in the Deuteronomic law) and judgment upon those who flout his revealed will. This means, on the positive side, that men must love Yahweh with heart, soul, and strength (Deut. 6:4), and, on the negative side, that anything smacking of idolatry has no place in the covenant community. To keep Israel's life pure from the con-

---

[9] See the discussion of the Deuteronomic History above, pp. 76-77. Notice that the Deuteronomic law is specifically mentioned in II Kings 14:6; compare Deuteronomy 24:16.

tamination of surrounding culture, the Deuteronomic historian advocated the centralization of worship in Jerusalem and the closing up of all outlying sanctuaries ("high places") where popular syncretism and idolatry flourished. In particular, he frowned on the independent shrines set up in the Northern Kingdom by Jeroboam I as blasphemy, and regarded all kings who tolerated these sanctuaries as the blackest sinners, regardless of how much they had to their credit on other points. The historian's perspective is set forth clearly in the summary found in II Kings 17:7-41, where he reviews events from the establishment of the monarchy and on.

Each northern and southern king is strictly judged by this Deuteronomic standard of covenant obedience. As in the case of the stories of the judges, the historian follows a stereotyped procedure which, in its skeletal outline, varies only slightly in the case of each king of Israel or Judah: [10]

JUDAH	ISRAEL
1. In the——year of so-and-so, king of Israel, so-and-so, king of Judah, began to reign.	1. In the——year of so-and-so, king of Judah, so-and-so, king of Israel, began to reign.
2. Facts about his age, duration of reign, name, and queen mother.	2. Facts about the length of his reign and the place of his capital.
3. Evaluation of his standing in comparison to "David his father."	3. Censure for the fact that "he did what was evil in the sight of Yahweh, and walked in the way of Jeroboam and his sin which he made Israel to sin."
4. "Now the rest of the acts of so-and-so . . . are they not written in the Book of Chronicles of the Kings of Judah"?	4. "Now the rest of the acts of so-and-so . . . are they not written in the Book of Chronicles of the Kings of Israel"?
5. Concluding statement that he slept with his fathers, and so-and-so reigned in his stead.	5. Concluding statement that he slept with his fathers, and so-and-so reigned in his stead.

The historian plainly tells his readers that if they are interested in learning more about these kings, they may go to the royal library and consult the archives. His purpose is to present to his own day the great lessons of the past in order that the people may understand why the nation was brought to ruin. He intends to show that these things did not happen by chance: rather, God was at work in the tragic career of Israel from the breakup of the Davidic kingdom to the final destruction of Jerusalem, punishing his people for their repeated faithless behavior in spite of prophetic warnings (II Kings 17:13). So he goes

---

[10] The word "Israel," which is basically a religious term referring to the tribes united by the covenant, now acquires a political meaning: the Northern Kingdom. Judah is the name for the Southern Kingdom, ruled by Davidic kings. Even after the division of Solomon's kingdom, however, Israel was often used to refer to the ideal unity of all the tribes within the covenant.

through the list of the kings, taking up a king of Israel and dating his reign in terms of the king of Judah who was reigning at the time; then he turns the spotlight on Judah and dates the Judean king's reign by cross-reference to the date of the reigning king of Israel. This seems a somewhat confusing procedure, but it was a necessary one, since there was no standard calendar in those days. Not one king of Israel escapes the historian's blacklist, and his judgment falls pretty severely on the kings of Judah too. Only two southern kings (Hezekiah and Josiah) come off with a clean record; six receive a grade of only "passing," because they failed to remove the high places; and ten "flunk," because they "did what was evil in the sight of Yahweh."

Fortunately, the Deuteronomist often clothes this historical skeleton with flesh and blood by choosing stories and traditions derived from other sources. In presenting Solomon, as we have seen, he evidently drew on the royal archives known as the Book of the Acts of Solomon, and he probably had access to temple archives as well. In his history of the divided kingdom he refers frequently to two other sources: the Book of the Chronicles of the Kings of Israel, and the Book of the Chronicles of the Kings of Judah. No trace of these royal annals has ever been found. They perished long ago, and survive only in the fragmentary quotations of the Deuteronomic History. In addition, this history incorporates certain legends that were drawn from popular tradition. The stories of Elijah and Elisha fall in the latter category, for they show no trace of Deuteronomic bias.

With this critical background, let us survey what happened after the long reign of Solomon came to an end.

THE DIVIDED KINGDOM

The story opens in I Kings 12. We are told that Rehoboam, the son of Solomon, made a trip into northern territory to be installed as "king of Israel," although he was already recognized as king in Jerusalem. Here the word "Israel" refers to the ten northern tribes—not to the larger unity that David had forged out of the remnants of Saul's kingdom and his own tribe of Judah. Clearly, the deep rift within the covenant community, evident earlier during the period of the Tribal Confederacy, had been healed only superficially by the policies of David. It is significant that the gathering took place at Shechem, which was hallowed by unforgettable memories. It was at Shechem, near a sacred tree, that Abraham had built an altar to Yahweh (Gen. 12:6). Moreover, in the Elohist narrative, which was treasured in northern circles, Jacob's first holding in Canaan was at Shechem (Gen. 33:18-20). And above all, Shechem was the place where the Tribal Confederacy had been established (Josh. 24). At this ancient tribal gathering place, the northern tribes—acting with a show of independence—gathered to make Rehoboam their king.

The tribes of Israel, smarting under the whiplash that Solomon had laid upon them in his labor gangs, demanded that the yoke be lightened.[11] Solomon's tyrannical policy had fallen most heavily upon the prosperous northern tribes. But Rehoboam, shunning the advice of his older counselors and swayed by "progressive" young men, answered the Israelite ultimatum by saying that his father had lashed them with whips, but that he would chastise them with scorpions.

This was the match that touched off the explosion. Again the call to revolution was sounded, as it had been in David's time under Absalom and Sheba. In the ancient cry there was a nostalgia for the old days of tribal independence:

> What portion have we in David?
>   We have no inheritance in the son of Jesse.
> To your tents, O Israel!   ·
>   Look now to your own house, David.
>   —I KINGS 12:16

When Rehoboam indiscreetly sent Adoniram, the taskmaster in charge of forced labor, to bring the situation under control, Adoniram was stoned to death. The king jumped into his chariot and hastily fled to Jerusalem. Only the oracle of a prophet, Shemaiah (I Kings 12:22-24), prevented him from declaring an immediate civil war.

Jeroboam the First

At some point in the revolutionary movement, Jeroboam I, the son of Nebat, joined the plot to overthrow the kingdom—to "lift up his hand against the king" (I Kings 11:26). Jeroboam was an Ephraimite—a northerner—who had once been Solomon's taskmaster over forced labor in the northern provinces (I Kings 11:26-28). It is important to notice that the prophet Ahijah, from the former confederate center of Shiloh, was a chief conspirator in this plot. His prophecy that Yahweh was about to tear the ten northern tribes from Solomon and give them to Jeroboam (I Kings 11:29-39) poured fuel upon the fires of rebellion. When Solomon crushed the first stage of the revolt, Jeroboam fled to Egypt, where he was given political asylum by Shishak, the pharaoh (I Kings 11:29-40). At the opportune moment after Solomon's death, Jeroboam returned and was proclaimed king over the northern tribes in about 922. Thereafter, these tribes were known as "Israel," as distinguished from

---

[11] In *The People of the Covenant* [109], p. 177, Murray Newman points out that the "yoke" which the northerners wanted lightened was theological, too. Unable to accept the royal covenant theology (II Sam. 7) which promised divine authorization for the Davidic throne and dynasty, they insisted upon limitation of the king's sovereignty in the north, in accordance with their Mosaic covenant theology.

"Judah," the tribe (along with Benjamin) that acknowledged allegiance to the Davidic dynasty.[12]

The political situation at the time favored the northern tribes in their secession. It is somewhat surprising that the empire of Solomon, fortified with the best military equipment of the day and policed by the king's officers, should collapse almost overnight. Rehoboam surely had the military power to strike against the revolutionaries before they had a chance to organize themselves and fortify their positions. He probably would have won had he acted quickly. The fact that he did not was undoubtedly due to a threatened attack from Egypt which caused him to forget about Israel momentarily and to divert his energies to the protection of his borders to the south and west. The fortifications described in II Chron. 11:5-12 were built, according to the Chronicler's inference, in the expectation of an Egyptian invasion (II Chron. 12:2-4).

Egypt was showing signs of awakening from the political lethargy that had paralyzed her for three centuries, ever since the death of Merneptah in 1216 B.C. A new pharaoh had seized the throne—Shishak (c. 935-914), the founder of the Twenty-second Dynasty. Dreaming of regaining Egypt's former position of prestige and power in the Fertile Crescent, he reversed the policy of diplomatic subservience that had been in force during the reign of David and most of the

---

[12] Sometimes the Northern Kingdom is referred to as Ephraim, after Jeroboam's tribe.

CHRONOLOGICAL CHART 3

B.C.	EGYPT	PALESTINE		MESOPOTAMIA
1000	Decline	**THE UNITED KINGDOM**		Assyrian Decline
		David, c. 1000-961		
		Solomon, c. 961-922		
	XXII Dynasty Shishak I (c. 935-914)			
		Division of the kingdom at death of Solomon, c. 922		
		THE DIVIDED KINGDOM		
		JUDAH	ISRAEL	
	Shishak invades Judah c. 918	DAVIDIC DYNASTY:		
		Rehoboam, c. 922-915	Jeroboam I, c. 922-901	
		Abijah (Abijam), c. 915-913		
900		Asa, c. 913-873	Nadab, c. 901-900	

(Iron Age)

THE TEMPLE OF KARNAK *had 134 of these massive pillars throughout its Hypostyle Hall. On the north wall of this temple, built by Rameses II in the thirteenth century* B.C., *appears the Karnak List, which refers to Shishak's invasion of Palestine.*

reign of Solomon, and began to meddle aggressively in Palestinian affairs. During Solomon's lifetime he had given refuge to political criminals, Jeroboam of North Israel and Hadad of Edom. The death of Solomon gave Shishak the opportunity to plot the disruption of Solomon's empire on the age-old political principle of "divide and conquer." So he gladly released Jeroboam to lead the seditionist movement, and began to prepare for the invasion of Palestine. Actually, Shishak was no more fond of Jeroboam than he was of Rehoboam, for when the Egyptian invasion came, just five years after the disruption of the United Kingdom (about 918 B.C.), it swept like an avalanche over Edom, Philistia, Judah, and Israel alike. In addition to the brief report in I Kings 14:25-28, we have the famous Karnak List of Asiatic countries that were conquered by Egyptian kings. This list was inscribed on the walls of the magnificent temple of Karnak, whose remains still stand outside Luxor.[13]

---

[13] See Pritchard, *Ancient Near Eastern Texts*, pp. 242-243, 263-264.

Jeroboam's Reform

While Rehoboam was busy with preparations for the threatened Egyptian invasion, Jeroboam took measures to strengthen his own kingdom. The Deuteronomic historian, who regards Jeroboam as a *bête noire*, gives only a minimum of information about his reign. Most of the account is devoted to damning him for his blasphemous act in setting up rival shrines in the Northern Kingdom (all of I Kings 13 and 14 are tirades against Jeroboam). But by a critical appraisal of what is left (12:25-33)—which is precious little—we come to a more sympathetic understanding of Jeroboam's accomplishments.

To begin with, he strengthened his temporary capital Shechem and fortified Penuel on the other side of the Jordan (see photos, pp. 90 and 184). Since both of these sites figured prominently in ancient sacred traditions of Israel, and were especially identified with the northern patriarch Jacob (Gen. 32:22-32; 33:18-20; chap. 34), it is likely that Jeroboam was also trying to capitalize on the religious significance of these places. It is hardly accidental that he turned to Shechem, the first center of the old Israelite confederacy. He realized that something more than military measures were necessary to consolidate his people. The pull toward Jerusalem, the seat of Solomon's temple, could easily counteract the political independence of the North. So, just as David had attempted to unify his kingdom by bringing the Ark of the Covenant to Jerusalem, Jeroboam determined to provide a religious foundation for his kingdom. He established two shrines, one at Dan in the north of his kingdom, and the other at Bethel on the southern boundary, both of which had been places of pilgrimage for a long time. Also, he established a priesthood which claimed direct lineage from the Mosaic period. Finally, he instituted an annual Fall festival (the Feast of Ingathering—that is, a Thanksgiving) comparable to a festival that was celebrated in Judah at a slightly different time.

The Deuteronomic historian was horrified at Jeroboam's innovations, especially the setting up of golden bulls in high places other than Jerusalem. Repeatedly in the book of Kings, Jeroboam is denounced as "the man who made Israel to sin." The language that he attributes to Jeroboam echoes the story of the worship of the Golden Calf in the wilderness period: "You have gone up to Jerusalem long enough. Behold your gods, O Israel, who brought you up out of the land of Egypt" (I Kings 12:28; see Ex 32:4, 8)—surely a slanted version of Jeroboam's religious reform. Probably the Judean historian, guilty of anti-northern propaganda, has changed the tradition from "Behold your *God*," for it is extremely doubtful that Jeroboam intended to introduce polytheism. Moreover, the setting up of the golden bulls probably did not have the sinister purpose that the historian saw in it. Jeroboam may have been returning to an old North Israelite tradition in which Yahweh was represented standing invisibly on the back of a young bull. Modern defenders of this king argue that the practice was "no more idolatrous than the equally symbolic representation

THE STORM GOD HADAD *stands on the back of a bull, holding in each hand a pronged fork representing lightning. This bas-relief, found at Arslan-Tash in northern Syria, comes from the eighth century* B.C. *Jeroboam I may have intended the golden bull to be not an idol but a pedestal on which Yahweh stood invisibly.*

of Yahweh in the Temple of Solomon as an invisible Presence enthroned on the cherubim." [14] In any case, Jeroboam's intention—as the Deuteronomic historian tacitly admits—was to connect the religion of the Northern Kingdom with the main stream of the Mosaic tradition, the chief theme of which was the Exodus from Egypt. As we shall see in Chapter 10, the traditions of the Tribal Confederacy—which was inaugurated in Shechem, the very place Jeroboam chose as his capital—were kept more alive in the North than in the Davidic circles of the South. Moreover, it has been plausibly suggested that in Jeroboam's time the northern (Elohist) version of the sacred history was written to express the nationalism of the independent state.[15]

---

[14] W. F. Albright, *The Biblical Period* [38], p. 31. See also his comments in *From the Stone Age* [59], pp. 203, 228-230. For a different view of Jeroboam's reform, see T. J. Meek, *Hebrew Origins* [94], chap. 5.

[15] This is the view of Walter J. Harrelson ([15], pp. 65, 199-200), who suggests that in re-telling the "true" story of Yahweh's saving deeds the E tradition often retained more ancient material than J.

Jeroboam, then, had no idea of introducing the worship of new "gods"; rather, his intention was to renew Israel's devotion to the God of the covenant. However, his action in setting up the golden bulls was fraught with serious dangers in an environment where Canaanite religion was all too attractive. In the Ras Shamra literature (see pp. 104-105), the chief god of the pantheon, El, took the form of a bull, and there are numerous references in these texts to the "Bull of El." Unwittingly, perhaps, Jeroboam was giving encouragement to the fusion of Israel's faith with Baal religion. It was a northern prophet, not a Deuteronomist from the South, who first denounced the calf of Bethel, seeing in it the seductive idolatry that had perverted Israel's faith ever since the entrance into Canaan. According to the prophet Hosea, Yahweh reacts with loathing and rage to the "Calf of Samaria," the official image of the cult of North Israel (Hos: 8:5-6; 10:5-6).

The Rise of the House of Omri

Having finished the story of Jeroboam, the Deuteronomic historian retraces his steps to summarize the reigns of two southern kings, Rehoboam and Abijah (or Abijam), who were contemporaries of Jeroboam. Finding nothing good to say about them, he finishes them off quickly with his characteristic Deuteronomic judgments (I Kings 14:21-15:8). However, he does excerpt from the Book of the Chronicles of the Kings of Judah the notice about Shishak's invasion, because it proves to him Yahweh's retributive action against Rehoboam for his sins.

Next the historian turns to the reign of Asa of Judah, which overlapped the reign of Jeroboam (I Kings 15:9-24). Asa's reign gives him a long date-line of about forty years on which to peg the reigns of contemporary kings of Israel— Nadab, Baasha, Elah, Zimri, Omri, and Ahab (I Kings 15:25-16:34). Thus the whole narrative leads up to the account of the reign of king Ahab, into which the Elijah stories have been inserted. (See Chronological Chart 4, p. 209.)

During these years (about 900-850 B.C.) political tensions were becoming more acute in Palestine. For fifty years—ever since the split of Solomon's kingdom—civil war had gone on between Israel and Judah. Egypt was continuing to interfere, and new dangers from the North were beginning to be felt. Most imminent was the threat of Syria (Aram), whose traditional rivalry with Israel is celebrated in the Jacob-Laban stories of Genesis. No longer under subservience to Israel as she had been during the reign of David and part of the reign of Solomon, Syria took advantage of her strategic location at the commercial crossroads of the Fertile Crescent. Syrian kings looked with envious eyes on Israel's territory, especially the territory in Transjordan just south of the Syrian capital of Damascus. And in the farther background—ultimately to be a threat to Syria, Israel, Judah, and all the small nations of the Fertile Crescent—the Assyrian lion was pacing restlessly in its Mesopotamian lair. At

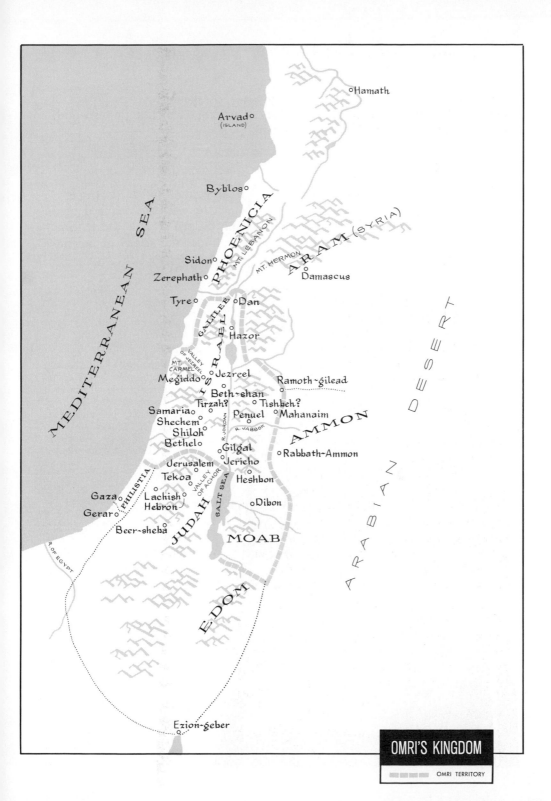

MEDITERRANEAN SEA

ARABIAN DESERT

oHamath

Arvado
(ISLAND)

Byblos o

PHOENICIA

Sidon o
Zerephath o

MT. LEBANON

MT. HERMON

ARAM (SYRIA)

oDamascus

Tyre o   o Dan

GALILEE

ISRAEL

o Hazor

VALLEY
OF JEZREEL

MT. CARMEL

Megiddo o   o Jezreel   Ramoth~gilead o

Beth~shan

Tirzah?   o Tishbeh?

Samaria o   Penuel   o Mahanaim

Shechem o

R. JORDAN

R. JABBOK

AMMON

Shiloh o

Bethel o

Gilgal o

Jerusalem o

Jericho o

Tekoa o

VALLEY
OF ACHOR

SALT SEA

Heshbon o

Rabbath~Ammon o

Gaza o

PHILISTIA

Lachish o

Hebron o

Gerar o

o Dibon

JUDAH

Beer~sheba o

MOAB

R. OF EGYPT

EDOM

Ezion~geber o

OMRI'S KINGDOM

OMRI TERRITORY

about 870 B.C., Ashur-nasir-apal (883-859 B.C.), awakening Assyria to her imperial ambitions after more than a century of lethargy, marched through northern Syria, and subjugated parts of Phoenicia.

Syrian Aggression

The trouble started during the reign of Asa of Judah (c. 913-873). Asa was interested in religious reforms, for which he won the qualified praise of the Deuteronomic historian, and he probably helped to halt the tendency toward syncretism which had been encouraged under the reigns of Solomon

THE STELE OF MESHA (king of Moab in the ninth century B.C.), on which the ruler boasts of his victory over the king of northern Israel. Discovered in 1868 at Dibon (Dibhan) in Transjordan, the stone was broken by some bedouin, and only fragments could be taken to the Louvre for restoration.

and his immediate successors. We are told that Asa shook himself free from the control of his mother, deposing her from her regency and banning the worship of Asherah, the Canaanite mother goddess that the queen mother had sponsored (I Kings 15:13). But Asa had other problems—problems that could not be solved by religious reform. Israel, with whom Judah had waged intermittent war from the time of the division of the monarchy, had become so strong that her king, Baasha, was able to blockade the northern avenues into Jerusalem. So Asa took a fateful step. He sent an appeal to Benhadad, king of Syria, to join him as an ally against Israel. The Syrian king gladly obliged by invading and devastating Galilee, and at the same time advancing his own political ambitions (about 878 B.C.).

In the resulting confusion, there was a rapid turn-over of kings in Israel, owing to assassination, suicide, and intrigue. (One king, Zimri, who had murdered his predecessor, held the throne only seven days!) As often happens in such circumstances, the commander of the army, Omri, emerged from the struggle the most powerful man. Omri came to the throne by a *coup d'état*.

The Deuteronomic historian is unusually severe with Omri, insisting that he "did more evil than all who were before him." The account of his reign is limited to six verses (I Kings 16:23-28), most of which consists of the usual Deuteronomic formulas. If we could look at the Book of the Chronicles of the Kings of Israel, to which we are referred, we would undoubtedly discover a man of tremendous political stature. He was able to do what none of his predecessors had done: to establish a dynasty of such prestige that Assyrian kings continued to refer to the Northern Kingdom as "the land of the house of Omri" for many years after his death and the downfall of his dynasty. He initiated a period of collaboration with Judah—a collaboration that was later strengthened by intermarriage between the two royal houses. Thanks to the work of archaeologists, we know a great deal more about Omri's reign than the scanty report in Kings tells us. In the Louvre Museum now stands the Moabite Stone, erected by Mesha, king of Moab (see II Kings 3:4), during the reign of the last king of the Omri dynasty. Boasting of his great accomplishments, Mesha says:

> As for Omri, king of Israel, he humbled Moab many years, for Chemosh [i.e., the god of Moab] was angry at his land. And his son [or, grandson] followed him and he also said, "I will humble Moab." In my time he spoke (thus), but I have triumphed over him and over his house, while Israel hath perished for ever! [16]

Not only was Omri successful against the Moabites in Transjordan, but he was able to keep the Syrians at bay, although at the price of ceding territory in Transjordan and granting the Syrians commercial concessions in Samaria (I

---

[16] See Pritchard, *Ancient Near Eastern Texts*, pp. 320-321.

Kings 20:34). His hand was strengthened, no doubt, by the close alliance he formed with Phoenicia, following the precedent of David and Solomon. This political union of two countries, whose common interest it was to hold Syria in check, was consummated by the marriage of Omri's son Ahab to the Phoenician king's daughter, Jezebel (I Kings 16:31). Here again he revived Solomon's policy of political marriage, although in this case—as we shall see— the marriage proved fateful for Israel.

So, in spite of the virtual silence of the book of Kings on Omri's reign, we have reason to believe that under his statesmanship Israel achieved great stability and prosperity. During his twelve-year rule, Israel's political power expanded toward the Mediterranean and into Transjordan. Something like an economic boom must have followed in the wake of his vigorous political exploits, with an inevitable widening of the gulf between the "haves" and the "have nots," which was to persist in Israel's society until the time of Amos, a century later. The monument to Omri's political astuteness was the city of Samaria, the new capital that he began to build on a hilltop, and that was completed by his son

THE HILL OF SAMARIA *on which Omri of Israel built his capital is seen in this southward-looking view. Because of the almost impregnable slopes of the hill and the strong fortifications surrounding it, the Assyrian armies had to lay siege to the city for three years before they were able to conquer it.*

A CHERUB OR SPHYNX *set in an ivory plaque found during the excavation of Samaria. Although this piece comes from the ninth century* B.C., *the composite figure of the cherub—half human and half beast—was a familiar motif of ancient art. The fragments of ivory carvings, which are Phoenician in style, witness to the splendor of king Ahab's "house of ivory" (I Kings 22:39).*

(I Kings 16:24).[17] The new site provided an excellent view of the surrounding landscape; furthermore, the steep slopes of the hill made it difficult to capture by ancient military maneuvers. Omri's purchase of the hill of Samaria was a wise decision, for his capital, astride the main north-south highway, was strategically situated to watch any advance from Judah and to gain easy access to Phoenicia, with whom Israel was bound by dynastic marriage. This luxurious city has come to light under the excavator's spade: the masonry, fortifications, the palaces of Omri and Ahab, and even the ivory inlaid in the furniture and walls (see I Kings 22:39; Amos 3:15; 6:4). Apparently Omri imported Phoenician craftsmen to execute the art and architecture, as Solomon had done, for the remains show strong evidence of Phoenician style. Henceforth, Samaria was to be the symbol of the Northern Kingdom, just as Jerusalem was the symbol of the Southern.

Under Omri's son, Ahab—who also receives strong censure from the Deuteronomic historian—Israel's material progress continued. But international troubles were beginning to mount. By this time, Egypt had sunk again into oblivion. But Syria was on the move, expanding south into Transjordanian territory traditionally claimed by Israel, and advancing up to the very gates of Samaria (I Kings 20). The southern king, Jehoshaphat (I Kings 22:41-46), reversed the

---

[17] Previously the northern capital had been located to the northeast at Tirzah (modern Tell el-Far'ah, which has been excavated under the direction of R. De Vaux). Because of military pressure one of Omri's predecessors, Baasha, had been forced to move the capital from Shechem to Tirzah (I Kings 15:16-21).

foreign policy of his predecessor, Asa, and joined forces with Ahab to fight the Arameans in Transjordan in order to recover Ramoth-gilead (I Kings 22). It was in this battle, according to the story, that Ahab lost his life.

The Threat of Assyria

Just a few years before Ahab's death, however, the necessities of politics made Syria and Israel bed-fellows. The Assyrians, intent on expanding to the Mediterranean, were beginning to pose a great threat to the petty kingdoms of Syria and Palestine. Syria, the nearest and most vulnerable, was the first to feel the threat of Assyrian expansion to the west. The Assyrian king, Shalmaneser III (c. 859-824 B.C.), believing that the small western states would be easy prey, prepared to strike in 853 B.C. The battle was fought at Qarqar near Hamath, not far north of Damascus, against a coalition of western states. Benhadad of Syria had accomplished the diplomatic triumph of organizing the states, including his enemy Israel, to stop Assyrian aggression. Joining strong contingents from Syria and Hamath, "Ahab the Israelite" brought 10,000 foot soldiers and 2,000 chariots—the greatest number of chariots contributed by any of the allies, according to Shalmaneser's annals.[18] In the usual manner of war communiqués, the Assyrian boasted an overwhelming victory. But apparently the victory was not nearly so decisive as he claimed, for he withdrew and did not appear again in the west for several years. This event, however, was a shadow of things to come. From then on, as we shall see more clearly in the next chapter, Assyria's ambition to rule the Fertile Crescent was the darkest cloud on the political horizon of Israel and Judah.

Against this political background, there arose a succession of prophets who stood in the spiritual lineage of Moses and Samuel. Some of them are mentioned only briefly—like Ahijah from Shiloh, who led the revolt against Solomon (I Kings 11:29-39), and Jehu ben Hanani, who pronounced doom against king Baasha of Israel (I Kings 16:1-4). Our attention will focus on three outstanding prophets who arose during the period of the Omri dynasty: Micaiah, Elijah, and Elisha.

ONE PROPHET AGAINST FOUR HUNDRED

One of the most vivid episodes in the history of prophecy is the story of Micaiah, the son of Imlah, a contemporary of Elijah. (Micaiah should not be confused with the later and better-known prophet Micah.) It comes from the closing years of Ahab's reign, and properly should be considered after the Elijah narratives. But we shall look at it here because it shows how much the prophetic

---

[18] See Pritchard, *Ancient Near Eastern Texts*, pp. 278-279.

"schools" or guilds had been nationalized during the historical period that we have considered in this chapter.

The story of Micaiah in I Kings 22 should be read in connection with I Kings 20. The Deuteronomic historian drew both these accounts from an independent source dealing with Ahab's wars. His purpose in including them was to show how divine retribution finally descended upon Ahab, one of the members of the Deuteronomic rogues' gallery. By describing the wars, he has given us a clear picture of the activity of "the sons of the prophets" (I Kings 20:35) at a time of military crisis, and has thrown into the foreground a great prophetic figure, Micaiah.

Chapter 20 takes us back to a time slightly before the battle of Qarqar, mentioned above. Even though Ahab's capital was besieged, he succeeded in turning the tables on the Syrian king at the battle of Aphek, forcing him to restore cities that Omri had ceded, and obtaining commercial concessions in Damascus. Ahab's act of mercy to the Syrian king was sharply rebuked by a member of a prophetic school who stood for a ruthless practice of holy war— the application of the sacrificial ban (*hérem*) against the enemy (see pp. 134-135). Despite this prophetic protest, it turned out that Ahab had been politically shrewd in making a covenant with Benhadad, for it was soon apparent

CHRONOLOGICAL CHART 4

B.C.	EGYPT	THE DIVIDED KINGDOM		SYRIA	ASSYRIA
		JUDAH	ISRAEL		
900		Asa,	Baasha,		Assyrian Revival
		c. 913-873	c. 900-877		
			Elah,		Adad-nirari II,
			c. 877-876		c. 912-890
			Zimri,	Benhadad I,	Ashur-nasir-apal II,
			c. 876	c. 880-842	c. 884-859
			(7 days)		
			Omri		
			Dynasty:		
			Omri,		
			c. 876-869		
	Egyptian	Jehoshaphat,	Ahab,		
	Weakness	c. 873-849	c. 869-850		
		Jehoram,	(Elijah,		
		c. 849-842	c. 850)		
		Ahaziah,	Ahaziah,		Shalmaneser III,
		c. 842	c. 850-849		c. 859-824
850		Athaliah,	Jehoram,	Hazael,	Battle of
		c. 842-837	c. 849-842	c. 842-806	Qarqar, 853

that the western nations needed to stand together if they were to halt the Assyrian advance.

Then came the battle of Qarqar (853 b.c.), which the Deuteronomic historian passed over in discreet silence because it did not serve his theological purpose. For three years the western military alliance against Assyria produced a truce between Israel and Syria (I Kings 22:1). But the friendship lasted no longer than the crisis. Shortly after the battle of Qarqar was fought to its indecisive finish, and after the Assyrians had withdrawn to face other problems, these two small nations resumed their bitter quarrel. The bone of contention was the city of Ramoth-gilead in Transjordan. Earlier, Omri had ceded this city along with others in order to hold Syria at bay. According to the agreement made after the battle of Aphek, Benhadad was to return them, but he had reneged. Ahab was eager to have possession of this city, which occupied a strategic position on the north-south commercial and military highway running through Transjordan.

As I Kings 22 opens, we see Ahab of Israel and Jehoshaphat of Judah taking counsel on a proposed joint military campaign. One of the accomplishments of the Omri dynasty had been to enter into friendly alliance with the Southern Kingdom, an alliance that was twice sealed by intermarriage. In this chapter, however, Jehoshaphat's position suggests that he was almost a vassal of the more powerful and wealthier Northern Kingdom.

Jehoshaphat declared his willingness to go along with whatever Ahab had in mind, but slyly hoped that an oracle from Yahweh would render the proposed campaign unnecessary. Hence, as was customary when important military decisions were to be made, he suggested that they "inquire first for the word of Yahweh." Ahab complied by summoning about four hundred ecstatic prophets. Verses 10-12 give a vivid picture of these nationalistic dervishes working themselves into an ecstatic frenzy (the verb for "prophesying" in verse 10 means "prophesying ecstatically") before the two kings seated in state. Meanwhile, the prophets' ringleader—a certain Zedekiah—performed a symbolic action that was intended to dramatize the inevitable defeat of the Syrians. The "sons of the prophets" spoke "with one accord" (literally "with one mouth," vs. 13). According to the clear-cut verdict of these yes-men, the will of Yahweh and the purpose of the king coincided perfectly. Without any question, they agreed, Ahab would be successful in a campaign against Ramoth-gilead.

Suspicious of this verdict, the Judean king, Jehoshaphat, asked whether all the prophets had been heard from. It turned out that there was another prophet, Micaiah ben Imlah, who had not been called—for obvious reasons. "I hate him," said Ahab, "for he never prophesies good concerning me, but evil" (vs. 8). A revealing confession! Nevertheless, Micaiah was haled into the presence of the kings, after having been given a stern reminder that the majority was unanimously in favor of the military venture.

With a tone of sarcasm, Micaiah at first mocked and mimicked the optimistic prophesy of the four hundred. But Ahab, knowing that Micaiah was acting out of character, put him under oath to speak the truth in the name of Yahweh. This the prophet did in two oracles: One was a vision of Israel in leaderless rout, "scattered upon the mountains, as sheep that have no shepherd"—a prediction of the death of the Israelite king and the utter failure of the Syrian expedition. The other was a vision of Yahweh presiding over his heavenly court and commissioning a "spirit" to fill the prophets with a lying ecstasy. The reactions to Micaiah's unpleasant prophecy were what we might have expected: a slap on the face from Zedekiah, and an order snapped out by Ahab to "put this fellow in prison." The story goes on to relate how Micaiah's prophetic word was later vindicated. In spite of Ahab's disguise, an archer "drew his bow at a venture" and the king, mortally wounded, had to withdraw from the battle. Thus, in a seemingly chance occurrence the word of Yahweh through his prophet was fulfilled. In the Israelite perspective, history is governed by providence, not by chance.

I Kings 22 gives us a glimpse of a transitional moment in the history of prophecy. Micaiah vowed that "what Yahweh says to me, that will I speak"— even though it was diametrically opposed to the royal view and to the voice of the majority. He proclaimed God's judgment *against* the nation—a message of doom—which in time was recognized as one of the badges of a true prophet of Yahweh (Jer. 28:8-9). With Micaiah, prophecy was no longer the echo of nationalism or the servant of popular desire. Here we have a break with the professional prophets—a break that became sharper later when Amos disavowed any connection with the "sons of the prophets" (Amos 7:14). But in a deeper sense, prophets of Micaiah's type did not break with Israel's true prophetic tradition; they were indeed more sensitive to that tradition than the ecstatic prophets themselves. In prophets like Micaiah the ancient Mosaic faith came alive in the present with new meaning and power. This is clear in the case of the greatest ninth-century prophet: Elijah (about 850 B.C.).

ELIJAH, THE TISHBITE

We now turn backward from the end of Ahab's reign, with which I Kings 20 and 22 deal, to the fateful domestic crisis at the beginning of his rule. Our source for this period is the Elijah cycle, found chiefly in I Kings 17-19 and 21. Like the stories of Ahab's wars, this cycle is an independent unit of tradition that was incorporated into the Deuteronomic History.[19] Notice that in this section the characteristic Deuteronomic language is lacking, and the narrative betrays no "Deuteronomic" concern over the fact that Elijah built an altar on

---

[19] The Septuagint, the Greek translation of the Old Testament, places chapter 21 immediately after chapters 17-19, showing that these four chapters belong together as a single unit.

a "high place" (Carmel). Nor is Elijah rebuked for not having denounced the bull cult of Bethel, a subject on which the prophet is completely silent. Here we have prophetic legends that were preserved, no doubt, in the prophetic community with which Elijah was associated (II Kings 2:1-18).

The Elijah stories were not told with the precise, factual interest that a modern historian would display, any more than the Yahwist's epic was. They were tinted with the dye of the imagination and faith of Israel as they were remembered and elaborated in the oral tradition. Although many of them are based on actual circumstances, primarily they mirror the *experienced history* of Israel in one of her great crises. Not only do these stories record the terrific impression made by Elijah, the man of God, but they also portray the deepest dimension of Israel's history—her encounter with Yahweh in the political and cultural crisis of the time. This crisis came to a head as a result of the aggressiveness of Ahab's wife.

The French writer Pascal once said that the whole course of Western history was changed by the shape of Cleopatra's nose. And we might say that the course of Israel's history was profoundly affected by the eccentricities of one woman: Jezebel. It will be recalled that Omri, in order to strengthen relations between Israel and Phoenicia, had brought about the marriage of his son, Ahab, to Jezebel, the daughter of Ethbaal, king of Tyre. Had Ahab married someone else, the whole story might have been different. The Deuteronomic historian leaves no doubt about his attitude toward the political marriage, for in marrying Jezebel, he says, Ahab actually out-sinned Jeroboam (I Kings 16:31)!

Ahab immediately tried to make his bride at home in the new capital, Samaria, where he was continuing the building program initiated by Omri. Just as Solomon built shrines in Jerusalem for his foreign wives, so King Ahab built a "temple of Baal," equipped with an altar and an image of Asherah, the mother goddess (I Kings 16:32-33). The Baal in this case was Baal-Melkart, the official protective deity of Tyre. This was the Phoenician version of the Canaanite nature religion, which we know best from the Ras Shamra literature. From the time of Israel's entrance into Canaan, this religion had been making subtle inroads into the covenant faith. But notice that Baalism had now acquired a political drive, for Phoenician imperialism was at its very height in the Mediterranean world. In antiquity, the way to acknowledge the political supremacy of another nation was to acknowledge and appropriate the religion of that country.

In fairness, though, Ahab seems to have had no idea of rejecting Yahweh, the God of Israel (contrary to the Deuteronomic judgment of I Kings 16:31), for he gave his children names containing the sacred element *Yah* (Atali*ah*, Ahaz*iah*, *Je*horam), and—as we have seen in the story of Micaiah—later on in his reign he consulted the prophets of Yahweh. His position was one of tolerance; he merely wanted to give his wife freedom of worship, as Solomon had done with his foreign wives. But Jezebel was not one to retire into privacy. She was a proud, domineering woman whose selfish passion would stop at nothing to achieve her desired purpose. A fanatical evangelist for her Phoenician religion, she inevitably came into conflict with the Yahweh prophets, who were equally passionate in their crusade for the covenant faith of Israel. She imported from Phoenicia a great number of Baal prophets, and supported them out of the public treasury (I Kings 18:19). Moreover, she began an aggressive campaign to "cut off the prophets of Yahweh." Taking advantage of the easy-going tolerance and naive syncretism of the people, she tried to liquidate every vestige of Israel's traditional faith. The altars of Yahweh were torn down, the prophets were killed, and the remaining loyal adherents were driven underground. It was at this time of crisis that Elijah appeared in Israel to speak "the word of the Lord."

The Contest on Carmel

The background of the first story in the Elijah cycle (I Kings 17 and 18) is a drought that paralyzed the country, as had happened periodically from time immemorial. Seen through a veil of legend, Elijah the Tishbite (that is, a native of the city Tishbeh in Gilead) suddenly appears on the scene like a meteor. The dramatic suddenness with which he is introduced suggests the impression he must have made on his contemporaries. Coming from across the Jordan, where he had lived a rough, semi-nomadic life on the edge of the desert, he must have been a strange sight in the cultured land of Israel— clothed in a garment of hair, wearing a leather girdle, and displaying his rugged strength (II Kings 1:8). His movements were so baffling that Obadiah, the king's servant, insisted that the spirit (or "wind") of Yahweh was wont to whisk him away to nobody-knows-where (I Kings 18:12). Elijah had a way of coming from nowhere to surprise people. According to the legend, his disappearance was just as mysterious as his lightning appearance, for—to use the language of the well-known spiritual—a fiery "sweet chariot," swinging low, carried him in a whirlwind to heaven (II Kings 2:11-12).

Elijah's first act was to announce a drought in the name of Yahweh—that is, to throw down the challenge to Baal in the sphere of his power—fertility (I Kings 17:1). The rest of chapter 17 is a series of vignettes showing the severity of the famine and the great miracles Elijah accomplished. These miracle stories, a favorite aspect of popular tradition that gathered around the prophet (see II Kings 1 and 2), are not to be taken literally. The central concern of the stories is to portray Yahweh's authority over the fertility of the land, and to affirm that men's lives are wholly in his hand. One of the most important features of this chapter is the claim that Yahweh controls fertility not only in Palestine but in Phoenicia as well—the special province of Baal-Melkart—for

MOUNT CARMEL *as seen across the plain of Acre from the north. On this range, which juts out toward the Mediterranean Sea, Elijah challenged the Baal prophets to a contest. The modern city of Haifa is nestled against the mountain.*

Elijah is shown ministering to a widow in the Phoenician town of Zarephath during the widespread famine.[20]

In I Kings 18, we have Elijah's encounter with Ahab the king. The king's first words were: "Is it you, you troubler of Israel?" He was thinking of the great disturbance that this prophetic "gad-fly" had brought about by his senseless prophecy of drought—a drought that had hit Samaria so hard that the king and his steward had to scour the countryside to find enough fodder to keep the chariot horses alive. Elijah, however, turned Ahab's words against him, reminding him that the trouble had been brought about by his policy of supporting the worship of the Canaanite "Baals" (I Kings 18:18), who are here regarded as local manifestations of the Phoenician Baal, lord of sky and weather. The prophet announced that it is Yahweh, not Baal, who controls fertility. He challenged the "four hundred and fifty prophets of Baal and the four hundred prophets of Asherah" to a contest on the promontory of Mount Carmel, which juts out toward the Mediterranean Sea.

The description of the contest between the Baal prophets and the solitary prophet of Yahweh is one of the most dramatic accounts in the Bible. Elijah

[20] That this famine has a basis in fact is suggested by the first-century Jewish historian Josephus, who quotes the statement of Menander of Ephesus that there was a year of drought in the time of Ethbaal, father of Jezebel (*Antiquities of the Jews*, viii, 13, 2).

accused the people of "limping with two different opinions." In Hebrew, the language suggests vacillation, but the exact meaning is uncertain. Possibly Elijah's question was: "How long will you hobble hesitatingly at the cross-roads?" Or, according to another view, the question conveys the picture of a bird hopping along a branch until it comes to the fork, then vainly imagines that it can go on by putting one foot on one branch, and the other on the second branch. Here the prophet says that the people have been hopping on one foot, then the other. They wanted to keep one foot in the traditional faith of Israel, and the other foot in the worship of Baal. This policy of syncretism had had a long history, and had been encouraged among the people by Jeroboam's religious innovations. But the program of Jezebel had brought the issue to a crisis. Israel finally had come to the fork of the road. Now it was a clear either-or question: either Yahweh, the God of the covenant, or Baal, the god of fertility. Elijah had no interest in discussing monotheism in theoretical terms, but in terms of life, of allegiance. "If Yahweh is God, follow him; but if Baal, then follow him." Deity makes a total claim upon men's loyalty. God is the One whom men serve with heart, soul, and the strength of their being. Israel, then, stood at the hour of decision. And in the prophet Elijah the Mosaic tradition was reaffirmed: Yahweh is the jealous God who will have no other gods beside him. The name Elijah—"Yah(weh) is (my) God"—was highly appropriate for the prophetic champion of this faith.

The object of the contest was to determine then and there who was Lord, who had the power to control rain and fertility. So both parties, the Baal prophets and the solitary Yahweh prophet, agreed to perform their respective rites with the understanding that "the God who answers by fire" is God. The Baal prophets lashed themselves into ecstatic frenzy as they performed their limping dance around the altar and shouted their ritual cries to Baal. With a touch of humor, the narrative portrays Elijah, serenely confident, laughing the Baal into meaningless unreality and taunting the Baal prophets with the jest that the heavens were unresponsive because, perhaps, Baal was relieving himself ("gone aside" is a euphemism), was on a business trip, or needed to be awakened from a reverie or from slumber. In spite of their carryings on, the ecstatic prophets were unsuccessful in ending the drought. The episode ends with the solemn words: "There was no voice; no one answered, no one heeded."

When Elijah stepped forward, his first act was to repair the abandoned altar of Yahweh—an act which signified a bold reclaiming of the cultic site for the God of Israel.[21] The ritual that followed (I Kings 18:32b-35) seems curious,

---

[21] Albrecht Alt, in his article dealing with the contest on Mount Carmel, "Das Gottesurteil auf dem Karmel," *Kleine Schriften zur Geschichte des Volkes Israel*, II (Munich, 1953), pp. 135-149, argues that this area had come under the control of the Phoenicians in the past, who devoted the cult-site to the worship of Baal. The Carmel contest, then, had political implications too: Elijah's victory dramatized the retaking of the territory in the name of Israel's God. For a discussion of the whole narrative, see H. H. Rowley, "Elijah on Mount Carmel," [144].

for why would the prophet pour water on wood if he expected it to be consumed with fire? There have been various fantastic attempts to "explain" this —for instance, by saying that the "water" was actually inflammable naphtha from an oil geyser nearby! But the purpose of the act was clearly to bring on rain by sympathetic magic—by imitating the falling of rain. So Elijah, in a three-fold ceremony, poured water on the wood until it filled the trench.

The upshot of Elijah's ritual is described in verses 36-40: the supernatural fire descended from heaven, the people were so awed by the spectacle that they exclaimed, "Yahweh, *he* is God," and the Baal prophets were condemned to the sacrificial ban (*hérem*). The real climax of the story, however, comes in verses 41-46, where the goal of the contest is realized: the drought is ended. Elijah proclaimed to Ahab that "there is a sound of the rushing of rain." Another rain ceremony, in which a servant was sent seven times to look toward the Mediterranean Sea while the prophet was prostrate in prayer, concluded with the announcement that a storm cloud—"a little cloud like a man's hand" —was approaching. So while the storm gathered and the rain began to descend, Ahab hurried through the Valley of Jezreel lest his chariot should bog down in the mud, and Elijah, with a terrific burst of ecstatic energy, ran before him.

The story of the drought belongs to the poetry of Israel's faith and should not be destroyed by modern rationalizations, such as construing the fire falling from heaven as the lightning of an electrical thunderstorm. In the Old Testament the symbolism of fire is frequently used to express the manifestation of God (for instance, the "burning bush"). Above all else, the narrator wants to communicate a sense of the active presence of Yahweh in that historical situation through his prophet. In the various episodes of the story, which accurately reflect the affairs of the day, we view a great crisis in Israel's history as interpreted by prophetic faith.

The Flight to Mount Horeb

The dramatic description of the contest on Carmel—the participation of "all Israel" (I Kings 18:19, 20), the people's unanimous confession of faith in Yahweh, and the massacre of the Baal prophets—could easily give the impression that Baalism was destroyed once and for all. Actually, Elijah's victory was not that impressive. A few years later, there were still enough Baal worshipers to fill a Baal temple (II Kings 10:21). The victory on Carmel was not the end of the war. And Elijah was reminded of this by the fact that Jezebel was still on the throne, threatening to track him down.

The sequel to the Carmel episode is related in the legend of Elijah's flight from the territory of Ahab and Jezebel into the wilderness of southern Judah, a day's journey south of Beer-sheba, where he threw himself down beneath a lonely juniper tree. Just as the Yahwist showed how God's promise was eclipsed by man's incapacity for faith (see pp. 181-186), so this narrator, with profound insight, portrays the despair that shadows faith. How could Yahweh really be Lord when Jezebel's power was undiminished? The Elijah portrayed in I Kings 19:4 is a broken and fatigued man, running for his life and wishing to die because, in his efforts to crush the power of tyranny and idolatry, he had been no better than his fathers. The intent of the miracle story in verses 5-8, however, is to affirm that in his darkest hour Yahweh did not desert him, but mercifully supplied him with strength for a long journey that would lead to a new and keener sense of the sovereignty of God.

We are told that Elijah traveled "forty days and forty nights" (the traditional number of years Israel journeyed in the wilderness) until he came to Horeb (Sinai), the sacred mountain of the covenant. On Horeb, a divine visitation (theophany) took place which the narrator describes with the revelation to Moses at Sinai-Horeb clearly in mind. The cave in which Elijah lodged recalls the cleft of the rock in which Moses was sheltered while Yahweh "passed by," showing his glory (Ex. 33:18-34:8). The Elijah narrative, too, says the Yahweh "passed by," and that his visitation was accompanied by earthquake, wind, and fire—the traditional phenomena of Yahweh's revelation on the sacred mountain (Ex. 19).[22]

Thus the whole narrative intends to say that Elijah was renewed at the sources of Israel's faith. But here there is an important difference, almost a reversal of the traditional theophany. It is stated that Yahweh was not in the earthquake, wind, or fire, but in the *lull* that followed the storm. Yahweh is lord of the storm, but, unlike Baal-Melkart—the sky-god of storm and fertility —he is not a nature god. The Hebrew words that are usually rendered "a still, small voice" really mean "a voice of a gentle stillness"—an awesome, vocal silence. In this silence, interpreted by the memories that hallowed the mountain spot, God's presence was made known to Elijah. When he heard this voice of silence, speaking to him out of Israel's sacred history, he moved to the entrance of the cave.

The dialogue too introduces new dimensions of meaning. The question addressed to Elijah seems to imply that he had no business out there in the quiet mountain retreat, a fugitive from the places where history was being made. The prophet protested that he had been very jealous (the Hebrew word means both to be jealous and to be zealous) for Yahweh. He had been a *zealot* for the Mosaic tradition, even though the people of Israel, under Jezebel's influence, had "forsaken thy covenant,[23] thrown down thy altars, and slain thy prophets with the sword." But Elijah's brooding over his loneliness and over

---

[22] Owing to some accident in the transmission of the text, verses 9b-10 have evidently been misplaced from the end of the description of the theophany, where they appropriately belong (see verses 13b-14).

[23] The Hebrew word translated "thy covenant" is textually insecure; important versions read simply "forsaken thee" (Yahweh) at I Kings 19:10, 14. Commentators admit, however, that the covenant tradition is implied in the whole narrative. See John Gray's commentary on I and II Kings [126], pp. 364-365.

the threat to his life was quickly challenged by three divine orders, two of which involved his fomenting political revolutions. Although these two commissions were carried out by Elisha, his prophetic successor, their mention here shows that Israel's faith finds expression in action rather than in mystic contemplation. As in the case of Moses at the "burning bush," Elijah realized afresh that Yahweh acts in the sphere of history and that he summons his prophet to take part in his plan of action. Yahweh's action called for returning to the land of Israel to incite a revolution. Elijah was told that though the revolution would make a clean sweep of the house of Omri and its supporters, Yahweh would nevertheless spare a faithful remnant—"seven thousand in Israel, all the knees that have not bowed to Baal"—with whom he would continue his purposive work in history.

It is significant that Elijah made a journey to Sinai, where Moses had received the revelation from Yahweh after the Exodus. In one sense, the whole prophetic movement, of which Elijah is the great exemplar, was a pilgrimage back to Sinai, to the source of Israel's faith. The prophets did not claim to be innovators—men who came forth with bright new ideas that would enable Israel to keep up to date in the onward march of culture. Rather, they demanded that Israel return to the wholehearted covenant allegiance demanded by the "jealousy" of Yahweh. They were reformers who took their stand on the ancient ground of Sinai. But in a deeper sense the prophetic movement was not a kind of archaism—a timid response to cultural crisis by retreating into the idealized past. In the message of the prophets the Mosaic past came alive in the present with new vitality and meaning, as we can see from the stories of Elijah. What was latent in the Mosaic tradition began to come to fullness, and Israel was given a deeper understanding of the implications of the covenant and of Yahweh's ways in history.

The Affair of Naboth's Vineyard

The third episode in the Elijah cycle (I Kings 21) apparently took place some years later. Ahab wanted to purchase the vineyard of Naboth, which adjoined his palace in the city of Jezreel (his second capital), so that he could enjoy more room. His terms were generous enough, but Naboth refused to sell, for one reason: it was a family estate. Properly speaking, it was not Naboth's "private property" to dispose of as he pleased. It belonged to the whole family or clan through whom it had been passed down from generation to generation as a sacred inheritance. His refusal—"Yahweh forbid that I should give you the inheritance of my fathers"—revealed an attitude toward land that was unique with Israel. According to this view, Yahweh himself was the owner of the land. Faithful to his promise, he had brought the Israelites into a cultured country and had given the land to various tribes and clans. They were to act as stewards of Yahweh's property, administering it for the welfare of the whole community. So land-grabbing and private speculation were ruled out by the very nature of the covenant community. Naboth was only reaffirming the ancient basis of Israel's land tenure when he insisted that he did not have the freedom to sell the inheritance of his fathers.[24]

Ahab recognized the validity of Naboth's position, although it made him very sullen. But Jezebel, who had been nurtured in the commercial civilization of Phoenicia, had other conceptions of property. Her Baal religion placed no limitations on the exercise of royal power. "Do you now govern Israel?" she asked Ahab. She promised to get Naboth's vineyard for him—in her own way. At her direction, Naboth was accused by two "good-for-nothings" of "cursing God and the king" (that is, of blasphemy and treason), and, with no word of defense spoken on his behalf, Naboth was stoned to death. Evidently Naboth's sons were done away with too (II Kings 9:26). The murder had a pretense of legality—enough to salve the conscience of those who had a hand in the treacherous deed. So with Naboth and his sons out of the way, Ahab thought he was free to take possession of the vineyard.

But Ahab had yet to stand before the highest tribunal, for "the word of Yahweh came to Elijah the Tishbite." In the vineyard that Ahab had gone to claim as his own, there occurred another dramatic face-to-face encounter of prophet and king. Like the ground stained with the blood of Abel, this outrageous crime was crying to Yahweh for requital, and the prophet thundered out the impending divine judgment. Stinging under the sharp words of the prophetic gad-fly, the king could only mutter, remembering his past associations with Elijah, "Have you found me, O my enemy?" The story concludes with a vivid description of Ahab's penitence, which reminds us of David's remorse after his encounter with Nathan (I Kings 21:27-29; most of verses 20b-26 are Deuteronomic comments).

The Naboth incident provides an excellent preface to the social message of the prophets of a later period. Here we see Baalism and the Yahweh faith in opposition, not in a dramatic contest on Carmel but in the field of social relationships. The great Israelite prophets were champions of the stern ethical demands of the ancient Mosaic tradition. As we saw in Chapter 2, Israel's covenant obedience was motivated by gratitude for the great acts of redemption that Yahweh had wrought on behalf of his oppressed people. Yahweh had created a covenant community in which every man stood equal before the law— whether he was rich or poor, king or private citizen. The whole community was responsible to the sovereign will of Yahweh as expressed in the absolute laws that had been handed down from the wilderness period and refined by legal usage. And when the justice of man was downtrodden by the powerful, Yahweh intervened to defend the weak and the defenseless and to restore the order and brotherly solidarity of the covenant community. Baalism tended to

---

[24] See Walter Eichrodt, "Revelation and Responsibility," *Interpretation*, III, 4 (1949), pp. 393-394.

support the *status quo*, with the aristocracy on top. But the Yahweh faith, as revived in the prophet Elijah, supplied the energy for a protest against the evils of a commercial civilization and for social reform.

ELISHA AND THE CLOSING YEARS
OF THE OMRI DYNASTY

At the opening of the Second Book of Kings (chapters 2-9; 13:14-21), we find the stories dealing with Elisha, upon whom Elijah's prophetic mantle had fallen. The Elisha cycle (and also the Elijah legends in II Kings 1) represent a type of prophetic tradition different from the great Elijah narratives we have been considering. Here is a popular lore that is filled with wonder-tales: the rolling back of the Jordan by Elijah's mantle, the magical sweetening of water, the deception of the Moabites with a mirage of blood-red water, the restoration of the Shunammite woman's child from the dead, the incident of the floating axe-head, and so on. Stories like these delighted the popular imagination and no doubt were told and re-told by the members of the prophetic order with which Elisha was intimately associated. Fanciful though they are, they show us Elisha as a prophet concerned for the people, and they record the conviction of those who knew from his deeds that "the word of Yahweh (was) with him" (II Kings 3:12).

The stories are told against the background of the political events in which Israel was involved during the closing years of the Omri dynasty, especially the reign of J(eh)oram, king of Israel. In this period (c. 849-842 B.C.), Moab revolted against Israel—a fact that is confirmed by the Moabite Stone (see p. 205), which makes the extravagant claim that Mesha, the Moabite king, subjected Israel to the sacrificial ban (*hérem*) of the god Chemosh, so that "Israel perished forever." [25] The Israelite account, though adorned with fanciful elements, is probably correct in reporting that the Moabite king sought victory by sacrificing his eldest son upon the city wall to the Moabite god Chemosh. As a result, so the historian interprets, "there came great wrath upon Israel" (II Kings 3:4-27).

Most of the stories, however, reflect the conditions of the continuing wars between Syria and Israel. A magnificent illustration is the charming story of Naaman, the commander of the Syrian army, who, at the suggestion of a little slave girl whom the Syrians had carried off from Israel during a raid, made the trip into Israelite territory to seek Elisha, and there became convinced that "there is no God in all the earth but in Israel" (II Kings 5). The story is doubtless no more than an expression of Israelite faith, but it shows how men could

---

[25] In the Moabite text, "son" probably means Omri's "grandson." The revolt occurred in Jehoram's reign, not Ahab's.

believe, even under the trying conditions of war, that the enemy was included within the sovereignty of Yahweh.

According to the account in II Kings 8:7-15, Elisha journeyed to Damascus. While he was there, Benhadad, suffering from sickness, sent one of his officers, Hazael, to ask the prophet whether he would recover. In a prophetic trance, Elisha predicted that Hazael would be the next king of Syria and that he would bring great military calamity to Israel. Under the authority of this prophetic word, Hazael murdered Benhadad the very next day, thus bringing about one of the revolutions that had been inspired by Elijah (I Kings 19:15-16). The second revolution was brought about when Elisha summoned one of the "sons of the prophets" to anoint Jehu as king over Israel (II Kings 9:1-13). With Jehu's rise to power, the Omri dynasty was brought to an end in a terrible bath of blood, and a new chapter in Israel's history began.

FALLEN

IS THE

VIRGIN ISRAEL

CHAPTER EIGHT   Today, we tend to value tolerance so highly that we sometimes advocate indifference toward competing religious loyalties. We are likely to sympathize with Solomon's cosmopolitanism, or even with the compromising attitude of Ahab's generation, who hopped back and forth between opposing views. But, as we have seen, Israel's prophets attacked the tolerant syncretism of the time and insisted on a fierce devotion to Yahweh. It has been rightly observed that "intolerance in religion was not a characteristic

Biblical readings: The books of Amos and Hosea, and the background material in II Kings 9-17. The account of II Kings is paralleled in II Chronicles 22-25.

of ancient peoples, and was only introduced into Israel by the prophets." [1] The flame of their conviction was kindled at the ancient sources of the Mosaic faith, and burst forth like a consuming fire at a time when the nation was in danger of being engulfed by Canaanite culture.

In the previous chapter we were primarily interested in the Northern Kingdom, whose prosperity and political power overshadowed that of Judah. To be sure, in the reign of Jehoshaphat, a contemporary of Omri, Judah enjoyed a resurgence of political and commercial power. The policy of peaceful collaboration with Israel, sealed by intermarriage between the royal houses, enabled Judah to recover from the enervating civil wars that had sapped her energies ever since the division of Solomon's kingdom. But Judah was still the weaker sister, especially during the period of the powerful Omri dynasty. In this chapter, our spotlight again falls on the kingdom of Israel during its next dynasty, that of Jehu. Toward the end of the Jehu dynasty, the star of Israel reached its zenith of glory, only to sink like a meteor into oblivion. The main sources for our study are found in a section of the Deuteronomic History (II Kings 9-17) and, above all, in the written prophecies of Amos and Hosea. We shall see how the reforming zeal of the prophets of the ninth century—Elijah, Micaiah, and Elisha —was continued and deepened by the prophets of the eighth.

THE REVOLUTION OF JEHU

Compared with the stability of the Southern Kingdom of Judah, which had a single dynasty from the time of David to its very end, the Northern Kingdom of Israel had a checkered political career. Political unrest and intrigue had kept both Jeroboam I and Baasha from founding a dynasty. And the dynasty of Omri lasted only for the reigns of four kings, to be superseded by the five-king dynasty of Jehu. Then political instability returned again, until the fall of the nation in 721 B.C. The political differences between the two kingdoms, as we have previously noticed, were rooted in different "ideologies." The continuity of the Davidic dynasty was supported by the view that Yahweh had made a covenant to maintain the Davidic throne. In the Northern Kingdom, however, there was greater political instability, owing to the persistence of the old "democratic" ideal of the Tribal Confederacy. Northerners believed that Yahweh's spirit was poured upon a man, but not a dynasty—and this view could foster revolution.

The story of the Jehu dynasty opens in II Kings 9. Elijah, as we have seen, set in motion the forces that were to overthrow the Omri dynasty by revolution. In this passage, Elisha commissions one of the prophetic band to seek out Jehu, the army commander who had resumed the attempt to take Ramoth-gilead

---

[1] T. J. Meek, *Hebrew Origins* [94], p. 169.

from Syria, and to anoint him king of Israel. The word of Yahweh coming from this ecstatic "madman," as he was called (II Kings 9:11), was all that was needed to light the fuse of revolt. Supported by the power of the mutinous army, Jehu was proclaimed king with great fanfare.

Jehu's purge of Israel after he took the throne was both thoroughgoing and brutal. The memory of the gory details, which are given in the old story that has been slightly touched up with Deuteronomic comments (II Kings 9:7-10a), sent a shudder through future generations, as we shall see in the book of Hosea. Riding furiously in his chariot—a trait that has become proverbial for modern speed demons ("sons of Jehu")—Jehu came to Jezreel, where Joram, the king of Israel, was nursing wounds received in the Syrian battle, and sent an arrow through the heart of the fugitive king. With a sense of poetic justice, Jehu ordered Joram's body to be cast into Naboth's vineyard—an act designed, no doubt, to win over the people, who had been suffering under the economic oppression of the nobility and merchant class during the time of the Omri dynasty. But Jehu was not satisfied to limit the purge to Israel; so he murdered Ahaziah of Judah, who had come to visit his sick uncle, and later massacred Ahaziah's brothers, who also had come for a visit. Then Jezebel, whose last queenly act was to paint her eyebrows and primp her hair, was tossed out of a window and mangled beyond recognition. Finally, to cap the gory climax, Jehu had all seventy sons of Ahab decapitated, thus removing all claimants to the throne. (See Chronological Chart 5, p. 244.)

The Religious Side of the Revolution

But this was more than a typical oriental *coup d'état*. Although the more sensitive Israelites must have cringed at Jehu's brutal excesses and brazen callousness (see II Kings 9:34: "He went in and ate and drank"), Jehu himself sincerely believed that he was carrying out the religious revolution called for by Elijah and Elisha. True, his butchery of the whole house of Ahab was motivated by political ambition, and he shrewdly capitalized on the revolutionary ferment within the army and the widespread economic unrest in the land. But he was also influenced by religious considerations, and undoubtedly intended the massacre as an application of the *hérem* against an evil family, as Achan's household had been destroyed in the time of Joshua (Josh. 7:24-26). Elijah himself, after all, had demanded the ruthless extermination of the prophets of Baal after the Carmel contest.

That the revolution was in part a religious development is clear, not only in Jehu's being anointed by an ecstatic prophet, but also in the collaboration of Jehonadab, the son of Rechab (II Kings 10:15-17). This man was the head of a family that was known for its passionate devotion to the tradition of the wilderness, in opposition to the agricultural ways of Canaan. He was a descendant of the Kenites (Midianites), the nomadic people who influenced and supported Moses during the wilderness period (see above, p. 41). And Jehonadab's descendants of a later generation, known as Rechabites (Jer. 35), perpetuated their ancestors' stern devotion to the wilderness ideal. Under a vow, which they had received from Jehonadab, they refused to drink wine, cultivate vineyards, build houses, or till the soil. Dwelling in tents as their nomadic ancestors had, they stood for the pristine purity of the Mosaic tradition of the wilderness—a purity which, they maintained, had been defiled by the agrarian culture of Canaan.

According to the story, Jehu invited Jehonadab to join him in his work of extermination. "Come with me," said Jehu, "and see my zeal for Yahweh." Jehu showed his zeal for the Yahweh faith by slaughtering the remnants of Ahab's house, according to the prophetic word of Elijah. And Jehonadab, a representative of the conservative, nomadic tradition of Israel, endorsed Jehu's purge by riding with him in his chariot.

Jehonadab also matched Jehu's zeal for Yahweh by joining in the extermination of the Baal worshipers (II Kings 10:18-27). With cunningly concealed sarcasm, Jehu announced that he was planning to make a great sacrifice to the Phoenician deity, Baal-Melkart, but the "sacrifice" turned out to be an application of the sacrificial ban (hérem) to the devotees assembled in the temple of Baal. The holocaust was completed by burning the "pillar" (perhaps this was the Asherah, image of the mother goddess), demolishing the temple, and converting the place into a latrine. Notice that the Deuteronomic historian is somewhat impressed by Jehu's zeal, and is not the least bit incensed at the ruthless destruction of the house of Ahab and the Baal worshipers. But he denounces Jehu, despite his fanatical devotion to Yahweh, for not removing the idolatrous shrines that Jeroboam I had established at Dan and Bethel.

Jehu's revolution had serious repercussions in the Southern Kingdom. The mother of the Judean king Ahaziah, who had been slain by Jehu, was Athaliah, the daughter of Ahab. Despite her Yahweh name, she was evidently a devotee of Baal-Melkart and, like Jezebel in the north, had helped propagate this religion in Judah (see II Kings 11:18). When she heard of her son's death, she liquidated the male members of the Davidic line and usurped the throne. But she missed one person: the infant Joash (or Jehoash), who was spirited away and hidden by the priests in the Temple. In the north, it was the prophets who led the revolution against the Phoenician Baal; in the south, however, it was fomented in the priestly circles of the Temple with the cooperation of "the people of the land"—that is, the conservative land-owners who lived outside Jerusalem. After a covenant ceremony involving Yahweh and his people on the one hand and the people and the king on the other (II Kings 11:17), the temple of Baal was destroyed, and both Athaliah and the Baal priest Mattan were assassinated. Thus Joash took his place along with Asa as one of the reforming kings of Judah, and thereby won the moderate praise of the Deuteronomic historian (II Kings 12:1-3).

THE BLACK OBELISK of *Shalmaneser III depicts these scenes of tribute being brought by representatives of various countries to the Assyrian king. In the second panel from the top, "Jehu, son of Omri" is shown kneeling before the king in the presence of Assyrian attendants. On the other faces of the Obelisk, in the panels of the second row, thirteen Israelite porters bear the tribute.*

Problems of Foreign Policy

Once the fires of revolution had died down in the north, Jehu was faced with political problems that proved too much for him to handle. His cold-blooded murder of Ahaziah and the rise of the new regime in Judah had alienated the Southern Kingdom, and his liquidation of the devotees of the Phoenician Baal had no doubt cut off any support from Phoenicia. Isolated from the political allies that the Omri dynasty had counted on for its foreign policy, the Northern Kingdom was now more vulnerable to attack from Syria than ever before. The Syrian king, Hazael, quick to take advantage of the situation, swept down through Transjordan (II Kings 10:32-33). In 841 B.C., Jehu sensed his hopeless plight and, anxious to save his throne at any cost, paid tribute to the Assyrian monarch, Shalmaneser III, who by that time had recuperated from the battle of Qarqar and was renewing his march into the west. This political event is ignored in the biblical account, but it is mentioned in the famous Black Obelisk of Shalmaneser III, which depicts Jehu, at the head of an Israelite delegation, kneeling before "the mighty king, king of the universe, king without a rival, the autocrat, the powerful one of the four regions of the world"—as Shalmaneser modestly described himself. The inscription records the "tribute of Jehu, son of Omri" (for the Assyrians continued to designate Israelite kings after the name of Omri).[2]

The Assyrian advance relieved the pressure on Israel for the time being, for Syria had to meet this threat to her Mesopotamian border. But within a few years, internal problems forced Assyria to shelve her plans for expansion into the west for a generation. Hazael capitalized on

---

[2] See Pritchard, *Ancient Near Eastern Texts*, p. 280.

this good luck (after 837 B.C.) and sent his armies in lightning thrusts to the south (cf. Amos 1:3). During the reign of Jehoahaz, son of Jehu, Israel's armaments were reduced to the barest minimum (II Kings 13:7), for, as the historian says with some exaggeration, "the king of Syria had destroyed them and made them like the dust at threshing." At the same time, during the reign of the contemporary Judean king Joash, the Syrians swept down the Philistine coast and were stopped from attacking Jerusalem only when the royal and temple treasures were turned over to them (II Kings 12:17-18).

Then, in the year 805 B.C., the tide turned. The Deuteronomic historian states that "Hazael king of Syria oppressed Israel all the days of Jehoahaz; but Yahweh was gracious to them and had compassion on them." As a result of this divine favor, when the new Syrian king, Benhadad, the son of Hazael, came to the throne, Jehoash of Israel (who had the same name as the contemporary Judean king) recovered from the Syrians the cities that previously had been lost in war (II Kings 13:22-25). This turn of affairs was due less to the energetic warfare of the new Israelite king than to another surge of Assyrian power into Syria. In 805 B.C., a new Assyrian monarch, Adad-nirari III, resumed the attack on Syria and in a short time so crippled her that she was no longer a threat to Israel. But the momentum of the Assyrian advance was spent in this campaign, and for fifty years Israel did not have to fear invasion from beyond the Euphrates.

So with Assyria having her troubles at home, and with Syria barely able to maintain herself as a state, Je(ho)ash of Israel inherited the most favorable political situation in the entire history of the Northern Kingdom. His program of political expansion was challenged only by the kingdom of Judah, whose king, Amaziah, riding high on the wave of victory over Edom, insisted on trying to settle a score with the Jehu dynasty. It was a foolhardy move, as the fable about the thistle and the cedar shows (II Kings 14:8-10). The Israelite king soundly whipped the Judean state and reduced it to vassalage, thus preparing the way for the glorious era of Jeroboam II, the greatest king of the Jehu dynasty.

THE AGE OF JEROBOAM II

The Deuteronomic historian dismisses the reign of Jeroboam II with a scant seven verses, most of which consist of the usual monotonous formulas (II Kings 14:23-29). He does excerpt from the Book of the Chronicles of the Kings of Israel the notice that Jeroboam "restored the border of Israel from the entrance of Hamath as far as the Sea of the Arabah." The "entrance of Hamath," the northernmost boundary of Solomon's kingdom (I Kings 8:65), refers to the pass between Mount Lebanon and Mount Hermon, which can be located on a map by drawing a line straight across from Damascus to Sidon. The "Sea of the

Arabah" refers to the Dead Sea, named after the low desert plain that extends from the Jordan valley to the Gulf of Aqabah. Thus Jeroboam II extended his kingdom northward into the orbit of Hamath and Syria, and southward into territory that encroached upon Judah.[3] Never before had an Israelite king held undisputed sway over so large a kingdom. And once again, this nationalistic revival was inspired by a prophet—a certain Jonah, the son of Amittai, under whose name the book of Jonah was later written (see pp. 524-526).

A blanket of Deuteronomic silence also falls upon the reign of Azariah (Uzziah), Jeroboam's contemporary in Judah (II Kings 14:21-22; 15:1-7). Under his reign and that of his son and co-regent, Jotham, however, Judah too experienced a national revival, as we know from the authentic report by the Chronicler (II Chron. 26). Having enlarged and modernized his army, Uzziah carried out conquests on both sides of the Jordan. The cities of the Philistine plain were subjected, as were the peoples of Transjordan. Moreover, the Negeb was brought into the orbit of Judean control, enabling Uzziah to build Elath (II Kings 14:22) near Ezion-geber, and to restore the avenues of commerce into the Arabian world that Solomon had opened up two centuries before. Thus under Jeroboam II and Uzziah the sister kingdoms of Israel and Judah controlled almost the full sweep of Solomon's empire "from the entrance of Hamath to the Brook of Egypt" (I Kings 8:65). Judah, however, did not reach the peak of her political and economic power until the stronger Northern Kingdom had begun to decline after the death of Jeroboam II. So we shall postpone further discussion of Judah until the next chapter, in order that we may consider the last and most glorious era of North Israel.

A Time of Prosperity

In spite of the silence of the Deuteronomic historian, we know a great deal about the long reign of Jeroboam II, not only from the books of Amos and Hosea, but from archaeological findings. A vivid picture of the material prosperity of this period has been provided by excavations at Megiddo and Samaria (see pp. 206-207).[4] At Samaria especially we see signs of the prosperity and cultural achievement that prompted Amos, a prophet of the mid-eighth century, to denounce "those who feel secure on the mountain of Samaria" (Amos 6:1). The beautiful ivories, the luxurious summer and winter homes (Amos 3:15), the impressive fortifications, the teeming marketplaces—all filled Amos with disgust, and led him to proclaim that Yahweh too loathed the whole spectacle:

---

[3] The statement in II Kings 14:28—"he recovered for Israel Damascus and Hamath, which had belonged to Judah"—is very obscure.
[4] See C. C. McCown, *The Ladder of Progress in Palestine* (New York: Harper, 1943), chaps. 12 and 13; Kathleen Kenyon, *Archaeology in the Holy Land* [54], chap. 11.

> The Lord God has sworn by himself
> (says the Lord, the God of hosts):
> "I abhor the pride of Jacob,
>   and hate his strongholds;
>   and I will deliver up the city and
>   all that is in it."
>   —AMOS 6:8

The books of Amos and Hosea provide a clear picture of the economic injustices that followed in the wake of generations of intimate cultural relations with the mercantile economy of Phoenica. During the reign of Jeroboam II, the commercial and colonial activity of the Phoenicians was at its peak in the Mediterranean world, and Israel shared in the profits that flowed from the exchange of goods and services. Moreover, Jeroboam's conquests in Transjordan (the cities of Lo-debar and Karnaim mentioned in Amos 6:13) put him in a position to control the trade route from Syria and evidently the commercial highways from Arabia. Thus Samaria, the luxurious capital, became a great center of wealth. But the price for this prosperity was high, for an oppressive social pyramid grew up with the royal courtiers and the merchant class at the top and the great mass of people ground into poverty at the bottom. The heinous crime committed by Ahab against Naboth was perpetrated on a wider scale, as economic tyrants—with the sanction of corrupt courts (Amos 5:10-13) —"sold the righteous for silver, and the needy for a pair of shoes" (Amos 2:6; cf. 8:4-6). Amos felt that these crimes would have been shocking to any of Israel's neighbors with an elemental sense of justice:

> Proclaim to the strongholds in Assyria,
>   and to the strongholds in the land of Egypt,
>   and say, "Assemble yourselves upon the mountains of Samaria,
>   and see the great tumults within her,
>   and the oppressions in her midst."
> "They do not know how to do right," says Yahweh,
> "those who store up violence and robbery in their strongholds."
>   —AMOS 3:9-10

The prophetic books of Amos and Hosea also give a clear picture of the popular religion of the time and tend to support the Deuteronomic judgment that the ways of Jeroboam I were perpetuated in his namesake. Baalism was too deeply rooted in the Northern Kingdom, which was directly exposed to the culture of the Fertile Crescent, to be eradicated even by measures as thoroughgoing as those of Jehu. Hosea, a contemporary of Amos, excoriated Israel for supposing that her prosperity sprang from the worship of the Baals, the local representatives of the Canaanite storm-god who allegedly granted the blessings of agriculture (Hosea 2:2-13). He poured scorn upon the Baal festivals (2:13), the practice of temple prostitution (4:14), sacrifice at the high places (4:13), and the worship of images in the form of bulls (13:1-2). Twice the golden bull, which Jeroboam I installed in Bethel as a symbol of Yahweh's presence (see pp. 200-202), came in for the strongest censure (8:5; 10:5).

The Northern Mosaic Tradition

The Yahweh faith was by no means dead, however. In the worship centers, the Mosaic tradition was kept alive through ceremonies of covenant-renewal like the one Joshua inaugurated at Shechem (Josh. 24). In the villages, a class of teaching priests, known as Levites, proclaimed and expounded the great convictions of Israel's faith. So when prophets like Amos and Hosea appeared in the Northern Kingdom, they did not speak in a vacuum, for they could appeal to the people on the basis of a common religious heritage. Indeed, these prophets did not claim to introduce the people to new doctrines that had never been heard of before. Rather, their task was to recall their hearers to the memory of events they had all but forgotten and to convictions that formed the basis of the whole community of Yahweh.

In the Northern Kingdom this religious heritage found expression in a northern version of Israel's sacred history which scholars call the Elohist narrative (E). Here we shall not go into the question of when this literature arose —whether in the time of Jeroboam I to express and justify the nationalism of the newly formed Northern Kingdom (see p. 201), or in the time of Jeroboam II to give expression to the nationalism of the Northern Kingdom in the eighth century B.C. (as most scholars hold). Clearly this epic goes back to an old oral tradition that was given a special stamp in the circle of the northern tribes. By the time of Amos and Hosea, this tradition was well known in Israel.

This tradition is designated by the symbol "E" because, as we have seen (pp. 40-41), it prefers to use the word *Elohim* (for God) instead of *Yahweh* in the stories dealing with the pre-Mosaic period. This is in contrast to the Yahwist, who uses Yahweh from the very first. That E comes from north Israelitic circles is indicated by the prominence given to northern figures like Joseph, his mother Rachel, and his son Ephraim (Gen. 48:20), and also by the interest in northern shrines like Bethel (Gen. 28:17-22) and Shechem (Gen. 33:18-20). Moreover, E shows peculiarities of vocabulary, like the use of "Horeb" for the sacred mountain (the Yahwist uses "Sinai") and "Amorites" for the natives of Canaan (the Yahwist uses "Canaanites").

Since the Pentateuch is based primarily on the Yahwist's epic, it is often difficult to reconstruct the E narrative as a continuous account. The Judean editors, who combined the northern and southern traditions after the fall of the Northern Kingdom in 721 B.C., usually gave preference to the J version and in many instances blended the accounts inseparably. Nevertheless, what is left of this tradition, though it now lacks the organic unity of J, stands out sharply enough for us to get some idea of its distinctive character.

The Elohist tradition lacks the universal and dramatic scope that the Yahwist epic shows in the stories of primeval history and in the interpretation of the choice of Israel as the agent of divine blessing to the nations. Instead of beginning with the Creation, E starts with the call of Abraham, and from this point follows the general outline of the Yahwist epic through the rest of Genesis, Exodus, Numbers, and Joshua. On the whole, it lacks both the theological breadth and depth, and the literary artistry, of J (see pp. 165-187). And yet it must be said that the story of Abraham's sacrifice of Isaac (Gen. 22) is a moving portrayal of the test of faith—as fine as anything that can be found in the Yahwist epic. The reader follows this man of faith along the path which obedience constrained him to tread, and sees him undergo the supreme trial of faith as he prepares to sacrifice Isaac—his only son, whom he dearly loved, and the child of the promise in whom lay the destiny of Israel.[5]

More so than J, the Elohist tradition is closely bound to the popular tradition of the ancient Tribal Confederacy which is summed up in the little confession of faith in Deuteronomy 26:5-10. E is essentially an elaboration of the themes of this confession: the call of Israel, the deliverance from Egypt, the wandering in the wilderness, and the conquest of Canaan. These themes are developed in such a way as to heighten the significance of Yahweh's revelation in the Mosaic period, and to glorify the figure of Moses. As we have seen in our study of the Exodus (pp. 47-48), E tends to exaggerate the miracles performed by Moses. Moreover, in this tradition, Moses is put in a special class as the prophet *par excellence.* Although Yahweh is said to reveal himself indirectly to ordinary prophets through dreams and visions, with Moses it is different: "With him I speak mouth to mouth, clearly, and not in dark speech; and he beholds the form of Yahweh" (Num. 12:7-8).

The unique position of Moses accounts for a noteworthy feature of the E narrative. At first glance, this tradition seems to emphasize the great distance of God from men, in contrast to the Yahwist's sense of the immediacy of God's presence in the world. E is reluctant to bring God into direct relation to the world. For instance, in the daytime the "angel of Yahweh" (or "the angel of Elohim") called from heaven (Gen. 21:17; 22:11, 15), and in the nighttime God's revelation came in enigmatic visions or dreams that had to be interpreted (Gen. 15:1; 20:3, 6; 28:12 [Jacob's dream]; and especially the dreams of the Joseph stories). So, according to E, the divine approach to man was made indirectly or through an intermediary. In this way the narrator throws into prominence the special status of Moses, with whom Yahweh spoke "mouth to mouth," and who "beheld the form of Yahweh." The emphasis upon Moses' uniqueness is found at the end of the book of Deuteronomy (probably an E passage): "There has not arisen a prophet since in Israel like Moses, whom Yahweh knew face to face, none like him for all the signs and the wonders

---

[5] An excellent exposition of this chapter is found in Gerhard von Rad's commentary on Genesis [133], *in loco.*

which Yahweh sent him to do in the land of Egypt" (Deut. 34:10-12). Hosea was consistent with this tradition when he affirmed that "by a prophet Yahweh brought Israel up from Egypt and by a prophet he was preserved" (Hos. 12:13).

Thus the Elohist narrative rehearses the sacred history of Israel, with special emphasis upon the revelation to Moses and the disclosure of the sacred name at the time of the Exodus. But aside from distinctive traits, manifested by both E and J, these two traditions agree on the fundamental convictions which bound together the sister kingdoms, Israel and Judah, in the common worship of Yahweh. Sharing these convictions, Amos, a southerner, journeyed to Bethel to hurl his protest against the distortion and repudiation of the covenant heritage, and to recall Israel to the God who had revealed himself in the time of Moses.

THE HERDSMAN FROM TEKOA

We know very little about Amos, for the book that bears his name stresses the "word of Yahweh" spoken by the prophet, rather than biographical facts about the man himself. The heading of the book of Amos (1:1), which was added by a later editor, tells us that Amos came from among shepherds of Tekoa, a village lying a few miles south of Jerusalem, and that he was active during the reign of two contemporary kings, Uzziah of Judah and Jeroboam II of Israel. We could date his career more precisely if we were sure of the meaning of the chronological reference, "two years before the earthquake" (cf. Zech. 14:5). In any case, Amos was active in the Northern Kingdom during the height of the reign of Jeroboam II, some time before Jeroboam's death in 746 B.C. A date of about 750 B.C. fits the conditions reflected in the book.

A clearer picture of Amos' background is given in the prose passage found in Amos 7:10-15, which records the dramatic encounter between Amos and Amaziah, the chief priest of the Bethel temple—the royal sanctuary which Jeroboam I had once established as one of the national shrines of the Northern Kingdom. Here we are told that Amos was a native of Judah where he had been a herdsman and a "dresser of sycamore trees." (The latter expression refers to the puncturing of the fig-like fruit so that the insects that form on the inside may be released.) The appearance of this southerner in the Northern Kingdom points out that the division between Israel and Judah was primarily political, and that the two nations were actually bound together as *one* covenant people with a common religious tradition. Amaziah, assuming that Amos was just another professional prophet who earned his living by his religious trade (cf. I Sam. 9:8; I Kings 14:2; II Kings 8:8), warned him to return to Judah and there "eat bread"—that is, seek fees for his prophetic oracles. Amos' reply is not transparently clear, but probably the Hebrew should be translated: [6]

---

[6] Translation by the author. Some scholars argue that the reply should be translated in the past tense, "I was no prophet, nor a member of a prophetic guild. . . ," implying that Amos

I am not a prophet [*nabi'*],
Nor one of the sons of the prophets;
rather, I am a herdsman,
and a dresser of sycamore trees.
However, Yahweh took me from behind the flock,
and Yahweh said to me:
Go! Prophesy to my people Israel.

—AMOS 7:14-15

In denying that he was a *nabi'*, Amos did not necessarily intend to disparage the prophetic orders. He believed that Yahweh had raised up prophets to warn the people (2:11; 3:7). And, of course, he himself had striking affinities with such prophets as Nathan, Elijah, and Micaiah. Rather, he insisted that he did not understand himself to be a prophet like the professional prophets of the day. He was only a layman, so to speak, whose work had been interrupted by a divine commission which came to him with irresistible power (see 3:8). In other words, this was prophecy of such a different type that the usual terms for "prophet" did not adequately express his understanding of his task.

Amos is the first in an extraordinary series of prophets whose oracles have been left to us in written form. The prophets who preceded him, like Elijah and Elisha, are known to us only through the oral tradition in which the memory of their words and acts was preserved. With Amos, however, we have the actual "words which he saw," as the heading of the book puts it. The book of Amos is a compilation of little units or "oracles," spoken by the prophet on different occasions, and compiled by Amos himself or by the circle of the prophets who treasured them. Amos delivered these oracles in various situations over a fairly brief span of time, during his preaching at Bethel (7:13) and possibly at Samaria (4:1). He directed his message primarily to the Northern Kingdom, but, since he was a southerner, the sister kingdom of Judah was also in his mind (6:1, 2; 8:14). He was concerned about "the whole family which Yahweh brought out of Egypt" (3:1).

Yahweh's Sovereignty over the Nations

In reading the book of Amos, we must remember the political situation at the time. As we have seen, in the age of Jeroboam II Israel was able to flex her military muscles and expand because Syria had been weakened and the Assyrian lion was confined to his distant lair. But the whole picture was soon

---

was not a member of a prophetic order when Yahweh called him but that he is actually one now by his own admission. See H. H. Rowley, "Was Amos a Nabi?" [151]; this position is also taken by R. E. Clements, *Prophecy and Covenant* [137], pp. 35-38. It is possible to translate the Hebrew that way, although the interpretation curiously inverts the negative statement of vs. 14a into positive agreement with Amaziah. However, this translation makes Amos' statement somewhat awkward as a reply. Amaziah had accused Amos of being a prophet, or seer (*hózeh*), in the present, not in the past, and Amos' reply to this charge would appropriately express his *present* self-understanding.

to change with the rise to power of an Assyrian usurper, Tiglath-pileser III (c. 745-727 B.C.). With amazing speed and energy he resumed the Assyrian advance, which had been slowed to a halt shortly after Assyria's crippling attacks on Syria in 805 B.C., and soon he was marching into Palestine, conquering everything before him. These events are clearly reflected in the book of Hosea. But in the time of Amos, Assyria's threat to Israel was still only a little cloud on the horizon the size of a man's hand. With great seriousness, which differed radically from the complacency and self-confidence of Samaria and Judah, Amos saw that trouble was brewing—not just because of Assyria's imperial ambitions, but also because Yahweh was at work in the political arena. Amos shocked his contemporaries with the hard-hitting language of history—of the sword's brutalities, captivity, desolate cities, political collapse. His role as a prophet was to interpret these ominous events in which Yahweh was acting, just as Yahweh had acted in Israel's history in the past.

As the book of Amos opens, we hear that Yahweh is at work among the nations. In the section on "Yahweh's Judgment Against the Nations" (1:3-2:3) Amos may have adopted a cultic "execration" form which was used in the temple to pronounce divine judgment upon the enemies who threaten Yahweh's chosen people.[7] If so, Amos has given the form a completely new twist. The prophet arouses attention by throwing the spotlight of divine judgment upon the small nations that surrounded Israel: Syria, Philistia, Tyre, Ammon, Moab.[8] Amos affirms that Yahweh is sovereign over these enemies and rivals of Israel. Because of their war atrocities a divine fire will break out against their proud palaces and fortifications. But then came the surprise. What Israel least expected or wanted to hear was the prophetic announcement that the same fire would consume the people of Yahweh's choice because of the atrocities committed in peace and prosperity. Thus the climax of the series of divine judgments is the startling announcement that Yahweh's wrath is also directed against his own people, Israel (2:6-8).

It is just at this point, where Amos is affirming the universal sovereignty of Yahweh, that we become most aware of the covenant tradition in which the prophet was rooted. He did not claim to say anything new, although certainly he spoke with a disturbingly new accent. Echoing Israel's ancient confessional affirmation (Deut. 26:5-10; Josh. 24:2-13), he recalled to Israel the memory of events in which Yahweh had made himself known. Just as Americans reflect on the meaning of the world crisis in the light of the memories of their past, so Amos interpreted Israel's crisis in the light of a common memory of the events that had made Israel Yahweh's people with a special task and destiny. He

---

[7] See especially A. Bentzen, *The Ritual Background of Amos 1.2-2.16*, Oudtestamentische Studiën, VIII (Leiden: Brill, 1950), pp. 85-99.

[8] Scholars question the originality of three oracles—those against Phoenicia (1:9-10), Edom (1:11-12), and Judah (2:4-5)—because they are cast in a somewhat different form and lack a specific portrayal of impending punishment. The oracle against Judah, however, may have replaced an earlier oracle, for it is hard to believe that the prophet would have omitted his own home country.

summoned the people to remember the events of their sacred history: how Yahweh had brought them out of the land of Egypt, had guided them in the wilderness, had enabled them to conquer and possess the "land of the Amorites," and had raised up prophets and Nazirites to keep his people faithful to their God (2:9-11).[9] In short, the prophet was proclaiming the "word of the Lord" within the context of Israel's historical memories. According to his witness, God speaks in the present through the remembrance of the events of a sacred past.

Covenant Promises and Threats

This appeal to the past, and to the great convictions that were stamped indelibly on the national epics of both North and South (J and E), shows that Amos was a vigorous upholder of the Mosaic tradition. That the conclusions which Amos and the people drew from their common convictions were very different, however, is seen in their contrasting attitudes toward Israel's election by Yahweh. The keynote of Amos' prophecy is struck in 3:1-8, a passage which begins by recalling the crucial event of Israel's history: the Exodus from Egypt. It was through Yahweh's action in this event that Israel has become a community, a "whole family" bound together by the bonds of religious loyalty. Israel was "the people of Yahweh." But it was also in that event that Yahweh had bound himself to Israel in covenant relationship. "You only have I known of all the families of the earth. . . ." The verb "know" here refers to the closest kind of personal relationship, comparable to the intimate union between husband and wife.[10] Yahweh, then, was "the God of Israel." As we have seen before, this covenant formula—"Yahweh the God of Israel, and Israel the people of Yahweh"—is the very heart of the covenant faith.

This conviction, however, led the people to an attitude against which Amos protested with all his might. Reasoning from Yahweh's special calling, the people felt that they could go on to say: "Therefore, Yahweh will give us prosperity, victory, and prestige among the nations." After all, they thought, the covenant-renewal ceremonies included Yahweh's promises of blessing! So, flushed with the national revival and economic boom of the age of Jeroboam II, they anticipated the "Day of Yahweh." Apparently this festal Day was celebrated annually during the Fall covenant festival, that is, at the turn of the year. In popular belief this New Year's Day was an anticipation and foretaste of the great Day of Yahweh, a final climax of history when Yahweh would realize his covenant promises and crown his people with glory and honor. This attitude shows through in the oracle found in 5:18-29, where it is said that the people were "desiring" the Day of Yahweh, confident that it would be a day of "light"

---

[9] The Nazirites (literally, "separated ones") were men who took special vows of consecration to Yahweh. Their abstinence from wine was a protest against Canaanite culture in the spirit of Israel's wilderness tradition.

[10] It is used in this sense, for instance, in Gen. 4:1.

—that is, a time of victory and blessing. Religion went hand in hand with nationalism. Indeed, in that time there was a great religious revival. Amos paints vivid pictures of a people who were thronging to the shrines to worship (4:4-5; 5:21-23), although they could scarcely wait for the services to be over so that they could get back to their money-making (8:4-6). Over and over again they were saying to one another that they were not really on "the eve of destruction."

According to the Mosaic tradition as remembered in the north, however, the covenant did not give an unconditional guarantee for the future. The covenant rested upon a fundamental condition: "*If* you will obey my voice and keep my covenant you shall be my own possession among all peoples" (Ex. 19:5, E). It included blessings for obedience, to be sure, but it also included threats in the form of curses upon disobedience (see above, pp. 95-97). Standing in this covenant tradition, and aware of the serious threats of divine wrath which it held forth,[11] Amos reversed the popular logic of his time, saying: Yahweh has known only Israel of all the families of the earth; *therefore*, Israel will be punished for her iniquities. Israel's special calling, said Amos, does not entitle her to special privilege, but only to greater responsibility. In fact, he censured Israel far more heavily than any of the surrounding nations precisely *because* Israel alone had been called into a special relationship with God and had received, through her historical experience, the teaching concerning God's will. Having seen the light, however, she preferred the darkness to cover her evil doings. Consequently, said Amos, "the Day of Yahweh" would prove to be a day of destruction:

> Woe to you who desire the day of Yahweh!
>   Why would you have the day of Yahweh?
> It is darkness, and not light;
>   as if a man fled from a lion,
>   and a bear met him;
> or went into the house and leaned
>   with his hand against the wall,
>   and a serpent bit him.
> Is not the Day of Yahweh darkness and not light,
>   and gloom with no brightness in it?
>   —AMOS 5:18-20; *cf.* 8:9-10

Since Yahweh controlled the movement of all nations, he would raise one of them to be the instrument of divine judgment (6:14).

So critical was Amos of the belief in Israel's election that in one passage he seems to renounce the doctrine altogether:

---

[11] R. E. Clements (*Prophecy and Covenant* [137], pp. 39-44) has an excellent discussion of "the curse of the law" which was rooted in the covenant cult and, under Amos' prophetic interpretation, was transformed into a message of doom. He argues that Amos has taken the covenant-threat and radically reinterpreted it to mean not just the purging of sinners within Israel, but the end of Israel absolutely.

"Are you not like the Ethiopians to me,
  O people of Israel?" says Yahweh.
"Did I not bring up Israel from the land of Egypt,
  and the Philistines from Caphtor and the Syrians from Kir?"
                                                    —AMOS 9:7

Two of the peoples referred to, the Syrians and the Philistines, had been Israel's worst enemies; and yet, says the prophet, Yahweh—the Lord of all the nations —has brought these peoples to their national homelands, just as he brought Israel out of Egypt into Canaan. In this instance the prophet repudiated Israel's notion that Yahweh is a national god, to be mobilized for the service of Israel's interests. In so far as the doctrine of election meant that God serves Israel, rather than that Israel is called to serve God, it was in error.

The two oracles about divine election just considered (3:2 and 9:7) were undoubtedly delivered at different times. Amos was not a systematic theologian, but a prophet who delivered the word that needed to be heard at the moment. Even so, it is doubtful whether there is a fundamental inconsistency between the two statements. What Amos says in 9:7 is that Yahweh is surely active in the histories of other nations, even though they are not aware that he leads them and judges them. Although they suppose that they are "known" by other gods, they are actually embraced within Yahweh's sovereign control. But with Israel it is different. Israel has been "known" by Yahweh himself in the personal contact of the covenant. Through her historical experiences she has come to know who God is, and what he demands. Therefore, because she could not plead ignorance, she must stand under a more severe judgment than any other nation.

The Threat of Doom

Amos spoke in accents of doom. Scarcely a ray of light breaks through the dark clouds he saw on the horizon. So certain was he of the impending catastrophe, which actually took place a generation later when the Northern Kingdom was destroyed by Assyria, that he sang a funeral dirge over Israel. This little lamentation (*qinah*) appears in a special 3-2 qinah-meter, and imitates the dirges that mourners wailed at the scene of death:

Fállen, no móre to rise,
  is the vírgin Ísrael;
forsáken on her land,
  with none to upraise her.

                —AMOS 5:1-2

The same theme is struck in a series of five prophetic visions, in which everyday objects are transfigured with religious significance. Four of the visions are introduced by the words, "Yahweh showed me." In the first, Amos is shown a locust plague about to consume the crop after the king has taken the first mowing for his tax (7:1-3). In the second, he sees a supernatural fire that has already licked up the subterranean waters which irrigate the earth and is about to consume the soil upon which man lives (7:4-6). In both cases, Amos is sensitive to the plight of Israel and intercedes on behalf of the people. So far, there still seems to be hope for Israel. But not in the remaining visions. A plumb-line, used by carpenters for construction, becomes the sign of the destruction that Yahweh will accomplish in the midst of "his people, Israel" (7:7-9). A basket of summer fruit (*qáyitz*), by a play on words, becomes a sign that "the end [*qetz*] has come upon my people Israel" (8:1-3). And finally a vision of Yahweh destroying the worshipers in the Temple (which reminds us of Jehu's purge of the Baal worshipers) fades into the judgment of Yahweh from which there is no escape, whether in the heights or the depths (9:1-4).[12] The last clearly authentic word in the book of Amos is one of utter doom:

> Behold, the eyes of Yahweh God
>   are upon the sinful kingdom,
> and I will destroy it from the
>   surface of the ground.[13]
>   —AMOS 9:8

This final prediction of the end of Israel had nothing to do with political fatalism. True, from a purely military point of view, Israel had no more chance of withstanding the Assyrian colossus than, say, Finland would have against Russia. But Amos was not thinking of comparative military strength. Nor did his message of doom spring from social despair, for the age of Jeroboam II was one of great political confidence. It rested solely on his conviction that although Israel seemed healthy outwardly, inwardly she was diseased with a malignant cancer. Israel was not merely guilty of social crimes; she stood accused of unfaithfulness to her calling as the people of Yahweh. In the economy of God, such a society could not long endure.

Symptoms of Sickness

To Amos this unfaithfulness was shockingly evident in the evils of the flourishing urban society. He pointed out the social injustices of his day with

---

[12] Some scholars (e.g., Gerhard von Rad, *Theology*, II [80], pp. 131-132) believe that the visions reflect the call of the prophet. After the second vision, he comes to sense the inevitability of divine judgment, and so he goes to Bethel, perhaps in time for the Autumn Festival. The trouble with this interpretation is that none of the visions mentions a summons to Amos, as we would expect in a "call." See further A. S. Kapelrud, *Central Ideas in Amos* [149], pp. 14-16.

[13] Verse 9:8 (beginning with "except I will not utterly destroy") to verse 10, which mitigates the force of Amos' word of doom, is usually regarded as a later addition. The conclusion of the book (9:11-15), which refers to the "fallen booth of David"—that is, the fall of the Davidic dynasty—comes from a later time. (See p. 379.)

such severity that Amaziah regarded his message as high treason and insisted that "the land is not able to bear all his words" (7:10). Wealthy merchants, lusting for economic power, were ruthlessly trampling on the heads of the poor and defenseless. Public leaders, reveling in luxury and corrupted by indulgence, were lying in beds of ease—unconcerned over "the ruin of Joseph" (6:1-7). The sophisticated ladies, whom Amos—in the rough language of a herdsman—compares to the fat, sleek cows of Bashan, were selfishly urging their husbands on. Law courts were used to serve the vested interests of the commercial class. Religion had no word of protest against the inhumanities that were being perpetrated in the very shadow of the temples at Bethel, Gilgal, Dan, and Samaria. To Amos, all these things were symptoms of a deep "sickness unto death": Israel's estrangement from Yahweh and the surrender of her covenant calling. Boldly, the prophet declared that Yahweh "hates," "despises," "abhors" the whole scene:

> Take away from me the noise of your songs;
>   to the melody of your harps I will not listen.
> But let justice roll down like waters,
>   and righteousness like an ever-flowing stream.
>   —AMOS 5:23-24

This passage shows us that Amos was opposed to the forms in which men acted out their worship of God, and other passages strengthen this impression. Turning back to the Mosaic period, Amos asks the rhetorical question (which seems to call for a negative answer): "Did you bring to me sacrifices and offerings the forty years in the wilderness, O house of Israel?" (5:25). He is merciless in his attack on the shrines, especially the royal shrine of Jeroboam II at Bethel (3:14; 7:7-9, 10-17; 9:1). It is very doubtful, however, that he intended a wholesale abolition of the system of worship. Rather, Amos was probably demanding that the cult be purified, for it had become so contaminated by pagan thought and practice that the people had become indifferent to the true worship of Yahweh and the demands of his *torah*. The prophet's standard—Yahweh's revelation in the Mosaic period—demanded that everything be swept away that did not conform to the proper worship of Yahweh. Amos felt that the existing cult was the source of Israel's sickness, and that divine surgery had to be applied radically to the source of the cancerous corruption: the temples and their system of worship (see the vision in 9:1). For the way men worship God, and their theological convictions concerning him, determine the attitudes and the relationships of the community.

A Call to Repentance

And yet the divine purpose was not that of mere destruction. Yahweh was active in the midst of his people, said Amos, in order that Israel might turn from her evil ways and "return" to Yahweh. This is the meaning of repentance:

it is a return (*teshubah*) to him who is the source of Israel's life, a redirection of the will in response to the jealous claim that Yahweh makes upon men's allegiance. In a striking series of oracles, each of which ends with the refrain "yet you did not return to me," Amos affirms that repentance had been the divine purpose behind the calamities that had befallen Israel (4:6-12). But Yahweh had failed in his attempts, for Israel was stubbornly set in her rebellious ways. The prophet warns that even more terrible events could be expected in the near future:

> Therefore thus I will do to you, O Israel;
>   because I will do this to you,
>   prepare to meet your God, O Israel!
>   —AMOS 4:12

Amos did not specify when or where this rendezvous would take place, but he was sure that it would take place soon, and in the arena of history. The end of Israel would be a great tragedy, but it would be a *meaningful* tragedy, and Israel herself would be responsible for it. Men can choose whom or what they will serve, but they cannot escape the consequences of their choice.

The purpose of Amos' preaching, then, was to give men an opportunity for the reformation and reorientation of their lives. He proclaimed what Yahweh was about to do in the the future in order to show how urgent it was to face the demand for covenant renewal—and face it now. Tomorrow, he said, might be too late; *today* is the time for decision, repentance, and change. The end is at hand! Therefore, "seek Yahweh and live"—this was his appeal as the approaching judgment thundered nearer and nearer.

There was little chance, however, that the people of Israel, enslaved by habit and blinded by complacency, would listen to Amos and mend their ways. But the prophet was no fatalist. He admitted that there was a slim possibility that a few (a remnant) might take his warnings to heart and "return" to Yahweh:

> Seek good, and not evil,
>   that you may live;
> and so Yahweh, the God of hosts, will be with you,
>   as you have said.
> Hate evil, and love good,
>   and establish justice in the gate;
> it may be that Yahweh, the God of hosts,
>   will be gracious to the remnant of Joseph.
>   —AMOS 5:14-15

This, however, was a "maybe," which rested on the unpredictable response of the people and, above all, on the incalculable grace of God.

Here is a slight indication that the message of doom was not Yahweh's last word, as later prophets recognized more clearly. In making his heavy emphasis upon doom, Amos leaned over backward to counteract the false optimism of his time. Later on, when the desperate political situation drove men to fanaticism or despair, the prophets were to proclaim a message of hope. But the age of Jeroboam II did not need to hear the divine promise, for the people already believed that "God is with us" (5:14).[14] What they needed to hear was the word of divine judgment that would shatter their complacency and false security. Then, perhaps, they would understand that the promise rests, not on the political and economic fortunes of men, but on the gracious dealings of God with his people.

THE PROPHECY OF HOSEA

Now let us take up the narrative in II Kings where we left off, and follow the thread of the history of the Northern Kingdom (II Kings 15-17). After the death of Jeroboam II in 746 B.C. came catastrophe. Shortly afterward (745 B.C.), Tiglath-pileser III, whose official throne-name was Pulu, and who is referred to as Pul in the biblical account, seized the Assyrian throne. He awakened Assyria from fifty years of lethargy and set a military program in motion that led ultimately to her conquest of Egypt. Under a line of vigorous rulers, Assyria moved toward a goal that had been in the mind of her kings from the time of the thirteenth century: the domination of the Fertile Crescent, the lifeline of the ancient world.

Tiglath-pileser lost no time in setting out on the path of conquest. After conquering Babylonia and incorporating it into his empire, he marched toward the Mediterranean and sent terror through all of Syria and Palestine. One reason for fear was his introduction of a new military policy, shrewdly calculated to crush nationalism and to hold captive countries firmly in control. This was the policy of uprooting conquered populations from their homeland and exiling them to remote parts of the Assyrian empire. Their land was resettled by foreign colonists and was incorporated into the system of Assyrian provinces. Israel, like other small nations, was destined to learn by bitter experience the meaning of the word "exile."

Neither Israel nor Judah could escape involvement in these political events, although Judah—as we shall see in the next chapter—managed to maintain far greater stability than the Northern Kingdom. Israel's political anxiety was reflected in the confused domestic events described briefly in II Kings with the usual Deuteronomic flourishes. Zechariah, the last king of the Jehu dynasty, was murdered after only six months on the throne. His assassin, Shallum, was struck down by Menahem after one month's reign, and cities that resisted this latest usurper were treated with savage ferocity. Menahem, after ten years of

---

[14] This is the literal meaning of Immanuel—the name that the prophet Isaiah later introduced (see pp. 272-274).

TIGLATH-PILESER III *recorded many of his activities in stone bas-reliefs such as this double-decker from the Assyrian monarch's palace at Calah. According to an inscription on the relief, the top portion shows the Assyrian deportation of the inhabitants from Astartu, the fortified hilltop city (east of the Sea of Galilee) called Ashtaroth in the Bible. In the bottom portion, Tiglath-Pileser rides in his royal chariot, accompanied by his driver and an umbrella-holding attendant; guards lead the horses.*

rule purchased by appeasement of Assyria, died in his bed, but his son Pekahiah held out for only two years before he fell victim to the conspiracy of Pekah, the army commander. Pekah held the throne for a few precarious years, only to be knifed by Hoshea.[15] And Hoshea, the last king of Israel, died in chains. (See Chronological Chart 6, p. 244.) Never before in the history of the Northern Kingdom had there been such a tangle of murder and intrigue. Hosea vividly describes the sorry situation:

> On the day of our king the princes became sick
>   with the heat of wine;
>   he stretched out his hand with mockers.
> For like an oven their hearts burn with intrigue;
>   all night their anger smolders;
>   in the morning it blazes like a flaming fire.
> All of them are hot as an oven,
>   and they devour their rulers.
> All their kings have fallen;
>   and none of them calls upon me.
>   —HOSEA 7:5-7 (see all of 6:11-7:7)

It was during the reign of Menahem (c. 745-738 B.C.) that Israel courted Assyrian favor. This was politically expedient, for in the very year that Menahem usurped the throne, Tiglath-pileser's armies began to invade the land. Menahem had to surrender the northern part of his kingdom (Galilee) and, in addition, he paid a heavy tribute to the Assyrian monarch "that he might

---

[15] According to II Kings 15:27, Pekah reigned for twenty years, but this figure is too high, as historians point out, for Samaria's fall occurred less than twenty years after the beginning of his reign. See John Bright, *History of Israel* [40], p. 256, footnote 8.

THE ASSYRIAN EMPIRE

CASPIAN SEA

BLACK SEA

MEDIA

URARTU

L.URMIAH

L.VAN

ELAM

Susa○

PERSIAN GULF

ASSYRIA

MESOPOTAMIA

Dur Sharrukin
(Khorsabad)
Asshur○
Nineveh○

BABYLONIA

TIGRIS R.

Nippur○

Babylon○

EUPHRATES R.

Ur○

PROBABLE
ANCIENT
SHORELINE

ARABIA

Carchemish○

Arpad○

Hamath○
Qarqar?

ARAM (SYRIA)

Damascus○

GILEAD

Samaria○
Bethel○
Jerusalem○
JUDAH

AMMON

MOAB

DEAD SEA

EDOM

Bozrah○

Elath○

CILICIA

CYPRUS
(KITTIM)

Arvad○
(ISLAND)

Byblos○
Tyre○

ISRAEL PHOENICIA

Ashdod○
Lachish○

MEDITERRANEAN SEA

AFTER ISAIAH'S
TIME, THE EMPIRE
EXTENDED
INTO EGYPT

Memphis○

EGYPT

help him to confirm his hold of the royal power" (II Kings 15:19). In his annals, Tiglath-pileser recorded that he received tribute from "Menahem of Samaria," along with gifts from numerous other peoples.[16] Menahem's policy of appeasement succeeded for the time being and the Assyrians marched away, allowing the Israelite king to keep his throne. But his capitulation was highly unpopular, for the wealthy class was heavily taxed to pay for it and the fires of resentment and revolt were fanned even more briskly. But before we consider the attempts to throw off the Assyrian yoke, let us turn to the prophet Hosea.

Hosea's Optimism of Grace

Hosea's prophetic career overlapped two eras: the last part of the age of Jeroboam II and the period of political instability that followed his death in 746 B.C. Hosea's earliest prophecy, found in Hosea 1-3, was apparently delivered in the very year of Jeroboam's death, for according to these chapters the dynasty of Jehu was still in existence (see 1:4). The heading of the book (1:1), which in its present form comes from a later Judean editor, states that Hosea prophesied "in the days of Jeroboam," and adds that his career embraced the reigns of four Judean kings, the last being Hezekiah (c. 715-687 B.C.). The latter statement is probably inaccurate, for it is doubtful whether Hosea was prophesying as late as the fall of the Northern Kingdom in 721 B.C. His career lasted for at least ten years after the death of Jeroboam, however, for the second major section of the book (chapters 4-14) reflects the turbulent conditions of

---

[16] See Pritchard, *Ancient Near Eastern Texts*, p. 283.

CHRONOLOGICAL CHART 5

B.C.	EGYPT	THE DIVIDED MONARCHY		ASSYRIA
		JUDAH	ISRAEL	
850	Decline	Athaliah, c. 842-837 Joash, c. 837-800 Amaziah, c. 800-783 Uzziah (Azariah), c. 783-742	*Jehu Dynasty:* Jehu, c. 842-815 Joahaz, c. 815-801 Jehoash, c. 801-786 Jeroboam II, c. 786-746 (Amos, c. 750) (Hosea, c. 745) Zechariah (6 mos.)	Shalmaneser III, c. 859-824 (Jehu pays tribute, 841) Shamshi-Adad V, c. 824-811 Adad-nirari III, c. 811-783 *Decline* Tiglath-pileser
c. 750			c. 745	III, c. 745-727

that period. According to these chapters, the dynasty of Jehu had fallen; kings followed one another in rapid succession as "the land devours its rulers"; and the country was filled with confusion, demoralization, and anxiety because of international developments.

Like the book of Amos, the book of Hosea is a compilation of little oracles delivered at different times and linked together in their present arrangement either by the prophet himself or by his disciples. Consequently, the same prophetic themes are repeated over and over again, with variations from situation to situation. The text has not been preserved as well as that of Amos. In chapters 4-14 the text is often so corrupt that the translator must turn to other ancient versions or resort to conjecture (see the footnotes of the Revised Standard Version). Moreover, several additions have been made to Hosea's oracles, the most obvious of which is the concluding exhortation in 14:9.

Hosea, like Amos, was a prophet of doom. But unlike Amos, who announced that the Day of Yahweh would be a day of pitch-darkness, Hosea balanced the word of judgment with the promise of restoration and renewal. He, too, saw the coming of the Day of Darkness, but he proclaimed that despite the total eclipse the sun was still shining. Hosea's qualified optimism was not due to any improvement in the political or religious situation since the time of Amos a few years earlier, for actually affairs had gone from bad to worse in the Northern Kingdom. Hosea insisted that Israel was prematurely senile and approaching death—"grey hairs" were scattered upon Ephraim (7:8-9). His message was an "optimism of grace," since Israel's hope was grounded solely in the constancy of Yahweh's love for his people. This was made clear to Hosea by his marriage experience, which became a "living parable" of the relation between Yahweh and Israel.

Hosea's Marriage

The key to the interpretation of Hosea's message is the story of his marriage with Gomer. This story, however, which is found in the first three chapters of the book of Hosea, presents one of the most difficult problems in Old Testament studies. For one thing, Hosea was not primarily interested in giving biographical data. Certainly he did not write a "true confession" after the manner of modern love romances. As in the case of Amos, the man recedes behind the word he proclaims. He gives only enough details about his marriage to symbolize the story of Yahweh's relation to Israel, which occupies the center of his attention.

What was the marital experience on which the prophet based his parable? Notice that there are different types of material in chapters 1-3: chapter 1 is written in the third person in the style of "biography," and chapter 3 is written in the first person in the style of "autobiography." The problem is this: Do chapters 1 and 3 represent a sequence of events in the prophet's experience with one woman, Gomer? Since the unnamed woman of chapter 3 is not explicitly identified with Gomer, some scholars think that the autobiographical chapter tells of Hosea's relation to another woman.

The balance of probability is on the side of the view that these chapters recount Hosea's experience with a single woman. If another woman were introduced in chapter 3, we would expect more explicit mention of it. We cannot escape the impression that the language of verses 1 and 2 takes it for granted that the woman has already been mentioned. Moreover, the analogy with Israel (3:1b) suggests that the prophet is to be reconciled with the estranged Gomer, just as Yahweh takes back the same Israel he has rejected. In chapter 1 the theme is the faithlessness of Israel; in chapter 3 it is the steadfastness of Yahweh's love in the face of infidelity. These themes are not based on one event of Hosea's life, but on a sequence of events in his relation with Gomer.

Forgetting for a moment the troublesome second verse of chapter 1, we may reconstruct the events as follows: In good faith, Hosea married a wife who bore him three children. Just as Isaiah gave symbolic names to his children (Is. 7:3; 8:3), so Hosea gave significant names to his, in order that they might be "walking signs" of Yahweh's word to Israel. The first son was named Jezreel, in recollection of the place where Jehu carried out his terrible blood purge (II Kings 9)—a sign that "in a little while" Yahweh would punish the house of Jehu for those monstrous atrocities. The second child, a daughter, was named "Not-pitied," a symbol that Yahweh's patience with Israel had been exhausted. And the third child, a son, was called "Not-my-people," a sign that Yahweh had dissolved the covenant bond and rejected his people. Then the prophet's attention shifted from the children to their mother, who had proved unfaithful to the marriage bond (as suggested in 2:2). Reading between the lines (for at this point we leave the biographical narrative and turn to the prophetic sermon in chapter 2 about Yahweh's rejection of his wife, the mother of harlotrous children), we must assume that Hosea divorced Gomer because of her unfaithfulness (2:2). But despite her disloyalty, Hosea was ready to go beyond the law and forgive. So, in chapter 3, we read that Hosea ransomed her and, after a period of discipline, restored her as his wife.

Hosea 1:2, then, which is a kind of second introduction, is the prophet's later interpretation of what had happened. When he married Gomer she was not yet a harlot, although—looking at the matter in retrospect—she was clearly destined to become one. Since in the prophetic view a divine purpose was discernible in all of life's experiences, Hosea insisted that all this had happened at Yahweh's command. He was ordered to take "a wife of harlotry and have children of harlotry." And once he had reflected on Israel's relation to Yahweh, the meaning of his own marriage became clear: "for the land commits great harlotry by forsaking Yahweh."

Since Hosea's only reason for mentioning his private life was to draw a living analogy of Yahweh's covenant with Israel, let us turn to the story of the "marriage" between Yahweh and Israel.

The Broken Covenant

No prophet was more profoundly aware of the Mosaic past than was Hosea. The memory of the Exodus, the sojourn in the wilderness, the covenant at Horeb, and the conquest of Canaan were always in his mind as he interpreted the events and conditions of his time. Since Hosea was a native of the Northern Kingdom, chances are that he was nurtured in the northern cycle of tradition represented in the Elohist epic. Notice that the book of Hosea, like the E tradition, lacks the broad perspective of Amos (and J). But what it lacks in breadth is more than made up by its depth of understanding.

To the prophet Hosea, one fact stood out from Israel's history: Yahweh's choice of Israel, which was most clear in the Exodus. In emphasizing the central importance of the Exodus, Hosea remembered a whole complex of events, including the flight from Egypt and the experiences of the wilderness, as a single event in which Yahweh revealed himself and constituted Israel as his people. Israel's God was known through this event: "I am Yahweh from the land of Egypt" (12:9; 13:4-5). And Israel could understand what it means to be God's people by remembering this same event. For the Exodus was the sign of God's decision to make Israel his people. Yahweh had *called* his son out of Egypt (11:1), and he had *found* Israel like grapes in the wilderness (9:10). This decisive historical event, stamped indelibly upon the Israelite memory, was the basis of the covenant relationship between God and people.

Hosea was the first Israelite prophet to interpret the covenant by comparing it with marriage. To be sure, the conception of sacred marriage was well known in antiquity. Mythological dramas in the fertility religions portrayed the loves and marriages of the gods and the goddesses, and in Canaanite temples the sacred marriage was enacted through ritual prostitution (see pp. 102-104). In a day when sex was glorified by nature religions, Hosea's use of the image of sacred marriage was a daring reinterpretation of Israel's faith. But the way Hosea used the comparison was completely new. Instead of explaining the divine marriage by referring to the cycles of nature, he spoke of a historical marriage made in the wilderness between God and a people. And the meaning of this marriage was disclosed to him, not by reflecting on the marriage of a god and a goddess, but by a deep understanding of his own relationship to Gomer.

Just as Gomer played the harlot, so Israel had broken the covenant. According to Hosea, this was the real historical tragedy, and all the contemporary troubles of Israel were only symptoms of it. The "wife" whom Yahweh had chosen and betrothed to himself had become a whore. A "spirit of harlotry" had inflamed the people, and they had become estranged from their God (4:12). Hosea's critique of Israel's society went far deeper than a mere condemnation of social immorality, political confusion, or religious formalism. He was concerned with men's motives, with the devotion of the heart, with the things in which men place their trust. Hence, echoing the criticism made by leaders of the old Tribal

Confederacy (see pp. 122-126), he condemned the institution of the monarchy, seeing in it a symptom of a harlotrous spirit. Saul's home-town of Gibeah and his coronation at Gilgal were evidences of Israel's determination to reject Yahweh as king (8:4; 9:15; 10:3, 9). The consequences of Israel's betrayal of the covenant were to be seen in the regicides (7:3-7), the feverish foreign policy aimed at courting Egypt or Assyria (7:11), and the foolish reliance upon arms and fortifications (8:14). Stubborn and determined, Israel had insisted on being "like the nations," and as a result she was "swallowed up" among the nations (8:8) and "strangers" were consuming her strength (7:8-9).

This harlotrous spirit had led the people into a false and idolatrous religion. Like the other great prophets, Hosea knew that religion was not necessarily a good thing, for it could be a way of betraying God, a manifestation of sin. In Hosea's time, popular religion, corrupted by the fertility cult of Canaan, provided a means of obtaining the good things of nature and tethering God to human interests. People thronged to the temples, not to acknowledge gratefully their utter dependence upon the God who had brought them out of Egypt, but to "get something out of religion"—harmony, security, prosperity, and peace. The priests and the prophets, exploiting the upsurge of religious interest, actually contributed to Israel's harlotry. Priests were "feeding on the sin" of Yahweh's people (4:7-10).

Israel's fidelity, then, was that of a fickle woman. It lacked the steadfastness, the trustworthiness of true covenant love. In Hosea's native language, Israel lacked *hésed*. This word is exceedingly difficult to render into English. (The Revised Standard Version usually translates it "steadfast love.") It is a covenant word that refers to the faithfulness or loyal love that binds two parties together in covenant. When a person shows *hésed* to another, he is not motivated merely by legal obligation but by an inner loyalty which arises out of the relationship itself. Such covenant love has the quality of constancy, firmness, steadfastness. In Hosea's vivid figure, Israel's *hésed* was like a transient morning cloud, or like the morning dew that evaporates quickly (6:4). Hence Yahweh scorned the existing forms of worship:

> For I desire steadfast love and not sacrifice,
>> the knowledge of God, rather than burnt offerings.
>>> —HOSEA 6:6

We probably should not press Hosea's words to mean that he was opposed to formal worship. But clearly he was opposed to forms that were devoid of the spirit of true faithfulness to the God of the covenant. Jesus twice asked his hearers to go and reread Hosea 6:6 when he was accused of breaking the formal rules of orthodoxy (cf. Matt. 9:13 and 12:7).

The Inner Flaw

In the key sentence Hosea 6:6, Hosea draws a poetic parallel between two important words. The first is *hésed*, which we have just mentioned. The second term, which overlaps in meaning, is "the knowledge of God." Hosea insisted that Israel did not *know* God (see 4:1, 6, 11), and that this deficiency was the root of her problem. Here we must be on guard against reading into the book of Hosea modern conceptions of knowledge. Hosea was speaking about a kind of knowledge that is intrinsic to the covenant relationship: a knowing God which is the response to being known (chosen) by him (Amos 3:2; Hos. 13:5). On the human side such knowledge has two aspects. On the one hand, this is a *theological* knowledge which can be taught by parents in the home (Deut. 6:20-25) or by cultic officials at the sanctuaries, especially at the covenant-renewal festivals. It is the knowledge of who God is (Hos. 13:4), what he has done for Israel, and what he requires of his people—in short, a knowledge of the covenant tradition.[17] When this understanding is lacking, the people turn to strange gods and break the laws of the covenant that are epitomized in the Ten Commandments.[18] Hosea lays the blame for this state of affairs at the door of the priests and prophets, whose duty it was to instruct the people in what the covenant means (4:5-6). On the other hand, this is a knowledge which includes the *will* as well as the mind. Hosea was talking about the knowledge of the heart [19]—that is, the response of the *whole person* to God's love. To know Yahweh means to respond to the claim he makes upon one's devotion, to obey his will in society where the poor and needy cry for help (see Jer. 22:16). So in observing that Israel lacked knowledge of God, Hosea affirmed that the people did not *acknowledge* God. The covenant was broken. Israel, the "wife," was estranged from her "husband."

> For the spirit of harlotry is within them,
> and they know not Yahweh.
> —HOSEA 5:4

In the end, when God's purpose wins out, the covenant will be restored, and then Israel will "know Yahweh" (2:20).[20]

Not only did Hosea expose the inner motives of Israel's contemporary life, but he also saw clearly that behind Israel's infidelity lay a pattern of thought and action that had been deeply ingrained in the people ever since their entrance into Canaan. In earlier chapters, we have described the transition from

---

[17] This theological dimension has been stressed by H. W. Wolff, " 'Wissen um Gott' bei Hosea als Urform von Theologie," in *Evangelische Theologie*, XII (1953), pp. 533-551. See also the discussion by James M. Ward in *Hosea* [154], in connection with Hosea 4.

[18] The Decalog is specifically referred to in 4:2 (prohibitions against lying, killing, stealing, and adultery). The whole passage (4:1-10) is cast in the form of a legal controversy or lawsuit, in which one covenant partner accuses the other for violation of the covenant. On this form see, for instance, Herbert B. Huffmon, "The Covenant Lawsuit in the Prophets," in *Journal of Biblical Literature*, LXXVIII (1959), pp. 285-295; also B. Gemser, "The *Rib*- or Controversy- Pattern in Hebrew Mentality" [223], pp. 120-137.

[19] In Hebrew psychology the heart inseparably incorporates thinking and willing.

[20] In the last days, according to Jeremiah's prophecy of the "new covenant" (Jer. 31:31-34), knowledge of Yahweh will come from the heart, not from teaching (see pp. 351-354).

semi-nomadic life of the desert to the agricultural life of Canaan—a transition that accentuated the problem of the relation between faith and culture. According to Hosea, Yahweh in the wilderness had entered into covenant with a bride who was destined to prove unfaithful. Indeed, the "honeymoon" in the wilderness, the time of Israel's fidelity, was all too brief. No sooner had Israel set foot on the soil of Canaan than she began to deck herself alluringly in a harlot's attire and to pursue her "lovers," the nature gods of Canaan who promised the "harlot's hire" of prosperity and security. This is the theme of the prophetic sermon in Hosea 2. The infiltration of Baal worship had taken place so slowly and subtly through the years that in popular religion Yahweh and Baal had become identified. No longer did the people see the difference between the worship of the god of fertility and the worship of the God of history! Israel did not realize that the very gifts she sought from the Baal had been mercifully provided by the God who had brought her up out of the land of Egypt!

So, from the very first, Israel's history was a sordid and shameful story of the betrayal of Yahweh's love. Throughout the years she had pursued the devices and desires of her own heart, and now she was caught in the coils of a sinful history from which she could not extricate herself. Israel was in bondage to habitual ways of thinking and to established patterns of behavior. "Their deeds," said Hosea, "do not permit them to return to their God" (5:4). So enslaved were the people to false loyalties that it was useless to appeal to them: "Ephraim is joined to idols, let him alone" (4:17). Every aspect of Israel's corporate life—politics, economics, religion—was tainted with the ideology of a false allegiance, a misdirected will, a vicious style of behavior. We might liken the situation to the plight of a person who is so completely enslaved by a habitual way of thinking and living that he lacks both the imagination and the will-power to change himself. And just as a great crisis in an individual's life sometimes makes possible a new beginning, so Hosea believed that the historical catastrophe that was about to befall the nation was intended by God as an opportunity for Israel to recover her health.

The Triumph of Love

Like Amos, Hosea spoke in accents of terrible doom as he described the threat from Assyria. The three children born to Gomer were given names that signified Yahweh's judgment, and the youngest child in particular stood for Yahweh's abandonment of his people. Moreover, the prophetic sermon in chapter 2 begins with Yahweh's announcement of divorce from Israel, the harlotrous mother of harlotrous children: "She is not my wife, and I am not her husband." Elsewhere, even stronger, fiercer language is used. Yahweh comes to "destroy" his people (13:9). Like a wild animal, he pounces on his prey (5:14; 13:7-8); like a moth or dry rot, he attacks his people (5:12). Indeed, the prophet even says that Yahweh will forget his people (4:6), that he will abandon them when they try to seek him (5:6), and that he will love them no more (9:15). A faithless people deserves a treatment no better than Gomer deserved: to be cast off.

Since the Hebrew mind expressed itself in concrete rather than abstract terms, we must try to understand the actual meaning of this language, even though some of it is offensive to modern taste. Hosea was speaking of God's judgment in the affairs of history. In one sense, the impending calamity would be the consequence of Israel's actions—her foolish determination to be a nation like other nations and to adopt the culture of the Fertile Crescent. "They sow the wind, and they shall reap the whirlwind" (8:7). But the prophets felt that God did more than just ordain moral laws which, like the law of gravity, men might break at their own risk. Rather, they believed that *God himself* was acting in the sphere of history, meeting his people in events, and using agencies (like Assyria) to bring his people to their senses. Like a New Testament writer, they knew that "it is a terrible thing to fall into the hands of the living God" (Hebrews 10:31). The absolute sovereignty of God in human affairs, on the one hand, and the full responsibility of men on the other, are equally important tenets of prophetic faith, even though the paradox may be difficult for us to grasp.

The deepest note struck in the book of Hosea is the proclamation that God's "wrath" or judgment is redemptive. God's purpose is not to destroy, but to heal. Through historical crises that shake the very foundations of human self-suffi-ciency, Yahweh acts to free his people from their enslavement to false alle-giances and to restore them to freedom in the covenant loyalty. Just as Hosea's love was greater and deeper than Gomer's infidelity, so Yahweh's love for Israel is truly steadfast. It is a divine love that will not let his people go, despite their fickleness and harlotry. His "wrath" is not capricious, vindictive, and destruc-tive; it is the expression of a holy love which seeks to break the chains of Israel's bondage and to emancipate her for a new life, a new covenant. According to Hosea, this new freedom will come only when God himself acts to destroy the idols in which Israel places her trust so that his "wife" may stand naked and humiliated in the presence of her lovers (see 2:2-13). Then Israel will have the opportunity to *be Israel*, to be the people of the covenant, living in grateful dependence upon the God who redeemed her from Egypt and who constantly supplies her needs in the land of Canaan.

As a Father Disciplines His Son

The holiness of Yahweh's love, which includes both judgment and mercy, is magnificently portrayed in Hosea 11, where the figure changes from the relationship between husband and wife to the relationship between father and son. There we read (verses 1-4) that Israel, Yahweh's "son" (see Ex. 4:22-23), has been called into being by divine love. The motive of Yahweh's love is behind and within Israel's history, giving meaning and purpose to everything:

> When Israel was a child, I loved him,
>   and out of Egypt I called my son.
>   —HOSEA 11:1

Like a father, Yahweh had taught his son how to walk, had taken him up tenderly in his arms, and gathered him in compassionate embrace. (In verse 4, the figure suddenly shifts to that of a man who gently leads and cares for an animal.) The theme of the next section (verses 5-7) is that Yahweh's patience is exhausted in dealing with his rebellious people. Israel must be punished by Egypt or Assyria, the very nations to whom they were turning for political salvation. But divine judgment is not the last word, as we read in the next section (verses 8-9). For even in the hour of catastrophe Yahweh does not abandon his people, nor does his love for them cease. It is not his will that Israel be destroyed as Admah and Zeboim were leveled during the holocaust of Sodom and Gomorrah (cf. Gen. 19:24-25; Deut. 29:23). Rather, the purpose behind Yahweh's judgment is love, like that of a parent who lovingly disciplines a wayward child. These verses passionately describe a struggle, as it were, within the heart of God—a struggle that doubtless reflects the agony of Hosea's experience with Gomer. But the triumph is on the side of the love that will not let Israel go. In the last analysis, mere words fail to plumb the depths of this holy love:

> for I am God and not man,
>   the Holy One in your midst,
>   and I will not come to destroy.
>   —HOSEA 11:9b

To us, the "wrath" and the "love" of God may seem contradictory, but to Hosea God's love surpasses human understanding. It has both the dark side of judgment and the promise of hope and renewal (see verses 10-11). Israel would learn, as did the poet Francis Thompson, that her gloom after all was but "the shadow of His Hand outstretched caressingly." [21]

The Renewal of the Covenant

Let us return, now, to the story of Gomer in Hosea 3. Hosea continued to love his wife even though she proved unfaithful. In this experience, Hosea found an analogy of the relation between Yahweh and Israel, for Yahweh too steadfastly loved his people even though they turned to other gods (3:1). (The "cakes of raisins" refers to food used in the Baal fertility cult.) So Hosea ransomed her and restored her unto himself, although he disciplined her "for many days." Israel too had to go through a period of discipline and quarantine

---

[21] See "The Hound of Heaven."

—"without king or prince, without sacrifice or pillar, without ephod or teraphim" (3:4). The deprivation would be primarily political and religious, the very areas that had been corroded by the culture of Canaan. Then, after "many days" of cleansing and purgation, there would be a new beginning, a new relationship. For Israel would return (or "repent") and seek Yahweh her God.[22]

This theme of discipline through suffering is developed at great length in Chapter 2. In vivid language Hosea speaks of the exposure of Israel's harlotry and the frustration of her attempts to pursue her "lovers." But Yahweh's purpose throughout is to reconcile his faithless people unto himself:

> Therefore, behold, I will allure her,
>   and bring her into the wilderness,
>   and speak tenderly to her.
> And there I will give her her vineyards,
>   and make the valley of Achor a door of hope.
> And there she shall answer as in the days of her youth,
>   as at the time when she came out of the land of Egypt.
>   —HOSEA 2:14-15

Just as Israel's life had been given to her in the ancient wilderness, so it will be in the wilderness—away from all the temptations of culture—that her life will be renewed. The Valley of Achor probably was located in the wilderness of Judah, on a plateau overlooking the Dead Sea. At its eastern rim, the river Qumran plunges through a gorge and descends abruptly to the Jordan Valley, passing by the site which, centuries after Hosea's time, was to be the headquarters of an Essene community which also spoke of a new covenant in the wilderness. Even today the visitor to the valley, just above the cliffs of Qumran, is impressed with the stark contrast between the elemental simplicity of this barren place and the fertility of the hill country where great cities once stood as proud symbols of man's culture. Life in the wilderness is precarious, and here the man of faith is reminded that his life depends on God's mercies. Significantly, Hosea saw the wilderness as the place of a new beginning. Yahweh himself, he prophesied, would lure his people into the wilderness. To Israel, stripped of all false securities and purged of all cultural pretensions, he would "speak tenderly," or, as the Hebrew says, "speak to her heart." There she would receive back her vineyards and learn that all the blessings of culture are gifts of God's grace. There she would enter a door of hope, leading into a meaningful and secure future within the love of God.

To sum up, the wilderness was to be the scene of the renewal of the covenant, and there the long history of the broken covenant would be ended. In the wilderness, Israel would *answer* Yahweh's overture of love, as she had responded

---

[22] In Hosea 3:5, the phrase "and David their king" is obviously a gloss by a later editor of the Southern Kingdom. Elsewhere the book has been touched up with Judean additions: 1:7, 4:15; 11:12b. Some scholars argue that all references to Judah are spurious. However, it is probable that Hosea, like Amos, applied his message both to Israel and Judah.

THE WILDERNESS OF JUDAH *with the Dead Sea in the background. This dry, barren plateau, which has been identified as the Valley of Achor, was a symbol to Hosea of the new beginning that Israel would make in the wilderness (Hosea 2:14-15). The author points to the approximate location of Qumran, which is situated below the bluffs ringing the near shore of the Dead Sea.*

in trust and gratitude at the time of the Exodus. And Yahweh would restore Israel to the relationship of a wife, betrothing her to himself in righteousness and in justice, in steadfast love (*hésed*) and in mercy. For Israel's persistent infidelity would be conquered by a love stronger and deeper than hers, and she would *know* Yahweh in the relationship of a new covenant (2:19-20).

THE FALL OF THE NORTHERN KINGDOM

Hosea's hope, as we have seen, rested on an "optimism of grace," not on political probabilities. To be sure, his message of doom was called forth by Israel's precarious position directly in the path of Assyria's advance across the Fertile Crescent toward Egypt. Politically, little Israel did not have a chance, especially when the leaders of the nation were pursuing suicidal foreign and domestic policies. But to Hosea the political crisis had another dimension. Within the events of the time he saw the activity of God in judgment and renewal.

We are not sure how long Hosea's prophetic career continued. Some scholars believe that he was active in 735-733 B.C. during the alliance between Syria and Israel (to be discussed in the next chapter), and suggest that the passage 5:8-14 reflects an invasion by the Southern Kingdom into Israel at that time.[23] In any case, his ministry, especially as reflected in chapters 4-14, extended into the turbulent period of the last days of the Northern Kingdom.

Events moved rapidly toward disaster. Tiglath-pileser's death in 727 B.C. gave Israel an opportunity to revolt. (See Chronological Chart 6, p. 271.) King

---

[23] This view has been advanced by Albrecht Alt, "Hosea 5, 8-6, 6"—an article which now appears in his *Kleine Schriften zur Geschichte des Volkes Israel*, II (Munich, 1953), pp. 163-187. See further James M. Ward, *Hosea* [154], on this passage.

SARGON II *was the conqueror of Samaria. Here he is shown wearing the royal headdress, long hair and curled beard, and a cruciform earring. This bust was found at Dur-Sharruken (Khorsabad), the city the ruler built as his residence a few miles east of Nineveh.*

Hoshea of Israel, hoping that the new Assyrian emperor would not be strong enough to keep his far-flung empire under control, and foolishly relying on the "weak reed" of Egypt, refused to pay tribute in about 724 B.C. But the new Assyrian king, Shalmaneser V (727-722 B.C.), quickly attacked Samaria. He died during the battle, and his successor Sargon II (722-705 B.C.) inherited the task of finishing the job. Then, in the first months of 721 B.C., after a three-year siege, Samaria fell. According to Sargon's annals, he deported 27,290 Israelites into the region of Persia (see II Kings 17:6) and repopulated Israel with colonists from Babylonia, Elam, and Syria.[24] The words of Amos' dirge had been translated into historical reality: "Fallen is the virgin Israel."

So far as we know, Hosea did not live through this final tragedy. But his prophecy was not forgotten. It was preserved in prophetic circles and eventually was edited and cherished in the Southern Kingdom of Judah.

---

[24] See Pritchard, *Ancient Near Eastern Texts*, pp. 284-287.

JUDAH'S COVENANT

WITH DEATH

CHAPTER NINE   All the great prophets we have considered up to this point—Elijah, Elisha, Micaiah, Amos, and
Hosea—were active in the Northern Kingdom, which parted
with the Davidic empire at Solomon's death. It is true that
prophets were active in Judah during the same period, for
the record speaks of obscure figures like Azariah (II Chron.
15:1-7), Hanani (II Chron. 16:7-10), and Jehu, the son of
Hanani (I Kings 16:1-4; II Chron. 19:2). But none of these
men could hold a candle to the prophets of the kingdom

Biblical readings: Of the prophetic literature dealt with in this
chapter it is especially important to read at least Isaiah 1-11 and 28-32,
and Micah 1-3 and 6:1-8. The historical background is sketched in
II Kings 18-20 (paralleled in II Chronicles 29-32).

of Israel, men whose spiritual stature matched the great crises of their time. It must have seemed that all the big issues were being decided in the north. Even Amos, a southerner, chose to deliver his message in Bethel, the seat of the royal sanctuary of Jeroboam II.

In politics, as well as prophecy, the kingdom of Israel stayed in the lead after the split of the United Kingdom. Occasionally, of course, when Israel was temporarily weakened by domestic troubles or by the intervention of a foreign power, Judah was able to achieve a position of equality. But on the whole Judah was overshadowed by her stronger and wealthier sister kingdom to the north. Whereas Judah was comparatively isolated in the hill country, off the main roads of the ancient world, Israel stood squarely in the path of history. Her position astride the crossroads of commerce between Egypt and Mesopotamia made it inevitable that she play a leading role in Palestine. It was providential that a succession of great prophets appeared on the stage of history at the very time when this nation was recognized as a leader among the small nations.

When "the wide land of the house of Omri," as Sargon II called the kingdom of Israel,[1] was swallowed up in the Assyrian empire, the prophetic succession was continued in Judah. Here too the story of the prophets is intertwined with the account of the political fortunes of the nation, down to the time when it collapsed under the attack of the Babylonian armies. Let us begin by considering the long and prosperous reign of Uzziah, or Azariah (c. 783-742 B.C.), which paralleled the glorious era of Jeroboam II in north Israel.

THE REIGN OF UZZIAH

In contrast to the political restlessness and economic discontent manifest during the history of the Northern Kingdom, Judah was able to achieve a remarkable degree of political and economic stability. A single dynasty, that of David, remained on the throne of Jerusalem throughout the whole period, while the sequence of Israelite kings was punctuated by violence and intrigue. Unlike Israel, where swift economic changes led to the erection of an unstable social pyramid, Judah moved fairly smoothly from the simplicities of the old tribal order to the more advanced economy of town life. And, in the process, she preserved an astonishing degree of social equality. True, the Northern Kingdom had no monopoly on evil. Judean prophets saw plenty of evidence that rapacious landlords were swallowing up the holdings of small farmers (Is. 5:8-10; Mic.

---

[1] This expression is used in Sargon's report of the conquest of Samaria (see Pritchard, *Ancient Near Eastern Texts*, pp. 284-285). As we noted earlier, it had been customary for Assyrians to name the land of Israel in honor of Omri. Even Jehu was called "son of Omri" in Assyrian records.

2:1-2), that the rich were skinning the backs of the poor (Is. 10:1-2; Mic. 3:1-4), and that flagrant social injustices were smoothed over with a veneer of religious piety (Is. 1:10-17). Nevertheless, the social order was relatively stable, and this stability—symbolized by the Davidic crown—is important to keep in mind as we approach the book of Isaiah. As we have already observed, this political stability was abetted by the theological conviction that Yahweh had made a special covenant with David, promising to uphold his throne and to establish his sons after him (see above, pp. 148-150).

Under Uzziah, Judah reached the very peak of her economic and military power. The brief report in II Kings 15:1-7, supplemented by the longer account in II Chronicles 26, gives us a picture of Uzziah's extraordinary accomplishments: the modernization of the army; his conquests in the Philistine plain, which put him in control of the main commercial highways; his commercial expansion into Arabia; his reconstruction of the trade-route seaport city of Elath (formerly Ezion-geber); and his development of agriculture, for, we are told, "he loved the soil."

To Judeans, the only disturbing event in Uzziah's reign was that in about 750 B.C. their beloved king was stricken with the dread disease of leprosy. He had to be confined to a separate house, and his son, Jotham, appeared in public as regent. But not even this loathsome disease, which the Judean historian interprets as a sign of Yahweh's disfavor, eclipsed the glory and fame of Uzziah. Even after his confinement, he continued to be the recognized ruler, and his name remained a symbol of the strength and stability of Judah (see Is. 6:1). As the kingdom of Israel swiftly declined after the death of Jeroboam II, Judah quickly rose to a position of power and influence second only to that of the era of David and Solomon. The only cloud on the horizon was the threat of Assyrian imperialism.

The Assyrian threat was, of course, no new development. As we have seen, the dominant theme of international politics, from the thirteenth century on, was the rise of Assyria and her ambition to establish an empire encompassing the whole Fertile Crescent. With the rise of Tiglath-pileser to power, this threat became an ominous reality. Once the Assyrian war machine was rolling, it did not stop until, under one of Tiglath-pileser's successors, it reached the valley of the Nile (see map, p. 243).

In such a time, filled with political promise and ominous with impending catastrophe, Isaiah was called to be a prophet. His call came in 742 B.C.—the year in which King Uzziah died and Tiglath-pileser finished his siege of Arpad, the capital of a province in northern Syria. Isaiah's prophetic career lasted more than forty years, and during that time the political map of the world was changed. Crisis followed crisis. The first major political event occurred in 735 B.C. when the armies of Syria and north Israel invaded Judean soil to force Judah to enter a coalition, organized for the purpose of stopping the Assyrian advance, after the manner of the western alliance that fought Assyria at Qarqar (see p. 208). It was a futile enterprise, for in 733-732 Tiglath-pileser conquered Syria and swept down through Gilead, Galilee, and the Plain of Sharon.

The second major event of Isaiah's career occurred when Shalmaneser V, the successor of Tiglath-pileser, was provoked by Israel's insurgence to visit Palestine again, this time to lay siege to Samaria, the capital of the Northern Kingdom

JUDAH
VASSAL STATE OF ASSYRIA

ASSYRIAN PROVINCES ✫

MEDITERRANEAN SEA

Sidon○
Damascus○ ✫
Tyre○
DIMASQU ✫
MT. HERMON ✫
QARNINI ✫
MAGIDU ✫
HAURINA ✫
Dor○
Megiddo○
Ramoth~gilead○
GALAZA ✫
DU'RU (PLAIN OF SHARON)
SAMERNA ✫
○Samaria
Joppa○
Bethel○
AMMON
ASDUDU
Ashdod○
Anathoth○
Jericho○
○Rabbath~Ammon
Libnah○
Jerusalem○○
Ashkelon○
○Moresheth~gath
Heshbon○
Gath○
○Tekoa
Lachish○
○Hebron
Dibon○
○Gaza
En~gedi○
MOAB
JUDAH
SALT SEA
ARABIA
Beer~sheba○

○Kadesh~barnea
○Bozrah

R. OF EGYPT
Sela○
EDOM

Elath○

GULF OF
AQABAH

Aiath?○   ○Rimmon
Migron?○Michmash
Ramah○   ○Geba
   ○Gibeah of Saul
NOB?△ ○Anathoth
   ○
Jerusalem

JORDAN R.
SALT SEA

SENNACHERIB'S INVASION AS IN ISAIAH 10:28-32

(722-721 B.C.). Then, later on, during the reign of the next Assyrian king, Sargon II, the Assyrian army marched down along the coastal highway of Palestine to put down another anti-Assyrian revolt, this time localized in the Philistine city of Ashdod (711 B.C.). And finally, toward the close of his ministry, Isaiah saw Judah's foolish attempt to conspire against Assyria and lived through the terrible days of Sennacherib's invasion in 701 B.C. (See Chronological Chart 6, p. 271.)

Through all these crises, the prophet maintained that an alliance against Assyria was a "covenant with death," as the kingdom of Israel had learned by bitter experience. And yet Isaiah was no mere political analyst. In the historical arena, where nations vied for power, he discerned the activity of Yahweh, the Sovereign of Israel and the nations. His task as prophet was to interpret what Yahweh was saying and doing through the tense political events of the time.

THE BOOK OF ISAIAH

Before we turn to the message of Isaiah, we must first consider the book itself. The present book of Isaiah has sixty-six chapters. It is commonly agreed, however, that not all this material comes from the eighth-century prophet. A nucleus of this big book does come from Isaiah, but a great deal of the material comes from others who were disciples and interpreters of the prophet. Again we must remember that our conception of "authorship" did not prevail in the biblical period. In a day when it was impossible to "publish" books for general circulation and when copyrights were unheard of, the only way to preserve prophetic material was to deposit it within a circle of followers who faithfully remembered the words of their leader and recorded the tradition for posterity.

Isaiah gives us a picture of how his message was handed on. Early in his ministry, when his message to Judah had fallen on deaf ears, he withdrew from public life in order to "bind up the testimony" and to "seal the teaching among [his] disciples" (Is. 8:16-18; cf. 30:8). If the present generation would not heed his words, then he would wait for Yahweh to make his purpose clear to a future generation that *would* listen! Apparently, then, Isaiah deposited his oracles for safekeeping within the faithful prophetic community. There they were treasured, revised in the light of Isaiah's later teaching, and, after his death, handed on by his disciples. So the tradition was kept alive. It included not only Isaiah's original words, but other accumulated materials which, in the conviction of his followers, were in keeping with his teaching. We have already seen that this is what happened with the teachings of Moses. The Mosaic tradition, finally compiled in the Pentateuch, included not only the original traditions of the Mosaic period but an accumulation of later traditions that had clustered around the great name of Moses.

In the Hebrew Bible the writings of the prophets are contained in four major scrolls: the book of Isaiah, the book of Jeremiah, the book of Ezekiel, and the book of the Twelve. Together, these scrolls make up the "Latter Prophets," as distinguished from the "Former Prophets" (see the table on p. 76). All four scrolls are approximately the same length. Apparently the size of a manageable scroll was one factor that controlled the amount of material to be included. The book of the Twelve, for instance, contains twelve small prophetic books— Hosea, Joel, Amos, Obadiah, Jonah, Micah, Nahum, Habakkuk, Zephaniah, Haggai, Zechariah, and Malachi. They are arranged in a single scroll, not on the basis of chronology or of relative importance, but because together the writings associated with the names of these prophets fill out a scroll. Like the book of the Twelve, the scrolls of Isaiah, Jeremiah, and Ezekiel are really prophetic anthologies, even though they are published under the name of a single prophet. One of the major tasks of biblical criticism is to ascertain the original nucleus of prophetic material and to answer, as far as possible, the questions of date, background, and authorship of any given passage. In many cases, however, the authorship of particular passages will never be known, since anonymous prophecies from various periods have clustered around great prophetic figures like Isaiah, Jeremiah, and Ezekiel.

A Breakdown of the Material in Isaiah

Let us examine the kinds of material included in the Isaiah anthology. First of all, it is generally agreed that chapters 40-66 do not belong to the Isaiah who prophesied in Jerusalem in the eighth century B.C. As we shall see in Chapter 13, these chapters reflect a historical situation that existed about two centuries later: when Judah had fallen, when the people were in exile, and when Babylonia—then the mistress of the world—was about to fall before the rising empire of Persia. This material, or at least much of it, is usually attributed to "Second Isaiah." This scholarly nickname does not mean that the writer was actually named Isaiah, but merely that this anonymous prophet's writings are included in the same scroll with those of "First Isaiah"—that is, Isaiah of Jerusalem.

The genuine writings of Isaiah, then, are found in the first thirty-nine chapters of the book. A variety of material is contained even in these chapters, however. Chapters 36-39 have been lifted, with some modifications, from II Kings 18:13-20:19, which relates incidents that happened during the latter part of Isaiah's ministry. Chapters 34 and 35, the first a passage of doom and the second a passage of hope, are more like the poems of Second Isaiah than like the preceding material in the book of Isaiah. Scholars generally agree that these two chapters, which deal with the end-time, do not come from Isaiah. Moving backward a bit further, chapters 24-27 (often called "the little apocalypse") seem to come from a period even later than Second Isaiah. So, by a process of elimination, we are left with three sections of the book of Isaiah that contain the genuine prophecies of Isaiah:

A. Chapters 1-11–a series of prophetic oracles and prophetic narratives. A later compiler added chapter 12, a hymn of praise (psalm), to round off this section.

B. Chapters 13-23–a series of oracles against foreign nations. Only a fraction of this material comes from Isaiah, however.

C. Chapters 28-32–a series of prophetic oracles. Chapter 33, which completes this section, is a late prophetic liturgy.

So the study of Isaiah is not so big a job as it would seem on first opening the book of Isaiah! At the most, we must tackle twenty-nine chapters, and, since for our purposes the section on the foreign nations (B) can be set aside temporarily, only eighteen chapters are left. Even then, not everything in the two remaining sections, (A) and (C), comes from Isaiah. The composition of the book of Isaiah is a rather complicated matter, and we shall refer to critical details only when absolutely necessary.

By narrowing our attention to these two sections—chapters 1-11 and chapters 28-32—our study of the long career of Isaiah is greatly simplified, for each of these sections comes from a fairly well-defined period in the prophet's ministry. In general, chapters 1-11 reflect the early period of Isaiah, from the death of Uzziah to the time of the Syro-Israelite alliance—or about ten years (742-732 B.C.). And chapters 28-32 reflect the later period of the prophet's career, from the accession of king Hezekiah of Judah to the great crisis brought on by Sennacherib's invasion of Judah—or about fourteen years (715-701 B.C.). These two major sections provide a convenient approach to the study of Isaiah. Let us look first at section A of our outline, beginning with the narrative material in 6:1-8:18, and then move on to the oracles of Isaiah's early career.

ISAIAH'S EARLY MINISTRY

Not very much is known about Isaiah's background. He was obviously a man of the city, which accounts for the great number of urban metaphors he used, and it may be that he grew up in the privileged circles of Jerusalem. Above all, the city of Jerusalem had a deep place in his affection. For Jerusalem was the place of Yahweh's Temple, the seat of David's throne, and the city hallowed with many sacred memories. Oddly enough, Israel's wilderness tradition, which loomed so large in the message of prophets like Amos and Hosea, seems to have had no great influence on Isaiah's prophecy. On the Exodus and the other great themes of Israel's sacred history he is silent, even though he was obviously aware of these traditions.[2] Isaiah seems to have been nurtured in circles that stressed the special relationship between Yahweh and the Davidic dynasty (see

---

[2] The Exodus is referred to explicitly in Is. 10:24-26 and 11:16, but most scholars doubt that these passages come from the prophet.

II Sam. 7). In view of his absorbing interest in Davidic theology, it is not surprising that he is regarded as the chief exponent of the hope for a coming Messiah (literally: "Anointed One") of David's lineage.

The Kingship of Yahweh

The account of Isaiah's call to be a prophet is one of the classic passages in prophetic literature (Is. 6). In a few verses of prose that verge on poetic sublimity we are ushered into the worship experience which provided both the motive and the content for his preaching. The account in its present form, of course, is written in retrospect. Although it points back to a time when he was a very young man, it carries the overtones of his later experiences, especially his bewilderment over the people's dullness and blindness. This, in part, is why the prophetic commission is described in such bleak and unpromising terms (6:9-13; see 29:9-12, an oracle from his later ministry). As a whole, however, the passage is an authentic account of the great moment of decision in Isaiah's life, an experience that was to persist at the center of his memory.

Notice the time and the place. It was a critical time, heavy with urgency and foreboding. That is the meaning of the reference to Uzziah's death. Uzziah had been a strong king, and even while his son Jotham was acting as regent Uzziah remained a pillar of strength for the people. Since kingship is more or less alien to our experience, it is difficult for us to appreciate the significance of the king in ancient society. "Just as the house is centered in the father," writes an eminent authority on Israelite life, "so the soul of the people is centered in the king." [3] From the king's person blessing and strength went out through the whole nation, like life-giving sap through the branches of a tree. Hence Uzziah's death was an event that touched the life of the people, especially in view of the weakness of his son Jotham and the menacing shadow of Assyria. In such an hour, says the prophet, "I saw the king." His testimony implies that his people were ultimately dependent, not upon the Davidic king enthroned in Jerusalem, but upon the true King, Yahweh of hosts.

The place of Isaiah's vision was the Temple of Solomon. Here, in a priestly setting of worship with which the prophet had grown familiar through the years,[4] he beheld a vision of Yahweh sitting on his heavenly throne, high and lifted up, while the chamber rang with the "holy, holy, holy" which is heard in anthems of worship even today. This theme of Yahweh's enthronement as king over the earth and the whole universe was especially at home in the Jeru-

---

[3] Johannes Pederson, *Israel* [69], I-II, p. 275.

[4] It has been suggested that Isaiah himself was a priest or a temple prophet (see R. B. Y. Scott, *Interpreter's Bible*, V, pp. 207-208). Since ordinary worshipers did not enter the Temple but stood outside before the high altar of sacrifice, this is possible; but it is sufficient to say that Isaiah, like other great prophets—Samuel (at Shiloh), Jeremiah, and Ezekiel—was influenced by the priestly tradition.

salem cult. The exclamation, "Yahweh is king!" sounded forth on the New Year's Day of the Autumn Festival, when worshipers sang hymns which portray Yahweh as robed in majesty, exalted in "the beauty of holiness," and enthroned over his whole creation as Judge and Arbiter of the destinies of men.[5]

The Prophet in the Heavenly Council

In this setting, the elements of the temple service—the antiphonal singing, the altar with its red-hot stones, the incense smoke that filled the sanctuary, the priestly attendants, the mysterious depths of the Holy of Holies—are transfigured.[6] Suddenly, in the prophet's vision the earthly temple enlarges and he finds himself standing in a spacious heavenly temple. He sees Yahweh himself seated upon a great throne, clothed in a majestic robe whose skirt fills the temple. A thrice-holy anthem resounds in the temple, and the visible radiance ("glory") of the King fills the whole earth. Yahweh is not only Israel's King, but the King *par excellence*, upon whose sovereignty the destinies of all men depend. In the vision, the temple priests, too, are transfigured. They are not ordinary men, but unearthly *seraphim*, like the strange figures—half-human and half-animal—which ancient people portrayed as attendants of the deity's sanctuary. Their three pairs of wings express symbolically the appropriate responses to Yahweh's presence: with one pair they shield their faces from the King's blinding glory, with the second pair they hide their nakedness from his holy purity, and with the third pair they fly to do their appointed tasks. With appropriate poetic reserve, the prophet makes no attempt to describe Yahweh's appearance. But the imagery communicates the overpowering and aweful effect of his sovereignty.

So the narrative suggests that the prophet, entering through the corridor of Solomon's Temple, stands in Yahweh's celestial throne-room, where the heavenly host surround the King. One of the recurrent themes in the Old Testament is the picture of the Heavenly Council presided over by Yahweh— as in Micaiah's vision, for example: "I saw Yahweh sitting upon his throne, and all the host of heaven standing by him on his right hand and on his left" (I Kings 22:19; see p. 211).[7] Yahweh's speech employs the plural "us" (Is. 6:8), for he is surrounded by his Council, his heavenly host, to whom and for whom

---

[5] The so-called Enthronement Psalms (Pss. 93, 96-99) will be discussed in Chapter 15.

[6] See the reconstruction of the interior of the Temple, p. 154. The assumption of Isaiah's vision is the ancient view that the Jerusalem temple was a microcosm of the macrocosm—that is, an earthly replica of the heavenly temple. This view enabled people to believe that Yahweh was truly present in Mount Zion and at the same time the transcendent God who is enthroned on high. See R. E. Clements, *God and Temple* [201], chap. 5.

[7] See the prologue to the book of Job, and also various Psalms where the angelic hosts are summoned to praise Yahweh as "a great King above all gods" (Ps. 82:5-7; 95:3; 103:19-22; 148:2). A good discussion of the Heavenly Council is found in G. E. Wright, *The Old Testament Against Its Environment* [125], pp. 30-41. See also H. Wheeler Robinson, "The Council of Yahweh," in *Journal of Theological Studies*, XLV (1944), pp. 151-157.

he speaks. Isaiah, then, is drawn into Yahweh's Heavenly Council where the divine decrees are announced and where messengers are sent forth to execute them.[8] In an ecstatic moment he is permitted to behold what is veiled to the sight of mortal man (see Ex. 33:20), for he exclaims that with his own eyes he has seen the King.

Called to Be the King's Messenger

His first response—already symbolized in the attitude of the seraphim in the King's presence—is to cry out that he is an "unclean" man and a member of an "unclean" people (verse 5). This response is evoked by the sense of God's holiness, a fundamental aspect of the experience of worship. To say that God is holy, means, first of all, that he is God and not man (see Hos. 11:9). Although he is active in the world, he cannot be imprisoned within it; nor can he be regarded as an object to be controlled and manipulated according to human purposes or understanding. He is the divine Thou, upon whom man's life is wholly dependent. But in Isaiah's message holiness means not only the sublimity of God as contrasted with man's creatureliness; it also means the awful contrast between God's purity and man's sinfulness. As "the Holy One of Israel"—a favorite expression of the prophet—Yahweh is exalted in righteousness (5:16). In his presence, nothing unclean, nothing unrighteous, nothing idolatrous can survive. So, in the moment when the threshold of the Temple shakes at the sound of the seraphim's anthem, Isaiah confesses that he is a member of a community in which there is no health (cf. 1:4-9), and he links himself with his people in a woeful cry of dereliction: "Woe is me! For I am lost!"

In his vision one of the heavenly "priests" (a seraph) takes from the altar a red-hot stone and purges his unclean lips:

> Behold, this has touched your lips;
>   your guilt is taken away,
>   and your sin forgiven.
>   —ISAIAH 6:7

Here a new note is introduced into prophecy: the prophet himself needs purification before he can be God's messenger. Amos had prayed that Yahweh would forgive his people (Amos 7:1-6), but Isaiah begins his prophetic career as a man who himself has been forgiven. And no sooner is he "consecrated"—that is, made holy or cleansed for God's service—than Yahweh, speaking in a manner which includes the whole Heavenly Council, says: "Whom shall I send, and

---

[8] The prophet understands himself to be God's messenger (see pp. 189-190), sent to deliver a message to the people. The prophet's source of authority, according to some passages, was located in Yahweh and his Heavenly Council (Jer. 23:18, 22). On this point see James F. Ross [136], pp. 102-106.

who will go for us?" Isaiah volunteers, only to receive a commission so un-
bearable that he cries out, asking how long it must go on. The answer is that
he is to proclaim Yahweh's word to a people whose heart [9] is fat (insensitive),   *foh leal*
whose ears are heavy (dull), and whose eyes are blind (verses 9-10).

This is a very puzzling command. As we have said, Isaiah's memory of his
call seems to be colored by his later feelings of failure. And yet more is expressed in this language than the mood of later discouragement. Isaiah, like
other prophets, believed that all events came from the hand of God. Although
we would regard the developments of Isaiah's career as stemming from human
sources, for which a cause-and-effect explanation could be found in the social
situation, the prophet insisted that these experiences happened within the
purpose and will of God, God was not taken by surprise, as it were. It was
known in advance that the prophetic word would have the effect that it did
among a *rebellious* people (see 1:2-3). For as excessive light can blind the eyes,
or excessive sound can be deafening, so the words and signs of the prophet would   ∨
increase the people's blindness to Yahweh's acts and their deafness to his words,
although, strictly speaking, that was not the intention of the prophet's activity.
Yet, if we are correct in interpreting the severe passage of doom (verses 11-13),
the darkness is illumined by a ray of light, for it is said that after the fire of
divine judgment has swept through the land a "stump" will remain. And just
as a new branch sprouts from a stump that stands in a burned forest, so new
life will begin in a remnant of the people.

The Day of Yahweh

Before going on to the prophetic memoirs in chapters 7 and 8, it is
appropriate to look back from chapter 6 to the preceding chapters, which, for
the most part, come from Isaiah's early ministry.[10] In these chapters the themes
of Isaiah's vision are elaborated. In various ways and situations the prophet
reaffirmed that Yahweh is enthroned, high and lifted up, above all the tumult
of history and the feverish strivings of men. As with Amos, the Day of Yahweh
will not be light, but darkness—a day of judgment against all the pride and
self-sufficiency of men: against silver and gold, horses and chariots, fortified   ∕
cities, and stately ships that sail to far-away places (2:6-21). These cultural
treasures are not bad in themselves; but when they are "lifted up" like the proud
cedars of Lebanon, men begin to place their trust in them, and they become

---

[9] "Heart" refers to the inward center of the person, not to mere feelings or emotions. In
Hebrew a man thinks in his heart, and loves with his heart.

[10] Not all of chapter 1 comes from this period, for verses 7-9 refer to the isolation of Jerusalem during the siege of Sennacherib. Also many scholars doubt whether the well-known poem
in 2:2-5 (found with a slight variation in Mic. 4:1-4) comes from Isaiah. If it is Isaiah's, it
comes from a later period.

objects of idolatry—for idolatry is trusting in anything less than God. The time will come, says the prophet, when men will cast their idols to the moles and the bats. The oracles of doom are punctuated with this refrain:

> And the haughtiness of man shall be humbled,
>   and the pride of men shall be brought low,
> And Yahweh alone will be exalted in that day.
>   —ISAIAH 2:17

That Yahweh comes to judge his people is the theme of Isaiah's famous Song of the Vineyard (5:1-7). The prophet begins by singing a vineyard song, like the popular ballads that were sung at the Fall vintage festivals. It is possible that Isaiah posed as a singer in order to catch the attention of the crowds on their way to the Temple to celebrate the gathering of the harvest. He tells about his disappointment. He had done everything possible to insure a good harvest, only to find that his vineyard yielded wild grapes. He asks his hearers what had gone wrong; after all, what more could he have done? Then he announces what he is going to do: he will tear down the vines and let the vineyard become a briar patch. Suddenly, the unexpected point of the song is plunged into the people's heart, for it turns out that Yahweh is the speaker and that the song is about his chosen people: "the vineyard of Yahweh of hosts." With a play on words, the prophet announces Yahweh's indignant disappointment:

> He looked for justice (*mishpat*),
>   and behold, bloodshed (*mispah*);
> for righteousness (*zedaqah*),
>   but behold, a cry (*ze'aqah*).

It is impossible to reproduce the force of the Hebrew assonance in English, but word-pairs like justice/distress and right/riot give a rough idea. The following oracles (5:8-24) elaborate further the woes of a people guilty of the most flagrant injustice and exploitation.

Isaiah's earliest message, then, was one of doom, in keeping with the commission given to him in chapter 6. Yahweh announces a covenant lawsuit (see p. 249) against his people Israel, summoning them to stand trial before their Judge (1:18-20; 3:13-15). Arraigned before his holy presence, the prophet had to say on their behalf that they were "unclean"—indeed, that there was no health in them (1:4-6). And yet, Yahweh's purpose was not just destructive: it was to restore Israel to health, to make her a holy people fit to serve the King. Just as Isaiah was cleansed by forgiveness, so—according to the prophet's interpretation—Yahweh was seeking to purify his people as by fire. Through the terrible sufferings of the time, he was purging away the dross and alloy so that Jerusalem might become the city of righteousness (1:24-26).

The Syro-Israelite Alliance

Now it is appropriate to return to the prophetic memoirs found in chapters 7 and 8.[11] A few years after Isaiah's call, his wife, the "prophetess" referred to in 8:3, gave birth to a boy, who was named Shear-yashub (7:3). Just as Hosea gave symbolic names to his children, so Isaiah's child was a living sign from Yahweh, a visible confirmation of the message of the prophet. Literally, the name means "A remnant shall return" (that is, "turn to God," "repent," as in 6:10). Although in one sense this phrase carried a negative meaning ("*Only* a remnant shall return," as in 10:22-23), in another sense it concealed a promise ("A remnant *shall* return"), just as doom and hope seem to be blended together in the concluding verses of chapter 6.

This sign-child figures prominently in a scene in the prophetic memoir found in chapter 7. The material in chapters 7 and 8 deals with the Syro-Israelite crisis that took place in 733-732 B.C., although the crisis had been in the making for some time. Jotham, Uzziah's regent, who had become king in his own right after his father's death, had been succeeded on the throne of Judah by Ahaz (c. 735-715 B.C.). This youthful king was no match for the political troubles he inherited. A plot was afoot among the small western states to stop the advance of Assyria. Apparently they hoped that by pooling their efforts they might duplicate the feat of the western allies more than a century earlier, when they temporarily turned back the Assyrian armies at Qarqar. This international conspiracy made the one-time enemies—Israel and Syria—bed-fellows, as we have observed (p. 255). Initially, the Assyrian king, Tiglath-pileser, was recognized by the western nations. Therefore, in 738 B.C., Menahem, king of Israel, joined with Rezin of Damascus to pay tribute to the Assyrian victor (II Kings 15:19-20). This capitulation to Assyria enabled Menahem and his son Pekahiah to stay in power, but it was highly unpopular, especially since the tribute was raised by heavy taxes on the rich. The time was ripe for revolution. An army captain, Pekah, the son of Remaliah, murdered Pekahiah in 737 B.C. and shortly thereafter, while Tiglath-pileser was occupied in the north, conspired with Rezin of Damascus to form an anti-Assyrian coalition. The two kingdoms joined in an attack on Judah in an attempt to replace Ahaz with a puppet king on the Judean throne (Is. 7:6).

Ahaz was in a tight spot, for he had come to the throne of Judah in one of the gravest crises of Judean history. From a purely political standpoint he deserves our sympathy, even though as a leader he was weak and vacillating. The presence of the invading armies on his soil filled him with panic: "his heart and

---

[11] These memoirs are found in the so-called "book of testimony," which Isaiah and his disciples may have composed after the events referred to in it (see 8:16). It includes: the account of Isaiah's call (chap. 6), his counsel to Ahaz (chap. 7), the consequences of his spurned counsel (chap. 8), and an oracle of promise to Judah (9:1-7).

the heart of his people shook as the trees of the forest shake before the wind."
Terror-stricken, he burned his son as an offering in the Valley of Hinnom (see
map, p. 143) just outside the city (II Kings 16:3), hoping by this pagan rite to
assuage the divine wrath that had come upon the city (compare the action of
the Moabite king, II Kings 3:26-27). The situation was desperate. As a responsible political leader, Ahaz had to choose between accepting defeat at the hands
of the invaders or appealing for outside help. Thoughts like these must have
been in his mind as he went out to inspect the city's water supply, which was
essential to Jerusalem's ability to hold out during a siege. It was at that moment
that Isaiah confronted Ahaz, accompanied by his little lad, "A remnant shall
return."

Harassed as he was, Ahaz must have regarded Isaiah's counsel as an irrelevant
interruption. But Isaiah's message was simple, apparently too simple: "Trust in
Yahweh; be quiet and keep calm." The appropriate response to the crisis, he
said, was faith, not feverish anxiety over the defenses of Jerusalem. Isaiah
evidently was thinking of the weakness of the Syro-Israelite alliance, whose kings
were "two smoldering stumps of firebrands," almost burned out; and he probably realized that for Judah to become involved in the international rivalries
of the time would be suicidal, as subsequent events were to show in the case of
the Northern Kingdom. But he viewed the crisis in a wider and deeper perspective than that of mere diplomacy and fortifications. For beyond the political
schemes of men was the sovereign activity of God, whose purpose shapes the
course of events. The head of Ephraim is Pekah, and the head of Damascus is
Rezin; but these are men, not God! Their plan to place a puppet king on Judah's
throne will fail unless Yahweh wills it. So Isaiah affirms that the greatest resource in time of trouble is faith—absolute trust in and dependence upon God.
He underscores his message of faith with a characteristic play on words (7:9b),
which may be paraphrased: "If your faith is not sure (ta'aminu), your throne
will not be secure (te'amenu)." [12] Abandon human alliance, exclaims Isaiah,
and place your reliance in Yahweh, whose sovereign will controls human affairs!
Such faith demands a complete and firm commitment of one's whole being to
God, in the confidence that he is the true King (see also Is. 28:16; 30:15).[13]

Specifically, Isaiah's advice in that political situation called for Ahaz to
cancel his plan to ask for Assyrian intervention on behalf of besieged Judah. It
was the prophet's conviction that Yahweh would overthrow the Syro-Israelite
alliance by bringing Assyria against these foolish nations. The word of faith,
then, was politically relevant in that situation. But Ahaz could not believe this.

---

[12] Both words are derived from the verb 'amen which means "to be firm, to be sure," from
which comes the meaning "to trust, to believe."

[13] Martin Buber's term for Isaiah's attitude is "theopolitics"—that is, the attempt to bring
Israel in a specific situation so completely under the divine sovereignty that it accepts its historical task: "to become the beginning of the kingdom of God." The Prophetic Faith [118],
p. 135.

DIVIDED MONARCHY

B.C.	EGYPT	JUDAH	ISRAEL	SYRIA	ASSYRIA
750	Decline	Jotham (regent), c. 750-742 Jotham (king), c. 742-735 (Isaiah, c. 742-700) Jehoahaz (Ahaz), c. 735-715 Invasion by Syro-Israelite Alliance, 735	Shallum (1 mo.), c. 745 Menahem, c. 745-738 Pekahiah, c. 738-737 Pekah, c. 737-732	Rezin, c. 740-732 SYRO-ISRAELITE ALLIANCE	Tiglath-pileser III, c. 745-727
				FALL OF SYRIA 732	Siege of Damascus, 732 Shalmaneser V, 727-722
		(Micah: before 722 to c. 701)	Hoshea, c. 732-724 FALL OF SAMARIA 722-721		Siege of Samaria, 722/721
	XXV Dynasty (Ethiopian) c. 716-663	Hezekiah, c. 715-687			Sargon II, 722-705 Siege of Ashdod, 711 Sennacherib, 705-681 Invasion of Palestine, 701
700					

So later on, when the king was mapping out a political strategy with his advisers, Isaiah came to him again with the offer of a "sign."

The Sign of Immanuel

Here it is appropriate to call to mind our earlier discussion about the meaning of signs (see pp. 48-49). According to the Exodus tradition, Moses performed signs in the sight of the pharaoh, and according to the New Testament Jesus performed signs (*semeia*). In the Bible a sign does not stand by itself; rather, it is closely linked to the prophetic word, as in Isaiah 7. The purpose of a sign is to make visible, to confirm dramatically, the truth and power of Yahweh's word spoken by his prophet. The sign does not have to be a stupendous "miracle," in our sense of the word, for its significance is not so much its unusual character as its power to confirm a prophetic word spoken in threat or promise. In other instances, Isaiah's symbolic act of going about naked and barefoot (Is. 20), or his children who were present with him (8:18), are called signs. The ability to see signs is an indication of something that we have found to be characteristic of Israel's faith, a vivid sense of divine activity in the realm of human affairs. God is *with us*—not aloof from the scene of history. Thus, not only can his word be *heard* through the prophetic message, but his action can be *seen* in signs that the prophet points to or acts out.

Remember that Isaiah was commissioned to speak to a people who could neither hear Yahweh's word nor see the signs of his activity (6:9). Ahaz had already failed to hear. So Isaiah said that Yahweh would confirm his word by any sign the king might choose. But evidently Ahaz had already decided to take another course of action, so he declined with a pretense of piety: he would not put Yahweh to the test. Exasperated by the king's sacrifice of faith on the altar of political expedience, Isaiah tersely announced that "Yahweh himself will give you a sign"—a sign that would confirm the prophetic word of doom upon the Syro-Israelite alliance.

The sign promised was the birth of a child whose name would be called Immanuel, which in Hebrew means "God [is] with us." The language presupposes that the mother is already, or soon will be, pregnant; the child will be born in the near future.[14] Even before he reaches the age of choosing between good and evil, the Syro-Israelite alliance will have been broken up and the king of Assyria will have wrought havoc upon Judah. (See the reference to Immanuel's land in 8:8b.) At that time Judah will be reduced to a primitive pastoral state in which the people will live on curds and honey. Yahweh will "shave" Judah with an Assyrian razor. In other words, Isaiah promised Ahaz that Yahweh would bring immediate relief from the Syro-Israelite threat, but announced that the deliverance would be followed by even greater disaster for Judah (7:15-24).

---

[14] The Hebrew is rendered in the American Translation as follows: "A young woman is with child and is about to bear a son." See the footnote to the Revised Standard Version.

A great deal of interest has centered in the Immanuel prophecy of Isaiah 7:14. In the New Testament period it was believed that the prophecy was fulfilled in Jesus Christ, to whom was given the name "God is with us." Moreover, in some circles the passage was appealed to in support of the Virgin Birth (Matt. 1:23). While it is beyond our purpose to consider the validity of this belief, we do want to understand what Isaiah meant in the concrete political situation we have been discussing. Let us consider briefly the meaning of Isaiah's words.

First of all, the sign is the child himself—not the manner of his birth. To be sure, the prophet had explicitly said that Ahaz could ask for anything—"let it be deep as Sheol or high as heaven" (7:11)—on the assumption that all things are possible with God. Ahaz refused to ask, so Isaiah announced the *timely* birth of a child to a "young woman" of marriageable age (see the Revised Standard Version).[15] The prophet, then, pointed to the advent of a child in the immediate future who would grow up among his people as a pledge that "God is with us."

The Davidic Heir Apparent

Moreover, Isaiah apparently indicated that the child would come from a particular family. In the Hebrew text he uses the definite article, saying, "*The* woman shall conceive," as though he were referring to a particular woman, already known to Ahaz. It has even been suggested that the woman was the queen and that the child was Hezekiah, destined to be the next king of Judah. Whether or not this is true, it seems that Isaiah was thinking of a son of the house of David, although surely the messianic implications of his prophecy were not fully developed until later in his ministry. The well-known poem in 9:1-7, perhaps written later in his career, clearly says that the wonder-child will sit upon the throne of David.

How, then, does the imminent birth of the Davidic child relate to the political crisis of the Syro-Israelite alliance? In contrast to Ahaz, the king who shows no faith, Isaiah pictures the advent of a child-king who in due time will *faithfully* exercise the task of government. Initially, the Immanuel child will live in a time of great woe, for before he is very old, the Assyrian invasion will sweep through the land, converting it into a wilderness (7:16-17).[16] And yet, to those who have eyes to see, his presence will be a sign, an assurance that God is leading his people through the fire of divine judgment to the dawn of a new

---

[15] This is the meaning of the Hebrew word *'almah*, which is used in the Old Testament without prejudice as to a maiden's virginity (for instance, Gen. 24:43; Ex. 2:8; Prov. 30:19). The word for "virgin" is *bethulah*. In this passage, the Septuagint translators render *parthenos*. Normally, this is the translation of *bethulah* in the Septuagint, but it is also used for *'almah* in Gen. 24:43; cf. 34:3. This simply shows that the Septuagint used the word freely, and did not necessarily imply literal virginity in Is. 7:14. Other Greek versions render "maiden" (*neanis*) here, which is more accurate.

[16] In 8:8 this devastated land is referred to as Immanuel's land. Here again the reference is to the child-king. See also the saying "God is with us" in 8:10.

word but
a puzzle?

day. The child will share his people's sufferings, will live with them in the wilderness of destruction. But, as in the prophecy of Hosea, "wilderness" will have a double meaning. It will be both the time of judgment, and the opportunity for a new beginning. The fact that the child will eat milk and honey—the food of Paradise which tradition associated with the Promised Land ("the land flowing with milk and honey")—suggests that he will be a sign of the promised future, which lies on the other side of the dark days ahead. For Yahweh's purpose is not to destroy, but to refine and cleanse a remnant of the people. Once the Assyrian yoke is removed, the child will ascend the throne as the agent of God's rule over his people. Then the meaning of his name, Immanuel, will be clearly understood.

So, although Isaiah was not looking into the distant future, it is difficult to resist the conclusion that he meant the child as a messianic figure. If so, the messianic poem in 9:1-7 fits in with the theme of his prophecy (see also 11:1-9). Like his initial prophecy to Ahaz, this passage begins with a picture of doom and darkness, a reminiscence of the terrible destruction wrought by Tiglath-pileser in 733-32 B.C. in the territory of Zebulun and Naphtali (Galilee) when these tribal areas were incorporated into the Assyrian empire (II Kings 15:29).[17] But the darkness is illumined by a great light:

> For to us a child is born,
>   to us a son is given;
> And the government will be upon his shoulder,
>   and his name will be called
> "Wonderful Counselor, Mighty God,
>   Everlasting Father, Prince of Peace."
> —ISAIAH 9:6

From Isaiah this prophecy passed into the stream of prophetic tradition and eventually was transposed into a higher key in the Christian gospel (see Matt. 4:15-16).[18]

The Waters of Shiloah that Flow Softly

We turn now to the rest of Isaiah's memoirs in chapter 8. At the outset of the chapter, Isaiah is still warning about the swift doom that will overtake

---

[17] The reference to Tiglath-pileser's conquest of Galilee places this oracle (9:1-7) early in the career of Isaiah, according to the judgment of Albrecht Alt in his article, "Jes. 8:23-9:6," now found in his *Kleine Schriften*, II (1953), pp. 206-225. Since the Assyrian king took this territory in 733-732 B.C., Alt dates the oracle sometime between the years 732-722. He believes that it was intended as a prophecy of the expulsion of Assyrian forces and the restoration of a United Kingdom under Davidic rule.

[18] It must be admitted that the interpretation of the Immanuel prophecy is exceedingly difficult and that a wide variety of views have been expressed. See the brief treatment of the problem by C. R. North, "Immanuel," in the *Interpreter's Dictionary* [11], and the literature cited at the end of the article.

the Syro-Israelite coalition. Some time after his encounter with Ahaz, a second
son was born to Isaiah's wife, to whom was given the frightening name: Maher-
shalal-hash-baz—that is, "The spoil speeds, the prey hastens." The prophet declared that before this sign-child would learn how to say "Daddy" and "Mama"
—to modernize a bit—the Assyrian king would plunder Samaria and Damascus.
Even before the child was born, this same ominous message was written conspicuously on a tablet and properly "notarized," in order to remind people in
the future, when the anti-Assyrian coalition was finally overthrown, that God
had given true words and signs to his prophet (8:1-4).

But the words and the signs were of no avail, for Ahaz lacked the kind of
faith the prophet called for. Ahaz had to be "practical" in facing the political
realities of the moment. Or so he would have said in self-defense. Already the
king of Edom, taking advantage of Judah's plight, had recovered the seaport of Elath, which Uzziah had won (II Kings 16:6). Action was imperative.
Only two alternatives were open, and neither one was desirable. Either Ahaz
could surrender to the forces of Syria and Israel, in which case he might lose
his throne and would surely risk being on the wrong side in a showdown with
Assyria; or else he could throw in his lot with Assyria, in which case Judah would
become a vassal state of the Assyrian empire. He chose the latter course. According to the record in II Kings 16, he appealed for help to the Assyrian king,
emptying the treasuries of the Temple and his palace to court his favor. Tiglath-
pileser was more than glad to come to the rescue. Damascus was overthrown,
Rezin was killed, and Syria was subdivided into provinces of the Assyrian empire.
A good part of the state of Israel was annexed (cf. Is. 9:1; II Kings 15:29),
leaving Israel only a strip of land from the plain of Jezreel to the Judean
frontier. Ahaz went to Damascus to pay homage to Tiglath-pileser and to con-
gratulate him on his victories. While there, he obtained the blueprint for an
Assyrian altar, which he promptly ordered constructed in the Temple at Jerusalem (II Kings 16:10-18). In a day when religion and politics went hand in
hand, there was no clearer way to demonstrate that Judah had become an
Assyrian vassal. The record in II Chronicles 28:16-27 shows further how greatly
the kingdom suffered under this royal weakling.

To Isaiah, Ahaz's action was final proof of the lack of faith for which Judah
would pay the consequences. In a vivid figure of speech, Isaiah denounced the
people for rejecting "the waters of Shiloah that flow softly" in order to show
their confidence in the mighty Euphrates of Assyria. Shiloah was a little aque-
duct that carried water from the Spring of Gihon to a pool inside the city wall
(see map, p. 143), probably the very waterworks that Ahaz was examining when
Isaiah went out to meet him (7:3). This gentle stream was to Isaiah a symbol
of quiet and confident faith in Yahweh, whose kingdom is more powerful and
everlasting than the mightiest empires. As he had warned, "If you will not have
faith, you shall surely not be established" (7:9). The Assyrians, like a flood

overflowing from the Euphrates, would sweep through the land, devastating not only Syria and Israel but Judah as well.

Binding up the Testimony

Isaiah, then, was met by the stubborn resistance of a faithless generation. The words that should have awakened faith fell on deaf ears. The signs that should have made the truth visible were held up before blind eyes. But the prophetic words and signs had not been given in vain, for the future was in God's hand. It was evidently at this time, just after Ahaz's overture to Assyria, that Isaiah separated himself from his unheeding countrymen and withdrew into the prophetic circle. According to Isaiah, the action was taken under Yahweh's pressure, for "Yahweh spoke to me with his strong hand upon me and warned me not to walk in the way of this people" (8:11). He told the prophetic community that they were to "conspire" with God, not to join the political conspiracy; and they were to "fear" the Lord of hosts, not to have the kind of fear that drives a nation to political suicide.[19] This faithful community, the prophetic remnant, was to be separated from the rest of the nation by a different allegiance. They were to trust in Yahweh and wait expectantly for the fulfillment of his purpose in history.

So Isaiah took his place within this "community," the nucleus of the New Israel. His prophetic *torah*, or teaching, was sealed, or entrusted, among his disciples until a future day when Yahweh would make its truth plain. The prophet himself, as well as his children, were signs that Yahweh had given, and some day these signs would be understood. In such a rebellious time, men of faith turned to the future in patient hope. "I will wait for Yahweh, who is hiding his face from the house of Jacob, and I will hope in him" (8:17). The command to "bind up the testimony" among Isaiah's disciples probably resulted in the composition of the Book of Testimony (6:1-9:7) which included not only the prophet's early memoirs but, as we have seen, the magnificent promise of the coming of a Davidic King and the dawning of a new day.

Evidently Isaiah emerged from the prophetic circle to address himself to the second great political crisis of his career, the imminent fall of the Northern Kingdom. As events rushed on toward the final Assyrian blow against Samaria in 722-21 B.C., he spoke out against "the fading flower of Ephraim's glorious beauty" in oracles that are now scattered in various parts of the book (9:8-10:4; 17:1-11; 28:1-4). Of these oracles the most forceful is the series found in 9:8-10:4, the conclusion of which has probably been displaced to 5:26-30. Blow after blow of divine judgment shatters the people, but in vain. They do not learn the severe discipline of history. Ending with a refrain, which grows omi-

---

[19] The verbs of verses 12 and 13 are in the plural, indicating that they refer to the prophetic circle.

nous with repetition, each strophe discloses that Yahweh's hand is poised, ready to strike:

> For all this his anger is not turned away,
>   and his hand is stretched out still.

Since we know very little about Isaiah's activity during the remainder of the reign of Ahaz, however, this is an appropriate point to turn to his great contemporary, the prophet Micah, whose earliest oracles were delivered before the fall of Samaria.

MICAH, A RURAL PROPHET

Other than the fact that Micah's hometown was Moreshath-gath, a small village in the hills about twenty-five miles southwest of Jerusalem, we know little about him. Unlike the city-bred Isaiah, Micah was a country prophet who spoke for the poor farmers who were suffering at the hands of the powerful landlords. In many respects he reminds us of Amos. But his message of judgment, evoked by the inexorable march of Assyria, also reminds us of the shattering message of doom proclaimed by Isaiah. Indeed, it has been conjectured that Micah was one of Isaiah's disciples. Although this is doubtful, we shall link the two prophets together in considering the fateful events that engulfed Judah toward the end of the eighth century B.C.

Micah's first oracle (1:2-9) is cast in the form of a covenant lawsuit (see pp. 249, 268), in which the earth and its peoples are summoned to hear Yahweh's complaint against his people. It is announced that Yahweh is coming from his heavenly temple to execute judgment upon both houses of his people, Israel and Judah. As he treads in majestic steps upon the high places of the earth, the mountains melt and the valleys divide. Micah sees that the approach of the Assyrian to destroy the proud and idolatrous kingdom of Israel is really the coming of Yahweh himself. With a revulsion that suggests the attitude of the early nomads toward the "tower of Babel," the proud symbol of Mesopotamian culture, the prophet insists that cities are the source of the evil that arouses Yahweh to come as Judge:

> What is the transgression of Jacob?
>   Is it not Samaria?
> And what is the sin of the house of Judah?
>   Is it not Jerusalem?
>
>   —MICAH 1:5

Micah was convinced that the cancerous corruption of Israel had spread into Judah (1:8-9). Filled with the divine charisma, in contrast to the professional prophets who preached a message that buttered their bread (3:5-8), this austere prophet felt compelled to announce the consequences of the people's behavior. Judah, as well as Israel, would experience the full impact of Yahweh's fearful judgment. In a vivid oracle, in which the Hebrew contains word-plays on the names of various cities and towns, the prophet portrays the Assyrian avalanche sweeping across cities west of Jerusalem, and engulfing his own home town of Moresheth near Gath (1:10-16). Moreover, the prophet insisted that "evil has come down from Yahweh to the gate of Jerusalem" (1:12). Unlike Isaiah, Micah did not believe that Jerusalem would be spared. Zion, he said, was "built with blood" (3:10)—it was the scene of outrageous social injustice, a place where people lay awake at nights devising wickedness (chapter 2). The civil and religious leaders were to blame for the sad state of affairs, for they should know what Yahweh demands of his people (chapter 3). What good is it, then, to "lean upon Yahweh" and to say that because he is "in our midst" no evil will come?

> Zion shall be plowed as a field;
> Jerusalem shall become a heap of ruins,
>   and the mountain of the house [i.e., the temple area]
>   a wooded height.
>
> —MICAH 3:12

This announcement was quoted a century later, when Jeremiah's life was in jeopardy because he made a similar prediction about Jerusalem and its Temple (see Jer. 26:18-19). According to the passage in Jeremiah, the oracle was first delivered in the time of king Hezekiah (c. 715-687 B.C.), who succeeded Ahaz to the throne of Judah.

Micah's bold prophesy against Zion cannot be explained wholly by saying that, unlike the city-bred Isaiah, he came from the country and therefore could criticize the Davidic City with cool detachment. There must have been also profound *theological* differences between the two prophets, despite the fact that both books bearing their names now contain the famous prophecy concerning the elevation of Zion "in the last days." [20] It is significant that in the indisputably genuine oracles of Micah there is not a single reference to the Davidic covenant theology, which guaranteed the permanence of the Davidic dynasty and the security of the Davidic City. Micah seems not to have been nurtured in court theology but rather in the Exodus tradition, which was kept alive in the rural areas of Judah. It is not surprising, therefore, that in the passage in Micah 6:1-8, which is often hailed as the epitome of the message of the eighth-century

---

[20] This oracle is found in both Micah 4:1-4 and Is. 2:2-4 with only slight variation. Isaiah clearly has the greater claim upon the oracle in view of his Zion-centered message. But it is possible that an independent oracle has been added to both prophetic books by compilers. (See above, p. 267, footnote 10.)

prophets, Micah turns to Israel's sacred history which centers in the Exodus.[21]

Notice the dramatic structure of this passage. Like the opening oracle of the book of Micah, it is built around a controversy in a law court, a familiar theme of prophecy, as we have seen. The trial opens with a summons by the prophet in the name of Yahweh (verses 1-2). The mountains are the witnesses: before them Israel is to present her case, and they are to hear the controversy between Yahweh and his people. Then Yahweh, the Plaintiff, gives his indictment (verses 3-5). Significantly, however, he appeals to Israel's memory—not to laws written in a statute book. He bases his case on events that have manifested his steadfast love for his people, beginning with the Exodus from Egypt and culminating in their establishment in the Land of Promise. These events constitute the very foundation of the covenant community. The clear implication is that because Israel has forgotten the great deeds that Yahweh has done on her behalf, she no longer knows what Yahweh requires of his people. The prophet is appalled at the incongruity between Yahweh's actions and Israel's conduct. At last, the defendant, Israel, speaks (verses 6-7). But before Yahweh, Israel has no case to plead, save to confess humbly that her actions are inconsistent with Yahweh's saving acts in history. Burnt offerings, rivers of oil, even the most costly sacrifice of the first-born—these things do not please Yahweh. In view of what Yahweh has done for Israel, such responses are empty mockery and wearisome offense. Finally, the passage reaches a climax as the prophetic voice proclaims that Yahweh himself has shown Israel what is good:

> What does Yahweh require of you
>   but to do justice, and to love kindness.[22]
>   and to walk humbly with your God?
>   —MICAH 6:8

Here we find, expressed in a single sentence, Amos' demand for justice, Hosea's appeal for the steadfast love that binds men in covenant with God and with one another, and Isaiah's plea for the quiet faith of the "humble walk" with God.

ISAIAH'S LATER CAREER

As we have seen, Isaiah seems not to have been very active in public after the Syro-Israelite crisis. Indeed, it has been suggested that during most of the re-

---

[21] Micah's prophecies are concentrated in chapters 1-3, though other oracles from him are found in chapter 6. The arguments for denying 6:1-8 to Micah are not decisive. The reference to child sacrifice (vs. 7), was not only familiar from tradition, like that of Gen. 22, but perhaps was immediately based on the action of King Ahaz under stress (II Kings 16:3). And the evangelical appeal of these verses is similar to passages in Amos (e.g., Amos 2:9-11), who also spoke in accents of doom.

[22] The word translated "kindness" is ḥésed, the same word that we have met in our study of Hosea (see p. 248). It refers to a covenant relationship that is steadfast and that finds expression in acts of brotherly kindness.

mainder of Ahaz's reign he withdrew into the circle of the prophetic community. However that may be, the death of Ahaz inaugurated a new period of his prophetic activity. It must have seemed to Isaiah, at least for a moment, that the time had come to break the "seal" from the prophetic testimony, in the expectation that Hezekiah would give a more favorable hearing than had his father.

The Age of Hezekiah

The accession of Hezekiah in 715 B.C. marked a turning point in Judean affairs. Ahaz had been a weak king, a servile and frightened vassal of Assyria. Hezekiah, however, was a wise and vigorous leader, whose policies brought about a religious reformation and a stiffening of Judah's attitude toward Assyria. In II Kings 18, the Deuteronomic editor gives unqualified approval to his reign, comparing him to David and saying that "there was none like him among all the kings of Judah after him, nor among those who were before him." This tribute, of course, was based on the Deuteronomic premise that the true worship of Yahweh must be centralized in Jerusalem.

One of Hezekiah's accomplishments was his great religious reform, which led to the suppression of local shrines ("high places"), the centers of the Canaanized popular religion that had threatened Israel's faith from the very first. Not satisfied with destroying the sacred objects in these local sanctuaries—the altars, the sacred pillars, and the Asherah—Hezekiah carried the reform right into the Temple of Jerusalem. At his orders, the copper serpent, Nehushtan, which had been an object of veneration for centuries, was shattered (II Kings 18:4). According to the tradition, it had been made by Moses himself (Num. 21:4-9). Hezekiah's aim was to purify Judah's worship and to concentrate it in the Temple at Jerusalem. His sweeping reform prepared the way for the Deuteronomic Reform, to be considered in the next chapter. Surprisingly, Isaiah makes no reference to Hezekiah's reform, though in all probability it was one of the factors that led the prophet to break his long silence and to reappear in public.

As in the case of other religious revivals in Israel, so here we find that Hezekiah's religious reform had certain political implications. When he ascended the throne, Judah was growing restive under the Assyrian yoke. Ahaz's appeasement policy, symbolized by the installation of an Assyrian altar in the Temple, had proved unpopular, especially among those who had to dig down into their pockets to pay heavy taxes for Assyrian tribute. Hezekiah's purification of worship, including no doubt the removal of Assyrian cult objects from the Temple, was a stimulus to Judean nationalism, for he was virtually declaring independence from Assyrian domination and throwing his weight behind the revolutionary spirit of the day. And he got away with this nationalistic policy for the time being, because Sargon, the Assyrian king, was busy waging war in the mountains of northern Mesopotamia.

A symbol of Hezekiah's political energy was the construction of the Siloam

THE SILOAM TUNNEL *was carved through 1,777 feet of solid rock for the purpose of bringing water from a spring outside Jerusalem to a pool inside the city wall. On the wall of the tunnel an inscription was found that described how the workers started at both ends and met in the middle after following a winding route.*

tunnel later in his reign, when political tensions were high (II Kings 20:20; cf. II Chron. 32:30). Ahaz, it will be remembered, had been worried about Jerusalem's fresh-water supply—one of the city's main defenses—during the Syro-Israelite crisis. So long as the city water had to be brought in through a conduit from the Spring of Gihon (or Virgin's Spring) outside the city wall, to the Pool of Siloam inside the wall, Jerusalem was vulnerable to the enemy. Hezekiah overcame this problem by a remarkable engineering feat. A tunnel more than 1,700 feet long was cut through solid rock from the spring to the pool. Workers equipped with wedges, hammers, and picks started boring at both ends simultaneously, and after some winding met in the middle. Today the visitor can walk through this tunnel, if he is willing to wade knee-deep in cold spring water, and can see the slanting pick marks where the workers met. The famous Siloam inscription, which has been cut from the wall and taken to the museum at Istanbul, tells the story of the boring, saying that "while there was yet three cubits to be bored through, there was heard the voice of one calling unto another." [23] Besides this work, Hezekiah extended the walls and strengthened the fortifications of Jerusalem (II Chron. 32:5; see map, p. 143).

Hezekiah was first tempted to join the rising rebellion against Assyria in the year 711 B.C. The revolution, instigated by Egyptian intrigue, broke out in the

[23] See Pritchard, *Ancient Near Eastern Texts*, p. 321.

Philistine city of Ashdod (Is. 14:28-32), which had been a hot-bed of revolution for several years. Afraid of being overrun by Assyria, Egypt fanned the fires of revolution. At this time, Isaiah was commanded to perform a sign to dramatize Yahweh's judgment against the conspiracy (chapter 20). He was to go naked and barefoot through the streets of Jerusalem, to signify that Assyria would lead Egypt and Ethiopia away into exile clad only in the loin cloth of prisoners of war.[24] As matters turned out, Isaiah's prophecy did not apply to Egypt, for Egypt left the Philistines in the lurch at the last moment. Sargon's armies pointed up the folly of revolution by destroying Ashdod and two other Philistine cities, and by converting the Philistine coast into an Assyrian province. Although Sargon accused Judah of having a hand in the revolt, evidently Hezekiah had avoided becoming deeply involved, possibly as a result of Isaiah's influence. In any case, Assyria did not invade Judah. The prophet Micah was still active

[24] Ethiopia is mentioned because the new Egyptian dynasty was Ethiopian.

A BOUNDARY STONE *named after Merodach-baladan II, the king who aspired to build a Babylonian empire in Isaiah's time. The king is presenting an official (the smaller figure) with a land grant. At the top are four shrines with the emblems of Babylonian deities. The triangular symbol at the right—resting upon a shrine and a straight-horned dragon—is that of the god Marduk.*

at this time. Ashdod and Gath, two of the Philistine cities sacked by the Assyrians, were only a short distance from his hometown. The distant sound of marching armies during this invasion prompted him to say that Moreshath-gath (near Gath) would fall to Assyria (Mic. 1:15; see above, p. 278).

Living in Revolutionary Times

The death of Sargon in 705 B.C. set off a chain reaction of revolution throughout the whole Assyrian empire. To a political observer of the time, it must have seemed that the empire, founded by the power of the sword and upheld by the ruthless suppression of nationalism, was about to explode into fragments. This time the revolution centered in the eastern part of the empire, in the province of Babylonia. The leader was the king of Babylonia, Marduk-apal-iddina, who is referred to in the Old Testament as Merodach-baladan (II Kings 20:12 = Is. 39:1). Something of a political genius, he might have established a Babylonian empire had the political situation been more favorable, but this dream was not realized until a century later.

Merodach-baladan, believing that the best way to win his political objectives was to stir up trouble for Sennacherib, kindled the fires of revolt throughout the whole Assyrian empire. He consolidated the revolutionary forces in his own area, and then sent embassies into Palestine. The story of the embassy to Hezekiah, and Isaiah's vehement protest against it, is given in II Kings 20:12-19 (= Is. 39:1-8). Egypt, too, was experiencing a national revival at the time, under the leadership of an energetic Ethiopian king named Shabako, the founder of the Twenty-fifth Dynasty. The oracle in Isaiah 18, which apparently comes from this period, speaks about the coming of Shabako's ambassadors to secure Hezekiah's participation in the general revolt. Egypt wanted to recover her ancient imperial glory, and through diplomatic intrigue she hoped to bring about Assyria's collapse.

When all Judah's neighbors, with few exceptions, were jumping on the revolutionary band wagon, Hezekiah simply could not resist the temptation to join in. This time he went all out for the revolution. He even threw his army against Philistia (II Kings 18:8) when several Philistine kings refused to join the conspiracy, and, as we know from Sennacherib's annals, took Padi, king of the Philistine city of Ekron, back to Jerusalem as a prisoner.

In this hour of fateful decision, Isaiah counseled the Judean king, as he had counseled Ahaz before, to stay out of the revolution. As we have said, most of the prophetic oracles found in chapters 28-33 come from this period, the last five years of the eighth century. Isaiah's advice was not based merely on the shrewd political calculation that Assyria would eventually win out. As a political observer, he was perhaps no wiser than others at the time who came to a different conclusion about the best course of action. Isaiah's greatness as a prophet does not lie primarily in his political astuteness but in the religious perspective with which he viewed the international scene.

In Quietness and Confidence Is Strength

Uppermost in his mind was the conviction that Yahweh was running history and that Assyria was called to serve his purpose. Isaiah elaborates this conviction in a magnificent oracle in the earlier section of the book of Isaiah, 10:5-19, where the Assyrian is hailed as "the rod of Yahweh's anger":

> Ah, Assyria, the rod of my anger,
>   the staff of my fury!
> Against a godless nation I send him,
>   and against the people of my wrath
>   I command him,
> to take spoil and seize plunder,
>   and to tread them down like the
>   mire of the streets.
>   —ISAIAH 10:5-6

To be sure, the Assyrian dictator does not realize that he is an instrument in the hand of God, for he supposes that he is pursuing his own political objectives. Nevertheless, behind the inexorable Assyrian advance is the overruling sovereignty of God, who, as one of the psalmists said, makes even the wrath of men to praise him. History is not governed by caprice or by the nation that possesses the largest battalions. The terrible havoc wrought by the Assyrian invader is the sign of God's judgment in human affairs, and particularly his judgment upon "a godless nation," the people of his choice. But "when Yahweh has finished all his work on Mount Zion and on Jerusalem, he will punish the arrogant boasting of the king of Assyria and his haughty pride" (10:12). It is folly for the axe to boast over the man who uses it, or for the rod to lord over the one who wields it! When Yahweh has carried out his judgment against his own people, he will overthrow the Assyrian tyranny (cf. 14:24-27). Even the most powerful empire must learn that it is Yahweh who is King, and that the tumultuous stream of history cannot escape the banks of his purpose. Hence the man of faith should willingly submit, not to the Assyrian yoke, but to the yoke of Yahweh's sovereignty. He should accept the judgment of God as a call to repentance for the flagrant wrongs of society, and should wait patiently for the time when Yahweh will humble the pride of the aggressor nation.

It was out of this conviction that Isaiah advised Hezekiah to shun the revolution against Assyria. Men cannot stay the Assyrian advance any more than they can prevent Yahweh's coming to judge and rebuke his people. Like Hosea, Isaiah condemned political alliances, calling them a "covenant with death." When the "overwhelming scourge" passes through the land, Judah will be inundated, for Yahweh will perform a "strange work," one that will utterly confound all human plans and hopes (28:14-22). In particular, Isaiah condemned the favorable reception given the Egyptian envoys mentioned in Isaiah 18, just as he had denounced Hezekiah's secret negotiations with Merodach-baladan (II Kings 20:12-19). He denounced those who went down to Egypt for help, trusting in "chariots because they are many" and "horsemen because they are very strong" (Is. 31:1-3), for

> the Egyptians are men, and not God;
>   and their horses are flesh, and not spirit.
> —ISAIAH 31:3

Such political efforts, according to the prophet, were clear evidence that men did not trust "the Holy One of Israel." In 30:1-15, he stresses the folly of taking refuge in "the shadow of Egypt." Echoing his earlier advice to Ahaz (7:9), Isaiah here gives the supreme summary of the meaning of faith:

> In returning and rest you shall be saved;
>   in quietness and in trust shall be your strength.
> —ISAIAH 30:15

Judah's security lies not in politics—in being a nation like other nations—but rather in returning to God (i.e., repentance) and in dependence upon his sovereign will, confident that deliverance will come from him alone in his good time. But to the prophetic summons the people answered a flat "No" (30:16). They wanted to ride on horses. They would ride, all right—in flight from swift horsemen. And if they could not hear the call to repentance in plain-spoken Hebrew, then they would have to listen to Yahweh speaking to them in the strange babble of a barbarian tongue (28:7-13). From the beginning to the end of his ministry, Isaiah was baffled by the people's inability to hear what Yahweh was saying in the events of the time. Yahweh had spoken of "rest to the weary" —the rest and repose of a steady and serene faith in a day of political anxiety and tumult; "yet they could not hear" (28:12).

More and more, however, Isaiah came to believe that a remnant of the faithful would hear and would be saved from the impending destruction. For Yahweh would lay in Jerusalem a foundation for "the faithful city" (cf. 1:26), a precious and well-tested cornerstone composed of a remnant whose strength is a quiet and patient trust in God:

> Behold, I am laying in Zion for a foundation
>   a stone, a tested stone,
> a precious cornerstone, of a sure foundation:
>   "He who believes will not be in haste."
> —ISAIAH 28:16

This appeal for faith in Yahweh, the King of Israel and of the world, was the prophet's central theme.

Shut up Like a Bird in a Cage

Sennacherib moved quickly to crush the rebellion that threatened his empire. First he decisively defeated Merodach-baladan of Babylonia and all his allies. Then, having restored order throughout Mesopotamia by the year 703 B.C., he launched a victorious campaign into the west. He marched triumphantly through Phoenicia and into the Philistine plain, where he destroyed a large Egyptian army at the Philistine city of Ekron. Micah 1:10-16 reflects the inexorable Assyrian advance, before which all the cities in his neighborhood—including the fortress of Lachish—fell one by one. Evidently one Assyrian army moved inland, through the hill country of Samaria and Judah, and approached Jerusalem from the north. The route of the Assyrian advance is reported in Isaiah 10:28-31, a passage that gives us a vivid impression of the lightning speed with which the cities were conquered. According to Sennacherib's annals, forty-six of Hezekiah's fortified cities were taken, as well as numerous small cities in the neighborhood, and 200,150 people were taken captive (cf. II Kings 18:13).[25] (See inset map, p. 260.)

During the invasion of 701, Jerusalem was cut off from all outside help. Sennacherib says that Hezekiah "like a caged bird, I shut up in Jerusalem, his royal city." In even stronger terms, Isaiah compared the catastrophe to the destruction of Sodom and Gomorrah. Isaiah 1:4-9 apparently springs from this crisis. Why, he asks, does Judah continue to revolt? The country is stricken, like a sick man, from head to toe; aliens are devouring the land; and Zion is left isolated and alone, "like a booth in a vineyard, like a lodge in a cucumber field."

But, strangely, Jerusalem did not suffer the complete destruction of Sodom and Gomorrah, for Yahweh in his mercy spared the city and left "a few survivors" (1:9). The story of this unexpected, marvelous turn of events is related in II Kings 18 and 19 (= Is. 36-37). During the siege of Lachish (see Plate 5), Sennacherib sent a delegation, led by the Rabshakeh (a title meaning "chief deputy"), to Jersualem to demand unconditional surrender. The story is told so vividly that we can almost imagine ourselves on the walls with the city's defenders, witnessing the episode. We see the Rabshakeh standing off at some distance, with a detachment of the powerful Assyrian army behind him. Through the tensely silent air comes the shrewd propaganda speech of the Rabshakeh, threatening to have a deadlier effect on the stout moral of the city's defenders

---

[25] See Pritchard, *Ancient Near Eastern Texts*, pp. 287-288. Certain difficulties in the biblical text have led scholars to advance the hypothesis that Sennacherib actually invaded Judah twice, once in 701 and again after 691 when another rebellion flared up in the west, and that it was on the latter occasion that Jerusalem was miraculously spared. John Bright (*History of Israel* [40], pp. 268-271, 282-287) favors this view, though he admits that Assyrian inscriptions do not mention the supposed second campaign.

than the Assyrian swords themselves. In alarm, the Judean officials ask him to speak in Aramaic, the language of international diplomacy, lest his unanswerable challenge be heard by the civilian population. But this confession of weakness only incites the Rabshakeh to press his arguments with greater force. In effect, he says that the people are fighting for a lost cause. They have everything to gain and little to lose by discarding Hezekiah and surrendering unconditionally to the powerful army of Sennacherib.

Isaiah's Message during the Invasion

pause here

Now comes a surprise: Isaiah counsels against capitulating to Assyria. In view of his earlier message that the Assyrian was the rod of Yahweh's anger, this may seem like a right-about face. But we must remember that Isaiah was not a politician who based his message on the relative strength of Assyria and the powers ranged against her. To us it seems reasonable that Judah, situated off the beaten path of world conquerors, could have escaped trouble by following a policy of non-interference. This may have been in the background of Isaiah's mind in earlier situations, but if so he gives no hint of it. His perspective was *religious*, not political. He believed firmly that Assyria was an instrument in Yahweh's hand. And although for a time Yahweh wielded that instrument to judge his people, Isaiah believed that Yahweh would lay it aside when he had finished his "strange work" in Jerusalem. Since Assyria's power was given to her by God, that power could be checked or taken away when God chose to do so.

Isaiah and Micah proclaimed different messages during the crisis of Sennacherib's invasion. With unyielding conviction, Micah insisted that Zion would be "plowed like a

SENNACHERIB'S CLAY PRISM announces his *victory over Palestinian forces and their Egyptian allies. The hexagonal artifact tells how he overran Judah and shut up Hezekiah "like a caged bird" in his royal city, Jerusalem.*

field" (Mic. 3:12). Isaiah, on the other hand, declared that Zion could not fall. This claim, however, must be viewed within the total context of Isaiah's prophetic ministry. As we have seen, he believed that Yahweh's saving purpose in history was tied up especially with the city of Jerusalem. For Jerusalem was the place of the Temple, in which the Ark rested. Jerusalem was the city that Yahweh had founded (14:32); Mount Zion was "the place of the name of Yahweh of hosts" (18:7). It was in Jerusalem's Temple that Isaiah had seen the vision of Yahweh, the King. Moreover, Jerusalem was the City of David. And the Davidic

THE SIEGE OF LACHISH *by Sennacherib is depicted on these reliefs. From towers along the wall of the city (top), the defenders shoot arrows and other missiles into the attackers. The main battle centers around the city gate (right). The Assyrians have thrown up a log incline for their siege engine, behind which archers advance upon the defending soldiers on the gate turret. From a doorway in the side of the tower, inhabitants of the city are escaping with their possessions, and in the lower right three victims have been hanged.*

dynasty, which had survived through three troubled centuries of history, was the sign of a social stability that Yahweh himself had given.

All these convictions, however, had their roots in a royal theology which developed in Jerusalem under the influence of Nathan's prophecy to David. This oracle (II Sam. 7), it will be recalled, announced Yahweh's *unconditional* promise to maintain the Davidic throne, regardless of the merit or demerit of Israel's kings. In Northern Israel, where the contingency of the Mosaic covenant was stressed, prophets like Amos or Hosea could announce that Israel's disobedience was sufficient ground for Yahweh to bring Israel's history to an end. Isaiah took his cue, however, from Yahweh's promises of grace to David and through the Davidic king, to the whole people. This did not mean soft-pedaling the call to repentance and reform. As we have seen, Isaiah, was the equal of Amos in his radical criticism of society and his urgent demand for reform. Yet he believed that in the last analysis the hope for the future rested not on the behavior of the people or the greatness of their king, but solely on the grace of Yahweh who, in his own way and in his own time, would fulfill his promises to David.

It is not surprising, then, for Isaiah to insist that Yahweh's purpose was not to eradicate Jerusalem, but to build a new Jerusalem on the foundation of a righteous and faithful remnant. Yahweh's purpose called for a holy people and a holy city. The doctrine of the remnant fundamentally had a positive meaning: a remnant shall return (repent) and "lean upon Yahweh" (10:20-21). Yahweh would spare Zion "for his own sake and for David's sake" (37:33-35), according to the tenets of the royal covenant theology.

So, when we consider Isaiah's message as a whole, his stand during the invasion of Sennacherib turns out to be religiously consistent. We must be on guard against forcing the prophets' pronouncements into our own patterns of logic, or even assuming that all prophets said exactly the same thing about Jerusalem. The prophets always addressed themselves to the situation at hand. And Isaiah, in 701 B.C., was called to speak to *that* situation, not to the earlier situation of the Syro-Israelite war or the later situation of Jeremiah's day. Experience had led him to realize, perhaps more deeply than in his earlier career, that behind and within Yahweh's judgment was his gracious will to deliver and renew. Hence the oracles from the stormy final years of Isaiah's ministry stressed Yahweh's saving power. The Assyrian shall fall "by a sword, not of man," for Yahweh "will come down to fight upon Mount Zion" and, like hovering birds, "will protect Jerusalem" (31:4-9). Since it is Yahweh himself who is encamped against Jerusalem, the proud nations that fight against Mount Zion will be like a hungry man who dreams that he is eating, only to awake and find that his hunger is not satisfied (29:1-8). Yahweh comes from afar to sift the nations with the sieve of destruction, and the Assyrians will be terror-stricken at the might of his arm and the fury of his voice (30:27-33). This appearance will be the final reminder that Yahweh, and not Assyria or any other human power, is the Lord of history.

SENNACHERIB'S CAMP AT LACHISH (II Kings 18:14): *against a background of palm trees and grapevines, the king is seated on his throne and fanned by servants. Immediately behind his officers, who present the booty of Lachish, hapless citizens of the town prostrate themselves (left). To the right of the throne is the royal tent, pitched on a wooded hill.*

The Deliverance of Jerusalem

According to the narrative in II Kings 19 (paralleled in Is. 37), when the challenge of the Rabshakeh was reported to Hezekiah the king was filled with despair. "This day is a day of distress, of rebuke, and disgrace; children have come to the birth, and there is no strength to bring them forth" (vs. 3). Isaiah, following an urgent word from the king, delivered an oracle against the arrogance of the Assyrian king (II Kings 19:20-28). To this prophetic word is linked another "sign," that a remnant will be saved and that after three years conditions in the land will return to normal (verses 29-31).

The oracle against Assyria is in keeping with the prophetic message of Isaiah in 10:5-16 but the rest of the story (verses 32-37) teems with difficulties. It is quite true that the Assyrian armies departed without laying siege to Jerusalem, precisely as Isaiah predicted in verses 32-34. However, this "answer to prayer" was explained on the basis of a legend: Sennacherib's army was decimated by the Angel of the Lord during the night, prompting Sennacherib to return to his capital, where he was assassinated by one of his sons (II Kings 19:35-37).

Possibly this refers to a disease or pestilence that spread through the Assyrian army, although Sennacherib's annals do not mention this. More likely, Sennacherib heard "a rumor," as Isaiah is said to have predicted elsewhere, which prompted him to hasten back to his home base (II Kings 19:7). The rumor proved to be word of a new uprising in Babylonia. So Sennacherib hastily withdrew to deal with a trouble spot that was potentially more dangerous than the little kingdom of Judah. Anyway, he had accomplished his objectives in Palestine. Egypt had been dealt a staggering blow; the anti-Assyrian coalition, inspired by Egypt, had been broken up. Hezekiah, secure in his mountain fortress, had seen his land diminished and had yielded to Assyrian demands by paying a handsome tribute to the Assyrian king during his stay at Lachish. The payment of the tribute is described in detail in II Kings 18:14-16 and is corroborated by Sennacherib's own account of his western campaign. So why should Sennacherib waste time and manpower on a costly siege of Jerusalem, especially when there were other more pressing matters to attend to?

Whatever the true explanation of Sennacherib's sudden withdrawal, the event made a deep impression upon Judean memory. The fact that Yahweh had spared Jerusalem in that crisis came to mean in popular thought that Yahweh would spare Jerusalem under any circumstances. Zion would stand forever! It is inconceivable that Isaiah would have agreed, for his message, like that of earlier prophets, included a condition:

> If you are willing and obedient,
>   you shall eat the good of the land;
> But if you refuse and rebel,
>   you shall be devoured by the sword.
>   —ISAIAH 1:19-20

It may be that Isaiah 22:1-14 comes from the time when the Assyrian armies withdrew from Jerusalem. If so, it gives us a picture of the wild abandon of those who went up to the housetop "full of shoutings." In the midst of the victory celebration, Isaiah stands alone, weeping for "the destruction of the daughter of my people."

After the tumultuous events of the end of the eighth century, Isaiah drops out of view. Whether he was active during the closing years of Hezekiah's reign (Hezekiah died in 687) we do not know. Tradition has it that he was martyred during the reactionary reign of Hezekiah's successor, Manasseh. It may be that Isaiah turned his attention to his disciples, giving fresh impetus to the extensive tradition that is associated with his name and within that prophetic community waiting patiently for God's purpose to be realized. In any event, long after the Assyrian empire had become a mere memory, Isaiah's conception of Yahweh's remnant—the "church" within the nation—exerted its influence upon Israel and eventually upon the community gathered around Jesus of Nazareth.

THE REDISCOVERY

OF MOSAIC TORAH

CHAPTER TEN   In times of insecurity, when the foundations of life are severely shaken, men often turn to the past to regain perspective and wistfully long for "the good old days gone by." In our time, for instance, the world crisis has stimulated an intensive study of the past and of the tradition in which we stand. The same situation arose in the kingdom of Judah during the seventh century B.C. At that

Biblical readings: The historical background is presented in the important chapters, II Kings 21-23 (paralleled in II Chron. 33-35). A great deal of literature comes from this period. We shall deal with the "Mosaic" sermon found in Deuteronomy 4:44 through chapter 26; read at least through chapter 11. Then read the following prophetic literature: Zephaniah 1-3; Jeremiah 1:1-4:4 (his early prophecies), Nahum, and Habakkuk 1-2.

time there was a "nostalgic revival of interest in the past." [1] This interest, which is clearly seen in the literature of the period, reflected a general tendency that was evident in the whole ancient Near East. The spirit of the times was well summed up by Jeremiah:

> Stand by the roads, and look,
>   and ask for the ancient paths,
> where the good way is; and walk in it,
>   and find rest for your souls.
>   —JEREMIAH 6:16

DIFFERING VIEWS OF THE COVENANT

We have already detected some of this nostalgia for the past in the prophet Isaiah, for whom the Golden Age was the glorious reign of David. Isaiah felt that the establishment of Jerusalem was "the beginning," the decisive time of the past, and that Yahweh's purpose in history was to restore Zion "as at the beginning" (1:26). Isaiah's concern for Davidic tradition was a unique development in prophecy, for he apparently paid little attention to the great formative period of the Exodus and the Sinai covenant. In this respect he differed from the prophets of the Northern Kingdom. Hosea, for instance, had traced Israel's beginning to the time of the Exodus and had affirmed that the goal of Israel's history would be a renewal of the covenant made in the wilderness. And Elijah's flight to Mount Horeb, the sacred mountain of the Mosaic covenant, was a symbol of the prophetic spirit in the Northern Kingdom.

In the kingdom of Judah, as we have observed at various points along the way, there developed a conception of the covenant that was fundamentally at odds with the northern Mosaic tradition.[2] David, the architect of the United Kingdom, had tried to unify the twelve tribes under his rule by taking over the religious traditions and symbols of the old Tribal Confederacy. But in the circle of the Davidic court a new theology developed, one that in the long run all but eclipsed the covenant faith that had been inherited from the Mosaic period. According to this view, Yahweh bound himself by a covenant oath to David, promising to preserve the Davidic line and to spare the Davidic kingdom "for the sake of my servant David," as Isaiah is reported to have said (Is. 37:35; see II Sam. 7). In short, Yahweh's sovereignty was *limited* by the covenant, since he was no longer free to choose or reject Israel, as Amos maintained, but was obligated to preserve her.

In past chapters, as we have surveyed the history of Israel and Judah, we have

---

[1] W. F. Albright, *From the Stone Age* [59], pp. 240-244.
[2] In what immediately follows, the author acknowledges indebtedness to the important study by George E. Mendenhall, *Law and Covenant* [108], pp. 44-50.

seen that the differences between the sister kingdoms were both political and theological. The theology of kingship, which centered in Yahweh's covenant with David, provided the theological foundation for the stability of Judah, with her unbroken succession of Davidic kings on the throne of Jerusalem. In the north, however, where no single dynasty was able to maintain itself throughout the history of the kingdom of Israel, the traditions of the ancient Tribal Confederacy were kept alive. There the remembrance of the old days of tribal independence contributed to the revolutionary ferment which brought about the downfall of kings; and there the accent fell upon the covenant made at Sinai, one that was based on the great saving acts of Yahweh which placed a grateful people under obligation to serve their covenant Lord.[3]

The most significant development within Judah during the seventh century B.C. was "the rediscovery of Moses," and the greatest literary monument to this revival of interest is the book of Deuteronomy and the whole Deuteronomic History from Deuteronomy through II Kings. "Ask now of the days that are past," is a characteristic appeal of Deuteronomy (4:32). But, as the context of this passage (verses 32-40)—one of the finest in Deuteronomic literature—indicates, the decisive period of the past was not the Golden Age of David's rule but the time of the Exodus when Yahweh made Israel his people "by trials, by signs, by wonders, and by war, by a mighty hand and an outstretched arm, and by great terrors, according to all that Yahweh your God did for you in Egypt before your eyes." The event of the Exodus, which fires the imagination and excites the wonder of the Deuteronomic writer, provided the source of Israel's knowledge of God, the foundation of the covenant community, and the motivation for fulfilling the obligations of the covenant.

MANASSEH, THE VILLAIN OF JUDAH

Let us look briefly at the historical background of the rediscovery of the Mosaic Torah or Teaching.

In recounting the events of Judah after the death of king Hezekiah, the Deuteronomic historian portrays Manasseh as the arch-villain of the whole gallery of Davidic kings. What Jeroboam I was to the kingdom of Israel, Manasseh was to the kingdom of Judah. It was he who reversed the religious reforms made under Hezekiah and "seduced" the people into doing more evil than the surrounding nations (II Kings 21:9). His long reign (687-642 B.C.) was painted as the darkest period of Judean history. Later historians, writing after the final fall of Jerusalem in the early sixth century B.C., held him responsible for pro-

---

[3] Recall at this point our discussion of the "suzerainty" covenant (pp. 61-62) in which Yahweh, instead of being limited by his relationship with Israel, was the author of a covenant that placed him under no obligation to continue the relationship if the people proved unfaithful.

voking Yahweh into bringing judgment upon the nation (II Kings 23:26-27; 24:3-4; cf. Jer. 15:4).

The reign of Manasseh, however, was an important transitional link between the great eighth-century prophets and the revival of prophecy at the end of the seventh century. So it should be viewed in a larger and perhaps a more sympathetic perspective than that of the critical report given in II Kings 21. This report makes no allusion to the great political fact that overshadowed the life and thought of Judah during Manasseh's entire reign: Assyria's victorious advance toward Egypt and her almost undisputed sway over the whole Fertile Crescent. It was during the reign of Manasseh that Assyria reached the very pinnacle of her imperial power and glory. To be sure, even in the early part of the seventh century, there were signs that the empire was built on shaky foundations. The murder of Sennacherib in 681 b.c. touched off a new revolution in Mesopotamia, and for a while it seemed as if the staggering empire, held together by the power of the sword and a system of vassal provinces, would fall. But the next Assyrian monarch, Esarhaddon (681-669 b.c.) proved up to the situation. After putting down all revolts, he marched into Egypt in 671 b.c., captured the city of Memphis, and took captive Tirhakah, the king of Egypt and Ethiopia. Esarhaddon's triumph is vividly portrayed on a stele in which he is represented standing before Assyrian religious symbols, while he holds two kneeling captives by ropes, one of whom is identified as Tirhakah.

The next Assyrian king, Ashurbanapal (669-c.633), was able to hold his father's empire together during the first part of his reign. The city of Thebes in Upper Egypt was destroyed and for a short while Egypt was held within the Assyrian orbit of power. Thus Assyria had at last succeeded in building the greatest empire in history. But as time passed it became clear that the sprawling empire was slipping out of control. In 652, revolt broke out again in Babylonia, this time under the leadership of a brother of the Assyrian emperor who had been appointed ruler of that vassal kingdom. With great effort, Ashurbanapal restored order, but not before the flames of revolution had spread throughout the Fertile Crescent. Other events conspired against Assyria. About 663 b.c. Egypt rose up under Psammetichus I (663-609 b.c.), founder of the Twenty-sixth Dynasty, and threw out the detested Assyrian army of occupation, thus inaugurating a brief Egyptian revival. To add to Assyria's troubles, hordes of invaders known as Scythians and Cimmerians were pouring into Mesopotamia from beyond the Caucasus mountains, and the Medes were beginning to consolidate their position in the highlands of Iran. Plainly Assyria's days of imperial rule were numbered. The time was not far off when the Judean prophet Nahum would vent his people's spleen against Assyrian oppression, announcing that the Assyrian capital of Nineveh would be overtaken by the same destruction that Assyria had visited upon Thebes (Nahum 3:8).

But all through the reign of Manasseh the powerful Assyrian empire was still intact. Like Ahaz before him, Manasseh believed that the best political policy was for Judah to play ball with Assyria as a faithful underling. There is some evidence that Manasseh was once taken captive to Babylon, presumably because of his part in an insurrection (II Chron. 33:10-13).[4] If he tried to revolt, however, he failed completely. In any event, most scholars doubt the historicity of this account, for which there is no parallel in II Kings or in the Assyrian annals. Chances are that Manasseh bought peace and at the same time made his own throne secure by playing the part of an obsequious vassal. This expedient policy

---

[4] The account in II Chronicles also states that while in exile the sinful king "humbled himself greatly before the God of his fathers" and repented. The reference to his prayer (II Chron. 33:19) prompted the composition, shortly before the Christian era, of "The Prayer of Manasseh." This is included in the Protestant Apocrypha; it is not contained in the Roman Catholic canon.

THE STELE OF ESARHADDON *was erected in northern Syria to commemorate that ruler's conquest of Egypt. With his right hand the king offers a libation to deities pictured (at top, riding on animals) next to their respective symbols—the crescent, winged sun disc, star, and lance. In his left hand he grips a mace and holds ropes on which two prisoners are leashed. The one kneeling is doubtless pharaoh Tirhakah, whose decisive defeat is described on the inscription written across the lower half of this stele, found at Zinjirli in North Syria.*

paid off, for while the Assyrian armies were marching up and down Palestine on their way to Egypt, the vassal state of Judah seems to have been left un-molested. (See maps on pp. 243 and 260.)

Judah's Dark Age

II Kings 21 points up Manasseh's domestic policy, which reflected the religious and social consequences of his capitulation to Assyria. Every one of his acts infuriated the minority who still remembered the great wave of religious enthusiasm created by Hezekiah's reforms. It is reported that "he rebuilt the high places which Hezekiah his father had destroyed"—that is, he re-opened the local pagan shrines in communities outside Jerusalem. He brazenly spon-sored a program to amalgamate the worship of Yahweh with Baal nature religion. Yahweh was worshiped at "altars of Baal"; an emblem of the mother-goddess, an Asherah, was made; and sacred prostitution was practiced (II Kings 23:7). Thus the Canaanization of Israel's worship, which had been a threat ever since the time of judges, was given free rein under royal sanction and patronage.

Moreover, the doors were thrown open to other pagan influences. The astral cult of Mesopotamia, referred to as "the worship of all the host of heaven" (the sun, moon, and stars were identified as deities) was introduced—clear evi-dence of the cultural influence that accompanied Assyrian political supremacy. To make matters worse, these pagan practices were admitted into the Temple of Jerusalem, the central sanctuary that Hezekiah had tried to purify of all alien defilement. Then, as if attempting to dredge up the foulest practices of the past, Manasseh revived the old cult of the dead (necromancy), which even Saul in his saner moments had suppressed and which Isaiah had vehemently condemned (Is. 8:19). In this respect too, Manasseh was showing his capitula-tion to Assyria, which gave official sanction to astrology, magic, and divination. And as a final concession to paganism, he resorted to the barbarous practice of human sacrifice. Following the precedent of Ahaz (II Kings 16:3), he "burned his son as an offering," evidently as an attempt to court divine favor (cf. Jer. 7:31).

The historian of II Kings compares Manasseh's reign with the time of Ahab and Jezebel, when paganism was sponsored and propagated by the crown. As in Ahab's time, the pagan practices were probably welcomed by many of the people, who saw no difficulty in worshiping Yahweh and at the same time ap-propriating practices that were fashionable throughout the Assyrian empire. But there was one great difference between the time of Ahab and that of Manasseh: in Manasseh's day there was no Elijah to rebuke the people for hopping on one foot and then the other, and to summon them to a renewed loyalty to the jealous God of the covenant. In part, this dearth of prophets may have been due to Manasseh's police-state measures, for we are told that

CHRONOLOGICAL CHART 7

B.C.	EGYPT	JUDAH	BABYLONIA	ASSYRIA
700	XXV Dynasty, c. 716-663 (Ethiopian) Tirhakah, c. 685-664 Invasion by Assyria, 671 Sack of Thebes, 663, by Ashurbanapal	Manasseh, 687-642		Sennacherib, 705-681 Esarhaddon, 681-669 Invasion of Egypt, 671 Ashurbanapal, 669-c. 633 Fall of Ashur to Medes, 614 Fall of Nineveh to Medes and Babylonians, 612 Babylonian defeat of Assyrians and Egyptians at Haran, 609 FALL OF ASSYRIA
		Amon, 642-640 Josiah, 640-609 First show of Judean independence, 629 (Zephaniah, c. 628-622) (Jeremiah, c. 626-587)	RISE OF BABYLONIA	
	XXVI Dynasty, c. 663-525 Psammetichus I c. 663-609	Josiah's "Deuteronomic Reform," 621	Nabopolassar, 626-605	
	Necho II, 609-593	Death of Josiah at Megiddo, 609		
		Jehoahaz II (Shallum), 609 (3 mos.) Jehoiakim (Eliakim), 609-598 (Habakkuk, c. 605)	Nebuchadnezzar, 605-562 Battle of Carchemish, 605	
600				

he "shed very much innocent blood, till he had filled Jerusalem from one end to another." Some have suggested that he tried to liquidate the prophets, and, as we have seen, Isaiah is said to have been martyred at this time. But this charge against Manasseh is only an inference, for which there is no real basis in the biblical record. It is hard to believe that if a prophet like Elijah had appeared, or if an organized purge of the prophets had been carried out, all record of such an event would have disappeared. Quite possibly the historian has exaggerated his account of Manasseh's reign somewhat in order to make him show up as badly as possible in comparison with the reforming kings, Hezekiah and Josiah. Nevertheless, after due allowance is made for the bias of the Deuteronomic historian, it is clear that his verdict is substantially correct. Manasseh's desertion of Yahweh plunged Judah into the "dark age" of her history, for he had bought peace at the terrible cost of surrendering Israel's distinctive religious heritage.

Anonymous Devotees of Yahweh

But the faithful devotees of Yahweh were far from inactive under Manasseh's rule. Not too many years after Manasseh's death, Jeremiah commended the Rechabites (see pp. 224-225) for their fidelity to their religious vows in protest against the sell-out of the ancient Mosaic faith (Jer. 35). This group, and others like them, must have annoyed Manasseh's party no end. Moreover, Manasseh's submission to Assyria must have galled all patriotic Judeans who were eager to throw off the Assyrian yoke. The smouldering fires of nationalism were kept alive, we may be sure, by prophets and priests who preserved and handed on the religious traditions of the past, especially by an order of teaching and preaching priests, known as Levites, who were active in the towns and the country area.[5] The Elohist epic (E), preserved in Judah after the fall of Samaria, was probably incorporated into the Yahwist epic (J) some time during Judah's vassalage to Assyria, perhaps in the last years of Hezekiah's reign. Thus throughout the "dark age" of Manasseh, the epic (JE) that included the traditions of the Northern and Southern Kingdoms continued to thrive and expand.

If we knew more about the period of Manasseh, we might find that many of the anonymous prophecies that are now mingled among the writings of the great prophets were composed at this time. For instance, portions of the book of Isaiah, which apparently come from a time before Second Isaiah, were probably produced then, and may well have come from the circle of disciples among whom Isaiah had deposited his original teaching. This was a reactionary period —a time when the prophets went into retreat; so it would have been appropriate for them to cherish and reflect upon the tradition, waiting and hoping for the

---

[5] The role of the Levitical priests in the country outside Jerusalem has been stressed by Gerhard von Rad, *Studies in Deuteronomy* [163].

time when Yahweh would once again show his face to Israel. If so, Manasseh's time was an age of anonymous prophecy when men of faith trusted in Yahweh's promise to overthrow the proud oppressors and to renew and restore his people.

NEW OUTBURSTS OF PROPHECY

So the reign of Manasseh, horrible as it appeared to the Deuteronomic historian, was not a time of complete decadence. Deep within the life of Judah a prophetic ferment was stirring, and men were turning to the past to rediscover the meaning of the Mosaic heritage. In anonymous circles, the way was being prepared for the national and religious renaissance that took place in Judah in the last quarter of the seventh century B.C. This Judean revival was made possible by changes in the international situation after the death of Assyria's last great king, Ashurbanapal, about 633 B.C.

Even before Ashurbanapal's death, trouble had been brewing for Assyria, as

ASHURBANAPAL'S HORSEMEN *battle camel-riding Arabs in this vivid action scene. Besides fighting wars on several fronts, Ashurbanapal was also a patron of culture, as shown by the excavations of his palace and royal library at Nineveh (see photo, page 321), where this artistic relief was found.*

was evident in the abortive revolt in Babylonia and the revival of Egyptian nationalism. With the speed of lightning, rumors of Assyria's weakness spread throughout the Fertile Crescent and excited great restlessness among satellite nations. When Manasseh died (642 B.C.), his son, Amon, continued his father's pro-Assyrian policy, but after a brief reign of two years he was murdered during a patriotic revolt. He was succeeded by the boy-king, Josiah (640-609 B.C.), who came to the throne when he was eight years old, about seven years before the death of Ashurbanapal. So by the time Ashurbanapal died, Josiah was ready to take over the reins of government. And the time was ripe for a radical change in Judah's policy.

The Prophet Zephaniah

Not long after the death of Ashurbanapal, the long prophetic silence that had lasted for three-quarters of a century was broken by two prophets who raised their voices publicly against the apostasy and degeneracy of Judah. The first was Zephaniah, possibly a descendant of the reforming king Hezekiah, according to the heading of the book that bears his name (1:1). It is impossible to date Zephaniah's career exactly, although his attack upon corruptions in worship suggests a time before Josiah's great reform in 621 B.C., to be discussed presently. He must have been a citizen of Jerusalem, for he mentions the districts of Jerusalem by name (Zeph. 1:10-11) and hurls his threats against the City (Zeph. 3).

Zephaniah's devastating message pierced the complacent atmosphere of Jerusalem like a trumpet blast.[6] The central theme of his prophecy, the nearness of the "Day of Yahweh," echoed a note struck earlier by Amos and Isaiah. Yahweh's Day would be "a day of wrath . . . a day of distress and anguish, a day of ruin and devastation, a day of darkness and gloom, a day of clouds and thick darkness, a day of trumpet blast and battle cry" (1:15-16). Isaiah had said that the Day of Yahweh would be ushered in by an Assyrian invasion; but by the time of Zephaniah the whole political situation had changed. The proud capital of Nineveh (see photo, p. 321) was about to be turned into a wilderness (2:13-15); Assyria would soon taste the bitter suffering she inflicted on others. At first it may seem strange that these two prophets should change the *political* focus of their messages. But remember that the prophets were not political forecasters, concerned only with tracing political developments. They viewed the historical scene from the perspective of faith in God, whose purpose is made known in, but is not identical with, political crisis at definite moments of history. Since they were concerned with what Yahweh was saying and doing in the concrete situation at hand, they did not think it was inconsistent for the

---

[6] Except for the concluding oracle (3:14-20), the present book of Zephaniah comes from the prophet himself. The concluding oracle seems to be a hymn of praise added later to round off the prophecy.

agent of divine judgment to vary from time to time. Notice that Zephaniah is rather vague about political details. Although he describes the invasion from the north in vivid terms, he does not clearly identify the aggressor, the new "rod" of Yahweh's judgment. Some scholars have felt that he may have had in mind Scythian hordes who, along with other peoples, contributed to the ferment of the time.[7] In any case, behind and within the whole political upheaval that hastened the downfall of the Assyrian empire, Zephaniah saw the judgment of Yahweh in the affairs of history.

Zephaniah spoke with a sense of urgency that was to be matched later by Jesus' proclamation that "the Kingdom of God is at hand." "The great day of Yahweh is near, near and hastening fast" (1:14). Events were hastening toward catastrophe; the clock was nearing midnight. Therefore, he summoned men to decision and repentance while they still had a chance. In scathing language he denounced the pagan practices which, under the influence of Manasseh, had defiled Judah and Jerusalem. He condemned Baal worship "in this place" (that is, in the city of Jerusalem); the astral cult—an importation from Assyria—which was practiced on the roof of the Temple; and the linking together of Yahweh and Milcom (the god of Ammon) (1:4-6). Even worse was men's easy-going complacency, based on the preposterous notion that Yahweh has no sway over history, that he is impotent to do either good or evil (1:12). In one breath Zephaniah condemned the whole leadership of the nation: politicians and judges, priests and prophets (3:3-4). Jerusalem, said Zephaniah, is a "rebellious city," impervious to Yahweh's word and lacking in faith. His prophetic task was to interpret the world crisis as God's action in history.

The prophet held out no hope that "the shameless nation," so deeply stained with paganism and so firmly entrenched in rebellion, would reform. Rather, Judah along with the other nations of the world would be consumed by "the fire of Yahweh's jealous wrath." Like Isaiah, he appealed for a remnant to repent and to seek refuge in Yahweh:

> Seek Yahweh, all you humble of the land,
>   who do his commands;
> seek righteousness, seek humility;
>   perhaps you may be hidden
>   on the day of the wrath of Yahweh.
>   —ZEPHANIAH 2:3

Since Yahweh's purpose was not utter destruction but the cleansing and renewal of his people, Zephaniah announced that a remnant would be saved from the holocaust (cf. 1:7)—"a people humble and lowly" who would live in sincerity and security (3:8-13).

---

[7] The theory of a Scythian invasion which swept as far as the border of Egypt is based on the Greek historian Herodotus' report (*Persian Wars*, I, 104-106) but, in the judgment of recent historians, this report must be taken with a grain of salt (e.g., John Bright, *History of Israel* [40], p. 293).

The Prophet Jeremiah

The second prophetic voice heard in the early years of Josiah's reign was that of Jeremiah. A full discussion of his long career will be postponed until the next chapter, but here we shall look for a minute at the early years of his ministry, which overlapped that of his contemporary, Zephaniah. According to the heading of the book of Jeremiah, he began to prophesy in the thirteenth year of Josiah's reign—that is, about the year 626 B.C. He was nurtured in the great traditions of Israel, for he is said to have come from a priestly family of Anathoth, a village about four miles northeast of Jerusalem. According to I Kings 2:26-27, Anathoth was the family residence of the priest Abiathar, a descendant of Eli whom Solomon expelled because of his complicity in Adonijah's attempt to seize the crown (I Kings 2:26-27). Possibly Jeremiah could trace his priestly ancestry back to Eli, the custodian of the Ark in the old confederate sanctuary of Shiloh. As we shall see later, the recollection of the fall of Shiloh, an event which virtually brought the former Israelite confederacy to an end (above, pp. 119-121), made a deep impression on Jeremiah's thought.

The materials in the first three chapters of the book of Jeremiah have been revised and reinterpreted in the light of later events in the prophet's ministry.

ASHURBANAPAL DRINKS A TOAST *to a victory in war. The last great king of Assyria, reclining upon a high couch while banqueting in his royal garden, is joined in the quaffing by his queen, seated facing him on a throne. Attendants fan the couple and provide music and delicacies. From the tree just in front of the harpist (left) hangs a man's head, perhaps that of the Elamite king just conquered. This mixture of culture and brutality was characteristic of Ashurbanapal's reign.*

But even so, these chapters (especially 2 and 3) give us important information about his career before the Deuteronomic Reformation of 621 B.C.

According to the introductory statement of the book of Jeremiah, the prophet's call to the prophetic ministry took place in the year 626 B.C. Evidently he was a very young man at the time, for he protested to Yahweh that he was a mere "lad" (1:6). The interior struggle recorded in the first chapter is played out under the ominous shadow of international events. It was a restless, uncertain time, yet pregnant with the hope of national liberation. Not long before, Ashurbanapal's death had set off a chain reaction of events. Babylonia, under Nabopolassar (626-605 B.C.), had at last gained independence after years of futile effort. Media had revolted under Cyaxares. Scythian hordes were on the move in the north. Egypt, like the famed Phoenix bird, was rising from her ashes. Great nations were stirring—watching for the opportune moment to strike a deathblow to the tottering Assyrian giant, each hoping to become the new master of the world. The old world order, which for over two centuries had been held together by Assyrian might, was crumbling. It was in this eventful hour of history that "the word of Yahweh" came to Jeremiah.

The Power that Destroys Rebuilds

In the story of Jeremiah's call, vividly presented in the form of a dialogue with Yahweh (1:4-19), we are told how irresistibly Yahweh's word came to him (see 5:14; 23:29). Throughout his career, Jeremiah himself had to struggle with the mighty power of Yahweh's word, but he could not refrain from speaking it. In retrospect, he saw that his whole life, right back to the time when he was still in his mother's womb, was part of Yahweh's plan. This was the meaning of his life: to be Yahweh's prophet, consecrated for a special task. Like Moses (see Ex. 3 and 4), he shrank from the great task, not only because he was too young—perhaps not yet twenty years old—but because he felt that he was the last man on earth to be chosen for such work. But his attempts at evasion were in vain. His strength, after all, did not lie in his youth but in the power of the One who spoke through him, of the Sovereign who sent him. He was to be the servant of Yahweh's word that "makes history," the word that is filled with power to destroy and to rebuild (1:10). In their feverish struggle to gain control of history, the nations had to know that Yahweh controls human affairs. So in vivid language the narrative portrays Yahweh putting forth his hand and touching the prophet's mouth, not to cleanse (as in Isaiah's vision), but to empower him to speak:

> And Yahweh said to me,
> "Behold, I have put my words in your mouth.
> See, I have set you this day over nations and over kingdoms,
> to pluck up and to break down,
> to destroy and to overthrow,
> to build and to plant."
>
> —JEREMIAH 1:9-10

In Jeremiah's message we are made aware, more clearly and deeply than in the case of any other prophet, that Yahweh's word is not only sovereign over the nations but also over the interior life of the prophet himself.

The ensuing passage relates two visions in a question-and-answer style that is reminiscent of the visions of Amos (cf. Amos 7:7-9; 8:1-3). The first one, like Amos' vision of the basket of summer fruit, employs the favorite prophetic device of a play on words. In Hebrew there is close similarity between "almond" (*shaqed*) and the participle "watching" (*shoqed*). According to some interpreters, the almond-branch, which in Hebrew means "waker" or "watcher" because it "wakes to blossom as early as February," suggests to the prophet that God is the Waker or Watcher, "who slumbers not nor sleeps, but proceeds to judgment." [8] The emphasis, however, probably is more on the sound of the words than on the association of ideas. The striking assonance of the Hebrew words was enough to evoke the conviction that Yahweh is "watching over his word"—that is, he is acting to bring his purpose to fruition (see Is. 55:10-11). It was as if someone today, gazing intently at a watch, were to realize that God is "watching" over his plan to bring it to historical reality.

The second vision brings out what is implicit in the first one: Yahweh's historical purpose is ominous for Judah, for judgment is at hand. The prophet sees an ordinary cooking pot. Although the details are not too clear, it may be that the pot is boiling in the north, with its mouth tilted south and pouring out an evil brew upon the land. In any case, the meaning is clear enough: It is from the north that an avalanche of evil will come upon the inhabitants of the land. Some think that in this passage, and in the original version of 4:5-6:26, the foe from the north was the Scythians (see, however, the foregoing discussion of Zephaniah). But whatever the historical agency, Jeremiah was convinced that Yahweh was the real foe who was coming to execute judgment against the whole land. Yahweh's word, spoken by his prophet, was *against* the kings of Judah, her princes, her priests, and the people of the land (verse 18).

Jeremiah's Early Preaching

The content of Jeremiah's message, delivered in the years between his call and the Deuteronomic Reformation, is set forth in a series of oracles now contained in 2:1-4:4.[9] Here the Mosaic tradition is revived with a depth of understanding that is matched only by the prophet Hosea. Indeed, the affinities between the second chapter of Jeremiah and the prophecy of Hosea are so striking that we may conclude that Jeremiah knew and was influenced by Hosea's message, which by that time had become the possession of the kingdom of Judah. Jeremiah's memory goes back to the great formative period of Israel's

---

[8] So H. Wheeler Robinson, *The Cross in the Old Testament* [232], p. 143.

[9] However, references to Egypt in 2:14-17 and 2:29-37 indicate that these passages were re-worked at a time after the year 609 B.C., when the Egyptians were victorious over Josiah at Megiddo.

past: the Exodus and the sojourn in the wilderness. This was the time of Israel's covenant faithfulness (*ḥésed*),[10] when the "bride" Israel was in love with her husband (verses 1-3). In the honeymoon of her "youth," Israel responded with her whole being to Yahweh's historical revelation. But her life in Canaan had been a history of unfaithfulness, with no sense of gratitude for Yahweh's past deeds of benevolence and his continuing providence (2:4-8). To the prophet the whole thing was fantastic—for no other nation had ever repudiated its gods, even though they were really not gods at all! It was just as appalling as if Jerusalem had rejected a supply of fresh water in order to store up water in cisterns that were no better than sieves!

> Be appalled, O heavens, at this,
>   be shocked, be utterly desolate, says Yahweh,
> for my people have committed two evils:
>   they have forsaken me,
> the fountain of living waters,
>   and hewed out cisterns for themselves,
> broken cisterns,
>   that can hold no water.
>   —JEREMIAH 2:12-13

Israel, said the prophet, is like a faithless wife who leaves her husband (3:19-20). Indeed, she is no better than a common harlot driven by lusts as strong as those of an animal in heat (2:20-25). The land, Yahweh's heritage, has been defiled, for Israel's harlotry is practiced "upon every high hill and every green tree" where men worship Baal at local sanctuaries. Like Lady Macbeth, the stain of her sin cannot be washed from her body even by the most powerful detergent; her skirts are soiled with "the life-blood of guiltless poor." Therefore, a divorce must take place (3:1-15). For Judah has not learned the lesson of the history of the Northern Kingdom, which ended in a decree of divorce written in the visible language of tragic events. "Faithless Israel has shown herself less guilty than false Judah!" She stands condemned for the most flagrant betrayal of the love that had called, redeemed, and sustained her throughout her history (3:6-14). Nevertheless, there is still time for repentance, said the prophet. For in the events of history Yahweh was pleading with his faithless people to return to him, to acknowledge their true Lord and Husband. It is Yahweh's purpose to heal the broken relationship (3:22) and to effect an inward transformation of the heart (4:1-4). When the covenant relation is restored, then the ancient promise to Abraham will come into effect: Nations will bless themselves in the name of the God of Israel (4:2; see discussion on pp. 179-180).

Thus Jeremiah, like his contemporary Zephaniah, protested against the syncretism that had all but erased the distinctive elements of Israel's faith. He

---

[10] In the Revised Standard Version of 2:2 *ḥésed* is translated as "devotion." On this covenant term, see above, p. 248.

called for a reformation—not just a superficial reform of traditional rites and practices, but a reformation that begins in the heart, the seat of men's loyalties and affections. He called for a "circumcision of the heart," [11] for a breaking up of the fallow ground that had encrusted the life of the people (4:3-4). In a time when Israel's sacred past was neglected and forgotten, the Mosaic faith of the ancient wilderness was revived with new depth and power through the message of Jeremiah.

THE DEUTERONOMIC REFORMATION

The break-up of the world order, expected by Zephaniah and by Jeremiah, did not take place overnight. Instead, the course of events in the decades after the death of Ashurbanapal seemed to favor a renaissance of Judean nationalism. The youthful Josiah, capitalizing on Assyria's impotence to restore order in the Fertile Crescent, took the initiative in removing every sign of Assyrian domination in Palestine. According to Chronicles, which seems trustworthy in this instance, Josiah's first efforts at reform began in the twelfth year of his reign (629 B.C.), six years before the Deuteronomic Reformation (II Chron. 34:3). At that time, he expanded his influence into the territory of the former Northern Kingdom, which had become the Assyrian provinces of Megiddo and Samaria. Evidently Judah's aspiration to restore a United Kingdom under a Davidic king was intensified by the political situation of the day, and Josiah was eager to translate this nationalistic dream into reality.

The Discovery of the Book of Torah

In the following years, Josiah probably stepped up his program of nationalistic reform, especially with the rise to power of Nabopolassar (625-605 B.C.), who led the Babylonians to independence. And just as Hezekiah expressed his stiffening attitude toward Assyria in an attempt to cleanse Judean worship of Assyrian and other alien elements, so Josiah's nationalism was accompanied by religious reform. In this reform he was supported by the conservative landowners of Judah, referred to in II Kings 11:14, 20 as "the people of the land," who had been hostile to Manasseh's appeasement of Assyria and longed for national independence (see II Kings 21:23-24).[12] Indeed, this reform was probably already under way when a remarkable discovery was made in the eighteenth year of his

---

[11] This expression, found also in Deuteronomy 10:16 and 30:6, is a metaphor for opening the "heart," the center of one's being, so that it may be humbly submissive to the will of God. The "uncircumcised heart" (Jer. 9:26) is one that is hardened in stubborn rebellion.

[12] Jehoash, in an earlier period, likewise had gained the support of this group. In cooperation with the High Priest, Johoiada, they elevated the king to the throne (II Kings 11:17-21; see p. 219).

reign—that is, 621 B.C. We miss the import of the account in II Kings 22 if we fail to read it in the political context of the time. According to the story, a manuscript—"the book of the Torah"—was found when repairs were being made on the Temple at Jerusalem. Perhaps these were not routine repairs, but repairs designed to remove from the Temple all traces of Assyrian and other alien influences. In any case, when Josiah's secretary came to the Temple to supervise the payment of the workers' wages, he was informed of this "archaeological discovery" and he immediately brought the matter to Josiah's attention.

When the contents of the document were read to Josiah, he tore his garments —an oriental gesture of consternation or despair. Urgently he demanded that the High Priest verify the authenticity of the manuscript. This was done, not by trying to determine its age and authorship (as we would do), but by consulting Huldah the prophetess. Her oracular response cut to the quick: Because of the violation of the words of the book, Yahweh would bring evil upon Jerusalem, making it "a desolation and a curse." At this point, Josiah summoned the people to the Temple for a ceremony of covenant renewal. He read "the book of the covenant" to them (the same book referred to above), and on the basis of this Torah the people made a covenant before Yahweh to walk after Yahweh and to be obedient to his commandments. The ceremony calls to mind the story in Joshua 24 about the convocation "before God" at Shechem, the ritual of covenant renewal, and "the book of the Torah of God" in which the Shechem covenant was recorded. It also recalls the ancient covenant ceremony in Exodus 24:3-8, when Moses read to the people "the book of the covenant."

This covenant ceremony was followed by a great royal reform, quite like that of Hezekiah almost a century earlier but carried out with greater energy and thoroughness (II Kings 23). The finding of the Book of the Torah at the opportune moment accelerated and gave direction to the royal reform that Josiah had initiated some years earlier. Behind Josiah's house-cleaning was the desire to recover Judah's vitality and strength and to avoid the curse that the Torah invoked upon the nation when it disobeyed Yahweh's commandments (cf. Deut. 11:26-32; ch. 28). Accordingly, the paganism against which Zephaniah had protested (Zeph. 1:4-6) was abolished: the Canaanite Baal worship, the Assyrian astral cult, and the worship of other deities such as the Ammonite Milcom. Into the ash heap went all foreign objects found in the Temple: the appurtenances of the male god Baal and the mother goddess Asherah, the horses dedicated to the sun, and the astral altars on the roof. The practices of sacred prostitution, child sacrifice in the Valley of Hinnom, and the consultation of mediums and wizards were discontinued. And Josiah's reform did not stop with the cleansing of the Jerusalem Temple. The outlying sanctuaries, or "high places," which had been hotbeds of pagan religion, were destroyed and defiled, and their idolatrous priests were deposed. Finally, Josiah's reform was carried into the area of the former Northern Kingdom, then nominally under Assyrian control. The rival temple of Bethel was destroyed, along with other outlying high places. Josiah's declaration of independence from Assyria could hardly have been made in clearer terms!

One feature of Josiah's reform deserves special attention. According to II Kings 23:8-9, the Yahweh priests in the cities of Judah were put out of business when the local shrines were abolished. We are told, however, that "the priests of the high places did not come up to the altar of Yahweh in Jerusealem, but they ate unleavened bread among their brethren" (verse 9). Clearly, the most drastic aspect of the reform, although it had been anticipated by Hezekiah, was that worship was to be concentrated in the Jerusalem Temple, the central sanctuary for all Judah, where it could be rigorously watched by the official priesthood. In this way the faith of Israel could be kept free from the defilement of pagan ways and practices.

Josiah's reform, then, represented a break with Assyria, whose cultural influence had been deeply impressed upon Judah during the reign of Manasseh. Religiously, it involved a repudiation of what in those days might have been called "modernism": the attempt to conform to the religious fashions of the Assyrian empire and to blend Israel's religion and other religions into a coat of many colors. Josiah's reform was essentially conservative, for it sought to return to and conserve the distinctive elements of Israel's faith, rather than capitulating to the cultural pressures of the world. The reform was based on the conviction that unless the people repudiated the syncretism that sapped their vitality, Judah would go the way of the Northern Kingdom, which had been destroyed because the sacred past—the past of the Exodus and the covenant of the wilderness—had been forgotten. So by means of the ancient ceremony of covenant renewal a serious effort was made to recover the past and to restore its meaning in the present. In keeping with this effort, Josiah ordered that the long-neglected feast of the Mosaic period, the Passover, be reinstituted (II Kings 23:22-23).

The Deuteronomic Basis of Josiah's Reform

We now come to a major question: What document was it that was discovered in the Temple and read in the ceremony of covenant renewal? Is the Book of the Torah still preserved somewhere in the Old Testament? It stands to reason—at least the "reason" of critical scholarship—that it could not be the Pentateuch, for this was not completed until quite a bit later than Josiah's reform. Other legal collections within the Pentateuch—for instance, the so-called Covenant Code in Exodus 20:23-23:19, or the Holiness Code in Leviticus 17-26 —hardly fit the situation. If the Torah found in the Temple during Josiah's reign is still extant, it must be a book that strongly condemns the paganism of the Manasseh era, demands centralization of worship in Jerusalem, and solemnly warns that unswerving loyalty to Yahweh alone is the sole basis of the nation's existence.

These specifications are met by a body of law that is now found in chapters

12 to 26 of the book of Deuteronomy. When we read these chapters through with the story of II Kings 22-23 in mind, we are immediately struck by the correspondence between this Deuteronomic Code and the reform measures of Josiah. This is clear, for instance, in chapter 12, where it is stated that all the local high places must be abolished, and that the worship of Yahweh must be confined to the central sanctuary, "the place which Yahweh your God shall choose." Moreover, the Deuteronomic Code stipulates that while animals can be slaughtered for meat in any city, sacrifice to Yahweh is confined to the central sanctuary (12:13-14; 16:5-6) and, further, that the people must make pilgrimages to the central sanctuary to celebrate the great religious festivals (16:1-5). In Deuteronomy 18:1-8 it is said that the country priests, who would lose their jobs with the closing of the local sanctuaries, are entitled to minister in the central sanctuary, although the writer in II Kings, who evidently knew that it was impractical for all these priests to join the Jerusalem temple staff, states that they found their livelihood by sojourning in the midst of their own people (II Kings 23:9). We cannot pursue these parallels any further at this point. Suffice it to say that since the early church fathers of the fourth century A.D. (Athanasius, Chrysostom, Jerome), and especially since scholarly advances made during the nineteenth century, it has been held that Josiah's reform was based on the Code of Deuteronomy in some form. For that reason, it is called the Deuteronomic Reformation. As we have seen in earlier chapters, a historian who took the theological convictions of the Deuteronomic Reformation seriously produced a comprehensive history of Israel from the Mosaic period to the final fall of the nation (Deuteronomy through II Kings).

Both in form and content the Deuteronomic Code shows dependence on an old legal tradition, although the tradition is re-cast and re-interpreted for the seventh century B.C.[13] Indeed, it is probable that Deuteronomic Torah goes back ultimately to a northern covenant tradition which had been preserved and interpreted by Levite teachers in North Israel. In the Deuteronomic Code, Jerusalem is not explicitly identified as the central sanctuary even though Josiah so identified it for his own reforming purposes. Originally, the Deuteronomic authors may have had in mind the city of Shechem, the scene of the covenant renewal under Joshua, and the city chosen by Jeroboam I as his first capital.

So the nucleus of Deuteronomy, chapters 12-26, has a long history behind it, even though it was kept in the Jerusalem Temple during the reactionary reign of Manasseh, and later was "found" at the appropriate time during Josiah's reign. If it also contained chapter 28, as it probably did, we can understand why the reading of "the blessings and the curses" led to Josiah's consternation and

---

[13] The laws in Deuteronomy 12-26 show many similarities to the Covenant Code of Exodus 20:23-23:19, as can be seen by consulting the table given in S. R. Driver's *Introduction* [25], pp. 73-75. Moreover, many of the laws are cast in the "conditional" (casuistic) style of Near Eastern jurisprudence which influenced Israel during the settlement in Canaan. See pp. 96-97.

contrition. Moreover, it is probable that other sermonic material was included in the book presented to Josiah, but this question necessitates a brief consideration of the structure and contents of the whole book of Deuteronomy.

THE BOOK OF DEUTERONOMY

The book of Deuteronomy merits special attention in view of its great importance in Judean faith and worship. The publication of this book under state sponsorship during Josiah's reign was the first serious step toward the creation of an official canon of sacred literature that would be binding upon the whole people in matters of faith and conduct. Later on, as we shall see, the concept of an authoritative Torah, or Teaching, was extended to include not only Deuteronomy but the priestly edition of JE—that is, the whole Pentateuch (see Chapter 12). Deuteronomy nourished and deepened faith in Yahweh during the critical period of the collapse of the Assyrian empire and in subsequent generations. Significantly, it is one of the Old Testament books most frequently quoted in the New Testament. The First Great Commandment, which Jesus affirmed to be the fulfillment of the whole Torah, is a direct quotation from Deuteronomy 6:5 (Mk. 12:30 = Matt. 22:37 and Lk. 10:27). And the Second Commandment, though it is quoted directly from Leviticus 19:18, is implicit in the Deuteronomic conception of brotherly love (cf. Deut. 10:19). Moreover, Jesus' answers to the Tempter, as recorded in the Gospels (Matt. 4:1-10 = Lk. 4:1-13), were couched in terms of Israel's trials of faith as recorded in Deuteronomy 6-8 (see 6:13, 16; 8:3).

In its present form, the whole book of Deuteronomy purports to be a sermon given by Moses to Israel in Moab, just before the people crossed over the Jordan River to take possession of the Promised Land. As they stand on the threshold of a new life, with all its opportunities and dangers, Moses exhorts them to remember Yahweh's gracious acts made known in the Exodus and the wilderness sojourn, and to hold firm to their covenant pledge when they are confronted with the paganism of the land of Canaan. This sermon is made all the more forceful and relevant because it actually reflects Israel's temptation to compromise her faith with Canaanite culture, from the earliest days of the Conquest to the most recent heyday of paganism under Manasseh.[14]

Closer inspection of the book shows, however, that it is not all of one piece. Around the nucleus of laws collected in chapters 12-26 are clustered no less than three "Mosaic addresses." The structure of the book may be outlined as follows:

---

[14] Remember that the term "Israel" actually embraces the two kingdoms of Israel, Ephraim and Judah, making it possible to refer to them as "the two houses of Israel" (cf. Is. 8:14). Thus, even after the Northern Kingdom had fallen, the term still applied to Judah.

A. The First Address (chapters 1-4)
   1. Introduction (1:1-5)
   2. Moses' summary of events since the departure from Mount Horeb (1:6–3:29)
   3. Moses' exhortation to Israel (4:1-40)
   4. Appendix (4:41-43)

B. The Second Address (chapters 5-26 and 28)
   1. Introduction (4:44-49)
   2. Moses' exhortation to Israel (chapters 5-11)
   3. The exposition of the Law (chapters 12-26)
   4. Conclusion (chapter 28)

C. The Third Address (chapters 29-30)

D. Supplements
   1. The Shechem covenant ceremony (chapter 27)
   2. Moses' last instructions (chapter 31)
   3. Old poetry: the Song of Moses (chapter 32) and the Blessing of Moses (chapter 33)
   4. Narrative of Moses' death (chapter 34)

The main address—the one on which we shall concentrate here—is section B of the above outline. It is generally agreed that this is the oldest edition of Moses' "sermon" to Israel, although we cannot be dead sure whether the sermonic material which surrounds the law code (chapters 12-26) was composed before or after Josiah's reform. Without attempting to go into this critical question, we shall assume that at least this section should be read as a unified whole and that probably this was substantially the book that was presented to Josiah.[15]

Moses' Sermon to Israel

One of the first things we notice in this passage is that Moses' farewell address is presented in a distinctive literary style. If we were to compare a Deuteronomic passage (for instance, 10:12-22) with a typical selection from either J or P, the differences would be apparent immediately. Here we find not the chaste style of a narrator or the pedantic prose of a priest concerned with cultic matters, but that of a preacher who uses skillful oratory to move his congregation to consider issues of life-and-death urgency. Very often the sentences are long flights of eloquent and impressive prose. As though trying to drive home his message to his hearers, the preacher piles clause upon clause in a manner that seems repetitious. Throughout the sermon appear characteristic turns of speech that we have already encountered in the Deuteronomic History: "To go

---

[15] See the critical discussion by G. E. Wright, *Interpreter's Bible*, II, pp. 311-330, who argues that Josiah's lawbook may have included virtually the whole of 4:44-30:20 (that is, sections B and C) and that most of the material in section A was added later as a preface to the Deuteronomic History of Israel, which extends from Deuteronomy through II Kings.

after (or serve) other gods"; "to hearken to the voice of Yahweh": "that you may prolong your days in the land"; "that it may be well with you"; "to do that which is evil (or good) in the eyes of Yahweh." The closest affinities to Deuteronomic style are found in the northern tradition designated as E—as evidenced, for example, by the fact that Deuteronomy, like E, calls the sacred mountain Horeb instead of Sinai (J and P), and refers to the natives of the Promised Land as Amorites rather than as Canaanites.

This new literary style, found in the Deuteronomic literature and the prose sections of Jeremiah, seems to have been characteristic of the late seventh and early sixth centuries B.C. The Lachish Letters, a series of inscribed potsherds found in 1935 and dating from the time just before the fall of Jerusalem, strengthen the opinion that this "rhetorical prose" was the literary fashion of the period.[16] Although the *style* belongs to the Deuteronomic period, however, the *content* is much older. At several points the pattern and content of the Mosaic sermon (especially chapters 29 and 30) suggest that this material has come out of a covenant-renewal ceremony, initiated by Joshua at Shechem, practiced at the old central sanctuary of Shiloh during the period of the Tribal Confederacy, and preserved in the Northern Kingdom. When it was used later as the basis of Josiah's reform, the old covenant tradition was written down and expanded in the language of the time.

Although the "author" of Deuteronomy remains anonymous, as is true of so much Old Testament literature, placing his address in the mouth of Moses is not a complete literary fiction. For Deuteronomy is essentially a revival of Mosaic teaching as it was understood in the seventh century B.C. To be sure, it does not contain the verbatim utterances of Moses; but the atmosphere is that of the Mosaic faith, though charged with the religious and ethical insights of the prophetic movement. Like the prophets themselves, the Deuteronomic Torah does not pretend to lead Israel forward to new heights of religious development, but to recall the people to the original faith of the Mosaic period. This is a program of reform, not innovation. Hence the address appropriately is ascribed to Moses.

The title of the book is evidently derived from the passage in 17:14-20, which stipulates that the king must have at hand "a copy of this law" all the days of his life and must conduct himself in obedience to it. The Greek translation (Septuagint), from which come our present names for the books of the Pentateuch, reproduces this phrase as "this second law" (*to deuteronomion touto*). The Hebrew title is simply "these are the words," the opening phrase of the book (1:1). So the Greek title designates the book according to its central theme: the "seconding" or repetition of the original law given by Moses. As the contents of Deuteronomy disclose, however, the modern word "law," which is based on Greek *nomos* and Latin *lex*, is inadequate to cover the full meaning

---

16 For the Lachish Letters, see Pritchard, *Ancient Near Eastern Texts*, pp. 321-322.

of the Hebrew word *torah*. Literally, *torah* means "teaching." Deuteronomy does contain what we would call "law," but the book is not narrowly confined to legal matters. It is fundamentally a teaching or "exposition" (cf. 1:5) of the basis and demands of Israel's covenant faith, and as such is directed not to professional administrators of law or to priests, but to the whole "lay" community of Israel. It is not a code of rules, but "a preaching, a proclamation and exposition of the faith of the nation," which includes both the "good news" (gospel) of what God has done and the requirements that are binding upon the people whom he has chosen and redeemed.[17] Therefore, the term Torah covers not only the so-called "code" in chapters 12-26 but the whole Mosaic address.

THE RENEWAL OF THE COVENANT

Let us glance briefly at the contents of the Address of Moses. It begins with an imperative that resounds like a trumpet call through the whole sermon: "Hear, O Israel" (5:1). A message is being proclaimed with great urgency, and the community is called to listen. Moses is speaking to the Israelite community in Transjordan when the memory of the Exodus is still fresh and when the people face the hazards of entering Canaan. But it is soon quite clear that the message is not addressed to a generation long ago, but to "this day" when Israel stands before God. Moses is speaking *today*. The present generation was actually *there* when the covenant was made, just as a Christian, singing the well-known spiritual, can testify that he was "there when they crucified my Lord." Notice the contemporary accent of the language:

> Yahweh our God made a covenant with us in Horeb. Not with our fathers did Yahweh make this covenant, but *with us, who are all of us here alive this day.*
>   —DEUTERONOMY 5:2-3 (*cf.* 29:10-15)

Every generation of Israel is involved in the covenant made at Mount Horeb. Therefore, when the covenant is renewed, the decisive moment of the past is "made present," contemporized. Deuteronomy does not advocate a retreat from the tumult of the present into a golden age of the past. Rather, it deals vigorously with the challenge of the present crisis, and with Israel's responsibilities and destiny in Yahweh's purpose. But, according to this sermon, the Mosaic past must come alive in the present if Israel is to have any future at all in the land that Yahweh has given. Hence the appeal for covenant renewal is made with life-or-death urgency. Another passage in the Third Address (30:15-20), which may have been used as a liturgy of covenant renewal, strikes the same serious and urgent note:

---

[17] See the excellent treatment of Deuteronomy by G. E. Wright, *Interpreter's Bible*, especially pp. 311-314.

> I call heaven and earth to witness against you this day, that I have set before you life and death, blessing and curse; therefore choose life. . . .
>
> —DEUTERONOMY 30:19

This is a forceful restatement of Joshua's message before the ancient assembly at Shechem: "Choose this day whom you will serve" (Josh. 24:15).

The Fulfillment of the Law

Having sounded this keynote, the speaker immediately turns his attention to the requirements that are binding upon the covenant community. These are summed up in the Ten Commandments (literally: "the ten words"), which are given in chapter 5 with slight variation from the version in Exodus 20. The essence of the commandments, however is given in 6:4-5, where the first commandment of the Decalogue is presented in a positive, rather than a negative, form. This terse summary—known as the Shema, from the opening Hebrew verb (*shema'* = "hear")—was regarded by the rabbis and by Jesus as the core of the Law. It states that Israel's first responsibility is to love God with her whole being—"with all your heart, and with all your soul ["self"], and with all your might." [18] This does not mean that one should love God in different ways, for these terms overlap in meaning. Israel is to love God in one way: with the unswerving, complete, steadfast loyalty that is the very foundation of the covenant community.

The emphasis upon love is one of the characteristic themes of Deuteronomy. In this respect, Deuteronomy, influenced in part by Hosea's message, returns to and deepens the meaning of the original Mosaic covenant.[19] Yahweh's gracious and undeserved love, manifested in his deeds of benevolence on behalf of Israel (6:20-23), should awaken Israel's response: love of God and, as a corollary, love of fellow-men. Notice, however, that Deuteronomy actually revives the original Mosaic tradition in which Israel's "gospel"—the good news of what Yahweh had done on behalf of a people in bondage (Ex. 1-24)—provided the motive for accepting the obligations of the covenant (see pp. 61-62). According to Deuteronomy, Israel is to love God, not for an ulterior motive, but solely because Yahweh first set his love upon his people. Love is "the fulfillment of the law." However, Israel's love of God must be combined with reverence ("fear"),

---

[18] The New Testament quotation of this commandment adds "the mind" in order to bring out what is meant by the Hebrew word "heart." As we have noticed before, the word *néfesh*, often translated "soul," does not mean soul in the Greek sense, but refers to the whole person, the self.

[19] William L. Moran, S.J., in an article on "The Ancient Near Eastern Background of the Love of God in Deuteronomy" (*Catholic Biblical Quarterly*, XXV [1963], pp. 77-87), argues that whereas Hosea spoke of Yahweh's love for Israel but never of Israel's love for Yahweh, Deuteronomy actually harks back to the ancient suzerainty covenant, within which the "vassal" was commanded to love the sovereign who had performed deeds of benevolence.

for Yahweh is a "jealous" God who will not tolerate turning to other gods (6:10-15). His love is a holy love, a wrathful love, that will become a consuming fire to those who are unfaithful to the covenant relationship.

The Choice of Israel

In the following chapters (7-9), the speaker shows what is meant by Yahweh's choice of Israel. Israel is a *holy people*. The basis of the community is a unique relationship to Yahweh, the Holy God. According to Deuteronomy, this is what makes Israel different from other nations:

> You are a people holy to Yahweh your God; Yahweh your God has chosen you to be a people for his own possession, out of all the peoples that are on the face of the earth.
> —DEUTERONOMY 7:6

Negatively, this means that Israel has been *separated from* the nations. Therefore, she is not to intermarry with them or to adopt their cultural ways, lest the gods of the nations seduce her from loyalty to Yahweh. This is put so strongly that Israel is enjoined to practice the *hérem* (see pp. 134-135)—that is, to consign the inhabitants of Canaan to total destruction as a sacrifice to Yahweh (7:1-5). Holiness demands purity, so the cult must be purified and all alien elements must be removed from the covenant community.

Positively, Israel has been *separated for* special service to Yahweh. Here the speaker presents one of the finest treatments of Israel's special calling in the Old Testament, although it lacks the universal breadth of the Yahwist (Gen. 12:1-3). Israel did not first choose; Israel was chosen (cf. Ex. 19:6). The initiative was with Yahweh. In his marvelous grace he selected this people, not because they were stronger or more numerous than others, but solely because he spontaneously set his love upon a small, insignificant band of slaves in Egypt. Therefore, Israel has no reason for boasting of her righteousness or superiority to other people. Election is an act of divine grace that should evoke consecrated service rather than the proud feeling of being God's favorite (7:6-11). The conquest and the inheritance of Canaan are reviewed in the light of this conviction (7:12-26).

As the sermon continues, we realize that Moses is speaking about the "temptations of culture" that Israel experienced throughout her history as an independent nation. One temptation was to suppose in *self-sufficiency* that "my power and the might of my hand have gotten me this wealth" (8:17). The community is urged to remember the wilderness sojourn, when Yahweh graciously led them for forty years, allowing them to hunger and feeding them with manna "that he might make you know that man does not live by bread alone, but that man lives by everything that proceeds out of the mouth of Yahweh" (8:3). In the spirit of Hosea, the speaker affirms that the sufferings of the wilderness period were a form of discipline, like the loving discipline that a father inflicts upon his son. The purpose was to "humble" Israel, to test the loyalty of Israel's heart. In this way the people were awakened to the realization that "life" is not something man controls, but is a gift received only by those who acknowledge their constant dependence upon God.

The second cultural temptation was that of *self-righteousness*, the proud belief of a victorious people that "it is because of my righteousness that Yahweh has brought me in to possess this land" (9:4). The speaker reminds Israel that her victory in Canaan does not rest upon her righteousness, but upon the corruption and wickedness of the peoples of the land, and especially upon Yahweh's faithfulness to the promise that he made to the patriarchs (9:5). Israel has no claim upon Yahweh because of her moral virtue or special religious insight. Indeed, the wilderness sojourn, contrary to Hosea's idealized treatment of it, was not a honeymoon of covenant faithfulness, but a time of ingratitude and rebellion. Israel is "a stubborn people" by nature. Moses is represented as saying: "You have been rebellious against Yahweh from the day that I knew you" (9:24)—a statement that is not intended to apply just to the generation of the wilderness but to the whole course of Israel's history from the Exodus to the time of Josiah. Had it not been for Moses' intercession on behalf of Israel, Yahweh would have destroyed the people in the wilderness and fashioned some better instrument for his historical purpose. Israel's preservation, so the speaker emphasizes, is due solely to Yahweh's freely bestowed grace and love (9:6-10:11).

Israel's Social Responsibilities

The climax and epitome of the sermon are reached in 10:12-22. Here the speaker again strikes the note with which he began, in a manner that is reminiscent of the great prophetic summary found in Micah 6:8. In answer to the question, "What does Yahweh require of you?," Israel is reminded that her calling is to be an obedient people, fearing Yahweh who is Lord of Heaven and earth and loving him who first loved them. Thus the basis for ethical responsibility is not dutiful obedience to a law code, but an inward, personal response to Yahweh's sovereign deeds of kindness and benevolence.

Moreover, Yahweh's righteous activity on behalf of the weak and oppressed has shown the way in which Israel herself should walk. In Yahweh's sovereign rule, love and justice are perfectly combined. Israel's God, "God of gods and Lord of lords, the great, the mighty, and the terrible God," has not only set his heart in love upon Israel, but he has manifested his love through his just dealings. He shows no partiality, for all men stand equal before him. He is the champion of those who are legally weak or helpless: the orphan, the widow, the resident alien. Because Yahweh acts in this way, Israel must imitate his manner of dealing with people. This is the basis of the "humanitarianism" that is noticeable in the laws found in Deuteronomy 12-26. The justice of the weak members of society must be defended, for Israelites must remember that they were once slaves in Egypt whom God set free (15:1-18). Every member of the community—high or low, rich or poor, bond or free—must stand in equality before the law (16:18-20). This emphasis puts Israelite legislation on a higher plane than other codes of the Near East, which favored the aristocratic class. Any exploitation of a fellow Israelite is ruled out, whether through murder, adultery, theft, dishonesty, false witness, or the taking of interest. The sanctities of the family are to be protected. Injustice in any form defiles the covenant community. The righteousness of God demands, negatively, the abolition of anything that defiles the community, even to the point of imposing the severest penalties, as in the case of idolatry (13:1-18; 17:2-7) or sexual abuses (22:13-25). And, positively, it means imitating God's dealings in order that a spirit of brotherly love and solidarity may pervade the community.[20]

In chapters 11 and 28, which are separated from one another by the exposition of specific laws, Israel is reminded that her future depends on how she responds to Yahweh's requirements. The people are confronted with a crucial decision, with the alternatives of the blessing or the curse. If Israel obeys faithfully, she will be strong in the land and will be blessed with fertility and welfare. But if Israel stubbornly turns aside to serve the gods of the land, Yahweh's anger will break forth and the people will be visited with all kinds of calamities and will quickly perish from the land.

Thus the governing purpose of Deuteronomy is to summon Israel to a renewal of the covenant with Yahweh. Although this literature has behind it a long tradition of covenant-renewal ritual, its immediate background is the cultural situation of the seventh century, when Israel's faith was corroded by the Canaanite nature cult and by Assyrian religious practices. The writer demands exclusive loyalty to Yahweh as the condition for national welfare and survival. In that situation, when powerful religious loyalties were contending for the devotion of men's hearts, the Deuteronomic writer summoned Israel to decision, to wholehearted commitment to Yahweh whose gracious love was made known in his "saving deeds" of historical deliverance and guidance.

THE INNER WEAKNESS
OF THE DEUTERONOMIC REFORM

For a while, the Deuteronomic Reformation made a deep impression upon the life and thought of Judah, as can be seen from the dominance of the Deuteronomic viewpoint in the Deuteronomic History of Israel that we have dealt with

---

20 See the perceptive essay by Lawrence E. Toombs, "Love and Justice in Deuteronomy," in *Interpretation*, XIX (1965), pp. 399-411. Here it is argued that the Deuteronomist's understanding of the law is one which avoids the Scylla of restricting law to the secular sphere, and the Charybdis of a legalism which identifies the Law with the whole will of God.

from time to time. The reform movement sincerely attempted to take prophetic teachings seriously and to return to the covenant faith of Moses. But we know that social reforms, even when sanctioned by the government and supported by popular approval, last only as long as the inward change in the hearts of the people persists. Josiah's reform, as we have seen, reflected the political climate of the time. Inspired to a great degree by the nationalistic spirit of rebellion against foreign rule, it could flourish only as long as the political situation that occasioned it.

Theological Flaws

Evidently Jeremiah supported the Deuteronomic Reformation for a time, although his attitude is not as clear as we might wish.[21] His interest in the reform movement would certainly have been in keeping with his concern for the Mosaic tradition. In Jeremiah 11:1-13 we are told that the prophet went through the streets of Jerusalem appealing for acceptance of "this covenant." The language of the passage strongly suggests that in his early career he supported the Deuteronomic Covenant, which was a renewal of the Sinai Covenant (cf. vs. 7). In the same chapter (verses 18-23), we are told that Jeremiah's kinsmen of Anathoth plotted to take his life. The reason may have been that this priestly family, which was associated with the local shrine, resented Jeremiah's support for a program that would put them out of their jobs by centralizing worship in Jerusalem, where the royal priesthood was in control.[22] Moreover, even in his later career, Jeremiah held Josiah in high esteem for his vigorous administration of justice (Jer. 22:15-16). In any case, if Jeremiah supported the reform at first, he must have soon turned against it. He came to see that it did not result in a circumcision of the heart or a breaking up of fallow ground, as Deuteronomy advocated (10:16), but yielded only a defiant nationalism and an external piety. Centralizing worship in Jerusalem only made people think that they were secure because Yahweh was dwelling in their midst. And the Torah was twisted into a way to "get something out of religion," to maintain the *status quo*. Jeremiah's fierce denunciation of the Torah,

> How can you say, "We are wise,
>   and the law of Yahweh is with us"?
> But, behold, the false pen of the scribes
>   has made it a lie.
>   —JEREMIAH 8:8

---

[21] For a defense of Jeremiah's support of the Reformation, see H. H. Rowley, "The Prophet Jeremiah and the Book of Deuteronomy" [165]. An opposite view is advocated by J. Phillip Hyatt, *Interpreter's Bible*, V, pp. 778-780.

[22] Deuteronomy 18:6-8 specifies that village priests had a right to be included on the Jerusalem staff, but this proved impractical (II Kings 23:9). The Jerusalem hierarchy would naturally oppose the intrusion of outside priests.

sounds like the outburst of a man disillusioned by a reform that had failed to achieve a genuine spiritual renewal of the covenant. His prophecy of the "new covenant," which we shall consider in the next chapter, must have been influenced partly by the failure of the Deuteronomic Reform.

One of the greatest defects of Deuteronomic theology was that it oversimplified the ways of God in history. The Deuteronomic doctrine of divine justice makes things too neat: obey Yahweh and all will go well; disobey him and hardship will come. It may be that the original version of Deuteronomy understood this truth more profoundly, but as it was worked out by the writer who left us the Deuteronomic History, it sounds suspiciously like the "success philosophy" which even today is the basis of much popular religion. Of course, the belief in divine reward (blessing) and divine punishment (judgment) had been fundamental in Israel's faith right from the very first. But Isaiah, like the other great prophets, put into the foreground an important qualification: "*If you are willing and obedient, you shall eat the good of the land*" (Is. 1:19). In Deuteronomy, however, something new was added—the belief that obedience or disobedience could be measured by a code of rules set down in a book, the Book of the Torah. Joshua, according to the Deuteronomic historian, was promised success in his invasion of Canaan *if* he would study faithfully "this book of the law"—the Deuteronomic Torah: "This book of the law shall not depart out of your mouth, but you shall meditate on it day and night, that you may be careful to do according to all that is written in it; for then you shall make your way prosperous, and then you shall have good success" (Josh. 1:8).

Now, in defense of Deuteronomy we must say that it was not the intention of the Mosaic address to encourage a bargain-counter religion. For this address is concerned primarily with man's personal relationship to Yahweh, rather than with personal profit gained by obeying religious rules. True, it was believed that the covenant relationship would result in concrete blessings in the daily life of the people. The Old Testament does not make our artificial distinction between "material" and "spiritual" blessings—the latter being confined to the inner blessings of peace of mind, fortitude, patience, and so on. There is a healthy spiritual "materialism" in Deuteronomy. Just as the marriage covenant yields the blessings of home life, so Israel's covenant with Yahweh yielded the divine promise of tangible blessings: security in the land, abundant crops, annual rainfall, long life. But the danger was that Israel would renew the covenant *for the purpose of* obtaining these blessings or—to use a recurring Deuteronomic phrase—"in order that it may be well with you," or "in order that your days may be long upon the land which Yahweh your God gives you." And because faith did not always bring men what they expected or wanted, a huge question arose with which later generations, influenced by the Deuteronomic view, had to struggle: If men obey the laws of God and are recompensed with suffering or hardship, how can God be just?

THE SITE OF ANCIENT NINEVEH *lies just across the Tigris River from modern Mosul. This mound (Tell Kuyunjik) is one of the two in the city limits, around which ran a wall nearly eight miles in circumference (compare Jonah 3:3!). Here, in the library of Ashurbanapal's palace, were found thousands of clay tablets, among which were the Babylonian Creation and Flood stories.*

A Period of Disillusionment

The easy moral logic of the Deuteronomic view was put to severe strain in the years following Josiah's reform. As we have seen, Josiah dreamed of restoring a United Kingdom under the single religious and political capital of Jerusalem. The Deuteronomic Reformation, viewed politically, was an attempt to consolidate and revitalize his expanded kingdom. Josiah evidently grew bolder and bolder as Assyria's star sank into political darkness. Thanks to the discovery of a Babylonian clay tablet, now in the British Museum, the story of the final death throes of Assyria can be told.[23] In 612 B.C., the Assyrian capital of Nineveh fell before the combined assault of the Babylonians, Medes, and Scythians. In retreat, the Assyrians tried to make a last-ditch stand at Haran, whence their capital had been moved, but this city too was captured by Scythian forces, thus fulfilling the prediction of Zephaniah (2:13-15).

The prophecy of Nahum, which comes from this period, gives powerful expression to the pent-up feelings of bitterness and hatred which Assyrian occupation had engendered in Judean hearts. Anticipating the fall of the capital city

---

[23] See J. Pritchard, *Ancient Near Eastern Texts*, pp. 303-305.

of Nineveh (612 B.C.), the prophet portrays Yahweh's coming in a storm to rescue his suffering people (chap. 1). He vividly describes the enemy attack upon the city as the battle rages through the streets (chap. 2), and he pronounces a terrible invective upon "the bloody city" (chap. 3). Nineveh, he says, is about to get the same treatment as Assyrian kings had once given to Thebes, the capital of Egypt (3:8), when Esarhaddon conquered the city in 669 B.C. and Ashurbanapal delivered the *coup de grâce* in 663. At last Assyria is going to taste to the full the suffering that she had inflicted upon other peoples, and there will be no one to feel sorry:

> Your shepherds are asleep,
>   O king of Assyria;
>   your nobles slumber.
> Your people are scattered on the mountains
>   with none to gather them.
> There is no assuaging your hurt,
>   your wound is grievous.
> All who hear the news of you
>   clap their hands over you.
> For upon whom has not come
>   your unceasing evil?
>   —NAHUM 3:18-19

Then came a sudden turn of affairs, the result of a political somersault on the part of Egypt. Pharaoh Necho (609-593 B.C.), the son of Psammetichus I, decided belatedly to come to the rescue of Egypt's former enemy, Assyria—the same enemy that had sacked Thebes not many years before. From Egypt's standpoint, it was expedient to have a weak Assyria as a buffer against more dangerous foes in the north, and, besides, Necho was eager to bring Syria and Palestine back into Egypt's orbit of power as in the days of her imperial glory. So in the year 609 B.C. Necho's army marched north to salvage the last remnants of the Assyrian empire. He was cut off at the pass of Megiddo (see p. 112) by Josiah, who gambled on achieving his goal of a United Kingdom by throwing in his lot with the Babylonians. In the ensuing battle, Josiah was defeated, and evidently was executed for his conspiracy with Babylonia. Judah was made a vassal of Egypt (II Kings 23:29-30), and Necho continued his march to the Euphrates to challenge Babylonia. The issue was decided in the year 605 B.C., at the battle of Carchemish, when Necho's army was decisively defeated by Babylonian forces under the command of the crown prince, Nebuchadnezzar II. (The name of the Babylonian prince is oftentimes spelled Nebuchadrezzar.) The Egyptian army, now in full retreat, was chased across Palestine to the borders of Egypt. Fleeing before her victorious enemies, Egypt made "a sound like a serpent gliding away" (Jer. 46). This was Egypt's last attempt to establish an empire in the Fertile Crescent. The fall of Nineveh and the victory at Carchemish made it clear that Babylonia was the new mistress of the world.

These developments must have shaken profoundly the morale of the people, whose hopes had been kindled by Josiah's reform. Good king Josiah, not yet forty years old, was dead. The nationalistic dream of a Davidic kingdom that would include both Israel and Judah was shattered. Temporary respite from the yoke of Assyrian oppression was followed, after a brief interval of Egyptian rule, by the imposition of a Babylonian yoke not a bit lighter or more merciful. In the popular view, Yahweh's justice meant that good consequences would come from good actions, that obedience would result in security on the land, victory against foes, and abundant life. But the cruel facts of history seemed to contradict this belief. No wonder that the first, fine rapture of the Deuteronomic Reform ended in disillusionment and reaction! Scarcely twenty years passed before the accomplishments of the reformers were erased, just as Hezekiah's reform had been eclipsed during the reign of Manasseh. As we learn from the prophets of this period, Jeremiah and Ezekiel, the Mosaic faith was forgotten, or compromised with the pagan ways of the world. Once again there was a reversion to the easy tolerance of syncretism. The tragedy of the time called for a deeper understanding of the meaning of Israel's covenant with Yahweh.

HABAKKUKS' WATCHTOWER OF FAITH

The strongest rebuke to a simple view of God's justice in history was given by the prophet Habakkuk. His prophecy, found essentially in chapters 1 and 2 of the book, dates from a time just after the battle of Carchemish in 605 B.C., the event that established Nebuchadnezzar as world ruler.[24] The prophet's poignant cry of anguish and perplexity is evoked by his realization that the new world power, Babylonia, represented a continuation of the monstrous, lawless evil which Assyria had unleashed:

> Why dost thou make me see wrongs
> and look upon trouble?
> Destruction and violence are before me;
> strife and contention arise.
> So the law is slacked
> and justice never goes forth.
> For the wicked surround the righteous,
> so justice goes forth perverted.
> —HABAKKUK 1:3-4

The prophet wonders whether history does justify the righteous, or whether instead brute power is really the factor that determines men's destiny. To him

---

[24] Most scholars believe that the psalm in chapter 3, though appropriate here, comes from another hand. Interestingly, the commentary on Habakkuk found among the Dead Sea Scrolls deals with only the first two chapters. W. F. Albright, however, regards the book as "substantially the work of a single author" in his study, "The Psalm of Habakkuk," in *Studies in Old Testament Prophecy* [165], pp. 1-18.

it is strange that when Yahweh is the Ruler of History, the Chaldeans (that is, the Babylonians) can sweep like a wild avalanche over men's lives, destroying all patterns of meaning and defying the most elementary human justice. These ruthless invaders rule by defining justice in their own terms (1:7); they are "guilty men, whose own might is their god" (1:11). Not that Yahweh's people are guiltless! But at least they are "more righteous" than this nation, which is a law unto itself. Divine judgment, which other prophets had proclaimed in times of invasion, makes no sense if the man of faith cannot discern some purpose in historical events. The prophet cries out:

> Thou who art of purer eyes than to behold evil
> and canst not look on wrong,
> why dost thou look on faithless men,
> and art silent when the wicked swallows up
> the man more righteous than he?
> —HABAKKUK 1:13

Habakkuk's question becomes even more acute if, as some scholars hold, he has in mind, especially in 2:5-20, not only the enemy without but the enemy within—namely, the wicked and worthless king Jehoiakim (cf. Jer. 22:13-19).[25]

No immediate answer is given to Habakkuk's question. But he takes his stand on his "watchtower of faith" and receives an answer to his prayer that lifts his eyes to the horizons of the future (2:1-4):

> Behold, he whose soul is not upright in him shall fail,
> but the righteous shall live by his faith.
> —HABAKKUK 2:4

According to this answer, the righteous man must face the enigmas of history in faith (or better, "faithfulness"), confident that the issues are in God's hands and waiting patiently for the time when his sovereignty will be made clear (cf. Is. 8:16-18). The answer to Habakkuk's question was to be pondered deeply in the tragic era that lay ahead, and eventually was reinterpreted in the New Testament by Paul in his great doctrine of "justification by faith" (Rom. 1:17; Gal. 3:11).

FAITH AND NATIONALISM

Looking back over this chapter, one fact stands out above all: the rediscovery of the Mosaic heritage was accompanied by an upsurge of nationalism. Josiah's

---

[25] This view is maintained in an extreme fashion by Paul Humbert, *Problèmes du livre d'Habacuc* (Neûchatel: Université, 1944), who argues that the prophet used international references to veil his attack against Jehoiakim. See the discussion by Walter J. Harrelson [15], pp. 375-378, who judiciously combines both the external and internal threats.

reform went far toward removing the religious influences of the Fertile Crescent which, like gangrene, had weakened Israel's vitality, making her the victim of Manasseh's reactionary policies. As in the period of the ancient Tribal Confederacy, Israel became strong when she was true to her own faith and loyal to the covenant pledge made at Sinai. But the Reform was infected with nationalism. The centralization of worship in the Jerusalem Temple, though it purified the land of pagan religious practices, actually led to a proud confidence that God was on the side of his people and that no evil could befall them. As we shall see in the next chapter, the pride of nationalism died hard in the turbulent events that rolled over Judah like an avalanche toward the end of the seventh century. And yet ironically it was the revival of the covenant faith in a time of nationalism that made possible the understanding of the death of the nation. Israel was a covenant community before the rise of the nation; and the nation would have to be dissolved before she could understand again the meaning of the covenant.

THE DOOM

OF THE NATION

CHAPTER ELEVEN   The reform of Josiah, as we have

seen, was borne on a wave of nationalism that swept through

Judah during the last days of the Assyrian empire. For a

while it seemed as though the people were standing on the

threshold of a Golden Age like the glorious era of David's

empire. But the patriots were awakened from their daydream

by the shock of a swift succession of events, beginning with

Biblical readings: Primary attention should be given to the prophecies of Jeremiah's later career found in Jeremiah 4-25. These oracles are supplemented by the biographical narratives of chapters 26-45. The history of the period is sketched in II Kings 24-25 (paralleled in II Chronicles 36), and the mood stimulated by the fall of the nation is poignantly expressed in the book of Lamentations.

the untimely death of Josiah and culminating in the fall of the nation and the carrying off into exile of part of the population. Nationalism died hard during those crowded years, for many prophets flourished by preaching a comfortable message of peace when there was no peace, by promising that affairs would soon return to the good old days of national glory. These prophets won great applause at the time for their wishful thinking. But in the long run the deepest impression was made by the prophets whose sharp words punctured the illusions of the time and summoned people to face the realities of their history.

We are fortunate to have the lengthy testimony of two great prophets who lived through this era of national cataclysm—Jeremiah and Ezekiel. Both men came from priestly families, and although they differed greatly in temperament and outlook, they supplemented each other as had Amos and Hosea, who also prophesied in a time of national downfall. Their task was to declare the meaning of the tragic events of their time—that is, to say what God was doing in the world crisis.

THE SUFFERING PROPHET

Postponing discussion of Ezekiel until the next chapter, we shall turn our attention first to Jeremiah, whose early career we have already traced. His prophetic activity spanned forty years (c. 626-586 B.C.), fateful years in the history of the Southern Kingdom. Later tradition tended to portray him as a "weeping prophet," a reputation that led to the invention of our word "jeremiad" for a doleful lament or complaint. But this portrait is overdrawn, for certainly Jeremiah's message had in it all the iron severity of Amos or Isaiah. Like his prophetic predecessors, Jeremiah announced that the Day of Yahweh, for which the people waited expectantly, would not be a day of victory and rejoicing, but a dark, bitter day of doom and gloom. But Jeremiah identified himself with his message in a more personal way than any other prophet. This helps to explain why we know more about Jeremiah *the man* than about any other Old Testament figure, with the possible exception of David. If Jeremiah was as staunch as "a fortified city, an iron pillar, and bronze walls" (Jer. 1:18), he was also as sensitive as a mother bereft of her children. His career was intimately tied up with the tragedy of Jerusalem, a tragedy that was intensified by the very words he felt compelled to speak in the name of Yahweh. The wound of his people cut deeply into his own heart, prompting him to mix with his prophecies of doom outcries of agony and grief (see 8:18-22). Although he was not the author of the elegies found in the book of Lamentations, which vividly reflect the mood of the time, it is appropriate that these poems were attributed to him.[1] His

---

[1] Several authors were evidently responsible for the book of Lamentations. Chapters 2 and 4 may have been written by eyewitnesses of the fall of Jerusalem; chapters 1 and 3 may have been inspired by the book of Jeremiah. With the exception of chapter 5, these poems were in the *qinah* or elegiac 3/2 meter (see p. 237) that Jeremiah and Ezekiel used effectively.

career was a Passion, a *via dolorosa*, and it is not without reason that some of Jesus' contemporaries thought that perhaps he was another Jeremiah.

THE BOOK OF JEREMIAH

Before turning to Jeremiah's later career, let us glance briefly at the book itself. The reader who turns to it for the first time may find himself in a maze of confusion. A modern novel on Jeremiah, like Franz Werfel's *Hearken Unto the Voice*, would tell the story in a more orderly fashion, following a chronological time-line throughout the prophet's career from beginning to end. And a modern theologian seeking to present the prophet's message would at least arrange the materials in a pattern according to subject or topic. But in the book of Jeremiah there is no clear principle of organization or development. There is some evidence that the compiler has tried to group materials according to the early, middle, and later periods of Jeremiah's career, but too often he has not bothered to date materials in sequence or to give dates at all. Nor was he governed by our desire to arrange subjects in a neat and logical manner. Hence the reader gets the impression, as he forges ahead chapter by chapter, that the book gets nowhere and that the same things are said over and over again to the point of monotony.

In view of these difficulties, we should realize at the outset that we are not dealing with a "book" in the modern sense, but with an *anthology*. As we have already noticed, prophetic literature is highly composite and bears the traces of a complicated history. Fortunately, however, it is possible to provide a rough map that will enable the reader to find his way through the fifty-two chapters of the book of Jeremiah:

A. Chapters 1-25. This section stands out as a separate block of material. In the main, it is composed of prophetic oracles, although now and then a biographical narrative is inserted.

B. Chapters 26-45. In contrast to the preceding section, this one is composed largely of biographical narratives about Jeremiah, interspersed occasionally with prophetic sermons. It falls into two subdivisions:
  1. Prophecies of judgment and hope (chapters 26-35).
  2. The "passion" of Jeremiah (chapters 36-45).

C. Chapters 46-51. This section consists of oracles against the nations. Although according to chapter 1 Jeremiah was called to be "a prophet to the nations," some of this material clearly comes from other writers.

D. Chapter 52. The story of the fall of Jerusalem, extracted from II Kings 24:18–25:30, is fittingly placed here as a historical conclusion.

For our purpose, sections A and B are relevant, and section A is the more important for a first reading.[2] Notice that, in general, the distinguishing feature of section A is its poetic form. Often these religious lyrics are cast in a 3/2 *qinah* meter (see 9:20-21), the mournful cadence so appropriate for expressing sorrow (see Amos 5:2; and Lamentations). On the other hand, section B is in prose. These narratives undoubtedly come from the hand of Baruch, Jeremiah's faithful disciple and secretary.[3] We have then, two main sources: Jeremiah's oracles and Baruch's Memoirs.

The Burning of the Prophet's Scroll

An interesting account found in Baruch's Memoirs (chapter 36) shows how the oracles in section A reached their present form. The story is placed in the fourth year of king Jehoiakim (605 B.C.), the son of Josiah whom the Egyptians had elevated to the throne after Josiah was killed at Megiddo (see p. 322). The battle of Carchemish in 605 B.C. had changed the political picture, and the time was ripe for the prophet to restate his message. Earlier—possibly under the influence of rumors about commotion caused by Scythian raiders in upper Mesopotamia [4]—he had spoken vaguely of a threat from the north; now he could identify the northern foe as Babylonia. He hoped that the publication of his oracles, which up to that time had been preserved in his memory and that of his followers, would awaken the people to the seriousness of their situation and encourage them to mend their ways. With this practical purpose in mind, Jeremiah dictated the oracles he had spoken during the twenty-three years that had elapsed since his call. His secretary, Baruch, took down the dictation, writing with ink on a scroll (cf. chapter 45).

Since Jeremiah was barred from the Temple at that time, Baruch was sent in his place to read the scroll before all the people who had assembled for a fast day. Jeremiah's warning that Yahweh would manifest his wrath against Judah by sending the Babylonian invader must have sounded like high treason. Alarmed, the royal officials advised Jeremiah and Baruch to go into hiding while the scroll was brought to the attention of king Jehoiakim. The haughty king's reaction was typical. We see him sitting in his luxurious winter palace, toasting himself before a fire burning in the brazier. As each few columns of the scroll were read, the king would reach over with his famous penknife, slash off the portion of the manuscript that had been read, and contemptuously toss it into

---

[2] That these are separate units of the book is suggested by the fact that the Septuagint places section C between sections A and B (that is, after 25:13).

[3] The book of Baruch is in both the Roman Catholic canon and the Protestant Apocrypha (see Chart, pp. 4-5); it represents itself as composed by Jeremiah's disciples in 582 B.C., five years after the fall of Jerusalem to the Babylonians. However, the book was written much later and indeed seems to reflect the destruction of Jerusalem by the Romans in A.D. 70.

[4] The question of the identity of the foe from the north is reviewed by H. H. Rowley in "The Early Prophecies of Jeremiah in their Setting" [172], pp. 206-220.

the fire. And so it went, despite the protest of some of the princes, until the whole scroll had been cut to shreds and burned. But this was not the end of the matter. Safe from arrest by the king, Jeremiah began his literary work all over. This time, we are told, he not only dictated the contents of the original scroll but produced an enlarged edition, for "many similar words were added" (36:32).

Besides giving us a glimpse into one of the episodes of Jeremiah's career, this story helps us to understand how the book of Jeremiah took shape. The nucleus of the book is the enlarged scroll, which is written in the first person, as we would expect if the oracles had been taken down at dictation. These oracles are dominated by the practical purpose of awakening the people to the meaning of the Babylonian threat. To be sure, the scroll contained numerous oracles from Jeremiah's early period; for instance, the oracles found in 1:1-4:4 (see pp. 303-307) and the account of Jeremiah's support of the Deuteronomic Reform in chapter 11. But these prophecies were reworked in the light of events that were fresh in Jeremiah's mind.[5] In addition, Jeremiah included many other oracles of more recent origin. In other words, the expanded scroll is one of the chief sources of the material in section A.

Of course, the literary process did not come to an end once the second scroll had been dictated. We may imagine that Jeremiah paused from time to time to dictate more oracles, thus expanding the scroll still further. And other oracles and narratives, now found in section A, were added subsequently by Baruch and later editors.[6] Finally, toward the end of Jeremiah's career, Baruch composed his biography of Jeremiah, using the third rather than the first person. As we have seen, most of the narratives are contained in section B, although some are found in the latter part of section A, beginning with chapter 19. In brief, then, this is the way the book of Jeremiah came into being.

IN THE REIGN OF JEHOIAKIM

The reading of Jeremiah's scroll before Jehoiakim was the turning point in the prophet's later career. It gives us a fixed point from which to consider first his message during the early part of Jehoiakim's reign, and then to deal with his career after he was driven into hiding by the king. Let us begin by considering the experiences that were still fresh in the prophet's memory as he revised and expanded his prophecies in 605 B.C. (See Chronological Chart 7, p. 298.)

A new phase of Jeremiah's career began in the year 609 B.C., when Josiah was

---

[5] For instance, the references to Egypt in 2:14-19 and 2:36-37 reflect the situation during 600-605 B.C., when Judah was temporarily a vassal of pharaoh Necho (see p. 322).

[6] For instance, 10:1-16 and 17:19-27 are usually regarded as later additions. Some also believe that the book of Jeremiah has been reworked by Deuteronomic editors. This position is vigorously defended by J. P. Hyatt, *Interpreter's Bible*, V, pp. 788-790, and is opposed with equal vigor by John Bright, "The Date of the Prose Sermons of Jeremiah" [162].

killed as a result of his attempt to halt the Egyptian army at Megiddo. Josiah's immediate successor to the throne was his son Jehoahaz (referred to as Shallum in Jer. 22:10-12). The reign of Jehoahaz need not detain us, however, for he was removed from the scene by the Egyptians after only three months. In his place, the Egyptians elevated to the throne another son of Josiah, and changed his name from Eliakim to Jehoiakim (II Kings 23:31-36). The fact that he was set up by a foreign conqueror shows that he was a puppet of pharaoh Necho. His first act in office was to impose a heavy tax upon the people of Judah in order to raise a tribute for Egypt (II Kings 23:35).

In almost every respect, Jekoiakim (609-598 B.C.) was a different man from his father, Josiah. If his father wanted to model his reign after David, then Jehoiakim's ambition was to be another Solomon. Jeremiah draws a sharp contrast between the two rulers in his oracle in 22:13-19. Jehoiakim was a typical oriental tyrant—cruel, selfish, and indulgent. Like Solomon, he subjected his people to forced labor to build his magnificent palaces (22:13). To him, being a king meant living in luxurious style (22:15). Heedless of the prophetic reminder that to "know" Yahweh is to do justice, he recklessly oppressed his people and shed much innocent blood (22:16-17). Those who opposed him courted death, for he feared neither God nor man. He was the only Judean king, so far as we know, who dared to put a prophet of Yahweh to death (26:20-23). During the brief interlude of Egyptian control of Palestine—that is, between the death of Josiah and the battle of Carchemish (609-605 B.C.)—Jehoiakim expediently followed a pro-Egyptian policy in order to keep himself in power.

The Temple as a Den of Robbers

Jeremiah stepped into the public arena at the beginning of Jehoiakim's reign. As a result of his growing disillusionment about Josiah's reform program, perhaps, he had been on the sidelines for several years. If so, he was at last "full of the wrath of Yahweh, weary of holding it in" (6:11). In the first year of Jehoiakim's reign (cf. 26:1), Jeremiah made a bold public appeal in the Temple —the very shrine that had become the center of religious zeal as a result of the Deuteronomic Reform. His Temple Sermon is given to us in two versions. The first, found in Jeremiah's scroll (chapter 7), gives a full account of what he said on the occasion. The second, found in Baruch's Memoirs (chapter 26), gives only a brief summary of Jeremiah's message and concentrates rather on biographical facts. We must read both chapters together if we are to see the complete picture.

In addition to playing the tyrant, Jehoiakim revived the paganism that his father had tried to get rid of. Evidently the people, disillusioned with the Deuteronomic Reform, were turning enthusiastically to the old ways. Every member of a man's family, we are told, had a part in making cakes for Ishtar, Queen of Heaven—the mother-goddess worshiped in Assyria and Babylonia (Jer. 7:18).

The barbarous rite of child sacrifice was practiced in the Valley of Hinnom (Topheth), south of the city (see map, p. 143), and pagan abominations (idols) were set up in the Temple (verses 30-31; cf. 19:5).[7] To make matters worse, social abominations were perpetrated in the very shadow of the Temple, and the people supposed they could get away with these crimes as long as they went through the formalities of worship (verses 8-10).

All these things rankled in Jeremiah's heart that day when he stood in the Temple court watching the people entering to worship. He began his message with a sharp summons: "Amend your ways and your doings!" There was no point in their chanting glib words about the Temple being a sanctuary of refuge (I Kings 1:50-51; 2:28) when it had become—as Jesus was to say many years later—a den to harbor thieves (Mark 11:17). After all, what had happened to Shiloh, the central sanctuary of the old Tribal Confederacy? (See above, pp. 119-121.) The Temple was no bulwark of security, no guarantee that "God is with us" to see that no harm would come. For, the prophet threatened, the Temple would fall and Judah would go into exile along with the Northern Kingdom. In another oracle, Jeremiah repudiated the practice of sacrifice. Yahweh, he said, had not commanded them to offer sacrifices on the day he brought them out of Egypt, but rather had asked for a loyal and obedient heart so that the covenant promise might be fulfilled: "I will be your God and you shall be my people" (verses 21-23). Faithfulness within the covenant relationship was fundamental.

According to chapter 26, Jeremiah's sermon created an uproar. Some people must have been shocked by the way he ignored the royal covenant theology, with its divine guarantee of support for the Davidic king and its assurance of Yahweh's presence in the Jerusalem Temple. Like some of his prophetic predecessors, he took his stand upon the covenant tradition rooted in the Exodus and the experiences of the wilderness. Had not some elders appealed to the precedent of Micah, who a hundred years before had prophesied the fall of Jerusalem and the Temple, Jeremiah would have lost his life like the hapless prophet Uriah. Even more important in saving Jeremiah from the wrath of the king was the support of Ahikam, son of Shaphan, a prince of great political influence (26:24). More than once, a member of the family of Shaphan stood on Jeremiah's side in a time of need.

The comparison with Micah was apt, for, like other prophets who had gone before him, Jeremiah also prophesied doom (see 28:8-9). The first effect of Yahweh's word—that is, his plan of action—was "to pluck up and to break down, to destroy and to overthrow" (1:10). To be sure, judgment was not Yahweh's last word, for he also showed his intention "to build and to plant." But the rebuilding would come only after the destruction. "Is not my word like fire, says Yahweh, and like a hammer that breaks the rock in pieces?" (23:29)

---

[7] The same picture is presented in Ezek. 16:20-21; 20:26, 31; 23:29.

The Balm of Gilead

Jeremiah's word of doom seemed incredible both to the king and the people. For they believed that their reliance upon Egypt was only a temporary device to protect them from the storm arising out of the north (cf. 2:16, 18, 36-37). It is not surprising, then, that Jeremiah's greatest adversaries were the popular prophets who promised a short cut to divine restoration without going through the valley of judgment. Like spiritual quacks, they were crying "peace, peace" when there was no peace and trying to "heal the wound of the people lightly" by remedies that did not touch the root of the trouble (6:13-15; cf. 5:12-13, 30-31; 14:13-16; 23:9-40). Jeremiah accused these prophets of lacking the proper credentials to speak, for they had not stood in "the Council of Yahweh," as had great prophets like Micaiah and Isaiah (see pp. 265-266). He said that they were filling the people with vain hopes, deceiving their hearers with lies, and stealing Yahweh's words from one another. Between them and the true order of Yahweh prophets there was no more similarity than between straw and wheat (23:28). For Yahweh's word brings not peace, but a sword— the sword that cuts like a surgeon's knife to the seat of the malignant cancer and makes possible a deep inward healing. To Jeremiah's poignant question, "Is there no balm in Gilead?"—a region famous for its healing ointments— came the answer that Yahweh's judgment was the beginning of restoration to health (cf. 8:22).

Jeremiah agonized over the people's incurable sickness. They were, he said, a people with "a stubborn and rebellious heart" (5:23). All Yahweh's discipline had failed. The word of the prophets had fallen on deaf ears; indeed, it had become an object of scorn to the people (6:10). With searching insight, antici- pated by Hosea, Jeremiah perceived that the problem lay *within*—in the heart. To be sure, Israel's "sickness unto death" showed itself outwardly in many ways. The people were putting their trust in institutions: the Ark (3:16), the rite of circumcision (4:4), the Law (8:8), sacrifice (7:21-26), the Temple itself (7:4). Moreover, the social bond of the covenant community was fractured. Every brother, said Jeremiah, was another deceitful Jacob (9:4-6). No one could be trusted, and oppression was heaped up like a pyramid. The people were like "well-fed stallions," each neighing for his neighbor's wife (5:8) and showing no concern for the defenseless victims of society (5:28). Blind nationalism, excited by the deceitful prophets, was rampant. And, to cap the climax, idolatry was practiced not only in the Temple but on every high hill and under every green tree.

But these were only the outward symptoms of a problem rooted in the heart, the seat of man's loyalties and devotion. Anticipating modern depth psychology, Jeremiah pointed out that the heart can cover up and justify ("rationalize") its real motives:

> The heart is deceitful above all things,
>   and desperately corrupt;
>   who can understand it?
>   —JEREMIAH 17:9

Yet, no man can hide himself in a secret place from God, for Yahweh is "at hand" and not "afar off" (23:23-24). He who "searches the mind and tries the heart" knows men's deepest motives far better than they understand themselves (17:10). In the awful exposure of God's revelation, man's real condition comes to light. Yahweh's eyes look for truth (5:3), for the inner integrity that comes from a true relationship to God and fellowman in the covenant. But instead, Yahweh finds inner deceit, a chronic falseness, evident throughout Israel's long history in Canaan. Shifting the figure of speech, Jeremiah stresses the deep-seated character of the problem. If one were to run through the streets of Jerusalem, like a Diogenes, seeking for even one just man, he would not find him (5:1-3). Every man recklessly follows his own course, like a horse plunging madly in battle (8:6). Although the birds follow their homing instincts, Israel does not seek rest in Yahweh's will (8:7). Yahweh has set a bound for the restless waves of the sea, but Israel's rebellion is beyond all bound (5:20-29). Israel's sin, Jeremiah declared, is deeply engraved upon the heart as with a pen of iron or a diamond point (17:1-4). The people can no more change their accustomed evil ways than the Ethiopian his skin or the leopard his spots (13:23). Sin has become so "natural" that the people do not even know how to blush for it (8:12).

The catharsis—to use the language of psychology—had to come through crisis and catastrophe. In the past, according to Jeremiah, Yahweh had tried to win his people back. Rising up early, he had sent his servants, the prophets. He had visited his people with calamities, his purpose being to bring them to their senses. But it was all in vain. Jeremiah insisted that the people's constant backsliding was a puzzle to God, for ordinarily if a man falls down he rises again, or if he turns away he comes back (8:4-7). Nothing had fazed Israel, however. The people had *refused* to return (that is, repent). At last Yahweh's patience was exhausted. He was "weary of relenting" (15:6). He would pour out his wrath against the people, destroying their idols and shaking the nation to its very foundations. For God is sovereign in history. This truth is vividly emphasized in the oracle that Jeremiah received in the potter's house, an oracle that may have formed the pungent climax of Jeremiah's scroll of prophecies (ch. 18). Seeing a potter seated in his pit, his feet spinning the wheel and his hands deftly molding the clay, Jeremiah was reminded that Israel was like clay in the potter's hand. If the vessel was spoiled, owing to some imperfection in the material, it could be reworked into another vessel as the potter saw fit. And so it was with Israel. If a nation refuses to be molded by the divine design, and insists on following its own plans, then Yahweh will repent of the good he has intended and will visit it with destruction.

Notice that the threatened catastrophe is to come as a result of human recalcitrance, not as a result of the arbitrary, capricious wrath of the potter. Again and again the prophet reminded the people that the imminent tragedy would be the consequence of their own actions:

> Your ways and your doings
> > have brought this upon you.
> This is your doom, and it is bitter;
> > it has reached your very heart.
> > > —JEREMIAH 4:18

In one sense, the "wrath of God" is not so much God's intervention to punish as it is his *withdrawal* from a rebellious people, leaving them to suffer the destructive consequences of their own actions and attitudes. It is, one might say, a kind of self-destruction. God's sovereignty in human affairs means that men cannot live with impunity, but the punishment is only "the fruit of their devices" (6:19). Therefore, in the very passage where Jeremiah proclaims the sovereignty of the potter over the clay, his word is accompanied by an urgent plea that the people mend their ways and doings while there is still time. Divine sovereignty does not erase human responsibility.

The Foe from the North

During the reign of Jehoiakim, Jeremiah saw the judgment of God taking political form in international developments. At the time of his call, when he had a vision of a boiling caldron pouring out evil upon Palestine, he spoke of some foe from the north. Beginning with the battle of Carchemish, however, the northern foe came clearly into focus: The caldron was boiling over from the land of Babylonia.

Scattered through chapters 1-18 are a number of prophetic oracles occasioned by the advance of Babylonia, most of them from the latter part of Jehoiakim's reign, after the battle of Carchemish. The cycle in chapter 4 is an excellent example of the poems on "the foe from the north." As expressions of intense feeling, these lyrics are unsurpassed in the Old Testament. With urgent voice Jeremiah sounds the battle alarm, crying to the people to flee to the fortified cities for safety (4:5-8). He sees the army approaching in chariots like the whirlwind and cries out to Jerusalem to repent while there is still time (5:13-18). His heart beats wildly as he hears the enemy trumpet and sees disaster suddenly overwhelm the land (5:19-22). He hears Jerusalem's death cry, like the piercing shriek of a woman in travail (4:29-31). Like Jesus later, he weeps over the fate of Jerusalem (see 8:18-9:3). Reading these moving poems, one has the impression that all the suffering of the people of Israel flowed through the channel of a single heart. No other prophet of the Old Testament period was more personally identified with his people or felt more keenly the "giant agony" of their tragedy.

Included with the poems of chapter 4 is a powerful lyric on "the return of chaos." In a terrifying vision, Jeremiah sees the world—"as if struck by a mighty nuclear bomb," as one commentator puts it—returning to chaos like that which prevailed before the Creation: the "waste and void" of Genesis 1:2: [8]

> I looked on the earth, and lo, it was waste and void;
>   and to the heavens, and they had no light.
> I looked on the mountains, and lo, they were quaking,
>   and all the hills moved to and fro.
> I looked, and lo, there was no man,
>   and all the birds of the air had fled.
> I looked, and lo, the fruitful land was a desert,
>   and all its cities were laid in ruins
>   before Yahweh, before his fierce anger.
>   —JEREMIAH 4:23-26

To Jeremiah, the catastrophe was of cosmic proportions, like the Deluge of Noah's time which threatened to convert the world into pre-creation chaos. His deep sense of universal disorder is echoed in modern literature that speaks of the wasteland, the threat of "non-being," the "Eve of Destruction," the void.

Signs of Doom

Jeremiah's words of impending doom were accompanied by signs, one of the most enigmatic of which is described in 13:1-11. According to the story, Jeremiah bought a linen waistcloth and wore it "to the Euphrates," [9] where he hid it in a cleft of a rock. Later, when he found that the cloth was spoiled and good for nothing, he was told that Yahweh would spoil the pride of the people, even though they had clung to him as closely as a garment. On another occasion, Jeremiah was commanded to buy a clay flask and to break it publicly in the Valley of Hinnom, the place where human sacrifice was practiced. In this way he dramatically demonstrated that Jerusalem would be broken into fragments, and that the destruction would be so great that the accursed valley would have to be used for a burial place (chapter 19). These signs or "enacted words" had an ominous significance, for Jeremiah portrayed *what Yahweh was about to do.* It is understandable that later, when Jeremiah repeated his message of doom against the Temple itself, Pashur, the priest seized him, beat him, and put him in stocks for the night (20:1-6). In spite of the people's heedlessness, however, Jeremiah believed that Yahweh's word was the power that shaped the course of

---

[8] The comment is that of Victor R. Gold, *Oxford Annotated Bible* [1], *in loco.* The expression "waste and void" in 4:23 (*tohu wa-bohu*) is exactly the same as in the P creation story (Gen. 1:2).

[9] It is difficult to understand this sign if it involves trips to the Euphrates (700 miles round trip). Probably Jeremiah went to Parah (modern 'Ain Farah), a short journey northeast from his home town of Anathoth. In Hebrew "to the Euphrates" and "to Parah" are spelled the same. See the commentary by John Bright [169], p. 96.

CASPIAN SEA

BLACK SEA

MEDIAN EMPIRE

LYDIAN EMPIRE

GREECE
Athens
Sparta

Sardis

LYCIA

CILICIA

CYPRUS

MEDITERRANEAN SEA

Arvad
(ISLAND)

Tyre

Megiddo
Ashdod
Ashkelon

Samaria
Jerusalem
AMMON
MOAB
EDOM

Elath

Damascus

Hamath
Riblah

ORONTES R.

PHOENICIA

Carchemish
Arpad
Haran

Nineveh
Asshur

TIGRIS R.

L.VAN

L.URMIAH

Ecbatana

ELAM

Susa

CHALDEA

BABYLONIA

EUPHRATES R.

Babylon
Nippur

Ur

PERSIAN GULF

Persepolis

PROBABLE ANCIENT SHORELINE

ARABIA

RED SEA

MT. SINAI

EGYPT

NILE R.

Memphis

Thebes

THE BABYLONIAN EMPIRE

612–539 B.C.

PROBABLE ROUTE OF THE EXILE

events. Yahweh was "watching over" his word, bringing his plan into historical reality (1:12).

Then came the battle of Carchemish, in which Egypt was decisively defeated and from which Babylonia emerged as the dominant world power.[10] From this fateful period comes the important prophecy of 25:1-14. In its present form, it is dated in the fourth year of Jehoiakim (605 B.C.), the same year the scroll was burned. Certain problems make it difficult to ascribe this passage to Jeremiah just as it stands, and the Septuagint (Greek) version, which is much shorter, may have a greater claim to authenticity. The Greek version makes no reference to Nebuchadnezzar or Babylonia, and concludes with the words of verse 13: "I will bring upon that land [Judah] all the words which I have uttered against it, everything written in this book, which Jeremiah prophesied against all the nations." Moreover, the Greek version has the oracles against the foreign nations right after this sentence, where they appropriately belong, rather than after Baruch's Memoirs (chapters 26-45) as in our Bible.

Aside from these differences between the Hebrew and Greek texts, the story rings true to the message of Jeremiah. In the shorter version, this story was probably the conclusion of the scroll that Jeremiah dictated to Baruch.[11] Astonished at the people's refusal to heed the warnings of his twenty-three year ministry, the prophet announced that Yahweh would send "a family from the north" (Septuagint) to devastate the whole region and reduce Judah to utter ruin. The people would serve the conqueror for seventy years—a round number (the proverbial span of a man's life) not intended to be taken literally. During this long period, the end of which would be seen by no man then living, the ordinary affairs of life would be interrupted, for Yahweh would banish "the voice of mirth and the voice of gladness, the voice of the bridegroom and the bride, the grinding of the millstones and the light of the lamp."

Evidently this dire prophecy of a Babylonian invasion, following closely in the wake of Babylonia's victory at Carchemish, was the theme of the scroll that infuriated Jehoiakim (Jer. 36:29). Certainly the king's feelings were not soothed by the announcement that he—an Egyptian vassal—would die a shameful death (36:30-31) and that, as Jeremiah said in another oracle, he would be buried "with the burial of an ass" (22:18-19). This was just more than a king could stand.

JEREMIAH'S CONFESSIONS

We have turned in a circle back to our earlier starting point: the burning of Jeremiah's scroll by Jehoiakim. The sequence of events that we have considered so far may be outlined as follows:

---

[10] Jeremiah's oracle against Egypt (46:1-12) was delivered shortly after the battle of Carchemish.

[11] For the short text, see John Skinner, *Prophecy and Religion* [173], pp. 240-241.

609 B.C.   Death of Josiah at Megiddo
            Jeremiah's Temple Sermon
605 B.C.   The Battle of Carchemish
            The burning of Jeremiah's scroll

Starting with the last episode, we have looked back over Jeremiah's ministry during these years and have considered the content of his enlarged scroll of prophecy. Now we shall move ahead from the year 605 B.C. to the last decades of Jeremiah's career.

Hunted as a public enemy and traitor to the king, Jeremiah may have gone into seclusion for some time. From this "period of silence" may have come a remarkable series of devotional lyrics, usually referred to as the Confessions of Jeremiah. Actually, these intimate outpourings of the prophet's restless heart, similar in type to the *Confessions* of Augustine and other devotional literature, came from several occasions in the prophet's career. It may be that Jeremiah dictated them to Baruch during the time when he was a fugitive from Jehoiakim's police. In any event, it is appropriate for us to consider them at this point.

Nothing like this personal diary can be found in the writings of any earlier prophet or, for that matter, in the other religious literature of antiquity. This is a unique type of prophetic literature that profoundly influenced the devotional hymns now preserved in the book of Psalms. Earlier prophets had been reticent about baring their interior struggles. Even Hosea, who spoke out of the personal suffering of a broken marriage, receded as a person behind the message he was called to proclaim. But it is different with Jeremiah. Not only does he proclaim the "word of the Lord" but, like the people who heard it, he struggles against it. He complains about his lot, cries out for vindication, and even hurls defiance at God. He undergoes the trials of faith—faith shadowed by doubt, rebellion, self-pity, and despair. Jeremiah is justly called the most human of the prophets.

Using the dialogue of prayer, Jeremiah poured out his interior life to God in the following confessions:

11:18-23	"Like a gentle lamb led to the slaughter"
12:1-6	"Why does the way of the wicked prosper?"
15:10-21	"I sat alone, because thy hand was upon me"
17:14-18	"Thou art my refuge in the day of evil"
18:18-23	"Is evil a recompense for good?"
20:7-12,14-18	"A burning fire shut up in my bones"

As a preface to these poignant outcries, we have an account of the prophet's call (1:1-12), a narrative that in its present form carries hints of his later experience. From the very first, Jeremiah is disclosed as a man quiet and sensitive by nature, a man who recoiled from the task to which he felt predestined even before birth. The message he was commissioned to deliver was sure to arouse the hostility of his people. He was to set himself *against* everyone, because God's judgment was against the whole land of Judah—its kings, princes, priests, and people. "They will fight against you," the prophet was warned. But in his loneliness he was to find a deeper resource than human approval: "I am with you, says Yahweh, to deliver you."

Jeremiah's Loneliness

Yahweh's commission went against Jeremiah's natural inclinations and sensitivities. More than anyone else, he seemed to need the affection and acceptance of his family and friends, and he would have been quite content to live peacefully on his ancestral estate in Anathoth. But his lot was to be that of a rejected man, constantly surrounded by enemies, and "sitting alone" because Yahweh's hand had been laid upon him. Even marriage and children were denied him, for, according to an ominous passage in 16:1-13, Yahweh forbade him to take a wife and to have children, or even to take part in social gatherings. The prophet's isolation was to be a sign of the impending catastrophe that would disrupt all family ties and silence the voice of mirth. The anguish of loneliness lay heavily upon his heart. Throughout his career he was torn on the one hand by his natural longing for peace and companionship, and on the other by the prophetic task that catapulted him into the arena of conflict.

Jeremiah's Vindication

The first two confessions apparently come from his early career. Both passages may belong to the time of the Deuteronomic Reformation and may reflect the fierce animosity of the people of his home town, Anathoth, who were aroused, perhaps, by his advocacy of a reform program that threatened to put local priests out of their jobs (see p. 319). The men of Anathoth plotted against his life, warning him not to prophesy in the name of Yahweh lest he die by their hand (11:21). Even the members of Jeremiah's immediate family joined in the conspiracy (12:6). This treachery evoked from the prophet a prayer for vengeance upon his persecutors and a passionate confession of his own innocence and integrity. To him it seemed inconceivable that Yahweh, who knows men's motives and judges their actions, should allow the wicked to prosper and even to get away with murder! Jeremiah's vindication was promised, but not without the reminder that far greater ordeals were ahead:

> If you have raced with men on foot,
>   and they have wearied you,
>   how will you compete with horses?
> And if in a safe land you fall down,
>   how will you do in the jungle of the Jordan?
>   —JEREMIAH 12:5

It was during the reign of Jehoiakim, as we have seen, that the plots against Jeremiah's life mounted in fury. After his Temple Sermon he narrowly escaped with his life, and his later message in the Temple court prompted Pashur to put him in jail for the night. Finally, Jeremiah was forced to hide from Jehoiakim's wrath. The fifth confession specifically refers to plots against his life that sprang from his alleged subversive activity against all the religious leaders— priests, prophets, and wise men (18:18). Incensed that they should treat him thus when he had interceded on their behalf before Yahweh, Jeremiah uttered a merciless prayer that Yahweh would not forgive them and that they be destroyed in divine anger.

These are the fierce outbursts of a deeply wounded heart. In another confession, the prophet protests violently against his destiny, like Hamlet bemoaning the fact that the times were out of joint and that he was born to set them right. Jeremiah's faith had brought him to the very brink of despair, to serious doubt about Yahweh's righteous government of the world. In the wild tumult of his spirit he cries out that Yahweh has deceived him, like a deceitful Palestinian wadi (brook) that overflows with water during the heavy spring rains and then quickly dries up (15:18). He accuses Yahweh of having overpowered him, making him a laughing stock all day long and filling him with an inward fire that would not allow him to be silent (20:7-9). And finally, in the deepest midnight of his soul, he curses the day of his birth (20:14-18) and castigates his mother for having born him as "a man of strife and contention to the whole land" (15:10).

Few men have suffered so deeply, and we must be careful not to criticize too easily the passionate queries and protests that Jeremiah hurled at God. And yet his prayers—like so many human utterances—express the self-pity and even the self-righteousness that arise when a man's faith is put to the severest test. His question, "Why does this happen to *me?*," suggests that he had been badly treated after all the sacrifices he had made for Yahweh's sake. He had not sat in the company of merrymakers, nor had he committed any injustice in borrowing or lending. He was innocent, "like a gentle lamb led to the slaughter." And self-pity is only the other side of self-righteousness. Hence Jeremiah pleads his case to the avenging God, knowing that his own righteousness will be vindicated and that the unrighteousness of his persecutors will be punished (11:20; 12:1-3; 17:17-18; 18:19-23; 20:11-12).

In answer to these prayers, Yahweh rebuked Jeremiah, for his bitter complaints were based on a self-centered attitude—the very attitude he had criticized in other people! The prophet who had summoned the people to repent (or to "return" to Yahweh) himself stood in need of inward purification:

> Therefore, thus says Yahweh:
> "If you return, I will restore you,
>   and you shall stand before me.
> If you utter what is precious, and not
>   what is worthless,
>   you shall be as my mouth."
>   —JEREMIAH 15:19

His prayers would be answered, but not exactly as he had hoped. For his vindication would not take place merely with the removal of external threats to his life. Instead, it would begin within—with a new heart, purged of self-centeredness. When he had repented and had learned to speak what is true, then he would know in a deeper sense the meaning of the divine promise: "I am with you to save you and deliver you."

IN THE REIGN OF ZEDEKIAH

Jehoiakim could afford to display contempt for Jeremiah's scroll, because there seemed to be no immediate threat to the security of his throne. The Babylonian king, Nabopolassar, had died shortly after the battle of Carchemish, and Nebuchadnezzar, the crown prince who had led the army to victory, returned to Babylon to assume the throne. About the year 601 B.C., his army swept through Palestine to the border of Egypt—an invasion that evoked some of Jeremiah's poems on the foe from the north. In the battle against Egypt, heavy casualties were suffered by both sides, and Nebuchadnezzar's crippled army had to return to Babylonia. The defeat of Babylonia and the weakness of Egypt gave Jehoiakim the opportunity he had been waiting for. About 600 B.C., he made a reckless bid for independence by withholding tribute to Babylonia. This rebellion was an invitation to Nebuchadnezzar to strike (II Kings 24:1-7).[12] See Chronological Chart 8, p. 353.)

The Good and Bad Figs

Since Nebuchadnezzar was unable to attend to Judah immediately, he first incited raiders from neighboring peoples to devastate the land. During these disturbances Jehoiakim died, leaving his eighteen-year-old son, Jehoiachin, to pay the penalty for his father's political folly.[13] The Deuteronomic historian, in typical fashion, charges Jehoiachin with doing evil as his father had done, despite the fact that his short reign hardly gave him a chance to do much of anything. In 598-597 B.C., Nebuchadnezzar mobilized his army for a full-scale invasion of Judah, and Jehoiachin, after only three months on the throne, was forced to capitulate. The Temple and royal treasuries were emptied and the young king and his queen mother were taken prisoners to Babylonia. Into exile with the king went the leading figures of Judah, including, as we shall see, a prophet named Ezekiel. Thus began the first chapter in the Babylonian Exile (II Kings 24:10-17).

---

[12] For a discussion of the historical developments during the last days of Judah, see David Noel Freedman, "The Babylonian Chronicle," *Biblical Archaeologist*, XIX, No. 3 (1956), pp. 50-60. Reprinted in *The Biblical Archaeologist Reader*, I [47,] pp. 113-127.

[13] Jehoiachin is otherwise referred to as Jeconiah or Coniah. See Jeremiah's oracle in 22:24-28.

PRISONERS OF WAR *are led into exile. Although this relief, found at the Assyrian ruler Ashurbanapal's palace in Nineveh, shows Assyrian soldiers carrying away war prisoners (see also the illustration on p. 242), scenes like these were duplicated by the Babylonians, who perpetuated the dread Assyrian policy. Notice the manacled captives, the youth riding pickaback (lower panel), the babe in arms, and the four women riding in the cart pulled by oxen.*

Nebuchadnezzar now placed Josiah's youngest son, Mattaniah, on the throne of Judah, changing his name to Zedekiah. Under this king, the last member of the Davidic dynasty to rule in Judah, Jeremiah spent the rest of his prophetic career in Jerusalem. A good deal of the material in chapters 1-25, especially chapters 21-24, comes from Zedekiah's reign (597-587 B.C.), as does most of the material in Baruch's Memoirs found in chapters 26-45.

In contrast to the despotic Jehoiakim, Zedekiah was mild and benevolent. But he was a weak and vacillating ruler, easily swayed by the advice of those around him. Although the new situation gave the princes a chance to control public policy in their own selfish interests, it also presented Jeremiah with a golden opportunity. Now that the tyrant was dead and a more benevolent regime had been inaugurated, the prophet could appear in public with new prestige, for his prophecies had been confirmed by history. On several occasions, Zedekiah sought the prophet's counsel behind closed doors, and evidently would have liked to follow it had he been more courageous. One can feel sympathetic toward Zedekiah and wish that he had appeared in a quieter period of Judah's history. Notice that Jeremiah's oracles against the royal house (22:1-23:6), did not include Zedekiah among the kings denounced for oppression and injustice. Rather, by a play on words, Jeremiah found in the name of Zedekiah (which in Hebrew means "Yahweh is my righteousness") the suggestion that the messianic king of the future would have a similar royal name: "Yahweh is our righteousness." [14]

Bereft of her first citizens, Judah was only a shadow of her former self. The cream of the leadership—the nobility, the artisans, the highest military ranks—had been shipped off to Babylonia. The nation was crippled at the very time when the need for resourceful leadership and stable traditions was greatest. Into this vacuum moved a new nobility, ill equipped for the heavy responsibilities of the hour and even less capable of perceiving the religious meaning of the crisis. Governed by a short-sighted nationalism and swayed by the emotional appeal of prophetic demagogues, these new leaders hastened the downfall of the nation (compare Ezekiel 11). Jeremiah saw no hope in people of such poor grade!

In a vision (chapter 24) he saw two baskets of figs placed before the Temple. One basket, containing good figs, ripe and freshly picked, represented the exiles whom Nebuchadnezzar had carried away. According to Jeremiah, the future lay with them, for Yahweh would restore them to the land and make them his covenant people. By contrast, the other basket, containing figs so bad they could not be eaten, represented Zedekiah, his nobles, and the remnant of people left in the land. Yahweh, said the prophet, would drive them out and make them a horror to all the kingdoms of the earth. Later on, Jeremiah sent a letter to the Babylonian exiles, advising them to plan on staying in the foreign land for a long time—until "seventy years are completed for Babylon" (29:10; cf. 25:11-12). Jeremiah saw the hope of Israel in these displaced persons, for, as he wrote in the letter, Yahweh had plans for them—"plans for welfare and not for evil, to give you a future and a hope" (chapter 29).

Plotting for Revolution

Zedekiah was under terrific pressure to break with Babylon. The new nobility was pro-Egyptian, and saw in Necho, or in his successor Psammetichus II, who came to the throne four years after Nebuchadnezzar's invasion (594 B.C.), the political potential that might restore a balance of power to the Fertile Crescent and allow Judah and other small nations to regain independence. Throughout this period, Egypt, following her ancient foreign policy, was stirring up discontent among these kingdoms. Moreover, the popular prophets in Judah, like the ancient ecstatics during the time of Micaiah, were beating the drums of nationalism. So it is not surprising that in the fourth year of Zedekiah's reign —the year of the accession of Psammetichus II—Egyptian agents encouraged

---

[14] Since the Hebrew word, here translated "righteousness," can also mean "salvation," the name may be translated: "Yahweh is our salvation."

the formation of an anti-Babylonian coalition consisting of Edom, Moab, Ammon, and Phoenicia. Envoys were sent to Zedekiah to get him to throw in his lot with the revolutionary movement (27:3).

But Jeremiah, with an accent similar to Isaiah's in the Assyrian period (see pp. 283-286), condemned the conspiracy. His word to the envoys was accompanied by a sign. At the command of Yahweh, according to the narrative in chapter 27, he made thongs and yoke bars and put them on his neck, thus dramatizing his prophecy that it was Yahweh's will for the nations to submit to Babylonia. He proclaimed to the conspirators that Yahweh is sovereign in the affairs of history. Since he has made the earth and all that is in it, he gives it into the temporary control of whomever he chooses. Jeremiah asserted that for the time being Nebuchadnezzar was Yahweh's "servant" (27:6-7), the agent of his historical purpose. Therefore, to revolt against Babylonia was to rebel against Yahweh himself. His message to Zedekiah and to the leaders of the people was this: "Serve the king of Babylon and live. Why should this city become a desolation?"

In a sense, this was a wiser political policy than the reckless nationalism of the Judean leaders. Jeremiah, however, did not view the situation in terms of ordinary politics. He was not a collaborationist who wanted to see his country under foreign domination; nor was he a pacifist who was opposed to war on principle. Rather, he saw the crisis as God's sovereign activity in history for the purpose of overthrowing and rebuilding, of judgment and renewal. Therefore the people were not confronted with a choice between two political alternatives —that is, whether to follow a pro-Egyptian or pro-Babylonian policy—but with a decision of faith that called for repentance and utter reliance upon God. Jeremiah's message was either too subtle or too offensive for the people of Judah, however. It made no political sense. Even when he had the ear of Zedekiah, he was misunderstood or repudiated. His advice that Judah should surrender to Babylonia brought him into head-on conflict with the "sons of the prophets," who were saying that Nebuchadnezzar's punitive measure of 597 B.C. was only a temporary setback, that the treasures taken from the Temple would soon be brought back, and that life would soon return to normal (see 27:12-22). This easy optimism, said Jeremiah, was based on a lie. The popular prophets had not stood in "the Council of Yahweh." They were filling the people with vain hopes and speaking "visions of their own minds, not from the mouth of Yahweh" (see the oracles against the prophets: 23:9-32).

Jeremiah's Clash with the Popular Prophets

Baruch has given us a vivid account of this clash between Jeremiah and the popular prophets, who were evidently attached to the royal court (Jer. 28). In the very year in which the foreign envoys came to talk Zedekiah into joining the anti-Babylonian movement, a prophet named Hananiah challenged Jeremiah publicly in the Temple. Hananiah announced that Yahweh would break the yoke of the king of Babylon, and that within two years the Temple treasures and the exiles, including Jehoiachin (Jeconiah), would be brought back. Evidently Hananiah and his prophets still believed that the exiled Jehoiachin—instead of his uncle Zedekiah, whom Nebuchadnezzar had elevated to the throne —was the legitimate king of Judah, and they pinned their hopes for national revival on his return. Jeremiah's sarcastic response was, in effect: Would that this nonsense were true! He reminded Hananiah and the assembled people that one thing had characterized Yahweh's prophets through the years: they all prophesied doom.

> The prophets who preceded you and me from ancient times prophesied war, famine, and pestilence against many countries and great kingdoms.
> —JEREMIAH 28:8

Any prophet who departed from this tradition and prophesied peace must accept the burden of proof. His prophecy must stand the test of historical reality. Incensed, Hananiah dramatically took the yoke bars, which Jeremiah was still wearing on his neck as a prophetic sign, and broke them before the people, repeating that in two years Yahweh would break the yoke of the king of Babylon from the neck of all the nations, and restore the exiled king to his rightful throne. Not to be outdone, Jeremiah proceeded to make a yoke of iron, for, he said, Yahweh had forged "an iron yoke of servitude to Nebuchadnezzar." The yoke could not be broken by human effort because the Babylonian king was the instrument of God's purpose. And it was futile to fight against God!

The Siege of Jerusalem

For various reasons, including perhaps the influence of Jeremiah, Zedekiah did not join the conspiracy in 594 B.C. But the political restlessness continued to mount, reaching its peak in 588 B.C. when a new Egyptian pharaoh, Apries (called Hophra in 44:30), came to the throne. Hophra's predecessor had confined himself to stirring up intrigue in Palestine, Phoenicia, and Transjordan, but Hophra revived the aggressive policy of Necho and began to organize an expedition into Asia. This turn of events gave new hope to the nations that were chafing under the Babylonian yoke. Revolution broke out anew, and this time the centers of revolt were Ammon and Judah. Nebuchadnezzar moved swiftly to put down the revolution, and established military headquarters at Riblah, Syria, on the Orontes River. In deciding whether to attack Ammon or Judah first, he resorted to divination, according to a vivid description in Ezekiel (21:18-23). In the year 588 B.C., Nebuchadnezzar's army laid siege to Jerusalem. From this period come the Lachish Letters, found by archaeologists during expeditions between 1932 and 1938.[15] These inscribed fragments contain, among other things, references to military activity in the vicinity of Lachish and Azekah (see Jer. 34:6-7) and throw light on conditions in the country during the Babylonian invasion. An even more vivid picture of the sufferings experienced during the siege of Jerusalem is given in the lyrical laments of the book of Lamentations, especially chapters 2 and 4.[16]

During the siege, Jeremiah never wavered in his conviction that the only course of action was surrender to Babylonia. This was the counsel that Zedekiah received when he sent a messenger to Jeremiah while the siege was on (chapter 21). The king was hopeful that Yahweh would perform a miracle and make Nebuchadnezzar withdraw, as had happened during the siege of Sennacherib in Isaiah's time. But he received no comfort from the prophet. Yahweh himself, said Jeremiah, would fight against the city "with outstretched hand and strong arm, in anger, and in fury, and in great wrath." Military resistance was futile. Indeed, he advised the citizens to desert to the Babylonians if they wanted to save their lives:

> Behold, I set before you the way of life and the way of death. He who stays in this city shall die by the sword, by famine, and by pestilence; but he who goes out and surrenders to the Chaldeans who are besieging you shall live and shall have his life as a prize of war.
> —JEREMIAH 21:8-9

15 See Pritchard, *Ancient Near Eastern Texts*, pp. 321-322.
16 See the discussion by Norman K. Gottwald, *Studies in the Book of Lamentations* [177].

A RECONSTRUCTION OF LACHISH *shows why that ancient city, here pictured from its west side (see Plate 5), was a powerful stronghold during the days of the Judean monarchy. Notice the double walls and gateways, and the citadel in the center of the city. The Lachish letters, written to the commander of Lachish by an officer of a nearby garrison, were found in the gate of the city.*

Zedekiah was desperate. Hoping to gain the favor of Yahweh, he tried to reinstate one feature of Deuteronomic law that had long been ignored: the prohibition against enslaving a fellow-Hebrew (see Deut. 15:12-18). According to Baruch's account in chapter 34, the king made a covenant with the people in Jerusalem to release all slaves, and the covenant was sealed by the ancient ceremony of cutting a calf in two and passing between the two halves (34:18-19). The upper class was undoubtedly motivated more by economic considerations than by religious conviction, for the emancipation meant that slave-owners would not have to provide slaves with food when rations were short. But when the political situation took a turn for the better, with the advance of pharaoh Hophra's forces and the temporary lifting of the Babylonian siege (37:5), the slaves were promptly taken back. To Jeremiah this was final proof, if more proof was needed, of the people's violation of the covenant, a violation for which they would suffer the judgment of God.

Jeremiah's Imprisonment

The withdrawal of the Babylonian army to face the troops of pharaoh Hophra seemed to be a hopeful sign (chapter 37). Again Zedekiah sent a messenger to Jeremiah, this time asking the prophet to pray to Yahweh on behalf of the people. But again, Jeremiah's response was infuriating. The Babylonian army, he said, would return, and even if the Babylonians were left with only wounded men in their ranks, they would rise up and destroy Jerusalem! This was the last straw. Jeremiah was clearly too dangerous to be left at large. As the princes later said to the king, in words that are used also in one of the Lachish Letters, the prophet was "weakening the hands" of the soldiers and the people by advising capitulation and even desertion to Babylonia (38:4-5).[17] So, as Jeremiah was going out to his home town of Anathoth on business, he was arrested, beaten, and thrown into prison (37:11-15). The pretext for the arrest was that Jeremiah was practicing what he preached: he was deserting to the Babylonians.

The scene that follows (37:16-21) is filled with pathos. The pitiful king, suspecting that Jeremiah might be right, yet not daring to go against the princes, summoned the prophet from his prison cell and brought him into his presence. Instinctively one feels sorry not for Jeremiah but for Zedekiah, "a king but much more bound than the prisoner who stands before him." [18] It was the king who was cowardly—a helpless puppet of his princes and a prisoner of circumstance. In the last hours, when darkness was falling upon Judah, he needed the help of the prophet. The meeting took place in secret. "Is there

---

[17] See Lachish Ostracon No. VI.

[18] The words are those of Bernhard Duhm, quoted by J. P. Hyatt, *Interpreter's Bible*, V, p. 1072.

any word from Yahweh?" the king whispered, doubtless knowing that Jeremiah would give the same word he had been proclaiming in season and out. This time Jeremiah spoke in a mild and friendly tone, tempered with the firm reminder that historical events had not vindicated the popular prophets. Zedekiah seems to have been almost persuaded. Yielding to the prophet's request to be moved to another jail, Zedekiah transferred him to the court of the guard.

Once again the princes intervened. Fearful that Jeremiah's words would ruin the morale of soldiers and people, to say nothing of undermining their own position, they demanded that he be put to death (chapter 38). Lacking the moral courage to be a king, Zedekiah yielded with the pathetic words: "Behold, he is in your hands; for the king can do nothing against you." So they let Jeremiah down by ropes into a cistern used to catch water during the rainy season, and there he was left to die in the mire. But he was rescued by an Ethiopian eunuch who, at the king's orders, drew him out of the pit and restored him to the court of the guard.

Once more Zedekiah sent for Jeremiah (38:14-28) and another secret conference took place, but with the same result. So far as we know, this was the last time the prisoner stood before the king. Shortly afterward, the Babylonian army made a breach in the city wall and poured through to destroy the Temple, burn the city, and carry off many of the population into exile. The story of Zedekiah was tragic to the bitter end. Trying to flee from Jerusalem, he was overtaken in the plain of Jericho and taken prisoner to Nebuchadnezzar's headquarters in Riblah. His sentence was terrible beyond words: His last sight was the execution of his own sons. Then his eyes were put out and he was carried in chains to Babylon. On orders from Nebuchadnezzar, Jeremiah was released from prison (chapter 39).

BEYOND THE DAY OF DOOM

At the time of his call, Jeremiah realized that the word of Yahweh had the double aspect of judgment and renewal, doom and promise. As the determining power in human affairs, it was released through the prophet both "to wreck and to ruin" and "to build and to plant." Much of Jeremiah's preaching, especially in the days when men were seeking the protection of false securities, was devoted to announcing the day of doom. But he never lost sight of the truth that God's purpose was not merely to destroy and overthrow. Jeremiah understood that the ground had to be swept clean of false foundations so that God might build and plant anew (see 24:6; 42:10; 45:4). So he would have been at odds with his deepest conviction and with the great prophets who preceded him had he not kept his eyes steadily on the vision of the New People and the New Age that lay on the other side of catastrophe. This theme of hope is prominent in a section of the book of Jeremiah that is often called "The Little Book of Comfort" (chapters 30-33).[19]

Jeremiah's Purchase of His Family Estate

One episode stands out clearly as the key to Jeremiah's message. Chapter 32, whose authenticity is beyond question, takes us back to the time when Jeremiah was imprisoned lest his words demoralize the people. The Babylonian army was pounding at the walls of Jerusalem. Bread was so scarce that the people had resorted to cannibalism (Lam. 4:10). Death stalked the streets and came in at the windows (Jer. 9:21). It was only a matter of hours until the sure doom would fall, "pitiless and dark." Clearly this was no time to think of the future, for most people, in despair, felt that there would be no tomorrow for Judah. But Jeremiah did something at this point that must have seemed like sheer madness. Word was brought to him that, as the next of kin, he had an opportunity to buy his cousin's field in the family city of Anathoth. While he was still in prison, he carried out the transaction according to the proper legal form and had the deeds put away in safekeeping. To him, the invitation to acquire the land was a sign from Yahweh that the people Israel would be given a future in the Promised Land, that "houses and fields and vineyards shall be possessed again in the land." This was the same promise Jeremiah had given the exiles in his letter, only now he expanded the promise to include other exiles who would undergo a baptism by fire and suffering on the occasion of the destruction of Jerusalem.

The New Community

Jeremiah is often called the prophet of individualism—a dubious tribute, if we have in mind the individualism of our own culture. Often we glorify the rugged individualist, the "lone eagle," who thinks for himself, acts on his own strength, and lives by a private religious faith. In this sense, Jeremiah was not an individualist. Certainly he plumbed the depths of personal faith more profoundly than any Old Testament prophet before or after him. He knew that in times of tragedy, when the whole social order was shattered, a person may sense with his whole being his utter reliance upon God. This kind of personal faith is magnificently expressed in his Confessions. But Jeremiah did not advocate an individualism detached from the traditions of a people, separated from the covenant community. Even in his isolation he knew that men have access to God and experience "healing" or salvation within a community. Hence when Jeremiah lifted his eyes to the horizons of God's future, he spoke of a New Community. The deepest cleavage of the history of the people—the tragic

---

[19] A great deal of the material in this section (for instance, the oracles in chapter 33) comes from later writers.

separation of the "house of Israel" and the "house of Judah"—would be overcome. As in the Tribal Confederacy of old, though on a higher plane, the people would become one in their one loyalty to the one God who had redeemed them (31:27-30).

It is not surprising, then, that some of the oracles now found in chapters 30 and 31 are addressed to Ephraim, the "house of Israel" that had gone into defeat and exile in an earlier period. To the people of the defunct Northern Kingdom is given this promise:

> Thus says Yahweh:
> "The people who survived the sword
>   found grace in the wilderness;
> when Israel sought for rest,
>   Yahweh appeared to him from afar.
> I have loved you with an everlasting love;
>   therefore I have continued my faithfulness to you.
> Again I will build you, and you shall be built,
>   O virgin Israel!"
>   —JEREMIAH 31:2-6

Rachel, the ancestress of Northern Israel, is heard weeping bitterly for her children and is asked to stop crying, for "there is hope for your future" (31:15-22):

> "Is Ephraim my dear son?
>   Is he my darling child?
> For as often as I speak against him,
>   I do remember him still.
> Therefore my heart yearns for him;
>   I will surely have mercy on him,"
>   says Yahweh.
>   —JEREMIAH 31:20

These passages echo Hosea's message of Yahweh's love that would not let his people go (Hosea 11:8). And as Hosea prophesied near the end of the Northern Kingdom, so Jeremiah stood on the brink of the abyss into which the Southern Kingdom was to plunge, affirming that Yahweh's love, working through his judgment, would make a new beginning for both Israel and Judah. It was a time of deep distress, Jeremiah said, and yet *out of it* the people would be saved (30:7).

The New Covenant

This vision of the ultimate restoration is profoundly expressed in the prophecy of the new covenant (31:31-34).[20] This prophecy was stamped more

---

[20] See the author's essay, "The New Covenant and the Old" [168].

indelibly upon later prophetic tradition than anything else Jeremiah said. Eventually it gave the name to the canon of Christian writings (New Testament means New Covenant). Like a finely cut jewel, this prophecy reflects light from several facets. Notice, first of all, that the new covenant, like the old, will rest upon the initiative and authority of God. Man's faith will be a response to what God does, not a bilateral bargain between equal partners. That is the meaning of the words, "I will make. . . ."

Second, this covenant will not be like the Mosaic covenant, for the history of the people had shown that to be a broken covenant. Even the attempt of the Deuteronomic Reformation to restore the Mosaic covenant had failed—a failure that must have been the background of Jeremiah's prophecy. History as it had been known—the history of the broken covenant—will come to an end and a new kind of history will be inaugurated.

Third—and this is the paradox—the new covenant will be new in the sense that it will fulfill the original intention of the Sinai covenant. The meaning of the original covenant had been eclipsed by religious ceremonies and written laws, as though God intended that the Law should be written on tablets of stone deposited in the Ark. In the new covenant, however, the Torah will be written upon the heart, the inward center of the being. It will find expression in a personal response to the God who says, "Obey my voice." This understanding of the inwardness of torah was to receive its supreme expression in the Sermon on the Mount (Matt. 5-7).

Fourth, the new covenant will bring into being a new community, Yahweh's *people*. "I will be their God and they shall be my people (verse 33)—this, as we have seen repeatedly, is the characteristic formula of the covenant (cf. 24:7; 32:39-40; etc.). Verse 31 correctly interprets it as embracing "the house of Israel and the house of Judah"—that is, the whole people that Yahweh brought out of Egypt. Individualism is far from Jeremiah's mind, for he stresses that this covenant formula will be true, personally true, for each member of the community from the least to the greatest. Moreover, the "knowledge of God" will not be mere knowledge *about* God in which men have to be instructed. As in the prophecy of Hosea, the "knowledge of God" will be an inward relationship, as when a friend knows another friend in the trust and tryst of personal relationship. (See above, pp. 248-250.)

Fifth, the new covenant will rest upon divine forgiveness. In the context of Jeremiah's whole message it is clear that pardon must be preceded by Yahweh's "discipline," which shatters men's pride and self-sufficiency and destroys the idols in which they place their trust. When men stand humbly before God, shamed by their sordid history and contrite about their betrayal of their Lord, then all things will be made new. "For I will forgive their iniquity, and I will remember their sin no more" (verse 34).

The sixth facet of the prophecy, though it appears first in the passage, has been left until this point in order that it may stand at the climax of our study.

CHRONOLOGICAL CHART 8

B.C.	EGYPT	JUDAH	BABYLONIA	PERSIA
600				
		Jehoiachin (Jeconiah), 3 mos., 598-597	Nebuchadnezzar, 605-562	
		First Deportation to Babylonia, 597		
		Zedekiah (Mattaniah) 597-587		
		FALL OF JERUSALEM		
		SECOND DEPORTATION, 587		
	Apries (Hophra), 588-569			
		BABYLONIAN EXILE		RISE OF PERSIA
		Ezekiel, c. 593-573	Nabonidus, 555-539 (his son: Belshazzar)	Cyrus II, 550-530
				Defeat of Media, c. 550
		Second Isaiah, c. 540		Invasion of Lydia, c. 546
				Conquest of Babylon, c. 539
			FALL OF BABYLON, 539	
		Edict of Cyrus, 538		
		THE RESTORATION		
		Return of exiles		Cambyses, 530-522
		Rebuilding of Temple, 520-515		Darius I, 522-486
		Haggai		
		Zechariah		
	Conquest by Persia 525			
500				

We have here a prophecy that pertains to "the last things," the consummation of the divine purpose in history. That is the significance of the opening formula, a characteristic preface to prophecies of the end-time: "Behold, the days are coming. . . ." The coming of the New Age cannot be dated on the calendar. This is the future for which men hope, knowing that the time of its coming is measured by God's activity and purpose.

As we shall see, the anticipation of the New Age assumed greater and greater significance in the years after the fall of the nation, and eventually it came to assume a central place in the New Testament. Jesus remembered Jeremiah's words on the last evening of his life when he said to his disciples, "This cup is the new covenant in my blood" (I Cor. 11:25; cf. Luke 22:20). The author of the Epistle to the Hebrews, quoting this passage from Jeremiah in full, affirmed that in Christ the new covenant had become a historical reality (Hebrews 8:8-12; cf. 10:16-17).

The Potter and the Clay

To summarize: The leading theme of Jeremiah's message is set forth in the story of his commission as a prophet to the nations. Throughout his career he came to understand more and more clearly that God's action in history had a two-fold aspect: tearing down and building up. In his time he saw the collapse of two great world powers, Assyria and Egypt, which had vied to be the master of the world; and he witnessed the rise of another nation, Babylonia, which in Isaiah's time had made a bid for power under Merodach-baladan. Judah, owing largely to her foolish nationalism, was caught in the political whirlpool, and was pulled under. But to the prophet this was the work of God, not of Babylonia. He interpreted the fall of Judah in the conviction that God, like a potter, shattered the imperfect vessel in order to create another of better clay.

Since Jeremiah came from a priestly family, it is rather surprising that the Temple had no place in his pictures of the future restoration. Perhaps this silence resulted from his reaction against the false confidence in the Temple that had been encouraged by the Deuteronomic policy of centralizing worship in Jerusalem. Perhaps it resulted partly from his being so preoccupied with the crisis of the present that he was not concerned about sketching the details of the future. In any case, his attitude toward Israel's worship contrasts with that of his contemporary, Ezekiel, the prophet-priest, with whom began a new phase of Israel's history.

Behold, the days are coming, says the Lord, when I will make a new covenant with the house of Israel.

—JEREMIAH 31:31

PART THREE

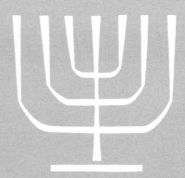

THE

COVENANT COMMUNITY

IS RENEWED

BY THE WATERS

OF BABYLON

CHAPTER TWELVE Although Jeremiah believed that the future lay with the exiles in Babylonia, he decided not to join them when Nebuchadnezzar's commanding officer gave him the chance. His decision to stay on in Jerusalem was clear proof to his accusers that he was not a deserter. The final phase of Jeremiah's career, however, as recorded by Baruch in Jeremiah 40-44, was interwoven with the troubles that beset the remnant left in the ruins of Judah. Gedaliah, whom

Biblical readings: In this chapter we shall consider first the message of the priestly prophet, Ezekiel; read Ezekiel 1-24 and 33-39. Then we shall consider the priestly teaching (P) of the Pentateuch in such passages as Genesis 1:1-2:4; 9:1-17; 17; 23; Exodus 6; 25-31; and 35-40.

the Babylonians had appointed governor of Judah, was assassinated by a certain Ishmael, an archpatriot whose Davidic blood was hot with the old nationalism. Ishmael's sword cut down many of Gedaliah's supporters and many of the Babylonian troops stationed at Mizpah. Fearing reprisals from Nebuchadnezzar, the Judean military chiefs, against Jeremiah's advice, fled to Egypt for refuge, taking the unwilling Jeremiah and Baruch with them. We last hear of Jeremiah in Egypt, where he was denouncing the colony of exiles for reverting to the worship of the Queen of Heaven, Ishtar. They justified themselves by recollecting that in the days before the fall of Jerusalem, when they worshiped the mother-goddess in Judah, everything had gone well: they had had plenty of food, had prospered, and had seen no evil. "But since we left off burning incense to the queen of heaven and pouring out libations to her, we have lacked everything and have been consumed by the sword and by famine" (Jer. 44:17-18). Jeremiah's last word to those blind to the meaning of their history was one of doom.

THE JEWISH DISPERSION

Egypt came to be one of the major centers of the Jewish Dispersion.[1] About a hundred years after the migration of Jeremiah and his fellow-Jews to Egypt, some of their descendants were settled at the first cataract of the Nile on the island of Elephantine (modern Aswan), as we know from papyri discovered there about the turn of the twentieth century.[2] In this Jewish colony there was a temple where Yahweh (or Yahu) apparently was worshiped along with a goddess, Anath. Despite this strange departure from orthodox Mosaic tradition, these Jews recognized their allegiance to the Temple in Jerusalem, which at that time had been rebuilt. Later, important Jewish settlements also sprang up in Alexandria and other Egyptian cities.

But Jeremiah was proved right: the future belonged not to the exiles in Egypt, but to those in Babylonia who preserved the traditions of their past and who eventually returned to Palestine to begin the work of reconstruction. One of the leaders of the Jewish colonies in Babylonia was the prophet Ezekiel. In order to review his career, we must turn back to 597 B.C., the year of Nebuchadnezzar's first deportation, and retrace some of the story we have already followed in speaking of Jeremiah. (See map, p. 337; Chronological Chart 8, p. 353.)

EZEKIEL THE PRIEST

Ezekiel, the son of Buzi, was one of the exiles who, along with Jehoiachin and other prominent citizens of Judah, was carried to Babylonia in the first captivity

---

[1] "Jew" (*Yehudi*) literally means a descendant of the Judeans who formerly occupied Judah. Even though Jews were "dispersed" or scattered in other countries (like Egypt or Babylonia), they continued to cherish their Judean ancestry and traditions.
[2] See Pritchard, *Ancient Near Eastern Texts*, pp. 222-223.

(Ezek. 1:2). The fact that he belonged to the first group of exiles is noteworthy, for Nebuchadnezzar's design was to take away the cream of the population (II Kings 24:14), leaving only the poorest people. We are justified in assuming, then, that Ezekiel belonged to the aristocracy of Jerusalem and perhaps that he was a member of the powerful priesthood that claimed descent from Zadok, the High Priest installed by Solomon.

With his fellow-exiles he settled by the banks of the river Chebar, a large canal that conducted water from the Euphrates through Nippur, a city that lay a short distance southeast of Babylon. In the village of Tel-abib, built on the edge of the canal, he received his call to prophesy five years after the deportation—that is, c. 593 B.C. The date given for his last recorded prophecy is c. 573 B.C. (40:1). Thus the twenty-year span of his ministry represents a transition between the periods before and after the fall of Jerusalem in 587 B.C.

Ezekiel's Babylonian environment undoubtedly exerted a great influence on his thought and imagination. It is likely that he visited the great city of Babylon, whose ancient glory is still dimly visible in the ruins that excavators have uncovered. Guarding the approach to the interior of the city was the magnificent Ishtar Gate—named in honor of Ishtar, mother-goddess and consort of Marduk. Through this gate one entered the processional street and advanced toward the ziggurat that rose above the city like a lofty mountain. Even yet the beautiful enameled brick, which throws into relief the figures of bulls and dragons, suggests splendor that must have dazzled Jewish visitors of old (see Plates 5 and 7).

This external influence, however, cannot account for the strange character of much of the book of Ezekiel. For Ezekiel *himself* was an unusual person whose psychic peculiarities make a fascinating psychological study. We read that his oracles often came to him in ecstasy or trance, when he was seized by "the hand of God" or transported by the Spirit. He was struck dumb, overwhelmed by cataleptic stupor, and seemingly gifted with second sight. But it should be emphasized that these psychic abnormalities throw more light on the *form* of his message than upon its *content*. In the final analysis, the truth of what he said cannot be measured by the unusual manner in which his message came to him, any more than a modern writer or artist can be dismissed because he happens to be odd. Like many of the ancient prophets, Ezekiel was eccentric. His unusual temperament is evidently reflected in some of the difficulties that are noticeable in the book of Ezekiel itself.

The Problem of Ezekiel

In the book of Jeremiah, we found that the greatest difficulty for the reader is the shapeless, disordered character of the materials collected there. At first glance, the book of Ezekiel presents no such difficulty. The oracles are precisely dated and arranged in good order, as though the prophet had planned and executed the work himself. Careful study of the book in the last generation or so, however, has brought to light many difficulties that lie beneath the surface.

ANCIENT BABYLON *as depicted in a reconstruction (see also Plates 5 and 7). A procession is entering the beautiful Ishtar Gate, the entrance through the city's double wall to the palace, which supported on its roof the famous "Hanging Gardens"—one of the seven wonders of the world, according to the Greeks. Beyond the gardens can be seen the ziggurat, Etemenanki, which Nebuchadnezzar rebuilt.*

One obvious problem is that in the first twenty-four chapters Ezekiel, though represented as speaking to the exiles in Babylonia, focuses his attention on Jerusalem and seems to have an intimate knowledge of what was going on there. For instance, in chapter 11 we are told that Ezekiel was "lifted up" by the Spirit and transported to the east gate of the Jerusalem Temple, where he saw twenty-five men plotting iniquity. Ezekiel was commanded by Yahweh to prophesy against them: "and it came to pass, while I was prophesying, that Pelatiah the son of Benaiah died" (verse 13). This seems to mean that Pelatiah, one of the twenty-five men, died at the time Ezekiel was speaking, presumably in Jerusalem. If we take seriously the geographical distance separating Babylonia and Palestine, this passage is baffling. It seems awkward to explain this and similar passages through clairvoyance, or, in Ezekiel's language, to say that God took him by a lock of his hair and spirited him away to Jerusalem (8:1-3). Hence it has been suggested that Ezekiel never did go to Babylonia at all, and that he was really a prophet who lived in Jerusalem during the final years of the kingdom of Judah.[3]

---

[3] For a brief summary of the various hypotheses that have been proposed for the book of Ezekiel, see H. G. May, *Interpreter's Bible*, VI, pp. 41-45. Another important commentary is that of Walther Zimmerli [181].

This view, however, is extreme. There is no convincing reason to doubt what is stated at the beginning of the book: that Ezekiel was carried away from Jerusalem in the first deportation, and that his call to prophesy occurred in Babylonia. It may be that some time after this experience he journeyed back to Jerusalem, believing that part of his prophetic commission was to warn Judah of the impending doom. If so, this would explain how he had such good information about Jerusalem during its last days and why he seems frequently to address his message to people in Palestine rather than Babylonia. On this hypothesis, he later returned to Babylonia and completed his career in the midst of the exiles. This is an attractive solution of the problem, but it raises other difficulties, which cannot be dismissed lightly. The most obvious is that Ezekiel was specifically commissioned to preach to the exiles (3:10-11).

At least some of the problems connected with Ezekiel's mission to the exiles are resolved when we consider, first of all, that he had been brought up in Jerusalem and that he knew the city and its environs intimately, especially the Temple. Again, there was undoubtedly fairly frequent communication back and forth between the Jews in Babylonia and the residents of Jerusalem. Ezekiel's oracles against Judah and Jerusalem, if given in Babylonia, could have been sent by letter, as was Jeremiah's message to the exiles (Jer. 29). And chances are that the exiles in Babylonia were kept posted on the latest developments in Jerusalem either by word of mouth or by letters. Of course, Ezekiel's lively religious imagination readily filled in many of the details, and his unusual psychic temperament found expression in his message. In addition, we should keep in mind that the book of Ezekiel, like other prophetic collections, is an anthology. It is conceivable that Ezekiel himself, like Jeremiah, revised his oracles during his career, and unquestionably the scroll was further revised and supplemented by later prophetic disciples, although by no means as extensively as some scholars have insisted. All this adds up to the probability that most of Ezekiel's work was carried on among the Babylonian exiles.

In its present form, the book of Ezekiel is arranged according to a clear outline:

A. Prophecies given before the fall of Jerusalem (593-587 B.C.)
    1. Ezekiel's opening vision and commission (chapters 1-3)
    2. Oracles of doom against Judah and Jerusalem (chapters 4-24)

B. Oracles against the neighboring nations (chapters 25-32)
    (The oracles against Tyre and Egypt are most clearly from Ezekiel.)

C. Prophecies given after the fall of Jerusalem (587-573 B.C.)
    1. Oracles of promise (chapters 33-39)
    2. The New Jerusalem (chapters 40-48)

In the following discussion, our attention will focus chiefly on sections A and C (1) of the above outline.

A PROTECTIVE GENIUS—*one of a pair which once guarded the gateway to the palace of Ashurnasirpal II (883-859 B.C.) at Nimrud. These winged figures, a prominent feature of ancient art (see picture, p. 207), help us to understand the imagery of Ezekiel's vision. The figure has the body of a lion, the wings and feathers of an eagle, and the head of a man. The clever sculptor cut the figure in both low and high relief, giving it an extra leg so that it presented a formidable appearance when viewed from either front or side. Viewers from oblique positions had to tolerate the fifth leg. A wide, corded band, tied in a tassel, encircles the creature's loins.*

Ezekiel's Call

Let us turn our attention first to the beginning of Ezekiel's prophetic career. The lot of the exiles, among whom he had been living for several years before his call, was not as bad as might have been feared. Many of the Jews deported in 597 were skilled craftsmen whose labor was evidently in great demand in Babylonia. Ezekiel, for instance, had a private house (3:24), in which he was visited by the elders of the people from time to time. The Jews must have been given a good bit of freedom to practice their religion, to live together in closely knit communities in the Babylonian cities, and to improve their economic status. Tablets from the reign of Nebuchadnezzar, discovered some years ago by archaeologists in the ruins of ancient Babylon, mention payments of rations in oil, barley, and so forth to foreign captives in exchange for skilled labor. Included in the list were Yaukin [Jehoiachin], king of Judah, five royal princes, and other men from Judah.[4] Evidently it was easy enough for the exiles to accept Jeremiah's advice to build houses and plant gardens, to raise families, and to show interest in the welfare of the city in which they lived (Jer. 29:4-7). So their life was fairly comfortable, even though many yearned to return to their homeland.

Ezekiel's call to be a prophet came as the result of an extraordinary vision in the fifth year of the exile of Jehoiachin. On that day, he says, "the heavens were opened, and I saw visions of God" (Ezek. 1:1). This overpowering experience convinced him that "the hand of Yahweh was upon him there." At the time, he was thirty years old, if that is the meaning of the mysterious opening words: "in the thirtieth year." The ancient rabbis, who were disturbed by the possibility of strange doctrines being based on the account of Ezekiel's vision, are said to have ruled that persons under thirty years of age were forbidden to read the opening of the book.

Ezekiel's call, like Isaiah's, came in connection with a vision of Yahweh seated upon his throne in ineffable glory and transcendent majesty. To understand this vision it is important to remember that, according to Jerusalem theology, Yahweh was enthroned within the Holy of Holies of the Temple, and that the wings of the guardian cherubim stretched out protectively over his throne-seat (the Ark). The imagery of the vision, described in chapter 1, is drawn both from Israel's priestly tradition, with which Ezekiel was familiar through his experience as a priest in the Jerusalem Temple, and the Babylonian religious emblems that had influenced his unconscious mind in exile. According to the narrative, he saw Yahweh's heavenly chariot approaching him from the north in a storm cloud flashing with lightning (cf. Ps. 29). On looking further, he saw that the throne-chariot was borne by four weird creatures (cherubim; cf. 10:18-22), half-animal and half human, like the figures familiar in Babylonian art, each moving in perfect coordination with the other because they were all animated by the divine Spirit. Alongside each cherub was a gleaming wheel—or rather, "a wheel within a wheel," as though set at right angles to each other to enable the chariot to move easily in any direction, as the Spirit directed. And above the creatures was something like a crystal platform or firmament (cf. Ex. 24:10), which was carried on the cherubs' wings with a roar like the sound of many waters. Looking still higher, the prophet saw above the firmament the likeness of a sapphire throne, and "seated above the likeness of a throne was a likeness as it were of a human form." In an ecstatic vision the prophet beheld Yahweh seated upon his lofty throne in dazzling radiance, or "glory." The holy God, whom Israel had once worshiped in the Temple at Jerusalem, had come to his people in exile!

Overwhelmed by the infinite distance separating the holy God from a mere mortal man, or a "son of man" (for that is the meaning of the latter expression),

[4] Pritchard, *Ancient Near Eastern Texts*, p. 308. See also W. F. Albright, "King Joiachin [Jehoiachin] in Exile," *Biblical Archaeologist*, V, No. 4 (1942), pp. 49-55. Reprinted in *The Biblical Archaeologist Reader*, I [47], pp. 106-112.

the prophet fell prostrate. Raised to his feet when the Spirit entered him, he stood to receive his commission. He was to speak to "a nation of rebels," a people "impudent and stubborn" who had been in revolt against Yahweh's sovereignty from the very first. Like a sentry posted on the city wall, it was his duty as a "watchman" to give them Yahweh's warning of approaching catastrophe, although there was little chance that a people with "a hard forehead and a stubborn heart" would respond (cf. 33:1-9). But whether they heard or refused to hear, at least they would know that a prophet had been among them. In the prophet's vision a hand was stretched out to him, holding a scroll—the message which the messenger was to deliver to the people. Strangely, Yahweh offered him the scroll to eat and digest. When he did so, he found that it was "sweet as honey" (2:9-10; 3:1-3), indicating that he not only appropriated the message but was in agreement with it, even though he would have to "sit upon scorpions." [5] This vivid account of the prophet's commissioning, related in chapters 2 and 3, recalls Isaiah's unpromising vocation (Is. 6:9-13) and Jeremiah's unhappy lot of being set like a fortified city against the whole people (Jer. 1:17-19). Awestruck at the vision of Yahweh's unearthly glory, and appalled by the fearsome task set before him, Ezekiel sat overwhelmed among the exiles for seven days.

WORDS OF LAMENTATION, MOURNING, AND WOE

In the days before the fall of Jerusalem, Ezekiel's oracles were, like the writing on the scroll he was given to eat, "words of lamentation, mourning, and woe" (2:9-10). Like his great prophetic predecessors, he prophesied doom. While Jeremiah was prophesying in Jerusalem, Ezekiel was speaking about the imminent downfall of the state and the captivity of the people. It is explicitly stated that he was to speak to "the house of Israel." Here "Israel" is used in its original sense of "the people of the covenant," and is applied to Jews, whether living in Judah or in Babylonian exile. At first glance, it would seem that his message would have been more immediately relevant to the people living in Judah. But granting that he spoke, at least during part of his early ministry, to Jews in exile, what relevance did a message of divine judgment have for them? To deal with this question, we must consider the situation of the Jewish captives.

Smouldering Nationalism

We know from modern history that a legitimate ruler, even when he is exiled from his own country, continues to be a symbol of nationalistic hope. And so it was with Jehoiachin, who would have continued to rule in the suc-

---

[5] Von Rad, *Theology*, II [80], pp. 223-224, interprets the symbolism to mean that, unlike Jeremiah, there was agreement between the prophet and his message. Certainly the passage should not be construed to mean that Ezekiel found a sadistic satisfaction in pronouncing judgment against Israel.

cession of Josiah and Jehoiakim had it not been for the intervention of the Babylonians in the affairs of Jerusalem. To the exiles of 597 B.C. Jehoiachin was the legitimate Davidic king. Moreover, he was called "king of Judah" in Nebuchadnezzar's tablets, so his captors recognized him as the legitimate ruler and Zedekiah as a regent. So long as the exiled king was alive to move about, and even given an allowance by the Babylonian government, there was hope for a revival of the Jewish nation. It seems, then, that Jehoiachin was a symbol for repressed nationalism among the exiles. We know that there was a party in Judah, suspicious of the Babylonian appointee Zedekiah, who pinned their hopes on the exiled king, for the prophet Hananiah opposed Jeremiah by predicting that within two years Jehoiachin and other exiles would return (see pp. 345-346). Apparently the revolutionary intrigue that centered about the legitimate king, both in Judah and in Babylonia, led to his subsequent imprisonment, although after the fall of Jerusalem he was freed from prison by Nebuchadnezzar's successor and given a regular allowance and a special place at the king's table (II Kings 25:27-30).

Ezekiel, then, faced a situation in which nationalism was still alive even in the exile. In Babylon there were popular prophets, of the same stripe as Hananiah, who were fanning the hope that the power of Babylonia would soon be shattered and the exiles would be able to return to the homeland. Every rumor from Jerusalem must have been followed with keen interest, especially the one about the intervention of pharaohs Psammetichus and Hophra. Jeremiah, as we have seen, even found it necessary to write a letter to the exiles, rebuking them for being deceived by the lies of their prophets and advising them to plan on settling in Babylonia for a considerable time (Jer. 29). Two of these fanatical prophets were seized by Babylonian agents and burned alive (Jer. 29:20-23).

So long as Jerusalem was still standing, Ezekiel's message—like that of Jeremiah—was almost wholly one of doom. It was his firm conviction that the fall of Jerusalem to Nebuchadnezzar was divinely ordained, and that rebellion against Babylonia was treason against God (Ezek. 17:20). In the imminent doom of the city he saw the coming of the Day of the Lord, the day of judgment. As though the event had already occurred, he announced that the end had come upon the land of Israel:

> The word of Yahweh came to me:
> "And you, O son of man, thus says the Lord God to the land of Israel:
>> An end! The end has come upon the four corners of the land.
>> Now the end is upon you, and I will let loose my anger upon you,
>> and will judge you according to your ways;
>> and I will punish you for all your abominations.
>> And my eye will not spare you, nor will I have pity;
>> but I will punish you for your ways,
>> while your abominations are in your midst.
>> Then you will know that I am Yahweh."
>>   —EZEKIEL 7:1-4

The Prophetic Signs

Ezekiel's prophetic word was accompanied by signs enacted with dramatic power. On a clay brick he drew a diagram of Jerusalem under siege, showing the siege-mounds, camps, and battering rams (4:1-3). He lay for 150 days on his left side, then for 40 days on his right side, to indicate the number of years that Israel and Judah respectively would be punished (4:4-8). While he was lying on his side, he weighed out small rations of food and water to show the privations of the coming siege (4:9-11). He cut off his hair with a sword and separated it into three parts to portray the three kinds of fate that would befall the people of Jerusalem (5:1-12). He packed his baggage and at night dug through the wall, suggesting a person trying to flee from the city under cover of darkness (12:1-16). He ate his bread with quaking and drank his water with trembling to symbolize the nervous fear that men would experience during the coming siege (12:17-20). When his wife—the "delight" of his eyes—died, he refrained from mourning as a sign to the exiles that the news of the fall of Jerusalem would fill them with sorrow too deep for tears (24:15-27).

Ezekiel's words and signs stirred up mild interest and curiosity, but they did not evoke repentance or even provoke hostility. His signs were performed before those who had eyes to see but saw not, and ears to hear but heard not (12:2). The people even seemed to "enjoy" his sermons, for to them he was like one who sings with a beautiful voice or plays well on an instrument (33:30-33)! The reaction was quite different from the one Jeremiah received, but it was no less indicative that Israel was a "rebellious house."

The History of Rebellion

According to Ezekiel, God's imminent judgment would be the harvest of a persistent apostasy that reached back to the very beginning of Israel's history. Hosea and Jeremiah, it will be recalled, had portrayed the ancient wilderness as the time of Israel's honeymoon, when the bride was faithful to her Lord (Hosea 2:15; Jer. 2:2). Not so Ezekiel. He advocated what may be called a doctrine of "original sin" in historical terms—that is, he insisted that there never was a time in Israel's history when she was sinless. Recapitulating the "sacred history" with a new twist, he traced Israel's unfaithfulness not only to the wilderness wanderings but to the sojourn in Egypt, for that was the time when her history began:

> Thus says the Lord God: "On the day when I chose Israel, I swore to the seed of the house of Jacob, making myself known to them in the land of Egypt, I swore to them, saying, I am Yahweh your God. On that day I swore to them that I would bring them out of the land of Egypt into a land that I had searched out for them, a land flowing with milk and honey, the most glorious of all lands."
>
> —EZEKIEL 20:5-6

But Israel's history was corrupted at the very beginning, for she responded to Yahweh's choice and promise by rebelling against him and turning to the idols of Egypt. Had it not been for Yahweh's restraint "for his name's sake"—that is, for the sake of his honor—he would have blotted out his people on the spot. For the holiness of God demanded a holy, faithful people, pure from the stain of idolatry. This is a fundamental theme that runs through all Ezekiel's sermons. His sense of the sovereign majesty of God, vividly expressed in his opening vision, made him deeply aware of the infinite distance of sinful, mortal man from the holy, righteous God.

Ezekiel's somber summary of the sacred history from the Exodus to the settlement in Canaan is supplemented by allegories of the two chief cities: Jerusalem and Samaria. In two eloquent sermons (chapters 16 and 23) he portrayed Israel's history in the figure of harlotry, a figure that had been used effectively by Hosea and Jeremiah. Jerusalem's origin, he said, was Canaanite: "Your father was an Amorite, and your mother a Hittite" (16:3; see verse 45). In a broad sense, this statement has some historical accuracy (see pp. 22-28); Israel did come to birth in the welter of the Canaanite culture. But in this context the prophet is talking in theological, rather than archaeological, language. He affirms that Israel's perversity can be traced to the fact that she was the offspring of a lustful union, thus justifying the proverb: "Like mother, like daughter" (verse 44). Yahweh, however, took pity on this illegitimate child whom others rejected, nurtured her to the beauty of maidenhood, and plighted to her his troth. The covenant, then, was based on Yahweh's grace and initiative. But the maiden "trusted in her beauty," forgetting that she owed her life and beauty to God. Wantonly she lavished her harlotries on any passer-by, for her lust was a wild power within her, like that of her passionate Hittite mother. Normally, said the prophet, men pay to go to a harlot; but this adulterous, "lovesick" wife was different—she actually bribed her lovers to come to her. Jerusalem had acted far worse than Samaria (the Northern Kingdom)—a point that is accented in the allegory of the twin harlots Oholah (northern Israel) and Oholibah (Judah) in chapter 23 —and had even out-sinned Sodom, whose corruption was proverbial! Therefore, the harlot must bear the disgrace of judgment and must become an object of reproach among the nations. Her history, the history of a broken covenant, must come to an end in order that Yahweh might renew the covenant he had made with her in the days of her youth (see 16:59-63).

The Deity of God

But before Israel could know Yahweh's forgiveness and enter into the new relationship of an "everlasting covenant," she had to know his judgment in history. Ezekiel's oracles of doom are punctuated with the refrain: "Then they will know that I am Yahweh." Yahweh would prove himself to be God by entering into judgment with his rebellious people, as he had done with their fathers in Egypt (Ezek. 20:33-38). On the basis of these historical demonstrations they would know the deity of God (compare I Kings 18:39!).

Ezekiel's sense of the holiness of God was accompanied by the realization that nothing unholy or profane could stand in his presence. In the view of this priestly prophet, cultic and ethical sins were on the same level. In an extraordinary vision, described in chapters 8-11, he was carried from Babylonia to the Jerusalem Temple, where he saw the abominations being practiced there: the women weeping for Tammuz (the Babylonian name for the dying-rising god of fertility), men worshiping the sun with their faces toward the east, the secret chamber filled with murals depicting beasts and idols, and the princes—the very men who had persecuted Jeremiah—making their evil plans. Then the prophet saw the Glory of Yahweh—the divine presence that was believed to tabernacle in the Holy of Holies—depart from the defiled Temple, borne on the very throne-chariot that the prophet had seen in his vision by the River Chebar (10:18-22). So great was the idolatry of the people, said Ezekiel, that even if three proverbially righteous men, Noah, Daniel, and Job, were to be found in the city, it would not escape destruction (14:12-20). The popular prophets came in for special censure, for they had misled the people by saying "peace" when there was no peace and had tried to whitewash the crumbling walls (chapter 13). In the important chapter 22, the indictment is made in terms of specific sins, including not only cultic abuses like the profanation of the sabbath but also ethical crimes: bloodshed, adultery, extortion, dishonor of parents, and the violation of the rights of the orphan, widow, and sojourner. Princes and prophets were linked in a conspiracy that had corrupted the whole people. No one was righteous.

> "I sought for a man among them who should build up the wall and stand in the breach before me for the land, that I should not destroy it; but I found none."
>
> —EZEKIEL 22:30

The Destiny of the Individual

Ezekiel's message, like the preaching of the prophets who preceded him, was addressed to the people as a whole—to the covenant community known as "the house of Israel." He declared that the community, from the beginning of its history down to his day, was so contaminated with evil that it could not endure. Within the political event of national ruin he discerned the judgment of God. But Ezekiel had to face the meaning of national calamity at another level. For the community, even though it deserved to suffer divine judgment, was made up of persons who were caught in the coils of the tragedy. What, then, about the destiny of the individual?

It must not be supposed that Israel's faith up to this time had stressed only the collective responsibility of Israel, without regard to the individual members of the community. Israel's faith was not totalitarian, if by this we mean that the individual was expendable in the interests of the whole. On the contrary, the covenant relationship, though binding the people together in brotherly solidarity, brought a sense of God's concern for each person. Within the community the individual had personal fellowship with God, and within the community his rights were legally protected. In the biblical view, man is truly a person only when he stands in a community—in relationship to God and to his fellow man. When he is isolated from the community, like Cain in his banishment, he suffers the greatest loneliness and misery.

Nevertheless, in a time of great suffering, when the community was temporarily dissolved and the people were uprooted from their homeland, the question of the destiny of the individual had to be faced more seriously than ever before. The question was not entirely new. According to a story in Genesis 18:22-33, Yahweh was so moved by Abraham's plea on behalf of Sodom that he vowed he would not destroy the city if ten righteous men could be found in it. And according to a story in II Samuel 24, David acknowledged his own guilt, but protested against Yahweh's smiting innocent people too with a plague: "Lo, I have sinned, and I have done wickedly; but these sheep, what have they done?" (verse 17). But in the time of Jeremiah and Ezekiel, when individuals were torn from the old social context that had given meaning and support to their lives, the suffering of the innocent came to be a burning issue. The popular complaint was expressed in the proverb: "The fathers have eaten sour grapes, and the children's teeth are set on edge." (Jer. 31:29; Ezek. 18:1-4). In other words, the people were saying cynically that they were victims of a situation inherited from their fathers. Insisting that they were not to blame for the evil that evoked God's judgment, they took the easy way out and shifted the blame to earlier generations. Ezekiel, then, was challenged to defend God's justice in bringing wholesale judgment upon the people.

It cannot be denied that in the course of human history the sins of the fathers actually are visited upon the children—say, the "children" who suffered or were killed in World War II for the mistakes and follies of the past. These children were apt to cry out bitterly, protesting against the misfortune that they should have been born when the times were out of joint. It was this mood of fatalism that Ezekiel sought to correct (18:25-29). His generation was caught in a *fateful* situation, to be sure; but he insisted that individuals should not respond *fatalistically*, saying "What's the use? God is not fair!" With some oversimplification, he argued that the acts of the past generations do not determine the response of the present generation, for a good father can have a bad son and a bad father can have a good son. He emphasized that each person is responsible for his own destiny—he is not the puppet of heredity, environment, or historical causation! He must answer for himself to God alone, and for no one else.

Had he been dealing with a case in a law court, Ezekiel would have denied the principle of "guilt by association" according to which, in ancient times,

Achan's whole family was put to death with him for his sin (Joshua 7). This practice, rooted in ancient religious taboos, had been abandoned by Ezekiel's time. King Amaziah had refused to liquidate the children of the murderers who assassinated his father (II Kings 14:6), and the Deuteronomic code had made it illegal to punish children for the sins of their parents (Deut. 24:16). But Ezekiel had to deal with the question of divine justice, not in a law court, but in the historical arena where the deeds and decisions of one generation do affect later generations, and where the retribution for past errors often falls not upon the fathers but upon their sons or grandsons.

Ezekiel did not advocate extreme individualism, any more than did Jeremiah (see p. 350), for—as we have seen—he was deeply aware of the solidarity of the Israelite community, the oneness of the people past, present, and future, in the covenant. How, then, did he try to answer the people's question? He turned the question of God's justice back on the questioners themselves, reminding them that they were not as blameless as they had supposed. They too were entangled in the sins of Israel, and had to accept full responsibility. Instead of proposing an explanation of the problem of suffering, he insisted that suffering provided occasion for repentance and faith (cf. Luke 13:1-5). According to Ezekiel, God himself was puzzled that the imminent danger did not awaken Israel to repentance:

> "Cast away from you all the transgressions which you have committed against me, and get yourselves a new heart and a new spirit! Why will you die, O house of Israel? For I have no pleasure in the death of anyone, says the Lord God; so turn, and live."
>
> —EZEKIEL 18:31-32 (cf. 33:10-20)

Ezekiel's attempt to vindicate God's justice may strike one as unsatisfactory. For one thing, bad men do not always suffer and good men do not always prosper. Primarily, however, the prophet urged the people to hear in the crisis God's call to repentance and to cast themselves in dependence upon his mercy. But his message only touched the edge of the mystery. In the centuries afterward, the problem of suffering was raised even more intensely as men sought to understand God's ways in history.

THE PROMISE OF A NEW BEGINNING

Ezekiel's appeal was in vain, for the people were too much enslaved by their false loyalties to be moved even by the threat of catastrophe. So the day of doom finally arrived. The prophet's oracles reflect the swift movement of events with which we have become familiar in the study of Jeremiah's career. In an allegory (chapter 17) Ezekiel tells of Zedekiah's revolt against the "great eagle" (Nebuchadnezzar) and his attempt to find refuge with "another great eagle"

(Egypt). He sees a great sword, polished and sharpened for slaughter (21:1-18), and portrays Nebuchadnezzar at the parting of the ways, waiting for the oracle's verdict on which rebel state he should attack first, Ammon or Judah (21:18-32). As long as Jerusalem was still standing, however, the exiles refused to believe that the nation would fall. They chose to believe that Ezekiel was talking about the far distant future, not about their own times. "The vision that he sees is for many days hence, and he prophesies of times far off" (12:27; cf. verse 22).

Israel's Resurrection

Then one day Ezekiel announced that Jerusalem was under siege (24:1-14). In the year 586 B.C., after an unexplained delay, a fugitive came with the news that the city had fallen (33:21). From then on, Ezekiel's accent became one of hope. Earlier, when nationalistic feelings ran high, his task had been to shatter illusions with hard-hitting words of doom; now, in the new situation, when the people were reduced to utter despair and remorse (33:1-11), his message was one of assurance. Apparently he believed that God makes known his sovereignty by speaking against man's self-confidence, whether it is expressed in high hope or in deep despair. So after disaster had struck, Ezekiel's recurring refrain, "You shall know that I am Yahweh," took on a new meaning. Yahweh demonstrates that he is God to his people, not by passing judgment upon them (compare pp. 367-368), but by acting in history to initiate a new beginning.[6]

This historical miracle is vividly portrayed in the famous vision of the valley of dry bones (chapter 37). Placed in the valley of death's shadow, Ezekiel was asked: "Can these bones live?" Then at Yahweh's command he prophesied to the bones, and suddenly they became living beings, clothed with sinews and animated by the divine Spirit. In the interpretation that follows, we are told that the bones symbolize Israel in despair. Israel as a community was dead, a historical nonentity. The cry was raised: "Our bones are dried up, and our hope is lost." Israel's extremity was God's opportunity, however, for he promised to raise up Israel from the grave (that is, from exile), restore her to the homeland, and give her new life by breathing his Spirit into the people. He would make them one nation, embracing both northern Israel and Judah, and would anoint one "prince" to rule over them. Then the ancient covenant formula would be fulfilled: "I will be their God and they shall be my people."

The Good Shepherd

The restoration is also portrayed in the image of the shepherd and his flock, an image that has an important place in both the Old Testament (Ps. 23;

---

[6] The "demonstration" of Yahweh's deity is treated in Walther Zimmerli's essay, "The Knowledge of God according to the book of Ezekiel," in his collected essays, *Gottes Offenbarung* (München: Kaiser Verlag, 1963), pp. 41-119. See also the companion essay on the *Erweiswort* (Demonstrative Word), pp. 120-132.

100:3; Is. 40:11) and the New (Luke 15:3-7; John 10:1-18). In contrast to the false shepherds who feed themselves instead of their sheep, Yahweh is the Good Shepherd who goes out to seek for sheep that are lost, crippled, or strayed, in order to restore them to their home pasture (chapter 34). He will take the initiative in gathering his flock together:

> For thus says the Lord God:
> "Behold I, I myself will search for my sheep, and will seek them out. As a shepherd seeks out his flock when some of his sheep have been scattered abroad, so will I seek out my sheep; and I will rescue them from all places where they have been scattered on a day of clouds and thick darkness. . . . And I will feed them on the mountains of Israel, by the fountains, and in all the inhabited places of the country."
> —EZEKIEL 34:11-13

After Yahweh has led his people back to their land, he will provide a good shepherd, a Davidic leader:

> "And I will set up over them one shepherd, my servant David, and he shall feed them: he shall feed them and be their shepherd. And I Yahweh, will be their God, and my servant David shall be prince among them: I, Yahweh, have spoken."
> —EZEKIEL 34:23-24 (cf. 32:24-25)

Notice that the prophet does not refer to a coming Davidic "king," but rather to a prince (nasi'), a term once used for a leader of the old Tribal Confederacy. Ezekiel seems to idealize the days before Israel became a nation—when Yahweh ruled as shepherd-king through a designated agent.

It was not because of Israel's goodness that Yahweh was about to act, Ezekiel insisted, but only because other nations had inferred from Israel's tragedy that he was powerless to save. This erroneous interpretation of Israel's defeat profaned God's honor, his holy name. Therefore, Yahweh would vindicate his holiness, for the nations would know that Yahweh was God when he restored a helpless and hopeless people. Moreover, his gracious and holy act would lead Israel to repentance. For Israel's heart must be changed, her inner life cleansed from the stain of idolatry:

> "A new heart I will give you, and a new spirit I will put within you; and I will take out of your flesh the heart of stone and give you a heart of flesh."
> —EZEKIEL 36:26 (cf. 11:19-20)

Then Israel would have the will to obey God's voice and in deep contrition would repent of her former evil ways. The affinities of chapter 36 with Jeremiah's prophecy of the "new covenant" (see above, pp. 351-354) are so close that some scholars think that Ezekiel must have seen or heard Jeremiah's oracle.

So Ezekiel proclaimed the gracious action of the Holy God in restoring a holy people to a holy land. Under the conditions of the New Covenant, God would dwell in their midst, laving the land with "showers of blessing" and multiplying the people in peace and security. One feature of the restoration was especially prominent with Ezekiel, the priest. Yahweh's dwelling place would be with his people, for "I will set my sanctuary in the midst of them forever more" (37:26). The Temple would stand at the center of everything. This theme is elaborated in the concluding chapters of the book (40-48).[7] In elaborate detail, Ezekiel portrays a new Temple in a new Jerusalem. In a vision that recalls the one he had seen at the beginning of his career by the river Chebar, he beheld the glory of Yahweh returning to tabernacle in the sanctuary. According to the prophet's lively imagination, the restoration of worship will have a transforming effect upon the land itself; for from the temple mount a life-giving river, whose source is the fresh-water Deep beneath the earth, will flow eastward into the wilderness and empty into the Salt Sea. Along its banks will grow trees that bear fresh fruit

---

[7] It is generally recognized that some of the material in chapters 40-48 comes from a later editor of Ezekiel's prophecies.

THE AREA OF EN-GEDI—*an oasis located on the western bank of the Dead Sea some thirty-five miles from Jerusalem. The climate in the depression of the Dead Sea—the lowest place on the earth's surface—is semitropical and the terrain is ruggedly desolate. En-gedi, fed by a strong spring, was famous for its fertility (see Song of Solomon 1:14). Ezekiel's vision pictures the fertilization of the whole region and the transformation of the Dead Sea into a fresh-water lake (Ezek. 47:1-12).*

every month, and in the region of En-gedi men will angle for fish, for the Dead Sea will become a fresh-water lake (47:1-12)![8] Ezekiel's vision of the New Jerusalem has had a profound effect upon later portrayals of the end-time, such as the vision of "the holy city Jerusalem coming down out of heaven from God" described in the last book of the New Testament (Rev. 21).

In Ezekiel's sketch of the new community, the relations between "church and state" are carefully regulated. The priests of the line of Zadok, assisted by the Levites, are to have jurisdiction in all religious matter. The responsibility of the civil leader, the prince (*nasi'*), is to support the religious community by providing sacrifices and by upholding law and order (45:7-46:13). The land will be re-apportioned among the twelve tribes, and they will find their unity in the service of the central sanctuary in Jerusalem, which will receive a new name: "Yahweh is there" (48:35). Thus Israel will become a worshiping community, modeled on the pattern of the ancient Tribal Confederacy. We shall see what a deep influence Ezekiel's priestly view had upon the Judaism that emerged out of the Exile.

LIFE UNDER CAPTIVITY

Although Ezekiel had envisioned a reunion of the two houses of Israel—the tribes of the north and the south—this dream did not materialize. The remnant of the Northern Kingdom (later known as Samaritans) and the descendants of the state of Judah were eventually divided by such deep rivalry that in New Testament times it could be said that "Jews have no dealings with Samaritans" (John 4:9). Jews claimed that they were the true "Israel"—using Israel not in a political sense but in its ancient religious meaning of "the people of the covenant."

Judaism—the word used at the end of the last section—is conventionally applied to the religion of the Judeans or "Jews," among whom the covenant faith came to new expression under the conditions prevailing after the collapse of the nation.[9] Hereafter, we shall apply the phrase "the faith of Israel" to Judaism, though recognizing that the Exile marked the beginning of a completely new chapter in the history of Israel's faith.

True to Jeremiah's prophecy, the future of the covenant people did not lie with the remnant left in Jerusalem. As a result of Nebuchadnezzar's blows, it was so disorganized and crippled that religious vitality must have been at a very

---

[8] See "The Geography of Ezekiel's River of Life" by William R. Farmer, in *Biblical Archaeologist*, XIX, No. 1 (1956), pp. 17-22. Reprinted in *The Biblical Archaeologist Reader*, I [47], pp. 284-289.

[9] The term "Judaism" is not found in the Old Testament. It seems to have been coined in later Hellenistic circles of the Dispersion (see Galatians 1:13-14).

low ebb. Even after the deportations of 597 and 587 B.C., Nebuchadnezzar had to intervene again, in 582 B.C., probably because of disturbances following in the wake of Gedaliah's assassination. At that time, another group of Jews was rounded up for exile to Babylonia. There is some confusion about the total number of people taken into captivity.[10] It is clear, however, that the Exile did not involve a wholesale movement of the Jewish population to Babylonia. Only the cream of Jewish leadership was taken, and the poorer elements of the population were left behind to harvest the crops (see Jer. 29:10; II Kings 25:12). By paralyzing the country in this manner, Nebuchadnezzar effectively removed the

[10] Jeremiah 52:28-30, which is probably fairly accurate, mentions three deportations and gives the total for all three as 4,600. II Kings 24:14 (compare verse 16) states that 8,000 to 10,000 were taken away in the first deportation of 597 B.C. No count is given for the deportation of 587 B.C., and the third deportation is not mentioned.

EXCAVATIONS AT NIPPUR *in modern Iraq reveal the two principal structures within the Sacred Enclosure: the Temple of Enlil in the foreground and the ziggurat in the background. These were constructed by Urnammu, the first king of the Third Dynasty of Ur, about 2100 B.C. and, though rebuilt several times, were in continual use throughout Neo-Babylonian times.*

threat of national revival. The land was left in such a wreck that even under favorable conditions it would have taken years to recover. The major fortified towns lay in ruins during the Exile, as archaeological discoveries have shown. The former state of Judah was partitioned, part going to the Babylonian province of Samaria and the rest absorbed by the Edomites (the later Idumeans), who had moved out of their homeland southeast of the Dead Sea into the area around Hebron. Many Jews, finding the economic and political conditions intolerable, migrated in a steadily increasing stream to Egypt to start life anew. Only a handful of Jews were left in the immediate environs of the ruins of Jerusalem.

Adjustment to the Babylonian Environment

Things were not going too badly for the exiles in Babylonia. As we have already noted in speaking of Ezekiel, the Jews were given a good bit of social freedom and economic opportunity. They proved to be so enterprising that a century later they held the controlling interest in the business concern of Murashu and Sons in the city of Nippur.[11] Certainly their lot in Babylonia was a great deal better than that of modern Jews who have been crowded into dingy ghettos or herded into concentration camps. In fact, "anti-Semitism" was quite unknown at that time. Babylonian Jews were permitted to move about freely, to live in their communities within or near the great cities, and to carry on their way of life.

The most serious adjustment that the Jews of Babylonia had to make was a religious adjustment. Their faith had been oriented to the land of Palestine, the inheritance Yahweh had given them, and to the Temple of Jerusalem, the place where Yahweh caused his "name" to dwell. The greatest danger was that in time the Jewish faith, torn from these historical moorings, would be drowned in the sea of Babylonian culture. For in every respect Babylonian culture was superior to the modest way of life the Jews had known in the land of Judah. Like modern visitors to the United States from some backward country, they must have been dazzled by what they saw on every hand. In contrast to the farming and grazing land of Judah, the rich land of Babylonia was a scene of thriving agriculture and teeming industry. The proud Temple of Jerusalem, gutted by Babylonian soldiers, paled into insignificance before the marvelous temples of Babylonia. Many Jews must have wondered whether the high level of Babylonian culture might not be due to the superiority of Babylonian religion over their traditional faith.

The problem faced by the Jews in Babylonia was fundamentally the same as the one faced by the nomadic Israelites in their transition from the wilderness to the new land of Canaan. They believed that Yahweh had manifested his

---

[11] A tax receipt (Late Babylonian) of Murashu and Sons is found in Pritchard, *Ancient Near Eastern Texts*, pp. 221-222.

lordship in Palestine; but could he be worshiped in a strange land where other gods seemed to be in control? Even the most devout Jews, who remembered the joy that they had once shared with worshipers in the Temple of Jerusalem, raised this question in despair. This mood is reflected in Psalm 137, which concludes (verses 7-9) with a terrible imprecation against the Babylonians who devastated Jerusalem and against the Edomites who gloated over its destruction:

> By the waters of Babylon,
>   there we sat down and wept,
>   when we remembered Zion.
> On the willows there
>   we hung up our lyres.
> For there our captors
>   required of us songs,
> and our tormentors, mirth, saying,
>   "Sing us one of the songs of Zion!"
> How shall we sing Yahweh's song
>   in a foreign land?
> If I forget you, O Jerusalem,
>   let my right hand wither!
> Let my tongue cleave to the roof of my mouth,
>   if I do not remember you,
>   if I do not set Jerusalem
>   above my highest joy!
>   —PSALM 137:1-6

Worship without a Temple

It is a tribute to Israel's tenacity and vitality that the Mosaic faith not only survived this transition but was immeasurably deepened and enriched thereby. In Babylonia, many Jews must have capitulated to the pressures of culture and were soon absorbed into the general population. But others were bound more closely to their Jewish past and to the Jewish community. Indeed, it is phenomenal that the faith of Israel was preserved with great purity and zeal in the Babylonian exile, in contrast to the Egyptian exile where the religious heritage was corroded with alien ideas and practices, as can be seen from the Elephantine papyri.

The great prophets had paved the way for the new expression of Israel's faith by insisting that Yahweh was not bound to the Temple of Jerusalem. In Jeremiah's letter to the exiles, he insisted that even in a faraway land, where there was no Yahweh temple, men could have access to God through prayer (Jer. 29:12-14). Ezekiel beheld a vision of Yahweh's coming upon his throne to his people in exile, just as the ancient ark had moved from place to place during the wanderings of Israel. And in a passage in Deuteronomy, written either in exile or more probably shortly before, we read:

> And Yahweh will scatter you among the peoples, and you will be left few in number among the nations where Yahweh shall drive you. . . . But from there you will seek Yahweh your God, and you will find him, if you search after him with all your heart and with all your soul.
>
> —DEUTERONOMY 4:27, 29

In the Exile, then, the people realized that they could turn to God anywhere with the confidence that he would be near, and that he would be their sanctuary in a foreign land (see Ezek. 11:16). Undoubtedly a number of the prayers now found in the book of Psalms were composed during the Exile by unknown men who, like Jeremiah in his Confessions, cried to Yahweh "out of the depths" (cf. Psalm 130). Moreover, during this period Jews undoubtedly came together in small groups, after the manner of the elders who consulted Ezekiel in his house, to be instructed in their scriptural traditions and to worship informally. It has often been suggested that the synagogue, the "gathering together" (as the Greek word "synagogue" means) for worship and teaching, may have originated during the Exile. There is no evidence, however, that there were any organized local assemblies. All that can be safely said is that the later synagogues, which came to be scattered throughout the countries of the Dispersion, arose in response to a need that was first experienced during the Exile, when Jews were separated from their land and their Temple.

THE PRESERVATION OF THE TRADITION

Surprisingly, the sense of belonging to the covenant community was intensified, rather than weakened, by the life under captivity. Even though the people were no longer held together by national allegiance, they did have a common history and they had received a tradition. Like Isaiah in his time of discouragement, they devoted themselves to preserving the Torah until Yahweh's face would no longer be hidden from Israel. They studied and searched the tradition intensively for its meaning and carefully preserved their sacred lore in writing for future generations. Of course, not all the exiles were trained for this special task. But some of them, like Ezekiel, were priests who either knew the tradition by heart, as was common in the ancient Orient, or who had brought along with them from Jerusalem some of the sacred writings as the most precious part of their light baggage. The people were accustomed to look to the priests for exposition of Israel's faith. They relied especially on a class of priests known as Levites, the descendants of Moses' tribe of Levi.[12] Before the Exile, these Levites had not always been priestly celebrants at the altar. Many of them, as we have seen

---

[12] The book of Leviticus is named after these Levites in the Septuagint, from which the title has come to us in our English Bible.

(above, p. 299), were "teaching priests" (II Chron. 15:3; 17:9; 35:3). Their task was to give the people torah, or teaching about the ways in which God was to be worshiped and served. Although the Levites lost some prestige as a result of Josiah's reform, which gave great power to the clergy of the Jerusalem Temple, it is safe to assume that priestly instruction was continued in the Temple and later was resumed during the Exile.

Interpreters of the Tradition

The Exile, then, was a time of religious activity, a time of concentrated and consecrated attention to Israel's religious heritage. Some of the "editing" of the prophetic and historical literature was done in this period by anonymous redactors, the forgotten men of much modern biblical study, who have too often been underrated. The editors were not just tampering with the tradition or touching it up for publication. They were interpreters who believed that the sacred heritage was relevant to their time. To them the tradition was not just a museum-piece out of the past, but a living tradition through which God spoke to their contemporary situation.

An illustration of the updating of prophecy is found at the end of the book of Amos.[13] In 9:11-12, the reference to the rebuilding of "the fallen booth of David" points to a time when the Davidic dynasty had come to an end; and the prophecy that Israel would possess "the remnant of Edom" reflects the resentment over Edom's grabbing a huge slice of Judah after the fall of Jerusalem. So the prophetic literature was read and interpreted in the light of what happened during the Exile. Increasingly it was realized that the prophetic message had been confirmed by historical events and that it provided a basis for future hope.

It was during the Exile that the Deuteronomic History was brought into final shape. Most of the work had been completed in the years before the fall of Jerusalem, perhaps around 600 B.C., slightly before the first captivity of 597 B.C. It is possible, however, that the first edition appeared around the year 610 B.C.—that is, just before the death of Josiah at Megiddo—and that it stopped at about II Kings 23:25. Since the reforming king, measured by Deuteronomic standards, was a paragon of virtue, it is hard to believe that the Deuteronomic historian would have dealt with the king's untimely death and thereby presented evidence to refute his central thesis that Yahweh rewards obedience. In any event, the first edition of the Deuteronomic History could not have concluded with the last verses of the present book of Kings, which refer to the elevation of the exiled king Jehoiachin in 561 B.C. This means that the final chapters of II Kings were added during the Exile, perhaps around the year 550 B.C.

---

[13] Today there is a tendency to defend Amos' authorship of some or all of the units found in the so-called appendix to the book of Amos (9:9-10, 11-12, 13-15). The passage 9:11-12 clearly comes from the exilic or early post-exilic period, and it is difficult to square the other two units with the message of Amos.

The Deuteronomic History had been addressed to the nation. The writer had taken for granted that the covenant community would be organized politically as a *kingdom*, ideally united under a Davidic king and centered in the Temple of Jerusalem. During the first years of the Exile, however, Ezekiel, a Jerusalem priest, had advocated a different view of the covenant community. Although Ezekiel's picture of the future left room for a "prince" (Ezekiel 44:3), he believed that fundamentally Israel would be a "kingdom of priests" (cf. Ex. 19:6), an ecclesiastical community presided over by the priestly hierarchy of the "sons of Zadok"—that is, the Jerusalem clergy who had been in charge of the Temple ever since the time of Solomon and who claimed direct descent from Aaron (Ezek. 44:13-15). This view was further developed by other members of the Zadok order who were carried into exile, especially in the second deportation of 587 B.C. when the Temple was destroyed and its treasures looted.

The Priestly Tradition

The priestly view of Israel's history is set forth in a large block of material found in the Pentateuch, especially in the books of Genesis, Exodus, Leviticus, and Numbers. After we take from the Pentateuch the traditions of the Yahwist (J) and the Elohist (E), and after Deuteronomy is subtracted, the residue belongs to the priestly tradition that is usually designated by the letter P. Although we have referred to the priestly writing from time to time, it is now appropriate to deal with it directly.

There was a time when it was believed that the priestly material was the oldest part of the Pentateuch, and that all other literary sources were built on it. But this view has been abandoned, for it is evident that in style and theological outlook P in its final form best fits the exilic and post-exilic community.[14] And yet the first impression of scholars was partially right. In the first place, P does preserve many ancient traditions. This does not mean that everything in P is as old as the Mosaic period, for clearly one of the motives of the writer was to authorize the views and practices of Jerusalem priests by showing that they had their origin at Sinai. Still, a good deal of the old tradition, which developed out of the cultic practice of the time of Moses and the Tribal Confederacy, has been preserved in P by the Jerusalem priesthood. Remember that the date of literary composition does not necessarily provide an index to the *age* of the material itself. No longer do we think of the Pentateuch being made up of sources that followed one another in chronological succession—J in about 950 B.C., E in 750 B.C. or earlier, D after 700 B.C., and finally P in the period of the Exile. Rather, these are *parallel* traditions stemming from ancient times, as can be seen by examining the chart on "Israel's Traditions" (p. 382).

---

[14] The major challenge to this scholarly consensus has come from the Jewish scholar Yehezkel Kaufmann. In his important book, *The Religion of Israel* [65] he maintains that the whole Pentateuch is pre-exilic and specifically that P came before D.

In writing down the priestly tradition, the writer quoted collections of priestly lore that had been preserved in Temple circles. An illustration is the Holiness Code of Leviticus 17-26, so designated because the exhortation to Israel to be a holy people even as Yahweh is holy, is the recurring theme of these ritual and ethical laws (20:26). This block of priestly teaching is really an exposition of Israel's faith. It is best known for the high ethical fervor of chapter 19, and especially for the law that is cited in the New Testament as the second great commandment:

> You shall not take vengeance or bear any grudge against the sons of your own people, but you shall love your neighbor as yourself: I am Yahweh.
>
> —LEVITICUS 19:18

The date of the Holiness Code is uncertain. The theme of holiness suggests the influence of Ezekiel, and the style at times resembles the exhortation of Deuteronomy (see 19:33-37). The Code may have been written in Jerusalem shortly before the fall of the nation, although it preserves older tradition as well.

So the priestly tradition did not originate in a single generation. Like the services of the Anglican Prayer Book, P is the end-product of many generations of temple usage. A study of the large mass of priestly instruction concentrated in the latter part of the book of Exodus (chapters 25-31 and 35-40), all of the book of Leviticus, and part of the book of Numbers would show the traces of a long history. This priestly tradition was available to the exiled priests of the Temple of Jerusalem, some of it in oral and some in written form, some of it early and some recent in origin.

The Formation of the Pentateuch

How, then, did the priestly editor unify the religious traditions? To begin with, he did not have to create unity out of a mass of diverse materials. Already a fundamental unity was manifest in the great epic of Israel which he received in enlarged form. After the fall of the Northern Kingdom, the northern (E) and southern (J) versions of this epic had been blended together (JE), probably in connection with the use of the tradition in worship. And shortly before the fall of the Southern Kingdom or not long after—the time cannot be pinpointed definitely—the book of Deuteronomy had been inserted into the JE epic just before the narrative of Moses' death (Deut. 34). Into this enlarged story (JED) the priestly editor inserted at various points the traditions of the Jerusalem Temple. These blocks of priestly material were "built into" the historical drama, just as if someone were to take a stirring account of American history and insert into it at key points the American Constitution or legislation of Congress. Priestly material has an integrity of its own, but it is dependent upon the JE epic for dramatic narration. Thus the Pentateuch finally took shape as a priestly edition of Israel's sacred history.[15]

ISRAEL'S TRADITIONS*

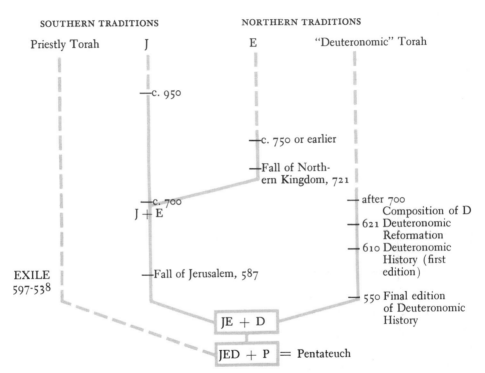

| SOUTHERN TRADITIONS | | | NORTHERN TRADITIONS | |

Priestly Torah   J   E   "Deuteronomic" Torah

c. 950

c. 750 or earlier

Fall of North-
ern Kingdom, 721

c. 700
J + E

after 700
Composition of D
621 Deuteronomic
Reformation
610 Deuteronomic
History (first
edition)

EXILE
597-538   Fall of Jerusalem, 587

550 Final edition
of Deuteronomic
History

JE + D

JED + P = Pentateuch

* In the above chart the broken lines signify oral tradition, and solid lines signify the transmission of the tradition in written form. Notice that all the traditions are parallel developments out of the ancient period, although each was subject to a special development in the circle that preserved it. Like several streams flowing into one river, these traditions were joined and unified in a priestly edition, thus forming the Pentateuch.

THE PRIESTLY POINT OF VIEW

With this background, we turn now to the scope and focus of the priestly writing in the Pentateuch. The first thing to notice is that the atmosphere of worship pervades the whole work. To enter sympathetically into this part of the Pentateuch is like standing in an ancient cathedral, whose symmetrical design and religious symbolism, hallowed by centuries of worship, produce a solemn sense of the holiness and majesty of God. To be sure, the modern reader may

[15] For a good discussion of the formation of the Pentateuch see the article "Pentateuch," by David N. Freedman, in *Interpreter's Dictionary* [11].

not get this impression at first as he plows through the prescriptions for various kinds of sacrifice, the elaborate specifications for the tabernacle and the altar, and the minute directions to priests and people. The book of Leviticus, to take one large example of priestly teaching, seems far removed from modern forms of worship. Nevertheless, all the details bear witness to a long history of worship and to a vital experience of the "tabernacling presence" of God in the sanctuary. In P we do not find dramatic narratives about human affairs, but rather torah or instruction about how God should be worshiped—as worship was understood by the priests of Jerusalem. P was intended primarily for the covenant community of Israel, conceived as a worshiping congregation—that is, a church. It was written with the sober conviction that Israel's whole life was to be a "liturgy," a service of God. Even today the solemnity of the priestly blessing entrusted to Aaron and his sons (the Zadokite Jerusalem clergy) brings a reverent hush over a worshiping congregation:

> Yahweh bless you and keep you:
> Yahweh make his face to shine upon you,
>   and be gracious to you:
> Yahweh lift up his countenance upon you,
>   and give you peace.
>   —NUMBERS 6:24-26

The Divine Plan in History

The priestly writer stands within the worshiping community of Israel, which had been called into being by God's marvelous deeds in the time of the Exodus, and looks backward to the very beginning, to the Creation. From this point of view, God's revelation follows a prearranged, systematic plan which unfolds in four successive eras, or "dispensations," each marked by the dispensing of certain privileges and duties. The scheme stands out clearly in the book of Genesis. Normally, P leaves the JE epic intact, adding only priestly notes or commentary to the flowing narrative. But in a few instances P departs from this procedure and introduces a priestly narrative, written in a measured, somber prose that contrasts with the picturesque, flowing style of J and E. Each of these P narratives is important for gaining an understanding of the priestly view.

(1) THE CREATION. The first dispensation began with the Creation and extended to the time of Noah. The priestly writer sets forth his understanding of the meaning of this era in the P creation story (Gen. 1:1-2:4a), placed right before the Yahwist's story of Paradise.[16] In majesty of style and sublimity

---

[16] For an exposition of this story see Gerhard von Rad's commentary [133] and his "Notes on the Priestly Account of Creation," pp. 61-65. Von Rad rightly stresses that the P account was added as a supplement to the earlier J version in order to provide a fuller picture. For further discussion of the biblical doctrine of creation, see the author's article, "Creation," in Interpreter's Dictionary [11].

of thought, the P story is excelled by few passages in the Bible. Its stately rhythms and sonorous refrains may reflect years of usage in worship services in the Temple, where it was solemnly recited and gradually assumed its present form of liturgical prose. In other words, although the story was written down during the Exile, it has a long history behind it and bears the marks of intense theological reflection over a period of many generations.[17]

Anyone who is looking for a scientific account of the origin of the world can find plenty of discrepancies in the priestly story. To the scientific mind it is odd to hear that the earth was created before the sun, or that light was created before the heavenly lights—the sun, moon, and stars. It is fruitless to try to harmonize this account with modern science by saying, for instance, that the six creative days correspond to geological periods, or that the creation of living things followed a pattern of evolution. The cosmology, or picture of the universe, presupposed in the story was inherited from Israel's cultural environment. Unlike

---

[17] The original version apparently was organized into eight creative acts, which are now compressed into the pattern of six working days of twenty-four hours each, following the scheme of the Israelite calendar. See the chart in R. H. Pfeiffer's *Introduction* [28], p. 195.

THE BABYLONIAN CREATION EPIC *is inscribed (in part) upon these seven tablets found in the ruins of the library of Ashurbanapal, the Assyrian king of the seventh century* B.C. *The epic, called* Enuma elish *after its two opening words ("when above"), probably dates back to the period of Hammurabi.*

the modern scientific cosmology, the universe was pictured as a three-storied structure: "heaven above, the earth beneath, and the water under the earth," as an editorial expansion of the Ten Commandments puts it (Deut. 5:8). The earth was conceived as having been formed by dividing "the waters from the waters," by raising up a solid substance, or firmament, to hold the primeval ocean back (1:6). Thus the habitable world was surrounded on every hand by the chaotic waters which, unless checked by God's creative power, would destroy the earth (see the story of the Flood; Job 38:8-11; Ps. 104:5-9). In this respect, the story has affinities with the picture of the universe presented in the Babylonian myth of _Enuma elish,_ although in the latter the creation of the universe resulted from a fierce struggle between the god Marduk and Tiamat, the dragon of watery chaos.[18]

But the priestly story is not a treatise on scientific origins. The issue lies, properly speaking, beyond the domain of science and is independent of any cosmology, whether ancient or modern. The purpose of the chapter is to declare that everything is dependent for its existence and meaning upon the sovereign God. Unlike ancient polytheistic myths, which depicted the birth of the gods out of the intermingling waters of chaos, P affirms the holy transcendence of the Creator. The heavens declare his glory, but he is not a part or a process of his creation. Nothing is independent, self-created, self-sustaining, but all things are dependent upon the sovereign will of God. If it were not for his power, which holds creation in existence, the world would revert to primeval and meaningless chaos.

The theme of God's sovereignty over all his works comes to its highest expression in the account of the creation of man. By placing this act last, P shows that man is the crown of God's creation, the noblest of the creatures. As a result of a decision made in the Heavenly Council (see the "us" and "our" of 1:26), man was made "in the image of God"—that is, he was to be a living representation of God's kingly rule on earth, just as the image of a king, set up in various provinces of an empire, is a visible token of the king's sway.[19] Man's nobility, then, is that he is given a special task: to be God's representative, exercising dominion within the empire of his King. This thought of man's special status in the creation excites the wonder of a psalmist in Psalm 8, a hymn of worship which is closely related to Genesis 1:

---

[18] See Pritchard, _Ancient Near Eastern Texts,_ pp. 60-72. The Hebrew word for "deep" (_tehom_) is equivalent to the Babylonian word Tiamat; here we have a distant echo of the mythology of the ancient world. For a discussion of the ancient mythology, see H. A. Frankfurt _et al., The Intellectual Adventure_ [123], pp. 169-183. For a discussion of how Israel "demythologized" the creation account, see Brevard Childs, _Myth and Reality_ [119], especially pp. 30-42.

[19] The figure of speech comes from Gerhard von Rad, ([133], pp. 55-59), who points out that the "image" should not be restricted to man's "spiritual" nature, but applied to his whole being, including his body, which is truly a work of divine art. Elsewhere the Hebrew word for "image" is used in referring to very concrete, visible things, like an idol (Num. 33:52) or a picture (Ezek. 23-14).

> When I look at thy heavens, the work of thy fingers,
>   the moon and the stars which thou hast established;
> what is man that thou art mindful of him,
>   and the son of man that thou dost care for him?
> Yet thou hast made him little less than God,
>   and dost crown him with glory and honor.
> Thou hast given him dominion over the works of thy hands;
>   thou hast put all things under his feet,
> all sheep and oxen,
>   and also the beasts of the field,
> the birds of the air, and the fish of the sea,
>   whatever passes along the paths of the sea.
>
> —PSALM 8:3-8

Created in the image of God, man was given a divine blessing that enabled him to multiply and to have dominion over all other living creatures (1:28). But this blessing was accompanied by a divine restriction: man's food was to be confined to fruits and vegetables. He was to be a vegetarian rather than a carnivore (1:29-30).

The priestly narrative comes to a conclusion with the creation of the sabbath (Hebrew: *shabbath*), for after six days God "rested" (*shabath*) from all his creative work (2:2-3; cf. Ex. 20:11; 31:17). Here we can see that, although the story deals with mankind (*'adam*), it concerns Israel in a special way. P anticipates the institution of a day of rest and gladness (Ex. 16) when Israel participates in the consummation of God's creative work, the "sabbath rest." [20] Thus the narrative shows that the days of man's week are not an empty cycle of "tomorrow and tomorrow and tomorrow" but times which are embraced within God's purpose for his creation. It is not surprising that even in our day the challenge to the biblical view of time and history has sometimes taken the form of a prohibition against observing the sabbath.

(2) THE COVENANT WITH NOAH.   In the priestly view, the Creation does not stand by itself, but sets the stage for history—the history that moves toward the climax of God's revelation at Sinai. So we come to the second stage of the divine plan: the covenant made with Noah at the end of the Flood (Gen. 9:1-17). According to P, the Flood came as a result of the corruption of mankind, for Noah alone was found righteous in his generation. The judgment of God, in the form of a flood, was of such catastrophic proportions that the world almost reverted to pre-creation chaos.[21] But God made a covenant with Noah

---

[20] On the "sabbath rest," see especially von Rad's exposition of the theme that "there is still a rest in store for the people of God," in his collected essays [100], pp. 101-108.

[21] In the Flood story (Gen. 6-9), P and J narratives are closely blended (see J outline, p. 170). In J, the Flood came as the result of heavy rain (7:4,12). According to P, "the fountains of the great deep (*tehom*)" and "the windows of heaven" were opened (7:11)—that is, the waters above and the waters below threatened a return to chaos.

and all living creatures, promising never again to destroy the earth. This covenant introduced a new privilege: animal meat might be eaten provided it was bloodless—that is, the animal had to be properly sacrificed or slaughtered, for blood, which was believed to have the potency of life, was sacred to God. This, according to P, was the origin of sacrifice, another basic institution of priestly religion (9:1-5).

Again, the new privilege was accompanied by a stringent prohibition—this one against the wanton shedding of the blood of any creature, especially man. Here again the command rests on the fact that man was made "in the image of God" (9:6). Priestly theology emphasizes that, despite the corruption of mankind at the time of the Flood, man still retained the divine image. Man's sin did not destroy the basic goodness of God's creation (cf. 1:31). With an exquisite touch, the P story of the Flood concludes by saying that every rainbow seen after a storm would be a "sign" or visible pledge of the covenant between God and man (9:8-17). In traditional Jewish theology, the privileges and prohibitions of this covenant (known as the Noachian Covenant) are regarded as binding upon all men, for the covenant was not made merely with Israel, but with Noah, the father of Shem (Semites), Ham, and Japheth (cf. Acts 15:20; 21:25). In the P genealogy, all the nations of mankind sprang from these three sons (10:32).

(3) THE COVENANT WITH ABRAHAM. The third dispensation began when God made a covenant with Abraham (Gen. 17). At that time the patriarch's older name Abram (meaning, "may the [divine] Father be exalted") was changed to Abraham, a name the writer takes to mean "father of a multitude." Thus the blessing came in the form of a promise that Abraham would be the father of many nations, and that to him and his descendants the land of Canaan would be given as an everlasting possession.

Like the covenant described in the older patriarchal tradition (Gen. 15:7-21; see above, pp. 28-29), the P version emphasizes that God graciously established a relationship with his people. This is an unconditional covenant, based solely on divine initiative, as Paul was later to say with Christian accent (Gal. 3:16-18). In the priestly scheme, the giving of the Law is not associated with God's covenant with Abraham but with his revelation in the Mosaic period. Membership in the covenant community, however, is attested by the sign of circumcision—one of the basic institutions of priestly religion, though it was criticized by prophets like Jeremiah because it engendered a false confidence in external rites and practices. P plainly states that any male who has not kept this "covenant in the flesh" is to be excluded from the Israelite community. By failing to be circumcised, a man breaks the covenant and has no claim upon the divine promise.

God's promise to Abraham is further emphasized in another priestly narrative found in Genesis 23, the story of Abraham's purchase of a cave at Hebron as a burial place. The burial of Abraham and Sarah in this place was to be a fore-taste or "earnest" of the fulfillment of God's promise that Israel would some day inherit the land. Even though Abraham did not live to see that day, he entered into it through his death and burial in the promised land. The Cave of Machpelah, as the traditional site of Abraham and Sarah's interment is known, also supposedly houses the remains of Isaac and Rebekah, and Jacob and Leah. (The traditional grave of Rachel is near Bethlehem.) Today a mosque, situated in the modern city of Hebron, rests upon what is claimed to be this cave; visitors may view the hallowed chamber through a small hole in the floor of the Islamic religious center. The mosque of Hebron is called the Haram el-Khalil, or "the sacred precinct of the friend" [of the Merciful One—i.e., God], in recollection of Abraham's standing as "the friend of God" (II Chron. 20:7; Is. 41:8).

(4) THE REVELATION AT SINAI.   All these passages lead up, step by step, to the supreme revelation in the Mosaic period. As we have seen, the priestly story begins with a canvas as wide as the whole creation. The scope of vision is universal: the creation story deals with mankind, and the covenant with Noah embraces all the nations. But from this universal scope the priestly vision nar-rows down until it comes to concentrate on the revelation at Sinai. Here, ac-cording to P, God's special revelation was given to Israel.

It is striking that whereas the old (JE) tradition stressed the making of the covenant at Sinai (see above, pp. 57-60), P contains no independent account of the Mosaic covenant. The reason for this undoubtedly is that, according to P *the Abrahamic covenant was the basis of God's relation to Israel*. It was an "everlasting covenant" (Gen. 17:7) which contained the promise that God would be with Israel and would give his people the land of Canaan as an in-heritance. In the Mosaic period, according to the view of P, this covenant promise was partially realized: God came to claim Israel as his people and to be to them God (Ex. 6:6-7; compare Gen. 17:7). The giving of the Law was a rati-fication of God's pledge: I will be your God, and you shall be my people.[22]

Like Ezekiel, P believed that Israel was called to be a holy community, sep-arated from all other nations in order that the holy God might take up his abode, or "tabernacle" in her midst (Ex. 29:43-46; Ezek. 43:7-9). That was the meaning of Israel's election. Therefore, no ethical or ritual impurity could be permitted to defile the people. The corporate group—the worshiping community —must be healthy and holy. Just as a doctor gives a patient a prescription to restore his health, so the priestly writer believed that God revealed laws and institutions so that Israel could be a holy people. It is important to realize that

---

[22] This explanation of the absence of a P account of the covenant in the Mosaic period was advanced by Walther Zimmerli, "Sinaibund und Abrahambund," an essay found among his collected essays entitled *Gottes Offenbarung* (Munich: Kaiser Verlag, 1963), pp. 205-216.

to the priestly mind there was nothing burdensome in the Torah. Rather, it
was a "means of grace" that God bestowed upon his people. Consequently,
knowing that the benevolence of God was behind all that was given, the priestly
writer moves toward the climax of the Mosaic revelation as one would hasten
to receive a great gift. He interrupts the Exodus story to give full treatment to
the institution of the Feast of the Passover (Ex. 12:1-20). When the people
arrive at Sinai, he introduces a large body of material dealing with the furnishings of the tabernacle, the construction of the Ark, various kinds of sacrifice,
laws related to "kosher" or permitted foods, the regulations for the sacred calendar, and so on. This Torah, which represents the official tradition handed
down by the Jerusalem priests, now stands between the old (JE) story of the
making of the covenant (Ex. 24) and the departure from Sinai (Num. 10:11ff.).

According to the priestly view, the successive periods of revelation were
marked by a sequence of names for the deity. In the first two eras, when all
mankind was in the range of the priestly writer's vision, the deity was known as
'Elohim (translated "God" in the Revised Standard Version). In the third
dispensation, Yahweh was known to Abraham by the special name 'El Shaddai
(often translated "God Almighty"). Not until the Mosaic period was the name
Yahweh introduced (Ex. 6:2-3), a name so holy that it must not be taken in
vain, and so ineffable that no layman could pronounce the sacred syllables. Thus
P shows how the disclosure of the sacred name, at the very climax of God's
historical design, inaugurated a new and special relationship between God and
his people.

This historical movement, from the cosmic scope of the Creation to the narrow focus of the Mosaic revelation, is rather like the action of a television camera
lens which begins with a wide view and gradually brings the central object closer,
until at last one sees only a close-up. The priestly scheme is illustrated by the
diagram which follows (p. 390).

The Priestly Understanding of Revelation

It can be seen from this sketch that P, like the JE epic, is interested in
God's revelation in history and his selection of a particular people, Israel. But
P differs in his understanding of the *nature* of this historical revelation. Even
when P writes narrative, as in the chapters of Genesis dealt with above, the
priestly work as a whole lacks the dramatic, dynamic character that is discernible in the epic narratives of J and E. P presents a historical scheme, structured
with the precision of a theological architect, rather than a history of the engagement between God and man in the affairs and crises of daily life. The priestly
tendency to view history in schematic terms reflects an emphasis upon revelation as something objectively given, rather than a concern for man as the subjective recipient. In the priestly view, revelation is not so much an event that

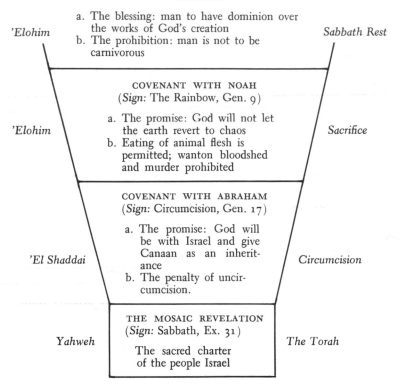

CREATION

'Elohim

a. The blessing: man to have dominion over
the works of God's creation
b. The prohibition: man is not to be
carnivorous

Sabbath Rest

COVENANT WITH NOAH
(*Sign:* The Rainbow, Gen. 9)

'Elohim

a. The promise: God will not let
the earth revert to chaos
b. Eating of animal flesh is
permitted; wanton bloodshed
and murder prohibited

Sacrifice

COVENANT WITH ABRAHAM
(*Sign:* Circumcision, Gen. 17)

'El Shaddai

a. The promise: God will
be with Israel and give
Canaan as an inherit-
ance
b. The penalty of uncir-
cumcision.

Circumcision

THE MOSAIC REVELATION
(*Sign:* Sabbath, Ex. 31)

Yahweh

The sacred charter
of the people Israel

The Torah

happens *between* God and man—a dialogue between "I and thou"—as it is something given *to* man in the form of laws and institutions. Hence the great figure in P is Moses, whose role is to mediate the Torah—received directly from Yahweh on Mount Sinai—to the people, with Aaron the priest always at his side. P's concentration upon the data of revelation led eventually to the belief that the whole Pentateuch had been delivered to Moses at Sinai. When revelation is viewed in this way, faith tends to become assent to what is written in an inspired book, as it is to many people today who in this respect are more "priestly" than "prophetic" in their religious understanding.

This objective view of revelation suggests that P is not very much interested in the human side of the drama of God's dealings with his people. Unlike the epic narratives, especially J (see pp. 182-187), P does not portray the subjective situation of faith—the conflicts, frustrations, anxieties, and doubts that arise when men respond personally to God's "word" or revelation. The priestly writer lacks the "human interest" that we find in the J story in Genesis 2 and 3, or in the naive touch, given in the J version of the Flood story, that Yahweh shut Noah in the Ark (Gen. 8:16b). Contrary to a good deal of opinion, this is not because P has gone beyond anthropomorphism—that is, thinking of God in human terms. True, the priestly theology is more sophisticated and refined than the naive imagery of J or the prophets, but P does not escape anthropomorphic language, as in the statements that God created man in his image, that he "rested" after six days of work, and that he speaks, thinks, acts, hates, rejoices, and so on. The real difference lies in the fact that P's interest centers in what God says and does, rather than in how men speak and act in response to the divine words and deeds. Consequently, the characters who appear in P are usually somewhat lifeless in comparison with those of the old epic tradition. Even the great Moses "is but a draped statue compared with the titanic Moses of the earlier narratives of J and E." [23]

It is sometimes said that the priestly writing is an "interpretation" that does not give us an accurate account of the past. It is true that P views the past through the tinted glasses of priestly bias, and we cannot take his dogmatic presentation of the Mosaic period as the factual report of an eyewitness. But can there be *any* history without interpretation? History is a narration of events that are meaningful in human experience, and biblical history is the narration of God's dealings with men. P is not history in the same way the J narrative is. This is not because the writer did not have accurate facts at his command; for more and more we realize the antiquity of many of the priestly traditions; nor is it because he was unconcerned about God's revelation in history, for after all P is a kind of commentary upon the JE epic. Rather, it is because the priestly writer was not really a narrator. For our word "history," P would probably use the word "genealogy," as in Genesis 37:2, which the Revised Standard Version renders:" This is the history of the family of Jacob." Instead of giving historical narrative, P divides his work into chapters that are headed with the titles: "These are the generations [that is, genealogy] of . . ." (Gen. 2:4a; 5:1; 6:9; 10:1; 11:10; 11:27; etc.). In this way he measures out the time span between the four successive dispensations.

The Interest in Genealogies

The priestly writer—like some of Israel's prophets—combined belief in God's universal sway with belief in God's special revelation to Israel. He affirmed that God, the Creator of all mankind and the Sovereign of the universe, chose Israel out of all the peoples and separated Israel for a special blessing by giving them the Law. We can see this increasing narrowing of attention in the genealogies or "family trees" that make up the skeleton of the priestly writing. With the exception of Jacob and Esau, the line is traced through the first-born son, and other offspring are left aside, as the chart on the following page shows.

Thus even in these dry genealogical tables (the "begats" of the King James

---

[23] Fleming James, *Personalities of the Old Testament* (New York: Scribner's, 1939), p. 431.

Version of the Bible) we can see that P is governed by a theological purpose. Just as—looking forward—the Creation sets the stage for the historical revelation that reaches its climax with the giving of the Law to Moses, so—looking backward—Israel's line can be traced back through the generations to the first man, Adam. In other words, the Creator has singled out Israel for special service in response to special revelation. The priestly writer did not believe that Israel's special place in God's plan was based solely on birth, for Esau as the first-born should have been the rightful heir, rather than Jacob. By departing in this instance from tracing the line through the first-born son, the writer recognizes that Israel's election rests solely upon the grace of God who chooses whom he will. Nevertheless, later on, when the Jews returned from the Exile, it was considered very important to be born in a Jewish family that could trace its ancestry back through the generations. Eventually, John the Baptist was to attack the false confidence in birth and genealogy, saying that God could raise up children for Abraham out of stones (Matt. 3:9)—a vivid way of saying that one's position in the chosen community is dependent on divine grace rather than on family ties or national allegiance.

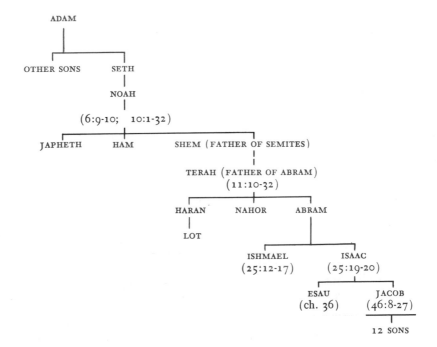

A Priestly Theocracy

In this chapter we have covered a good deal of ground. During the Exile, as we have seen, the people sought for a new understanding of the community that still bound them together despite national disaster. As they searched their scriptural tradition, they were reminded that the covenant community originated at a time when Israel was not a nation and had no king, except Yahweh himself. To this ancient theocracy the priests sought to return. Ezekiel, a member of the Zadokite clergy of the Temple, was influential in establishing the view that Israel was fundamentally a worshiping community—a holy people, living in a holy city, and worshiping in a holy Temple. Judaism had its major roots in the Exile. As we shall see later (Chapter 14), Ezra brought with him from Babylonia the Law that priests had compiled in Babylonia and made it the basis of the post-exilic community. But before we consider further these priestly developments, we must turn to another figure of the Exile, one in whom Israel's prophetic movement reached its highest and deepest expression.

THE DAWN

OF A NEW AGE

CHAPTER THIRTEEN   According to the historian
Charles A. Beard, one of the lessons of history can be summarized in the proverb: "The bee fertilizes the flower it
robs." This is particularly true of the history of Israel during
the Exile. Although the experience seemed bitter to many at
the time, they came to realize that in it God was working
for good. As prophets like Hosea prophesied, Yahweh led
his people into the wilderness—not just the desert, but the

Biblical readings: The most essential reading for this chapter is
Isaiah 40-55. This may be supplemented with the closely related chapters 56-66, and with the "enthronement psalms," Psalms 47 and
93-100.

"wasteland" of despair—so that he might speak to their heart. Had it been possible to bypass this journey—this new pilgrimage "round about by way of the wilderness"—Israel's political situation might have been better at the time, but her faith would have been immeasurably impoverished. For although the nation had been robbed and plundered by conquerors, Israel's experience of historical tragedy fertilized and deepened the soil of her religious understanding.

NEW WORLD HORIZONS

We know from our own experiences in the twentieth century that worldshaking events often have a double—and seemingly contradictory—effect on man's lives. They bring about both a renewal of national loyalties and a wider vision of "one world." This two-fold attitude came to expression during Israel's exile. The collapse of the nation brought about an intense awareness of the uniqueness of Israel's calling, a point of view that was championed, as we have seen, by Ezekiel and by the Jerusalem priests who produced the priestly edition of the Pentateuch. The surrounding culture was regarded as a threat to Israel's faith, as it had proved to be throughout Israelite history. Israel was called, therefore, to be a worshiping community and to build her whole life upon God's Torah. She was to be a holy people separated from the rest of the nations by the purity of her life and her complete submission to God's rule. But the Exile also awakened a new world-consciousness. Israel's faith was enlarged by the vision of new horizons that had never been seen so clearly before, not even in the cosmopolitan age of Solomon. Israelites realized that they must look beyond their own circumscribed community to the whole civilized world if they would behold the glory and majesty of Yahweh's purpose in history. The time was ripe for a deeper understanding of the Yahwist's affirmation that Yahweh's purpose spans the ages from the beginning of history, and that Israel was called to be his agent in the redemption of mankind (see pp. 169-187).

The Second Isaiah

The new understanding of Israel's special place in world history was magnificently expressed during the Exile by an unknown prophet, whose writings are found in the latter part of the book of Isaiah, beginning with chapter 40. In contrast to Jeremiah, with whom this prophet had close inward affinities, or even to Ezekiel, whose message also influenced him, we know absolutely nothing about his life or the events of his personal career. He is known to us only through the impact of his words, which, in the last analysis, are the best approach to the interior life of any person. For want of a better title, he is usually called Second Isaiah (or Deutero-Isaiah), because his writings are bound up in the scroll of Isaiah of Jerusalem. In spite of his anonymity, many acclaim him as one of the greatest, if not the greatest, prophet of the Old Testament.

Troubles in Babylonia

Before turning to the poems of Second Isaiah, let us look for a moment at the sweeping historical changes that took place about the middle of the sixth century B.C. To appreciate these changes, we must remember that for centuries the center of world civilization had been the Fertile Crescent. This area had been under the domination of Semitic empires ever since the time of Hammurabi in the eighteenth century B.C., with the exception of the interval of Hittite and Egyptian ascendancy in the middle of that millennium. The old Babylonian empire, which held sway about the time of Abraham, was succeeded eventually by the Assyrian empire, which rose to power in the time of Amos and Hosea. After more than a century of Semitic rule under the Assyrians, the Fertile Crescent next came under the sway of the Neo-Babylonian (or "Chaldean") empire. But this empire lasted not much longer than its first and greatest emperor, Nebuchadnezzar (605-562 B.C.). His death set off a reaction of murder and intrigue, and the throne changed three times in the space of seven years. One cause of the unrest was an attempt by the Babylonian priesthood, whom Nebuchadnezzar had sought to keep under the control of the crown, to regain power. Rumors of these troubles spread throughout the vast empire, and to many it must have seemed that the end of Babylonian tyranny was near.

In spite of the tolerable conditions in exile, the Jews' hope for a return to Jerusalem (Zion) burned intensely. The Deuteronomic History, which was completed after the fall of Jerusalem in 587 B.C., was dominated by the conviction that even the fall of the Temple and the exile of the people would not eclipse Yahweh's promise to David (cf. I Kings 9:1-9), and so it concludes with the news that one of David's descendants, Jehoiachin, was still alive in exile. According to this historian, the successor of Nebuchadnezzar, Amel-Marduk (called Evil-merodach in the Old Testament), did something that must have kindled "Zionist" hopes. Jehoiachin, the legitimate claimant to the Davidic throne, was released from prison in the year 561 B.C. and was given a position of prestige in the Babylonian court (II Kings 25:27-30). The name of the exiled Jewish king probably stood as a symbol to the nationalists who still dreamed of a restored Jewish state in Palestine under Davidic rule. Sheshbazzar, the man who later negotiated permission for the Jews to return to their homeland, was one of the sons of Jehoiachin.[1]

The favorable moment for Jewish "Zionism" came very soon. After the seven years of instability referred to above, Nabonidus came to the throne of Babylon

---

[1] According to W. F. Albright, Sheshbazzar appears as a son of Jehoiachin under the name Shenazzar in the genealogy in I Chronicles 3:18. See *The Biblical Period* [38], pp. 48-49.

(556-539 B.C.). He was an unpopular king, especially with the priests of Marduk, who hated him for constructing a rival sanctuary to the moon god Sin. Nabonidus went off on a distant expedition to Tema in Arabia, and, after conquering the city, established it as his royal residence. The rule of his empire was shared with his son, Belshazzar, about whom we shall hear more when we come to study the book of Daniel. Political troubles started in the plateau of Iran (Airyana), the home of Aryan-speaking people. In the middle of the sixth century B.C. the Iranian highland was divided into three areas: Media, Persia, and Elam, although Elam was actually under the control of Persia. Thus the two peoples of the region were the Medes and the Persians, and the Medes enjoyed political ascendancy. The Medes had joined with the Babylonians earlier to give the death-blow to the Assyrians, and the two allies had divided the spoils of the Assyrian empire between them (see p. 321).

The Rise of Cyrus of Persia

Belshazzar must have seen the handwriting on the wall as he considered with envy and apprehension the growing Median kingdom, which stretched from central Asia Minor into the territory now known as Iran. When Cyrus, a Persian king from the Elamite city of Anshan, challenged the power of his Median overlord in 553 B.C., he was probably encouraged by Babylonia. After all, it was to Babylonia's advantage to cut down the power of her former ally. But in the unpredictable game of politics, events took an unexpected turn. Within three years Cyrus had defeated the Median king, Astyages (550 B.C.). On the crest of this victory, he pressed on to further triumphs beyond the Median borders in Asia Minor. In the year 546 he conquered the kingdom of Lydia (now the western part of Turkey), ruled by Croesus, whose vast wealth is still proverbial. As a result of these smashing victories, Cyrus controlled a vast empire, extending from the Persian Gulf to the Aegean Sea. Finally, Nabonidus, realizing the gravity of the situation, returned to Babylon to celebrate the New Year's festival. But it was too late to check the internal disorder within his empire and to halt the momentum of the Persian advance. In the year 539 B.C., the Persians and the Babylonians fought a great battle at Opis on the Tigris River. The Persians won, and serious Babylonian resistance came to an end. A few weeks later, the city of Babylon capitulated to Cyrus without a struggle. (See Chronological Chart 8, p. 353.)

Cyrus' account of his Babylonian triumph is recorded on the famous Cyrus Cylinder—an inscription written on a clay barrel.[2] The account begins with a condemnation of Nabonidus for ignoring the temple of Marduk and for subjecting the Babylonian people to slave labor. It was for this reason, we are told, that "the lord of the gods [Marduk] became terribly angry" and, accompanied

---

[2] See Pritchard, *Ancient Near Eastern Texts*, pp. 315-316.

by his retinue of gods, withdrew from Babylon. Seeing the terrible ruin of the country, however, Marduk abated his anger and showed mercy on Babylonia.

> He scanned and looked (through) all the countries, searching for a righteous ruler willing to lead him [Marduk] (in the annual procession on New Year's Day). (Then) he pronounced the name of Cyrus, king of Anshan, declared him the ruler of all the world.

The account goes on to say that Marduk ordained Cyrus to march against Babylon, "going at his side like a real friend," for Marduk was pleased with the conqueror's kind treatment of his subjects. Hence, it is reported, Cyrus was allowed to enter Babylon "without any battle," and the whole population of Marduk's city "greeted him as a master through whose help they had come

(again) to life from death." Cyrus boasts of his efforts to obtain peace in Babylonia. He claims to have abolished forced labor, improved housing conditions, and enjoyed the affection of the people. The account concludes by referring to the renown of his name throughout the world, owing to his power and benevolence. Explicitly, it is stated that he returned the sacred images to the peoples from whom they had been taken and rebuilt their sanctuaries, that he gathered together foreign exiles and returned them to their former homes, and that he restored the idols of Sumer and Akkad that Nabonidus had displaced from their own chapels.

This, of course, is the victor's story, and it undoubtedly contains a good bit of propaganda. Nevertheless, in contrast to other oriental conquerors, especially the Assyrians and the Babylonians, Cyrus was extraordi-

THE FAMOUS CYRUS CYLINDER *tells of Cyrus' conquest of Babylon "without any battle" and of his policy of allowing captives to return to their homelands and rebuild their temples. Although Second Isaiah claims that Cyrus was Yahweh's agent, this inscription affirms that Marduk, the god of Babylon, selected Cyrus to become "the ruler of the world" and then went by his side "like a real friend."*

narily benevolent and humane. Instead of executing Astyages of Media and Croesus of Lydia, he permitted each of them to retain a royal retinue. He protected the treasures of Babylon, and respected traditional forms of religion. He abrogated the Assyro-Babylonian policy of deporting captive populations to a foreign land, and even permitted exiles to return to their homelands. He has rightly been called one of the most enlightened rulers in human history.

So began the great Persian empire, an empire that was destined to last for two hundred years, until the rise of Alexander the Great. It is against the background of these momentous international developments, which sent a wave of expectancy throughout the ancient world and which widened men's horizons of thought as never before, that we must understand the prophecy of Second Isaiah.

THE POEMS OF SECOND ISAIAH

For many years it was held that the latter part of the book of Isaiah (chapters 40-66) was written in the Assyrian period by Isaiah of Jerusalem. But today there is universal agreement among scholars that "First Isaiah" did not write this section.

First Isaiah and Second Isaiah

The most obvious reason for this verdict is the different historical circumstances that are presupposed in the two main sections of the book of Isaiah. In the writings of Isaiah of Jerusalem, the people are still living in Judah under Davidic kings, Jerusalem is regarded as Yahweh's City which he will not allow to fall, and the Temple—the scene of Isaiah's inaugural vision—is still standing. But when we turn to the section beginning with Isaiah 40, a radical change in the historical situation is apparent: the cities of Judah are desolate, the Temple lies in ruins, and the people are in Babylonian exile. Clearly the Israelite monarchy is a thing of the past. These historical circumstances are not predicted for some time in the future, but are assumed to be existing in the *present* (see, for instance, 44:26; 49:19; 51:3). Moreover, the Assyrians, whose advance across the Fertile Crescent Isaiah mentions specifically, are ignored. Instead, Babylonia is the mistress of the world (chapter 47), although the end of her rule is at hand (48:14, 20; 52:11-12). Cyrus of Persia is mentioned twice (44:28; 45:1). He is hailed as Yahweh's "shepherd" who will soon decree the rebuilding of Jerusalem and the Temple, and he is called Yahweh's "messiah"—that is, the one who is anointed to fulfill the divine purpose.[3]

---

[3] At that time, "messiah" was not a technical term for the future messianic king. The Hebrew word literally means "anointed one," and before Second Isaiah could be used of a king or a priest. Second Isaiah was using the term in a new way in applying it to Cyrus.

THE PERSIAN EMPIRE
550-336 B.C.

SCYTHIA

CASPIAN SEA

MEDIA

PERSIA

EMPIRE EXTENDS
EAST TO INDIA

Pasargadae
Persepolis

PERSIAN GULF

BLACK SEA

ARMENIA

L. URMIAH

Ecbatana

BEHISTUN
ROCK

L. VAN

ARABIAN DESERT

PROBABLE
ANCIENT
SHORELINE

LYDIA

CAPPADOCIA

Pteria

Arbela

ASSYRIA

TIGRIS R.

OPIS

SUSIANA

Susa

Babylon

Nippur

BABYLONIA

EUPHRATES R.

Haran

Damascus

Dumah

Tema

Sardis

CYPRUS
(KITTIM)

Sidon

Tyre

Samaria

Jerusalem

Gaza

Elath

RED SEA

AEGEAN SEA

THRACE

MEDITERRANEAN SEA

GREECE

Athens

Sparta

CAPHTOR

Cyrene

LIBYA

EGYPT

Memphis

NILE R.

Thebes

Elephantine

The study of vocabulary, poetic structure, and meter gives further support for the view that some or all of the poems in Isaiah 40-66 were written by an author other than Isaiah of Jerusalem. Literary style is always an important criterion of authorship. Even in the English translation the literary difference between the two sections of the book of Isaiah is noticeable. The oracles of Isaiah of Jerusalem, for example, are expressed in a balanced, stately, poetic form that was appropriate to the seriousness of his warnings of the impending day of disaster. In the last section of the book, however, we encounter poetry of great beauty and power. Commanding a Hebrew vocabulary that depends somewhat on First Isaiah but that is really a new idiom, the poet breaks forth into lyrical strains of triumphant song. Prophecy and poetry are merged in such a matchless synthesis that we are justified in calling Second Isaiah one of the greatest poets of all time.

Accompanying this rhapsodic language is a new theological emphasis that gives the poems an entirely different tone from that found in the message of First Isaiah. While Jerusalem was still standing and the nation of Judah was involved in the political storm of the time, it was appropriate for Isaiah to speak in the language of warning and rebuke. To him the Day of Judgment was at hand, and he appealed to the people to repent while there was still time. But Second Isaiah strikes a different note. According to him, the divine judgment had already taken place; Israel had received from Yahweh's hand double punishment for all her sins (40:2). Second Isaiah's commission was to "speak tenderly" to Jerusalem, proclaiming to a despairing people that Yahweh was coming not to judge but to release Israel from her bondage and to restore the shattered foundations of the homeland. Pardon, deliverance, restoration, and grace are the characteristic notes of his message of comfort and hope.

These three lines of argument—historical setting, literary style, and theological perspective—lead to the conclusion that the author of much of the material found in Isaiah 40-66 was a prophet of the Exile who lived more than 150 years after Isaiah of Jerusalem. His writings presuppose that Cyrus was already a prominent political figure, perhaps as a result of his victory over Croesus, king of Lydia, in 546 B.C., or of his early triumphs in northern Babylonia shortly after. In fact, Cyrus' victorious campaign is actually described (see 41:2-3, 25). Since the fall of Babylon (539 B.C.) had not yet taken place, though it was expected at any moment, it is safe to date the beginning of Second Isaiah's prophetic career at approximately 540 B.C.

The prophecy becomes much more meaningful when we read it in the context of these stirring events. As we have seen before, the prophets addressed themselves to immediate historical circumstances. They were not clairvoyants who gazed into a crystal ball, as it were, and predicted the details of a political situation far in the future. Their predictions about the future were oriented to the present situation of Israel. It is noteworthy that nowhere in Isaiah 40-66 is it claimed that Isaiah was the author of the poems, nor is his name mentioned even once. To be sure, the New Testament attributes quotations from this section to "the prophet Isaiah" (Matt. 3:3; Luke 3:4; 4:17), but this can hardly be used as evidence of authorship. In a day when scripture was not yet divided into chapter and verse, this was simply a convenient way of indicating where the passage was to be found. And above all, the New Testament writers were not concerned with the critical question of authorship, but with the theological meaning and fulfillment of the prophecy.

In the Tradition of Isaiah

It is doubtful, however, whether *all* these chapters belong to Second Isaiah. Chapters 56-66 apparently presuppose a different historical setting from that of chapters 40-55. Whereas Second Isaiah addressed himself to exiles in Babylonia, chapters 56-66 presuppose that the people had returned to Jerusalem and that they were facing some of the difficulties of the Restoration. True, these chapters are much more closely related to Isaiah 40-55 than the latter are to the oracles of Isaiah of Jerusalem. Some passages, like 57:14-19 and 61:1-3, sound so much like Second Isaiah that it is not difficult to believe that he wrote them. The prevailing view, however, is that chapters 56-66—often called "Third Isaiah"—were written by a disciple or disciples of Second Isaiah shortly after the return from Babylonia. So we shall not consider them further at this point.

It seems strange to us, who inevitably think in terms of Western conceptions of authorship, that the prophet could write poems of such great literary charm and theological depth without giving any inkling of his identity. But we must remember what has been said before about these prophetic collections. By and large, the major prophetic scrolls are anthologies that clustered around the name of a major prophetic leader. This is particularly true of the book of Isaiah. Indeed, it is possible that there was a school of Isaiah that extended over several generations. We know that Isaiah at one point in his career had gathered his disciples around him in order to "bind up" and "seal" the teaching for a future time when Yahweh would no longer hide his face from Israel (Is. 8:16). It has even been suggested that Second Isaiah believed himself to be one of Isaiah's later "apprentices" whose task was to give a fresh exposition of his master's teachings in the new time when Yahweh was showing his face to his weary and despairing people. This would explain why Second Isaiah's oracles are not represented as being spoken directly to him, as were those of First Isaiah, and why the prophet's personality recedes into the background. And, too, it would explain why the poems of Second Isaiah are attached to Isaiah's teachings as an interpretive supplement. For it was Second Isaiah who broke the seal on Isaiah's prophecy and gave the contemporary sense of his master's words, which had been preserved in the tradition and hearts of the disciples.[4]

---

[4] This is the view of Martin Buber, *The Prophetic Faith* [118], pp. 202-205.

If all this is so, we have here a classic example of the student surpassing his teacher. But Second Isaiah did not limit himself to a re-interpretation of Isaiah of Jerusalem. He was also the heir of a larger prophetic tradition, including especially Jeremiah and Ezekiel. And he was not just an expositor of ancient prophecy; he was fresh and original in his prophetic insight. In him, prophecy reached a new height of poetic elevation, and plumbed a profounder depth of historical understanding than ever before.

A HERALD OF GOOD TIDINGS

From beginning to end, the prophecy of Second Isaiah is an exultant proclamation of good news. The people who dwell in darkness hear that a new day is dawning. Captives are told that deliverance is on the way. The brokenhearted are comforted. Every poem is filled with the excitement and expectancy of great events about to come to pass. When we enter this arena of faith, "it is as if the hell and the horror had been left behind, and one is moving up a high, sun-drenched summit to the very doors of the Kingdom of God." [5] No wonder the message of Second Isaiah was appropriated in the New Testament to proclaim the "good news" that "the Kingdom of God is at hand!" (Mk. 1:15).

In the Heavenly Council

The setting of the opening poem (40:1-11) is placed in heaven, where Yahweh's Council is assembled. Several times before, we have noticed that prophetic authority rested upon a direct commission given to the prophet standing in this Council (cf. Jer. 23:18), as, for instance, in the case of Isaiah's vision in the Temple.[6] So the prophecy of Second Isaiah begins with good news heard in the Heavenly Council. Then the poetry moves from heaven to earth. Since the first poem serves as a prologue to the whole poetic cycle, we shall give it special attention.[7]

In the ancient view, the decisions affecting men's destiny were made in the Heavenly Council. The Babylonian creation myth (*Enuma elish*; see p. 385), which was recited at the New Year's Festival, relates that in the assembly of the gods Marduk was invested with supreme authority and acclaimed with the shout: "Marduk has become king!" His victory over the monster Tiamat and her allies, which the myth vividly portrays, assured worshipers that for the coming

---

[5] John Bright, *The Kingdom of God* (New York: Abingdon, 1953), p. 137.

[6] See above, pp. 265-267. In addition, see Frank M. Cross, Jr., "The Council of Yahweh in Second Isaiah," in *Journal of Near Eastern Studies*, XII (1953), pp. 274-277.

[7] See the excellent discussion by James Muilenburg, *Interpreter's Bible*, V, pp. 422 ff., whose insights have contributed to this discussion.

year the world would be subject to the high god's sovereign decrees. Perhaps Second Isaiah, who was undoubtedly familiar with Babylonian myth and ritual, was influenced by this religious background as he portrayed Yahweh's kingship over the world. His deepest debt, however, was to the prophets who preceded him, and to the great convictions that were celebrated in Israel's worship. He was heavily dependent upon the hymns and liturgy of the pre-exilic worship services of the Jerusalem Temple, especially the services of the Fall festival when a number of psalms (47, 93, 96-99) were used to extol Yahweh as King of the nations and of the whole universe (see Chapter 15, pp. 481-484). So Second Isaiah was speaking primarily out of Israel's tradition in his portrayal of Yahweh, the King *par excellence*. Thus his first poem begins with two imperatives, "comfort, comfort." These imperatives are in the plural, because God is speaking to his heavenly servants, announcing the destiny of Israel and the nations.

The Coming of God's Kingdom

The opening words are arresting. When the first Isaiah stood in the Heavenly Council, he was commissioned to proclaim a message of judgment upon an unresponsive people (Is. 6:9-13). But according to 40:1-2, the declaration that Yahweh now makes to the Council is a message of consolation to weary and despairing exiles. The note of divine judgment is scarcely more than an echo from the past, for it is announced that Israel's "time of service" in exile is completed. The people have suffered heavily under the hand of Yahweh's punishment (42:24-25; 48:17-19). But all that is past. Now the time has come of which Hosea spoke when he said that in the wilderness Yahweh would "speak to the heart" of Israel. So Yahweh commissions his servants to speak tenderly to (literally, "speak to the heart of") his people in the desolation of their bondage. Israel, moreover, will be released from a heavier bondage than that of foreign captivity: she will be released from the bondage of her guilt. Yahweh's message is one of pardon and grace. Israel's past has been forgiven, not because sin and punishment have been balanced on the divine books, but only because the free gift of God's forgiveness makes a wholly new beginning (see Jer. 31:34). Israel stands on the threshold of the new age. The decisive moment has come. The time is fulfilled and the kingdom of God is drawing near.

In First Isaiah's temple vision, the seraphs had antiphonally "called out" or "proclaimed" that Yahweh's glory fills the whole earth. And in this poem too an unidentified speaker—evidently one of the Heavenly Council—responds to the divine decree announced in verses 1-2. From the New Testament (Mk. 1:3) we are accustomed to the translation (which is derived from the Septuagint) that makes this a "voice crying in the wilderness." But the perfect poetic parallelism of the Hebrew has been restored in the Revised Standard Version:

A voice cries:
> "In the wilderness prepare the way of Yahweh,
> make straight in the desert a highway for our God."
> —ISAIAH 40:3

The first main strophe, then, portrays Yahweh coming, like a conquering king, to lead his people from exile to their homeland. All obstacles are to be removed from his path. Along "the highway of God" the people will be led through the wilderness, in a manner reminiscent of Yahweh's deliverance of Israel from Egyptian bondage. The "new exodus," says the speaker, will be a disclosure of "the glory of Yahweh" unto all mankind. Ezekiel had said that the glory that had departed from the Temple would return to a New Jerusalem. Now it is announced that Yahweh's glory will be visible to all in the marvelous event that opens the new age.

The Word of God Stands Forever

In the next strophe (verses 6-8), a second speaker, presumably another member of the Heavenly Council, resumes the proclamation. But suddenly another voice breaks in, indicated by the words "and I said" (verse 6b).[8] Probably the "I" is none other than the prophet himself. If so, the passage suggests that the prophet is standing within the Heavenly Council, where he receives his "call" from the King (compare Isaiah 6). In response to his commission he asks, "What shall I proclaim?" The earlier announcement that "all flesh" would see Yahweh's glory awakens the melancholy thought that "all flesh" is transient. Man's days are like the grass of the field or the wayside flower—green and lovely in its season, but withered when the hot desert wind blows over it. Taken by itself, this is a cry of despair, based on the gloomy but realistic view that man is finite, his achievements evanescent, his life merely temporal. But the prophet's despondent observation is the preface to a climactic affirmation of faith:

> The grass withers, the flower fades;
> but the word of our God will stand forever.
> —ISAIAH 40:8

Here we have an exposition of what it means for all flesh to behold Yahweh's glory. Yahweh is active in history, but he is eternal—above history. His word is not subject to the change and decay that can be seen all about, although it serves as the dynamic power of history (see 55:8-11). Second Isaiah understands profoundly one of the crucial tenets of Israelite and Christian faith: the revelation of the eternal God in time.

---

[8] The received Hebrew text reads "and he said" (see the King James Version). The Revised Standard Version translates "and I said" on the basis of the Septuagint, the Vulgate, and a manuscript of the book of Isaiah found among the Dead Sea Scrolls (photo on p. 6).

Good News

In exultant language, which has been set to music in Handel's *Messiah,* the poem sweeps toward its climax and conclusion (verses 9-11). The poet's thought moves from heaven to earth as he contemplates Yahweh's purpose in history. He sees that purpose concentrated in a particular City, which represents the people of Israel. This concrete language is significant, for according to Davidic theology Yahweh had elected the mountain of Zion as his dwelling-place, the seat of his active presence in the midst of his people. So Jerusalem, though in ruins, is summoned to be a herald of "good news." [9] Ascending to a high mountain, she is to announce loudly and clearly to the stricken cities of Judah that Yahweh, her God, is coming in might. Once again he will display the "mighty hand and outstretched arm" which, according to Israel's ancient confession of faith, delivered the people from Egyptian bondage. With consummate skill the prophet fuses the two major theological traditions of Israel— the election of Israel in the Exodus and the election of Zion (and David)—to announce the gospel of the Kingdom.

To the ordinary observer, the imminent collapse of Babylonia and the rise of Persia was a political event with a political result: the release of exiles to return to their homeland. But this event, like the Exodus, is seen in a deeper dimension by Second Isaiah. Behind and within the event, he affirms, is the activity of God, who is advancing as a conqueror to inaugurate in Zion his kingly rule over Israel and the whole world. The poem ends (verse 11) on the same tender accent with which it began. Blending the figure of the conquering king with that of the Good Shepherd, the poet proclaims that Yahweh will gather and feed his flock with tender care. The range of Second Isaiah's thought spans the whole of heaven and earth, but his view never loses its central focus on the redemption of Israel.

THE CREATOR AND REDEEMER

As a Bach fugue introduces a major theme and subjects it to complex contrapuntal development, so the poems of Second Isaiah are an elaboration of the theme announced in the prologue: Yahweh's imminent coming to inaugurate his kingdom. In the remaining poems, this central theme is artistically blended and enriched with other motifs as the work dramatically moves toward its climax. There is no substitute for reading the literature itself, and we can only call attention to a few of the major movements in the poet's composition.

Of all the titles that Second Isaiah ascribes to God, two of the most signifi-

---

[9] The meaning of the New Testament word for "gospel," *evangel,* is undoubtedly derived through the Septuagint from the verb used by Second Isaiah.

cant are Creator and Redeemer. Creation and redemption are the two manifestations of Yahweh's kingship over Israel and the nations. It is only for the
sake of discussion, however, that we separate these two functions, for in the
message of Second Isaiah they are linked together inseparably.[10] Of course, the
connection between the Creation and Israel's sacred history was not original
with this prophet. We have found it already in the J epic, in which the call of
Abraham is seen against the spacious background of "the first things" (Genesis
2-11); and we have seen it in the priestly writing, in which the Creation provides the foundation for Yahweh's special revelation to Israel. Second Isaiah
was influenced profoundly by the Yahwist, and the creation story of Genesis 1
was undoubtedly familiar to him. But he grasped the connection between God's
activity in the Creation and his redeeming work in history more profoundly
than anyone before or after him in the Old Testament.

Like the priestly writer of Genesis 1, Second Isaiah affirms that the Creation
is the manifestation of God's sovereignty. Being the Creator, Yahweh alone is
Lord and there is none beside him. This theme is stressed in the magnificent
poem found in 40:12-31. In contrast to the God who has measured the waters
in the hollow of his hand and marked off the heavens with the span of his hand,
the nations are "like a drop from a bucket." Their proud claim to manage the
affairs of history is absurd when contrasted with the sovereignty of the God who
holds the world in his grasp. Having seen idols made in Babylonia, Second
Isaiah pokes fun at the notion that these products of human craftsmanship
have any control over men's destinies. Enthroned above the vault of the
heavens, Yahweh is incomparable in power and majesty. No image or likeness
can be made of him, as the Mosaic commandment had affirmed from ancient
times. Yahweh is God and not man. He is "the Holy One of Israel"—an expression of First Isaiah to which Second Isaiah gave great emphasis.

Creation as the Foundation of History

The purpose of this appeal to Yahweh's power as Creator was to comfort Israel, who in the desolation of Babylonian exile was thinking that Yahweh
did not see or care what had happened to his people. There must have been
many Jews who watched the procession of the idols in the Babylonian festivals,
and all but conceded that Babylonian victory was historical proof that Marduk
was king. Against this mood of despair the prophet raises his voice:

> Have you not known? Have you not heard?
> Yahweh is the everlasting God,
>   the Creator of the ends of the earth.

---

[10] See Carroll Stuhlmueller, C.P., "The Theology of Creation in Second Isaias," in
Catholic Biblical Quarterly, XXI (1959), pp. 429-467; also Gerhard von Rad, "The Theological Problem of the Old Testament Creation-faith," in his volume of collected essays [100].

A GATE RELIEF *from Cyrus' palace at Pasargadae, the city which he established as his royal residence. This is the one detail which has survived from the monumental gateway into the palace area. The relief of the four-winged figure on whose head is the triple crown seems to reflect cultural influences from as far away as Egypt. The door-jamb once carried the superscription: "I, Cyrus, the King, the Achaemenian." The winged figure may have been intended as a guardian genius or as an unusual representation of Cyrus himself.*

He does not faint or grow weary,
   his understanding is unsearchable.
He gives power to the faint,
   and to him who has no might he increases strength.
                 —ISAIAH 40:28-29

Second Isaiah's argument rests upon the conviction that the God of Israel is Creator and Lord; therefore, the weary exiles should wait expectantly for Yahweh's coming to redeem them from their bondage and to inaugurate his kingdom. And waiting for his imminent appearance, they will be filled with new vitality, mounting upon the buffeting winds with wings like the eagle's (40:30-31). Although Israel was seemingly powerless in the grip of massive international forces, she could trust Yahweh whose purpose overarches history from beginning to end, from the Creation to the consummation of history.

It is clear, then, that Second Isaiah does not treat the Creation in isolation, as many of us tend to today. According to him, the Creation sets the stage for history. It is the beginning of the historical drama that presses toward the goal God has in view. Human affairs are not governed by historical processes, human ambitions, fate, or chance; they are controlled by the "everlasting God," the Creator of the ends of the earth. Second Isaiah views history in the light of the divine purpose that moves from beginning to end. The Creator is the Redeemer and the Redeemer is the Creator.

It is in this wide perspective that Second Isaiah understands the events of his time. Vividly he describes the advance of "one from the east whom victory meets at every step of the way"—a reference to the far-flung victories of Cyrus in Media and as far west as the Aegean (41:2-4, 25-29; cf. 46:11). In a remarkable poem, which is cast in the form of a court trial (chapter 41), he challenges the nations to produce evidence that their gods had been able to anticipate and bring about the rise of Cyrus, an event that brought new hope to the peoples living under the Babylonian yoke. Emphatically he affirms that it was Yahweh who aroused the victor from the east. The event was part of his historical plan. It did not catch Yahweh by surprise, so to speak, but was announced ahead of time; for Yahweh directs the course of history and has been working purposively for the day of redemption and release.

For Israel, however, the event has a special meaning, according to Second Isaiah. Israel may be pitifully weak and insignificant in the eyes of the nations. But this "worm" is the object of Yahweh's love and concern (41:14). Yahweh is Israel's champion, her "redeemer." [11] He had chosen this "family" and would not forget their "justice" (40:27)—that is, their rightful place. Hence the prophet predicts Israel's restoration. Yahweh, he says, will gather his sons from the north and the south (43:6-7). He will send to Babylon and break the bars of their captivity (43:14-15; cf. 48:14, 20). And finally, after this theme has been subjected to rich variation, Cyrus is mentioned by name (44:28-45:6). Isaiah of Jerusalem had said that the Assyrian conqueror was to be "the rod of Yahweh's anger." Second Isaiah, however, affirms that Cyrus, though he will not realize it himself, will be the historical agent by whom Yahweh will redeem his people. There are striking affinities between the language of the Cyrus Cylinder and Isaiah 45:1-6 (see also verse 13), so much so that some scholars have conjectured that Second Isaiah must have been acquainted with the Persian document. The cylinder says, for instance, that Marduk searched the countries for a righteous ruler, that he accompanied Cyrus as a friend, and that he called him by name. Second Isaiah, for whom Marduk is a powerless idol, ascribes these things to Yahweh, who "anointed" the Persian to serve his purpose.

The New Exodus

One of the central motifs in Second Isaiah's message is that of the New Exodus.[12] In his thinking the Exodus was the decisive event of Israel's past. It

---

[11] The word "redeemer" (go'el) comes out of ancient family law. It was the duty of the redeemer to vindicate the right of another member of the family. In the case of murder, he obtained blood-revenge; and in the case of mortgaged property, he championed the family's right of ownership. The nearest male relative had the obligation to vindicate family rights.

[12] See the author's development of this motif in his essay, "Exodus Typology in Second Isaiah," in Israel's Prophetic Heritage [136], pp. 177-195.

was the time of Israel's creation, even as it was the time of her redemption. Hence, he portrays Israel's imminent liberation from the bondage and despair of exile in imagery drawn from the Exodus tradition: the flight from Egypt, the deliverance at the "Red Sea," the march through the wilderness, the triumphant journey toward the Promised Land. Moreover, he blends with this historical tradition imagery drawn from the old creation myth, according to which Creation was the outcome of a fierce conflict between the Dragon of Chaos (called Tiamat) and the Creator. As we have pointed out before, this myth (found in *Enuma elish*) figured prominently in Babylonian religion, and was transmitted to Israel through the Canaanites. But in Israel's faith the mythology is transformed by being blended with the remembrance of Yahweh's deeds *in history*. According to Second Isaiah's poetic imagination, the waters of the Red Sea, through which Israel crossed long ago, were the waters of Chaos, hostile to Yahweh's creative and redemptive act. And just as Yahweh's arm was victorious in that conflict, so in the present historical situation he comes as the victor on behalf of his fainting people. To the Deep he says, "Be dry," and through the midst of the waters he prepares a way for the people to pass over (44:27). The poetry rises to a pitch of exultation as Second Isaiah contemplates the New Exodus:

> Awake, awake, put on strength,
>   O arm of Yahweh;
> awake, as in days of old,
>   the generations of long ago.
> Was it not thou that didst cut Rahab in pieces,
>   that didst pierce the dragon?
> Was it not thou that didst dry up the sea,
>   the waters of the great Deep [*tehom*],
> that didst make the depths of the sea a way
>   for the redeemed to pass over?
> And the ransomed of Yahweh shall return,
>   and come with singing to Zion;
> everlasting joy shall be upon their heads;
>   they shall obtain joy and gladness,
> and sorrow and sighing shall flee away.
>   —ISAIAH 51:9-11 [13]

So the approaching redemption is viewed as a new beginning, a New Creation. According to Second Isaiah, the Creation was not just an event of the past. In the new age, which the prophet heralds, God will make all things new. In God's creative work there is no boundary between "nature" and "history," for both men's lives and the natural setting will be marvelously transformed (41:17-20).

---

[13] In this passage the word *tehom* is equivalent to Tiamat, the Babylonian name for the Chaos monster. Rahab is the Western Semitic name for the same mythical dragon. See further the author's article, "Water," in the *Interpreter's Dictionary* [11].

The wilderness, which the prophet identifies with the waste places of Judah, will be converted into a garden like Eden (51:3; cf. 41:17-20; 43:19-21). Above all, there will be a New Israel, bound to Yahweh in a new relationship (54:4-10), and with a "new song" on her lips (42:10-12).

A LIGHT TO THE NATIONS

We have seen that Second Isaiah's perspective is as wide as the Creation and as long as the whole sweep of history. These spacious horizons reflect the immense vistas opened to the Jewish people, who had been thrust out of the narrow corridor of Palestine into a larger world. Cyrus' conquests had carried him to the Aegean shores. Second Isaiah's frequent references to the "coastlands" or the "isles" (that is, the shores of the Mediterranean area) show that men were thinking of the world in wider terms than the Fertile Crescent. There is a broad universality in Second Isaiah's message, and yet never does he surrender the conviction that Israel occupies a special place in Yahweh's historical plan. The prologue begins by referring to Israel as "my people," and by announcing that Yahweh is Israel's God ("your God," 40:1). The ancient motif of the covenant faith, "I am your God and you are my people," runs through all the poems. So the great hymn of redemption found in 51:1-16 concludes with Yahweh's assurance:

> I have put my words in your mouth,
>   and hid you in the shadow of my hand,
> stretching out the heavens
>   and laying the foundations of the earth,
>   and saying to Zion, "You are my people."
>   —ISAIAH 51:16

In Second Isaiah's message, however, Israel's redemption was part of the redemption of all the nations. This theme had already been anticipated by the Yahwist, who, viewing the call of Abraham (that is, Israel) in the perspective of universal history, proclamied that from Israel blessings would issue for all the families of the earth (Gen. 12:1-3). Second Isaiah appropriated this theme, which had been largely ignored in the intervening years, and transposed it into a new key. According to him, God's choice of Israel was not only the sign of divine initiative and grace, but also evidence of Israel's special task in God's world-embracing purpose. It was Yahweh's intention that Israel should be a "light to the nations," illumining the darkness of the world. Given by Yahweh as "a covenant to the nations," Israel was to demonstrate that the Gentiles— that is, the non-Jewish peoples—were also included within the divine promise (42:5-9). Chosen as the special agent of the sovereign God, Israel's calling was to testify that Yahweh alone directs the course of history and that he alone is the Savior of all men (45:20-21). To Yahweh, every knee shall bow and every tongue shall swear, for he alone is Lord (45:22-23).

The Critique of Idolatry

There was a time when scholars tried to trace an ascending evolution in Israel's thought, from the supposed polytheism of the early period to the heights of reflective monotheism in Second Isaiah. But it is being recognized more and more that this reconstruction, which reflects the perspective of Western rationalism, does not do justice to Israel's religious development. Israel's approach to the theological question—that is, the question of God— was not "reflective." The question of "the existence of God," for instance, is not asked in the Bible. The primary concern there is with God's activity, his purpose, his will. From the very first, the Mosaic Decalogue had declared that Israel's life was solely and absolutely dependent upon one God—the God who revealed his redemptive power and purpose in the Exodus and who disclosed his name (that is, his identity) to the people of Israel in the decisive moment of their history. Later on, prophets contended with the problem of "polytheism," seeing behind the idols the seductive power of loyalties and ideologies that captivated men's allegiance. The prophets condemned the worship of the gods of Canaan and the Fertile Crescent, not because these religions were intellectually indefensible, but because following "strange gods" was a fundamental breach of the covenant, a rebellion against the one God whose power and purpose sustained Israel's history.

Second Isaiah expands and deepens this prophetic teaching—found classically in the Yahwist, Amos, Isaiah, Deuteronomy, Jeremiah, and the priestly writing —with the result that it becomes relevant not just for Israel alone but for all the nations. Fundamentally, his critique of the idols is that they are *powerless* in history, and therefore they are nothing. Again and again he challenges the nations to bring proof that their gods have been able to announce a plan in history and carry it through (42:5-17; 43:8-13; 44:6-8, 21-23; 44:24-45:13; 48). With some caricature of Babylonian worship, he pokes fun at the idol-making industry (see 40:18-20; 44:9-20), arguing that these artifacts are mere expressions of human cleverness and power. Man-made idols do not have the divine power to control the issues of history, nor can they sustain the meaning of life from birth to old age. With fine satire, he ridicules the Babylonian idols, Bel and Nebo—the very gods whom, according to the Cyrus Cylinder, Cyrus restored to their sacred cities—who have to be loaded on the backs of dumb animals, causing them to strain and stoop under the burden. These pathetic gods have to be carried, but—says the prophet—Yahweh carries his people and lifts their burdens. He alone has the power to save and to accomplish his purpose in history (chapter 46).

A Theology of World History

Second Isaiah, then, advocated a historical monotheism—that is, he perceived that the whole course of history is under the control of Yahweh, who alone is Creator and Lord. This prophet has been called "the originator of a theology of world history." [14] This statement may seem a bit exaggerated when we consider the broad perspective of the Yahwist, but it is certainly true in the sense that really for the first time the vision of history's unity under the purpose of one God is made the basis of an appeal to all mankind. To be sure, Yahweh is Israel's redeemer, but closely allied with Israel's redemption is the redemption of mankind. Therefore, although the prophet first speaks a word of comfort to Israel in her despair and bondage, he addresses the same message to other nations who in faith may see in the rise of Cyrus and the imminent return of Jewish exiles the approach of the new age in which they too will participate. As the nations must acknowledge Yahweh as the Creator of the ends of the earth, so too they must know that there is no Savior in history other than he. His revelation is the source and ground of the meaning of all history. His power emancipates all nations from spiritual bondage (42:7). Hence the prophet addresses his message to the farthest boundaries of the world of that time:

> "Turn to me and be saved,
>   all the ends of the earth!
> For I am God, and there is no other."
>   —ISAIAH 45:22

This universalism is reminiscent of a poem found in both the book of Isaiah (2:2-4) and Micah (4:1-5), which announces that in the end-time the Temple will be the highest mountain, and "all the nations" will stream to it so that Yahweh may teach them his torah. When the nations recognize Zion as the spiritual center of the world, it is said, they will beat their swords into plowshares and their spears into pruning hooks. Second Isaiah's universalism runs deeper than this, however. He proclaims that Yahweh actively achieves this world-salvation through Israel, his chosen agent. In other words, Israel's redemption—which includes the forgiveness of her past sins, the release from her fears, the deliverance from exile, the return to Zion, and the beginning of a new age—is not an end in itself. Israel is to be a light to the nations. Her mission is to be the servant of God's wide-reaching historical purpose. Through her life all the families of the earth will know divine blessing. This is the true meaning of her election.

---

[14] Martin Buber, *The Prophetic Faith* [118], pp. 208 ff.

THE SERVANT OF THE LORD

We come now to the most difficult, and at the same time the most important, problem in the interpretation of Second Isaiah's message. Several times there appears in the poems a mysterious figure designated as "the servant of Yahweh." In at least four passages, the Servant is described, though he is not clearly identified:

1. 42:1-4   "He will bring forth justice to the nations."
2. 49:1-6   "Yahweh called me from the womb." [15]
3. 50:4-9   "Morning by morning he wakens my ear."
   (Notice the reference to the Servant in verse 10.)
4. 52:13–53:12   "A man of sorrows, and acquainted with grief."

The last poem is best known in Christian circles because it was appropriated as a portrayal of the Passion of Jesus, the Christ. From the Christian standpoint, this is the deepest meaning and fulfillment of the prophecy. But instead of putting the cart before the horse by committing ourselves in advance to a "messianic" interpretation, let us try to understand the Servant poems within the context of the message of Second Isaiah.

At the outset it should be recognized that some scholars question this procedure, because they believe that the Servant poems had an independent origin. They argue that these poems stand by themselves, even interrupting the context, and that they display a conception of the Servant not to be found elsewhere in the writings of Second Isaiah. Hence, they allege that the poems have been introduced into Second Isaiah's writings from another source. These arguments are not conclusive, however. The Servant poems are written in the style that is typical of Second Isaiah's poetry, and they fit well into their context. So we shall approach the question from the premise that the poems belong to Second Isaiah and see where our investigation leads.

The Servant as Israel

One of the Servant poems gives an important clue to the mystery. In 49:3, the Servant is explicitly identified with Israel:

> And he said to me, "You are my servant,
>   Israel, in whom I will be glorified."

To be sure, the mystery does not vanish, for in the same poem it is stated, at least according to the usual interpretation of the Hebrew, that the Servant has a

---

[15] The extent of this Servant poem is disputed. It may end with verse 7, verse 9, or verse 13, according to various views.

mission to Israel (verses 5-6). Nevertheless, this poem provides a bridge to another series of poems in which Israel is addressed as Yahweh's servant. In these cases the role of the Servant is associated with Israel's task as Yahweh's chosen people, as is clear from the recurring parallelism: "Israel, my servant—Jacob, whom I have chosen" (41:8-10; 43:8-13; 44:1-2; 44:21; 45:4; cf. 48:12). All these passages give the impression that in some sense Israel's task is that of the Servant.

The figure of the Servant first appears in the poem dealing with "the trial of the nations" (chapter 41, concluding with 42:1-4). The nations are summoned to a court trial before Yahweh, the Creator and Lord of history, and are asked to interpret the meaning of the rise of Cyrus (verses 1-4). When they can give no answer, except to encourage one another in their pitiful idol-making (verses 5-7), Yahweh turns to Israel:

> But you, Israel, my servant,
>   Jacob, whom I have chosen,
>   the offspring of Abraham, my friend;
> you whom I took from the ends of the earth,
>   and called from its farthest corners,
> saying to you, "You are my servant,
>   I have chosen you and not cast you off";
> fear not, for I am with you,
>   be not dismayed, for I am your God;
> I will strengthen you, I will help you,
>   I will uphold you with my victorious right hand.
>   —ISAIAH 41:8-10

Here the prophet is speaking out of Israel's covenant tradition. The covenant, as we have seen repeatedly, was the relationship between the Lord who had manifested his deeds of benevolence, and the servant Israel whose responsibility was to serve Yahweh in gratitude and reverence. The conception of *service* was the heart of Israel's faith from the very first.

In a later section of the poem, the nations are summoned once again to present their case before Yahweh, and in particular to give evidence that their gods have been able to foretell the new age initiated by Cyrus' victories. Again there is no answer (verses 21-29); so Yahweh turns a second time to his Servant.[16] This time the Servant is not explicitly identified with Israel, but in the context of the whole poem (41:1-42:4) there is a strong prejudice in favor of this view:

> Behold my servant, whom I uphold,
>   my chosen, in whom my soul delights;

---

[16] James Muilenburg convincingly shows that 42:1-4 is the climax of the last strophes (and indeed of the whole poem), just as the earlier poem on the Servant (41:8-10) is the climax of the first arraignment of the nations. See his whole discussion, *Interpreter's Bible*, V, pp. 406-414, 447-466.

> I have put my spirit upon him,
>   he will bring forth justice to the nations.
> He will not cry or lift up his voice,
>   or make it heard in the street;
> a bruised reed he will not break,
>   and a dimly burning wick he will not quench;
>   he will faithfully bring forth justice.
> He will not fail or be discouraged
>   till he has established justice in the earth;
>   and the coastlands wait for his law [torah].
>   —ISAIAH 42:1-4

Here something is added to the portrait of the Servant in the previous poem. Not only does Yahweh "uphold" or "hold" his Servant (41:10 and 42:1), but he is Yahweh's agent, endowed with his spirit, who in a quiet way will bring justice to the nations. Israel's election is for responsibility. Like Cyrus, the Servant too is the agent of Yahweh's historical purpose, but his way of conquest, as described in this poem, contrasts sharply with the methods of a military conqueror, even one as benevolent as Cyrus.

So far, it would seem that Second Isaiah identifies the Servant with the covenant community of Israel. Plumbing the meaning of the intense suffering occasioned by the fall of the nation, he affirms that in "the furnace of affliction" (48:11) Yahweh has refined his people for greater service. In one sense, the national catastrophe came as God's judgment upon Israel's foolishness and disobedience, just as prophets of the past had prophesied (see 42:18-25). But, according to this prophet, Israel has paid the penalty for the past, and is now accepted and renewed by Yahweh's freely offered forgiveness (40:1-2; 43:22-44:5). As iron is tempered by fire and shaped on the anvil, so Yahweh re-creates his people through sufferings so that they may be a more effective instrument of his sovereign purpose in history.

The Servant as an Individual

There are, however, difficulties in this interpretation. The poems also suggest that the Servant is an individual. The second poem (49:1-6) is crucial. Although in this passage it is emphatically said that the Servant is Israel (verse 3), it is also said that he has a mission to Israel, implying a distinction from the covenant community. The Servant affirms that Yahweh has called him from the womb to gather Israel to Yahweh.[17] And, lest this task should appear "too light," he is also given the mission of being a light unto the nations in order that

---

[17] Some scholars, however, contend that the verbs in verse 5 refer to Yahweh rather than Israel. See the American Translation (University of Chicago, 1939):
>   And now Yahweh,
>   Who formed me from the womb to be his servant,
>   Says that he will bring back Jacob to himself,
>   And that Israel shall be gathered to him. . . .

Yahweh's salvation may reach to the ends of the earth (verses 5-6). In this poem (see verses 1-4) one is struck by the similarity of the Servant's testimony to the Confessions of Jeremiah. The "I" who speaks appears to be an individual, and this impression is strengthened by the concrete, personal description of "the man of sorrows" in Isaiah 53. So we are confronted with a singular problem: On the one hand, in many cases the similarities between Israel and the Servant are so close as to indicate that they are the same; and, on the other, the differences seem to be so sharp as to indicate that Israel is not the Servant. Some of these likenesses and differences are summarized in the following table.

THE SERVANT OF THE LORD

THE SERVANT ISRAEL	THE ANONYMOUS SERVANT
Likenesses:	
1. Chosen by Yahweh 41:8-9; 45:4; 43:10; 44:1; 49:7	1. Chosen by Yahweh 42:1
2. Formed by Yahweh in the womb 44:2; 44:21, 24	2. Formed by Yahweh in the womb 49:1, 5
3. Upheld and comforted by Yahweh 41:10; cf. 42:6	3. Upheld and comforted by Yahweh 42:1
4. Hid in the shadow of Yahweh's hand 51:16	4. Hid in the shadow of Yahweh's hand 49:2
5. Endowed with Yahweh's spirit 44:3	5. Spirit-endowed 42:1
6. Honored by Yahweh 43:4	6. Honored by Yahweh 49:5
7. A light to the nations 42:6; cf. 51:4	7. A light to the nations 49:6
8. Gives torah and justice to the nations 51:4-8; cf. 42:21, 24	8. Gives torah to the nations, establishes justice 42:4
9. Yahweh glorified in Israel 44:23	9. Yahweh glorified in the Servant 49:3
Differences:	
1. Israel despairs 40:27; 41:8-10; 49:14, etc.	1. The Servant is undiscouraged 42:4; 50:7-9 (*But see* 49:4)
2. Israel is rebellious, sinful 48:4; cf. 43:27	2. The Servant is not rebellious but faithful 50:5; 53:4-6, 12
3. Israel is blind and deaf 42:18-25	3. The Servant is attentive, responsive 50:4-5
4. Israel suffers unwillingly, seeks vindication 41:11-13; 51:21-23, etc.	4. The Servant suffers patiently, willingly 50:6; 53:4-9 (*Notice* 50:7-9)
5. Israel suffers for her own sins 42:24-25; 43:22-28; 47:6; 50:1	5. The Servant innocently suffers for the sins of others chap. 53
6. Israel is to be redeemed 43:1-7, etc.	6. The Servant's mission is to redeem Israel 49:5

Some interpreters believe that the differences outweigh the similarities. If the Servant is interpreted in a corporate sense, they say, either as the holy community of Israel or as a faithful remnant, this does not account for the fact that the Servant has a role to perform on behalf of Israel, as well as on behalf of the nations. Nor does it do justice to the concrete detail of the Servant's portrait, which is modeled after that of an individual, especially in Isaiah 53. Hence a long list of candidates for the Servant has been proposed, beginning with Moses and coming down to Second Isaiah himself. Others, believing that no historic person of ancient Israel fits the picture, propose that the figure is one who appears on the horizon of God's future—that is, the Messiah. Still others, impressed with the Babylonian background of Second Isaiah's thought, believe that the portrait of the Servant is influenced by the role of the oriental king who acted as the representative of the people in the Tammuz cult (the Babylonian fertility religion), suffering ritual humiliation for them and taking upon himself their sins.[18]

The One and the Many

Two questions emerge out of our discussion: Did Second Isaiah understand the Servant in a corporate or in an individual sense? Did the prophet understand that the work of the Servant was to take place in his time or in the messianic future (the "last days")? A sympathetic study of Isaiah 40-55 will disclose that these are alternatives that have no real basis in the prophet's message.

A great deal of light is thrown on the first question by considering how the relationship between the individual and the community is understood in the Old Testament. Again and again we have seen that an individual may incarnate the whole community of Israel or, vice versa, the community may be addressed as an individual who stands in direct, personal relation to God. According to our way of thinking, the alternative is either collectivism or individualism, but in Israel's covenant faith the issue is not an either-or. Take the case of Abraham. He was certainly an individual. But his "biography" is also a representation of the whole community of which he is the ancestor. Abraham the man and Abraham the community, are inseparably fused in psychic unity.[19] So when Yahweh speaks to Abraham, Israel in every age is involved in the call and the promise. In the man Abraham, Israel sees its whole life mirrored and condensed, for the father lives on in his sons. The "one" includes the "many" in a spiritual

---

[18] For a review and analysis of the various theories on the identity of the Servant, see C. R. North, *The Suffering Servant in Deutero-Isaiah* [187]; also H. H. Rowley, *The Servant of the Lord* [188], pp. 3-60.

[19] J. Pedersen, *Israel*, I-II [69], p. 476. See especially the discussion of the Israelite sense of community, pp. 52-60, 263-279. See also J. Muilenburg, *op. cit.*, pp. 410-412.

unity that binds all generations together. Therefore Second Isaiah exhorts Israel to turn to her ancestors, in whom the contemporary meaning of her history is represented:

> Look to the rock from which you were hewn,
>   and to the quarry from which you were digged.
> Look to Abraham your father
>   and to Sarah who bore you;
> for when he was but one I called him,
>   and blessed him and made him many.
>   —ISAIAH 51:1-2

Looking at the same matter from the other side, the community of Israel is often personalized or regarded as a "corporate personality." [20] Yahweh does not deal with a collection of individuals but with a *people,* bound so closely together by a common history and single covenant obligation that Israel is addressed in the dialogue of "I and Thou." The covenant tradition, as we have seen, is cast in the form of personal address. Moreover, the most individualized images are applied to the community: a son in relation to his father, a wife in relation to her husband, a servant in relation to his lord (see Is. 46:3-4 and 54:4-8 for examples of this personal imagery). In other words, the community is considered as an individual. This throws light on something that is confusing to the modern mind—the fluctuating use of singular and plural verbs and pronouns. For instance, in Hosea 11 Yahweh begins by addressing Israel in the singular: "I loved him . . . I called my son." But in the very next line (verse 2) the language suddenly shifts to the plural: "The more I called them, the more they went from me."

So it is unnecessary to choose between an individual and a corporate interpretation of the Servant of Yahweh, for both are true to the Israelite sense of community. The conception oscillates between the servant Israel and the personal servant who would perfectly fulfill Israel's mission. The portrait of the Servant is painted with colors drawn from many sources in Israel's history. Some scholars have emphasized that the prototype of the Servant is Moses, who, especially in Deuteronomic tradition, was portrayed as the true prophet: the covenant mediator who made intercession for his people and who finally died vicariously for their sins (Deut. 3:23-27; 4:23, etc.). Thus Second Isaiah, whose message is dominated by the "new exodus," envisions the rise of a prophet *like Moses* to lead Israel into the new age.[21] Doubtless this was a major

---

[20] See H. Wheeler Robinson, "The Hebrew Conception of Corporate Personality," in J. Hempel, ed., *Werden und Wesen des Alten Testaments* (Beiheft 66, *Zeitschrift für die alttestamentliche Wissenschaft* [1936], pp. 49 ff.).

[21] This view is presented persuasively by von Rad, *Theologie*, II [80], pp. 264-274. He calls attention to the expectation of a prophet like Moses in Deut. 18:15-19, and to the "suffering prophet" tradition which developed especially in the time of Jeremiah and Ezekiel.

influence upon Second Isaiah's thought, but he also drew upon other recollections in shaping the portrait of the Servant. In his prophecy the Servant is a person, although no single person, past or contemporary, corresponds completely to the type. For the person also includes and represents Israel, the community that is explicitly designated as Yahweh's servant.

The Servant Who Is To Come

The second question—whether the Servant's work was thought of as present or future—must be considered from the standpoint of Second Isaiah's proclamation that the New Age was beginning. The prophet was not looking ahead into the distant future, envisaging the coming of a Servant who was not yet visible on the horizon. His prophetic task was to interpret the contemporary political situation occasioned by the rise of Cyrus and the imminent collapse of the Babylonian empire. In the political ferment of the time he saw the sign of Yahweh's coming to liberate his people and to inaugurate his kingdom. And with the advent of Yahweh, according to the prophet, the Servant would appear upon the world-stage, born out of the travail of Israel's history, to be Yahweh's agent for bringing salvation to the ends of the earth. In the past, Yahweh had called the Servant, had tested and refined his life by suffering, and had hidden him like an arrow in his quiver. But now the time was fulfilled. The work of the Servant was about to begin. Yahweh's victory through his Servant was coming near.

In a sense, then, the Servant was a future figure, but he was also a figure of the present age. He stood in the dawn—when the darkness of the old order was lingering and the light of the new day was breaking on the horizon. This seems paradoxical to us, for we insist on measuring time as a chronological progression from present to future. Hence, we say, the work of the Servant must be *either* present or future, *either* today or tomorrow. But in prophetic literature historical time is not measured by the calendar, but by God's activity, God's purpose. From this perspective, the future can enter the present, the power of the coming kingdom can be felt in the old order. The task of the Servant, then, must be considered in relation to Second Isaiah's gospel concerning the "last things" or the consummation of history. Within this theological perspective, the prophet perceived the meaning of Israel's suffering and the role of the "suffering Servant" depicted in the Servant poems.

VICTORY THROUGH SUFFERING

Throughout the poems of Second Isaiah runs the theme of Israel's exaltation. With this exultant note the message of the prophet begins in chapter 40 and ends in chapter 55. Israel's *mishpat*—her "justice" (40:27)—was not disregarded by her God. Rather, God's people were invited to walk along a royal highway leading from bondage into the glorious freedom of a new life. Had Second Isaiah's message been stated *only* in the language of deliverance from captivity, it would have been no more than a lofty nationalism inspired in the heart of a poet by the stirring international developments of his time. But the prophet proclaimed that Yahweh would glorify himself through the mission of Israel— a mission that must reach unto the ends of the earth. Israel's nobility was her task, her service. She had to learn what her greatest son was to say later, that the least are the greatest in God's kingdom, for he that loses his life for the sake of the gospel will find life abundant.

Second Isaiah affirmed that Israel would be highly exalted through suffering. This was the deepest mystery of her calling. The mystery is illumined by the figure of the Servant who, unlike Cyrus or any great nation, would tread a path leading through defeat to victory.

The four Servant poems depict the unusual character of the Servant's task. His method is extraordinary: a bruised reed he will not break, and a dimly burning wick he will not quench, but quietly, gently, he will persist until he has established *mishpaṭ* ("justice") in all the earth (42:1-4). Despite his discouragement, he believes that Yahweh has hidden him like an arrow in a quiver until the appointed time when he will be sent forth victoriously to accomplish his mission, a mission that will go far beyond the confines of Israel (49:1-6). Like a disciple schooled in suffering, his close fellowship with God enables him to bear affliction submissively: the lash of the smiters, the disgrace of the plucking of the beard and being spat upon (50:4-9). In all his suffering he knows that Yahweh has chosen him to walk this *via dolorosa*, at the end of which will be vindication and exaltation. *And it is through the suffering of the Servant that God inaugurates his kingdom.* The nations will share with Israel the good news of the herald: "Your God reigns"—that is, Yahweh is King (cf. 52:7).

The Man of Sorrows

The theme of the exaltation of the Servant rises to a tremendous climax in the fourth Servant poem, which portrays "the man of sorrows" (52:13-53:12). In view of the dramatic power of the poem, as well as its far-reaching influence upon Israelite and Christian thought, it deserves special attention, strophe by strophe. It is divided into five poetic units. At the beginning and end of the poem Yahweh is the speaker. When Yahweh speaks, he gives the verdict that the Servant will be exalted through suffering.

In the first strophe (52:13-15), Yahweh introduces his Servant and announces his triumph and elevation. Although the promise is spoken primarily to Israel, for whom the prophet's words are meant most immediately, the attention centers on the nations. The Servant has an international role, as is indicated in two other Servant poems where it is said that "the coastlands wait for his torah" (42:4) and where the Servant addresses himself to the peoples from afar (49:1). The mystery of the Servant's suffering, it is said, will finally be understood by the peoples. His garb of humiliation will be removed, and they will come to know who he really is. And the contrast between his ultimate triumph and his present form—"marred beyond human semblance"—will be so overwhelming that the nations will be astonished, kings will bow in reverent silence before him. Thus the strophe deals with a motif that runs through the entire message of Second Isaiah: the reversal of Israel's position of distress and humiliation and the recognition of her *mishpaṭ*, her proper and just place in Yahweh's world order.

The new understanding of the nations is elaborated in the following three strophes, in which the rulers of the nations are represented as speaking for their peoples. In the second strophe (53:1-3), the kings express their astonishment at what they finally see and hear. To them the whole thing is fantastic and unbelievable. The Servant had grown up before Yahweh (or perhaps, "before us"—that is, the nations) like a young sapling, like a root out of dry, unpromising ground. Some interpreters find here an allusion to the Messiah, who elsewhere is called a "branch" or a root from the stock of Jesse (see Is. 11:1, 10; Jer. 23:5), but it is more likely that the kings are describing Israel's unpromising career. Possibly with the figure of leprosy in mind, the poet portrays the Servant's "form" (cf. 52:14) as so marred that men hide their faces from him (Lev. 13:45). The kings are utterly amazed that such an unlovely, despised, revolting figure is actually the chosen agent of God through whom his "arm" or redemptive power is revealed. The Servant had appeared among them *incognito*, unrecognized in his disguise of humiliation.

The kings continue to speak in the next strophe (verses 4-6). Although they formerly had no esteem for the Servant, their eyes are suddenly opened to perceive the true meaning of his suffering. In their previous understanding, the Servant was stricken, smitten, and afflicted by God for his own sins. But it turned out that all along he had been suffering in their stead—taking upon himself the consequences of their transgressions and restoring them to "wholeness" (*shalom*, which means "peace" or "well-being"). Astonishingly, the man who seemed to be diseased was the source of their health and healing! It was not Israel's sins that the Servant was bearing, for according to the initial proclamation of the prophet Israel had suffered more than enough for her own sin. The "overplus" of Israel's suffering was vicarious—for the nations. The nations confess that the Servant's sacrifice was Yahweh's redemptive act for their welfare, their salvation:

> All we like sheep have gone astray;
>   we have turned every one to his own way;
> and Yahweh has laid on him
>   the iniquity of us all.
>   —ISAIAH 53:6

Here is a profound insight into the meaning of suffering, for which there is no parallel elsewhere in the Old Testament.

In the fourth strophe (verses 7-9), the nations are still speaking. This passage emphasizes the way the Servant endured his suffering (cf. 42:1-4; 50:4-9). Unlike most sufferers—even Jeremiah, according to his Confessions—he did not cry out in bitterness or self-pity when affliction fell upon him. He bore his cross silently, without any complaint or vindictiveness, "like a lamb that is led to the slaughter, and like a sheep that before its shearers is dumb" (see Jer. 11:19, where the same figure appears with a slightly different nuance of meaning). The speaker goes on to describe the character of the Servant's affliction, although the details are not too clear. Evidently the meaning is that the Servant was imprisoned, brought to trial, and led away to death (verse 8a). He died in complete loneliness, for no one gave a thought to his "generation"—that is, the posterity in whom his life would continue.[22] He was "cut off from the land of the living" for the sake of other peoples (each king is represented as speaking of his nation as "my people," verse 8d). And to add insult to injury he was buried in a criminal's grave. The strophe ends by repeating the theme of the sacrificial lamb: he was meek and innocent through the whole ordeal.

But the Servant typifies the meek who will inherit the earth. In the concluding strophe (verses 10-12), as in the opening one, Yahweh is the speaker. The tones of all the preceding strophes are blended together in this great climax in which the glorification of the Servant is announced. Here it is apparent that the Servant was not just a martyr who bore "the slings and arrows of outrageous fortune." His stroke of affliction was not just a fate that men or circumstance had imposed upon him. It was a divine event. It was enfolded in Yahweh's purpose. That is the meaning of the words, which sound harsh to modern ears: "It was the will of Yahweh to bruise him; he has put him to grief." Here the thought is not that Yahweh was punishing the Servant or taking out on him the anger that should have been displayed toward others who deserved it. Rather, the intention is to say that God was identified with, involved in, the Servant's voluntary sacrifice (compare Hosea 11). God himself was active in the Servant's career. The Servant's sacrifice was an activity within the activity of God. Thus the poet stresses that the Servant is, in one sense, the subject of the action: "He makes himself an offering for sin" or "his life shall make an offering for sin." There is no divine arbitrariness in a situation where God's purpose and man's voluntary action meet and coalesce.

Vicarious Sacrifice

The conception of the Servant's sacrifice set forth here has exerted a profound influence on Christian theology. Christians cannot read this poetry without thinking of many passages in the New Testament—for instance, the

---

[22] The translation "generation" is advocated by a number of scholars. Others translate the Hebrew word (dor) as "fate"—that is, "Who considered his fate?" See the American Translation (University of Chicago Press, 1939).

important saying of Jesus found in Mark 10:45: "For the Son of man also came not to be served but to serve, and to give his life as a ransom for many." In Isaiah 53:10 it is said that the Servant offers himself as a "guilt offering" ('asham; cf. Lev. 5:1-19; 7:1-38; 14:1-57; I Sam. 6:3), and that his offering will bring acquittal or justification to "many" (verse 11). This conception of vicarious sacrifice—a sacrifice on behalf of others—was widely prevalent in the ancient world, and the belief underwent a special development within Israel's cultic tradition. One thinks, for instance, of the famous Israelite ceremony of the scapegoat who was driven into the wilderness after the sins of the community had been put upon him (Lev. 16:8-26). Moreover, the belief was widespread that animal sacrifice was a means of sustaining life and overcoming a broken relationship with the deity. As we have indicated earlier, some of the language of the Servant poems suggests the ritual drama of the Babylonian Tammuz cult, in which the king, on behalf of his people, subjected himself to humiliation and pain.

Undoubtedly Israel appropriated much of her sacrificial practice and liturgical language from others. But a profound transformation took place in the process of borrowing. In other religions of the ancient world, sacrifice was a powerful technique for controlling the will of the gods. When rightly performed, sacrifice was effective, for it was filled with magical power. Israel's theology of sacrifice, however, as developed in the priestly writing of the Pentateuch, was based on an entirely different conception. It was believed that God himself, in a sovereign act of mercy, graciously approached men, providing the means for overcoming guilt and maintaining the holiness of the community. Sacrifice was an avenue which carried "a two-way traffic"—that is, it was the channel of God's approach to man in grace and man's approach to God in responsive faith.[23] At its best— although it seldom reached this level, according to prophetic critics—sacrifice was a "sacrament," a visible means of grace.

In Second Isaiah's portrait of the Suffering Servant the theology of sacrifice attained its highest expression in the Old Testament. The Servant is led like a lamb to the sacrificial slaughter, but his sacrifice has a far greater power than any animal sacrifice. It is a willing self-sacrifice, made for others. The sacrifice moves the nations to confess that power is made available for their healing. Through it they are made whole, pronounced righteous (or "justified"), transformed into new persons. This is because the Servant's sacrifice, in the conviction of the prophet, represents God's gracious approach to men with power. The Servant is not a mere scapegoat upon whom men can cast their sins and lightly dismiss the burden of responsibility for their actions. On the contrary, the Servant poem shows that the sacrifice is powerful only when it moves the nations to confess that, like sheep, they have followed their own self-centered way and that the Servant suffered on their behalf. Above all, the poem stresses

---

[23] H. H. Rowley, *The Unity of the Bible* [74], p. 56. The whole chapter (pp. 30-61) deserves attention.

the central point that back of and within the Servant's suffering is the initiative and activity of God. The Servant is the agent through whom God overcomes men's broken relations and reconciles the world unto himself.

The Exaltation of the Servant

Let us return to the concluding strophe of the poem. Yahweh announces that the outcome of the Servant's mission will be victory and exaltation. According to Second Isaiah, this follows from the fact that the power of God is manifest in the Servant's sacrifice. The Servant is not a victim, but a victor. For Yahweh will reverse the Servant's position of humiliation and disgrace and will establish his "justice" before the whole world. In Yahweh's determination the Servant will have a posterity and a long life (verse 10)—both of which, to the Israelite mind, were signs of God's favor. The purpose of God will prosper in the career of the Servant, and the Servant himself will look with satisfaction upon the successful result of his travail.

At first glance, it would seem that the prophet had in mind an individual Servant, whose resurrection from the grave is implied in this passage. But this is by no means certain. The doctrine of the resurrection of the individual appeared later in Israelite tradition, as we shall see in a subsequent chapter. A doctrine as revolutionary as that of individual resurrection surely would have been introduced here in less veiled language, if that were the meaning intended. The only instance of resurrection that we have found so far is Ezekiel's vision in the valley of dry bones, and Ezekiel was speaking of the resurrection of Israel from the grave of exile. Probably this is the meaning in Isaiah 53. The prophet portrays the victorious destiny of Israel in language that oscillates between the conception of the Servant as an individual and the conception of the Servant as the community.

The poem ends with a reference back to the beginning. Just as it was said in the opening that great kings and many nations would be astonished at the Servant, so Yahweh announces in the conclusion that he will make his Servant great. His greatness is described in the concrete terms characteristic of the Israelite mind. The Servant will receive a portion with the great and will divide the spoil of conquest, for he is the true conqueror who advances along the royal road of God's kingdom.

THE SERVANT AND THE MESSIAH

To summarize: In this chapter we have seen that the belief in Israel's election is the basic conviction of Second Isaiah. Understanding this belief more profoundly than any of his predecessors, Second Isaiah expounds its universal implications for the whole of human history. But he never wavers from his central premise that Yahweh has chosen Israel for a special task in his world-embracing plan. Second Isaiah's message begins with the "good news" of Yahweh's comfort and grace to Israel, and after many variations of this theme his poems reach a mighty climax on the same note (chapters 54 and 55):

> For a brief moment I forsook you,
>   but with great compassion I will gather you.
> In overflowing wrath for a moment
>   I hid my face from you,
> but with everlasting love I will have compassion on you,
>   says Yahweh, your Redeemer.
>   —ISAIAH 54:7-8

It is striking that nowhere does Second Isaiah include the Davidic king in his portrayals of the coming kingdom of God. This is particularly surprising when one considers the resurgence of messianic hope among Jews who returned from exile to Jerusalem, as we shall see in the next chapter. His thinking is so dominated by the sacred history which centered in the Exodus that he seems to have found it necessary to modify the royal theology based as it was on the twin pillars of Yahweh's election of Zion and his covenant with David. Although he frequently refers to the Holy City, he mentions the Davidic covenant only once, in connection with Yahweh's invitation to an eschatological banquet (Is. 55:1-5). In this instance, however, the "everlasting covenant" is not made with the Davidic king but with all Israelites who respond to the call: [24]

> Incline your ear, and come to me;
>   hear, that your soul may live;
> and I will make with you an everlasting covenant,
>   my steadfast, sure love for David.
> Behold, I made him a witness to the peoples,
>   a leader and commander for the peoples.
> Behold, you shall call nations that you know not,
>   and nations that knew you not shall run to you,
> because of Yahweh your God, and of the Holy One of Israel,
>   for he has glorified you.
>   —ISAIAH 55:3-5

Thus Second Isaiah affirms that Yahweh's promises of grace to David do not guarantee the continuance of a dynasty but rather support Israel, whose suffering will bring divine blessing to the world.

Jewish thought did not usually identify the Messiah with the Suffering Servant. This revolutionary identification was carried out mainly in Christianity,

---

[24] This point is discussed by Otto Eissfeldt in "The Promises of Grace to David in Isaiah 55:1-5," in *Israel's Prophetic Heritage* [136], pp. 196-207. In this essay Eissfeldt contrasts the motif of the Davidic covenant in Psalm 89 with the use of the same motif by Second Isaiah.

PLATE 5

Above: The mound of Lachish, a Judean city which lay on the western slopes of the hill country between Jerusalem and Gaza. Strong defenses once ringed the city which, along with Jerusalem, was conquered by Nebuchadnezzar. Below: A reconstructed temple stands back of the ruins of the famous Ishtar Gate at the site of ancient Babylon.

PLATE 6

The eastern portal of the Gate of Xerxes at Persepolis, the main Persian capital, was guarded by colossal human-headed "bulls." An inscription on the gate reads: "King Xerxes says: By the grace of Ahura Mazda, I constructed this gateway called All-Countries." This splendid piece of architecture was a casualty of Alexander's conquest.

Above: The processional street of Babylon which led
through the Ishtar Gate to the great "Tower of Babel"
ziggurat was adorned with sacred dragons and bulls of
Hadad. Below: A relief carved on the Behistun Rock commemorated Darius I's victory over rebels who seized the
Persian throne.

PLATE 7

Above: "*Seleucia by the Sea*" (see I Macc. 11:8), site of
the port built by Seleucus Nicator, a general under Alexander the Great, to serve the new Seleucid capital, Antioch. In the background is Casius, the sacred Mount of the
North mentioned in ancient Canaanite literature. *Below:*
A portion of the ruins of Qumran on the Dead Sea shore
show where an Essene community flourished early in the
Christian era.

PLATE 8

although the way had been prepared in some Jewish circles, like the Essene community which occupied the site of Qumran on the northwestern shore of the Dead Sea at the beginning of the Christian era (see pp. 552-553). However, even in the message of Second Isaiah the ground was prepared for a messianic interpretation, as we have seen in our discussion of the prophet's gospel of the New Age. A distinguished Jewish interpreter affirms that "in the essential point" the messianic interpretation "approximates closely" the intention of Second Isaiah.[25] For the Servant represents true Israel. Whenever the humble worshiper lives in such close fellowship with God that his suffering is borne willingly, thereby becoming God's power for restoring and renewing mankind, then Israel is fulfilling her task. Then, this Jewish authority continues, "God's purpose for Israel has put on skin and flesh." The kingdom makes its beginning.

In the Acts of the Apostles (8:26-39) there is a story about an Ethiopian eunuch who, riding along in his chariot, was reading from the book of Isaiah, specifically the description of the Suffering Servant in Isaiah 53. Perplexed about the meaning of the passage, he asked Philip, the Christian apostle, a question that we have been raising in this discussion: "About whom, pray, does the prophet say this, about himself or about someone else?" The story goes on to say that Philip, "beginning with this passage" (Is. 53), told him "the good news of Jesus." In the New Testament, and throughout the history of the church, Christians understand the mission of Jesus in the light of the Servant poems of Second Isaiah.[26] Christians are convinced that the vocation of the Servant is realized in Jesus. He is the true Israelite—"Israel reduced to one." Through his vicarious sacrifice, a new Israel is gathered around him, and the doors of the kingdom are thrown open to all nations. The whole of Israel's history comes to focus and fulfillment in him. According to Christian tradition, Jesus opened his ministry in Nazareth by reading a passage from the scroll of Isaiah and announcing that "today this scripture has been fulfilled in your hearing" (Luke 4:16 ff.). The passage was the opening of Isaiah 61—a passage that some scholars believe was written by Second Isaiah and that was probably understood as a Servant poem in Jesus' day:

> The Spirit of Yahweh God is upon me,
>   because Yahweh has anointed me
> to bring good tidings to the afflicted;
>   he has sent me to bind up the brokenhearted,
> to proclaim liberty to the captives,
>   and the opening of the prison
>   to those who are bound;
> to proclaim the year of Yahweh's favor,
>   and the day of vengeance of our God;
>   to comfort all who mourn. . . .
>   —ISAIAH 61:1-2

[25] Martin Buber. *The Prophetic Faith* [118], p. 218; see also, p. 232.
[26] See *The Servant of God* [191], by Walther Zimmerli and J. Jeremias.

A KINGDOM

OF PRIESTS

CHAPTER FOURTEEN In our modern political experience, we have had many vivid illustrations of peoples who have gone wild with joy at the approach of an army of liberation. The Cyrus Cylinder (see pp. 397-398) is a first-hand historical witness to the jubilation produced by the advance of the Persian army in the middle of the sixth century B.C. Cyrus' benevolent policy was a welcome relief from Baby-

Biblical readings: The period of the return from Babylonian captivity is dealt with in the books of Ezra and Nehemiah. To keep the story in sequence, read first Ezra 1-6, then Nehemiah 1-7, 11-13, and then Ezra 7-10 and Nehemiah 8-10. For further understanding of the period, read the small prophetic collections of Haggai, Zechariah 1-8, Malachi, Obadiah, and Joel. The meaning of the Torah for Judaism is expressed in Psalms 1; 19:7-14; 119.

lonian tyranny both to the Babylonians themselves, who in high anticipation opened the doors of their cities and their hearts to him, and to the many captive peoples under his rule. Apparently Cyrus understood the futility of trying to lash people of diverse backgrounds and national traditions into subservience—a policy that had been the foundation of the empires whose lands he inherited. To be sure, he did not relax his political power. The Persian army had proved itself to be a powerful fighting force, and the Persian government soon developed a swift system of communications—a forerunner of the American "pony express." This system made it possible to supervise the far-flung empire, which was efficiently divided into satrapies or provinces. But Cyrus seems to have understood the limitations of power, or perhaps he realized that the emperor who enjoys honor and loyalty from his people also enjoys an increase of power.

CYRUS' EDICT OF LIBERATION

In one passage of the Cylinder, where Cyrus is speaking of various regions that he has conquered, he says: "I returned to (these) sacred cities on the other side of the Tigris, the sanctuaries of which have been in ruins for a long time, the images which (used) to live therein and established for them permanent sanctuaries. I (also) gathered all their (former) inhabitants and returned (to them) their habitations." [1] Clearly, Cyrus chose to abandon the "scorched-earth" tactics of the Assyrians and Babylonians, who had destroyed cities and temples, looted sacred treasuries, and transported idols and people into captivity. With a political right-about-face, he permitted the subject peoples to carry on their customs, to worship their gods, and to settle in their homelands. (See Chronological Chart 8, p. 353.)

It is against this background that we should read the account of the edict of liberation that Cyrus proclaimed to the Jewish exiles in the first year after Babylon's fall (538 B.C.). This edict is preserved in two versions: one is written in Hebrew, the traditional language of Israel (Ezra 1:2-4), and the other is written in Aramaic (6:3-5).

First, a word about the Aramaic language, which gradually became the common tongue of the Jewish people during the post-exilic period. Although Aramaic became particularly popular at this time, actually it is at least as old as Hebrew, and both belong to a common family of Semitic languages. The differences and resemblances between them are like those between such modern Romance languages as Spanish and Italian. The close relations that existed between the Aramean (Syrian) and Hebrew people as recorded in the patriarchal stories of Jacob and Laban, existed between the two languages as well. Like Jacob and Laban, Aramaic and Hebrew are relatives. In the ancient world,

---

[1] Pritchard, *Ancient Near Eastern Texts*, p. 316.

Aramaic commanded great international prestige, for like English today it was used as a *lingua franca* in international relations. Remember that when the Rabshakeh came to demand the surrender of Jerusalem in Isaiah's day (Is. 36: 11), he was asked to speak in Aramaic rather than in the native tongue of the Judeans. During and after the Exile, the Persian authorities' use of Aramaic as an international language in speaking to their satrapies enhanced its popularity. Gradually, the Jews came to think of Hebrew as a literary or classical language, and in Palestine and throughout the Dispersion (for instance, at Elephantine) their spoken language was Aramaic. Well before the Christian era, Hebrew scripture had to be accompanied by a "targum," a free translation into Aramaic, to enable ordinary Jews to understand it.

The very fact that Cyrus' edict is preserved in two versions speaks in favor of its authenticity. Although some scholars believe that the Aramaic version is the original account, there are no fundamental discrepancies between the two.[2] According to the Hebrew version, Cyrus claimed that "Yahweh, the God of heaven" had given him all the kingdoms of the earth and had charged him to build Yahweh a temple in Jerusalem. This claim reminds us of Second Isaiah, who regarded Cyrus as Yahweh's agent by whom Jerusalem would be rebuilt (Is. 44:28; 45:1-3, 13). It is not improbable that the Jewish historian has touched up the edict theologically, for in his Cylinder Cyrus had claimed that it was Marduk who gave him world dominion. Still, the Hebrew report is not inconsistent with Cyrus' policy, for he regarded himself as the patron of the gods of conquered peoples, restored sacred images to their sanctuaries, and supported the rebuilding of their temples. Both versions of the edict say that he permitted the Jews to return to their homeland, ordered the Temple of Jerusalem to be rebuilt with support from the Persian treasury (Ezra 6:4) and commanded that the vessels taken by Nebuchadnezzar from the Temple be returned (1:7-11).

The Return under a Davidic Prince

To head up the whole Jewish return from exile, Cyrus appointed a man named Sheshbazzar. This was a particularly significant appointment. Admittedly, Sheshbazzar made no great mark on his age, for he was overshadowed by other leaders. But he was a son of Jehoiachin, the exiled king whom many had regarded as the legitimate king of Judah. In effect, then, Cyrus handed over the leadership of the Jews to a prince of the Davidic line (Ezra 5:19). And Sheshbazzar was succeeded by an even more important figure: Zerubbabel, a descendant of Jehoiachin (I Chron. 3:19). Evidently the Persian policy was not only to permit the observance of religious customs but, in a limited degree,

---

[2] It has been argued that the Hebrew version rests on the oral proclamation of a herald, and the Aramaic version represents the official document. See R. A. Bowman, *Interpreter's Bible*, III, pp. 571-573.

to permit the nation to be restored. These developments must have stirred the hearts and kindled the hopes of many Jews. It must have appeared that the New Age, in the dawn of which Second Isaiah stood, was about to break into the full light of day.

But Second Isaiah's picture of the New Age was so elevated in grandeur, so transfigured in the light of eternity, that no ordinary historical era, least of all the post-exilic period of Judaism, could measure up to his vision. He spoke, not of a Davidic king, but of the Servant exalted through suffering. He pictured no ordinary Jerusalem, but a New Jerusalem which would be a sign to all mankind that Yahweh is King. He described a marvelous transformation that would begin in men's hearts and that would be mirrored in the whole drama of history and the vast scenery of nature. His message had to do with "last things," the consummation of all history in the redemptive purpose of God. But the exiles who chose to return to Jerusalem under the protection of Cyrus experienced not the poetry of Second Isaiah but the prose of a grim and bitter struggle.

To tell the story of the return as briefly as possible, we shall concentrate on three figures and three events: first, Zerubbabel and the rebuilding of the Temple; second, Nehemiah and the rebuilding of the walls of Jerusalem; and third, Ezra and the renewal of the covenant. We shall also look briefly at prophets

THE TOMB OF CYRUS *at Pasargadae, his royal residence. According to Plutarch, a Roman writer of the early Christian era, it bore this inscription: "O man, whosoever thou art and whencesoever thou comest, for I know that thou wilt come, I am Cyrus, and I won for the Persians their empire. Do not, therefore, begrudge me this little earth which covers my body." Alexander visited Cyrus' tomb on his return from India and, Plutarch reports, was deeply moved by the inscription.*

like Haggai and Zechariah, and try to understand the character of the Judaism that emerged with Ezra.

THE WORK OF THE CHRONICLER

Before turning to the period of post-exilic Judaism, we must consider the major historical source for our knowledge of Jewish life in Palestine during the Persian period—that is, from the rise of Cyrus to the coming of Alexander the Great (332 B.C.). The only biblical history of the Persian period is found in two seldom-read books, Ezra and Nehemiah, and even this history covers no more than half the period. Admittedly, after the stirring poems of Second Isaiah these two books come as an anticlimax; it is like leaving the vistas of a lofty summit to descend to a flat lowland. Yet this period of Judaism is an important chapter in Israel's life-story, far more important than is often realized. Without it we would not have received the spiritual heritage that has profoundly influenced Western civilization.

The Books of Ezra and Nehemiah

The books of Ezra and Nehemiah tell the story of Israel's history from the return to Jerusalem to the end of Nehemiah's second term as governor of Judah (538 to shortly before 400 B.C.). Apparently, though, the material was first split up into two books by Jerome, who about the last of the fourth century A.D. produced the Latin translation known as the Vulgate, which came to be the authoritative translation of the Roman Catholic Church. Before that time, the account was treated as one book in the earliest Hebrew and Greek manuscripts.[3] During the early centuries of the Christian era, the standard text (called the *Masora*, or "tradition") was meticulously preserved by Jewish scholars known as Masoretes, who counted all the words in order to be sure that no one would ever add or take away a single one. On the basis of their count, they indicated that the exact middle of the account of Ezra and Nehemiah was at what we would designate as Nehemiah 3:32. This, of course, is not the middle of our present book of Nehemiah, but of the single book Ezra-Nehemiah, which was one scroll when the rabbis did their counting. So, since we are dealing with a single book, we can understand why the story of Ezra is found partly in our book of Ezra and partly in Nehemiah (Neh. 7:73b-10:39).

In the original Hebrew, the scroll of Ezra-Nehemiah was part of a large historical work, the first part of which was I and II Chronicles. The whole work is governed by the same theological point of view, is written in the same style, and displays such an over-all unity that it undoubtedly came from the hand

---

[3] In the Greek translation of the Old Testament (Septuagint), the single work is known as "Ezra" (Esdras B); see Chart, pp. 556-557.

of a single author, known as "the Chronicler." [4] His identity is unknown. He must have been a member of the Temple staff, probably one of the priestly order known as Levites.

Thus we add one more major historical work to those that we have already investigated in earlier chapters. Leaving out the J and E narratives, which belong in the category of historical epics, the list includes:

1. The Deuteronomic History (Deuteronomy through II Kings).
2. The Priestly Work (found in Genesis through Numbers).
3. The Chronicler's Work (I and II of Chronicles, Ezra-Nehemiah).

The list probably should be reduced by one, for, as we have found, the Priestly Work is actually an expanded version of the ancient Israelite epic. We are left, then, with two major works that recount the history of Israel. The Deuteronomic History is written from the standpoint of the Deuteronomic theology, and in its final form concludes with the fall of the nation and the exile of the people. The Chronicler's Work is written from the standpoint of the priestly interests of post-exilic Judaism, and carries the story down to about 400 B.C.

The Chronicler's Priestly Perspective

It would be interesting to compare in parallel columns the Deuteronomic History and I and II Chronicles. (The remainder of the Chronicler's history—Ezra, Nehemiah—is not paralleled at all in the Deuteronomic History, which concludes with the Exile.) A comparison of the David story, for instance, as given both in I Samuel 15 to I Kings 2 and in I Chronicles 10-29, would reveal how the Chronicler re-viewed the past. Sometimes he excerpted passages from Samuel-Kings word for word—another indication that our conceptions of authorship (or plagiarism!) did not apply in antiquity. At other times he ignored or changed the tradition according to his interests. For instance, in II Samuel 24:1 Yahweh moved David to number Israel, whereas in I Chronicles 21:1 Satan provoked the action. This seems a cavalier way of writing history. But in defense of the Chronicler it must be said that he was primarily an *interpreter* of the past, and he selected the materials that would emphasize certain aspects of the tradition. Of course, when any historian deals with a sweep of 600 years —a much longer span than the whole of American history—he cannot avoid selecting and weighting his materials. Obviously he cannot include everything, especially in a work of about 100 pages, the extent of the Chronicler's Work. We can see the theological bias of the Chronicler clearly when we observe how, in dealing with the tradition of Samuel-Kings, he selects, omits, adds, modifies. This is propaganda, not in the derogatory sense that the word has acquired in

---

[4] The concluding verses of II Chronicles are identical with the opening verses of Ezra. This is the ancient scribe's way of connecting the narrative and saying that I-II Chronicles and Ezra-Nehemiah are one book.

our time, but in its primary meaning of an effort to spread particular doctrines.[5]

It is erroneous, however, to suppose that this work, just because it was written in a late period and from a priestly point of view, is pure fiction. The Chronicler relied not only on Samuel-Kings, but also on source material that either was not included in the Deuteronomic History or was not available at the time it was written. An excellent example of the Chronicler's use of good historical sources is found in Ezra-Nehemiah, where he excerpts almost verbatim the autobiographical Memoirs of Nehemiah—one of the most trustworthy historical sources for Jewish history in the Persian period. The autobiographical Memoirs of Ezra, though more open to question, are also a very important historical witness. These two sources are found in the following places:

1. Nehemiah's Memoirs: Nehemiah 1:1–7:73a; 11:1-2; 12:27-43; 13:4-31.
2. Ezra's Memoirs: 7:27-9:15.[6]

The Chronicler's Work is fundamentally a revision—or reinterpretation—of Israel's history. So it is important for us to understand his over-all purpose, for the story of Ezra-Nehemiah is the final phase of the unfolding history that begins with David. The Chronicler was dominated by one central conviction: Israel was called to be a "church," a worshiping community. In a broad sense, Israel was to be "a kingdom of priests and a holy nation"—that is (as the phrase means in Ex. 19:6), a people whose whole life was to be a "liturgy" or divine service. But in a special sense the community was to have its center in the Temple, where priests and especially Levites had an indispensable place in the conduct of worship. This liturgical interest is one of the major motifs of the Chronicler's Work. In fact, the Chronicler's Work is essentially a history of Israel's worship centering in Zion, the Holy City.[7]

David as a Churchman

In Samuel-Kings, David is presented as a political leader, a man with strengths and weaknesses that endeared him to his people as the first and greatest king of all Israel. But the Chronicler was not particularly interested in David's political genius, for by the time he wrote Israel had ceased to be a nation. To

---

[5] It needs to be added, however, that not all of the deviations can be explained on the basis of the Chronicler's tendentious interests. Werner E. Lemke shows that in many instances the differences arise from the fact that the Chronicler was using a different version of the original text (*Vorlage*) than that presupposed in the received Masoretic text. This *Vorlage*, he argues, lies back of the Greek translation known as the Septuagint and is presupposed in some manuscripts from Qumran. See his article, "The Synoptic Problem in the Chronicler's History," in *Harvard Theological Review*, LVIII (1965), pp. 349-363.

[6] It is difficult to determine how much of the Ezra narrative (Ezra 7:11-10:24; Neh. 7:73b-9:5) belongs to the Ezra Memoirs. One of the problems is that sometimes Ezra speaks in the first person and sometimes he is spoken of in the third person.

[7] See Jacob M. Myers' commentary, I [194], especially "The Intention of the Chronicler," pp. xviii-xl, where he deals with the continuity of true worship in Jerusalem.

be sure, the Chronicler gloried in David's military accomplishments and the splendor of his kingdom. And he emphasized the covenant with David (II Sam. 7; cf. I Chron. 17) that guaranteed the continuation of the Davidic house. But for him David was primarily the one who organized Israel as a worshiping community. It was David who had made Jerusalem, the Holy City, his religious capital; who had planned the building of the Temple according to a plan alleged to have come directly from Yahweh (see I Chron. 28:19); who had organized the music of the Temple and had assigned the Levites their duties. The ecclesiastical robes with which the Chronicler invested David tend to cover up David the man.

Hence the Chronicler chose to ignore aspects of the tradition that might detract from David's ecclesiastical stature, such as the story of David's earlier career as an outlaw, his adultery with Bathsheba, Absalom's rebellion, and much of the material in the Court History. Most striking of all, he glorified David's last words. Suppressing David's death-bed instructions to liquidate Joab and Shimei (cf. I Kings 2:5-9), the Chronicler affirmed that David's mind was engrossed to the very last with the dream of the future Temple (I Chron. 28-29), and placed on his lips one of the finest prayers to be found in the Old Testament (I Chron. 29:10-19). No one tried more earnestly than the Chronicler to encircle David's head with a halo.

And yet the Chronicler did not make all this up out of whole cloth, for there is considerable basis in the tradition for David's "churchly" interest. After all, David had brought the Ark to Jerusalem, had purchased Araunah's threshing-floor to build an altar (II Sam. 24), and had set in motion plans for building a temple. Moreover, David's interest in temple music was well established in Israelite tradition. He was "a skillful player on the lyre" (I Sam. 16:14-23; cf. Amos 6:5) and was noted as a composer of songs and laments, like the exquisite lament over Saul and Jonathan (II Sam. 1:17-27). Surely it is wrong to regard David as the author of the whole book of Psalms, which contains hymns, laments, and supplications from many times and poets.[8] But in view of David's reputation as a poet-musician, we can understand how later generations attributed the Psalter to him. Probably there is a strong element of truth in the Chronicler's claim that David instituted changes in Israel's worship service, especially in instrumental music (I Chron. 23-27). But after all this has been said, it is still true that the Chronicler's ecclesiastical portrait of David was colored by the interests of post-exilic, priestly Judaism.

Israel's Ecclesiastical History

From the account of the origin of the worshiping community under David, the Chronicler proceeds to tell the history of Israel in ecclesiastical terms. Agreeing with the author of II Samuel 7, he affirms that Yahweh's blessing

---

[8] Less than half of the psalms are attributed to David in the headings. The Davidic Psalter is discussed further in Chapter 15.

rested upon the Davidic dynasty. (Since there was only one legitimate kingship, he even passes over the tradition about the anointing of Saul!) The Northern Kingdom fell because, owing to the sin of Jeroboam I, it had separated itself from the true community of worship. The Southern Kingdom, too, eventually proved to be so corrupt that Yahweh brought severe judgment upon it. Thus the Holy City fell, the Temple—which David planned to be "exceedingly magnificent, of fame and glory throughout all lands" (I Chron. 22:5)—was destroyed, and the priests and people were taken into exile.

At this point the Chronicler begins the story found in Ezra-Nehemiah. He tells how the edict of Cyrus enabled faithful Jews to return to Jerusalem, where they immediately built an altar on which to offer burnt offerings to the God of Israel, and some years afterward rebuilt the Temple. But the Jewish community was threatened by the paganism that had precipitated the destruction of the first Temple. So next—according to the Chronicler's scheme—Ezra the priest came from Babylonia with the Law of Moses in his hand, and initiated a great religious reform aimed at maintaining the holiness of the community. And shortly after, if we follow the present order of the narratives, Nehemiah came from Babylonia to Jerusalem, and as governor of the Jews supervised the rebuilding of the walls of Jerusalem and instituted various social and religious reforms.

So Israel came back from exile, not as a nation, but as a religious community. This account is in keeping with the historical situation of the post-exilic period, as we shall see. The Chronicler's intention, however, is to show that this profound change in Israel's life was not just a response to the political vicissitudes of the period. Rather, it was a return to the charter of Judaism handed down from David.

ZERUBBABEL, THE BRANCH

Now that we have seen the place of the books of Ezra and Nehemiah in the Chronicler's history, let us turn to the pioneers who responded to Cyrus' edict and set their faces toward the homeland. We must not suppose that there was a mass exodus from Babylonia. The list given in Ezra 2 (cf. Neh. 7) puts the number at about 50,000; but this is undoubtedly an expanded census list from the time of Nehemiah several generations later. For in Nehemiah 7:5 it is explicitly stated that Nehemiah published the list.[9] The number of those "whose spirit God had stirred to go up to rebuild the house of Yahweh in Jerusalem" (Ezra 1:5) was unquestionably much smaller, and the immigration took place over a period of several generations. Many of the Jews were comfortably settled and were doing well in business; so Josephus (A.D. 37 to after A.D. 100), the

---

[9] See W. F. Albright, *The Biblical Period* [38], p. 49, and note 122.

famous Jewish historian, was correct in saying that many were loath to leave their possessions.[10] To many Jews it must have seemed sheer recklessness to start out on a long, hazardous, and costly journey that could end only in uncertainty and insecurity in the impoverished environs of Jerusalem.

Tension between Samaritans and Jews

Some time later, however, we do find a small community of people in Jerusalem under the leadership of the High Priest Jeshua (or Joshua) and Zerubbabel, the latter having succeeded Sheshbazzar as the recognized civil authority. Among the first acts of this community, according to the Chronicler's account in Ezra 3, were the building of an altar, the installation of the Levites, and the laying of the foundation of a new temple. The worship was carried out "according to the directions of David king of Israel" (Ezra 3:10), which, of course, shows the Chronicler's interest in the Davidic charter for Judaism.

During the remaining years of Cyrus' reign, however, the work was interrupted by trouble with "the people of the land" and also with the neighboring people to the north who lived in the province of Samaria. Here we see the first sign of the tension between Samaritans and Jews that eventually led to outright hostility and the building of a rival Samaritan temple on Mount Gerizim overlooking Shechem. From the Jewish standpoint, the Samaritans had been corrupted by mixing with the foreign peoples whom the Assyrians had settled in that area (see Ezra 4:2). But the Samaritans themselves felt that they were faithful adherents to the Mosaic tradition and shared the Jewish interest in rebuilding the Temple at Jerusalem. Besides, as inhabitants of the area of the former Assyrian province of Samaria, they looked with apprehension and resentment upon the possible revival of a Jewish state on their very doorstep.

The Samaritans offered to cooperate with the Jews in rebuilding the Temple, but their offer was spurned by Zerubbabel. So the hand of friendship curled into a fist. Samaritan hostility was not prompted by the Jewish rebuff alone, however, for there was undoubtedly economic and political rivalry between the two peoples. In any case, the Samaritans did everything in their power to stop the building of the Temple, which they regarded as a symbol of revived Jewish nationalism. These were the political troubles, then, that led to the suspension of the work during the remainder of the reign of Cyrus (he died in 530 B.C.), during the reign of his successor, Cambyses II (530-522 B.C.), and on into the reign of Darius I, the Great (Ezra 4:4-5:24).[11] (See Chronological Chart 8, p. 353.)

---

[10] *Antiquities of the Jews*, xi, 1, 3.

[11] Ezra 4:6-23 obviously is out of place, for the passage deals with the reigns of Xerxes (Ahasuerus) and Artaxerxes I, kings who succeeded Darius. See the summary of Persian history in J. Finegan, *Light from the Ancient Past* [42], pp. 193-205.

The Time of Haggai and Zechariah

Then, after a lapse of about eighteen years, in 520 B.C., the second year of the reign of Darius I (522-486 B.C.),[12] the work of rebuilding the Temple was resumed. We must understand Zerubbabel's leadership at that time in the context of the events that shook the Persian empire to its foundation. Cambyses, Darius' predecessor, went insane and committed suicide. His death was followed by murder and intrigue within the court and by nationalistic uprisings in the Persian provinces. After a time, Darius managed to quell the far-flung revolution, and celebrated his triumph by carving a huge relief and tri-lingual inscription high on the Behistun Rock (see Plate 7).* But in the second year of his reign revolt broke out in Babylonia under the leadership of a certain Nebuchadnezzar, a namesake of the ruler we have met previously in our study of Jeremiah. Scarcely a month after the Babylonian uprising, the Jews started to rebuild the Temple under the Davidic leadership of Zerubbabel and the High Priest Joshua.

According to Ezra 5:1, the work was inspired by two prophets, Haggai and Zechariah, whose brief writings are preserved in the Old Testament.[13] Encouraged by the apparent success of the Babylonian revolution in 520 B.C., Haggai preached with the fire of nationalism in his words. He reminded the people that economic conditions in the land were precarious because they had left Yahweh's house lying in ruins while they lived in fine, paneled houses. His very first oracle aroused the Jews to action. Hoping that Yahweh would favor them if they put first things first, the people fell in behind the leadership of Joshua the priest, and Zerubbabel the governor (Haggai 1). A month later, when the people became downcast over the contrast between their inferior structure and the splendor of Solomon's Temple, Haggai fired their imaginations with the dream of a temple whose glory would outshine that of the former temple. He announced that divine intervention would soon come, and prophesied that Yahweh would shake the heavens and the earth, as well as all nations (2:1-9), so that the treasures of all nations would be brought into the new temple. Evidently Haggai was looking forward to the downfall of the Persian empire. His final oracle, which struck the same nationalistic note, was addressed to Zerubbabel, and announced in

---

[12] The Chronicler has mistakenly dated the laying of the foundation of the Temple in the second year of Cyrus (Ezra 3:6-13) rather than the second year of Darius (Haggai 1:1-6).

* The relief portrays Darius, followed by two attendants, putting his foot on the prostrate rebel chief and pointing to the winged disc, symbol of the Zoroastrian god, Ahura Mazda. Before him stand nine rebel leaders, their necks tied together by a rope and their hands manacled behind their backs. The accompanying cuneiform inscription—written in three languages: Old Persian, Elamite, and Akkadian—opened up new vistas of knowledge, for by deciphering the Old Persian, scholars were able to translate the other two languages.

[13] The authentic prophecies of Zechariah are found in chapters 1-8; the rest of the chapters come from the circle of his later disciples.

veiled language that the Jewish governor—a descendant of Jehoiachin—was Yahweh's Anointed One, the Davidic Messiah (2:20-23).

The prophecy of Zechariah, dated slightly later, expresses the same hope for a restoration of the Jewish state under the co-leadership of the High Priest and the Davidic prince. The oracles are cast in a bizarre form that was popular in Judaism in the late post-exilic period. Like the prophecy of Second Isaiah, this new type deals with the end-time, the consummation of history in Yahweh's sovereign purpose; but unlike the earlier prophecy, it is couched in cryptic language, abounds with marvelous visions of the future, and foresees the coming of a dramatic finale when the foes of Yahweh will be shattered and his kingdom will be established.[14] In the conviction that the might of the nations will be broken by Yahweh in a miraculous fashion (see Zech. 4:6-10), the prophet Zechariah names Zerubbabel as the Davidic Messiah. Speaking to the High Priest Joshua, to whom was given charge over the Temple, Yahweh says through the prophet: "Behold, I will bring my servant the Branch" (3:8; cf. 6:12). The word "messiah" (anointed one) is not used here, for it was only in the later period of Judaism that the term took on the special meaning of *the* Anointed One, the Messiah (Greek: *Christos*). In the earlier tradition of messianic prophecy, the future Davidic king is referred to as "a shoot from the stump of Jesse," "the branch" that will "grow out of his roots" (Is. 11:1). In Zechariah, the word "branch" is a term for the messianic king, the descendant of David's line. According to the prophet, the sign of Zerubbabel's messianic authority is that he will complete the building of the Temple:

> Thus says Yahweh of hosts: "Behold, the man whose name is the Branch; for he shall grow up in his place, and he shall build the temple of Yahweh. It is he who shall build the temple of Yahweh, and shall bear royal honor, and shall sit and rule upon his throne. And there shall be a priest by his throne, and peaceful understanding shall be between them both."
>
> —ZECHARIAH 6:12-13; *cf.* 4:6-10

Possibly the name Zerubbabel once stood in the passage from which this quotation is taken (verses 9-15), but for some unknown reason it was deleted. In any case, the prophecy of Zechariah leaves no doubt that the symbol of the Branch referred to Zerubbabel.

The Second Temple

In spite of attempts by the satrap of Syria and the leaders of Samaria to obstruct the project, the Temple was finished in the year 515 B.C. When the

---

[14] This type of prophecy is known as an "apocalypse," a Greek term meaning "revelation"— that is, revelation of the shape of things to come. Since the book of Daniel is the best Old Testament example of apocalyptic literature, discussion of this kind of thinking will be postponed until the final chapter of this book.

project is viewed in light of the troubles of the Persian empire in the first years of Darius' reign, it is apparent that the Jews were motivated by the hope for the revival of the Jewish state. Zerubbabel mysteriously vanished from the scene at this point. What happened to him we do not know. It has been conjectured that the Persians spirited him away, fearing that the messianic movement centering in him was a symptom of revolution. In any event, we hear no more of attempts to revive the Davidic state during the Persian period. The leadership of the community was now vested in the High Priest, Joshua, and his successors, and henceforth Israel was to be a temple-centered community, a kingdom of priests, patterned after the instructions which, according to the Chronicler, were given by David.

The second Temple did not compare in splendor to the Temple of Solomon, which had been a product of the artistry of Phoenician architects. We are told that when the old men who remembered the former Temple saw the foundations of the second Temple laid, they wept with a loud voice (Ezra 3:12-13). And yet the modest new Temple served as the center and bulwark of Israel's life in the post-exilic period. What was lacking in architectural beauty was covered over by the great devotion that the people lavished upon it, and above all, by the conviction that it was the place where Yahweh was enthroned in the midst of Israel.

As we have seen, the Chronicler was right in emphasizing the importance of music and praise in the history of Israel. To be sure, his writing reflects the interests of the post-exilic Temple, but he was fundamentally correct in believing that the continuity of worship extended back to David. In a profound sense, the foundation of the second Temple was the religious devotion of the people. As a worshiping community Israel was a singing people, and instrumental and choral music had an important place in their life. Both in the Chronicler's Work and in the headings of the Psalms we hear of leaders of musical guilds—men like Heman, Asaph, and Ethan or Jeduthun—who had a special role in the worship service. And, according to the Chronicler, the main function of the Levites was to lead the worshiping congregation in praise and prayer.

Israel's life and thought were nourished in the Temple until its final destruction in the Roman period (A.D. 70). Since it was not always possible for Jews living outside Jerusalem to attend the Temple services, however, synagogues began to dot the Palestinian countryside during the post-exilic period and eventually were found throughout the Dispersion, as, for instance, during Paul's missionary travels. The synagogue made a deep impression upon Israel's life and thought, and in the long run out-lived the Temple. But during the post-exilic period there was no real substitute for the Temple. Devout Jews made pilgrimages to Jerusalem to participate in the drama of priestly sacrifice and congregational praise. In the services of worship, as we can sense from the book of Psalms —sometimes called "the hymnbook of the second Temple"—they found comfort in their sorrow, forgiveness in their guilt, and hope in time of trouble. A day in Yahweh's courts, said a psalmist, was better than a thousand spent elsewhere.

> How lovely is thy dwelling place,
>   O Yahweh of hosts!
> My soul longs, yea, faints
>   for the courts of Yahweh;
> my heart and flesh sing for joy
>   to the living God.
>   —PSALM 84:1-2

The Disciples of Second Isaiah

We shall defer further consideration of the Psalms until the next chapter. But before turning to the activities of Nehemiah and Ezra it is appropriate to say a word about the disciples of Second Isaiah whose writings are found at the end of the book of Isaiah (chapters 56-66). This miscellaneous collection of poems, often put under the rubric of "Trito-Isaiah," seems to reflect the early post-exilic period when returning exiles awakened from Second Isaiah's glorious dream of the imminent Kingdom of God to the sober and somber realities of history. When one reads these chapters with this struggling, disillusioned community in mind, the shift of accent from the message of Second Isaiah becomes understandable. Second Isaiah had announced that Israel's vocation was to be a light to the nations, mediating through her sufferings the blessing of God upon all mankind; but here there is more of a disposition to cry out for vengeance against Israel's enemies and to portray Yahweh's gory vindication. Second Isaiah had summoned all Israelites, without exception, to seek Yahweh and cast themselves upon his forgiving mercy; but here there is more of a tendency to segregate the righteous and the wicked by the standards of sabbath observance, offering of sacrifices, avoidance of eating pork, and so on.

Yet there are also echoes of the master's teaching in this collection—showing that the spirit of prophecy was not dead. No finer interpretation of the demands of the covenant can be found anywhere in the Old Testament than in this exposition of the meaning of fasting (58:1-12):

> Is not this the fast that I choose:
>   to loose the bonds of wickedness,
>   to undo the thongs of the yoke,
> to let the oppressed go free,
>   and to break every yoke?
> Is it not to share your bread with the hungry,
>   and bring the homeless poor into your house;
> when you see the naked, to cover him,
>   and not to hide yourself from your own flesh?
>   —ISAIAH 58:6-7

And Second Isaiah could well have written this solemn reminder of Israel's dependence upon the grace which forgives and renews:

> Thus says the high and lofty One
>   who inhabits eternity, whose name is Holy:
> "I dwell in the high and holy place,
>   and also with him who is of a contrite and humble spirit,
> to revive the spirit of the humble,
>   and to revive the heart of the contrite."
>
> —ISAIAH 57:15

Recall that when Jesus began his ministry in Nazareth he turned to a Servant passage found in this part of the book of Isaiah (Is. 61:1-3; see Luke 4:16-30).

RECONSTRUCTION UNDER NEHEMIAH

From the completion of the Temple (515 B.C.) to the appearance of Nehemiah in Jerusalem (445 B.C.) there is a span of about three generations. In this period, Persian culture reached its greatest height, as evidenced by the impressive ruins standing at Persepolis, the main capital of the Persian empire (see Plate 6). Both Darius I and Xerxes, builders of this magnificent capital, waged campaigns against Greece, only to be defeated at the famous battles of Marathon (490 B.C.), Thermopylae, and Salamis (480 B.C.).

Since the Chronicler leaps over this period in order to come as quickly as possible to the great cultic reform of Ezra, we must turn to other sources for the meager information about Jewish affairs that is available. The Elephantine papyri, to which we have alluded before, come from the fifth century, but they are chiefly important for an understanding of Judaism in the Egyptian Dispersion. There are, however, several minor prophecies that throw some light on conditions in Palestine during this period.

Obadiah's Denunciation of Edom

The prophecy of Obadiah is a bitter outcry against Edom, the nation which—it will be remembered—had seized part of the territory of Judah after the fall of Jerusalem (cf. Mal. 1:2-5). Obadiah denounced the pride and treach-

DARIUS ON HIS THRONE *holds a scepter in one hand and a lotus blossom in the other. Behind him stands the crown prince, Xerxes—the Ahasuerus mentioned in Ezra 4:6 and in the book of Esther. The king is receiving a foreign dignitary, whose hand is raised to his mouth in a gesture of respect. This relief was found at Persepolis.*

ery of Edom, which was traditionally related to Israel according to the story of the twin brothers, Jacob and Esau. Yahweh, said the prophet, was about to summon the nations to destroy Edom for the violence done to "Jacob." The date of Obadiah's prophecy cannot be determined exactly. The reference to Edom's malicious actions in the day of Judah's ruin (vss. 11-14) dates it after the fall of Jerusalem in 587 B.C. Yet since the destruction of Edom is presented as a future threat, not a description of what was happening (vss. 1-10), it must have been written before the fifth century B.C. when Arab tribes began pressing into Edomite territory from the Arabian Desert. By the fourth century these invaders, known as Nabateans, had claimed this cultivated area as their own and had made Petra their splendid capital.

Malachi's Plea for Sincere Worship

Other evidence on conditions in the Jewish community is provided by the book of Malachi, which was probably written a generation or so before the

THE MOUNTAIN FORTRESS OF SELA *dominates the basin in which the Nabateans (successors of the Edomites) carved the "rose city" of Petra into the red limestone cliffs. Since the Hebrew word* sela' *means "rock," there is probably an allusion to the Edomite acropolis (modern Umm el-Bayyarah) in Obadiah, verse 3: "The pride of your heart has deceived you, you who live in the clefts of the rock, whose dwelling is high. . . ." On the Nabateans see Nelson Glueck,* Deities and Dolphins *(Farrar, Straus & Giroux: 1965).*

arrival of Nehemiah. At this time the Jewish community was ruled by a Persian governor (see Mal. 1:8). The second Temple had been completed, but the people's heart was no longer in their worship. Echoing Obadiah's outcry against Edom, this prophet began by giving a bitter twist to the patriarchal story of the twin brothers: "I have loved Jacob, but I have hated Esau"—in this way stressing Yahweh's favor for Israel (1:2-5). Yet, said the prophet, this divine favor only throws into sharp relief the people's faithless and ungrateful actions. He accused them of dishonoring Yahweh by placing polluted food on the altar and by offering sacrifices—blind, lame, sickly animals—that would not even be accepted by their governor. The people were going through the motions of ritual, but clearly they found the whole thing boring and wearisome (1:13). It would be better, said the prophet, to close the doors of the Temple than to go on like that, for Yahweh deserved nothing but the best gifts and the most sincere worship of men's hearts. With a note of universalism, he pointed out that even the Gentiles magnified Yahweh's name (1:11; cf. 2:10), whereas Israel was profaning it by inadequate and insincere worship. The priests were not guarding the true torah, men were divorcing their Jewish wives to marry foreign women, and social injustices abounded. And to make matters worse, the people were complaining that serving God did not "pay off," for it was evident to them that it was the evil-doers who came out on top. "Where is the God of justice?" they asked (2:17). Why serve God if religion yields no tangible benefits (3:13-15)?

Despite the vigor of Malachi's critique, the prophet himself does not measure up to the stature of his predecessors. He suggested that if men would only present a tenth (tithe) of their income, and stop "robbing God" of what was due him, then Yahweh would pour upon them a great blessing, and Israel would be great among the nations (3:6-12). In a vivid passage—later interpreted by Christians to refer to John the Baptist, the forerunner of the Christ—he announced that the Messenger [15] would appear to prepare the way for the coming of Yahweh. Suddenly, he said, Yahweh would come to his Temple, and on "the day of his coming" men would shrink back in fear, for "he is like a refiner's fire." Yahweh's purpose, first of all, is to refine the priests, purifying them until they present "right offerings" to Yahweh; and then his judgment will fall upon sorcerers, adulterers, false witnesses, and those who oppress the poor and defenseless (3:1-5). Even now, said the prophet, the segregation of the righteous from the wicked is beginning, for the names of those who fear Yahweh are recorded in a "book of remembrance," and they will be spared on the day of judgment (3:16-18). The writing ends with the prophecy that Yahweh will send Elijah, the prophet *par excellence*, to summon Israel to repentance and to prepare the people for "the great and terrible day of Yahweh" (4:5).

---

[15] The expression "my messenger" in 3:1 is *mal'aki* in Hebrew—that is, the name of the prophet as given in 1:1. Probably this is the source of the name attributed to the prophet. Actually, we know nothing about the author of the book.

Joel and the Army of Locusts

The prophecy of Joel may come from this same period, although it is difficult to assign any precise date to it. It is generally believed that Joel lived some time in the period from 500 to 350 B.C. Whatever the date, the occasion of his preaching was a plague of locusts that had devastated the country, not an uncommon scourge in ancient Palestine. Moreover, the land had suffered a great famine. To Joel, the "army" of invading locusts, whose attack he described with extraordinary vividness, was the sign of the impending Day of Yahweh.[16] Urgently the prophet summoned the people to a great fast, perhaps in connection with the festival of the New Year in the Fall, for repentance and lamentation.

> "Yet even now," says Yahweh,
> return to me with all your heart,
> with fasting, with weeping, and with mourning;
> and rend your hearts and not your garments."
> —JOEL 2:12

Then, with a sudden shift from warning to promise, he announced that beyond the judgment was the day when Yahweh would restore "the years which the swarming locust has eaten" (2:25) and would pour out his spirit upon young and old (2:28-29; cf. Acts 2). Joel's prophecy is reminiscent of pre-exilic preaching concerning the Day of Yahweh, but it also contains descriptions of cosmic upheavals like those found in post-exilic apocalyptic literature (2:30-32).

Thus the books of Obadiah, Malachi, and Joel present a picture of a struggling Jewish community, threatened from the outside by neighboring peoples and the pressures of foreign culture, and weakened from within by poverty, discontentment, and religious apathy. This was the situation when Nehemiah and Ezra made their appearance.

The Coming of Nehemiah

Before proceeding further, we must mention briefly one of the major critical problems of the Old Testament. Who came to Jerusalem first—Ezra or Nehemiah? The date for the beginning of Nehemiah's first term as governor is definitely fixed as the twentieth year of the reign of Artaxerxes (Neh. 1:1; 2:1). It is generally agreed that this must refer to Artaxerxes I Longimanus (see Chronological Chart 9, p. 449) and that therefore we can pinpoint the date of

---

[16] Some scholars believe that the locust army is a veiled description of an invading foreign power. See the discussion by Arvid S. Kapelrud, *Joel Studies* [193], pp. 14-17.

Nehemiah's arrival as 445 B.C.[17] Beyond this point, however, the chronological picture becomes blurred and confused. The Chronicler, believing that Ezra came first, dated his appearance in Jerusalem in the seventh year of Artaxerxes I— that is, 458 B.C. (Ezra 7:7-8). Hence the Chronicler proceeded immediately from the completion of the Temple in 515 B.C. (Ezra 6) to the account of Ezra's return from Babylon (Ezra 7-8). Believing that Ezra's career overlapped that of Nehemiah, who arrived a few years later, he inserted part of the Nehemiah story (Neh. 1-7) into the middle of the account of Ezra's career (Ezra 7-10 and Neh. 8-10). But the Chronicler did not always keep the historical record straight. He seems to have written more than a century later, when memories had become dim about the sequence of things. Probably he reasoned that Ezra should have come first since his task was more urgent and had greater priority. It is strange, however, that if Ezra and Nehemiah were working together no mention is made of it in the Chronicler's sources: the Memoirs of Nehemiah and those of Ezra.

A number of historians believe that the Chronicler was broadly right in dating Ezra and Nehemiah under the reign of Artaxerxes I. He was wrong only in

---

[17] Archaeological evidence enables us to fix this date. One of the Elephantine letters, dating from the year 408 B.C., mentions "the sons of Sanballat, the governor of Samaria" (Pritchard *Ancient Near Eastern Texts*, "Petition for Authorization to Rebuild the Temple of Yaho," p. 491). Governor Sanballat was a contemporary of Nehemiah, a fact which precludes dating Nehemiah under a later Persian king bearing the name Artaxerxes.

TOMBS OF PERSIAN KINGS *were hewn into the solid rock of this cliff face near Persepolis. At right is the tomb of Darius I, who authorized the rebuilding of the Temple (Ezra 3:5-6); the center tomb is that of Artaxerxes I, possibly the king who appointed Nehemiah as his cupbearer; the one at the left is that of Darius II.*

failing to locate Ezra in the latter part of this monarch's reign. One plausible view is that Ezra came in the thirty-seventh year (the word "thirty" having dropped out of the text of Ezra 7:7 by a scribal mistake) of Artaxerxes I, in which case the date would be 428 B.C.[18] If this view is correct, the story may have gone something like this. During his first term as governor, Nehemiah worked on the wall of Jerusalem and made some attempt at reform. Since he carried only political authority, however, he was unable to bring about the sweeping religious reforms needed. So he returned to the Persian capital and persuaded the authorities to send someone with proper religious credentials. Nehemiah returned for his second term as governor in 432 B.C., and about five years later came Ezra, the priest, with the Law as a basis for reform.

Admittedly, this reconstruction is at best a probability. Some scholars, who also recognize that Ezra followed Nehemiah, argue that the Persian king referred to in Ezra 7:7-8 is not Artaxerxes I (465-424 B.C.) but Artaxerxes II (404-358). In this case, Ezra would have appeared in Jerusalem in 398 B.C., after Nehemiah's terms as governor had concluded.

Here we shall assume that the Nehemiah-Ezra sequence is the proper one, and go no further into the complex historical problem. Incidentally, this approach will give us an opportunity to treat the great reform of Ezra as the climax of this chapter.

With the exception of chapters 8-10—the materials dealing with Ezra—the book of Nehemiah is based largely on the Memoirs of Nehemiah, which were written by his own hand.[19] This is the only example of the continuous story of a man's career, written in the style of autobiography, that we have in the Old Testament. It is a historical record of the greatest importance; and as a narrative it is written in a fresh and interesting manner. Here we can only summarize what the reader should pursue in detail for himself. The story tells how Nehemiah, a cup-bearer to Artaxerxes I in the court at Susa, the Persian winter capital (see photo, p. 525), heard of the dismal conditions within Jerusalem; how he prevailed upon the king to send him there with the authority of a governor; how, after an inspection tour of the walls at night, he roused the people to undertake the rebuilding of the city's defenses; how the project was completed in fifty-two days, even though some of the workers had to carry a tool in one hand and a weapon in the other because of the hostility of neighboring peoples; and how at last, amid scenes of singing and thanksgiving, the walls were dedicated.

---

[18] See W. F. Albright, *The Biblical Period* [38], p. 53 and note 133; also John Bright, *History of Israel* [40], chap. 10, especially the excursus on "The Date of Ezra's Mission to Jerusalem," pp. 375-386. On the date of Ezra there is essential agreement between the Albright school and Martin Noth. See the latter's *History of Israel* [44], pp. 315-335.

[19] The Memoirs, found in the passages listed on p. 434, have been supplemented by lists and other material added by the Chronicler.

Nehemiah's Reforms

Throughout his first term as governor, as well as during the second term, which began in 432 B.C. (Neh. 13:6-7), Nehemiah introduced various reforms to bind the Jews into a closely knit community. When we remember the powerful pressures that threatened to erase Israel's identity, it is clear that this policy was necessary, even though today we might look at it askance. During the days when the walls were being rebuilt, Sanballat, the governor of Samaria, and his allies did everything in their power to frustrate the project. Sanballat laid claim to the Jewish territory, for it had been assigned to the province of Samaria by the Babylonians after the destruction of Jerusalem. Moreover, the Ammonites of Transjordan and the Edomites to the south of Jerusalem looked with a jealous eye upon the Jews' activities. First these enemies accused the Jews of plotting a revolution against Persia; then they ridiculed the feeble strength of the walls; and finally they threatened to attack. Clearly their design was to break the morale of the workers. And some of the Jews themselves, especially members of the wealthier class, took an easy-going attitude toward their neighbors, even to the point of mingling and intermarrying with them. To meet these circumstances, Nehemiah introduced and enforced a stiff policy of exclusivism, thereby sharpening the division between Jew and Gentile, and between Jew and Samaritan.

Membership in the Jewish community, according to Nehemiah, was determined by two standards. The first was birth. We are told that when the walls were built God put it into Nehemiah's head to enroll all the citizens according to genealogy (Neh. 7:5-69; cf. Ezra 2). In the context of the rest of Nehemiah's work, this can mean only one thing: It was important to be born into the right family and to be able to trace one's ancestry to a Jewish father, grandfather, and so on. During his second term, Nehemiah strictly prohibited intermarriage, on the basis of Deuteronomic Law (Neh. 13; cf. Deut. 23:3 ff.), and even banished a priest from office when it was discovered that he was married to a

CHRONOLOGICAL CHART 9

B.C.	EGYPT	JUDAH	MESOPOTAMIA
500	Egypt under Persian rule, 525-401	(Malachi, c. 500-450) Ezra's mission, 458(?) Nehemiah arrives, 445 Ezra's mission, c. 428(?)	Persia Xerxes I (Ahasuerus), 486-465 Artaxerxes I (Longimanus), 465-424 Xerxes II, 424-423 Darius II, 423-404
400		Ezra's mission, c. 398(?)	Artaxerxes II (Mnemon), 404-358

daughter of Sanballat, the Samaritan governor. Nehemiah was especially angered by the fact that children of mixed marriages could not even speak the Hebrew tongue. Later on, Ezra carried these reform measures even further. Not only did he denounce mixed marriages, but he forcibly broke up any that had already been made (Ezra 10:2-5).

It was probably in this period that the book of Ruth was written. This charming short story, which the narrator placed in the rural setting of the ancient Tribal Confederacy, tells how Ruth, a Moabitess, was providentially led from her home country to Bethlehem of Judah, where she married an influential citizen, Boaz, and became the great-grandmother of David, Israel's greatest king. So intent is the author on telling an entrancing story that his purpose is not altogether clear. Many scholars believe that the story is a subtle piece of "propaganda" against the view that one's position within Israel was dependent upon purity of blood or correctness of genealogy. For God's greatest favor was bestowed upon Israel through a mixed marriage—the very thing that Nehemiah and Ezra frowned upon! Even if the author did not intend a direct attack upon the policy of Ezra and Nehemiah, his delightful story, with its human interest and its spacious view of Yahweh's sovereignty, shows that tendencies other than narrow exclusivism were at work in post-exilic Judaism.

The second qualification for being a Jew, according to Nehemiah's policy, was that of loyalty to the Torah and faithful support of the Temple. The purity of the people demanded strict observance of the sabbath. When he found that work and commercial activity were being carried on during the holy day, he threatened that divine wrath would fall upon the people if the abuse were not stopped. He organized a regular service of worship in the Temple and demanded that the people support the Temple staff with their tithes. Thus a strong wall was built around the Jewish community—not just the wall of Jerusalem but the wall of an exclusiveness based on birth and religious loyalty.

What was the real motive behind these severe measures? Political factors were present, to be sure. But more was involved than just a question of Jewish survival or of restoring prestige to Jerusalem. The desire to maintain Jewish purity was fundamentally a struggle to preserve the identity of the people Israel and the distinctiveness of Israel's faith in the face of the tremendous cultural pressures at work during the Persian period. With some justification, Nehemiah reminded the people of the folly of Solomon's cosmopolitanism, especially the influence of his foreign wives. The sympathetic student will agree that the work of Ezra and Nehemiah did not rest on nationalism or racialism, but upon a passionate loyalty to Israel's religious heritage, for, "they feared that the faintly burning flame of Judaism might be quenched altogether." [20]

We have seen that the problem of syncretism had haunted Israel ever since the time of the occupation of Canaan. During the Exile, when the people lived

---

[20] H. H. Rowley, *The Rediscovery of the Old Testament* (Philadelphia: Westminster, 1946), p. 164.

an uprooted existence, the problem was intensified. And in the post-exilic period
the threat of cultural assimilation persisted, especially with the conscious effort
after the rise of Alexander the Great to absorb all religious and cultural differences into the synthesis known as Hellenism. The mystery is that Israel resisted
assimilation, and creatively transformed what was borrowed from others into a
vehicle for expressing her own faith. Israel's calling was not to be "like the
nations," eventually to be swallowed up in whatever empire ruled the earth, but
to be a "peculiar" people, set apart from the nations. It is easy to criticize the
narrow theological focus of Judaism under Nehemiah and Ezra. The spacious
vista of Second Isaiah was clouded over, and there was an intense concentration
upon participation in the holy community through family descent and obedience to the Law. But it was this circumscribed community that preserved the
spiritual heritage which eventually burst with transforming power upon nations
and cultures and turned the course of Western civilization into a new channel.

EZRA, THE FATHER OF JUDAISM

Some years after Nehemiah began his second term as governor in Jerusalem, if
our chronology is correct, a priest named Ezra received permission to conduct

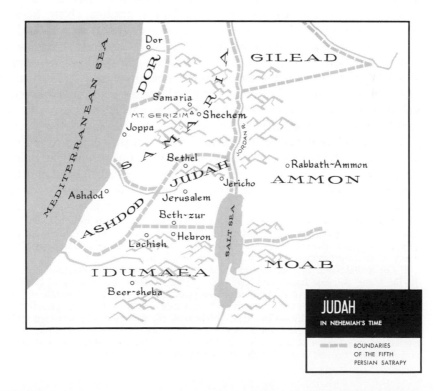

a caravan of exiles from Babylonia to Palestine.[21] Unlike Nehemiah, Ezra was not sent to Palestine by the Persian king as a political authority; rather, with Persian permission, given perhaps as a result of Nehemiah's influence, he went to investigate religious matters in Jerusalem. He is pictured as "a scribe skilled in the law of Moses, which Yahweh, the God of Israel, had given" (Ezra 7:6). Elsewhere, he is referred to as "Ezra the priest, the scribe of the law of the God of heaven" (7:12, 21).

A Ceremony of Covenant Renewal

One of the important items in the baggage that Ezra brought from Babylonia was a copy of "the book of the law of Moses" (Neh. 8:1). In the month of the Fall harvest festival, which was known as the Feast of Taber-nacles,[22] the people gathered "as one man" in a public square in Jerusalem to hear what was in Ezra's book of the Law (Neh. 8:1-8). Ezra climbed up to a specially constructed wooden pulpit and, while the people stood in rapt atten-tion, read to them from early morning until noon. Levites stood at his side to give "the sense" in order that the people could "understand the reading." The next day the people began the celebration of the Feast of Tabernacles accord-ing to the directions of the Law (see Lev. 23:42-43): they cut branches and built booths ("tabernacles") to live in during the seven-day festival, and during this whole time the readings from the Law continued (Neh. 8:13-18). The climax of the ceremonies came in a solemn act of covenant renewal (Neh. 9) when the people confessed their sins and Ezra, as a covenant mediator, offered a prayer on behalf of the people, ending with the words of covenant renewal (Neh. 9:38). The covenant document was officially signed by the representatives of the people,[23] and all the rest of the people joined with them and took an oath under penalty of a curse "to walk in God's law which was given by Moses the servant of God" (Neh. 10).

This procedure is strikingly similar to the covenant ceremony of Josiah's time as related in II Kings 23:1-3. The same features are present: the public reading of the Law, the confession of sin, the cultic and social reform, and the solemn covenant to follow the divine commandments under penalty of a curse. The

---

[21] The Ezra story, which is now out of order, should be read in the following sequence: Ezra's journey (Ezra 7-8); the reading of the Law (Neh. 8); the expulsion of foreign wives (Ezra 9-10); the renewal of the covenant (Neh. 9). The section on the expulsion of foreign wives seems to presuppose that the Law had already been read.

[22] For a discussion of this festival which was celebrated at the beginning of the year, see R. De Vaux, *Ancient Israel* [62], pp. 495-502. He explains the building of booths (*sukkoth*) by referring to the ancient custom, which survives to the present in Palestine, of erecting huts made out of branches in the orchards and vineyards during fruit and grape harvest.

[23] According to the Chronicler's text, "Nehemiah the governor" was a co-signer (Neh. 10:1). If one adopts the later date for Ezra's arrival (398 B.C.), these words would have to be re-garded as an addition. Admittedly, the Memoirs of Ezra (at least those written in the first person) make no reference to Nehemiah's presence in Jerusalem.

covenant ceremony under Ezra, as well as that under Josiah, was based on an ancient tradition of periodic covenant-renewal at the sanctuary. At such times it was the function of the Levites to act as interpreters of the Law when it was read in the public assemblies, for the Law was not just special direction to the priests but teaching for the whole community. Thus the distinction arose between the "priest" and the "Levite," as we find it, for instance, in the parable of the Good Samaritan (Luke 10:30-37). The priests who claimed descent from Aaron were in charge of the sacrifice at the altar; the Levites who claimed Moses as an ancestor (Ex. 2:1) had the task of giving an exposition of the meaning of Israel's faith (II Chron. 15:3; 17:8-9; 30:22; 35:3), just as they are described as doing when Ezra read the Law.[24]

Ezra's Book of the Law

What was "the book of the Law" that Ezra read to the people? On this question there is no agreement. A variety of suggestions has been made, including the Holiness Code, the Priestly Code, Ezekiel's plan of restoration (Ezek. 40-48), Deuteronomy, and the Pentateuch. The problem could be solved, some think, by figuring out how long it took Ezra to finish his reading. But this is a difficult task, since the Levites used up some unknown amount of time in giving their interpretations. And it is not explicitly stated that Ezra read the whole "book of the Law" from beginning to end. Perhaps he selected certain key passages as a prelude to the covenant-renewal ceremony. The Deuteronomic Law is a good possibility, especially in view of the place given to the Levites in Deuteronomic tradition, but Ezra's reform seems to presuppose instruction in matters of a more priestly character. The P Code is often suggested, but this view assumes that P had an independent existence at this late time, which is dubious (see pp. 380-392). So we come to the view that was evidently held by the Chronicler himself—namely, that the "book of the Law" that Ezra read was the Pentateuch, as edited by priests during the Babylonian exile.

If this is true, Ezra's greatest contribution was to establish the Pentateuch as the authoritative canon for Jewish faith and practice. The word "canon," which is Greek in origin, refers in its primary sense to any measurement or yardstick—a carpenter's rule, for example. In a metaphorical sense, the Greeks referred to their classics as *kanones*—that is, standards of excellence. But as applied to the Old Testament the word does not refer to the literary excellence of "classics," even though parts of the Old Testament do rate high according to literary standards. Rather, the claim is made that this literature is *sacred* scripture and as such constitutes the community's rule for faith and conduct. In the time of Ezra and later, the authority of the Pentateuch was underscored by the dogma that this was none other than the "book of the Law of Moses" that had been

---

[24] See Gerhard von Rad, *Studies in Deuteronomy* [163], pp. 13-14, and G. Ernest Wright, *Interpreter's Bible*, II, pp. 315-316.

delivered by God to Moses on Mount Sinai. Ezra probably introduced the Pentateuch as the officially recognized Mosaic tradition and, by his cultic reforms, brought Israel's life into conformity with this norm. He is rightly called "the father of Judaism," for under his inflence the life and religion of the Jews were molded by the sacred Torah.

The Samaritan Pentateuch

The Jews had no monopoly on the Pentateuch, however. It was also the scripture of the Samaritan community, who followed Mosaic tradition too. The tension that developed between Jew and Samaritan was not over the authority of the Law (Pentateuch), but over the interpretation of its meaning, and particularly over the issue of who the true people of the Law were. Created originally by political and economic factors in the early post-exilic period, the split between the Jews and the Samaritans gradually widened until eventually, perhaps in the middle of the fourth century, the Samaritans built their own temple on Mount Gerizim (see photo, p. 90).[25] According to a New Testament story, when Jesus paused at Jacob's well while passing through Samaria, a Samaritan woman reminded him that the Jews had no dealings with the Samaritans, for they worshiped God in separate places (John 4:4-29). Even today a colony of Samaritans lives near Mount Gerizim. Their priests proudly display to visitors their scrolls of the Pentateuch, which is the sole scriptural basis of their religion.

THE LAW AND THE PROPHETS

Ezra, then, gave great impetus to the development of "legalism"—the strict conformity to Law—which came to be one of the major characteristics of post-exilic Judaism. In Christian circles, legalism is a "loaded" word, largely because of the Christian protest against the view that man's relation to God, his "justification" or rightness with God, is based on his righteous deeds in obedience to the Law (see the parable of the Publican and the Pharisee in Luke 18:9-14, and Paul's discussions of justification by faith, Gal. 2:16; 3:11). In time, a sharp antithesis grew up between grace and Law, and in some Christian circles it was believed that the whole Old Testament was under the dominion of Law. Although we cannot go into the issue as presented in the New Testament, in fairness to post-exilic Judaism we must correct certain one-sided views about the place of the Law in Jewish faith.

To begin with, Ezra did not invent the emphasis on obedience to the Law.

---

[25] The Gerizim temple was destroyed by the Jewish leader John Hyrcanus in 128 B.C., 200 years after it was built, according to Josephus (*Antiquities*, xiii, 9, 1; *Jewish Wars*, i, 2, 6). If Josephus' reckoning is correct, it must have been built about the middle of the fourth century B.C.

As we have seen time and again in earlier chapters, the giving of the Law had an important and indispensable place in Israel's covenant faith from the very first. Man's relation to God, according to the Israelite faith, lays upon him obligations in the area of worship and social relations within the covenant community. The Ten Commandments, which probably go back to the Mosaic period, are the ancient witness to the divine demand. And, as we have seen, the Law was expanded and refined as Israel faced in new historical situations the question: "What does Yahweh require of you?" The detailed prescriptions found in the Pentateuch are the end result of a legal development that had its source in the ancient covenant of Sinai.

Grace and Law

Second, there is no basis in Israel's faith for the notion that the Law is just a code to be obeyed, as we dutifully obey the laws of a city or a state. Back of the specific laws stands the Law-giver, who is none other than the God who has graciously redeemed his people and guided them in their historical pilgrimage. The preface to the Ten Commandments, "I am Yahweh your God who brought you out of the land of Egypt, out of the house of bondage," is the introduction to all the laws of Israel. As we have seen repeatedly, the Law is set within the context of the "good news" of what Yahweh has done for his people. His deeds of benevolence, his *grace*, stirred the people to contrition and gratitude, and provided the motive for serving him with heart, being, and strength. The book of Deuteronomy, which was the basis for a great legal reform, is one of the most eloquent expressions of Israel's understanding that grace was more important than Law. In Israel's faith, the gospel of what God has done precedes the exposition of what men must do.

The relationship between gospel and law comes to clear expression in the covenant-renewal ceremony of Ezra's time. According to Nehemiah 9, the making of the covenant was preceded by a long prayer, which is essentially a confession of Israel's faith. The public prayer is unique in that it is a recital of the whole history of Israel—or, better, the history of Yahweh's dealing with his people. It articulates the community's remembrance of her unique history, her life-story. Here is an outline of the salient aspects of the prayer:

1. Yahweh, the only God, is creator and sustainer of all that is (verse 6).
2. He called Abraham out of Ur of Babylonia and promised to give his descendants an inheritance in Canaan (vss. 7-8).
3. When Israel was oppressed in Egypt, Yahweh kept his promise. He manifested his presence in their midst by various signs and wonders, and by giving the Law to Moses on Mount Sinai (vss. 9-15).
4. In spite of Israel's incapacity for faith, Yahweh showed himself

as "a God ready to forgive, gracious and merciful, slow to anger and abounding in steadfast love." Rebellious Israel was sustained in the wilderness by divine grace (vss. 16-21).

5. Yahweh gave Israel kingdoms and peoples, and brought them victoriously into Canaan. Thus the people prospered and increased (vss. 22-25).

6. Nevertheless, Israel continued to be rebellious. So Yahweh disciplined his people, raising up prophets to warn them and giving the people into the hand of enemies when they refused to listen. However, Yahweh graciously spared a remnant (vss. 26-31).

7. Especially since the time of the kings of Assyria, the hardships have been grievous. Yet Yahweh has been just in all these events. He has been faithful; the people have been unfaithful (vss. 32-34).

8. Because of their sins the people are now slaves (i.e., vassals of Persia) in the very land that Yahweh gave them, and its rich yield is taken away by heavy taxation (vss. 35-37).

This prayer is a stirring recital of past events in which, according to the confession of faith, Yahweh had been active in Israel's history. It resounds with the note of Yahweh's initiative, his grace, his redemptive activity. On the basis of this declaration the people renewed the covenant and dedicated themselves to serve Yahweh according to "the Law which was given by Moses."

Rejoicing in the Law

Third, we must not get the idea that the Law, conceived of as a gift from Yahweh, was regarded as burdensome. Later on, it is true, the Law was hedged about by so many casuistic rules—for instance, on the subject of what constitutes work on the sabbath—that the common people found difficulty in keeping it. However, in the Old Testament period, and even more so in the rabbinic period that followed, the Jewish attitude toward the Law was one of great rejoicing. To obey the Law was, to use a later rabbinical expression, to take upon one's self "the yoke of the Kingdom"—that is, to surrender to the sovereignty of God. But, according to testimonies found in the Psalms, the yoke was easy and the burden was light. The devout Jew took great delight in the study of the Law, for it was the source of life and blessing (see Ps. 1). Its precepts, rejoicing the heart, were "more to be desired . . . than gold" (Ps. 19:7-14). The longest psalm in the Psalter is devoted to a praise of the Law (Ps. 119).

Finally, we must not suppose that there was a sharp antithesis between the Law and the prophetic tradition. To be sure, the corpus called the Prophets—the second division of the present Hebrew Bible (see Chart, p. 556)—was not canonized until considerably later. But it was preserved, read, and interpreted during the post-exilic period. Indeed, instead of opposing prophecy, the post-exilic priests wanted to take the prophetic demands seriously, as can be seen by a careful study of Ezra's prayer. They realized that the prophetic message of divine judgment had been confirmed by the events of history. The remnant, whom Yahweh had spared from national destruction and exile, took to heart the lessons of history as interpreted by prophets. Far from repudiating the ethical demands of the prophets, the priests of Judaism attempted to "put teeth" into prophetic teaching. "It is very doubtful," says a British scholar, "if Ezra thought of this religion [Judaism] as in any way the antithesis of prophetic religion. He doubtless thought he was serving the ideals of the prophets, and embodying them in the Law, that they might achieve more than the preaching of the prophets had hitherto achieved." [26]

Prophet and Priest

This is a good opportunity to review the relation between prophet and priest in Israel's tradition. Many modern religious people have tended to "play down" the priestly emphasis of Judaism, even to the point of affirming that prophetic religion was fundamentally opposed to priestly religion. There can be no doubt that prophets like Amos, Hosea, and Jeremiah were radical in their criticism of the rituals of worship. But every religion must have a cultus—that is, forms in which faith and worship can find expression. A non-cultic religion is a contradiction in terms. Cultic forms were particularly important in Israel's faith, which, by its very nature, required participation in the community that had been called to serve Yahweh, both by proper worship and by social responsibility. Indeed, the Mosaic tradition was transmitted as a living faith through the services of worship. At the great festivals the people engaged in rites that recalled their past; the Law was read and expounded; the priests performed the sacrifices that displayed Israel's grateful obligation to God; and worshipers acknowledged what God had done for them by acts of praise. The little "confession of faith" that provided the theological basis of the Yahwist's epic was made in connection with a "cultic act" at the sanctuary: the presentation of the first fruits of the harvest (see pp. 9-10). And as the context of the confession makes clear (Deut. 26:1-11), this solemn recital was an act of worship.

Israel's prophetic movement emerged out of the cultus. Many of the early prophets were "cultic prophets," intimately associated with the sanctuary. And it is no exaggeration to say that all the great prophets were dependent upon the cultus, even those who criticized it most radically.[27] Isaiah and Ezekiel were especially indebted to the Temple, although both criticized the kind of worship that was an abomination unto Yahweh, and insisted that the Temple service would be brought to an end by the fall of Jerusalem. We must, of course, be aware of the difference in emphasis between prophet and priest, but it is no more necessary to regard the two as fundamentally incompatible than to say

---

[26] H. H. Rowley, *op. cit.*, p. 166, and the whole discussion, pp. 161-186.
[27] See R. E. Clements, *Prophecy and Covenant* [137], especially chap. 1.

that a "liturgical" and "prophetic" ministry are mutually exclusive in modern churches.

The priestly conception of sacrifice reached its supreme expression in the Suffering Servant poems of Second Isaiah. In Israel's faith, sacrifice was not understood as a means of appeasing the wrath of God or of controlling divine caprice in man's interests, as it was in pagan religions. Rather, sacrifice was in some cases a joyful gift to God in gratitude for his great goodness, and in others it was a means of atonement—that is, of healing the breach of the covenant relationship and reuniting the people with God. It was believed that sacrifice was efficacious in atonement (that is, in having power to overcome sin), not because there was anything magical about sacrifice, but because *God had provided the means* by which guilt was pardoned and holiness restored. Largely because of the prophetic preaching concerning divine judgment, Judaism was deeply sensitive to the persistence of sin that contaminated the health of the community. One of the great holy days on the sacred calendar, the Day of Atonement, provided an occasion for releasing the people from a sense of guilt, and enabling them to approach God in penitence and sincere faith. And lest sacrifice should become just an end in itself, leading a person to suppose that he could have the benefits of divine grace and still continue in his stubborn, rebellious, and self-centered way, the priestly Law affirmed categorically that sacrifice is not effective in the case of deliberate sin—sin "with a high hand" (Num. 15:30). Sacrifice, said the priests, is effective only in the case of "hidden sins"—the sins that come to light when one's life is exposed to the light of God's revelation. And even then it must be accompanied by confession and repentance.

This priestly conception of atonement has influenced the portrait of the Servant in Isaiah 53 (see pp. 423-425). The Servant's sacrifice is offered not to appease the anger of God, but to win the nations to Yahweh. It is *the* efficacious sacrifice, for it reconciles men to God in a new relationship. It makes men whole and healthy; it frees them from guilt; it establishes them in right relation with God. Second Isaiah viewed Israel's life as a temple, as it were, within whose holy of holies the perfect sacrifice is made by the Servant. And yet this sacrifice, to be effective, must prompt a confession of sin in the full sincerity of faith.

It is true, as we have noticed in this chapter, that the world mission of the Servant was ignored during the post-exilic period of biblical Judaism. But had the people of Israel been absorbed by the surrounding culture, the Servant's mission could not have been achieved. So the leaders of Judaism turned to the laws, rituals, and cultic acts of priestly religion, believing that the foundation of Israel's life was the pure worship of God, for this too was Israel's "service." In doing so, they were restoring what was most basic in Israel's life from the very first. For before Israel became a nation, before prophets were raised up to proclaim Yahweh's word, before the world was confronted with the mystery of the Servant, Israel was a worshiping community.

The Weaknesses of Judaism

But Judaism had its weaknesses, and they became increasingly apparent through the years. The rituals of the Temple too often became—as they had in Malachi's day—empty forms, devoid of the deep contrition, sincerity, and joy of worship. Devotion to the Law easily lapsed into legalism, the fruit of which was a complaining bitterness about one's lot or a proud self-righteousness— notes that sometimes are heard in the Psalms. The Law could become so over- laden with minutiae or so twisted by clever legal interpretation that it could be used as a means of escaping from God's demand—an accusation that Jesus made against the scribes and Pharisees of his day. Moreover, the exclusive policy of Nehemiah and Ezra later developed into a narrow and rigid outlook and even into a snobbish attitude toward "the lesser breeds without the law." It was too easy to assume that men—rather than God—could determine the boundaries of the chosen community on the basis of a genealogical list or the scrupulous observance of circumcision, sabbath, and the many details of the Law. We have only to read the New Testament to become aware of this weakness in Judaism. And it should be added that the rabbis of the post-Old Testament period at times were just as severe in their criticism of the dangers and corruptions to which the Jewish faith was exposed.

Moreover, it is noteworthy that prophecy at this time almost ceased. There were, to be sure, a few prophets—men like "Third Isaiah," Haggai, Zechariah, Obadiah, Malachi, and Joel—but they were mostly second-rate in comparison with the great prophets who had gone before. Preoccupation with the Law seemed to stifle the spirit of prophecy. And understandably so, for if the basis of the holy community was the Law, regarded as directly revealed to Moses and written in a book, the greatest need was for scribes (like Ezra) who could study it, expound its meaning, and preserve it carefully. In the Chronicler's history the prophets are, for the most part, good churchmen. Instead of viewing their role as interpreters of the events of the time, as was true of all the major prophets we have studied, the Chronicler affirmed that the prophets' chief function was in the worship service. They were definitely "cultic prophets," like many of the professional prophets of the pre-exilic period. They "prophesied" by leading the congregation in music (I Chron. 25:1). And, in addition, they may have taken part in the liturgical recitation of some of the psalms. After Ezra's time the belief emerged that the age of charismatic prophecy was over until the coming of the messianic age.

And yet in one sense prophecy did continue within Judaism. The writings of the prophets were preserved and eventually canonized, which shows the great importance that the men of Judaism attached to the prophetic message. The Pentateuch, the charter of Judaism, contains many "prophetic" elements, as we have seen in connection with our study of the J, E, D, and P traditions. Although Judaism regarded cultic and ethical offenses as equally serious, insisting that the most trivial offenses were as blameworthy as important ones, there was not the slightest intention of disregarding the great exhortation that Yahweh requires men to do justice, to practice steadfast love, and to walk humbly with God (Micah 6:8). The two great commandments, singled out by rabbis as the quintessence of man's obligations (Mk. 12:28-34), are from the Law. And, lest we think of the post-exilic period as sterile, we should remember that Christianity burst with prophetic power out of the heart of Judaism.

In the post-exilic period prophecy found a new form of expression in the literature known as "apocalyptic." Although this type of literature was anticipated by Ezekiel and Zechariah, it flourished in the later years of Judaism, beginning with the Maccabean period. The chief example in the Old Testament is the book of Daniel. But before we turn to this new expression of prophecy, we must pause to give special attention to two matters that have been slighted up to this point: Israel's worship as reflected in the book of Psalms (Chapter 15), and the reflections of the wise men of Israel (Chapter 16).

THE PRAISES

OF ISRAEL

CHAPTER FIFTEEN   Looking back over the ground we

have traveled so far, one thing stands out clearly: Israel un-

derstood her history to be a theophany, a manifestation of

the presence and activity of God. In the time of the Exodus

Yahweh acted to create a people "out of nothing" and to

bind this people to himself in a covenant relationship. With

many signs of his grace and goodness, he led Israel through

the wilderness and into the Promised Land. In the course of

Biblical readings: Read at least selected hymns and laments such as the following: Hymns (psalms of praise): 8, 19, 33, 92, 93, 95-100, 103, 105, 135, 136, 145-150. Laments (psalms of supplication): 3, 7, 10, 22, 25, 27, 31, 38, 44, 51, 73, 77, 88, 130, 137, 143.

time he acted anew by raising up David to be king and by opening up to Israel wider horizons than had ever been seen. Prophetic interpreters declared that Yahweh was active in the secular sphere of politics, punctuating Israel's life-story with historical events which manifested his active presence in the midst of his people. Even the most catastrophic event—the end of Israel as a nation—was interpreted as Yahweh's coming to judge and to renew his people and to mediate, through Israel's suffering, blessing for all nations. This view of history as the narrative of God's deeds was a new breakthrough in the field of the religions of mankind. "It may be said with truth," writes an authority on comparative religions, "that the Hebrews were the first to discover the meaning of history as the epiphany of God." [1]

But the other side of Yahweh's revelation, as we have seen throughout our study, is the response of his people. When Yahweh speaks, Israel answers. Although it is appropriate for the accent to fall primarily on what Yahweh has done, the Old Testament shows that—to quote a leading Old Testament theologian—when these "mighty acts" of Yahweh occurred, "Israel did not keep silent:"

> Not only did she repeatedly take up her pen to recall these acts of Yahweh to her mind in historical documents, but she also addressed Yahweh in a wholly personal way. She offered praise to him, and asked him questions, and complained to him about all her sufferings, for Yahweh had not chosen his people as a mere dumb object of his will in history, but for converse with him.[2]

THE PSALTER

The finest examples of Israel's "converse" with Yahweh are found in the book of Psalms, often called the Psalter.[3] In previous chapters we have found it necessary to refer to the book of Psalms frequently in discussing the various phases of Israel's history. Just as the hymnbooks of church or synagogue unite the voices of many generations, so the Psalter is a condensed account of the whole of Israel's history with God from the time of David down to the late period of the Old Testament. The trouble is, however, that it is practically impossible to deal with the Psalms in their proper historical periods or life-situations. Unlike modern hymnbooks, no reliable indication of the date or occasion of a particular psalm is provided at the beginning or end.[4] Moreover, with the exception of

---

[1] Mircea Eliade, *Cosmos and History* [121], p. 104.

[2] Gerhard von Rad, *Theology*, I [80], p. 354. His discussion of the Psalter is placed under the rubric, "Israel Before Yahweh (Israel's Answer)."

[3] The term Psalter comes from the Greek *psalterion* (a stringed instrument), the title given to the collection in some manuscripts of the Greek Old Testament (Septuagint). The prevailing Greek tradition has the title *psalmoi*, "songs" (for stringed music).

[4] It is generally recognized that the few superscriptions or headings which associate psalms with particular events in David's career were added later. Such superscriptions are found at the head of thirteen psalms: 3, 7, 18, 34, 51, 52, 54, 56, 57, 59, 60, 63, 142.

THE BLIND HARPER *of Leiden is one of a group of musicians portrayed on a tomb in a temple of Hatshepsut at Karnak, dating from the Amarna period (c. 1400-1350 B.C.). In Israel the "harp" and "lyre" were used to accompany religious songs (Pss. 92:3; 150:3), but we have to turn to the art of other countries, like Egypt, to visualize what these stringed instruments were like.*

Psalm 137, which clearly presupposes a situation in the Babylonian exile (see above, p. 377), the content of particular psalms tells us very little about the time and circumstance of their composition. So even though the book of Psalms reflects a long history of worship it is appropriate to begin our study of it within the context of the period of Judaism, when the hymns and prayers of many generations were compiled for use in the Second Temple (completed in 515 B.C.).

Enthroned on the Praises of Israel

In Jewish tradition the 150 psalms found in the Hebrew book of Psalms are placed under the caption *Tehillim*, a word which means "praises." This is a most appropriate title for these songs of adoration and thanksgiving, confession and supplication, with which Israel responded to Yahweh's active presence in her history. Through the entire Psalter sounds the steady diapason of man's joyful dependence upon the God who is the source and center of his being. Doubtless the psalmists would have agreed with the statement of the old Calvinistic catechism that "man's chief end is to glorify God and enjoy him forever." Whether the mood was elation or sorrow, bewilderment or confidence, these songs were intended as anthems to the glory of God. They usher us into the sanctuary where, as one psalmist put it, Yahweh was "enthroned on the praises of Israel" (Ps. 22:3). The faith of the Psalms has rightly been described as "theocentric piety." [5]

From the very first, Israel was a covenant *community* whose primary bond of unity was the worship of Yahweh. The twelve-tribe Confederacy, instituted by Joshua, had its focal point in the central sanctuary to which the people gathered for the great festivals, especially the festival of covenant renewal. During the time of David, Jerusalem became the worship center of the new nation, and Solomon contributed further to the centrality of Zion by building a great temple. So strongly did the people feel the pull to go to Jerusalem to worship Yahweh that, after the disruption of the monarchy, Jeroboam I found it necessary to establish pilgrimage shrines in his own territory, especially at Bethel. When the exiles returned from Babylon after the destruction of Jerusalem, their first thought was to rebuild the Temple. The history of Israel shows, then, that the fundamental reality, through all social changes and historical vicissitudes, was *Israel as a worshiping community*. For this reason the book of Psalms lies at the very heart of the Old Testament.

More and more we are coming to realize that the religion of the Psalms is "cultic"—that is, it is the faith of this community at worship, especially on the occasions of temple festivals. It is quite true that many of these hymns and laments were composed by individuals who spoke out of their concrete life-situations. Even so, it is not necessary to suppose that in every case these individual psalms were composed as private meditations; some may have been intended for use in connection with a liturgical act or for recitation at a temple festival. In any case, the treasury of psalms was appropriated by the worshiping community, precisely as songs of various origins are incorporated into modern hymnbooks. Thus when the pronouns "I" and "my" are used, as in the well-known Shepherd's Psalm (Ps. 23), we must think of the whole community joining to express its faith.[6]

One of the great difficulties that stands in the way of understanding the Psalter is the modern individualism which assumes that worship is a private affair between the individual and his God, and that God is accessible apart from the established means of public worship. Starting from this premise, the first step would be to divide the psalms into those that reflect public worship and those that reflect personal piety. But this contrast between the individual and the community is completely alien to Israel's covenant faith, according to which the individual is related to God as a member of a community. God, in his sovereign freedom, can deal with any man when and as he chooses (invariably to the surprise of the one who receives the theophany); but if men would have access to God, they must come to the place which he has chosen and seek him according to established cultic means. It is only as a member of the

---

[5] See Helmer Ringgren *The Faith of the Psalmists* [216], chap. 3.
[6] See the discussion of "The One and the Many" in Chapter 13, pp. 417-420.

community that the individual shares in the promises and obligations of the covenant. To be a solitary individual, cut off from the established means of grace and therefore, as fugitive David said, having "no heritage of Yahweh" (I Sam. 26:19), was the greatest calamity imaginable. According to Israel's faith, Yahweh is present—enthroned on the praises of his people—when the congregation worships together at the sanctuary on the occasion of appointed holy days or festivals.[7] The individual praises God *with* the worshiping community:

> O magnify Yahweh with me,
>   and let us exalt his name together!
>   —PSALM 34:3

The Hymnbook of the Second Temple

The book of Psalms in its present form is the product of the post-exilic community of Israel. Insofar as the Psalter reflects the liturgical practice of this period, it is proper to speak of it as "the hymnbook of the second Temple." The staff of this Temple undertook the task of arranging the hymns and supplications of the ages into suitable form, and provided them with musical and liturgical notes which survive to puzzle the modern reader. Although their notations clearly suggest that the psalms were to be sung in public worship, we cannot be sure of the details. For example, the term *selah*, which occurs repeatedly in some psalms (e.g., Ps. 46), apparently was the signal for a musical interlude and the singing of a refrain. In other instances, a note at the beginning indicates the kind of musical accompaniment, whether stringed instruments or flutes (e.g., Ps. 5); and it may be that some of the superscriptions indicate the tune to which the psalm is to be sung.[8] A clearer picture of the place of the psalms in post-exilic worship is provided by the Chronicler. For instance, the bringing of the Ark to Jerusalem is climaxed with a worship service which is rather post-exilic in style (I Chron. 16:7-36): the Temple choir chants certain psalms (portions of Psalms 105, 96, and 106), and the people respond at the appropriate point with "Amen."

The Psalter, however, did not receive its final form overnight. The process of completion took place in several stages, extending from about the fourth to the second centuries B.C. The Psalter is composed of five collections or "books,"

---

[7] On the cultic character of Israel's worship, see for instance R. E. Clements, *Prophecy and Covenant* [137], pp. 86-102; also H. Ringgren [216], pp. 1-19. Claus Westermann, in *The Praise of God in the Psalms* [219], is critical of an excessive emphasis upon the cultic character of the psalms of Israel, though he is equally critical of reading into them individualistic piety. He prefers to speak of the "forensic character of the praise of God" (p. 10), by which he means that praise occurs "in public" and makes the individual conscious that he is "a member of a congregation." See especially pp. 15-25.

[8] For instance, "according to The Hind of the Dawn" (Ps. 22:1) may refer to a well-known tune. It has been suggested that the Israelite community appropriated secular tunes for its hymnody, just as the Christian church has sometimes done.

each of which concludes with a doxology (see the arrangement in the Revised Standard Version). Psalm 1 now serves as an introduction to the whole Psalter, and Psalm 150 is the concluding doxology for the whole compilation.

Introduction:	Psalm 1
Book I	Psalms 2-41
Book II	Psalms 42-72
Book III	Psalms 73-89
Book IV	Psalms 90-106
Book V	Psalms 107-150
(Conclusion:	Psalm 150)

This fivefold arrangement is undoubtedly patterned after the five books of the Torah.

An important clue to the origin of the Psalter is found in the postscript which follows Book II: "The prayers of David, the son of Jesse, are ended" (Ps. 72:20). This means that at one stage in the formation of the Psalter it was felt that the "Davidic" collection ended here. It is of note that in these first books almost all of the psalms are prefixed with the words *leDawid*, which means "to David" or "belonging to David." This collection is undoubtedly the oldest, and probably goes back to the liturgical usage of the pre-exilic Temple in Jerusalem. To this old nucleus other collections gravitated, until eventually the fivefold arrangement of the Psalter came into being. Yet these successive editions were all issued under the aegis of David. Despite the fact that only 73 out of the 150 psalms are attributed explicitly to David, while others are assigned to Moses (Ps. 90), Solomon (Psalms 72, 127), and others, the view was popularly held that David was the author of the entire Psalter. Probably this view was intended to enforce the prestige of temple worship in Jerusalem and at the same time to refute the Samaritan claims for the primacy of the Shechem area.[9] Yet it is not a complete fiction for, as we have previously observed (p. 145), David undoubtedly gave impetus to Israel's music and hymnody, and it is not unlikely that Davidic psalms are embedded in the Psalter. Thus the relation of David to the Psalter is analogous to the relation of Moses to the Pentateuch.

The Worship of Pre-Exilic Israel

It is one thing to speak of the creation of the present book of Psalms as the hymnbook of the second Temple; it is quite another thing, however, to deal with the origin and use of individual psalms contained in this compilation. A generation or so ago it was stylish in scholarly circles to date most of the psalms in the post-exilic period or even in the Maccabean period near the dawn

---

[9] This tendency to legitimate worship in the Jerusalem Temple by capitalizing on the prestige of David is found in the work of the Chronicler. See above, pp. 436-443; and further, Jacob M. Myers' commentary on I Chronicles [194], pp. lxxxi-lxxxiv.

of the Christian era. However, our increasing knowledge of the worship of Israel during the period of the monarchy, as well as our wider understanding of the psalmody of the ancient Near East, has led us to believe that a great number of psalms were composed and used liturgically during the pre-exilic period.[10] In fact, there is now a scholarly disposition to say that, although the Psalter received its final shape at the hands of the staff of the second Temple, most of the psalms reflect the official, pre-exilic worship of Israel.

The origin and earliest use of many of the psalms are beyond recovery, just as the authorship of many of the hymns in modern hymnbooks is unknown. However, through the application of the method of study known as form-criticism it is possible to gain a deeper understanding of the pre-exilic worship of Israel as reflected in the Psalms.[11] Two things are uppermost in this approach: first, the classification of psalms according to their form or literary *genre*; and, second, the attempt to place these literary types within their cultic *Sitz im Leben*, or setting of worship. It is assumed, furthermore, that the psalms were not free literary creations but were composed according to poetic canons which were followed throughout the ancient Near East when men wrote for cultic situations; therefore a study of extra-biblical literature may throw light on the Bible. One goal of form-criticism of the Psalter would be to classify the psalms according to their liturgical use, perhaps on the analogy of certain Christian hymnbooks whose songs are arranged according to the seasons or festivals of the ecclesiastical year.

When analyzed in terms of form, many psalms fall into two, or perhaps three, major categories. First, there is the *hymn*, in which the worshiping community praises God for who he is and what he has done. The second category is the *lament*, which presupposes a problematic situation in which God's sovereignty is temporarily eclipsed. Many scholars identify a third form, the *thanksgiving*, although it is admitted that this form is often blended with the lament and overlaps with the hymn.[12] In the following discussion we shall consider

---

[10] For the Babylonian hymns, see Pritchard, *Ancient Near Eastern Texts*, pp. 383-392; for Egyptian literature, pp. 365-381. See also the works by Charles Cumming [202] and George Widengren [209]. On the other hand, the study of hymns found at Qumran, as well as other late literature such as the Psalms of Solomon (eighteen psalms issued under the name of Solomon about 60 B.C.), indicates that "the psalms of the Maccabean period are much developed beyond the latest of Old Testament psalms" (Frank M. Cross, Jr., *The Ancient Library of Qumran* [250,] pp. 165-166).

[11] The pioneer in form-critical study of the Psalms was Hermann Gunkel; see especially his *Einleitung in die Psalmen* [cited under No. 212]. His work has been advanced by Sigmund Mowinckel; see his *The Psalms in Israel's Worship*, I-II [213]. Whereas Gunkel stressed the setting of the psalms in the sacrificial worship of the temple, Mowinckel maintains that many psalms are connected with temple festivals, especially the New Year's festival.

[12] Artur Weiser in his commentary on the Psalms [218], pp. 52-91, follows the usual major distinctions: hymns, laments, and thanksgivings. Claus Westermann, however, in his *The Praise of God in the Psalms* [219], insists that "thanksgiving" should be subsumed under "praise" and therefore there are only two major types: hymns and supplications. See also H. Ringgren [216], pp. 76-91, who maintains that "thanksgiving is simply one way of praising God."

only the hymn and the lament, and then turn our attention to the Temple festivals in which various psalms were used liturgically.

ISRAEL AT WORSHIP

A people's worship is inevitably the expression of its conviction about who God is and how he is related to the world. If the gods are part of nature's cycle of decay and renewal, as in archaic societies, then worshipers leave the profane sphere of everyday life and enter a sacred realm where they experience the divine renewal of the world.[13] If God is the One who is beyond everything, the unnamable Ultimate Reality—as in much modern piety—then the worshiper takes the path of withdrawal from the world in order to enter into mystic communion with him (or "it"). According to Israel's faith, however, Yahweh is the God who acts, who makes history, who intervenes to deliver the oppressed and to humble the proud and mighty. Therefore the beginning of praise is the meditation upon what God has done and continues to do.

> One generation shall laud thy works to another,
>   and shall declare thy mighty acts.
> Of the glorious splendor of thy majesty,
>   and of thy wondrous works, I will meditate.
>   —PSALM 145:4-5

These "mighty acts" which evoke praise undoubtedly include things that the psalmist had experienced in his own life. But the psalmist mainly refers to the great events of the past, right back to the creation of the world, in which Yahweh displayed his greatness and goodness. Indeed, one of the characteristic features of Israel's worship is the remembrance of the tradition. This remembrance, however, is not just the recollection of what happened once upon a time. Rather, it is a "cultic remembrance" in the presence of Yahweh which makes the past present, so that worshipers become contemporary with the historic events which are crucial for the community of faith. "The *magnalia* [great events] of Israel's past," writes one scholar, "are present whenever she appears before the God who creates history, attends it, directs it to its goal, and calls men to accountability in it." [14] As we have observed earlier (see p. 8), even today the Passover ritual emphasizes that the believing Jew is to regard himself as a contemporary of the event of the Exodus.

---

[13] On this archaic view see especially M. Eliade, *The Sacred and the Profane* [122].

[14] James Muilenburg, *The Way of Israel* [68], p. 107. On the theme of making the past present ("actualization" or "re-presentation"; German *Vergegenwärtigung*), see Martin Noth, "The 'Re-presentation' of the Old Testament in Proclamation," in *Essays on Old Testament Hermeneutics*, ed. by Claus Westermann [83], pp. 76-88. Also Brevard Childs, *Memory and Tradition* [200].

Hymns of Praise

The hymn is a song which extols Yahweh for his greatness and good-ness as manifest in his deeds.[15] In a group of hymns which have been labeled "imperative psalms," the structure can be seen clearly. These psalms begin with an imperative call to worship; then comes a section which gives the ground for praising Yahweh; and sometimes they conclude with a renewed summons to praise, thus echoing the note sounded at the first. Psalm 100 is a good example of this literary type:

> *Introduction: Call to worship*
> Make a joyful noise to Yahweh, all the lands!
>> Serve Yahweh with gladness!
>> Come into his presence with singing!
>
> *Main section: The ground for praise*
> Know that Yahweh is God!
>> It is he that made us, and we are his;
>> we are his people, and the sheep of his pasture.
>
> *Recapitulation:*
> Enter his gates with thanksgiving,
>> and his courts with praise!
>> Give thanks to him, bless his name!
>
> *For* Yahweh is good;
>> His steadfast love [ḥésed] endures forever,
>> and his faithfulness to all generations.

This structure is found with various modifications in a number of hymns con-tained in the Psalter, such as Psalms 95, 117, 145, 148, 149, and 150.

In the psalm discussed above, the praise of Yahweh is grounded in his work as Creator. In previous chapters we have noticed, however, that Israel's earliest credo (Deut. 26:5-9) was a recitation of the events of Israel's history in which Yahweh had manifested his saving power. The poetic couplet composed by Miriam to celebrate the crossing of the Reed Sea (Ex. 15:21) is a terse example of a hymnic cry of praise to Yahweh: the first line is a summons to praise, and the second grounds praise in Yahweh's deed at the Sea. In line with this an-cient tradition, a number of psalms extol Yahweh by reciting his marvelous historical deeds according to the general outline of the old credo: the Exodus, the deliverance at the Reed Sea, the wandering through the wilderness, and

---

[15] Westermann [219] distinguishes two kinds of praise: "descriptive praise," which extols God's deeds in general terms, and "declarative praise," which refers to special acts of God which may have been performed in answer to prayer. The latter category he uses to replace the so-called "songs of thanksgiving." See the discussion of this analysis by Roland E. Mur-phy, O. Carm., "A New Classification of Literary Forms in the Psalms," *Catholic Biblical Quarterly*, XXI (1959), pp. 83-87.

the conquest of the land. In these *Heilsgeschichte* psalms, or psalms of sacred history (e.g., 78, 105, 106, 135, 136), the psalmists re-present Israel's history as the story of Yahweh's actions which centered in the deliverance from Egypt.

Psalm 136 is an excellent illustration of how Israel's praise (or thanksgiving) [16] is evoked by the recitation of what Yahweh has done. The invocation, which appears in the same form at the beginning and end, strikes the keynote:

> Sentence: O give thanks to Yahweh, for he is good,
> Response: for his steadfast love endures for ever.

This pattern of call to praise followed by liturgical response runs through the whole psalm, sentence by sentence. The first three sentences (vss. 1, 2, 3) re-present the summons to worship, with which hymns characteristically begin. The concluding sentence (vs. 26) rounds off the whole by recapitulating the theme struck at the beginning. The remaining portion of the psalm gives the ground for this praise by reciting the marvelous acts of Yahweh. In Hebrew, each of these sentences usually begins with a participle. For instance:

> to him who smote the first-born of Egypt,
> *response*
> and brought Israel out from among them,
> *response*
> with a strong hand and an outstretched arm,
> *response*
> to him who divided the Red Sea in sunder,
> *response*
> and made Israel pass through the midst of it,
> *response*
> . . . etc.
>
> —PSALM 136:10-14

In this section of the psalm (vss. 10-22), the psalmist is elaborating the old covenant credo.

It is striking, however, that in this recitation of Yahweh's mighty acts the psalmist begins with Creation:

> to him who alone does great wonders,
> *response*
> to him who by understanding made the heavens,
> *response*
> to him who spread out the earth upon the waters,
> *response*

---

[16] Though this psalm seems to begin with a call to thanksgiving, it is actually a hymn, as Weiser correctly recognizes ([218], p. 53). Here we have further evidence that there is no sharp difference between praising God and thanking God.

to him who made the great lights,
> *response*

the sun to rule over the day,
> *response*

the moon and stars to rule over the night,
> *response*.

—PSALM 136:4-9

Here Creation is not an independent article of faith but is the *beginning of history*—that is, the first of the series of divine acts which unfold into the story of God's dealings with Israel. Looking at it another way, Israel expanded her own sacred history by tracing Yahweh's actions back to the very beginning. Thus the community confessed that Yahweh's gracious purpose, revealed in Israel's history, underlies all historical times and embraces all mankind, as the Yahwist had affirmed in his great epic (see above, Chapter 6). In the religions of other ancient peoples, Creation was tied up with a mythical view of reality which motivated men to escape via the cult from the sufferings and terrors of history. Only when Creation had been "demythologized"—that is, divorced from the mythical world-view—and understood to be the initiation and basis of God's saving work in history, was it possible for it to become a vital part of Israel's worship.[17] Then Israel could sing hymns (like Psalms 33 and 135) to Yahweh in the confidence that the Lord of history is the Creator, upon whom Israel and all peoples depend for life and meaning. The magnificent "Creation psalms" (Psalms 8; 19:1-6; 104; 148) underscore this conviction.[18]

Laments in Distress

The remembrance of Yahweh's deeds can also have the effect of plunging an individual or the whole Israelite community into bewilderment about the present situation of suffering and distress. Although "theoretical atheism" was unknown in the Old Testament period, Israel was afflicted from time to time with the feeling that Yahweh had abandoned his people. When one considers that Israel, situated in a storm-center of world politics, so often suffered deeply, it is not surprising that fully one third of the Psalter consists of laments in which a suppliant cries to God "out of the depths" (Ps. 130:1). The surprising thing is that psalms of this type display so little whining self-pity

---

[17] See especially Gerhard von Rad, *Theology*, I [80], pp. 136-139; also "The Theological Problem of the Old Testament Creation Faith," in his volume of collected essays [100]. Israel's response to pagan mythical views is discussed in the excellent study by Brevard Childs, *Myth and Reality in the Old Testament* [119].

[18] Psalm 104 has been influenced by the Egyptian "Hymn to Aton," the deity symbolized by the sun disc whom the reforming king Akhnaton worshiped in the fourteenth century B.C. (see above, pp. 79-80). The text of this magnificent hymn is found in Pritchard, *Ancient Near Eastern Texts*, pp. 369-371.

or vindictive bitterness and that the praise of Yahweh reverberates through human sorrows.

The lament is composed according to a characteristic form, though there is some variation in the details.[19] The suppliant a) begins with an invocation to God; b) he presents his complaint; c) he confesses his trust in God; d) he offers his supplication for help or forgiveness; and e) he concludes with a vow that he will praise God. (The latter element is usually lacking in community laments.)

A good example of a community lament is Psalm 44. In the "invocation" (vss. 1-8) the community recalls how Yahweh performed mighty acts in the past:

> We have heard with our ears, O God,
>   our fathers have told us,
> what deeds thou didst perform in their days,
>   in the days of old:
> thou with thy own hand didst drive out the nations,
>   but them thou didst plant;
> thou didst afflict the peoples,
>   but them thou didst set free;
> for not by their own sword did they win the land,
>   nor did their own arm give them victory;
> but thy right hand, and thy arm,
>   and the light of thy countenance;
> for thou didst delight in them.
>   —VERSES 1-3

Then the community raises its complaint (vss. 9-16) as it contrasts former days with the present:

> Yet thou hast cast us off and abased us,
>   and hast not gone out with our armies.
> Thou hast made us turn back from the foe;
>   and our enemies have gotten spoil.
> Thou hast made us like sheep for slaughter,
>   and hast scattered us among the nations.
> Thou hast sold thy people for a trifle,
>   demanding no high price for them.
>   —VERSES 9-12

In the following section (vss. 17-22) the community confesses its trust in God:

> All this has come upon us,
>   though we have not forgotten thee,
>   or been false to thy covenant.
> Our heart has not turned back,
>   nor have our steps departed from thy way,
> that thou shouldst have broken us in the place of jackals,
>   and covered us with deep darkness.
>   —VERSES 17-19

---

[19] See especially the work by Claus Westermann [219], pp. 52-81.

The lament concludes with the community's fervent supplication:

> Rouse thyself! Why sleepest thou, O Yahweh?
>   Awake! Do not cast us off for ever!
> Why dost thou hide thy face?
>   Why dost thou forget our affliction and oppression?
> For our soul is bowed down to the dust;
>   our body cleaves to the ground.
> Rise up, come to our help!
>   Deliver us for the sake of thy steadfast love!
>   —VERSES 23-26

Other community laments are found in Psalms 10, 74, 79, 106, and 137—to mention just a few.

Many of the laments are the cries of individuals in distress. In these cases the suppliant's suffering is veiled in traditional imagery, so that it is next to impossible to determine the concrete situation out of which he speaks. The heart of his complaint is that he feels abandoned by God and that the powers of death (often described as Sheol or the subterranean waters surrounding it) are about to engulf him. As an example of an individual lament we may take the moving Psalm 22, whose opening words, according to Christian tradition,

SUPPLIANTS APPEALING *to a royal servant are depicted on a tomb relief of Hor-em-heb at Memphis (c. 1349-1319* B.C.). *Such gestures of prostration were also appropriate to express man's humble and fearful adoration of God (see Psalm 95:6).*

became Jesus' cry of dereliction from the Cross. The suppliant begins with a poignant invocation:

> My God, my God, why hast thou forsaken me?
>> Why art thou so far from helping me, from the words of
>>> my groaning?
> O my God, I cry by day, but thou dost not answer;
>> and by night, but find no rest.
>>>> —VERSES 1-2

As a member of the worshiping community, he confesses confidence in the "faith of our fathers" which lives on in spite of fire and sword:

> Yet thou art holy,
>> enthroned on the praises of Israel.
> In thee our fathers trusted;
>> they trusted, and thou didst deliver them.
> To thee they cried, and were saved;
>> in thee they trusted, and were not disappointed.
>>> —VERSES 3-5 (also 9-10)

However, his recollection of the past, when Yahweh's mighty acts were made known to the fathers, is only "an island of comfort in the midst of the ocean of his suffering" (Weiser). He lays his complaint before God in ever-shifting figures of speech:

> I am poured out like water,
>> and all my bones are out of joint;
> my heart is like wax,
>> it is melted within my breast;
> my strength is dried up like a potsherd,
>> and my tongue cleaves to my jaws;
>> thou dost lay me in the dust of death.
>>> —VERSES 14-15

To describe the attack upon his life he turns to different imagery: he sees himself set upon by a pack of dogs, or by brigands who divide his garments as booty (vss. 16-18). His complaint reaches a climax when out of the depths of his despair he cries for help:

> But thou, O Yahweh, be not far off!
>> O thou my help, hasten to my aid!
> Deliver my soul from the sword,
>> my life from the power of the dog!
> Save me from the mouth of the lion,
>> my afflicted soul from the horns of the wild oxen!
>>> —VERSES 19-21

Then suddenly in the following verses (vss. 22-31) the whole mood changes from dire lament to praise. The suppliant believes that Yahweh "has not hid his face from him" but has favorably accepted his prayer (vs. 24); so he vows to tell the congregation about Yahweh's saving work, and he ends on notes of praise. How can one account for this abrupt shift from a minor to a major key, here and elsewhere (e.g., Psalm 28:6)? Many scholars believe that in the interval beween the final parts of the psalm a minister of the temple, perhaps a priest or a cultic prophet, uttered comforting "words of assurance" to the effect that God had heard the suppliant's prayer and that he would graciously grant deliverance, whereupon the worshiper responded with a vow of praise: [20]

> I will tell of thy name to my brethren;
>   in the midst of the congregation I will praise thee;
> You who fear Yahweh, praise him!
>   all you sons of Jacob, glorify him,
>   and stand in awe of him, all you sons of Israel!
> For he has not despised or abhorred
>   the affliction of the afflicted;
> and he has not hid his face from him,
>   but has heard, when he cried to him.
>
> —VERSES 22-24

This interpretation helps us to understand more clearly the place of individual psalms of lament within the Israelite cult. It also shows how lament does not stand by itself but, like the second movement of a symphony, moves through the minor to the major key of the final movements, from petition out of distress to joyful praise of God. Other individual laments—to mention a few—are found in Psalms 3, 13, 31, 54, 56, and 102.

In a number of laments the suppliant pleads that he is righteous and passionately cries out for God's vindication against the wicked (e.g., Psalms 7, 17, 26, 59) who mockingly question: "Where is your God?" (see Psalms 42-43, which is one psalm, and especially Ps. 73). These psalms reflect a growing concern about theodicy, or the justice of God's administration of earthly affairs, which came to be a burning issue in Judaism. On the other hand, there are great penitential psalms, especially Psalms 51 and 130, in which the cry *de profundis* comes from one who has plumbed the human problem at its deepest level and who knows that there is no solution apart from divine forgiveness (Ps. 130:4). Psalm 51, for instance, is composed in the typical pattern of the lament. The suppliant begins with an invocation to God:

> Have mercy on me, O God, according to thy steadfast love,
>   according to thy abundant mercy blot out my transgressions.

---

[20] For an exposition of this view see Weiser [218], pp. 219-226; Westermann, *op. cit.*, pp. 64-81.

> Wash me thoroughly from my iniquity,
>   and cleanse me from my sin!
> —VERSES 1-2

He then proceeds to state his complaint (vss. 3-5):

> Against thee, thee only, have I sinned,
>   and done that which is evil in thy sight.
> —VERSE 4

He makes his supplication for purification, forgiveness, and inner renewal (vss. 6-12):

> Create in me a clean heart, O God,
>   and put a new and right spirit within me.
> Cast me not away from thy presence,
>   and take not thy holy Spirit from me.
> —VERSES 10-11

And finally he vows that he will help other transgressors to know God's ways and that he will offer the sacrifice which is acceptable to God: "a broken and contrite heart" (vss. 13-17).[21]

WORSHIP DURING PILGRIMAGE FESTIVALS

From the time when Israel was organized as a federation of twelve tribes it was customary to make pilgrimages to the central sanctuary (see I Sam. 1:3 ff.). "Three times in the year shall all your males appear before Yahweh . . . God of Israel," the covenant law stipulated (Ex. 23:14; 34:23). These three pilgrimage feasts, adopted from the old Canaanite calendar, were the feasts of Unleavened Bread, of Weeks, and of Tabernacles.[22] In the course of time these agricultural feasts were historicized—reinterpreted in terms of Israel's sacred history. The spring feast of Unleavened Bread, held at the beginning of the barley harvest, was connected with the Passover, and both became commemorations of the Exodus. The feast of Weeks, held seven weeks later at the time of wheat harvest, may have been observed in a special way at Gilgal, the threshold of the Promised Land, where it commemorated Yahweh's gift of the land to Israel.[23] And the Fall festival, known as the feast of Ingathering or Tabernacles, and held at the turn of the year (New Year), came to be a time for the renewal

---

[21] It is generally recognized that verses 18-19 were added in the early post-exilic period by editors who believed that when the Temple was rebuilt, Yahweh would then delight in animal sacrifices.

[22] For a discussion of the festivals, see R. De Vaux, *Ancient Israel* [62], pp. 484-506.

[23] This theory, first advanced by Gerhard von Rad, has been developed by H. J. Kraus, *Gottesdienst in Israel* [206], pp. 179-193.

of the covenant with Yahweh. The ancient custom of making pilgrimages to the central sanctuary was perpetuated throughout the period of the monarchy and was revived after the completion of the second Temple. The little collection of psalms comprising Psalms 120-134, each of which is titled "a song of ascents," appears to have been a handbook used by pilgrims who went up to Jerusalem for the great festivals. One of these songs expresses the joy of going to Jerusalem, the city which was decreed as the pilgrimage shrine for the tribes of Israel:

> I was glad when they said to me,
>   "Let us go to the house of Yahweh!"
> Our feet have been standing
>   within your gates, O Jerusalem!
>   —PSALM 122:1-2

Do the Psalms tell us anything, directly or indirectly, about worship during these great festivals?

Covenant Renewal Festivals

Although our knowledge of the history of Israelite worship is very limited, there is good reason to suppose that the ancient covenant renewal festival, first held at Shechem during the period of the amphictyony, was revived in the Northern Kingdom. We are told that Jeroboam I, the first king of North Israel, instituted a Fall festival in his domain "like the feast that was in Jerusalem" (I Kings 12:32-33), in order to counteract the custom of making pilgrimages to the Jerusalem Temple. Apparently the Jerusalem covenant festival had acquired important features of Davidic theology, as we shall see presently; the northern festival, however, must have been quite like the old covenant renewal festival that had been popular during the days of the Tribal Confederacy. In both cases the festival in question is the great annual festival (the Feast of Tabernacles) that was held in the Fall at the turn of the year. As we have noticed previously (pp. 235-236), the prophetic message about the "Day of Yahweh" may have presupposed this cultic celebration.

Form-critical studies of the Psalter have led scholars to classify various psalms as belonging to this festival.[24] But of all of those proposed, Psalm 81 is one of the best candidates. It has close affinities with the classic account of covenant renewal found in Joshua 24, which tells of the gathering of the tribes to Shechem, the recitation of Yahweh's saving acts, the challenge to give undivided allegiance to Yahweh, and the promulgation of the covenant law in connection with the covenant pledge (see above, pp. 94-97). In this psalm the initial verses (vss. 1-5) present a summons to worship "the God of Jacob" at the sanctuary "on our feast day." The next section (vss. 6-10) is a recitation of the

---

[24] In his commentary on the Psalms [218], pp. 35-52, Weiser classifies a great number of psalms in this category. Walter Harrelson, in *Interpreting the Old Testament* [15], pp. 421-424, more conservatively lists as covenant renewal psalms: 50, 76, 78, 81, 82, 89, 105, 111, 114.

deeds of benevolence performed by Yahweh, the God who brought his people up out of the land of Egypt. It is noteworthy that the announcement "I am Yahweh" is associated with the first commandment, precisely as in the Decalog. The psalm reaches a climax with an appeal to the community to hear Yahweh's voice and receive his blessings (vss. 11-16). It has been suggested that cultic prophets may have taken part in the service, particularly at the point where the challenge to renew loyalty to the God of the covenant was presented.

It is quite possible that the psalm we have just discussed is a psalm from the northern covenant renewal festival. Doubtless there are a number of northern psalms, once used in the sanctuary at Bethel, which after the fall of the northern kingdom found their way into the south, where they were adapted for use in Zion festivals. Psalm 50 is another good illustration of a covenant psalm, though in this case the old Sinai theophany has become a theophany on Mount Zion (verse 2). This psalm presupposes the form of the "covenant lawsuit" which we have discussed from time to time (see, for instance, pp. 249, 277). In the first part (vss. 1-6) Yahweh is described as coming to judge his people in the presence of heaven and earth as witnesses. The main part of the psalm (vss. 7-21) contains the charge: Israel's failure to live up to the requirements of the covenant in daily life invalidates ritual and sacrifices—a note which the prophets had struck. The conclusion (vss. 22-23) is a reminder to those who "forget God" that God shows salvation only to those who order their way aright.

The Festival at Jerusalem

As we have already indicated, the covenant festival celebrated in the south was unique in some respects, owing to profound changes brought about by the Davidic monarchy. It will be remembered that David, in order to centralize power in Jerusalem, had brought the old amphictyonic symbol, the Ark of the Covenant, to his capital with the intention of installing it in a temple. This decisive act called for a reinterpretation of Yahweh's covenant with Israel. With the support of the prophet Nathan, the Davidic court circle advanced a royal covenant theology, the substance of which was that Yahweh had elected the Davidic king as his son and had elected Zion as his dwelling-place (see above, pp. 148-150). Yahweh the King, whose glory filled the Jerusalem Temple, had made a covenant with the Davidic king, and through him with the people! The effect of this Davidic-Zion theology was to suppress the old Sinai covenant tradition, or at least to reduce it to a secondary place in the liturgical tradition of the Jerusalem Temple.[25] It was not until the great reformation of Josiah that the Mosaic covenant tradition was "rediscovered."

---

[25] See the excellent discussion of the Exodus-Sinai tradition and the Davidic-Zion tradition in R. E. Clements, *Prophecy and Covenant* [137], pp. 45-68. Pertinent in this connection is the study of northern and southern covenant traditions by Murray Newman, *The People of the Covenant* [109], especially his discussion of "The Kingship at Jerusalem," chap. 6.

In view of this southern theology, which is reflected in the prophet Isaiah of Jerusalem, it would be natural for the Jerusalem Fall festival to take on a character of its own. From various psalms we glean fragmentary references to cultic activities. In an "entrance liturgy" (Ps. 24) we read about the command to the gates of Jerusalem to lift up their heads so that Yahweh, the King of Glory (presumably enthroned invisibly on the Ark), may come in. We read about festal processions into the sanctuary, led by singers and musicians (Psalms 68:24-25; 118:27), about dancing and making melody to Yahweh (Ps. 149:3), about the blowing of trumpets and the raising of "the festal shout" (Ps. 89:15). Even when these details are read in the light of extra-biblical sources, such as texts dealing with the New Year celebrations of other peoples in the ancient Near East, there is much that remains obscure.[26] But there is increasing agreement that a major aspect of the festival was the processional bearing of the Ark into the Jerusalem Temple, where Yahweh was acclaimed as King of the universe and where he reaffirmed his covenant with the house of David.

Psalm 78, which undoubtedly reflects pre-exilic worship in Jerusalem, is an interesting example of how the Exodus-Sinai tradition and the Davidic-Zion tradition were related in the south. Most of the psalm (vss. 1-66) is a long summary of Yahweh's historical acts, beginning with the Exodus. The purpose of this recitation is to show how Yahweh's people, especially the north Israelites, did not keep the covenant. Then the psalmist shifts to the Davidic covenant tradition:

> He rejected the tent of Joseph,
>   He did not choose the tribe of Ephraim;
> but he chose the tribe of Judah,
>   Mount Zion, which he loves.
> He built his sanctuary like the high heavens,
>   like the earth, which he has founded for ever.
> He chose David his servant,
>   and took him from the sheepfolds,
> from tending the ewes that had young he brought him
>   to be the shepherd of Jacob his people,
>   of Israel his inheritance.
> With upright heart he tended them,
>   and guided them with skilful hand.
>
> —PSALM 78:67-72

Here the psalmist affirms that the old sacred history which centered in the Exodus and the Conquest has come to an end. Yahweh has made a new beginning by raising up David and selecting Mount Zion as the divine abode.

The Zion festival is clearly reflected in Psalm 132, which is based on the events narrated in II Samuel 6 and 7: David's bringing the Ark to Zion, and

---

[26] Sigmund Mowinckel has pioneered in the study of the bearing of Babylonian and other Near Eastern cultic ceremonies upon the Israelite cult. See his *The Psalms in Israel's Worship*, I-II [213].

Nathan's oracle to David.[27] In the first part of the psalm (vss. 1-10) it is announced, in words that recall the ancient Song to the Ark (Num. 10:35-36), that Yahweh has already found a dwelling-place.

> Arise, O Yahweh, and go to thy resting place,
>   thou and the ark of thy might.
> Let thy priests be clothed with righteousness,
>   and let thy saints shout for joy.
> —VERSES 8-9

The second part of the psalm (vss. 11-18) is based on Nathan's oracle:

> Yahweh swore to David a sure oath
>   from which he will not turn back:
> "One of the sons of your body
>   I will set on your throne.
> If your sons keep my covenant
>   and my testimonies which I shall teach them,
> their sons also for ever
>   shall sit upon your throne."
> For Yahweh has chosen Zion;
>   he has desired it for his habitation:
> "This is my resting place for ever;
>   here I will dwell, for I have desired it."
> —VERSES 11-14

A similar point of view is expressed in Psalm 89. The first part of this psalm is a hymn (vss. 1-37) to Yahweh, who manifested his steadfast love by electing the house of David. The second part (vss. 38-52) is a lament in which the psalmist complains that the promise has been violated by the defeat of the king. He appeals to Yahweh to reaffirm, by removing the calamity, the steadfast love which he once swore to David.[28]

The twofold emphasis upon the election of Zion and the election of David helps us to understand the importance of two other groups of psalms in the Psalter. One group is the so-called Zion psalms (Psalms 46, 48, 76, 84, 87, 122). These psalms are based on the conviction that Zion is the place of Yahweh's presence in the midst of his people. The well-known Psalm 46 takes up this theme, elaborating it with the mythological motif of the river of God which flows down from the sacred mountain to water the earth (see pp. 373-374):

> There is a river whose streams make glad the city of God,
>   the holy habitation of the Most High.

---

[27] H. J. Kraus has argued that the story in II Sam. 6-7 is a cultic legend which was recited at the Jerusalem festival to dramatize the election of Zion and the election of David as king. See his *Gottesdienst* [206], pp. 210-272.

[28] Otto Eissfeldt has a good discussion of this psalm in his essay on "The Promises of Grace to David," *Israel's Prophetic Heritage* [136], pp. 196-207.

> God is in the midst of her, she shall not be moved;
>   God will help her right early.
> The nations rage, the kingdoms totter;
>   he utters his voice, the earth melts.
> Yahweh of hosts is with us,
>   the God of Jacob is our refuge.
>
> —PSALM 46:4-7

The other group, often called royal psalms, consists of prayers on behalf of the king, Yahweh's Anointed (Psalms 2, 20, 21, 45, 72, 110). Unlike other nations who absolutized monarchy or deified kings, Israel affirmed that the reigning king was the elected agent of Yahweh and was completely dependent upon him.[29]

> For the king trusts in Yahweh,
>   and through the steadfast love of the Most High
>   he shall not be moved.
>
> —PSALM 21:7

The King of the Universe

In Jerusalem it was not felt as a contradiction to affirm that Yahweh, whose glory fills the Holy of Holies in the Jerusalem Temple, is—to recall Isaiah's vision—enthroned "high and lifted up" as King of the universe (see above, pp. 264-267). A number of psalms belong together because they are characterized by the motif "Yahweh is king" or "Yahweh reigns" and develop the theme that he is the Creator of heaven and earth and the judge of all the nations (Psalms 47, 93, 96, 97, 98, 99). One of the perplexing issues of Old Testament study is the question of the place of these hymns in the pre-exilic cult.

For a number of years scholars, influenced by the creative work of Sigmund Mowinckel, have described these hymns as "enthronement psalms." [30] Under the assumption that a common pattern of "myth and ritual" prevailed in the ancient Near East, it has been argued that the enthronement psalms belonged in the cultic setting of a "throne-ascension festival," held every New Year, when Yahweh's kingship over Israel, the nations, and the cosmos was celebrated in song, ritual, and pageant. In the Babylonian cult, for instance, hymns of praise had an important place. Every New Year, when the cycle of the seasons returned to its beginning, the worshipers re-experienced and re-actualized the victory of the powers of life over the powers of death. The creation myth of *Enuma elish* depicted the victory of the god Marduk over the dragon of chaos,

---

[29] On this point see especially Martin Noth's essay on "God, King, and People" in his volume of collected essays [111].

[30] Mowinckel [213]. See also the writings of the British "myth and ritual" school: Bibliography, Nos. 203, 204, 205.

Tiamat.[31] Not only was the myth recited, but the battle was re-enacted during the festival. At the climax of the celebration worshipers joined in the acclamation, "Marduk has become king!" This is interpreted to mean that he had re-ascended his throne for another year.

At first glance, it is tempting to understand the biblical psalms in the light of this mythological drama, and to suppose that at the New Year festival in Jerusalem, Israelites celebrated with hymn-singing Yahweh's victory over hostile powers and his ascension to his throne. Psalm 93, for instance, begins with the festal shout: *Yahweh malak,* which some propose to translate "Yahweh has become king!" Our accepted English translation (RSV) reads:

> Yahweh reigns; he is robed in majesty;
>   Yahweh is robed, he is girded with strength.
> Yea, the world is established; it shall never be moved;
>   thy throne is established from of old;
>   thou art from everlasting.
>   —PSALM 93:1-2

While it is grammatically possible to translate the opening Hebrew exclamation as either "Yahweh has become king" or "Yahweh is king (reigns)," exegetically there is only one possibility. Israel's historical faith cannot be squared with the pagan belief that man's life is caught up in the cycle of nature which ever returns to its beginning, when there is a new creation and when God ascends his throne once again. Yahweh, the God of Israel, is acclaimed as "the Living God" —not the god of nature who undergoes the cycle of death and resurrection. It is proper, then, that the Revised Standard Version translates "Yahweh reigns." Yahweh's throne is established "from of old," his kingship is "from everlasting." He does not have to claim his throne anew at every turn of the year.

Nevertheless, scholars have been right in suspecting that the mythical view has influenced Israel's hymns of worship. In the realm of worship, as in other areas, Israel borrowed from her cultural environment, but what was borrowed was transmuted in the alchemy of her covenant faith so that it enriched the praise of Yahweh as King. The ancient myth of a divine victory over the "floods" or the "sea" (that is, the rebellious "waters of chaos" which threaten the security of the world) was employed to express the faith that Yahweh is triumphant over all powers, especially historical enemies which threaten to convert the world into dark and meaningless chaos.[32]

> The floods have lifted up, O Yahweh,
>   the floods have lifted up their voice,
>   the floods lift up their roaring.

---

[31] See Pritchard, *Ancient Near Eastern Texts,* pp. 60-72.

[32] Recall that in Is. 51:9-10 the victory over the chaos-dragon Rahab is reinterpreted as a historical event: Yahweh's victory at the Reed Sea. See the author's essay, "Water," in *Interpreter's Dictionary* [11].

Mightier than the thunders of many waters,
   mightier than the waves of the sea,
   Yahweh on high is mighty!
                     –PSALM 93:3-4

It is not surprising that Jerusalem, which came to be a metropolitan center under David and especially Solomon, was hospitable to cultural influences of this sort. Indeed, the theologians who developed the royal covenant theology seem to have capitalized on the doctrine of creation to buttress the stability of Yahweh's sanctuary in Zion (Ps. 78:69) and the permanance of the Davidic dynasty (Ps. 89:2-4). The writer of Psalm 89 is completely consistent with Davidic theology when, to emphasize the firmness of the covenant with David, he praises Yahweh's power as Creator and even portrays his victory over the primeval powers of chaos, Rahab and her allies.

O Yahweh, God of hosts,
   who is mighty as thou art, O Yahweh,
with thy faithfulness round about thee?
Thou dost rule the raging of the sea;
   when its waves rise, thou stillest them.
Thou didst crush Rahab like a carcass,
   thou didst scatter thy enemies with thy mighty arm.
The heavens are thine, the earth also is thine;
   the world and all that is in it,
      thou hast founded them.
                  –PSALM 89:8-11

All of this adds up to the conclusion that the hymns to Yahweh as King belong essentially to the New Year's festival celebrated in Jerusalem during the pre-exilic period.[33] Impressive testimony to the ancient cultic celebration is found in Psalm 24, which in all probability goes back to the time of David when the ceremonial bringing of the Ark into Jerusalem was re-enacted in the cult.[34] The psalm opens with an ascription of praise to the Creator:

The earth is Yahweh's and the fulness thereof,
   the world and those who dwell therein;
for he has founded it upon the seas,
   and established it upon the rivers.
                  –VERSES 1-2

---

[33] This view is opposed by H. J. Kraus, in *Gottesdienst* [206], who maintains that the so-called enthronement psalms come from the post-exilic period and show dependence on Second Isaiah (e.g., Is. 52:7-8). See also his work, *Die Königsherrschaft Gottes im Alten Testament* (Tübingen: J. C. B. Mohr, 1951), pp. 99-112. Claus Westermann's form-critical studies ([219], pp. 145-151) have led him to the same conclusion.
[34] See Aage Bentzen, "The Cultic Use of the Story of the Ark in Samuel," in *Journal of Biblical Literature*, LXVII (1948), pp. 37-53, for an attempt to connect the whole story of the Ark (not just II Sam. 6) with the ritual presupposed in Psalm 132 (and Ps. 24).

It comes to a <u>climax as the procession reaches the gates of Zion</u>, where voices sing responsively:

> Lift up your heads, O gates!
>   and be lifted up, O ancient doors!
>   that the King of glory may come in!
>   Who is this King of glory?
>   Yahweh of hosts,
>   he is the King of glory!
>   —VERSES 9-10

Beyond and above the earthly king is the King *par excellence*—Ruler of the universe and the Lord of history (Is. 6:1). Yet Yahweh has appointed the Davidic king to be his agent for the execution of his rule. He has promised to maintain the Davidic throne in the face of all foes who are arraigned against the Anointed. Hence the Zion festival was not only a time when Israel acclaimed Yahweh as King everlasting but when the people heard anew Yahweh's promises of grace to David.

MEDITATING ON THE TORAH

Up to this point we have been considering the Psalter as a collection of hymns and prayers for use in temple worship, mainly in connection with the great festivals. Of course, the faithful Israelite expressed his reverence and gratitude at other times and places, especially in the family circle, but there was no substitute for the temple, for it was believed that Yahweh was present there in the "beauty of holiness."

> One thing have I asked of Yahweh,
>   that will I seek after;
> that I may dwell in the house of Yahweh
>   all the days of my life,
> to behold the beauty of Yahweh,
>   and to inquire in his temple.
>   —PSALM 27:4

Moreover, as indicated in this psalm (verse 6) and numerous other psalms (see especially Ps. 66:13-15), the service of worship at the Temple included animal sacrifices. Some psalmists were critical of burnt offerings and other sacrifices, particularly when they were performed without true covenant obedience (e.g., Ps. 40:6-8); but there was no thought of abandoning the "means of grace," which provided for communion and reconciliation with God, in favor of a spiritual, noncultic religion.[35]

---

[35] See the discussion of sacrifice in the previous chapter, pp. 457-458. In addition, consult R. De Vaux, *Studies in Old Testament Sacrifice* [192], especially chaps. 2 and 4; also his *Ancient Israel* [62], pp. 415-456.

There are some psalms, however, which do not presuppose the worship of Yahweh in the Temple and in this sense may be called noncultic. Illustrative of psalms of this sort is a group whose central theme is that of meditating upon and delighting in the Torah (Psalms 1; 19:7-14; 119). One of these psalms (Ps. 119), whose chief distinction is that it is the longest in the Psalter, is organized according to a rather artificial plan. It is an "acrostic," or alphabetical study, consisting of as many eight-line stanzas as there are letters in the Hebrew alphabet. Each of the eight lines begins with the same Hebrew letter, according to the position of the stanza in the alphabetical sequence. Here it is plain that the Torah has become an object of study and devotion. Psalms of this kind (especially Psalms 1 and 119) probably have their setting in the post-exilic period when another institution, the synagogue, came to have increasing influence. The synagogue did not, of course, replace the Temple—at least not until the Temple was finally destroyed by the Romans in A.D. 70. But it began to develop a distinctive pattern of worship in which the reading and study of the Torah had a central place.

One of the striking things about the Torah psalms is the theme that the study of the Torah makes one wise and happy ("blessed"). This idea is expressed in Psalm 19:7-14, a passage which now forms the appropriate conclusion to an old creation hymn (Ps. 19:1-6).

> The law of Yahweh is perfect,
>   reviving the soul;
> the testimony of Yahweh is sure,
>   making wise the simple;
> the precepts of Yahweh are right,
>   rejoicing the heart;
> the commandment of Yahweh is pure,
>   enlightening the eyes;
> the fear of Yahweh is clean,
>   enduring forever;
> the ordinances of Yahweh are true,
>   and righteous altogether.
> More to be desired are they than gold,
>   even much fine gold;
> sweeter also than honey
>   and drippings of the honeycomb.
>   —PSALM 19:7-10

At one point in the acrostic Psalm 119 it is emphasized that the Torah is the source of wisdom which should be sought by a young man:

> How can a young man keep his way pure?
> By guarding it according to thy word.
>   —PSALM 119:9

Above all, this wisdom theme is developed in Psalm 1, the psalm which now introduces the whole Psalter.[36] Just as Jesus told a story about a wise man who built his house on a rock and a foolish man who built on sand (Matt. 7:24-27), so this psalmist, though with a different intention, divided men into two types, as was customary in the wisdom schools. The righteous man, who meditates on God's law day and night, is likened to a tree planted by running water, which yields fruit in season and is ever green. The wicked, on the other hand, are likened to chaff blown away by the wind, for their success is evanescent and their doom sure.

In the Torah psalms the sharp contrast between the righteous and the wicked, the wise and the foolish, is too neat and simple. As we shall discover in the next chapter, Israel's wisdom movement had to probe to a much deeper level of understanding to deal adequately with the problem of life's imbalances.

---

[36] The question as to whether it is proper to speak of "wisdom psalms" (psalms such as 1, 32, 34, 37, 49, 112, 128) as a distinctive literary form is considered by Roland E. Murphy, O. Carm., "A Consideration of the Classification, 'Wisdom Psalms'" in Supplement to *Vetus Testamentum*, Congress Volume IX (Leiden: Brill, 1963), pp. 156-167.

THE BEGINNING

OF WISDOM

CHAPTER SIXTEEN   Philosophy literally means "the love of wisdom," as can be seen from the elements making up the word (*philo-sophia*). Among the ancient Greeks, from whom we have received our philosophical tradition, the search for wisdom reached its greatest maturity and refinement, especially in the age of Pericles (460-429 B.C.) with Socrates, and in succeeding generations with Plato and Aristotle. But the Greeks knew that the love of wisdom is

Biblical readings: To read all the wisdom literature would be a big assignment. Read at least Proverbs 1-9, Ecclesiastes, and Job (omitting chapters 32-37). Also Psalms 1, 32, 34, 37, 49, 112, and 128 belong to this type of literature. If one were to go beyond the limits of the Hebrew Bible, the Wisdom of Ben Sira (or Ecclesiasticus) and the Wisdom of Solomon would deserve first attention.

not bounded by culture, nation, or race. Wisdom is the concern of man as man: Greek or Jew, Babylonian or Egyptian, male or female, king or slave. The quest for wisdom is the quest for the meaning of life. And this quest is the basic interest of every human being.

THE WISDOM OF THE EAST

Long before the meeting of East and West in the Hellenistic empire founded by Alexander the Great (332 B.C.), the search for wisdom was carried on in the Fertile Crescent, especially in Egypt and Babylonia.[1] Since wisdom writings circulated far beyond the country of their origin, and Israel was situated at the cultural crossroads of the ancient world, the wisdom of the East early influenced her thought. Though wisdom writings date back to the Egyptian Pyramid Age (c. 2600-2175 B.C.) and to the Sumerian era in Mesopotamia, wisdom had a timeless quality. The sage seemed to detach himself from the limitations of his time and culture. To be sure, he reflected on problems of society as he knew them, but these were essentially problems found in varying forms in all societies. Thus the wisdom movement was in essence international.

The Sage's Individualism

Another trait of wisdom literature is its focus on the individual. The sage was interested in Everyman—more concerned, it appears, with Man ('adam), as in the J story in Genesis 2-3, than with peoples identified by particular histories and societies. This is hardly a fair comparison, however, for the Yahwist portrays the human problem in terms of a historical drama that moves from the beginning toward the fulfillment of the divine purpose. But wisdom literature did not usually have this kind of historical perspective. The sage brought history to a standstill, so to speak, so that he could analyze microscopically the problem of human existence.

Wisdom literature falls into two classes. The first consists of practical advice to the young on how they may attain a successful and good life. This "prudential literature" is illustrated by the Egyptian *Teaching of Amen-em-opet*, the Babylonian *Counsels of Wisdom*, and the maxims found in the Old Testament book of Proverbs. The second consists of reflective probing into the depth of man's anguish about the meaning of life, often in a skeptical mood. This "reflective literature" is well illustrated by the Egyptian *Dispute over Suicide*, the Babylonian composition entitled *I will Praise the Lord of Wisdom*, and the biblical books of Ecclesiastes and Job. But both types of wisdom literature

---

[1] See Pritchard, *Ancient Near Eastern Texts*, pp. 405-440 for Egyptian and Babylonian literature. A brief introduction to "International Wisdom and its Literature" is found in R. B. Y. Scott's commentary on Proverbs and Ecclesiastes [228], pp. xl-lii.

isolate the human problem from the particularities of history, and in this respect they stand in contrast to most of the literature of the Old Testament.

Most of us are more at home in the wisdom literature than in the historical literature of the Bible. For although the Hebrew-Christian faith has given Western civilization a dynamic sense of history, as shown in the doctrines of Progress or the Marxist view of history, modern men are profoundly indebted to the "love of wisdom" inherited from Greeks, Egyptians, Babylonians, and others. It is more natural for us to think of man as a "citizen of the world" than in the context of a particular history, especially the history that begins with Abraham. Modern sages insist that the way to solve the problem of world unity is to concentrate on Man, whose needs and aspirations are fundamentally the same in all situations, and to rule out the memories, loyalties, and cultural peculiarities that make for human diversity and conflict.

ISRAEL'S WISDOM LITERATURE

A certain amount of wisdom literature is included in the Hebrew Bible, and with it comes the tension that exists between these two ways of viewing man—in a particular historical context or simply as a human being. The three wisdom

AN EGYPTIAN SCRIBE *from the Fifth Dynasty (c. 2500-2350 B.C.) holding on his lap a partly opened papyrus roll. After the invention of writing in the early third millennium B.C., the scribe came to be regarded as a man having special skill and intellectual power, and often held an influential post at a royal court. From the Pyramid Age come several wisdom writings, such as the* Instruction of Ptah-hotep *(c. 2250 B.C.), principal minister of a king of the Fifth Dynasty.*

writings in the Hebrew Bible are Proverbs, Ecclesiastes, and Job.[2] In addition, there are a number of poems, now included in the Psalter or the prophetic collections, which apparently came from the circle of Israel's sages.

The wisdom literature of the Old Testament seems to stand apart from the rest of the books. All the literature we have considered so far is marked by Israel's awareness of having a unique history. This historical sense, as we have seen, is the very heart of Israel's faith, and is summed up in the confession that Yahweh is the God of Israel, and Israel the people of Yahweh. To be sure, prophet and priest did not always understand history in the same way, but both agreed that Yahweh had made himself known to Israel uniquely and had entered into a special relationship with his people. Yet when we turn to Israel's wisdom literature, we find that these distinctive features of Israel's faith are lacking. The prophetic themes that dominate the Pentateuch and the prophetic writings—Israel's election, the Day of Yahweh, the covenant and the Law, the priesthood and the Temple, prophecy and the messianic hope—are dealt with hardly at all.

Although much of the wisdom literature was produced in the post-exilic period, when Israel was deeply conscious of being a worshiping community, there are strikingly few references to acts of worship, and what few there are say little of the centrality of worship (Prov. 3:9-10; Eccles. 5:4-5; Job 12:19; cf. 1:5; 42:8-9). Also, the personal name Yahweh is not used in Ecclesiastes or (with a couple of exceptions) in the poem of Job, for the writers of these books prefer to use a general name for deity. Even when the name is used, as in Proverbs, nothing is made of the special relationship between Yahweh and Israel. Yahweh is not identified as the One who brought his people out of Egypt or who made himself known in the long history of Israel. Indeed, there are no explicit allusions to Israelite history or to outstanding Israelite personalities, with the single exception of Solomon who ruled in Jerusalem (Eccles. 1:1, 13-14). The form of address, "my son" (as in Prov. 1-7), follows the ancient tradition of the wisdom schools in which the sage counseled his pupils in this fashion.

Israel's wisdom literature, then, stands by itself—so much so that some theologians have great difficulty in understanding how it relates to the mainstream of Israel's faith. Yet it is difficult to believe that these books were forced into the Jewish canon as one drags a story into a speech by its heels.[3] Later on,

---

[2] Outside of the Hebrew Bible, but included in the Roman Catholic and Orthodox canons, are the important wisdom books called Ecclesiasticus or the Wisdom of Ben Sira (dating from the early second century B.C.) and the Wisdom of Solomon (from the first century B.C.). Both books are included in the Protestant Apocrypha. (See chart, pp. 4-5.)

[3] See Lawrence E. Toombs, "Old Testament Theology and the Wisdom Literature," in *Journal of Bible and Religion*, XXIII (1955), pp. 193-196. Gerhard von Rad includes wisdom literature (as well as the Psalms) under the rubric of "Israel before Yahweh"—that is, Israel's response to Yahweh's activity in her history (*Theology*, I [80]); but this strikes many as a theological *tour de force*.

Israel's wisdom literature was "nationalized"—that is, it was specifically related to Israel's history and Yahweh's revelation of his Law.[4] This full baptism of Wisdom into Israel's historical faith was accomplished during the so-called "inter-Testamental period"—the period, speaking generally, between the composition of the last book of the Old Testament and the literature of the New Testament. It is clear in two books found outside the Hebrew Bible: the Wisdom of Ben Sira (about 180 B.C.) and the Wisdom of Solomon (about 50 B.C.). But it was probably in the earlier period that the process started which culminated in the assimilation of wisdom literature into Israel's heritage. For although Israel borrowed wisdom materials from her cultural environment, she stamped what she borrowed with her own faith and experience.

What was the place of the sage in Israel's life? And how did the wisdom literature of the Bible, which drew deeply on the wisdom of the East, ultimately come under the sway of Israel's distinctive religious tradition?

The Counsel of the Wise

One confession of Jeremiah refers obliquely to the three important classes of religious leaders in Israelite society. The conspiracy against Jeremiah, we are told, sprang from the conviction that "the law [torah] shall not perish from the priest, nor counsel from the wise, nor the word from the prophet" (Jer. 18:18; cf. 8:8-9; Ezek. 7:26). This passage clearly implies that all three leaders spoke with authority derived from Yahweh—an authority that Jeremiah allegedly was trying to subvert. But the passage also indicates that each leader had a different spiritual gift. The prophet spoke the "word of Yahweh," for he stood in Yahweh's Council and was able to communicate the divine will in specific situations. The priest gave the people torah or instruction, based on the Mosaic tradition. The wise man, however, gave counsel, with the insight derived from his keen observation of life, from years of experience, and from wide acquaintance with the fund of ancient wisdom.

It is sometimes said that the sage's counsel was based on "rational" or "empirical" observation, in distinction from the priest and the prophet who relied on "supernatural" sources of insight. But this logical distinction was not made by ancient peoples, for they believed that wisdom was a divine gift, not just a human attainment that could be won through superior intelligence, serious study, or long life. The divine gift, they believed, was bestowed chiefly upon the leaders of the people: the elders who sat at the gate (Prov. 1:20-21), the scribes and other members of the educated class, and above all the ruler of the people. According to Israelite tradition, the gift of wisdom was bestowed in greatest measure upon Solomon, who was such a wise ruler that his fame for wisdom spread far beyond the boundaries of his nation.

---

[4] On the baptism of wisdom literature into Israel's faith, see especially J. C. Rylaarsdam, *Revelation in Jewish Wisdom Literature* [225].

The prophets were from time to time critical of "wisdom" (cf. Is. 29:14; Jer. 8:9), an indication that the wisdom movement was strong enough to warrant their attack.[5] In fact, in Israel the wisdom tradition preceded and outlasted the prophetic movement, and reached its peak of development only after prophecy had declined. The origin of Israel's wisdom movement is lost in the haze of the early oral tradition. Probably there was a vigorous wisdom movement among the Canaanites, from whom it was carried over into Israel in the period before the monarchy. The many affinities between the book of Proverbs and the Ras Shamra literature suggest that Israel did assimilate wisdom material from her Canaanite environment. Balaam, the Babylonian diviner, was related in some sense to Israel's early wisdom movement. Moreover, it is from the earliest period of Israel's oral tradition that we have the proverb, the riddle (see Judges 14:14), and the fable (Judges 9:8-15)—ancient types of oriental wisdom that were gradually integrated into Israel's heritage. Also, Egyptian wisdom motifs have been detected in the Joseph stories.

In any event, by the time of the early monarchy the sage was a well-known and respected leader in Israelite society. We are told that the counsel of Ahithophel, one of David's court advisers, was "as if one consulted the word of God" (II Sam. 16:23)—that is, it was virtually filled with prophetic power. During Absalom's rebellion a wise woman from Tekoa, the home town of Amos, was summoned to use her influence on David (II Sam. 14:1-21), and later during the same crisis another wise woman negotiated with Joab (II Sam. 20:14-22). The remark that the wise woman went to the people "in her wisdom" indicates that she was a recognized leader with professional standing, perhaps like the "wise women" who were found in the Canaanite court, according to the Song of Deborah (Judges 5:29). Certainly women were found among Israel's sages, just as they were sometimes found among the prophets (Judges 4:4; II Kings 22:14).

Solomon, Israel's Patron Sage

Israel regarded Solomon as the fountainhead of her wisdom. Just as the Pentateuch was ascribed to Moses, and the Psalms to David, so it was believed that a great deal of the wisdom literature had stemmed from Solomon. To him are ascribed the books of Proverbs, Ecclesiastes, the Song of Songs, and Psalms 72 and 127; and, outside the Hebrew Bible, the Wisdom of Solomon, the Psalms of Solomon, and the Odes of Solomon are attributed to him. Undoubtedly there is a solid basis for crediting Solomon with an avid interest in wisdom.[6] He was a skillful diplomat in his negotiations with Hiram of Tyre (I

---

[5] See William McKane, *Prophets and Wise Men* [221].

[6] The origin of wisdom with Solomon is defended by Albrech Alt, "Die Weisheit Salomos," in his *Kleine Schriften*, II (Munich, 1953), pp. 90-99. However, R. B. Y. Scott, in his article "Solomon and the Beginnings of Wisdom in Israel," *Wisdom in Israel and in the Ancient Near East* [223], pp. 262-279, traces the origin of the Israelite movement to the time of King Hezekiah (ca. 700 B.C.).

Kings 5:12; cf. 5:7), and he showed wisdom in other areas as well. His great wisdom is traditionally illustrated by his decision in the case of the two women who claimed the same baby (I Kings 3:16-28). The story goes that Solomon proposed to settle the argument by cutting the baby in two with a sword, giving half to one woman and half to the other. At this point the real mother of the child offered to surrender the baby, and Solomon, with psychological understanding of a mother's love, rendered the verdict in her favor. This folktale, one of the finest in the wisdom tradition, is rounded off with a statement of the community's response to the king's act:

> And all Israel heard of the judgment which the king had rendered; and they stood in awe of the king, because they perceived that the wisdom of God was in him, to render justice.
>
> —I KINGS 3:28

Here we have an excellent example of a popular story that must have circulated orally for many years before the editor of Kings picked it up as evidence that Yahweh had bestowed the gift of wisdom upon Solomon in answer to his "Deuteronomic" prayer (I Kings 3:3-14). The story is important for understanding the place of wisdom in ancient Israel. In our way of thinking, Solomon was a shrewd judge of character and knew how to use a little practical psychology when the need arose. But in Israel's view psychological insight did not come simply with maturity or as a result of keen observation of human behavior. Rather, it was believed that Yahweh bestowed wisdom upon the wise man, just as he gave torah to the priest or put his "word" into the mouth of the prophet.

The editor of Kings has preserved other information, less legendary in character, about Solomon's famed wisdom. One passage (I Kings 4:29-34) says that "Solomon's wisdom surpassed the wisdom of all the people of the east [that is, the bedouin Arabs], and all the wisdom of Egypt," as well as the wisdom of the sons of Mahol, who may have been Edomite sages.[7] People from all lands came to hear the wisdom of Solomon, for "he was wiser than all other men":

> He spoke of trees, from the cedar that is in Lebanon to the hyssop that grows out of the wall; he spoke also of beasts, and of birds, and of reptiles, and of fish.
>
> —I KINGS 4:33

Now this does not mean that Solomon was a biologist. Rather, the wise man, by studying the behavior of what we would call "nature," was given insight into correct human behavior, for ancient peoples did not draw the sharp distinction that we do between nature and human nature. Remember that Jeremiah contrasted the homing instincts of the birds with the rebellious conduct of Israel, implying that the birds could teach Israel how to behave (Jer. 8:7; see Is. 1:3).

---

[7] W. F. Albright, however, regards the sons of Mahol as Canaanite sages; see *Archaeology and the Religion of Israel* [50], pp. 127-128.

The sage turned to the natural scene, rather than to the historical drama of Israel, to gain wisdom. Jotham told the fable of the olive, fig, and bramble bush to show the folly of Abimelech's attempt to make himself king (Judges 9: 8-15). And the industry of the ant is offered as food for thought:

> Go to the ant, O sluggard;
>   consider her ways, and be wise.
> Without having any chief,
>   officer or ruler,
> she prepares her food in summer,
>   and gathers her sustenance in harvest.
>   —PROVERBS 6:6-8

In studying the behavior of animals, however, Israel's sages were not just trying to find moral lessons or clever figures of speech; they were trying to fathom the meaning of existence (see Prov. 30:24-31). And this attempt meant letting their interest range over every aspect of experience:

> Three things are too wonderful for me;
>   four I do not understand:
> the way of an eagle in the sky,
>   the way of a serpent on a rock,
> the way of a ship on the high seas,
>   and the way of a man with a maiden.
>   —PROVERBS 30:18-19

This is the sense, then, in which Solomon was reputed to have talked of trees, beasts, birds, reptiles, and fish.

Solomon's Songs and Proverbs

The historian reports that Solomon uttered three thousand proverbs and one thousand and five songs (I Kings 4:32). The last part of that statement supported the later tradition that the "sweetest" of Solomon's songs, about twenty-five of them, are found in the Song of Songs. The two lovers mentioned in these songs are the glorious King Solomon himself and apparently the famed Shulammite or Shunammite beauty who, according to I Kings 1:1-4, was brought to David to minister to him and to keep him warm during his declining days. There is no clear evidence that Solomon took Abishag as his wife (cf. I Kings 2:13-25), and there is still less basis for the claim that Solomon composed these sensuous love lyrics. Nevertheless, their association with Solomon and their popularity at wedding festivities established them so firmly in Israelite life that eventually they were admitted to the rank of sacred scripture, on the ground that the songs present an allegory of the covenant love between Yahweh and his people. Quite apart from this rather strained interpretation, the songs accent truths that are basic to Israel's faith: God's intention that man should live before him as a total personality, that man and woman should find fulfillment in their union with each other, and that married love should partake of the goodness of God's creation. Hellenistic notions of a dualism of "body" and "soul" find no support in the Old Testament, certainly not in the Song of Songs!

The other part of the historian's statement, which refers to Solomon's proverbs, became the basis for the claim that Solomon was the author of the book of Proverbs. In English the word "proverb" refers to a maxim or aphorism, like "A word to the wise is sufficient." The Hebrew word *mashal* may have this meaning, but it can also refer to a longer unit like the "parable" of the New Testament. Solomon may have spoken some of the proverbs found in the oldest section of the book of Proverbs (Prov. 10:21), but we cannot be sure of what comes from him. Probably most of the treasury of Solomonic wisdom has passed imperceptibly into the reservoir of Israel's wisdom tradition.

It was appropriate for Israel's sages to ascribe the whole fund of Israelite wisdom to Solomon, for, as we have observed (see pp. 150-159), his reign was characterized by a cosmopolitan outlook. When the Queen of Sheba came on a visit from far-off Arabia, Solomon displayed his wisdom by propounding and solving riddles (I Kings 10:1-10). And it is said that God gave Solomon "largeness of mind like the sand of the sea-shore" (I Kings 4:29). This claim is confirmed by the historical record, which shows that Solomon was extremely hospitable to the cultural influences of the Fertile Crescent, and established close relations with Phoenicia and Egypt. It was in the age of Solomon that Israel's horizons were first enlarged beyond the boundaries of her own heritage. The spirit of the time was reflected in one way by the Yahwist, who reinterpreted Israel's calling in terms of Yahweh's world-embracing purpose. It was expressed in quite a different way in the development of the wisdom tradition, which was concerned less with Israel's history than with the wide expanse of human experience. By both temperament and interest, Solomon was admirably qualified to be the patron of wisdom. Although Israel's wisdom literature flourished in written form chiefly after the fall of the nation, there is good reason to believe that the wisdom tradition received its greatest impetus during Solomon's reign.

Egyptian wisdom made a deep impression on Israel's thought from at least the time of Solomon, who established diplomatic ties with Egypt. The close parallels between the *Instruction of Amen-em-opet* and Proverbs 22:17-24:22 indicate that the Israelite writing depended heavily on the Egyptian writing (dated during the period 1000-600 B.C.).[8] There are only a few verses of this section of Proverbs that have no counterpart in the Egyptian source. The subject matter, the form of presentation, and even the telescoping of the thirty

---

[8] See Pritchard, *Ancient Near Eastern Texts*, pp. 421-424.

chapters of the Egyptian work into thirty sayings in the book of Proverbs (cf. Prov. 22:20) provide eloquent proof of Israel's contact with the wisdom of Egypt.

AN ANTHOLOGY OF PROVERBS

The history of Israel's wisdom movement is condensed in the pages of the book of Proverbs. It is generally agreed that this book, in its final form, comes from the period of Judaism, probably after the time of Ezra, when the wisdom schools were flourishing. But like the Pentateuch, the book of Proverbs represents the final stage of a tradition that goes back at least to the time of Solomon, who may have composed or collected the original nucleus. As the following headings indicate, several wisdom collections are contained in this one book:

1. Chs. 1-9: "The proverbs of Solomon"
2. 10:1–22:16: "The proverbs of Solomon"
3. 22:17–24:22: "The words of the Wise"
   24:23-34: "These also are sayings of the Wise"
4. Chs. 25-29: "The proverbs of Solomon collected by the men
            of king Hezekiah"
5. Ch. 30: "The words of Agur the son of Jakeh"
6. 31:1-9: "The words of Lemuel king of Massa"
7. 31:10-31: An alphabetic poem on the good housewife

A glance at this material is enough to show the diversity of the book. Notice that, in general, numbers 1-4 belong to the tradition of Solomon, while the remainder of the book is of foreign origin. And within these four, most scholars regard the second collection as the oldest portion of the book of Proverbs. The first collection is often regarded as the latest, but in view of the Canaanite elements in this section some scholars regard at least part of it as belonging to the pre-exilic tradition. All we can say for sure is that the book of Proverbs represents a complex tradition, extending throughout almost the whole of the Old Testament period.

Common-sense Proverbs

The wisdom sayings of this anthology are usually short, crisp, two-line sentences dealing with some aspect of experience. In some instances, the second line of the proverb runs parallel to the thought of the first. An example of this "synonymous parallelism" is found in Proverbs 22:1:

A good name is to be chosen rather than great riches,
    and favor is better than silver and gold.

Often the lines are a balanced pair of opposites. This type of "antithetic parallelism" is illustrated by 10:1:

> A wise son makes a glad father,
>   but a foolish son is a sorrow to his mother.

And sometimes the second line of the pair completes the thought of the first, in a kind of "ascending parallelism," as in 11:22:

> Like a gold ring in a swine's snout
>   is a beautiful woman without discretion.

Many of the proverbs give the impression of being rather "secular," although this term may be too modern to do full justice to the ancient appeal to common sense. It is true that the oldest proverbs show a positive, healthy view toward worldly affairs. Reflecting on various courses of human conduct, the sage suggests that the good life can be won through diligence, sobriety, and prudence, and that the marks of the good life are success, well-being, and a long and fruitful life. In this respect, the proverbs are quite similar to the prudential advice given by sages in Babylonia, Egypt, and elsewhere. Many of the biblical proverbs deal with ordinary problems that hinder a man from attaining fullness of life: laziness (6:6-11; 24:30-34), drunkenness (23:20-21, 29-35), relations with harlots (5:9-10), unwise business dealings (6:1-5), and so on. Judged by the frequency of the nagging-wife theme, the sage seems to have been greatly troubled by this problem:

> A continual dripping on a rainy day,
>   and a contentious woman are alike;
> to restrain her is to restrain the wind
>   or to grasp oil in his right hand.
>   —PROVERBS 27:15-16;
>   cf. 17:1; 19:13;
>   21:9, 19; 25:24

But beyond all this "secular" advice, there is a tendency to affirm that religious faith is the necessary foundation of the good life. The Deuteronomic historian, it will be recalled, applied the doctrine of rewards and punishments to Israel's history, and tried to show that obedience to Yahweh's Torah insured prosperity and success, whereas disobedience brought hardship and disaster. The wise men of Israel, building on the earlier common-sense view that success is the fruit of prudent living, insisted that the Deuteronomic dogma could be applied to the life of the individual. Thus the way was paved for the identification of Wisdom with Torah in the latest phase of Israel's wisdom literature.

The Fear of the Lord

The characteristic teaching of Israel's sages is summed up at the beginning of the first collection: "The fear of Yahweh is the beginning of knowledge" (1:7; cf. 1:29; 2:5). The same theme is repeated at the conclusion of the collection:

> The fear of Yahweh is the beginning of wisdom,
>   and the knowledge of the Holy One is insight.
> > —PROVERBS 9:10; *cf.* 15:33;
> > JOB 28:28; PSALM 111:10

In this affirmation we have the most direct contact between the wisdom teaching on the one hand, and Israel's prophetic and priestly tradition on the other. According to Israel's sages, wisdom comes not just by observing human conduct or by reflecting on sayings handed down in the wisdom schools. Rather, true wisdom comes only to the man who acknowledges the sovereignty of Yahweh— who "fears" or reverences the Holy One. Religious faith is the "beginning"—that is, the foundation or the heart—of wisdom. From faith the wise man is led into an understanding of the meaning of life. The "fool," on the other hand, gropes in confusion, regardless of how learned or technically skilled he may be.

You will remember that this same theme had been emphasized by Israel's religious leaders. According to the prophets, "knowledge of God" was the heart of the covenant faith. Hosea had insisted (see p. 248) that Israel's lack of this knowledge was the fundamental flaw in her history. Similarly, Jeremiah contrasted folly with true wisdom:

> Thus says Yahweh: "Let not the wise man glory in his wisdom, let not the mighty man glory in his might, let not the rich man glory in his riches; but let him who glories glory in this, that he understands and knows me, that I am Yahweh who practice kindness, justice, and righteousness in the earth; for in these things I delight, says Yahweh.
> > —JEREMIAH 9:23-24

Yahweh's great acts in history, the prophets insisted, were intended to correct folly and to awaken faith. The New Covenant, according to Jeremiah and Ezekiel, would be a new relationship in which Israel would "know Yahweh." In late Old Testament times, "the fear of the Lord" became a conventional expression for religious faith, and the "God-fearer" was the pious, humble worshiper of God. But in the period of the prophets, "the fear of Yahweh" and "the knowledge of Yahweh" were almost synonymous. Both phrases point to the deepest concern of man's life: his relationship to God.

Wisdom as God's Gift

Thus under the influence of Israel's faith a change took place in the traditional conception of wisdom. In early times, the wise man was regarded as one who had professional skill, owing to his uncanny insight into human affairs (cf. Prov. 6:6; 20:18; 21:22; 24:3-6; 30:24-28). Broadly speaking, this skill was regarded as a divine gift. A wise woman, addressing David in extravagant language, could say that "my lord has wisdom like the wisdom of the angel of God to know all things that are on earth" (II Sam. 14:20). But in actual practice wisdom meant only extraordinary skill or insight, as in some of the maxims of the book of Proverbs (e.g., 21:22; 24:3-6; 30:24-28). Just as the prophet advanced from the status of a professional seer to that of a religious interpreter of Israel's calling and destiny, however, so the wise man came to be an interpreter of life in its broadest and deepest terms. As the wisdom tradition was adapted to Israel's faith, it yielded a conception of wisdom with which the prophets would have agreed:

> Trust in Yahweh with all your heart,
>   and do not rely on your own insight.
> In all your ways acknowledge him,
>   and he will make straight your paths.
> Be not wise in your own eyes;
>   fear Yahweh, and turn away from evil.
> It will be healing to your flesh,
>   and refreshment to your bones.
>   —PROVERBS 3:5-8

In a manner reminiscent of Jeremiah (Jer. 10:12) or Second Isaiah (Is. 40:14, 28), Israel's sages affirmed that wisdom belongs pre-eminently to God:

> Yahweh by wisdom founded the earth;
>   by understanding he established the heavens;
> by his knowledge the deeps broke forth,
>   and the clouds drop down the dew.
>   —PROVERBS 3:19-20

This wisdom is more than just the key to proper ethical behavior, as in many of the proverbs (e.g., 4:10-19). Rather, it is the key to the divine plan behind the whole creation (30:2-4). That is why the fear of Yahweh is the only beginning of wisdom. Earlier sages had supposed that wisdom helped man to acquire wealth or influence, but later sages affirmed that wisdom far excels the greatest wealth and the most precious treasure. Wisdom comes from God. In exquisite language, the sage portrays wisdom standing at the gate of the city or in the crowded market place, crying to men to turn aside from folly and follow her footsteps (Prov. 1:20-33). Wisdom is God's gift, and blessed is the man who wins it (3:13-20). Indeed, Wisdom is personified as the agent of God's creation (Prov. 8-9).

The Wise and the Foolish

Despite all this refinement of the conception of wisdom, the book of Proverbs is governed by a neat doctrine of rewards and punishments. To be sure, the older view that wisdom brings success was superseded by the notion that wisdom itself is the highest good of life. But, according to the sages, this blessing is bestowed upon the good people. The wise are identified with the pious (see 9:9; 10:31; 23:24) and are contrasted with the scoffers (9:8, 12; 13:1; 14:6; 15:12; 21:11; 29:8). The Deuteronomic doctrine of the Two Ways (Deut. 11:26-28; 30:15-20) was a forceful and urgent appeal for decision in a time of historical crisis; but when it was applied to individuals, as in Proverbs (2:13; 5:5-6; 12:28), it gave rise to certain difficulties. Too easily the sages separated people into two camps—the wise (righteous) and the fools (wicked)—and claimed that rewards and punishments were meted out by Yahweh according to this formula.[9] Psalm 1, which some scholars think was written by a member of the wisdom schools, sets forth the Two Ways (see above, p. 486). The righteous man is like a tree planted by streams of water; the ungodly man is like the chaff that the wind blows away. The inadequacy of this doctrine was apparent to other wise men, who wrestled more profoundly with the riddle of life's meaning.

THE SKEPTICISM OF ECCLESIASTES

As we have seen, the distinctive contribution of Israel's sages was their teaching that wisdom is a gift of God, not a human achievement:

> No wisdom, no understanding, no counsel,
>   can avail against Yahweh.
> The horse is made ready for the day of battle,
>   but the victory belongs to Yahweh.
>   —PROVERBS 21:30-31

Men can prepare themselves by seeking diligently, but wisdom itself comes from Yahweh. The sages believed that this divine gift was available to men, particularly to the righteous who fear Yahweh. And they were convinced that wis-

---

[9] Notice that the opposite of "wise" is not "ignorant," but "foolish." Several words are used to describe the fool: he is "the evil one," "the self-confident one," "the empty person," and "the thick headed one." Regardless of how much he knows or how skilled he is, he is a fool if he has not found the key to life's meaning.

dom could not only show the right course of action, but could enable men to understand the riddle of life, indeed to comprehend the divine plan underlying the Creation.

This optimistic view was challenged by the author of the book of Ecclesiastes. Unlike the book of Proverbs, which is a "collection of collections" covering a long period of wisdom tradition, the book of Ecclesiastes is fundamentally the work of one sage who wrote during the late post-exilic period, perhaps between 250 and 200 B.C. His bold challenge to orthodox Judaism was regarded as dangerously close to heresy. Consequently, the book was touched up here and there to make it more palatable to orthodox taste.[10] Also, two conclusions were added. One disciple, who wrote the appendix in 12:9-11, praised the sage for his genius in weighing, studying, and arranging proverbs. But another editor, who wrote 12:12-14, cautioned the reader to take the teaching with a grain of salt, for "of making many books there is no end, and much study is a weariness of the flesh." According to this editor, the fundamental tenet of Judaism still stands unscathed in spite of the book's teaching: fear God and keep his commandments.

Had it not been for these pious revisions, and the tradition that Solomon had written the book, it is doubtful whether it would have found its way into the Old Testment canon. In fact, Ecclesiastes was one of the three books whose right to be included in the Bible was seriously questioned by the rabbis during the Tannaitic period (first century B.C. to third century A.D.).[11] Today the Jews read Ecclesiastes on the third day of the Feast of Tabernacles, in order to add a serious note to the festivity by reminding the congregation that the joys of life are transient and that man should number his days so that he may acquire wisdom (see Psalm 90:12).

The Melancholy Preacher

The word "Ecclesiastes" comes to us from the Greek Old Testament (Septuagint) by way of Jerome's translation, the Latin Vulgate. The Greek translator used the word *ekklesiastes* to render the Hebrew *qohéleth*, a participle related to the noun meaning "assembly, congregation" (Hebrew: *qahal*; Greek: *ekklesia*). Apparently the Hebrew word refers to "one who speaks to an assembly"—that is, a speaker or preacher. Thus Ecclesiastes is not a proper name, but a description of a function. It was believed that this function was performed by Solomon, who "assembled" the leaders of Israel in Jerusalem (cf. I Kings 8:1) and showed himself to be the preacher *par excellence* (see Eccles. 1:1). Having been "king over Israel in Jerusalem," Solomon is represented as saying that all through his career he has tried to search out by wisdom the meaning of human experience (1:12-13; cf. 2:4-11).

---

[10] Among the passages that are held to come from orthodox editors are 2:26; 3:17; 5:19; 7:18b, 26b; 8:11-13; 11:9b; 12:1a.

[11] The other two questionable books were Esther and the Song of Songs.

The word "preacher" may be misleading, however, for the book is not a sermon in the usual sense, but rather a rambling lecture on the meaning of life given by a professional wisdom teacher. The book as a whole is not arranged according to any pattern or scheme of development. Indeed, the reader gets the impression that the main point of the discourse has been made by the end of the second chapter. The thesis of the lecture, announced at the beginning and again at the end, is that all human activity is vanity and a striving after the wind:

> Vanity of vanities, says the Preacher,
> vanity of vanities! All is vanity.
> —ECCLESIASTES 1:2; 12:8

Writing in the melancholy vein of Omar Khayyám's *Rubáiyát*, the sage announces that man's wisdom cannot "grasp the sorry scheme entire." Wisdom, he admits, does have some value, for it enables men to walk circumspectly, aware of the limitations of mortal life. "The wise man has his eyes in his head, but the fool walks in darkness" (2:14). Indeed, wisdom is the source of strength greater than ten rulers (7:19). But the advantage won through practical wisdom is doubtful (2:12-23; 7:7-8), for with wisdom comes increase of sorrow (1:18) and in the end death comes alike to the wise man and the fool (2:14-17). Ecclesiastes advises his pupils to make the best of life while they are alive, enjoying the present and not trying to prove the future (2:24-25; 3:12-15; 7:14). For the grim truth is that, despite its practical value, wisdom cannot penetrate the mystery of life and deal with the ultimate questions; yet it is on the answers to these questions that man's very existence hangs. Unable to gain access to the divine wisdom that underlies the Creation, the wise man is thrown back upon himself to define the meaning of life. As a result, he feels despair over the emptiness of life, or even develops a hatred for life (2:17) that reminds one of the nausea expressed by some modern existentialists.

God's Hidden Purpose

Some scholars believe that the author of Ecclesiastes, living in the Hellenistic period inaugurated by Alexander the Great, was influenced by Greek philosophy and by the sense of fate (*moira*) that obsessed Greek culture. There is at least a superficial resemblance to the philosophy of Epicureanism, for the sage advises "seizing the day" (*carpe diem*) and enjoying momentary pleasures while they last (8:15-9:9; cf. I Cor. 15:32). Moreover, there is a kind of determinism in the outlook of Ecclesiastes—a realization that whatever happens has been foreordained long ago. The sage knows how to accept the joys and sufferings of life with an inner serenity, undisturbed by the ebb and flow of fortune (6:10-11; 9:1). It is often pointed out that this teaching is reminiscent of the philosophy of Stoicism, and some have suggested that several of the words used

by Ecclesiastes are taken from a Greek context. For instance, the word translated "chance, accident" (2:14; 3:19; 9:2-3) is said to be the philosophical equivalent of Greek *tyche* ("chance").

It seems clear that Ecclesiastes was influenced in some degree by the spirit
of Greek culture. This was the atmosphere that he breathed, and he could no
more escape the Hellenistic spirit than a modern writer can avoid the influence
of the scientific spirit of the twentieth century. But it is doubtful that Greek
concepts influenced Ecclesiastes in any fundamental way. In spite of his "tragic
sense of life," he never surrenders the conviction that God is sovereign over
human affairs. The tragedy of life is not that the inexorable power of fate gov-
erns both man and God, as in Greek culture, but rather that God's wisdom is
so inscrutable that, from the human angle of vision, life has no rhyme or reason.
Since man cannot know the ways of God, everything seems to happen by chance.
Indeed, says Ecclesiastes, "there is nothing new under the sun," for to all ap-
pearances the weary course of life turns back in a circle to the beginning (1:4-
11). Nevertheless, he emphatically affirms that everything is "in the hand of
God" (9:1). The trouble is that God's sovereignty is so completely hidden to
human view that men are left in the dark about the divine plan, if indeed there
is one. Therefore, to human wisdom events are matters of caprice. The days
turn in a circle, rather than moving toward the fulfillment of purpose.

The Times of Man's Life

This world-outlook of Ecclesiastes is disclosed in a very important discussion of the nature of time (chapter 3). We might compare Ecclesiastes'
sense of time with that reflected in a modern hymn:

> Time like an ever-rolling stream
>   Bears all her sons away;
> They fly forgotten as a dream
>   Fades at the break of day.

Like the hymn-writer, Ecclesiastes was poignantly aware of the transience of
life. But to him life's tragedy is not that men are caught in an inexorable
process of time that mechanically grinds out the days and years. He does not
speak of time abstractly. Rather, he writes of concrete "times"—that is, times
that have a specific content or purpose. "For everything there is a season," he
writes, "and a time for every matter under heaven" (3:1). There is a time to
be born and a time to die, a time to plant and a time to harvest, a time to
weep and a time to laugh, a time to embrace and a time not to embrace, a time
to keep silence and a time to speak, a time for war and a time for peace, and so
on (see Eccles. 3:2-9). A time is an opportunity that invites a particular
action, just as we say "now the time is ripe" or describe an action as "timely."
Ecclesiastes speaks of times in the plural—man's times. Moreover, he believes

that somehow man's times are in God's hands. Each time is an opportunity sent from God, for "he has appointed a time for every matter, and for every work" (3:17).[12]

The problem of life is that man, with his limited wisdom, cannot discern any over-all purpose running consistently through life's experiences; as a result, the times just come one after another, and everything seems to turn in a circle of futility. Ecclesiastes acknowledges that God in his wisdom can see the whole movement from beginning to end. But man is not God. Man is like the animal, for he must die; but he is more miserable than the animal, for—to use a phrase from Matthew Arnold—he longs to "see life steadily and see it whole." Ecclesiastes testifies that "He [God] has put eternity [?] [13] into man's mind, yet so that he cannot find out what God has done from the beginning to the end" (3:11). Mortal man cannot peer beyond the veil that hides the purpose of the Eternal God from human understanding. Consequently, he is overwhelmed with the ultimate meaninglessness of human existence. For if man cannot discern the thread that binds the times together purposefully, the verdict of futility must be pronounced upon all human thought and activity.

The Problem of Death

For Ecclesiastes the tragedy of life is heightened by the intense realization that the problem of existence must be answered within the brief span between birth and death (cf. 8:6-8). The problem of death—the most universally human experience—hangs like a dark shadow over the whole book. The death of the individual had not loomed as a serious problem in the early period of Israel, for then it was believed that the individual's life was given meaning by his participation in the covenant community. The father lived on in his son, and all generations were bound together in the psychic solidarity of Israel. Unlike the Egyptians, who developed elaborate preparations for the after-life, Israel was not preoccupied with death. The doctrine of the resurrection of the self (body) emerged very late in the period of Judaism, as we shall see in the next chapter. Ecclesiastes, however, is governed by the individualistic spirit of the Hellenistic age, rather than by the covenant thinking of the priests and prophets of Israel.[14] Separated from a historical community that bears life's meaning, the destiny of the individual becomes an acute problem. Ecclesiastes does not evade the

---

[12] The Hebrew word is equivalent in meaning to the New Testament word *kairos*, as found, for instance, in Mark 1:15.

[13] The word which the RSV translates as "eternity" is very difficult to interpret in this context. In his commentary on Ecclesiastes [228], pp. 220-221, R. B. Y. Scott maintains that the word means "enigma" (or "darkness," "obscurity"), and he translates: "Yet he has put in their minds an enigma, so that man cannot discover what it is that God has been doing, from beginning to end."

[14] The word "Israel" appears only once (1:12), and refers to the people over whom Solomon ruled.

problem by affirming the survival of the individual beyond death, for he knows too well the limitations of human nature. Man is a mortal being. There is nothing in him that is immortal or "deathless." In this respect, man is no better than the animal (3:18-22), for at death "all go to one place" (3:20). Only in this life is there hope, for "a living dog is better than a dead lion" (see 9:5-6). Because Ecclesiastes takes death seriously, he takes life seriously.

The sage, then, looks upon the world with a pessimistic eye. Unable to see in nature the handiwork of God, he complains that the sun, wind, and sea follow an aimless course, for "all things are full of weariness" (1:5-8). According to him, orthodox Judaism, summed up in the doctrine of the Two Ways, does not ring true to experience, for the righteous are rewarded with suffering and the wicked are chastened with success. Ironically, a man who has toiled with wisdom has to leave everything to a man who did not work for what he received (2:18-23). The dead, says the sage, are more fortunate than the living, but better than both is not to be born at all (4:1-3; cf. 2:17; 6:3-5). He advises discreet reverence in the house of God, "for God is in heaven, and you upon earth; therefore let your words be few" (5:1-7). He recommends moderation in both wisdom and folly, for too much of either may lead to disaster (7:15-18). He counsels enjoying marital bliss and finding satisfaction in work, for all too soon one must go to Sheol, the land of the dead, where there is "no work or thought or knowledge or wisdom" (9:9-10). He broods over the accidents of life that make it absurd to plan for the future:

> Again I saw that under the sun the race is not to the swift, nor the battle to the strong, nor bread to the wise, nor riches to the intelligent, nor favor to the men of skill; but time and chance happen to them all.
> —ECCLESIASTES 9:11

Man does not know his "time"—that is, the time of his death; for, like a bird caught in a snare, the evil time suddenly "falls upon" him. Ecclesiastes concludes by exhorting men to enjoy life while they are young, before the infirmities of age or death take their toll (11:9-12:8).

The Shadow of Despair

This skepticism, however, is fundamentally religious. To be sure, Ecclesiastes does not pretend to give divine teaching, after the manner of prophets or priests, but rather to set forth the lessons derived from experience and reflection (see 1:13; 7:23; 9:1). And yet his conception of God is fundamental to his world-outlook, even though he uses the general name Elohim instead of the special Israelite name, Yahweh. The basic tenet of his theology is that God is hidden. But there is a precedent for this theme in Israel's religious heritage, for from ancient times it had been affirmed that the God who reveals himself also conceals himself. God had revealed his name (that is, his identity), but

Yahweh also was the Holy One hidden from human sight. He helped and delivered, but he also performed the "strange deed" that plunged men into bewilderment and even despair. He gave "signs" of his presence and power, but never provided proofs that eliminated the possibility of doubt. In the epic of the Yahwist and the Confessions of Jeremiah, to take two examples, we have found a picture of the despair that accompanies faith like a shadow. Ecclesiastes writes within the shadow of despair. For him God is transcendent, completely other, separated from man by an infinite gulf (see 5:2). No other writer puts more emphasis on the sovereignty of God. He orders and controls, but his sovereignty is completely hidden to human understanding (3:10-11; 8:17; 11:5). Even when men cannot understand, however, he has no ground for questioning God's sovereignty, for "who can make straight what God has made crooked?" (7:13).

The book of Ecclesiastes is a vigorous repudiation of the claim that wise men can discern the purpose of God. The sages of the book of Proverbs had claimed optimistically that wisdom, beginning with "the fear of Yahweh," could chart the Two Ways and even identify the travelers along each road. But Ecclesiastes insisted that wisdom can do none of this, for man's mind cannot fathom the wisdom of God:

> When I applied my mind to know wisdom, and to see the business that is done on earth, how neither day nor night one's eyes see sleep; then I saw all the work of God, that man cannot find out the work that is done under the sun. However much man may toil in seeking, he will not find it out; even though a wise man claims to know, he cannot find it out.
>
> —ECCLESIASTES 8:16-17; cf. 8:23-24

Since religious people are prone to settle down comfortably in their faith, supposing that they possess the answer to life's questions under their hats, it is fortunate that the rabbis finally decided to include Ecclesiastes in the canon. For, as one of the editors of Ecclesiastes wrote, "the sayings of the wise are like goads" (12:11). Like the prophets, they awaken men from complacent orthodoxy and stimulate the struggle for faith that can stand all the tests of doubt and despair.

THE BOOK OF JOB

We turn now to the greatest monument of wisdom literature in the Old Testament, the book of Job. Through the centuries, this book has received the highest of praise. Luther extravagantly said that Job is "magnificent and sublime as no other book of Scripture." Tennyson called it "the greatest poem of ancient and modern times," and Carlyle declared that "there is nothing written, I think, in the Bible or out of it of equal merit." Philosophers, supposing that the book is concerned with the problem of evil, have manifested great interest in it.[15] In our day the writer has been acclaimed as "the Shakespeare of the Old Testament." And recently Archibald Macleish has attempted to interpret the meaning of the biblical book for our time in his play, *J.B.*[16]

The Impatience of Job

The strange thing is that many who celebrate Job have only a faint understanding of what the book is about. This ignorance is clearest among those who refer to the "proverbial patience" of Job (cf. James 5:11). In the popular mind, Job is a model of piety—a man who patiently and serenely suffered "the slings and arrows of outrageous fortune" without losing his faith. But this portrait holds true only in the prologue (1:1-2:13) and the epilogue (42:7-17), both of which are written in prose. The main part of the book is in poetic form, and here Job is anything but a paragon of patience. He begins by cursing the day of his birth, and his spirit gathers the fury of a tempest as he hurls his protests to God. Only at the very last, after Yahweh has rebuked him, does he repent of his wild and impatient charges, lapsing into something like the lull that follows a storm.

Before we go into the relation between the prose and poetic sections of this book, let us summarize the contents of the prologue and epilogue. The narrative tells the story of Job, a man renowned for his piety and blessed with the divine favor that accompanied his righteousness. But Job's sincerity was suspect to one of the members of the Heavenly Council—"the Satan." Notice that the definite article is used with *satan*, a Hebrew word which literally means "adversary." In the prologue, the Satan is not represented as the Arch-enemy of God, as in later Jewish and Christian thought (where "Satan" becomes a proper name), but rather is an angel in good standing in the Heavenly Council (see Zech. 3:1ff.) whose special function is to investigate affairs on earth.

When Yahweh boasted to the Council about his servant Job, the prosecuting Angel, suspecting that Job's service was motivated by self-interest, cynically asked: "Does Job fear God for nought?" Thereupon he made a wager with Yahweh that if Job's prosperity and family were taken away his faith would be destroyed. These losses did not shake Job's faith, however, for in his sorrow he patiently murmured: "Yahweh gave, and Yahweh has taken away; blessed be the name of Yahweh." So the Satan proposed a more severe test. Job was stricken with loathsome sores from head to foot, making it necessary for him to sit alone in the city refuse ground. Ignoring his wife's advice, he still refused to "sin with his lips" by cursing God. Then his three friends—Eliphaz, Bildad, and Zophar—came to comfort him in his plight. In the end, according to the

---

[15] Immanuel Kant, in his monograph *On the Failure of All Philosophical Attempts in Theodicy*, devoted considerable space to interpreting the book of Job.

[16] Archibald Macleish, *J.B.: A Play in Verse* (Cambridge, Mass.: Riverside Press, Sentry Edition, 1961).

epilogue, Yahweh accepted Job's prayer and restored to him twice as much as he had before. And, as in all good folktales, Job lived happily ever after.

The Relation between the Prose and Poetry

It is generally agreed that the author of the poetic sections did not compose the story that appears in the prologue and epilogue. Not only is there the difference between prose and poetry, but the portrait of Job himself differs, as we have noticed. Moreover, the author of the narrative uses the name Yahweh, whereas the author of the poems uses general terms for deity, such as *'Eloah* (God) or *Shaddai* (The Almighty).[17] And finally, the narrative is written in the charming manner of a folktale, whereas the poetic sections resemble the wisdom literature in Proverbs and Ecclesiastes. It follows, then, that if we are to understand the viewpoint of the author of Job we must rely on the poems rather than on the prologue and epilogue.

This does not mean, however, that the prose narrative is unrelated to the poetic meditations. In fact, the effectiveness of the poems is due largely to their being framed within the context of the folk story. Since the story is located in Edom, the area southeast of the Dead Sea on the border of the Arabian desert, it is possible that the Job legend originated in Edomitic territory around Teman (1:1; 2:11; cf. Hab. 3:3). In any case, the author of the poems appropriated the old story as a literary framework within which to place his poetry. The story provides the life-situation that occasions the poetic meditations. Intending to address himself to the deepest problem of every man, the poet wisely bases his meditation upon the experience of one man whose legendary righteousness was well known in antiquity. As we noticed in an earlier chapter, Ezekiel mentions Job together with Daniel as legendary wise and righteous men (Ezek. 14:14, 20). Daniel (or Dan'el) was celebrated in Canaanite legend now known to us in the Ras Shamra literature. Similarly, the story of Job must have circulated orally for many years before it was written down as we now have it. In short, the author took a well-known story and placed his poetic meditations between the first part and the conclusion, substituting his own poetry at the point where Job's friends come to console him. As a result, the prose and poetic sections constitute a unified work that elaborates a single theme. Because the author's distinctive theological outlook is found only within the poetic section of the book (3:1-42:6), however, he must not be held accountable for the theological problems raised by the narrative, such as the Satan's wager with Yahweh.

The Poetic Pattern

Let us glance briefly at the material found in the poetic sections. Unlike

---

[17] Outside the prologue, the name Yahweh occurs only in the headings in chapters 38-42. It also occurs in 28:28, which many scholars regard as a later addition, and in 12:9 where the text is not certain.

other wisdom literature, such as Proverbs and Ecclesiastes, the poetry is devoted to a single theme, which is developed in the exchange between Job and his friends. Job speaks first, uttering a terrible lament over the day of his birth (Job 3). Then Eliphaz responds (chs. 4-5), and Job gives his rebuttal (chs. 6-7). Next, Bildad joins the discussion (ch. 8), and Job replies (chs. 9-10). The third friend, Zophar, adds his advice (ch. 11), to which Job again responds (chs. 12-14). Here we have a complete cycle, during which Job has answered each of his friends. The discussion then goes back and forth in the same manner until three full rounds are completed. After a final monologue by Job (chs. 29-31), Yahweh answers him out of the whirlwind, and Job repents (38:1-42:6).

It is clear that what we have here is a carefully planned literary scheme. The third cycle (chs. 22-27), however, has been thrown out of order by revisers who tried to tone down Job's heretical utterances, and the poem on wisdom (ch. 28) has been inserted into its present context by later editors. Another irregularity is the presence of a long poetic rebuke of Job by Elihu (chs. 32-37), which is definitely an intrusion into the literary scheme. Elihu is not mentioned as one of Job's friends in either the prologue or epilogue. He has nothing to say during the three rounds of discussion, and his advice comes as an afterthought, following the statement that "the words of Job are ended" (31:40). It is generally held that the Elihu speech was added by a later Jewish writer who sought to uphold orthodox Judaism even more vigorously than the three friends.

To summarize, the book of Job falls naturally into the following outline:

1. The prose prologue (1:1–2:13)

2. Three cycles of discussion
   a. Job's lament (ch. 3)
   b. First cycle:
      Eliphaz (chs. 4-5)
         Job's answer (chs. 6-7)
      Bildad (ch. 8)
         Job's answer (chs. 9-10)
      Zophar (ch. 11)
         Job's answer (chs. 12-14)
   c. Second cycle:
      Eliphaz (ch. 15)
         Job's answer (chs. 16-17)
      Bildad (ch. 18)
         Job's answer (ch. 19)
      Zophar (ch. 20)
         Job's answer (ch. 21)
   d. Third cycle: [18]

---

[18] Various reconstructions of the third cycle have been attempted. In the above outline, the proposal of Samuel Terrien, *Interpreter's Bible*, III, p. 888, is followed. Notice that according to the confused state of the received text the speech of Zophar is missing, that of Bildad is curiously short, and Job inconsistently seems to endorse the view of his friends (see 24:18-24; 26:5-14; 27:13-23). Evidently, editors have tried to correct Job's statements by rearranging the text.

Eliphaz (ch. 22)
    Job's answer (23:1–24:17, 25)
Bildad (25:1-6; 26:5-14)
    Job's answer (26:1-4; 27:1-12)
Zophar (24:18-24?; 27:13-23?)
    Job's answer is displaced by the chapter on wisdom (28)
e. Job's final defense (chs. 29-31)

3. Yahweh's answer from the whirlwind
   a. The first speech (chs. 38-39), followed by Job's submission (40:1-5)
   b. The second speech (40:6–41:34), followed by Job's repentance (42:1-6) [19]

4. The prose epilogue (42:7-17)

The Author of Job

The date and authorship of the poem of Job are exceedingly difficult to determine, for the writer gives us no hint of the historical circumstances of his time. Like Ecclesiastes, he displays no interest in the traditional motifs of Israel's faith, such as Yahweh's activity in history or the election of Israel. The hero of the book is not an Israelite, but an Edomite sheik from the land of Uz, which was evidently in the southeastern part of Palestine around Edom (cf. Gen. 31:2; Jer. 25:19-24; Lam. 4:21), the area from which Job's friends came (2:11). The locale of the book is not the city of Jerusalem, but the edge of the desert. All these facts, together with certain peculiarities of language, have led to the conjecture that the author was not an Israelite at all. According to one theory, the author was an Edomite.[20] But the hypothesis that the author of Job was a foreigner has yet to be proved. It is plausible to assume that the author was an Israelite sage who lived perhaps on the outskirts of Palestine.

The fact that the Edomites are pictured in a favorable light seems to indicate that the Hebrew version of the Job folktale arose in the pre-exilic period, for beginning with the sixth century B.C., when the Edomites encroached upon Judean territory, the Jews viewed their southern neighbors with bitter hatred (cf. Obad. 10-14). The prose story, at least, probably would not have been written during this period of animosity. As to the poetic section of Job, however, there is no general agreement on whether it should be assigned to the period of the Exile or to some time in the post-exilic period. A possible clue is the relationship of the poems of Job to Second Isaiah, for between the two books there are numerous parallels of thought and language. Did Second Isaiah

---

[19] The Yahweh speeches apparently have been expanded, perhaps by the addition of the poem on the ostrich (39:13-18) and some of the description of Leviathan (41:12-34). Some scholars regard the descriptions of Behemoth (hippopotamus) and the Leviathan passage (40:15-41:34) as later additions.

[20] See Robert Pfeiffer, *Introduction* [28], pp. 678-683.

depend upon Job or vice versa? If the author of Job knew the poems of Second Isaiah, it is strange that as he explored all the possible answers to the mystery of suffering he made no allusion to Second Isaiah's treatment of suffering as a sacrificial witness for others. On the other hand, it is possible that the suffering of Job influenced Second Isaiah's portrayal of the Suffering Servant. These considerations lead some scholars to the conclusion that Job preceded Second Isaiah, and that the book was written between the time of Jeremiah and Second Isaiah, speaking in general terms.[21]

The date of Job is not decisive for the interpretation of the poem, however, for, like the wisdom literature in general, it deals with a human situation that cannot be confined to any particular time. Even the Edomite locale of the story is incidental, for the writer deals with human existence as such, whether the man in question be an Edomite, Israelite, Egyptian, or of some other nationality. Not that the author is unconcerned with historical existence, though. His concrete portrayal of the hero Job is evidence enough that he was dealing with the stuff of daily experience—with human life as it is lived in history. And yet the author raises the historical question in such a way that it has universal relevance, regardless of a man's social background, historical milieu, or religious tradition. In the last analysis, the historical question is the religious question raised with infinite concern: What is the meaning of *my* life—this solitary person who thinks and loves, remembers and hopes, lives and dies? The poet looked intensively into the depths of one man's existence, and in so doing exposed the *human* question. This intensive concentration gives to the book of Job a dramatic quality—not in the sense that it was intended for stage performance like a Greek drama, but in the sense that, like any great drama, the reader knows that the hero is undergoing his own interior struggles. Job is Everyman.

Job and Other Wisdom Literature

Behind the writing of the book of Job was the wisdom literature of many generations, not only that of Israel but of the whole Near East. The author may have been acquainted with a Babylonian writing often referred to as the "Babylonian *Job*." [22] According to this story, a man who was originally rich and influential was suddenly stricken with great illness and trouble. Bitterly he complained that his prayers and sacrifices had been in vain. Like Job, he protested his innocence, and insisted that the will of the god was beyond human understanding:

---

[21] See Marvin H. Pope, *Job* [231], pp. xxx-xxxvii, who judiciously discusses the problem and inclines to a date in the late pre-exilic period: the seventh century B.C. Pfeiffer (*op. cit.*, p. 677) dates Job about 600 B.C. Terrien (*op. cit.*, pp. 888-890) proposes a date between 580 and 540 B.C. Other scholars favor a later date in the fifth or fourth century B.C.

[22] It is entitled *I Will Praise|the Lord of Wisdom*, after its opening words. See Pritchard, *Ancient Near Eastern Texts*, pp. 434-437.

Oh that I only knew that these things are well pleasing to a god!
What is good in one's sight is evil for a god.
What is bad in one's own mind is good for his god.
Who can understand the counsel of the gods in the midst of heaven?
The plan of a god is deep waters, who can comprehend it?
Where has befuddled mankind ever learned what a god's conduct is?

—LINES 33-38; *cf.* JOB 9:1-12

Finally, when the hero was on the verge of death, the god Marduk suddenly rewarded him for his virtue and restored him to health.

Even more interesting is the Babylonian *Dialogue about Human Misery* [23] between a skeptic who, having known nothing but suffering, questions the justice of the gods, and a pious friend who advocates humble surrender to the divine will and faithful performance of religious obligations. As in the book of Job, the conversants speak in turn. The skeptic begins, the pious man responds, and so on. This dialogue resembles the book of Job so strikingly, both in form and content, that it is tempting to believe that the author of Job was influenced by it.

From Egypt come other examples of the literary form used in the book of Job. For instance, in the *Protests of the Eloquent Peasant*, the poetic discussion is framed between a prose prologue and epilogue. Also, Egyptian pessimism is illustrated by the *Dispute with His Soul of One Who Is Tired of Life*, otherwise known as the *Dispute over Suicide*.[24]

It is impossible, of course, to prove that the author of Job was directly dependent on these or other writings of antiquity. Since apparently he was a man of wide travel and learning, he was probably acquainted with literature from many places. And certainly he was influenced by currents of thought from Mesopotamia, Egypt, Arabia, Edom, and elsewhere. But he was not an eclectic who borrowed indiscriminately from a variety of sources. He stamped what he received with his own distinctive and highly original thought and experience. Moreover, even though he displayed no interest in the traditional themes of Israel's faith, his outlook was profoundly influenced by the Israelite heritage.

FROM DESPAIR TO FAITH

Many people assume that the purpose of the book of Job is to discuss the problem of suffering (evil), or to raise the philosophical question of how absolute goodness and absolute power are reconciled in the nature of God (theodicy). But the reader who approaches the book expecting to find an answer to these questions will be disappointed. Indeed, it is doubtful whether the author had

[23] See Pritchard, *op. cit.*, pp. 438-440.
[24] *Ibid.*, pp. 407-410 for reference to the former (*Protests*), and pp. 405-407 in the case of the latter (*Dispute*).

any intention of trying to answer them. To be sure, he wrestles with an in-escapable problem of human life: the suffering of the innocent. But the problem of suffering—and its counterpart, the question of divine justice—provide the occasion for probing a much deeper question, namely, *the character of man's relationship to God.* This issue is first introduced in the prologue, where the Satan insinuates that Job's relation to God is not one of unqualified trust "for better or for worse," but a fair-weather service of God in order to obtain the blessings of health, reputation, family, and long life. In the poetic sections, the nature of Job's faith is explored at a much deeper level. Finally, after the discussion has ranged through the whole realm of experience, Yahweh gives an answer out of the whirlwind. Job then submits in silence and *repents,* where-upon his life is put on a new axis. In order to understand the book of Job, we must view the poetic meditations in the light of the whole composition, which reaches its climax when Yahweh speaks and Job humbly repents.

The Dialogue between Job and His Friends

Let us consider briefly the dialogue between Job and his friends. Under-lying the friends' argument is the doctrine of rewards and punishments that was widespread in the wisdom literature of antiquity. According to this view, virtue was rewarded with prosperity, health, and long life; and, conversely, sins were punished by poverty, sickness, and untimely death. This doctrine, as we have seen, was applied to Israel's national history by the Deuteronomic his-torian and was applied to the individual in Proverbs and, later on, in the Wis-dom of Ben Sira. The three friends claim to understand the meaning of life in terms of this doctrine.

The dialogue is introduced by Job's lament, one of the most poignant pas-sages in the Bible. No doubt influenced by one of Jeremiah's confessions (Jer. 20:14-18), it expresses the aching misery of existence in language of rare im-aginative power. Notice that Job's death-wish springs from his sense of the emptiness of life when he is estranged from a meaningful relation to God. He does not question God's sovereignty; rather, he laments that his sovereignty is so completely eclipsed that life has no meaning (cf. 9:11; 13:24). Job's outcry is an expression of the anxiety that afflicts the most sensitive sufferer: the anxiety of meaninglessness. Such suffering, more terrible than the torment of physical pain, can be assuaged only by death, "the king of terrors" (cf. 18:14), or, better, by not coming through birth to consciousness. With a fine poetic touch, Job wishes that the light had never dawned upon his natal day, and that the night of his conception had never seen "the eyelids of the morning."

Eliphaz tries to comfort Job by suggesting that the flaw lies in Job himself. At first, Eliphaz is courteous in offering his advice. All men have sinned, he points out; therefore Job should humbly confess his sin rather than hurl his protest at God. Since the fault really lies within Job, as the friends agree, the remedy also is within his power (see 11:14 ff.; 22:21). But as Job stubbornly insists on his innocence, the friends become vehement in their accusation. Attempting to defend the majesty of God, they use every argument available to demonstrate that God is just in his dealings according to the orthodox formula of rewards and punishments. They accuse Job of pride, charging that he does not accept the finite limitations of manhood. They say that if he were really honest he would have to admit that God had punished him more lightly than he actually deserved. Again and again they entreat him to surrender his haughty defense of his righteousness and to make supplication to the Almighty.

The poet portrays the three friends in such a manner that they are more to be pitied than Job, the sufferer. Although they are sincere in their stand, and at times speak of the meaning of faith in eloquent language, they cling desperately to their orthodoxy, and sense in Job's dangerous words a threat to their own security. Orthodoxy has invariably feared the heretic, as the history of Western civilization amply shows. In a truly prophetic spirit, the author of Job championed the creative power of heresy, for faith is often most vigorous when it dares to break with theological dogmas—yes, even with "religion"—and to enter into unchartered areas. The three friends were too smug in their orthodoxy, too sure of the answers to life's enigmas, too confident that God was bound by their logic. In the face of opposition, they could answer only with clichés. Eventually their rigidity prevented them from having any real sympathy for Job. They supposed that they had grasped the wisdom of God. "It is not God they defend," writes a modern interpreter, "but rather their own security. Indeed, it is their pride which they uphold when they condemn Job, and it is their sin which they reveal when they pay tribute to divine sovereignty." [25]

Job's Promethean Defiance

Job retorts that the friends speak only "windy words" that bring poor comfort to him in his search for the meaning of life. Despite their claim that they have diagnosed his malady, they are "worthless physicians." Annoyed by their pious taunts, he maintains his innocence and integrity with increasing passion. He admits that he may have sinned, as all men do, but insists that he is comparatively righteous and, in any case, that the punishment does not fit the crime (14:1-6). At first he contented himself with cursing his miserable existence, or wishing that God would crush him instantly instead of prolonging his torture (6:8-9). But soon his words break beyond all restraint. The flaw, he cries, is not in himself but in God, who is responsible for his misery. He accuses God of appearing as a sinister enemy. Instead of caring for his creature, God is like a capricious tyrant (9:18-19), a savage beast (16:7, 9), a treacherous assailant (16:12-14). In a display of wild imagination, he likens himself to the

---

[25] The quotation comes from Samuel Terrien ([233], p. 900), whose insights have influenced this whole discussion.

mythical sea-monster (Tiamat or Rahab), the arch-enemy of God, over whom God has set a watch (7:11-12). In utter misery, he wishes that God would let him alone, even long enough for him to swallow his saliva, for if he could only escape God his spiritual agony would end.

> What is man, that thou dost make so much of him,
>   and that thou dost set thy mind upon him,
> dost visit him every morning,
>   and test him every moment?
> How long wilt thou not look away from me,
>   nor let me alone till I swallow my spittle?
>   —JOB 7:17-19

In the prologue, as we have seen, Job is a very submissive man who, despite the enormity of his misfortune, does not "sin with his lips." But in the poems Job is a different person altogether. His accusations are so wildly defiant that they must have appeared heretical to any orthodox Jew, which undoubtedly accounts for the fact that the third cycle of poems was rearranged and the Elihu speeches added. Jeremiah in his Confessions had hurled bold questions to God; but Job goes even further in challenging the Almighty. Clinging adamantly to his integrity (27:6; 31:36), he virtually sets himself up as the judge of God. In one mood he wishes that he could escape God's clutch, and in another he wishes that he could meet God in a fair debate, even as an equal, in order that his integrity could be vindicated (31:37). Like Prometheus, Job is a titanic figure who doubts, rebels, and shouts defiance at God.

Job's Plea for Vindication

Throughout his spiritual struggle, Job is tortured by the remoteness and hiddenness of God—the God who "hides his face" (13:24). His poignant cry is: "O that I knew where I might find him!" (23:3). As Job's thought hovers uncertainly between doubt and hope, he considers the possibility that God will not finally abandon him, but will seek him only to discover, too late, that he is in the grave (7:21). With increasing clearness he sees that a great gulf is fixed between the Creator and the creature, between the righteousness of God and the righteousness of man, and that man is foolish to try to span the chasm (9:32-33). At times, he admits that the wisdom of God so surpasses the wisdom of men that men may know God only if God chooses to speak and reveal himself. He knows that God is "God and not man"—the Wholly Other, the Transcendent One, the Absolutely Sovereign. And by contrast he knows that man is an earth-bound creature, held under the power of sin which taints his nature (4:17-21; 14:4; 15:14-16; 25:4-6) and subject to the dominion of death (4:19; 7:6).

Although Job finds no access from man to God, he dares to hope that some day, somehow, a reconciliation will take place. Then the impassable gulf will be bridged, and the contradiction between God as he now appears and God as he really is will be resolved. Apparently this is the meaning of the well-known passage in which Job affirms that his Vindicator (*Go'el*) will restore him to fellowship with God: [26]

> I know that my redeemer [Vindicator] lives,
>   and at last he will stand upon the earth;
> and after my skin has been thus destroyed,
>   then without my flesh I shall see God,
> whom I shall see on my side,
>   and my eyes shall behold, and not another.
> My heart faints within me!
>
> —JOB 19:25-27

Unfortunately the Hebrew text is so uncertain, especially in verse 26, that no reliable translation can be given. For instance, the meaning of the phrase translated "without my flesh" is very obscure. Does the phrase refer to a vindication before death or after? If after death, this passage may be the earliest reference in the Old Testament to the resurrection of the body. But even assuming that the thought of life beyond the grave occurred to Job, it is clear that he rejected it as a solution to his problem. To him, death was a tormenting issue precisely because it was the end, beyond which there could be no satisfactory answer to the enigma of life (see 14:7-15). Probably the meaning of the above passage is that the Vindicator in heaven (cf. 16:19) would effect Job's reunion with God, which had been his deepest longing during the dark days of estrangement and loneliness. For, as the writer of the Seventy-third Psalm affirmed, the nearness of God is man's greatest good (Ps. 73:21-28).

Job's search for the meaning of life has carried him to the very limits of thought, where momentarily his vision is enlarged. However, his stance is not changed. Still he is concerned primarily with his own self-vindication. Still, his questions betray his stubborn self-sufficiency, his determination to find the meaning of life on his own terms. To the very end he asserts his integrity. In answer to his friends' accusations, he reviews his life with the conviction that the record is unblemished:

> Far be it from me to say that you are right;
>   till I die I will not put away my integrity from me.
> I will hold fast my righteousness, and will not let it go;
>   my heart does not reproach me for any of my days.
>
> —JOB 27:5-6

Job's concluding defense is a long declaration of the high ethical standards by

---

[26] For the meaning of the word *go'el*, see p. 409, footnote 11. Marvin Pope ([231], pp. 134-135) compares this mediator or arbiter, who will prove Job's innocence, to the personal god in Sumerian tradition who acts as a defender in the Council of the gods.

which he has lived, and a vivid portrayal of the righteous man (chapters 29 and 31). His final word is a ringing challenge: "Let the Almighty answer me!" (31:35).

The Voice from the Whirlwind

Then Yahweh answers Job out of the whirlwind—but not in response to Job's cry for vindication or as an endorsement of Job's innocence. In fact, the speech of Yahweh is not so much an answer as a series of ironical questions that make Job's questions irrelevant. The effect of the questions is to remind Job that he is a creature whose finite standards are ineffective for judging the Creator:

> Who is this that darkens counsel
> by words without knowledge?
> Gird up your loins like a man,
> *I will question you*, and you shall declare to me.
> —JOB 38:2-3

Then follows a superb account of God's work as Creator, Sustainer, and Provider. God's questions are designed to remind Job of the deity of God and the humanity of man. Was Job present at the time of the Creation,

> . . . when the morning stars sang together,
> and all the sons of God shouted for joy?
> —JOB 38:7

Job had been talking as if he knew exactly how God should run the world. His sense of integrity had been the basis of his presumptuous claim that God should have treated *him* better. Outraged that he could not square his innocence with his fate, Job had dared to challenge and judge his Creator. His religious quest had been motivated by a Promethean defiance. Therefore, Yahweh's answer came in the form of a rebuke—an overwhelming reminder that the first religious obligation of the creature is to acknowledge and glorify the Creator.

Job's Repentance

Yahweh's speech raised questions that Job could not answer. He had presumed to know too much, to be more than he was. Silenced, he admits that he has no ground for arguing with God (40:1-3). As his final word, he retracts his rash charges and casts himself humbly and repentantly before God:

> Therefore I have uttered what I did not understand,
> things too wonderful for me, which I did not know. . . .

> I had heard of thee by the hearing of the ear,
>   but now my eye sees thee;
> therefore I despise myself,
>   and repent in dust and ashes.
>   —JOB 42:3, 5-6

Along with Job's confession of his sin of self-sufficiency went a new consciousness of fellowship with God—not the God of traditional religion, but "the Living God." This in itself was a form of "vindication," but not the kind that Job had asked for. Although the author of Job did not compose the prose epilogue, he appropriately placed it just after the statement regarding Job's repentance, with the implication of Job's restoration to a new and more meaningful life through the grace of God.

To some readers it is disconcerting that the book of Job does not end with an attempt to resolve the problem of suffering, or to cast light on the goodness and omnipotence of God. Assuming that the book is concerned primarily with these questions, some interpreters believe that Yahweh's speech was beside the point and that Job finally had to admit that the problem of God's justice was too great for his understanding. *But the key to the book of Job is Job's repentance,* and the preceding discourses which come to a climax with the voice from the whirlwind. From the very first, the fundamental issue is Job's relationship to God. The climax of the poem occurs at the very end, when a false relationship based on self-sufficiency is converted into a relationship of personal trust and surrender. In the words of Job, formerly he had heard of God by hearsay—that is, he was related to a conception of God received from tradition. But "now my eye sees thee." Job in the moment of repentance was related to *God himself* in an act of personal faith. Instead of a total eclipse, the divine light shone directly upon him, giving meaning to all his sufferings. By repudiating the smug orthodoxy of his friends, his life was open to receive the gift that God bestows to those who truly seek him with all their heart. It is appropriate that in the epilogue, Job, rather than his friends, receives Yahweh's approval for having spoken rightly, and that Job offers a prayer of intercession for his friends, whose orthodoxy was a barrier separating them from genuine faith.[27]

The mystery of suffering is left rationally unanswered, as it is finally unanswered in the Bible as a whole. For the crux of the human problem, according to Israel's faith, is not the fact of suffering but the character of man's relationship to God. Outside the relationship for which man was created, suffering drives men to despair or to the easy solutions of popular religion. Within the relationship of faith, suffering may be faced in the confidence that man's times are in God's hands and that "in everything God works for good with those who love him, who are called according to his purpose" (Rom. 8:28).

---

[27] For a different interpretation of "the philosophy of Job," see R. H. Pfeiffer, *Introduction* [28], pp. 692-707. There it is argued that the book deals exclusively with the problem of God's justice (theodicy).

THE PERSONIFICATION OF WISDOM

Before concluding this chapter we must refer to one of the most important developments in the wisdom tradition. As we have seen, the sages believed that wisdom is not mere human insight, but is the divine purpose by which the universe is directed and in obedience to which man should order his life. From this conviction it was an easy step to regard wisdom as having a special and an almost independent status in God's Creation. We have noticed that in the book of Proverbs wisdom is personified as a woman who stands in the market place, summoning men to follow her ways (Prov. 1:20-22). At first consideration this may appear to be the Hebraic way of describing abstract concepts in concrete, personal terms. But the glorification of wisdom was carried further, as can be seen from a superb lyric in Proverbs (3:13-20), where it is affirmed that wisdom is the most precious of treasures, for

> Yahweh by wisdom founded the earth;
>   by understanding he established the heavens.
>   —PROVERBS 3:19

Wisdom's Cosmic Status

A hymn to wisdom, found in Proverbs 8 and 9, depicts wisdom as a distinct personality who was present with Yahweh at the time of the Creation. Wisdom, it is said, was created by Yahweh as his first creative act and was "beside him like a master workman" as he did his work.[28]

> When he established the heavens, I was there,
>   when he drew a circle on the face of the deep,
> when he made firm the skies above,
>   when he established the fountains of the deep. . . .
> then I was beside him, like a masterworkman;
>   and I was daily his delight,
>   rejoicing before him always,
> rejoicing in his inhabited world
>   and delighting in the sons of men.
>   —PROVERBS 8:22-31 (in part)

In these cases wisdom has a cosmic status. Wisdom is, or is moving toward becoming, a hypostasis—that is, a distinct entity.

---

[28] This translation, which has the support of the principal ancient versions, is challenged by R. B. Y. Scott, "Wisdom in Creation: the 'āmōn of Proverbs vii 30," Vetus Testamentum, X (1960), pp. 213-223. See also his commentary on Proverbs [228], p. 72. Scott proposes to read the term as a participle, "uniting, binding together" and to translate: "Then I was beside him binding [all] together." This translation, he maintains, knocks the props out from under the view that wisdom is hypostasized in Proverbs 8.

This lofty conception of wisdom was not original with Israel, but the conception was subjected to a special development in the Israelite tradition. In the magnificent hymn to wisdom found in Job 28 it is affirmed that wisdom, the plan of the universe, is hidden from men.[29] Search as men will, wisdom cannot be found in the sky, the earth, or the Deep. God alone knows the path to wisdom, for he established it at the time of the Creation:

> God understands the way of it,
>   and he knows its place.
> For he looks to the ends of the earth,
>   and sees everything under the heavens.
> When he gave to the wind its weight,
>   and meted out the waters by measure;
> When he made a decree for the rain,
>   and a way for the lightning of the thunder;
> then he saw it and declared it;
>   he established it, and searched it out.
>   —JOB 28:23-27

Later Reflections on Wisdom

Beyond the boundaries of the Hebrew Bible the cosmic significance of wisdom received even greater attention. In the book known as the Wisdom of Ben Sira (or Ecclesiasticus), written in the early second century B.C., wisdom is compared to the breath issuing from the mouth of God—an emanation that penetrates all things:

> I came forth from the mouth of the Highest,
>   and like vapor I have covered the earth;
> I have made my abode in the heights,
>   and my throne on a pillar of cloud.
>   —ECCLESIASTICUS 24:3-4

Here, too, it is said that wisdom was created before all things and poured out upon all that God made (Ecclesiasticus 1:1-20). However, wisdom is said to have found rest only in Israel, where she was associated with the Temple of Jerusalem and the Law of Moses (Ecclesiasticus 24).

In another writing, the Wisdom of Solomon (c. 50 B.C.), wisdom is clearly a hypostasis, almost identified with God himself. In a portion of the relevant passage (Wisd. Sol. 7:22-8:1) it is written:

> For Wisdom is more mobile than any motion,
>   and she penetrates and permeates everything
>   because she is so pure;

---

[29] Clearly out of place in Job's mouth before Yahweh's speech reminded him of the limitations of human understanding, the poem has obviously been inserted into its present context. It may have been written by the author of Job and placed here by later editors.

for she is the breath of the power of God,
    and a pure emanation of his almighty glory;
therefore nothing defiled can enter into her,
    for she is a reflection of the everlasting light,
and a spotless mirror of the activity of God,
    and a likeness of his goodness.
Though she is one, she can do all things,
    and while remaining in herself, she makes everything new.
                            —WISDOM OF SOLOMON 7:27 ff.

Thus wisdom came to be regarded as a semi-independent power—the agent of God's creation and the intermediary between God and the world. Israel's sages had become aware of the chasm between man and God, between human wisdom and the wisdom possessed by God. But their reflection also led them toward the understanding that the gulf is spanned from God's side, through the agency of the divine wisdom that dwells among men.

We have noticed that the wisdom literature of the Old Testament manifests no interest in the revelation of God in Israel's history. The sage was interested in man as a human being, rather than in the unique historical drama in which God had made himself known to a particular people, Israel. In the late period of biblical Judaism, however, wisdom was understood in relation to God's redemption of Israel. An excellent witness of this is the Wisdom of Ben Sira. Here a Jewish sage, by identifying Wisdom and Torah, brought the wisdom literature into the central stream of the Mosaic tradition. Wisdom was "nationalized," that is, related positively to the redemptive activity of God in history. In order to gain Wisdom, said Ben Sira, one must keep the commandments of the Torah (Ecclesiasticus 1:26).

For the Christian church, the wisdom movement came to its fulfillment in Jesus Christ. Paul identified Wisdom with Christ, through whom redemption came to all mankind (I Cor. 1:24, 30). Moreover, it is probable that the prologue to the Fourth Gospel, which begins with the words, "In the beginning was the Logos [Word], and the Logos was with God, and the Logos was God," should be understood in the light of the wisdom of the East, especially that of Israel's sages. Thus the Christian church received from Israel a conception of cosmic, pre-existent wisdom in terms of which the significance of God's revelation in Jesus Christ could be understood.

THE

UNFULFILLED

DRAMA

   Looking back over a nation's past, it seems that there are times when the river of history flows quietly, smoothly, like the wide waters of the St. Lawrence, and at other times cascades with a thunderous roar like the falls of the Niagara. This figure of speech may be applied to Israel's history in the new period inaugurated by Cyrus' edict releasing Jews from exile in Babylonia. Despite the troubles faced by the struggling Jewish community dur-

Biblical readings: After brief consideration of the books of Esther and Jonah, our attention will focus on the book of Daniel, whose historical background is presented in the book of I Maccabees. The "little apocalypse," found in Isaiah 24-27, and so-called Second Zechariah (Zech. 9-14), belong to the same type of literature as Daniel.

ing the Reconstruction, there is considerable reason for believing that through-out most of the Persian period the Jews of Palestine enjoyed great security. To be sure, this inference is drawn from silence. The story of the Jewish community, which breaks off with the Chronicler's account of reconstruction under Nehemiah and Ezra, is not resumed until I Maccabees, a book (outside the Hebrew Bible) which covers events of the second century B.C. (175-132 B.C.). Much of the interim, especially the fourth century, is obscure or totally blank. This historical silence may mean that Judah was relatively secure for a century or more after Nehemiah and Ezra. But the times were destined to change. Before the Old Testament closes, we see the stream of Israel's history plunging and swirling along a turbulent course.

TENSIONS WITHIN JUDAISM

So long as the remarkable stability of the Persian empire persisted (539-332 B.C.), the Jewish community in Palestine was not molested by external political threats. At the height of its power, this empire included the whole Fertile Crescent and extended beyond to the Aegean on the west, the Indus Valley on the east, the steppes beyond the Caspian Sea on the north, and Egypt on the south (see map, p. 400). Long before the rise of Alexander the Great, the Persians had created a far-flung political regime that encouraged citizens to widen their horizons, to lengthen their trade arteries, and to jostle with people and ideas from other lands. Even though there was no attempt to superimpose Persian religion upon the whole empire, we may be sure that the influence of Zoroastrianism was felt in Judah.

Thus Judah's problem was no longer that of being caught in the rip tide of rivalry between the two power centers of the Fertile Crescent, Mesopotamia and Egypt. Her problems were more local. We have already referred to the increasing tension between Jews and Samaritans (p. 437), which led to the building of the rival Samaritan temple on Mount Gerizim, probably in the middle of the fourth century. In the future, we may expect more light from archaeology on these local affairs of the post-exilic community.

But there were also tensions within Judaism itself. We must not think of Judaism as a monolithic structure, fashioned by the great reforms of Nehemiah and Ezra. True, the reconstruction along the lines of an exclusive community, with the Temple as its center and the Torah as its constitution, was carried out with great vigor, for Nehemiah's position as a Persian governor gave great prestige to his leadership, and Ezra too enjoyed the blessing of the Persian government. But there were also other currents within Judaism, currents that are reflected in the book of Psalms and other anonymous literature composed in this period. At the very time when Jewish exclusivism was developing, wisdom teachers were reflecting on the meaning of life in an atmosphere of thought that was more international than Israelite. And in some circles spacious views were expressed which contrasted with the narrow exclusivism of Nehemiah and Ezra, as we have already noted in the case of the book of Ruth (p. 450).

The Story of Jonah

A prophetic universalism, reminiscent of Second Isaiah, finds expression in the book of Jonah, which stands in the collection of the Twelve (see Chart on p. 76). Like so many authors of the post-exilic period, this writer does not disclose his name. Instead, he presents his message in the guise of a story concerning a prophet who lived at a time when prophets were still active—back in the days of Jeroboam II (see II Kings 14:25). This is not a biographical account of what actually happened in the experience of the prophet—Jonah, son of Amittai—but a short story told to drive home a prophetic message to the writer's generation. In the judgment of many scholars, it was written in the post-exilic period, no earlier than the fifth century B.C. and perhaps toward the end of the Persian period in the fourth century.

Many people think of Jonah as a "fish story"—perhaps the biggest one ever told. Modern literalists ingeniously search the seven seas for a "whale" whose belly is big enough to accommodate a man, and they try to produce documentary evidence that there have been other instances of persons who have come out alive after a sojourn in a whale's stomach. Once we recognize that this is a short story, however, all this speculation is beside the point.

The story tells how Jonah was commissioned by Yahweh to go to Nineveh, the Assyrian capital (see photo, p. 321), and preach that the city would be destroyed if it did not repent. No task could have been more distasteful, for the Assyrians, who had oppressed Israel cruelly, were bitterly detested (see Nahum). So Jonah ran as fast as he could go in the opposite direction. From Joppa, the fugitive took a ship bound for Tarshish, in the western Mediterranean, whereupon Yahweh hurled a great wind upon the sea. The panic-stricken sailors cried out to their gods to discover the cause of the divine anger that was on the verge of destroying the ship. The lot fell on Jonah, who was sleeping peacefully in the hold, and he was arraigned before the captain. After some discussion, it was agreed to throw Jonah overboard—and suddenly the sea became calm. Yahweh, however, prepared a great fish (the narrative says nothing about a whale) to swallow Jonah, and after three days and nights in the fish's belly, he was vomited forth upon the land.[1]

Once again the commission was given to preach to Nineveh—a city so expansive, according to the writer's exaggerated description, that it took three days to walk through it. This time Jonah began to preach to the wicked city, only to be shocked that his preaching was successful. The whole city was converted

---

[1] It is generally agreed that the psalm (2:2-9), which Jonah is represented as reciting in the fish's belly, has been inserted into the Jonah story by an editor.

and Yahweh "repented" of the evil he had planned. Like Elijah but for just the opposite reason, Jonah was so discouraged and angry about this turn of events that he wished to die. On the outskirts of the city he made a booth for himself, and sat down beneath its protective shade to observe what would happen. Yahweh then commanded a gourd to grow up as an umbrella over Jonah's head; but the next day he sent a worm to wilt it, thus exposing Jonah to the merciless heat of the sun. When Jonah expressed pity for the gourd, Yahweh rebuked the prophet for not being able to understand that Yahweh would show at least as much pity toward the city of Nineveh, with its 120,000 infants and many cattle.

The point of the parable is that Yahweh's sovereignty is not circumscribed by the boundaries of the chosen community; for in his freedom he has mercy upon whom he will (cf. Ex. 33:19!) and shows his salvation in the most unexpected places. The Jewish people were rebuked for supposing in their pride that Yahweh's purpose was restricted to the preservation of the Jewish community, even at the cost of the destruction of Jewish enemies, and they were reminded that other people—yes, even the enemies of the Jews—were embraced within Yahweh's mercy. At the very time when the policies of Nehemiah and Ezra were fostering a narrow nationalism, the unknown prophetic writer of the book of Jonah proclaimed that Israel's call was not a guarantee of privilege and prestige but a responsibility: to bear witness to the God whose salvation reaches to the ends of the earth.[2]

The Book of Esther

At the opposite extreme to the book of Jonah is another story—a novel —the book of Esther. Found in the third section of the Hebrew Bible (the Writings; see Chart, pp. 556-557), Esther is one of five festal scrolls that are read even yet on important festivals of the Jewish calendar. Despite the fact that it does not contain a single explicit reference to God or the religious practices of Judaism, the scroll of Esther came to be regarded as the scroll *par excellence,* and in later Jewish tradition it was given a place second only to the Torah.[3] Because of its seemingly non-religious character, and because its nationalistic spirit might be misunderstood, various rabbis of the Tannaitic period (first century B.C. to third century A.D.) expressed uncertainties about its right to be included in the canon. But owing to the popularity of the Feast of Purim, with

---

[2] This view, supported by the majority of scholars, has been challenged by Yehezkel Kaufmann in *The Religion of Israel* [65], pp. 282-286. He maintains that the point of the story is not Israel's vocation in the universal setting of God's purpose but Yahweh's readiness to forgive his people.

[3] The Greek Old Testament (Septuagint) contains several extra passages which give the story a more religious tone. The translator of the Vulgate, Jerome, placed these additions to the Hebrew scroll at the very end of the story (after Esther 10:3). They are included in the Protestant Apocrypha under the title: "The Additions to the Book of Esther."

THE MOUND OF ANCIENT SUSA *as seen from the air. Once
the capital of ancient Elam, Susa was inhabited as early
as the fourth millenium* B.C. *Under Cyrus, the city was
one of several capitals of the Persian empire (see Neh. 1:1;
Esth. 1:2); it later served as a winter residence for Persian
kings. The mound is situated on roads leading to the sites
of other former Persian capitals: Ecbatana (a summer capital), and Persepolis (the main capital). The chateau visible in the center of the picture was built by archaeologists
whose work in the nineteenth century uncovered the Code
of Hammurabi and the Stele of Naram-Sin (pp. 22, 24).
The cone-like building to the left is a mosque which, according to Moslem tradition, covers the tomb of Daniel.*

which the book was associated, these doubts eventually proved too weak to have
any lasting effect and faded away.

The story is placed during the reign of Ahasuerus—that is, Xerxes I (486-465
B.C.). The scene opens in Xerxes' winter palace at Susa, whose remains, once
comparable with the beautiful architecture of Persepolis (see photo, p. 442; and
Plate 6), have been excavated. When Vashti the queen refused to show off
her beauty at the king's lavish wine banquet, she was deposed and a search was
made throughout the empire for the most beautiful girls from whose number
the king might select a new queen. Esther (or Hadassah—her Jewish name)
took part in the beauty contest. Her loveliness was so natural that, without having to go through the year of beauty treatments required by the other maidens,
she captured the king's affections. Her position as queen of Persia enabled her
to avert a plot to liquidate her Jewish people.

The writer has subtly constructed the story around the ancient hostility between Israel and the Amalekites, which began in the time of Moses (Ex. 17:16; cf. Num. 24:20; Deut. 25:17-19) and which blazed up in Saul's day when the Israelite king was commanded to subject king Agag and his Amalekite tribesmen to the sacrificial ban or *ḥérem* (see pp. 134-135). This hostility is embodied in two of the principal figures of the story: Mordecai the Jew, who is regarded as a Benjaminite descendant of Kish, the father of Saul (I Sam. 9:1); and Haman, described as the son of Hammedatha, "the Agagite"—a descendant of the Amalekite king conquered by Saul. Because Mordecai refused to pay him the proper courtesies, Haman the grand vizier planned to liquidate the Jews scattered throughout the empire. When Haman pointed out to Xerxes that the Jews refused to be assimilated, choosing instead to live by their own laws (3:8), Xerxes granted him permission to issue an edict for a wholesale massacre of Jews on the thirteenth day of the month Adar (February-March).

Mordecai, however, persuaded Esther, his cousin, to risk her life on behalf of her people by going to the king, even though an unsummoned visit was punishable by death. Favored by a remarkable series of coincidences, the tables were now turned on the enemies of the Jews. The *ḥérem* was executed on Haman, who, ironically, was hung on the towering gallows (83 feet high) that he had constructed for Mordecai. Haman's ten sons were also executed—thus bringing the last of the "Amalekites" to an end. Moreover, by royal decree the thirteenth of Adar became a day on which the Jews of Susa were permitted to slaughter their persecutors, and on another day—the fourteenth of Adar—the Jews in the provinces of the empire were authorized to continue the bloodshed. At the end of the *ḥérem* a festival of rejoicing was held, which came to be known as Purim in remembrance of the lot (*pur*) that Haman had cast to determine the day of vengeance. The story not only purports to explain the origin of this popular festival but also to account for its celebration on two days.

There are, of course, numerous elements of fiction in the story—like the irrevocable royal decree that a husband should be boss in his own house (1:21-22), and the fabulous bribe that Haman promised to raise (the equivalent of $18,-000,000; cf. 3:9). The story of how Haman was duped into proposing the way Mordecai should be honored by the king (chapter 6), and how he was trapped in an absurd situation that resulted in his death on the very gibbet he had prepared (chapter 7), was unquestionably designed to tickle Jewish humor. It is quite possible, however, that the story rests on the historical memory of a real threat to Jews of the Dispersion. If this is true, Esther is a historical novel that dates from the latter part of the Persian period, when the memories of Xerxes' reign were dim, and when Jews were subject to persecution owing to their refusal to be assimilated.[4] In any event, the story of the origin of Purim came to be very popular during the Maccabean period, when the stubborn separation

---

[4] A number of scholars, however, believe that the book of Esther reflects the persecution of Jews during the Maccabean period. For a discussion of the question, see Bernhard W. Anderson, *Interpreter's Bible*, III, pp. 825-828.

of Jews from heathens occasioned violent persecution. And throughout the tumultuous Jewish history since then, Haman has been the symbol of a number of wicked leaders (like Adolf Hitler) who have carried out vicious programs of anti-Semitism.

Esther is unique among the books of the Jewish Bible in that it studiously avoids religious matters. The author seems to go out of his way to avoid direct mention of God, as for instance in 4:14 where the reference to deliverance coming "from another place" is often regarded as a veiled allusion to help from God. This theological reticence was probably motivated by the fear that the Name of God might be profaned in connection with the carefree festival of Purim when, as we learn from the Talmud (*Megillah* 7b), it was permissible to drink wine freely, until the difference between "Blessed be Mordecai" and "Cursed be Haman" became blurred! However, beneath the heady worldliness of the book of Esther—as the Septuagint version rightly interprets—is the conviction that God has called his people to be separate from the world (see 3:8) and to be exclusively loyal to him. True, the book of Esther lacks the wide vistas of Second Isaiah or Jonah; its provincial and vindictive spirit is much closer to the prophecy of Nahum. But in a time of foreign domination and aggressive cultural influence, when the vitality of Israel's tradition was threatened, it seemed that the only course of action was a narrowing of loyalty. In its own way the book of Esther intended to say with Elijah: "I have been very jealous for the Lord God of hosts" (I Kings 19:10). This jealousy, or "zealousy," became religiously articulate in another writing composed under foreign domination: the book of Daniel. Before turning to Daniel, however, we must sketch the political changes brought about by the rise of Alexander the Great.

THE HELLENISTIC ERA

The westward expansion of the Persian empire had resulted in a series of clashes between Greeks and Persians in such famous battles as Marathon, Thermopylae, and Salamis. The courageous Greeks fought hard to keep the Persians from their soil. Then, in the latter part of the fourth century, the political tide turned with the rise to power of one of the greatest military leaders in the history of civilization, Alexander of Macedon (336-323 B.C.). Twenty years of age when his father, Philip of Macedon, was assassinated, he set out on a dramatic military career in which victory followed victory—at the Granicus in Asia Minor (334), at Issus in upper Syria (333), at Tyre and Gaza (332), and at Arbela in Mesopotamia (331). From these triumphs his armies swept on through Persia and Afghanistan, and by 326 had reached the Indus River in present-day Pakistan. Never before had a military leader been crowned with such dazzling victories.

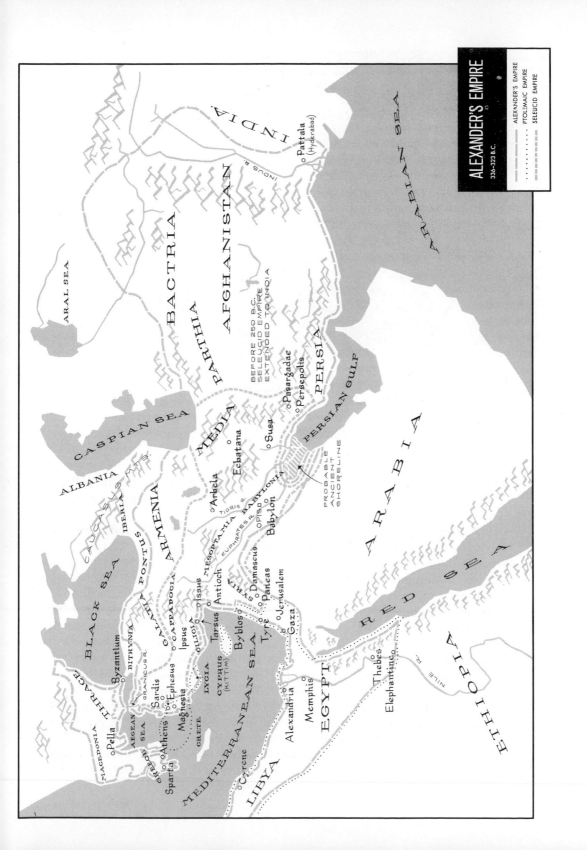

ALEXANDER'S EMPIRE
336–323 B.C.

ALEXANDER'S EMPIRE
PTOLEMAIC EMPIRE
SELEUCID EMPIRE

INDIA

Pattala
(Hyderabad)

ARABIAN SEA

BACTRIA

PARTHIA

AFGHANISTAN

ARAL SEA

BEFORE 250 B.C.
SELEUCID EMPIRE
EXTENDED TO INDIA

Pasargadae
Persepolis

PERSIA

PERSIAN GULF

CASPIAN SEA

MEDIA

Ecbatana

Susa

ALBANIA

CAUCASUS MTS.

IBERIA MTS.

PONTUS

ARMENIA

Arbela

TIGRIS R.

MESOPOTAMIA

EUPHRATES R.

BABYLONIA

OPIS

Babylon

PROBABLE
ANCIENT
SHORELINE

ARABIA

BLACK SEA

THRACE

BITHYNIA

GALATIA

CAPPADOCIA

GRANICUS R.

Byzantium

Sardis

Ephesus

Magnesia

CILICIA

Ipsus

Tarsus

LYCIA

CYPRUS (KITTIM)

Issus

Antioch

Damascus

Paneas

Tyre

Byblos

Gaza

Jerusalem

RED SEA

MACEDONIA

Pella

AEGEAN SEA

GREECE

Athens

Sparta

CRETE

MEDITERRANEAN SEA

Cyrene

LIBYA

Alexandria

Memphis

EGYPT

Thebes

Elephantine

NILE R.

ETHIOPIA

ALEXANDER THE GREAT *presents an offering to the Egyptian god, Amon, in this relief on a wall of the Temple of Karnak. Although Alexander himself (left, holding tray of objects) never visited Thebes, he had no difficulty appropriating the ancient Egyptian belief that a king is the son of a god. The blending of Occidental and Oriental culture in Hellenism is also symbolized by the Greek inscription underneath the Egyptian hieroglyphic.*

According to legend, Alexander stood weeping on the banks of the Indus River because there were no more worlds to conquer. (See Chronological Chart 10, p. 541.)

Having studied under the Greek philosopher, Aristotle, Alexander was interested not only in military conquest, but also in spreading the best fruits of Greek culture. The city of Alexandria, Egypt, which was named after him, came to be a monument to the Greek way of life in all its aspects: intellectual, athletic, artistic. Alexander dreamed of "one world"—a world bound together by Greek culture. Believing that Greek learning was superior to all other, he considered it to be his divine mission—for he was honored as a god—to leaven ancient civilization with Greek scholarship, art, and manners.

Alexander did not live to see his dream fulfilled, for he died in the year 323 B.C. before he reached his thirty-third birthday. His vast empire was partitioned among his generals, two of whom inherited the eastern domains. Mesopotamia and Syria eventually went to Seleucus, and Egypt came under the sway of Ptolemy. Once again, Palestine was caught in a struggle between the powers of the Fertile Crescent, this time with the capitals located at Antioch (Seleucid) and Alexandria (Ptolemaic). Alexander's policy of spreading Greek culture through the world was continued by the leaders of these two sections of his empire, despite the political rivalry between them.

The Struggle for Cultural Unity

The term "Hellenism" is applied to the Greek-like culture that was fostered by Alexander's successors. Derived from Hellas, the ancient name for Greece, it refers to the perpetuation of the Greek spirit within the countries of the Alexandrian empire. Just as the American visitor to the Middle East today can see signs of the spread of western civilization—for instance, advertisements for Pepsi-Cola, Socony Vacuum, or Hollywood movies—so in the Hellentistic period a visitor to the same area would have found gymnasiums, theaters, stadiums, and so on. Moreover, Greek dress became fashionable, especially among the more well-to-do. And an obvious sign of the spread of Hellenism was the widespread use of the Hellenistic vernacular known as *koine* Greek —that is, the spoken language of international business and political affairs as distinct from the classical Greek of the age of Pericles. Like English today, Greek was the *lingua franca*. Hellenism, then, represents a synthesis of the Occident and the Orient.

The rivalry between Seleucids and Ptolemies was not just military: both Antioch (see Plate 8) and Alexandria vied to become cultural capitals as great as Athens had been in the past. The "school of Antioch," however, was surpassed by Alexandria. The Ptolemies, patrons of the arts and sciences, built up a famous museum at Alexandria, with a huge library that would compare favorably with the best libraries of today. Under their sponsorship, research was carried on by a band of notable scholars, including the mathematician Euclid and the physicist Archimedes. The cultural ascendancy of Alexandria was enhanced by the city's strategic commercial relations with the Mediterranean world on the one hand, and with Arabia and the Fertile Crescent on the other.

At first, the Jews apparently did not regard Hellenism as a serious threat to their faith. No problem was felt in Alexandria, for ever since the days of the founding of the Elephantine colony, Egyptian Jews had been receptive to foreign influences. In this part of the Dispersion, Aramaic was superseded by *koine* Greek, and under the aegis of Ptolemy II (285-246 B.C.) scholars began the task of translating Jewish scripture into Greek. Thus, over a period of years, the Septuagint was produced, the translation to which we have referred from time to time. Since a language inevitably conditions one's manner of thinking about the world, it is not surprising that Greek-speaking Jews produced a number of books, like the Wisdom of Solomon, which were influenced by a Hellenistic world-view.[5]

Shortly after the partition of Alexander's empire, Palestine came within the orbit of the Ptolemies. These Egyptian rulers, rather easy-going in contrast to

---

[5] On the Wisdom of Solomon, see the remark in Chapter 16, footnote 2.

the aggressive Seleucids, made no attempt to coerce Jews into cultural conformity. It is said that Ptolemy III (246-221 B.C.), on a visit to Jerusalem, deferred to Jewish custom and presented a thank-offering at the Temple. Under the mild, patronizing rule of the Ptolemies, undoubtedly many modernistic Jews welcomed Hellenism, seeing no contradiction between the new cultural fashion and their traditional faith. Many of these modernists were found in the upper classes, whose education and commercial interests exposed them to the attractions of Hellenism.

The Resistance Movement

The spread of Hellenism, then, posed anew the problem with which Israel had had to wrestle ever since the entrance into Canaan: the relation between faith and culture. Again and again, when Israel's faith was on the verge of being sold out in the world's markets, individuals arose who rigorously protested in the name of the jealous God of the covenant. Like Elijah, these champions were zealots—men who were zealous to uphold the covenant faith and to bring about its renewal in times of degeneration. As we have seen repeatedly, this protest against the seductiveness of foreign culture was often accompanied by the revival of Israelite nationalism, as in the case of the Deuteronomic Reform. In the Hellenistic era, the stage was prepared for another revival, kindled by both conservative religious loyalty and by the nationalistic hope for the re-establishment of a Davidic state. The revival caught fire in the circle of a sect known as the Hasidim (the "loyal, or pious ones"), the forerunners of the later Pharisees. Although the Hellenizers tended to be found among the Jewish upper classes, the Hasidim in many (but certainly not all) instances came from a rural background, where they were more or less isolated from the allurements of the Hellenistic world. Filled with great zeal for the Torah, they frowned upon the modernism of fellow Jews who were welcoming Hellenistic styles of thought and behavior, and they clung conservatively to the faith of their fathers. Although this resistance movement must have started very early in the Hellenistic period, it did not appear on the scene of history until a dramatic turn in political affairs, which ended the rule of the Ptolemies in Palestine.[6]

The Outbreak of Jewish Persecution

Although the Seleucids of Syria had repeatedly tried to gain control of the Mediterranean coastland, which they claimed belonged to them by right,

---

[6] Ancient sources for the history of the Maccabean period are I-II Maccabees—works found outside the Hebrew Bible. They are included in the Roman Catholic canon and found in the Protestant Apocrypha (see Chart, pp. 4-5). In addition, there are the important works by the first-century A.D. Jewish historian, Josephus. For modern studies of the period, see Bibliography, Nos. 238-243.

Palestine remained under the control of Egypt during the third century B.C. But in 223 B.C., Antiochus III (the Great) came to the Syrian throne in Antioch. After more than two decades of war with Egypt, in 198 B.C. the Syrian king won a decisive victory over Ptolemy V at Panias (or Paneas), near the source of the Jordan River, thereby bringing Palestine into his political orbit.

Antiochus the Great was a vigorous apostle of Hellenism. His policies were fanatically upheld by one of his successors, Antiochus IV (175-163 B.C.), known as Antiochus Epiphanes because he claimed to be god (Zeus) manifest (*theos epiphanes*). The coins that bore his image were inscribed with *theos* (god). His pretensions to divinity, though in line with the claims of Alexander and others, prompted him to rule with absolute authority, and to stop at nothing in imposing Hellenistic culture upon his realm. He did not object to people having other gods and following local religious customs. But the test of political loyalty was the worship of Zeus, and this meant submission to the absolute authority of the king—"god manifest." No policy could have been better calculated to stir up trouble in Palestine. For the cardinal tenet of Israel's faith from the very first was the jealousy of Yahweh—his determined refusal to have a place beside any other god, and his ardent intolerance of idolatry in any form.

Antiochus' enthusiasm for Hellenism, however, was not the only, or even the initial, reason for his intervention in Jewish affairs. He needed money badly, for

ANTIOCHUS IV *in profile according to a coin bearing his image. The reverse side carries the Greek words:* Basileos Antiochou, Theou Epiphanous, Nikephorou—"(coinage) *of King Antiochus, God Manifest, Bearer of Victory." The king represents himself as Zeus, seated on a throne, holding in his left hand a royal staff and in his right the figure of the goddess of victory, Nike, who holds in her hand the laurel wreath, symbol of victory.*

the protracted wars with the Ptolemies and the staggering expense of keeping the sprawling Seleucid kingdom under control had drained his treasury. Jewish resentment against Antiochus was first felt at the economic level—in stepped-up taxation. But it rose to a pitch of rioting when the most sacred office, that of the High Priest, was auctioned off to the highest bidder. This scandal involved two Jewish "Hellenizers," Jason and Menelaus, both of whom bore Greek names. Jason handsomely bribed Antiochus to depose his brother, Onias III, and to give him the high priesthood, and in addition he offered to build a Greek-type gymnasium in Jerusalem in honor of Antiochus (I Macc. 1:11-15). While Jason was attending the Greek games held at Tyre in honor of Heracles, however, Menelaus out-bid his rival and was given the office. In the ensuing riots, Jason returned and banished Menelaus, who, naturally enough, appealed to Antiochus for help. So Antiochus came to Jerusalem with his army, reinstated Menelaus, and punished the populace by plundering the Temple and shedding Jewish blood (II Macc. 4-5).

This action only made matters worse. Infuriated over the Jews' stubborn defiance of his will, and smarting under a defeat that his army had received in an Egyptian campaign, Antiochus determined to "get tough" with the rebels. He issued orders for the outlawing of Jewish religion and the complete Hellenization of Jewish life. According to the edict, mothers who circumcised their children were to be put to death, copies of the Torah were to be burned, and observance of the Sabbath or possession of a copy of the Torah were made capital offenses. To carry out his plan to exterminate Judaism, in 168 B.C. he marched his troops into Jerusalem. The Temple was desecrated by the erection of "an abomination of desolation"—the Jewish description of an altar to Zeus —over the altar for burnt offerings in the Temple court; and it was further defiled by sacrificing swine upon it—the most unclean animal of all, according to Jewish law (I Macc. 1:54; cf. Dan. 9:27; 11:31; 12:11; Mk. 13:14). Pagan altars were built in the land; Jews were forced to make sacrifices to Zeus and to eat swine's flesh. And Antiochus' troops policed the country to see that the royal edict was obeyed.

The Maccabean Revolt

During this reign of terror, many Jews—not only the Hellenizers but the weak-hearted as well—yielded to the king's decree. Others, refusing to surrender their faith at any cost, went to their death or fled into hiding. The tinder for revolution was ready, needing only a spark to ignite it.

The spark was struck one day in Modein, a little town in the hill country a few miles northwest of Jerusalem. When a Syrian officer demanded that local citizens comply with his order to make a pagan sacrifice, Mattathias, a village priest, flatly refused. Filled with rage at the sight of a Jew who had come forward to make a sacrifice, Mattathias killed both the Jew and the Syrian officer who had issued the order. He and his five sons fled to the hills, where they gathered around themselves a band of loyal Jews. What they lacked in numbers and weapons, they hoped to make up for by guerrilla tactics, and, above all, by their zeal. Their battle cry was the shout of Mattathias: "Let everybody who is zealous for the Law and stands by the covenant come out after me" (I Macc. 2:27).

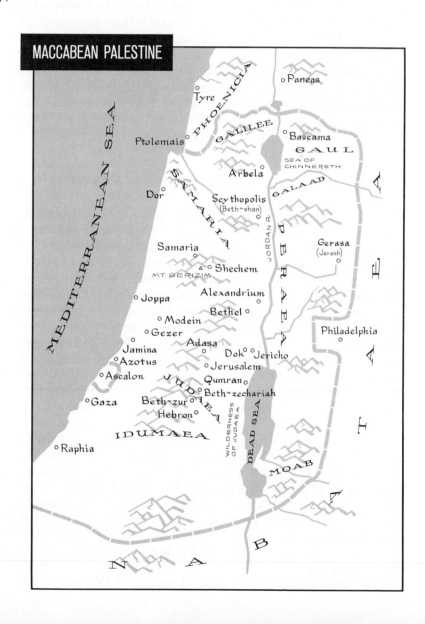

MACCABEAN PALESTINE

On his deathbed in 166 B.C., the aged Mattathias commissioned his oldest son, Judas, to carry on. So vigorous a fighter was Judas that he was given the title "Maccabeus," a word that is sometimes interpreted to mean "hammer," in reference to his hard-hitting blows against the enemy, both Jewish assimilationists and Syrians. Despite overwhelming odds, Judas and his band of recruits soon won a surprising victory over Antiochus' general and demanded a peace treaty. On the twenty-fifth day of the month of Kislev (December), 165 B.C., he rebuilt the altar of the Temple and restored the service of Jewish worship, thereby inaugurating the Hanukkah (Rededication) feast, or the Feast of Lights, which Jews still celebrate around Christmas time.

Thus began the Maccabean wars, carried on successively by the brothers Judas, Jonathan, and Simon. What began as a resistance movement eventually flared up into a full-scale war. Favored by international developments, especially Rome's increasing intervention in eastern affairs, the energetic, zealous Jews were able to achieve a century of independence that lasted until the coming of the Roman ruler, Pompey, to Jerusalem in 63 B.C.

THE APOCALYPSE OF DANIEL

Shortly after the outbreak of the Maccabean wars, an unknown writer composed the book of Daniel. Undoubtedly he was one of the Hasidim, who felt a revulsion for the ways of Hellenism and the tyranny by which it was imposed upon the Jews. His purpose was to rekindle the faith of Israel, which was in danger of being extinguished by the aggressive and severe policies of the Seleucids, and to summon the Jewish people to unyielding loyalty even in the face of persecution. Affirming that the course of history was completely under Yahweh's sovereignty, he summoned his people to courageous faith. For when men believe that the issues are in the hands of God, rather than in human hands, they can act without fear of the consequences. The book of Daniel, then, sets forth the theology of the Maccabean revolution. It has been rightly called "the Manifesto of the Hasidim."

Some people have been misled by the author's portrayal of incidents and visions experienced by Daniel during the Babylonian exile. Supposing that the book of Daniel was written during the Exile, they have regarded it as a prophetic preview of several centuries of future history and, indeed, of the divine program for a future that still lies ahead. Thus the book has become a happy hunting ground for those who are fascinated by "biblical prophecy" and who look for some mysterious blueprint of the future hidden in its pages. We have already questioned this view of prophecy (see pp. 188-190), pointing out that although the prophets looked to the future, they were concerned primarily with the meaning of the present. This observation holds true for the book of Daniel, even though, properly speaking, it is not classed with the Prophets in the Hebrew Bible but in the catalogue of the Sacred Writings, or Hagiographa (see

Chart, pp. 556-557). The author of Daniel spoke to his time in the guise of a writing that was pre-dated in the Babylonian period, as though one were looking forward into the future rather than backward from the present. In the late post-exilic period, when prophecy was believed to have ceased, it was common to release writings under the name of some figure of ancient Jewish tradition.[7] In this case, the author chose the name of Daniel—a traditional, pious Israelite, according to Ezekiel (14:14, 20; 28:3), and a legendary hero of the Ras Shamra literature.

Prophecy and Apocalyptic

The book of Daniel belongs to a special class of literature known as apocalyptic (from the Greek word *apokalyptein*, "to uncover, reveal"), of which there are many examples in the late post-exilic and Christian period.[8] To take one outstanding illustration, the last book of the New Testament—called the Revelation, or the Apocalypse—is written in an idiom that is strikingly similar to, and even dependent upon, the book of Daniel. Apocalyptic literature abounds with bizarre visions, strange symbolism, and supernatural happenings. Written in times of persecution, it employs a kind of spiritual code that makes it a "sealed book" (Dan. 12:4) to those outside the circle of faith.

The central theme of the apocalyptic literature is God's revelation concerning the end-time, the coming of the Kingdom of God. Even though this literature arose in a time when prophecy supposedly had ceased, it continues and gives new expression to the prophetic message. From the very first, Israel's faith had been oriented toward the future—toward the fulfillment of the promise that Yahweh had given his people. Yahweh's work in history, according to Israel's faith, was *purposeful*, and events were pressing toward the realization of his goal for Israel and the nations. History was not spinning in circles, like the cycle of the seasons; nor was it governed by blind fate or chance. Israel understood that her life was involved in a great drama which, under the direction of God, was moving toward a final consummation.

In the pre-exilic period, this hope found expression in the popular doctrine about the coming "Day of Yahweh"—the Day when Yahweh would vindicate Israel by humbling her foes and raising her to a position of prestige and blessing in the world. This is what the people derived from the confessional affirmation that Yahweh had chosen Israel out of all the nations, and that "God is with us" (Immanuel). The great prophets, as we have seen, challenged this popular view. They too believed that Yahweh had chosen Israel and that he was with

---

[7] A collection of late writings called the Pseudepigrapha (spurious writings) contains works issued under the names of various biblical characters, such as the Assumption of Moses, the Testament of the Twelve Patriarchs, and so on. Writings of this type are found in R. H. Charles, *The Apocrypha and Pseudepigrapha of the Old Testament* [238], although the literature has been increased with the discovery of the Dead Sea Scrolls.

[8] See D. S. Russell, *The Method and Message of Jewish Apocalyptic* [249], for a full discussion of this type of literature.

his people, tabernacling in their midst and guiding them in their historical pilgrimage. But with one voice they insisted that his presence gave no justification for pride or complacency; on the contrary, God's activity in history was for the purpose of shocking his people into an awareness of their unfaithfulness to the covenant and bringing about a "return" or repentance. Therefore, the prophets stood up in the market place, in the Temple, or in the presence of kings, and rebuked the people for their failure. Speaking to the present situation, they interpreted the meaning of political events—such as the rise of Assyria or the destruction of Jerusalem—in the light of God's judgment and mercy. Convinced that Yahweh was about to act in the historical arena, using some historical agent as his instrument, they preached to the people with great urgency to mend their ways while there was still time.

These prophets, then, were also concerned about the end-time, the divine consummation of history. Beyond the darkness of the Day of Judgment they saw the dawn of a new era which Yahweh, in his mercy, would introduce. They proclaimed that the Kingdom was near at hand, for the King was coming both to judge and renew his people. Sometimes they portrayed the New Age in glorious colors. In the last day, they said, the political schism of the Israelite monarchy would be healed, the blessings of fertility would be poured out abundantly, nations would beat their swords into plowshares, and the wilderness would blossom like a rose. But in general the great prophets did not speculate on the diagram of the New Age, for their concern was with the future as it impinged upon the present. Even their portrayal of the coming Kingdom was a kind of mirror of the transformation that they believed God would work within men: the new heart, the new covenant, the new people. They did not expect that the course of human affairs would come to an end, but rather that the course of Israel's rebellious history would be ended. Then Israel would be living in the Kingdom of God—that is, under his sovereign sway—as the covenant had required from the very first.

Prophecy in a New Idiom

Beginning with the Exile, however, a shift in prophetic emphasis gradually took place. We can see this change in the prophet Ezekiel, who stood on the boundary between the old national era and emerging Judaism. Although he spoke in accents of doom and hope like his prophetic predecessors, his message was cast in a new style of bizarre visions and weird symbolism. Looking beyond the Day of Judgment, he produced a diagram of the New Age, drawn according to the pattern of a priestly utopia. If the oracles found in chapters 38-39 came from Ezekiel himself, he believed that this New Age would be preceded by a final assault on Jerusalem by Gog from the land of Magog. In that day, Yahweh would intervene decisively, shaking nature itself with his power, and destroying the mysterious hosts of Gog with a great slaughter. Thus the earlier prophets' vision of the coming of a foe from the north (as, for instance, in Jeremiah) was transformed into the prophecy of the final battle of history that would usher in the Kingdom of God.

The overthrow of Gog, a symbolic foe, is a good illustration of how apocalyptic literature tends to shift the prophetic emphasis upon God's judgment in the present through historical agencies to a final judgment portrayed in extravagant language. To be sure, the apocalyptic writer never surrenders the prophetic conviction that God's warfare with evil powers is waged in the arena of history. But to him the struggle is not merely with flesh-and-blood enemies, but with a kingdom of evil of which Israel's oppressors are only the tools. Since the historical struggle is blown up into super-historical or cosmic proportions, the final battle must also be super-historical. Eventually, apocalyptic writers, influenced by Zoroastrian dualism, affirmed that God's arch-enemy is Satan, a fallen angel, who is at the head of a whole kingdom of evil. God's final victory, then, must take the form of the overthrow of Satan, as in the Apocalypse of the New Testament.

Outside the book of Daniel, a number of passages in the Old Testament are written in the apocalyptic idiom. One example is found in the last part of the book of Zechariah, particularly chapters 12-14.[9] Here an unknown apocalyptist portrays the last great conflict, when all nations will gather to Jerusalem for battle (cf. Joel 3:9-21), and when Yahweh himself will overthrow them and become King over all the earth. Perhaps from about the same time comes a section of the book of Isaiah often called "the little apocalypse" (Is. 24-27). The writer portrays the Last Judgment, when Yahweh will judge all the nations by bringing about a cosmic catastrophe. The earth will be turned upside down and will reel to and fro like a drunkard, the sun and the moon will be eclipsed, and universal chaos will reign. But in the midst of this catastrophe, Israel—"the righteous nation that keeps the truth" (26:2)—will remain secure, with her mind stayed on Yahweh. The righteous of earlier generations will be raised from the dead in order that they too may participate in the consummation of history (26:19). Here we have the first clear reference in the Old Testament to the resurrection of the individual. Ezekiel had spoken of the resurrection of Israel (Ezek. 37), but the doctrine was first applied to the individual in apocalyptic literature. Eventually, the doctrine was extended to that of a general resurrection at the end-time, in order that the wicked might not escape the final judgment and that the righteous might receive the reward of their faithfulness.[10]

---

[9] Zech. 9-14, often called Deutero-Zechariah, consists of prophecies that are usually assigned to a period much later than that of the prophet Zechariah, perhaps in the last of the third century B.C.

[10] Notice that in the Bible the hope for the future life of the individual beyond the grave is expressed in terms of the resurrection of the body—that is, the self. The doctrine of the immortality or deathlessness of the "soul"—a deathless substance imprisoned within the body —rests upon an extra-biblical view of human nature.

The apocalyptic literature, then, is prophecy in a new idiom.[11] Although it represents a shift in emphasis, it expresses the prophetic convictions that Yahweh is King, that his Kingdom is near at hand, and that men are called to be faithful under all circumstances. It is not surprising that in our time, when many people have been subjected to the cruelest suffering, and when it often seems that history is controlled by reckless men or demonic forces, the message of an apocalyptic writing like Daniel has spoken with new relevance.

THE KINGDOM THAT IS GOD'S

The book of Daniel naturally falls into two sections: chapters 1-6, which relate stories about Daniel and his companions; and chapters 7-12, which contain Daniel's visions.[12] Part of the book is written in Aramaic rather than Hebrew, but, oddly enough, the Aramaic portion overlaps the two main sections (2:4b-7:28). Probably the author has drawn upon earlier materials, adapting them for his purpose. In any case, the book in its present form is fundamentally a unity, issued during Antiochus Epiphanes persecution – probably about 165 B.C.

By placing the narratives in the time of the Babylonian exile, the author has made numerous blunders on historical details. The book begins with a glaring historical error, for Nebuchadnezzar did not take Jerusalem in the third year of king Jehoiakim (606 B.C.), and it was Jehoiakim's son—Jehoiachin—who was borne away to captivity (see II Ki. 24). The author did not have his history of the Persian empire straight, as is shown by his confusion about the sequence of kings (see 5:31; 9:1) and his telescoping of historical periods (11:2). These, and other, errors indicate that the writer was looking back over four centuries of history from a time when memories were blurred or distorted by popular views. After all, his purpose was not to give a correct history, after the manner of Thucydides or Herodotus, but to proclaim a religious message to his embattled fellow men. Writing in a cryptic code that the enemy could not understand, he veiled his references to contemporary historical events and personalities in narratives and visions that allegedly originated at a time long past.

Loyalty to the Torah

The author of Daniel belonged to the Hasidim, whose religious faith demanded loyalty to the Torah at any cost. As we read the stories in chapters

---

[11] See the discussion of this matter by Bruce Vawter, C.M., "Apocalyptic: Its Relation to Prophecy," in Catholic Biblical Quarterly, XXII (1960), pp. 33-46. Gerhard von Rad, however, denies that apocalyptic has its roots in prophecy and argues that its primary connection is with the Wisdom tradition (Theology, II [80], pp. 301-315).

[12] The Greek (Septuagint) version of the book of Daniel is longer than the Hebrew-Aramaic text. It contains at the beginning "The Story of Susanna" and at the end "The Story of Bel and the Dragon," as well as "The Song of the Three Children" (see below, footnote 13). This surplus material is included in the Roman Catholic canon, and is found in the Protestant Apocrypha as Additions to Daniel.

1-6, we should keep in mind that he was speaking at a time when even the possession of a copy of the Torah was a capital offense. We do not have to do much reading between the lines to guess whom he had in mind when he described the tyrants of the past—men who did everything in their power to destroy the faith of Daniel and his friends.

The book opens by relating how Daniel and his friends were brought to Nebuchadnezzar's court in Babylon and trained for royal service (chap. 1). But even in foreign surroundings, where they were under great pressure to eat

CHRONOLOGICAL   CHART   10

B.C.	EGYPT	JUDAH	MESOPOTAMIA Persia
			Artaxerxes II, 404-358 Artaxerxes III, 358-338 Arses, 338-336 Darius III, 336-331
400 to 300	EMPIRE OF ALEXANDER THE GREAT, 336-323			
	Ptolemaic Kingdom	Egyptian Control	*Seleucid Kingdom* (Mesopotamia and Syria)
	Ptolemy I, 323-285		Seleucus I, 312-280
300 to 200	Ptolemy II, 285-246 Ptolemy III, 246-221 Ptolemy IV, 221-203	Egyptian Control	Antiochus I, 280-261 Antiochus II, 261-246 Seleucus II, 246-226 Seleucus III, 226-223 Antiochus III, 223-187
200 to 100	Ptolemy V, 203-181 Ptolemy VI, 181-146 Ptolemy VII, 146-116	Syrian Conquest, 200 MACCABEAN REVOLT, 167 Judas, 166-160 Jonathan, 160-143 Simon, 143-134 John Hyrcanus, 134-104 Conquest of Shechem, 128	Seleucus IV, 187-175 Antiochus IV (Epiphanes), 175-163 Antiochus V, 163-162 Demetrius I, 162-150 Alexander Balas, 150-145 Demetrius II, 145-138 Antiochus VI, 145-141 Antiochus VII, 138-129
100 to A.D.	Roman Conquest, 30	Pompey captures Jerusalem, 63	Roman occupation of Syria, 63
	THE EMPIRE OF ROME			

the king's sumptuous fare, they were faithful to the dietary regulations of the Jewish Torah. Even though they ate nothing more than vegetables and water, they proved stronger than anyone else in the training program. Moreover, God gave them wisdom that put to shame all the magicians and enchanters of the kingdom. Here we see how in the period of Judaism "wisdom" was identified with understanding and obeying the Torah (see pp. 485-486, 497-500).

Daniel proved that his wisdom far surpassed that of all the wise men of Babylonia by performing an impossible task set by the king: not merely to interpret his dream, but to guess what it was (chap. 2). Nebuchadnezzar was so impressed by this feat that he confessed faith in Daniel's God, "a revealer of mysteries" of the future (here we see the meaning of "apocalypse"; 2:47), and elevated Daniel to the position of governor of the province of Babylon and leader of all the Babylonian sages.

There follows a series of familiar stories on the theme of faithfulness to Yahweh under the most severe ordeals. When Nebuchadnezzar commanded that all his subjects must either bow down and worship a huge golden idol or else be thrown into a fiery furnace (a veiled reference to the forced worship of Zeus), everyone complied except Daniel's three friends (chap. 3). Their courageous faith reflects the spirit of the Hasidim of the Maccabean Revolution:

> If it be so, our God whom we serve is able to deliver us from the burning fiery furnace; and he will deliver us out of your hand, O king. But if not, be it known to you, O king, that we will not serve your gods or worship the golden image you have set up.
>
> —DANIEL 3:17-18

In a fit of rage, Nebuchadnezzar (Maccabean readers would inevitably think of Antiochus Epiphanes) ordered that the furnace be heated seven times hotter than usual. Once again, the astonished king was moved to have faith in the God of Israel when he saw the three men, joined by an angel, walking around in the furnace unsinged by the roaring fire.[13] The outcome was that the king promoted the three Jews to a higher rank.

Another story (chap. 4) tells how one day Nebuchadnezzar bragged about his imperial glory as he surveyed from his palace roof the new Babylon, which, as archaeology has confirmed (see pp. 359-360; also Plates 5, 7), was his very own creation. But just as Daniel had predicted in his interpretation of the king's dream, in which an angel chopped down a huge tree (verses 4-27), the proud king had a great fall. A voice from heaven spoke, reminding Nebuchadnezzar of who really runs history; at this point, the king went insane and lived a beastly

---

[13] In the Septuagint, after 3:23, there is an account of how one of the friends, named Azariah (Abednego), prays to God for deliverance from the fiery furnace; when deliverance comes, the three friends sing a song of praise. This addition to the Hebrew Bible ("The Song of the Three Children" and the accompanying prayer of Azariah)) was incorporated into the Vulgate. It is included in the Protestant Apocrypha under Additions to Daniel.

existence, eating grass like an ox. After seven years of this humiliation, he was restored to sanity. In a hymn of praise, he confessed that the kingdom, power, and glory belong to the God of Israel alone.

We are told that Belshazzar, supposedly Nebuchadnezzar's successor to the Babylonian throne, held a great banquet for a thousand nobles of his kingdom (chap. 5).[14] While they were carousing, they decided to drink wine out of the sacred vessels that Nebuchadnezzar had taken from the Temple of Jerusalem. But a great hush fell on the scene of merriment when "the fingers of a man's hand appeared and wrote on the plaster of the wall of the king's palace." When the king saw the ghostly hand write "Mene, Mene, Tekel, and Parsin," he was overcome with great fright, and summoned the wise men of the realm to interpret the mysterious message. When they failed, Daniel was called. He interpreted the words as a message of doom upon Belshazzar's kingdom: the king had been "weighed in the balances and found wanting." Daniel was given the highest honors for his success in de-coding the message, but that very night Belshazzar was slain and the kingdom passed to "Darius the Mede." (Notice that Cyrus and Cambyses actually followed after Nabonidus/Belshazzar).[15]

Darius was so pleased with Daniel that he made him one of three presidents over the 120 satraps of his empire (chap. 6). Fearing that Daniel would soon become the chief administrative officer of the realm, the jealous presidents and satraps persuaded the king to sign an irrevocable decree that anyone, except the king himself, who made a petition to a god or man during a thirty-day period would be thrown to the lions. When Daniel was found praying to his God in his upper chamber, the king reluctantly commanded that he be cast into the den of lions, although he expressed the hope that Daniel's God would deliver him because of his faithful obedience to the Torah. To the king's great joy, Daniel was found unharmed the next morning, and his accusers were then thrown to the lions. Orders were issued for everyone in the empire to reverence the God of Daniel. Daniel prospered during the reign of his presumed successor, Cyrus the Persian. (See Chronological Chart 8, p. 353!)

---

[14] Actually Belshazzar never reigned as king of Babylon, and the statement that he was the son of Nebuchadnezzar (5:2,11) is a glaring error. It is true, however, that when Belshazzar's father, Nabonidus, went off into Arabia to spend his final years at Teman, the empire was left temporarily in Belshazzar's control. See the discussion above, pp. 396-397, and Chronological Chart 8, p. 353. It is interesting to note, however, that in a fragmentary document from Qumran, designated as "The Prayer of Nabonidus," a story similar to that of Daniel 4 is told of Nabonidus, rather than Nebuchadnezzar. This seems to suggest an older tradition in which Nabonidus was regarded as the father of Belshazzar (cf. Dan. 5:2). "The change of names," writes Frank M. Cross, Jr., "as well as the development of the elaborate details of Nebuchadnezzar's theriomania, is best attributed to the refracting tendencies of oral transmission, in this case the shift of a legend from a lesser to a greater name" ([250], pp. 166-168).

[15] The idea of a Median kingdom *between* the Babylonian and Persian regimes is a historical inaccuracy. It is true that in the Babylonian period the Medes were a formidable power; indeed, they joined with Babylonia to overthrow Assyria (see above, p. 321). But they never established themselves as imperial successors to the Babylonians. Rather, their leader, Astyages, was vanquished by Cyrus, who established the Persian empire as the successor to Babylonia.

In all these stories, the faith of the Hasidim during the trials of the Macca-bean period finds magnificent expression. Men must be loyal to the Torah at all costs, for God is able to deliver his faithful ones. God's kingdom is an ever-lasting kingdom, in contrast to the kingdoms of the world, which are symbolized in a dream (2:31-36) by a colossal statue with a head of gold (the Babylonian kingdom), chest and arms of silver (Median kingdom), abdomen of brass (Persian kingdom), legs of iron (Alexander's kingdom), and feet of iron mixed with potsherds (the Hellenistic kingdoms of Syria and Egypt). Though tyrants strut and boast, their days are numbered; their power is nothing when measured against the Lord of history. Like "the stone cut without hands" which shattered the statue and became a great mountain, God's kingdom—with its center in the holy community of Judaism—will vanquish all earthly kingdoms and endure forever.

Visions of the End-Time

The second part of the book of Daniel consists of four visions that portray the dramatic movement of historical events toward the final consum-mation when God will overthrow the tyrannical rule of men and establish his kingdom on earth, as in heaven. Four successive empires are pictured—the Baby-lonian, Median, Persian, and Greek, each surpassing the preceding one in evil and brutality. In this view, the accumulated evil of history was finally concen-trated in one kingdom (the Seleucid) and in one depraved king (Antiochus Epiphanes). To the writer, this increase in evil meant that history was hasten-ing toward the final show-down, when men would know that God is King.

In the first vision (chap. 7), Daniel saw four beasts arising out of the "great sea"—that is, the watery chaos which was regarded as the source of powers hostile to God's creation. The last of these beasts was the worst: it was "terrible and dreadful and exceeding strong," and it had ten horns. An angel explained that these beasts were four successive empires (verses 15-17): the Babylonian (a lion with eagle's wings), the Median (a bear with three ribs in its mouth), the Persian (a leopard with four wings and four heads), and the Hellenistic or Seleucid (the ten horns refer to Seleucid kings, and the little horn "speaking great things" is Antiochus Epiphanes).[16] "The Ancient of Days," presiding over the Heavenly Council at the Last Judgment, sentenced the fourth kingdom to destruction, and the other three, whose rule had not been so monstrously evil, were deprived of their dominion and permitted to survive for a time. Then, with the clouds of heaven, in contrast to the beasts' origin from the depths of the sea, came "one like unto a son of man"—that is, a figure with a human rather than a beastly countenance. The angel interpreted this heavenly figure to sym-

---

[16] In a passage from the Sibylline Oracles (3:381-400), written about 140 B.C., the expres-sion "ten horns" refers to the ten kings who preceded Antiochus Epiphanes. As a matter of historical fact, Antiochus was the seventh in the series of Seleucid kings after Alexander's death.

bolize the holy community of Israel—"the saints of the Most High." [17] Instead of a transient kingdom, they would be given everlasting and universal dominion which was to be inaugurated after "a time, two times, and a half a time" of the little horn—a cryptic reference to the three and a half years when Antiochus Epiphanes persecuted the Jews (168-165 B.C.).

The same theme is developed in the second vision (chap. 8), whose interpretation was given by Gabriel, the patron angel of the Jewish people (cf. 12:1). A two-horned ram (the Medo-Persian empire) was charging to the west, north, and south. He held undisputed sway until a he-goat (the Greek empire), with a conspicuous horn between his eyes (Alexander the Great), came to engage him in battle and decisively defeated him. But when the he-goat was strong, the "great horn" was broken (the death of Alexander), and in its place came up four horns (the partition of Alexander's empire into four kingdoms). Out of one of these horns (the Seleucid kingdom) sprouted "a little horn" (Antiochus Epiphanes), whose power extended southward and eastward. In his pride, this horn exalted himself against the heavenly host, and challenged the authority of the Prince of the host (God) by defiling his Temple, casting down truth to the ground, and interrupting the daily sacrifice. The celestial being announced that the power of the boastful tyrant would be broken, though "by no human hand." The daily sacrifice would be resumed after 2,300 evenings and mornings—that is, the three years and two months from Antiochus' proscription of Jewish worship in 168 B.C. to Judas' rededication of the Temple in 165 B.C. Daniel was reminded that "the vision was for the time of the end," for it would be fulfilled "many days hence."

In the third vision, however, Daniel came to see that the "many days" were not too far away, for according to the divine timetable, the Kingdom of God was near at hand (chap. 9). Daniel was puzzled by Jeremiah's prophecy that seventy years must pass before the desolation of Jerusalem would be ended (Jer. 25:11; 29:10), and he prayed to God for light on this mystery. His prayer, like that of Ezra (Neh. 9), gratefully acknowledged Yahweh's great deeds of mercy, beginning with the deliverance from Egypt, and humbly confessed Israel's persistent covenant disloyalty for which great calamity had fallen on the people. His petition for speedy relief was not based on Israel's faithfulness to the covenant, but solely on Yahweh's steadfast and gracious goodness:

---

[17] The vision of Daniel 7 introduces a motif which has important implications for the Christian gospels. In an apocalyptic writing known as the book of Enoch, which is based on a tradition reaching back into the pre-Christian period (first century B.C.), there are references to an eschatological figure, the Son of Man, who comes to establish God's kingdom (Enoch 46:1-6; 48:2-10). In the Jewish apocalypse called Fourth Ezra or Fourth Esdras [II Esdras in the Protestant Apocrypha], from the close of the first century A.D., a vision is described in which Ezra sees emerging out of the sea "as it were the likeness of a man" who flies on the clouds of heaven (chap. 13). This Man is understood to be the heavenly agent of God's judgment in the last days. For these writings, see R. H. Charles, *Apocrypha and Pseudepigrapha* [238].

> For we do not present our supplications before thee on the ground
> of our righteousness, but on the ground of thy great mercy. O Lord,
> hear; O Lord, forgive; O Lord, give heed and act. . . .
>
> —DANIEL 9:18-19

It is worth noting that Judaism, even when it concentrated on the works of the Law, affirmed that in the last analysis Israel had no ground for boasting—except the incalculable mercy of God. The parable that portrays the Pharisee boasting before God that he is better than other men (Luke 8:11) is a caricature of Judaism, although devotion to the Law often did lead to self-righteousness.

While Daniel was praying, confessing his sin and the sin of his people Israel, the angel Gabriel came to interpret the seventy years (verses 20-27). In the prophecy of Jeremiah, as we have seen (pp. 338, 344), the figure seventy apparently referred to the full span of a man's life; but here it comes to mean "seventy weeks of years" (490 years), at the end of which the Jews will have atoned for their sins and the desolation of Jerusalem will have ended. This period falls into three periods: seven weeks, sixty-two weeks, and one week. The first seven weeks (49 years) apparently extend from king Zedekiah to Joshua the High Priest (587-538 B.C.), who was in office in the days of Cyrus; the sixty-two weeks (435 years) extend from the return from Exile to the assassination of the High Priest Onias III (538-171 B.C.); and the last week covers the reign of Antiochus Epiphanes. During the first half of this week (171 -168 B.C.), Antiochus showed some lenience toward the Jews; but during the last half (168-164), in which the author of Daniel was living, Antiochus attempted to abolish Jewish religion and desecrated the Temple by installing an altar to Zeus of Olympus. In Hebrew, this altar was ascribed to the "Lord of heaven" (*Baal shamáyim*), which came to be, by a malicious pun, "the abomination of desolation" (*shiqqutz shomem*; see 11:31; 12:11).

According to this view, history follows a prearranged timetable in which the length of each period is set by divine decree. Once we realize that the author was not really looking forward from the time of the Babylonian Exile, but looking backward over the ages from the Maccabean period, this mathematical calculation, even though too mechanical, has religious meaning. The writer believed that he was living in the "last days," in the final moments of the second half of the last week of years. The days of Antiochus were numbered, for he had insulted God. The clock was beginning to strike midnight. The time was near when God, through a mighty act, would win his victory, would end Israel's long years of desolation, and would introduce the messianic age. Unfortunately, this chronological calculation has led to many attempts, ancient and modern, to predict the date of the coming of God's Kingdom (but see Acts 1:7).

The author's backward glance from the Maccabean period also explains why his historical knowledge about the period before the rise of Alexander is blurred, and why his historical information becomes more exact and detailed as he comes closer to his own time. This point is illustrated in the final vision (chapters 10-12). Although it is dated in the third year of Cyrus of Persia (10:1), the Persian period is sketched in only one verse (11:2)—enough space, however, to make a major historical blunder, for ten Persian kings (not three) succeeded Cyrus. The author knows of Alexander's triumph over Persia (11:3; cf. 8:6-8, 21; 10:20), and the fact that, since he had no heir, his empire was divided (11:4; cf. 8:8, 22). From this point on, the author's historical memory improves, as the following explanatory summary of the biblical text (11:5-19) shows.

Ptolemy I (323-285), the king of the south, will establish a strong kingdom, but even stronger will be that of Seleucus I (312-280), the king of the north, whose kingdom will include Syria and Mesopotamia (11:5). Ptolemy II (285-246) will make an alliance with the Seleucid kingdom by marrying his daughter, Bernice, to Antiochus II (247 B.C.; cf. 2:43). This will anger Laodice, Antiochus' former wife, and she will conspire to have the couple and their son murdered (11:6). To avenge his sister Bernice, Ptolemy III (246-221) will march triumphantly against Seleucus II (246-226), the son of Laodice, but after a few years the latter will counterattack and a truce will be declared (11:7-9).

The seer's vision then focuses on the shift in the balance of power under two sons of Seleucus II—Seleucus III (226-223) and especially Antiochus III, the Great (223-187). The latter will be successful at first in a war against Egypt (11:10), but the king of the south, Ptolemy IV (221-203), will successfully counterattack at Raphia in 217 B.C. (11:11-12). Then, in the see-saw struggle, Antiochus will overrun Palestine by defeating the Egyptians at Gaza in 201 B.C. (11:13-15) and Panias in 199 B.C. (11:16). Hoping to secure his grip on Egypt, Antiochus will marry his daughter Cleopatra (not the same woman whose charms proved irresistible to Julius Caesar and Mark Antony) to Ptolemy V, but this move will not work to his political advantage (11:17). When he attempts to conquer "the coastlands" (Asia Minor and Greece), he will be defeated by a Roman general at Magnesia in 190, and on his return to his own country will die as a result of his plunder of a temple (11:18-19). Seleucus IV (187-175) will be assassinated by the very tax-collector he had appointed to raise money for the reparations owed to the Romans after the battle of Magnesia (11:20).

The rest of chapter 11 deals with prophecies concerning "a contemptible person," Antiochus IV Epiphanes. Pushing aside his brother, who legally had title to the throne (11:21), he will plot the assassination of "the prince of the covenant," the High Priest Onias III, in 171 B.C. (11:22), and will plunder the riches of the provinces (11:23-24). After his first campaign against Egypt (170 B.C.), he will return in triumph to Palestine and set his heart against "the holy covenant," thus initiating his anti-Jewish program (11:25-28). His second campaign against Egypt (168 B.C.), however, will be frustrated by the interference of "ships of Kittim" (the Romans) and, on his return, he will vent his spleen on the Jews, sparing only those who desert their faith (11:29-30). He will station his troops in the Temple area, abolish the daily sacrifices prescribed by the Torah, and set up "the abomination of desolation" on the altar (11:31). At this time, the lines will be drawn between the Jews who betray the covenant, and the Hasidim who stand firm under persecution, receiving "a little help" through the brave leadership of Judas Maccabeus (11:32-35). Antiochus will magnify himself above every god by taking the title Epiphanes, and will honor the Olympian Zeus, a Greek deity strange even to his own Syrian countrymen (11:36-39). Finally, "at the time of the end," Antiochus will attack the king of Egypt and win a decisive victory (11:40-43), but on his way home will die "by no human hand" (cf. 8:25) while encamped in Palestine between Jerusalem and the Mediterranean Sea (11:44-45).

Although Daniel's historical summary is cast in the form of a vision of events to come which are written down in God's "book of truth" (10:21), actually very little of it is prediction in the proper sense of the word. Rather, it is a résumé of past events. The only example of pure prediction is the prophecy concerning the death of Antiochus (11:40-45), an event that had not yet transpired in the author's time. And this prediction lacks the accuracy of the author's treatment of past events of the Maccabean period, for Antiochus did not die near Jerusalem (the setting of the final apocalyptic battle), but in Persia in 163 B.C. (I Macc. 6:1-16; Josephus, *Antiquities*, xii, 9, 1). The author's haziness about this event is the basis of the scholarly view that the book of Daniel was written before the death of Antiochus in the East, yet after the outbreak of the Maccabean revolution—in other words, between 168 and 164 B.C.

Thus the writer tells the story of the past so that persecuted Jews may see their sufferings in the perspective of God's purpose in history. He insists that none of these events happened by accident. Like a master chessman, God knew in advance every play that would be made and he let the game run its course. Even the tyranny of Antiochus was part of God's preordained plan. "He shall prosper till the indignation is accomplished; for what is determined shall be done" (11:36). This extreme emphasis on God's absolute sway in human affairs was not intended to encourage complacency, any more than the Marxist vision of the inevitable movement of history toward the classless utopia is meant to discourage revolutionary activity. On the contrary, the confidence that history moves inevitably and by prearranged plan toward the Kingdom of God fired the zeal of a small band of Jews, and enabled them to act and hope when everything seemed against them. "The people who know God shall stand firm and take action" (11:32). If God was for them, what did it matter how many battalions were against them? And who cared how many battles were lost, so long as the saints were fighting on the winning side, which God would soon crown with victory? Here is expressed the dynamic faith of courageous men who lived and died to the glory of God, confident that their martyrdom would "cleanse" and "refine" the community and somehow prepare for the coming of God's kingdom (11:35).[18]

---

18 This view of martyrdom, which came to have great importance in Jewish circles and in later Christian history, is stressed in II Maccabees (chaps. 6-7), a book later than I Maccabees, probably dating from about the dawn of the Christian era.

The Messianic Hope

In the book of Daniel there is no mention of the Anointed One (Messiah) who, in the last days, would appear as God's agent, either to execute judgment on Israel's oppressors or to rule over God's people in righteousness. To be sure, the expression "one like unto a son of man" was soon interpreted to mean a heavenly ruler whom God would send to shatter the powers of evil and to inaugurate the Kingdom.[19] In the New Testament the symbol of the Son of Man is often used in a messianic sense (see Mark 8:31). In Daniel 7, however, the heavenly figure symbolizes the covenant community—"the saints of the Most High"—as the interpretation of Daniel's dream makes clear. Yet in a broad sense this is a messianic passage, for the Hasidim are the standard-bearers for the Kingdom of God. In their faithful martyrdom they bear witness to the Kingdom that God will inaugurate with power and glory at the end of the times. They live and die in anticipation of the messianic age, which, the writer believed, would soon dawn—indeed, according to one passage, in three and a half years (12:7), the time of the cessation of the regular sacrifices in the Temple (9:27; cf. 7:25).[20]

According to one strand of tradition, found in the Old Testament and later literature, the Messiah would be of David's lineage and would come to restore David's kingdom (see Is. 9:1-7; 11:1-9). This political messianism, which filled the air in Jesus' day, is illustrated in a psalm from the late Maccabean period:[21]

> Behold, O Lord, and raise up unto them their king, the son of David,
> At the time in which thou seest, O God, that he may reign over Israel, thy servant.
> And gird him with strength, that he may shatter unrighteous rulers,
> And that he may purge Jerusalem from nations that trample her down to destruction.
>
> —PSALMS OF SOLOMON 15:21-25

In the book of Daniel, however, the coming Kingdom is not portrayed in terms of political realities such as inspired the messianic movement in Zerubbabel's time (see pp. 438-439). Rather, the consummation is to be a divine victory, transcending and transfiguring the ordinary realities of history. So Daniel's last vision finally leaves the sphere of politics, where the Seleucids and the Ptolemies vie for power, and moves on to a higher plane (chapter 12). The goal of history is *God's* Kingdom—not a human kingdom of any description or a utopia of any

---

[19] See the previous reference to Enoch and IV Ezra (above, footnote 17). For further discussion, see Sigmund Mowinckel, *He That Cometh* [207], chap. 10.

[20] Later editors extended this time to 1,290 days (12:11) and to 1,335 days (12:12).

[21] The Psalms of Solomon, found in a body of literature known as the Pseudepigrapha, date from about 50 B.C.

social planning. It will come solely by God's miraculous power and in his good time. According to Daniel, the Kingdom will be preceded by "a time of trouble" —the birth pangs of the messianic age (12:1). The faithful whose names are written in "the book" will be rescued from the trouble. Moreover, many who have already died will be raised up in order that they too may share in the grand fulfillment of the historical drama:

> And many of those who sleep in the dust of the earth shall awake, some to everlasting life, and some to shame and everlasting contempt. And those who are wise [the Hasidim] shall shine like the brightness of the firmament; and those who turn many to righteousness, like the stars for ever and ever.
>
> —DANIEL 12:2-3

This doctrine of the future life, one of the great contributions of apocalyptic literature, was late in coming. And yet, unlike the Greek doctrine of the immortality of the soul, it is infused with the Israelite sense of history. According to Israel's way of thinking about the future, the individual cannot experience the fullness of life without participating in the redeemed community, the Kingdom of God. Therefore, the resurrection of the body (that is, the self) is portrayed as occurring in the end-time, at the very consummation of the historical drama, when God's victory over the powers of evil is complete. In one sense, the apocalyptic literature is other-worldly, for it proclaims that the historical drama points beyond the tragic strife to God's ultimate kingdom. But in another equally important sense, it is profoundly this-worldly, for the sufferings of this world are to be fulfilled in history's grand finale. Unlike some forms of oriental mysticism, it does not encourage a repudiation of this world, but appeals to men to face present suffering in the confidence that the whole historical drama, from the beginning to end, is embraced within the sovereign plan of God.

BEYOND THE OLD TESTAMENT

With the book of Daniel the Old Testament period comes to a close—if we limit our attention to the books included within the Hebrew Bible.[22] Israel's life-story, as recorded in the pages of the Old Testament, ends on a note of intense expectation that soon the time would come of which the prophets had spoken: the dawning of God's Kingdom. But the apocalyptic vision of the speedy arrival of the messianic age—a vision that stirred faithful Jews to resist the tyranny of Antiochus Epiphanes—did not become a historical reality in the years that followed. Contrary to Daniel's dating of the time of the Kingdom,

---

[22] As we shall see, other books found in the Greek Old Testament (Septuagint), such as I-II Maccabees and the Wisdom of Solomon, actually date from a slightly later period. In the arrangement of the Hebrew Bible, Daniel is found before the works of the Chronicler with which the list ends (see Chart, pp. 556-557).

history moved on in its usual course. To be sure, the Maccabean revolution was successful for a time. But the successors of the Maccabees lost the religious zeal that had initially inspired the revolution, and turned to the old political game of intrigue and deceit—in which the reward for the successful schemer was the office of the high priesthood. Finally, after about a century of Jewish independence, the Jews were subjected to an empire that had not been envisioned in Daniel's scheme—the empire of Rome. This phase of the story of Israel lies beyond the province of our discussion.

Party Movements within Judaism

In the period between the outbreak of the Maccabean revolution and the dawn of the Christian era, the religious struggle continued. There were, to be sure, external sources of conflict, such as the rivalry with the Samaritans that exploded in 128 B.C. when one of the Maccabees, John Hyrcanus, conquered Shechem. And throughout the period the shadow of Rome was lengthening across the world. But the struggle also went on in the very heart of Judaism. All devout Jews subscribed to what is central in the book of Daniel: the authority of the Torah, the sacrificial services of the Temple, and the promise that God's Kingdom would have its center in the Holy Land. Party differences arose, however, over how the devout Jew should interpret these tenets of faith in the daily world.

One group, known as the Sadducees, advocated a policy of tolerance and compromise—an understandable attitude, since they came from families of priestly prestige and political influence. They claimed to be strict devotees of the Torah (the Pentateuch)—so strict that they would not accept the body of oral law that gathered around it. They rejected the doctrine of the resurrection because they found no support for it in the Torah (see Mk. 12:18), and for the same reason they opposed other aspects of apocalyptic thought, such as the belief in angels and demons, and predictions about the end-time. Their view of history was essentially that of the P writing of the Pentateuch (pp. 382-392), according to which the divine plan came to fulfillment in the establishment of a theocratic community, patterned after the Law revealed to Moses. Instead of looking to the future, they sought to maintain this existing holy community by strict fidelity to the Law, especially the regulations dealing with sacrifice and priestly prerogative. Since they were interested in the priestly *status quo*, they advocated a policy of collaboration with foreign rulers and even a certain degree of compromise with Hellenism, provided the Temple services were permitted to continue.

On the other side were various religious groups who stood in the tradition of the Hasidim, men whose zeal for the Torah brought them into conflict with Hellenistic culture and with all Jews who wanted to collaborate with foreign rulers. Like the author of the book of Daniel, they believed that the present age was under the dominion of wicked powers, and they anticipated the time when God would intervene and establish his Kingdom, thus restoring the Holy Land to his people. Out of the circles of the Hasidim there eventually arose a party known as the Pharisees. Like Daniel and his friends, they practiced strict devotion to the customs that separated Jews from Gentiles: dietary rules, circumcision, fasting, prayer. Although in one sense they were stricter than the Sadducees, in another sense they were more liberal, for, unlike the latter, they accepted the teachings found in books outside the Torah, such as the Prophets. In addition, they believed that Moses had not only promulgated the written Torah but also a body of oral law that interpreted the meaning of what was written. This oral law, called "the tradition of the elders," was eventually codified in the Mishnah (c. A.D. 200) and finally came out in an expanded edition known as the Talmud.[23]

The Pharisees, then, were able to adapt the rules and teachings of the written Law to the changing conditions of life, and even to accept doctrines not found therein, like the resurrection of the body and the apocalyptic Kingdom. Most Pharisees opposed fanatical revolt against foreign rulers. They preferred to maintain the strictest separation from the contaminations of the world, waiting for the time when God would establish his Kingdom. But closely related to the Pharisees was another group, known as the Zealots, whose views on political action were more in line with the Maccabean revolutionists.

In recent years, public attention has been aroused by the discovery of the Dead Sea Scrolls and the excavation of the ancient community headquarters of Essenes (or a closely related sect) located toward the northwest end of the Dead Sea near the mouth of the Wadi Qumran (see Plate 8). The fascinating story of this community—its history, practices, and religious beliefs—would carry us far afield.[24] Suffice it to say that this group, regarding itself as the community of "the new covenant," separated itself from the world in order to practice a monastic devotion to the Torah and to await the end of the historical drama, when God would overthrow the powers of evil and inaugurate his Kingdom. In many respects these covenanters resembled the Hasidim of the early Maccabean period. Their zeal for the Torah and their hope for the apocalyptic Kingdom led them to revive the ancient conception of holy war (ḥérem), by which the land would be purified of the contaminations of pagan culture and converted into the Holy Land.[25] There are close affinities, and at the same time significant differences, between the eschatological beliefs of this Jewish sect and those of the early Christian community.[26]

It can be seen, then, that many currents were moving through Judaism in

---

[23] See H. Danby, The Mishnah, translated from the Hebrew with introduction and brief explanatory notes (Oxford: Clarendon Press, 1954). The Talmud is a large library. See H. L. Strack, Introduction to the Talmud [242].

[24] See especially Frank M. Cross, Jr., The Ancient Library of Qumran [250].

[25] See William R. Farmer, Maccabees, Zealots, and Josephus (New York: Columbia University Press, 1956), Chapter 7, for a discussion of "the war of the sons of light against the sons of darkness."

[26] See Frank M. Cross, Jr., op. cit., pp. 216-230.

the two centuries preceding the Christian era. The book of Daniel is only one sample of the great amount of religious literature produced in this creative period. Some of this literature has been known for years, such as the writings found in the Apocrypha and the Pseudepigrapha. The manuscripts of Qumran include not only portions of our Old Testament and manuals for the sect, but also a whole library whose fragmentary remains were found in caves near the community center.

But of all the types of literature coming from this period—wisdom literature, history, short stories, psalms, interpretation of Torah—the most popular was the apocalypse. In troubled times, when faith was put to the severest tests, men hoped for the coming Kingdom. And since it came to be believed that "the exact succession of the prophets" ended in the time of Ezra (Josephus,

CAVE NUMBER FOUR *is located in a cliff overlooking the Wadi Qumran. In this cave were found many fragments of manuscripts that belonged to the library of the monastic community of the ancient Essenes (see Plate 8). Some eleven caves in the area have yielded materials, including the famous Isaiah Scroll pictured on p. 6.*

Against Apion, i, 8) and even that prophecy had ceased altogether (see I Macc. 9:27), anonymous writers couched their prophecy in the form of a revelation (that is, apocalypse) given to a figure of ancient times, like Adam, Enoch, Noah, or Moses, or to a figure who lived in the centuries just before the cessation of prophecy, like Jeremiah, Baruch, Daniel, or Ezra. The apocalyptic hope for the Kingdom was one of the major influences upon the early Christian community.

The Old Testament Canon

Clearly, devotion to the Torah was the unifying factor within Judaism. Within this unity there was great richness and diversity, as evidenced by the literature of the period and by the sectarian movements. The new horizons opened up by the study of the Qumran community show that "the tree whose trunk was the Old Testament had then many branches which later were lopped off or withered away." [27] This "lopping off" and "withering away" occurred during the terrible ordeals of Judaism in the Roman period, especially the smashing blow struck against Jewish nationalism by the war of A.D. 66-70, when the Temple was destroyed, never to stand again, and when Jews were scattered or reduced to an insignificant remnant in Palestine. The Sadducees, whose religion was inseparably bound to the Temple, were shorn of their *raison d'être* by this catastrophe. Many of the covenanters of Qumran perished in the conflict, and their headquarters was destroyed, as we know from archaeological excavation. Only the Pharisees survived with strength. Their flexible interpretation of the written Torah, and their support of synagogue worship, enabled them to meet this crisis and to place the stamp of Pharisaic thought upon subsequent Judaism.

The crisis of Judaism, resulting from the fall of Jerusalem and the destruction of the Temple, gave new impetus to discussions about the inspiration of scripture and the extent of the Jewish canon. The loss of Judaism's vital center posed the threat that the tradition would be distorted or weakened by Hellenistic influences and that the Jews, scattered out from the Holy Land, would lose their sense of identity. In this situation a major role in the reorganization of Judaism was played by an academy established at Jabneh, or Jamnia (the name used in Christian circles), on the coast of Palestine. This school was founded by a certain rabbi Johanan ben Zakkai, who had escaped from Jerusalem during the bitter siege of the city. By attracting to it some of the ablest and most learned Jewish leaders, Jamnia came to be a great center of Pharisaic Judaism. The closing of the Jewish canon is usually dated to discussions which took place in the "Council of Jamnia" about A.D. 90.[28]

---

[27] Millar Burrows, *The Dead Sea Scrolls* (New York: Viking Press, 1955), p. 345.

[28] Jamnia, however, must be viewed as a phase of a discussion which took place over a considerable period of time and thus as a symbol of the crystallization of rabbinical views. In

JEWISH CATACOMBS *at Beth She'arim (Sheikh Ibreiq) located not far from modern Haifa. After the fall of Jerusalem in A.D. 70, and especially from the second to the fourth centuries, a loyal group of Jews lived here. Tombs were cut into the solid rock and arranged in stories. Of all the symbols carved in the interior, the menorah, or seven-branched candlestick, was the most important and apparently had a significance to Jews comparable to the cross in Christian catacombs. (See further the article "Lampstand" [11] by L. E. Toombs.)*

Long before this, however, the main structure of the canon had already been established. The Torah (Pentateuch), as we have seen in an earlier chapter, was promulgated by Ezra as the basis of the post-exilic covenant community, and from that day on it had a unique place in Jewish life. Shortly after 200 B.C., the collection known as the Prophets was regarded as scripture—for instance, in the prologue to Ecclesiasticus (c. 130 B.C.). By the time of the New Testament, "the Law and the Prophets" was a standing expression for Jewish scripture (Matt. 22:40). In addition, a third collection of miscellaneous literature, called the Writings, was gradually taking shape. One of these books, the Psalms, gained a place of special scriptural importance owing to the use of psalms in worship (see Luke 24:44). Thus, well before the Academy of Jamnia, the religious community had been registering its verdict on the authority of certain books by making them central in its life and worship. A list of accepted writings had already come into being through practical use.

There was, however, considerable uncertainty about the scriptural boundary

this connection see Jack P. Lewis, "What Do We Mean by Jabneh?" in *Journal of Bible and Religion*, XXXII (1964), pp. 125-132. The Jewish scholar Samuel Sandmel, in *The Hebrew Scriptures* [20], warns against the notion that Jamnia was a kind of modern convention during which rabbis debated an agenda and reached binding decisions by vote. "Canon," he says, "was a matter of the evolution of opinions which converged over a period of decades, 90 being a likely terminal date, but far from a definite one" (p. 14, footnote 6).

beyond the authoritative nucleus of the Law and the closely attached collection of the Prophets. Striking evidence of the fluidity of Jewish scriptural tradition has come from Palestine itself, namely from Qumran. The library of the Essene community, founded during the life of the Maccabean brothers, contained—as we would expect—"biblical" books such as the famous Isaiah manuscript, and numerous commentaries on biblical books such as Psalms, Hosea, Habakkuk, Nahum. But in addition the library contained a rich variety of apocryphal and pseudepigraphical writings, some of which were scarcely known before.[29] Even when we take into account that the Essenes were a separatist and somewhat "off-beat" group, their monastery has demonstrated that at the dawn of the Christian era Jewish "scripture" was an umbrella which covered more than what we would normally think of as the Old Testament.

Further evidence of this uncertainty about the bounds of scripture is found in the Greek version of the Old Testament (Septuagint) which was produced by Hellenistic Jews in Alexandria. As can be seen from the accompanying chart,

JEWISH SCRIPTURAL TRADITIONS

Items found in the Protestant Apocrypha are italicized. Compare this list with the one found on pp. 4-5, where deuterocanonical books of the Catholic canon are indicated.

PALESTINIAN (*The Hebrew Bible* *or Masoretic Text*)	ALEXANDRIAN (*The Septuagint* *or Greek Version*)
I. THE TORAH The five books of Moses, each designated according to opening words.	PENTATEUCH Genesis Exodus Leviticus Numbers Deuteronomy
II. NEBI'IM (Prophets) Former Prophets: Joshua Judges I-II Samuel I-II Kings Latter Prophets: Isaiah Jeremiah Ezekiel The Twelve: Hosea, Joel, Amos, Obadiah, Jonah, Micah, Nahum, Habakkuk, Zephaniah, Haggai, Zechariah, Malachi	HISTORICAL BOOKS Joshua Judges Ruth I-II Kingdoms (I-II Sam.) III-IV Kingdoms (I-II Kings) I-II Paralipomenon (I-II Chron.) *Esdras A* [a] Esdras B (Ezra-Nehemiah) Esther (plus *Additions to Esther*) *Judith* *Tobit* *I-II Maccabees* III-IV Maccabees [b]

[29] See Frank M. Cross, Jr. [250], pp. 30-47.

PALESTINIAN	ALEXANDRIAN
III. KETHUBIM (Writings)	POETRY AND WISDOM
Tehillim (Songs of Praise)	Psalms
Job	Odes of Solomon including the *Prayer*
Proverbs	*of Manasseh* c
The Festal Scrolls:	Proverbs
Ruth, Song of Songs, Ecclesiastes,	Ecclesiastes
Lamentations, Esther	Song of Solomon (Song of Songs)
Daniel	Job
Ezra-Nehemiah	*Wisdom of Solomon*
I-II Chronicles	*Ecclesiasticus* (Wisdom of Ben Sira)
	Psalms of Solomon

PROPHETIC WRITINGS
The Twelve: Hosea, Amos, Micah,
Joel, Obadiah, Jonah, Nahum,
Habukkuk, Zephaniah, Haggai,
Zechariah, Malachi
Isaiah
Jeremiah
Baruch
Lamentations
Epistle of Jeremiah d
Ezekiel
Daniel, plus additions:
The Story of Susanna
The Song of the Three Children
The Story of Bel and the Dragon

a Esdras A is I Esdras in the Protestant Apocrypha and III Esdras in the Vulgate tradition. The Protestant Apocrypha also includes an apocalyptic book called II Esdras from the close of the first century A.D. Since the Council of Trent, these works have been printed in the Roman Catholic Vulgate as appendices to the New Testament, where they are called III and IV Esdras. The Greek text of the main part of II (IV) Esdras (chaps 3-14) has been lost.

b Though popular in parts of the ancient church, these never gained canonical recognition.

c This beautiful prayer, based on a late tradition in II Chron. 33:11-13, is found as a separate entry in the Protestant Apocrypha. It is not part of the Roman Catholic canon but, since the Council of Trent, has been included as an appendix to the Vulgate.

d This letter, supposedly the one Jeremiah sent to Jewish exiles in 597 B.C., is often attached to the book of Baruch. It is included as a separate entry in the RSV of the Apocrypha.

the Egyptian Jews translated or adopted a larger number of books than we find in the received Hebrew Bible. Some scholars have attempted to explain the differences between these two lists of sacred writings by the hypothesis that in the liberal atmosphere of Alexandria a larger canon was adopted.[30] However that may be, the differing scriptural usage of Jews in Palestine and Jews in Alexandria points to an uncertainty about the extent of accepted writings which existed before the period of the Jamnia Academy and even after. It is not surprising, then, that the fathers of the early Christian church were not clear about the extent of the Old Testament. Jerome (c. A.D. 342-419), the great scholar

[30] This hypothesis has been vigorously challenged by Albert C. Sundberg, Jr., *The Old Testament of the Early Church* [255]. He argues that "the scriptures received from Judaism were not limited to either the Hebrew canon or even to the larger so-called Alexandrian canon, but a still larger collection of Jewish holy writings without fixed bounds is reflected in the usage of these two groups" (p. x).

who translated the Latin Vulgate, was inclined to follow the Palestinian tradition and to relegate the extra writings found in the Septuagint to a secondary place. But his contemporary, Augustine (A.D. 354-430), insisted that the catalog of Old Testament books also includes books found in the Septuagint scriptural tradition which had been established in the usage of the Christian church. For a long time uncertainty about the extent of the Old Testament continued in the Christian community.[31]

Within the Jewish community it was increasingly felt necessary, especially after the fall of Jerusalem in A.D. 70, to end the uncertainty about the circumference of Jewish scripture and to fix the limits of the canon so definitely that nothing could be added or taken away. Jewish leaders were motivated to face this question by several considerations, such as suspicion of the excessive popularity of apocalyptic writings, and the challenge posed by the circulation of Christian "messianic" writings. A decisive phase in the discussion, as we have already observed, was the so-called Council of Jamnia in A.D. 90. But we must not think of this as an ecclesiastical council which arrived at official decisions binding upon the community. Rather, the opinions expressed were "unofficial," though they came to be accepted as a general judgment because of the influence of the academy and because of the appeal to criteria recognized to be valid.[32]

Since the text of the Law had been fixed earlier, and since there was general agreement on the number of books in the prophetic collection, the major problem was to decide which books belonged to the Writings. One of the rabbis' principles, of course, was harmony with the written Torah. The book of Esther, for instance, posed difficulties, for besides its seemingly secular character, it deals with a festival (Purim) for which there is no explicit provision in the Torah. Even the book of Ezekiel was questioned by some rabbis, for at some points it conflicts with prescriptions of the Torah (compare, for instance, Ezek. 46:6 with Num. 28:11). According to the Talmud, one rabbi filled three hundred jars of oil and, as modern students would say, "burned the midnight oil" until he solved the problem. The Pharisaic freedom of interpretation, based on the oral law, meant that the principle of harmony with the written Torah could be applied flexibly.

Another principle applied by the rabbis was a doctrine of prophetic inspira-

---

[31] The issue came to the fore in the sixteenth century. The Protestant Reformers, insisting upon a return to the Bible, called for the elimination of the extra books not found in the Hebrew Bible. The disputed writings were put in a separate section, entitled "Apocrypha," either at the end of the Old Testament or of the entire Bible, with the note that they deserve to be read but are not equal with canonical books. The Roman Catholic Church at the Council of Trent (A.D. 1545-1563) officially adopted a larger canon, which included both protocanonical and deuterocanonical books (see above, p. 3, footnote 4). The acceptance of deuterocanonical books was based on long use of these books in Christian liturgy.

[32] See Alfred C. Sundberg, Jr. [255], chap. 8, on "The Jewish Canon." Aage Bentzen maintains, in his *Introduction*, I [23], pp. 27-31, that discussions at Jamnia dealt "not so much with acceptance of certain writings into the Canon, but rather with their *right to remain there*."

tion which assumed that prophecy ceased in the post-exilic period, just after the time of Ezra. According to this view, Haggai, Zechariah, and Malachi were the last of the prophets, for—as the rabbis said—with their death "the Holy Spirit departed from Israel." Therefore, only writings coming from the period before the cessation of prophetic inspiration were regarded as having religious authority. This criterion may have been adopted because the rabbis believed that the more recent prophetic (apocalyptic) movement, closely associated with the Maccabean revolt and the war of A.D. 66-70, had finally been proved false by historic tragedy in Palestine. In any case, this principle automatically excluded books that were known to have arisen in the Hellenistic period, like the Wisdom of Ben Sira or I and II Maccabees. The rabbis had serious questions about the Song of Songs and Ecclesiastes, but these books were admitted on the supposition that Solomon had written them. Finally, the rabbis rejected books written in Greek, since that language was not employed in the period of prophetic inspiration. On this basis, writings like the Wisdom of Solomon were rejected, even though they had been published under the name of great figures of Israel's tradition.

These principles may strike us as being rather arbitrary. It would certainly not have detracted from Jewish scripture if, for instance, some reason had been found to substitute the Wisdom of Ben Sira or some of the psalms from the Qumran community for the Song of Songs or Esther. We must remember, however, that the question of the authority of most of the writings now found in the Hebrew Bible had been answered before the Academy of Jamnia, especially in the worship practice of the community. Those writings were preserved and used devotionally which spoke authoritatively to the community of faith.

ISRAEL'S PILGRIMAGE

Pausing for a concluding moment to survey the ground covered in this book, one point stands out clearly: the Old Testament represents the memories and interpretations of the historical experiences of Israel, from the formation of the community to the time of its great test of faith in the Maccabean period. It is Israel's life story—a story that cannot be told adequately apart from the conviction that God had called this people in his grace, separated them from the nations for a special responsibility, and commissioned them with the task of being his servant in the accomplishment of his purpose. Because Israel remembered her sacred past, she was able to live in the present with her face set toward the future—the time of the new covenant, the new creation, the Kingdom of God. The Old Testament ends like an incomplete drama, an unfinished symphony. According to Pharisaic Judaism, Israel's pilgrimage leads through the Old Testament to the Talmud and to a continued life of messianic expectancy. According to the New Testament, Israel's pilgrimage leads to Jesus, the Christ, who came not to destroy, but to fulfill the Law and the Prophets.

SELECTED BIBLIOGRAPHY

No attempt has been made to mention all important books on Old Testament subjects or even to include everything referred to in footnotes. Rather, the list includes selected basic works which will be valuable to the student who for the most part is confined to what is available in English. To facilitate footnote references, the various items are listed by number. Titles available in paperback editions are indicated by PB.

GENERAL READINGS

Tools for Bible Study

1. *The Oxford Annotated Bible with the Apocrypha,* ed. by Herbert G. May and Bruce M. Metzger (New York: Oxford, 1965). Based on the Revised Standard Version and provided with brief articles, notes, maps, and other aids. A most valuable tool for the student.
2. *Ancient Near Eastern Texts Relating to the Old Testament,* 2nd ed., edited by J. B. Pritchard (Princeton University Press, 1955). This tool should be within easy reach.
3. *Documents from Old Testament Times,* ed. by D. Winton Thomas (New York: Nelson, 1958). PB: Harper Torchbook. This volume is easier to reach financially than the above item, but contains a smaller collection of texts.
4. *The Ancient Near East in Pictures Relating to the Old Testament,* ed. by J. B. Pritchard (Princeton University Press, 1954). *Note:* Items 2 and 4 are combined in *The Ancient Near East: an Anthology of Texts and Pictures,* ed. by J. B. Pritchard (Princeton University Press, 1965). PB.

5. *The Westminster Historical Atlas to the Bible*, rev. ed., edited by G. Ernest Wright and Floyd V. Filson (Philadelphia: Westminster, 1956). Highly recommended both for accuracy of discussion and cartography.
6. *Atlas of the Bible*, by L. H. Grollenberg, O.P., trans. by J. Reid and H. H. Rowley (New York: Nelson, 1956). A first-rate atlas by a Roman Catholic scholar. The value of the text and maps is enhanced by magnificent pictures.
7. *Geographical Companion to the Bible*, by Denis Baly (London: Lutterworth, 1963). See also his earlier book, *The Geography of the Bible* (New York: Harper & Row, 1957).
8. *A Catholic Commentary on the Holy Scriptures*, ed. by E. F. Sutcliffe and B. Orchard (New York: Nelson, 1953; new edition in preparation). A one-volume commentary prepared by Roman Catholic scholars.
9. *Peake's Commentary on the Bible*, rev. ed., edited by Matthew Black and H. H. Rowley (New York: Nelson, 1962). A standard one-volume commentary updated.
10. *Encyclopedic Dictionary of the Bible*, ed. and trans. by Louis F. Hartman (New York: McGraw-Hill, 1963). A comprehensive work by Roman Catholic scholars; not all the articles are of the same quality.
11. *The Interpreter's Dictionary of the Bible*, in 4 vols., ed. by G. A. Buttrick and others (New York: Abingdon, 1962). The best Bible dictionary in English.

TRANSLATIONS.   The best translation now in general use is the Revised Standard Version (Division of Christian Education, National Council of Churches, 1946-1952). See also the officially sponsored Roman Catholic work, the American Confraternity Translation (1952 on). The translation, made from the original languages, is in good modern English. Attention should also be called to the fresh translations in the Anchor Bible, and to the forthcoming New English Bible (Old Testament).

COMMENTARY SETS.   See especially *The Interpreter's Bible*, ed. by G. A. Buttrick and others (New York: Abingdon, 1952-1957). Some of the outstanding contributions are listed below. To date there is no thorough, exegetical commentary series in English which deserves to be considered the successor to the older *International Critical Commentary* series. Of the various nontechnical series that have appeared, note especially the *Torch Bible Commentaries* published by the SCM Press, 1952 onwards; an orthodox Jewish series, *Soncino Books of the Bible*, ed. by Abraham Cohen, 14 vols. (London: Soncino Press, 1945-1952); and the Roman Catholic *Old Testament Reading Guides* (Collegeville, Minn.: Liturgical Press), a series of booklets containing text and commentary which began to appear in 1965. The Paulist Fathers' *Pamphlet Bible Series* (New York: Paulist Press, 1960 onwards) introduces and stimulates the study of Biblical books.

MAGAZINES.   The best way to keep abreast of biblical research is by reading the journals. A good nontechnical magazine is *Interpretation*, published quarterly at 3401 Brook Road, Richmond, Va.; also *The Expository Times*, published monthly by T. & T. Clark, Edinburgh. The revival of interest in biblical studies in the Roman Catholic Church is reflected in *The Bible Today*, published bimonthly, a popular magazine (Collegeville: Liturgical Press). Other important professional journals are: *The Catholic Biblical Quarterly*, *The Journal of Biblical Literature*, and *Vetus Testamentum*—to mention just a few.

Introductions to the Old Testament

12. Charlier, C., *The Christian Approach to the Bible*, trans. by H. J. Richards and B. Peters (Westminster: Newman, 1958). An introduction for the general reader, written by a Roman Catholic.

13. Ellis, Peter, C. Ss. R., *The Men and Message of the Old Testament* (Collegeville, Minn.: Liturgical Press, 1963). A Roman Catholic survey.
14. Gottwald, Norman K., *A Light to the Nations* (New York: Harper & Row, 1959). A thorough treatment based on a synthesis of Old Testament introduction, history, and theology.
15. Harrelson, Walter, *Interpreting the Old Testament* (New York: Holt, Rinehart & Winston, 1964). Essentially a one-volume commentary based on the structure of the Hebrew canon; displays judicious scholarship and theological sensitivity.
16. Hunt, Ignatius, O. S. B., *Understanding the Bible* (New York: Sheed & Ward, 1962). A popular introduction by a Roman Catholic writer.
17. Moriarty, Frederick L., S. J., *Introducing the Old Testament* (Milwaukee: Bruce, 1960). A popularly written book which stresses major personalities in Israel's history.
18. Napier, B. Davie, *The Song of the Vineyard* (New York: Harper & Row, 1962). A vigorous, informative book introducing the student to the Old Testament.
19. Rowley, H. H., *The Growth of the Old Testament* (London: Hutchinson, 1950). One of a number of important writings (see entries elsewhere in this Bibliography) by the dean of Old Testament studies in Great Britain.
20. Sandmel, Samuel, *The Hebrew Scriptures: An Introduction to their Literature and Religious Ideas* (New York: Knopf, 1963). A presentation by an eminent Jewish scholar.
21. Tos, Aldo J., *Approaches to the Bible: The Old Testament* (Englewood Cliffs, N.J.: Prentice-Hall, 1963). An outline for a survey, written by a Roman Catholic.

More Technical Introductions

22. Anderson, G. W., *A Critical Introduction to the Old Testament* (London: Duckworth, 1959). A fairly detailed examination of each book or group of books; includes a short history of the canon.
23. Bentzen, Aage, *Introduction to the Old Testament*, I-II, 2nd ed. (Copenhagen: G. E. C. Gad, 1952). A balanced presentation by a Scandinavian scholar.
24. Bewer, Julius A., *The Literature of the Old Testament*, 3rd ed., revised and expanded by Emil G. Kraeling (New York: Columbia University Press, 1962). A valuable literary history from an older generation.
25. Driver, S. R., *Introduction to the Literature of the Old Testament*, rev. ed. (New York: Scribners, 1913). PB: Meridian, 1956. In many ways this old work is still valuable.
26. Eissfeldt, Otto, *Introduction to the Old Testament*, 2 vols., trans. from the 3rd German edition by P. R. Ackroyd (New York: Harper & Row, 1965). For many years this has been a pre-eminent work.
27. Kuhl, Curt, *The Old Testament: Its Origins and Composition*, trans. by C. T. M. Herriott (Richmond, Va.: John Knox, 1961). A brief technical introduction. Note the bibliography at the end.
28. Pfeiffer, Robert H., *Introduction to the Old Testament*, rev. ed. (New York: Harper & Row, 1949). A thorough, almost encyclopedic work which for years has been the best of its type in English. An abridged version, more suitable for the general reader, is available in PB: *The Books of the Old Testament*.
29. Tricot, A., and A. Robert, eds., *Guide to the Bible*, I and II, trans. from the 3rd French edition by E. P. Arbez and M. R. P. McGuire (New York: Descleé; I, 2nd ed., 1960; II, 1st ed., 1955). A scholarly Roman Catholic introduction which deals with general and special matters.
30. Weiser, Artur, *The Old Testament: Its Formation and Development* (New

York: Association Press, 1961), trans. from the 4th German ed. by Dorothea M. Barton. A major commentary in English which takes full advantage of form-criticism.

31. Young, Edward J., *An Introduction to the Old Testament*, rev. ed. (London: Tyndale Press, 1960). A conservative Protestant work which rejects the application of the so-called "scientific" method to Scripture.

Critical Methodology and the History of Recent Biblical Criticism

32. Alonso-Schökel, Luis, S. J., *Understanding Biblical Research* (New York: Herder & Herder, 1963). A brief statement about the development of the modern biblical movement, by a Roman Catholic scholar.
33. Coppens, J., *The Old Testament and the Critics*, trans. by E. A. Ryan, S.J., and E. W. Tribbe, S.J. (Paterson, N. J.: Guild Press, 1942). A judicious evaluation of biblical criticism from a Roman Catholic point of view.
34. Hahn, H. H., *The Old Testament in Modern Research* (London: SCM Press, 1956). An interestingly written and discerning history of biblical criticism.
35. Kraeling, Emil G., *The Old Testament Since the Reformation* (New York: Harper & Row, 1955). A valuable survey of the history of historical criticism.
36. Levie, Jean, S. J., *The Bible, Word of God in Words of Men* (New York: Kenedy, 1961). An excellent Roman Catholic treatment of the origins of the modern biblical movement.
37. Rowley, H. H., ed., *The Old Testament and Modern Study* (New York: Oxford, 1951). PB: Oxford, 1961. A valuable collection of essays dealing with various aspects of Old Testament research.

History of Israel

38. Albright, W. F., *The Biblical Period from Abraham to Ezra* (Pittsburgh: Biblical Colloquium, 1950). PB: Harper, 1963. A first-rate, concise history of Old Testament times.
39. Albright, W. F., "The Old Testament World," in *Interpreter's Bible*, I (New York: Abingdon, 1952), pp. 233-271.
40. Bright, John, *A History of Israel* (Philadelphia: Westminster, 1959). One of the standard works in the field, by a scholar of the so-called Albright school. A first-rate piece of work.
41. Bright, John, *Early Israel in Recent History Writing*, Studies in Biblical Theology, No. 19 (London: SCM Press, 1956). A vigorous criticism of the historical approach of Martin Noth (see below, No. 44).
42. Finegan, Jack, *Light from the Ancient Past*, 2nd ed. (Princeton University Press, 1959). An excellent treatment of ancient history as it bears on the Bible.
43. Mendenhall, George, "Biblical History in Transition," in *The Bible and the Ancient Near East: Essays in Honor of W. F. Albright*, ed. by G. Ernest Wright (New York: Doubleday, 1961), pp. 32-53. PB: Anchor.
44. Noth, Martin, *The History of Israel*, 2nd ed., English trans. by Stanley Godman from 2nd German edition and revised by P. R. Ackroyd (London: Adam & Charles Black, 1960). One of the major works in the field, by a leader of the German school of tradition-history.
45. Orlinsky, Harry M., *Ancient Israel* (Ithaca, N.Y.: Cornell University Press, 1964). A brief but valuable history of ancient Israel. PB.
46. Robinson, H. Wheeler, *The History of Israel*, Studies in Theology, No. 42 (London: Duckworth, 1957). A very good short history.

Archaeology

The best way to keep up with current archaeology is to read the quarterly issues of *The Biblical Archaeologist*, published by the American Schools of Oriental Research, New Haven, Conn. Selected articles from past issues have been published separately under the following titles.

47. *The Biblical Archaeologist Reader*, I (1961), ed. by G. Ernest Wright and David N. Freedman. PB: Anchor.
48. *The Biblical Archaeologist Reader*, II (1964), ed. by E. F. Campbell, Jr. and David N. Freedman. PB: Anchor.
49. Albright, W. F., *The Archaeology of Palestine*. PB: Pelican, 1961. A fully revised publication by a distinguished American archaeologist (see comment below, No. 59).
50. Albright, W. F., *Archaeology and the Religion of Israel*, 2nd ed. (Baltimore: Johns Hopkins Press, 1946).
51. Burrows, Millar, *What Mean These Stones?* PB: Meridian, 1957. A valuable introduction to the field, first issued in 1941.
52. Gray, John, *Archaeology and the Old Testament World* (New York: Nelson, 1962). PB: Harper.
53. Heaton, Eric W., *Everyday Life in Old Testament Times* (New York: Scribners, 1956).
54. Kenyon, Kathleen M., *Archaeology in the Holy Land* (New York: Praeger, 1960). PB.
55. Pritchard, James B., *Archaeology and the Old Testament* (Princeton University Press, 1958).
56. Williams, Walter G., *Archaeology in Biblical Research* (New York: Abingdon, 1965).
57. Wright, G. Ernest, *Biblical Archaeology*, 2nd ed. (Philadelphia: Westminster, 1962). Abridged ed. in PB: Westminster, 1960. A first-rate introduction by an eminent authority.
58. Wright, G. Ernest, *Shechem: The Biography of a Biblical City* (New York: McGraw-Hill, 1965). A vivid account of the results of excavation at the former center of the Tribal Confederacy.

Religion and Theology

59. Albright, W. F., *From the Stone Age to Christianity* (Baltimore: Johns Hopkins, 1940). Rev. ed. available in PB: Anchor, 1957. A monumental work by the American scholar whose research has profoundly influenced modern biblical studies.
60. Barr, James, *The Semantics of Biblical Language* (London: Oxford, 1961). A trenchant criticism of the following book by Boman.
61. Boman, Thorleif, *Hebrew Thought Compared with Greek*, trans. by Jules L. Moreau (Philadelphia: Westminster, 1960). This book and the response by Barr represent a major contribution to discussions of biblical theology.
62. DeVaux, Roland, O. P., *Ancient Israel: Its Life and Institutions*, trans. by John McHugh (London: Darton, Longman & Todd, 1961). Also PB: McGraw-Hill, 1965. A monumental study by the director of the Dominican École Biblique in Jerusalem.
63. Gelin, Albert, S. S., *Key Concepts of the Old Testament* (New York: Paulist Deus Paperback, 1963). In this PB, Old Testament themes are treated concisely.

64. Johnson, Aubrey, *The Vitality of the Individual in the Thought of Ancient Israel* (Cardiff: University of Wales Press, 1949). An important essay on Israelite psychology. See also his essay, *The One and the Many in the Israelite Conception of God* (Cardiff: University of Wales Press, 1961).

65. Kaufmann, Yehezkel, *The Religion of Israel,* trans. and abridged by Moshe Greenberg (Chicago: University of Chicago Press, 1960). An illuminating and provocative study by a highly original Jewish scholar who departs from many of the accepted tenets of present-day scholarship.

66. McKenzie, John, S. J., *The Two-Edged Sword* (Milwaukee: Bruce, 1956). A discerning presentation of Old Testament theology by a leading Roman Catholic scholar.

67. Muilenburg, James, "The History of the Religion of Israel," in *Interpreter's Bible,* I (New York: Abingdon, 1952), pp. 292-348. A perceptive summary of Israel's religious development.

68. Muilenburg, James, *The Way of Israel* (New York: Harper & Row, 1961). Also PB. An illuminating study built around a central biblical motif.

69. Pedersen, Johannes, *Israel: Its Life and Culture* (New York: Oxford), I-II (1926); III-IV (1940). An indispensable book for dealing with the psychological characteristics of ancient Israel.

70. Robinson, H. Wheeler, "Hebrew Psychology," in *The People and the Book,* ed. by A. S. Peake (New York: Oxford, 1946). An excellent study which supplements No. 69 above.

71. Robinson, H. Wheeler, *Inspiration and Revelation in the Old Testament* (New York: Oxford, 1946). Also PB: Oxford, 1962. Valuable chapters intended originally as the basis for an Old Testament theology.

72. Snaith, Norman, *Distinctive Ideas of the Old Testament* (London: Epworth, 1947). PB: Schocken, 1965.

73. Wright, G. Ernest, "The Faith of Israel," in *Interpreter's Bible,* I (New York: Abingdon, 1952), pp. 349-389. An excellent essay.

74. Rowley, H. H., *The Unity of the Bible* (Philadelphia: Westminster, 1953). Another series of lectures by the same author is *The Faith of Israel: Aspects of Old Testament Thought* (London: SCM Press, 1956). PB: SCM Press.

Works Specifically on Old Testament Theology and Hermeneutics

75. Anderson, Bernhard W., ed., *The Old Testament and Christian Faith* (New York: Harper & Row, 1963). An international symposium in response to an essay by Rudolf Bultmann.

76. Eichrodt, Walther, *Theology of the Old Testament,* I, trans. by J. A. Baker from the 6th German edition (Philadelphia: Westminster, 1961). *Theologie des Alten Testaments,* II-III, 4th ed. (Stuttgart: Klotz, 1961)—to be translated into English.

77. Jacob, Edmond, *Theology of the Old Testament,* trans. by A. W. Heathcote and P. J. Allcock (New York: Harper & Row, 1958). An important work by a French theologian, whose approach is like No. 79 below.

78. Knight, George A. F., *A Christian Theology of the Old Testament* (Richmond, Va.: John Knox, 1959). PB: SCM Press, 1965. As the title indicates, this book assumes the unity of the whole Christian Bible.

79. Koehler, Ludwig, *Old Testament Theology,* 3rd ed. (Philadelphia: Westminster, 1958). Structured systematically (doctrines of God, man, salvation), but contains many valuable insights.

80. Rad, Gerhard von, *Old Testament Theology*, I: *The Theology of Israel's Historical Traditions*, trans. by D. M. G. Stalker (New York: Harper & Row, 1962); II: *The Theology of Israel's Prophetic Traditions* (1965). A fresh, incisive work which is based on *Heilsgeschichte*, or sacred history.
81. Smart, James, *The Interpretation of Scripture* (Philadelphia: Westminster, 1961). An excellent introduction to biblical hermeneutics.
82. Vriezen, Th. C., *An Outline of Old Testament Theology*, trans. by S. Neuijen (Oxford: Blackwell, 1958). A discerning work by a Dutch theologian.
83. Westermann, Claus, ed., *Essays on Old Testament Hermeneutics*, English trans. ed. by James Luther Mays (Richmond, Va.: John Knox, 1963). Important essays by a number of outstanding German scholars.

READINGS CHAPTER BY CHAPTER

Introduction: Israel's Sacred History

84. Herberg, Will, "Biblical Faith as Heilsgeschichte: The Meaning of Redemptive History in Human Existence," in *The Christian Scholar*, XXXIX (1956), pp. 25-31. An excellent introduction to the meaning of sacred history by a Jewish philosopher.
85. McKenzie, Roderick A., S. J., *Faith and History in the Old Testament* (Minneapolis: University of Minnesota Press, 1963).
86. Niebuhr, H. Richard, *The Meaning of Revelation* (New York: Macmillan, 1941). PB. Chapter 2 is especially valuable in this connection.
87. Rowley, H. H., *The Biblical Doctrine of Election* (London: Lutterworth, 1950). A helpful treatment of a central biblical motif.
88. Wright, G. Ernest, *God Who Acts*, Studies in Biblical Theology, No. 8 (London: SCM Press, 1952). An excellent exposition of Israel's historically oriented faith.

See relevant sections of von Rad's *Theology* [80], especially pp. 106-128.

Chapter One: The Beginnings of Israel

See relevant sections of von Rad's *Theology*, I [80], especially pp. 106-128.

OTHER BOOKS ON HISTORICAL BACKGROUND

89. DeVaux, Roland, O. P., has written an important series of articles on the patriarchs which appeared in the *Revue Biblique*, LIII (1946), pp. 321-348; LV (1948), pp. 321-347; LVI (1949), pp. 5-36.
90. Gurney, O. R., *The Hittites*, 2nd ed. PB: Pelican, 1954. An authoritative discussion.
91. Holt, John, *The Patriarchs of Israel* (Nashville: Vanderbilt University Press, 1964). A discussion of the background of the patriarchs in the light of archaeology.
92. Kramer, S. N., *The Sumerians: Their History, Culture, and Character* (University of Chicago Press, 1963). One of the definitive works in this field.
93. Kramer, S. N., ed., *Mythologies of the Ancient World* (Chicago: Quadrangle Books, 1961). PB: Anchor.
94. Meek, T. J., *Hebrew Origins*, rev. ed. (New York: Harper & Row, 1950). Also PB: Harper Torchbook, 1960. Chapter 1 is especially relevant in this connection.

95. Rowley, H. H., *From Joseph to Joshua* (London: Oxford University Press, 1950). An important treatment of the historical problems.
96. Steindorff, George, and Keith C. Seele, *When Egypt Ruled the East*, 2nd ed. (University of Chicago Press, 1957). PB: Phoenix, 1963. Reliable, interestingly written, beautifully illustrated.
97. Vergote, J., *Joseph en Egypte* (Belgium: University of Louvain Press, 1959). An illuminating discussion of Genesis 37-50 in the light of recent studies of Egyptian history.
98. Wilson, John A., *The Burden of Egypt* (University of Chicago Press, 1951). An excellent exposition of Egyptian history and culture. See especially chaps. 7-10.

ON LITERARY CRITICISM

Source-analysis at a technical level is presented in S. R. Driver's *Introduction* [25]. Books of this period are out of date in that they take no account of developments in form-criticism or tradition-history. A brief discussion of current issues is found in the book by Walter Harrelson [15], pp. 28-40, and there is a helpful source-analysis of the Pentateuch in the appendix, pp. 487-492; see also Norman Gottwald [14], pp. 103-114. In the field of Roman Catholic biblical studies, special attention is called to the introduction to *La Genèse* by R. de Vaux, O. P., Bible of the École Biblique of Jerusalem, 2nd ed. (Paris: Editions du Cerf, 1962), pp. 9-24. See the important article by Christopher R. North, "Pentateuchal Criticism," which appeared in 1951 [37].

Two important German studies in form-criticism and tradition-history are:

99. Noth, Martin, *Ueberlieferungsgeschichte des Pentateuch* (Stuttgart: Kohlhammer, 1948).
100. Rad, Gerhard von, "Das formgeschichtliche Problem des Hexateuchs," in his volume of collected essays, *Gesammelte Studien zum Alten Testament* (Munich: Kaiser, 1958), pp. 9-86. Now available in trans. under the title *The Problem of the Hexateuch and Other Essays* (New York: McGraw-Hill, 1966). Von Rad's thesis is summarized in his commentary on Genesis [133], pp. 1-23.

The following readings set forth the position of the "Scandinavian School":

101. Anderson, G. W., "Some Aspects of the Uppsala School of Old Testament Study," in *Harvard Theological Review*, XLIII (1950), pp. 239-256.
102. Nielson, Edward, *Oral Tradition*, Studies in Biblical Theology, No. 11 (London: SCM Press, 1954). A representative statement from a Scandinavian scholar.

For a completely different view, see the important work by Yehezkel Kaufmann [65], pp. 153-211, who accepts literary sources but reverses the order of D and P.

Chapter Two: Revelation and Response

103. Baltzer, Klaus, *Das Bundesformular*, 2nd ed. (Neukirchen Kreis Moers: Neukirchener Verlag, 1965). An important study of the treaty or covenant form. See also Nos. 107 and 108.
104. Beyerlin, Walter, *Herkunft und Geschichte der ältesten Sinaitraditionen* (Tübingen: J. C. B. Mohr, 1961). Available in trans. by Stanley Rudman,

Origins and History of the Oldest Sinaitic Traditions (Oxford: Blackwell, 1965). An argument that the Exodus and Sinai traditions have a common origin.

105. Buber, Martin, *Moses* (London: East & West Library, 1946). Selections from this study appear in *The Writings of Martin Buber*, part III, ed. by Will Herberg (PB: Meridian Book, 1956).

106. Huffmon, Herbert B., "The Exodus, Sinai and the Credo," in *Catholic Biblical Quarterly*, XXVII (1965), pp. 101-113.

107. McCarthy, Dennis J., S. J., *Treaty and Covenant, a Study in Form in the Ancient Oriental Documents and in the Old Testament* (Analecta Biblica 21; Rome: Pontifical Biblical Institute, 1963). Another important investigation of the relationship between Israel's covenant form and the treaty form of Hittite (also pre-Hittite and non-Hittite) documents.

108. Mendenhall, George, *Law and Covenant in Israel and the Ancient Near East* (Pittsburgh: Biblical Colloquium, 1955), reprinted from *The Biblical Archaeologist*, XVII, 2 (May 1954), pp. 26-46; and No. 3 (Sept. 1954), pp. 49-76. An excellent discussion of Israel's covenant tradition, analyzed in the light of Hittite parallels. See also his later article on "Covenant" in the *Interpreter's Dictionary* [11].

109. Newman, Murray Lee, Jr., *The People of the Covenant: A Study of Israel from Moses to the Monarchy* (New York: Abingdon, 1962). An illuminating analysis of the two major covenant traditions, showing their bearing upon Israel's history.

110. Noth, Martin, *Exodus*, The Old Testament Library, trans. by J. S. Bowden (Philadelphia: Westminster, 1962). This commentary is too brief to do justice to Noth's work.

111. Noth, Martin, "The Laws in the Pentateuch," in his volume of essays, *Gesammelte Studien zum Alten Testament* (Munich: Kaiser, 1957), pp. 9-141. Now available in trans. under the title *The Laws in the Pentateuch and Other Essays* (New York: McGraw-Hill, 1966).

112. Rad, Gerhard von, *Moses*, World Christian Books (London: Lutterworth, 1960). A profound little book, simply written.

113. Rylaarsdam, J. Coert, "Introduction and Exegesis to the book of Exodus," in *Interpreter's Bible*, I (New York: Abingdon, 1952). A good introduction followed by brief commentary.

Chapter Three: The Promised Land

On the geography of Canaan see especially Nos. 1, 5, 6, 7.

114. Bright, John, "Introduction and Exegesis to the book of Joshua," in *Interpreter's Bible*, II (New York: Abingdon, 1953). A good introduction which seriously takes archaeology into account.

115. Kaufmann, Yehezkel, *The Biblical Account of the Conquest of Palestine*, trans. by M. Dagut (Jerusalem: Magnes Press, Hebrew University, 1955).

116. Noth, Martin, *Das Buch Josua*, Handbuch zum Alten Testament, I, 7, 2nd ed. (Tübingen: Mohr, 1953). This little book, not yet available in English, is the antithesis to the article by Bright [114]. Noth's view is summarized in his *History* [44], especially pp. 68-84.

117. Noth, Martin, *Ueberlieferungsgeschichtliche Studien*, I (Halle: Niemeyer, 1943). A fundamental work on the "Deuteronomic History" (and also the Chronicler's History).

See also the works cited under "Archaeology," especially No. 57 by G. Ernest Wright.

Chapter Four: The Struggle Between Faith and Culture

An excellent treatment of the background of the period in the light of archaeology is that of Albright [50], chap. 4.

118. Buber, Martin, *The Prophetic Faith*, trans. by Carlyle Witton-Davies (New York: Macmillan, 1949). PB: Harper & Row, 1960. See especially the discussion of the Song of Deborah and of the clash between Israel's faith and Canaanite religion, pp. 8-12 and 70-80.

119. Childs, Brevard S., *Myth and Reality in the Old Testament*, Studies in Biblical Theology, No. 27 (London: SCM Press, 1960). An excellent study of the way Israel responded to and transformed the pagan view of reality.

120. Driver, G. R., *Canaanite Myths and Legends* (Edinburgh: T. & T. Clark, 1956).

121. Eliade, Mircea, *Cosmos and History: The Myth of the Eternal Return*. PB: Harper Torchbook, 1954. This work, and the one listed next, are important studies of the religious mentality of the so-called archaic societies.

122. Eliade, Mircea, *The Sacred and the Profane: The Nature of Religion*. PB: Harper Torchbook, 1961.

123. Frankfurt, H. and H. A., *et al.*, *The Intellectual Adventure of Ancient Man* (University of Chicago Press, 1946). Reprinted as *Before Philosophy* (PB: Penguin, 1949). The chapters on Egypt and Babylonia are very good.

124. Gray, John, *The Legacy of Canaan*, 2nd ed. (Leiden: Brill, 1965). A study of the Ras Shamra texts and their bearing on the Old Testament. A popular study by the same author is *The Canaanites* (London: Thames & Hudson, 1964).

125. Wright, G. Ernest, *The Old Testament Against Its Environment*, Studies in Biblical Theology, No. 2 (London: SCM Press, 1950).

Chapter Five: The Throne of David

126. Gray, John, *I and II Kings*, Old Testament Library (Philadelphia: Westminster, 1963).

127. Hertzberg, H. W., *The Books of Samuel*, Old Testament Library, trans. by J. S. Bowden (Philadelphia: Westminster, 1964).

128. Montgomery, James A., and Henry S. Gehman, *The Books of Kings*, International Critical Commentary (New York: Scribners, 1951). A thorough, critical commentary in the tradition of the series.

129. Rost, Leonhard, *Die Ueberlieferung von der Thronnachfolge Davids*, Beiträge zur Wissenschaft vom Alten und Neuen Testament, 42 (Stuttgart: Kohlhammer, 1926). This fundamental study of the Davidic Court History or "Succession Document" is discussed by von Rad in his *Theology*, I [80], pp. 312 ff.

Chapter Six: Israel's National Epic

130. Buber, Martin, "Saga and History," in *The Writings of Martin Buber* [see above, 105], pp. 149-156. A valuable aid to understanding the character of the biblical narratives.

131. Gunkel, Hermann, *The Legends of Genesis* (PB: Schocken Book, 1964). This little book, which has a preface by W. F. Albright, is a reprint of the introduc-

tion to Gunkel's monumental commentary on Genesis, dating to the year 1901 (*Genesis*, 5th ed. [reprinted as 6th ed., 1964] in the Handkommentar zum Alten Testament, I, 1 [Göttingen: Vandenhoeck & Rüprecht, 1922]), which provided the foundation for modern form-critical studies.

132. Hooke, S. H., *In the Beginning* (New York: Oxford, 1947). An interesting treatment of the Genesis stories in the light of ancient mythology.

133. Rad, Gerhard von, *Genesis*, Old Testament Library, trans. by John Marks (Philadelphia: Westminster, 1961). A fresh and perceptive interpretation in the light of form-critical studies. Very important.

134. Speiser, E. A., *Genesis*, Anchor Bible (New York: Doubleday, 1964). A new translation with helpful notes, many of which deal with Near Eastern parallels.

135. Vawter, Bruce, C. M., *A Path Through Genesis* (New York: Sheed & Ward, 1956). See also his excellent little article, "Understanding Genesis," in *Studies in Salvation History*, ed. by C. Luke Salm, F. S. C. (Englewood Cliffs, N.J.: Prentice-Hall, 1964), pp. 57-67.

Chapter Seven: Prophetic Troublers of Israel

136. Anderson, Bernhard W., and Walter Harrelson, eds., *Israel's Prophetic Heritage*, Essays in honor of James Muilenburg (New York: Harper & Row, 1962).

137. Clements, R. E., *Prophecy and Covenant*, Studies in Biblical Theology, No. 43 (London: SCM Press, 1965). This fine study brings the reader up to the frontier of research in this field.

138. Gottwald, Norman K., *All the Kingdoms of the Earth* (New York: Harper & Row, 1965). A fresh, perceptive study of prophecy in ancient Israel.

139. Heschel, Abraham J., *The Prophets* (New York: Harper & Row, 1963). A discerning work by a Jewish philosopher.

140. Hyatt, J. P., *Prophetic Religion* (New York: Abingdon, 1947).

141. Johnson, Aubrey R., *The Cultic Prophet in Ancient Israel*, 2nd ed. (Cardiff: University of Wales Press, 1962). This valuable study traces the connection of many early prophets with the cult.

142. Lindblom, Johannes, *Prophecy in Ancient Israel* (Philadelphia: Muhlenberg Press, 1963). An extremely valuable work by a Swedish scholar.

143. Mowinckel, Sigmund, *Prophecy and Tradition*, Avhandlinger utgitt av det Norske Videnskaps-Akademi (Oslo: Jacob Dybwad, 1946). A discussion of a traditio-historical approach to the study of the prophets.

144. Rowley, H. H., "Elijah on Mount Carmel," in *Bulletin of the John Rylands Library*, XLIII (1960-1961), pp. 190-210.

145. Scott, R. B. Y., *The Relevance of the Prophets* (New York: Macmillan,, 1947). This book continues to have great value.

146. Vawter, Bruce, C. M., *The Conscience of Israel* (New York: Sheed & Ward, 1961). A good discussion of pre-exilic prophecy.

147. Westermann, Claus, *Grundformen prophetischer Rede*, 2nd ed. (Munich: Kaiser, 1964). An important study of the basic forms of prophetic speech. Announced for publication in 1967 by Westminster (trans. Hugh K. White) under the title *Basic Forms of Prophetic Speech*.

See also the work of Martin Buber [118], the summary of research on prophecy made by Otto Eissfeldt [in No. 37, pp. 115-161], and T. J. Meek's discussion of the origin of the prophetic movement [No. 94, chap. 2].

Chapter Eight: Fallen Is the Virgin Israel

See the general books on prophecy listed in the preceding chapter.

ON AMOS

148. Bentzen, Aage, "The ritual background of Amos 1:2-2:16," in *Oudtesta-mentische Studiën,* VIII (Leiden: Brill, 1950), pp. 85-99.
149. Kapelrud, Arvid S., *Central Ideas in Amos* (Oslo University Press, 1961; first printed 1956).
150. McCullough, W. S., "Some Suggestions About Amos," in *Journal of Biblical Literature,* LXXII (1953), pp. 247-254.
151. Rowley, H. H., "Was Amos a Nabi?", in *Festschrift Otto Eissfeldt,* ed. by J. Fueck (Halle: Niemeyer, 1947), pp. 191-198. A provocative interpretation of Amos 7:10-15.
152. Smith, George Adam, *The Book of the Twelve Prophets,* I, rev. ed. (New York: Harper & Row, 1940). This is a great classic. Smith's treatments of Amos and Hosea deserve special attention.

ON HOSEA

153. Rowley, H. H., "The Marriage of Hosea," in *Bulletin of the John Rylands Library,* XXXIX, 1 (1956), pp. 200-233. A good survey of views on the central problem of the book of Hosea.
154. Ward, James M., *Hosea: A Theological Commentary* (New York: Harper & Row, 1966). An illuminating theological exposition of the whole book, along with a fresh translation. Note the bibliography at the end.
155. Wolff, Hans Walter, *Dodekapropheton, I: Hosea,* Biblischer Kommentar (Neukirchen Kreis Moers: Neukirchener Verlag, 1961).
156. Wolff, Hans Walter, " 'Wissen um Gott' bei Hosea als Urform von Theologie," in *Evangelische Theologie,* XII (1953), pp. 533-551. An important study of Hosea's use of the expression "knowledge of God."

Chapter Nine: Judah's Covenant with Death

157. Blank, Sheldon H., *Prophetic Faith in Isaiah* (New York: Harper & Row, 1958). A leading Jewish scholar attempts to disengage the original Isaiah from traditions that gathered around him.
158. Kissane, Edward J., *The Book of Isaiah,* 2nd ed., 2 vols. (Dublin: Browne & Nolan, 1960).
159. Scott, R. B. Y., "Introduction and Exegesis to Isaiah 1-39," in *Interpreter's Bible,* V (New York: Abingdon, 1956).
160. Smith, George Adam, *The Book of Isaiah,* rev. ed. (London: Hodder & Stoughton, 1927). Though old, this is still worth reading.
161. Vriezen, Th. C., "Essentials of the Theology of Isaiah," in *Israel's Prophetic Heritage* [136], pp. 128-146. An illuminating essay.

Chapter Ten: The Rediscovery of Mosaic Torah

162. Bright, John, "The Date of the Prose Sermons of Jeremiah," in *Journal of Biblical Literature,* LXX (1951), pp. 15-35. Opposes the view, maintained for

instance by Hyatt [170], that the book of Jeremiah has been radically reworked by Deuteronomic editors.

163. Rad, Gerhard von, *Studies in Deuteronomy*, Studies in Biblical Theology, No. 9 (London: SCM Press, 1953). An important form-critical discussion.

164. Rad, Gerhard von, *Das fünfte Buch Mose: Deuteronomium*, Das Alte Testament Deutsch (Göttingen: Vandenhoeck & Ruprecht, 1964).

165. Rowley, H. H., "The Prophet Jeremiah and the Book of Deuteronomy," in the book edited by the same author, *Studies in Old Testament Prophecy* (Edinburgh: T. & T. Clark, 1950), pp. 157-174. Also in Rowley's *From Moses to Qumran* (London: Lutterworth, 1963), pp. 187-208.

166. Welch, A. C., *The Code of Deuteronomy* (London: J. Clarke & Co., 1924), and *Deuteronomy: The Framework to the Code* (London: Oxford, 1932). Old works but still important.

167. Wright, G. Ernest, "Introduction and Exegesis to Deuteronomy," in *Interpreter's Bible*, II (New York: Abingdon, 1953). One of the best treatments of Deuteronomy.

Chapter Eleven: The Doom of the Nation

168. Anderson, Bernhard W., "The New Covenant and the Old," in the book edited by the same author [72], pp. 225-242. A discussion of Jer. 31:31-34.

169. Bright, John, *Jeremiah*, Anchor Bible (New York: Doubleday, 1965). A fresh translation with valuable notes.

170. Hyatt, J. Philip, "Introduction and Exegesis to Jeremiah," in *Interpreter's Bible*, VI (New York: Abingdon, 1956). See also his book, *Jeremiah, Prophet of Courage and Hope* (New York: Abingdon, 1958).

171. Leslie, Elmer A., *Jeremiah* (New York: Abingdon, 1954). PB: Apex.

172. Rowley, H. H., "The Early Prophecies of Jeremiah in their Setting," in *Bulletin of the John Rylands Library*, XLV, 1 (1962), pp. 198-234.

173. Skinner, John, *Prophecy and Religion* (New York: Cambridge, 1922). This has long been a standard book on Jeremiah.

174. Welch, A. C., *Jeremiah, His Time and His Work*. The original 1928 edition has been reprinted (Oxford: Blackwell, 1951).

ON HABAKKUK

175. Albright, W. F., "The Psalm of Habakkuk," in *Studies in Old Testament Prophecy* [cited under No. 165], pp. 1-18.

176. Humbert, Paul, *Problèmes du livre d'Habacuc* (Neûchatel: Université, 1944).

ON LAMENTATIONS

177. Gottwald, Norman K., *Studies in the Book of Lamentations*, Studies in Biblical Theology, No. 14 (London: SCM Press, 1954). A helpful monograph for understanding the biblical book.

178. Meek, T. J., "Introduction and Exegesis to Lamentations," in *Interpreter's Bible*, VI (New York: Abingdon, 1956).

Chapter Twelve: By the Waters of Babylon

179. May, Herbert G., "Introduction and Exegesis to Ezekiel," in *Interpreter's Bible*, VI (New York: Abingdon, 1956). An excellent study.

180. Noth, Martin, *Leviticus*, Old Testament Library, trans. by J. E. Anderson (Philadelphia: Westminster, 1965). Helpful for understanding priestly tradition and Israel's cultus.
181. Zimmerli, Walther, *Ezechiel*, Biblischer Kommentar (Neukirchen Kreis Moers: Neukirchener Verlag, 1955).
182. Zimmerli, Walther, "Sinaibund und Abrahambund," in his volume of collected essays, *Gottes Offenbarung* (Munich: Kaiser, 1963). An important contribution to the understanding of P.

In connection with the Creation story, refer especially to von Rad's commentary [133]. Also the works by Eliade [121, 122], Hooke [132], and Frankfurt [123] will prove helpful. In addition, see the author's article, "Creation," in *The Interpreter's Dictionary of the Bible* [11].

Chapter Thirteen: The Dawn of a New Age

183. Anderson, Bernhard W., "Exodus Typology in Second Isaiah," in *Israel's Prophetic Heritage* [136].
184. Knight, George A. F., *Deutero-Isaiah: A Theological Commentary on Isaiah 40-55* (New York: Abingdon, 1965).
185. Muilenburg, James, "Introduction and Exegesis to Isaiah 40-66," in *Interpreter's Bible*, V (New York: Abingdon, 1956). One of the best commentaries on Second Isaiah.
186. North, Christopher R., *Isaiah 40-55* (New York: Macmillan, 1964).
187. North, Christopher R., *The Suffering Servant in Deutero-Isaiah*, 2nd ed. (New York: Oxford, 1956). A good discussion of interpretations of the Servant passages.
188. Rowley, H. H., *The Servant of the Lord and Other Essays on the Old Testament*, 2nd ed. (Oxford: Blackwell, 1965), pp. 3-60. A good review of the subject.
189. Smart, James D., *History and Theology in Second Isaiah: A Commentary on Isaiah 35, 40-66* (Philadelphia: Westminster, 1965).
190. Stuhlmueller, Carroll, C. P., "The Theology of Creation in Second Isaias," *Catholic Biblical Quarterly*, XXI (1959), pp. 429-467. A perceptive essay.
191. Zimmerli, Walther, and J. Jeremias, *The Servant of God*, Studies in Biblical Theology, No. 20 (London: SCM Press, 1957). The translation of an important article from Kittel's *Theologisches Wörterbuch zum Neuen Testament*.

See also some of the books listed under Chapter 9, and Buber's *The Prophetic Faith* [118], pp. 203-235.

Chapter Fourteen: A Kingdom of Priests

192. DeVaux, Roland, O. P., *Studies in Old Testament Sacrifice* (Cardiff: University of Wales Press, 1964). A perceptive discussion of how sacrificial worship was transformed by Israel's historical faith.
193. Kapelrud, Arvid S., *Joel Studies* (Uppsala: Almquist & Wiksells, 1948).
194. Myers, Jacob M., *I and II Chronicles*, 2 vols., Anchor Bible (New York: Doubleday, 1965). See also his Anchor volume on Ezra-Nehemiah (1965).
195. Rad, Gerhard von, *Das Geschichtsbild des chronistischen Werkes* (Stuttgart: Kohlhammer, 1930). The results of this important work are summarized in his *Theology*, I [80], pp. 347-354.

196. Ringgren, Helmer, *Sacrifice in the Bible*, World Christian Books (New York: Association Press, 1962). A small but valuable study.
197. Rowley, H. H., "The Meaning of Sacrifice in the Old Testament," in *Bulletin of the John Rylands Library*, XXXIII (1950-1951), pp. 74-110. Reprinted in *From Moses to Qumran* [cited under No. 165], pp. 67-107.
198. Rowley, H. H., "Nehemiah's Mission and Its Background," in *Bulletin of the John Rylands Library*, XXXVII, No. 2 (1955), pp. 528-561.
199. Rowley, H. H., *The Rediscovery of the Old Testament* (Philadelphia: West-minster, 1964). Chapter 7 gives an appreciative treatment of the ethos of Judaism.

Chapter Fifteen: The Praises of Israel

ON ISRAELITE CULT AND NEAR EASTERN INFLUENCE

200. Childs, Brevard, *Memory and Tradition in Israel*, Studies in Biblical Theology, No. 37 (London: SCM Press, 1962). An important discussion which bears on "making the past present" (actualization).
201. Clements, R. E., *God and Temple* (Philadelphia: Fortress Press, 1965). A study of the Jerusalem Temple as the center of Yahweh's presence in ancient Israel.
202. Cumming, Charles G., *The Assyrian and Hebrew Hymns of Praise* (New York: Columbia University, 1934). Treats formal parallels to Israel's psalmody.

See also the extra-biblical psalms translated in J. B. Pritchard [2], pp. 365-401.

203. Hooke, S. H., ed., *Myth and Ritual* (London: University of London Press, 1933); *The Labyrinth* (London: SPCK, 1935); *Myth, Ritual, and Kingship* (New York: Oxford, 1958). These books contain important contributions from the British "myth and ritual" school.
204. Johnson, Aubrey R., *Sacral Kingship in Ancient Israel* (Cardiff: University of Wales Press, 1955).
205. Johnson, Aubrey R., "The Psalms," in *The Old Testament and Modern Study* [37], pp. 162-209.
206. Kraus, Hans-Joachim, *Gottesdienst in Israel*, 2nd ed. (Munich: Kaiser, 1962). An important outline of the history of Israelite worship. (Announced for pub-lication in English as: *Worship in Israel: A Cultic History of the Old Testa-ment*.)
207. Mowinckel, Sigmund, *He That Cometh*, trans. by G. W. Anderson (New York: Abingdon, 1956). One of the most important works on Israelite eschatology.
208. Noth, Martin, "Gott, König, Volk im Alten Testament," in his collected essays [cited under No. 111], pp. 188-229.
209. Widengren, George, *The Accadian and Hebrew Songs of Lamentation* (Uppsala: Almquist & Wiksell, 1936). Helpful for understanding the genre of the lament.

ON THE BOOK OF PSALMS

210. Kissane, Edward J., *The Book of Psalms*, 2 vols. (Dublin: Browne & Nolan, 1952 and 1954).
211. Kraus, Hans-Joachim, *Psalmen*, Biblischer Kommentar, 2nd. ed. (Neukirchen Kreis Moers: Neukirchener Verlag, 1961). A major work on the Psalms.

212. Leslie, Elmer A., *The Psalms* (New York: Abingdon, 1949). This and other modern works show the influence of the pioneering form-critical study of the Psalter by Hermann Gunkel (with Joachim Begrich), *Einleitung in die Psalmen*, Göttinger Handkommentar zum Alten Testament (Göttingen: Vandenhoeck & Ruprecht, 1933); also by Gunkel, *Die Psalmen*, Handkommentar zum Alten Testament, II, 2, 4th ed. (Vandenhoeck & Ruprecht, 1926).

213. Mowinckel, Sigmund, *The Psalms in Israel's Worship*, I-II, trans. by D. R. Ap-Thomas (New York: Abingdon, 1962). See also his earlier *Psalmenstudien*, I-VI (1921-1924), reprinted photomechanically by P. Schippers, Amsterdam, 1961. The works of Mowinckel and Gunkel are fundamental to all modern study of the Psalter.

214. Oesterley, W. O. E., *The Psalms* (New York: Macmillan, 1939).

215. Paterson, John, *The Praises of Israel: Studies Literary and Religious in the Psalms* (New York: Scribners, 1950).

216. Ringgren, Helmer, *The Faith of the Psalmists* (London: SCM Press, 1963). PB: SCM Greenback. An excellent study of the religious aspects of the Psalms which utilizes the results of recent cultic research.

217. Terrien, Samuel, *The Psalms and Their Meaning for Today* (Indianapolis: Bobbs-Merrill, 1952). A good, nontechnical exposition.

218. Weiser, Artur, *The Psalms*, Old Testament Library, trans. by Herbert Hartwell (Philadelphia: Westminster, 1962). An important work which stresses the place of many psalms in covenant-renewal festivals.

219. Westermann, Claus, *The Praise of God in the Psalms*, 2nd ed., trans. by Keith R. Crim (Richmond, Va.: John Knox, 1961). In this important form-critical study, Westermann suggests a new approach to classifying the types of psalms.

220. Worden, Thomas, *The Psalms Are Christian Prayers* (New York: Sheed & Ward, 1961). A good introduction to motifs in the Psalms by a Roman Catholic writer.

Chapter Sixteen: The Beginning of Wisdom

221. McKane, William, *Prophets and Wise Men*, Studies in Biblical Theology, No. 44 (London: SCM Press, 1965).

222. Murphy, Roland, O. Carm., *Seven Books of Wisdom* (Milwaukee: Bruce, 1960).

223. Noth, Martin, and D. Winton Thomas, eds., *Wisdom in Israel and in the Near East*, Supplement to *Vetus Testamentum*, III (Leiden: Brill, 1955).

224. Rankin, O. S., *Israel's Wisdom Literature* (Edinburgh: T. & T. Clark, 1936). An older standard work.

225. Rylaarsdam, J. Coert, *Revelation in Jewish Wisdom Literature* (University of Chicago Press, 1946). This valuable little book shows how Wisdom was eventually incorporated into Israel's faith.

ON PROVERBS AND ECCLESIASTES

226. Gordis, Robert, *Koheleth, the Man and His World* (New York: Jewish Theological Seminary of America Press, 1951). A fresh translation and good commentary.

227. Rankin, O. S., "Introduction and Exegesis to Ecclesiastes," in *Interpreter's Bible*, V (New York: Abingdon, 1956).

228. Scott, R. B. Y., *Proverbs and Ecclesiastes*, Anchor Bible (New York: Doubleday, 1965). A fresh translation with valuable notes.

229. Whybray, R. N., *Wisdom in Proverbs: The Concept of Wisdom in Proverbs 1-9*, Studies in Biblical Theology, No. 45 (London: SCM Press, 1965).

ON THE BOOK OF JOB

230. Kissane, Edward J., *The Book of Job* (Dublin: Browne & Nolan, 1939).
231. Pope, Marvin H., *Job*, Anchor Bible (New York: Doubleday, 1965). A fresh translation with illuminating notes.
232. Robinson, H. Wheeler, *The Cross in the Old Testament* (Philadelphia: Westminster, 1955). A fine study of Job, Jeremiah, and the suffering servant. PB: SCM Press, 1960.
233. Terrien, Samuel, "Introduction and Exegesis to Job," in *Interpreter's Bible*, III (New York: Abingdon, 1954). An excellent commentary, with respect to both literary analysis and theological interpretation.
234. Terrien, Samuel, *Job: Poet of Existence* (Indianapolis: Bobbs-Merrill, 1958). A good nontechnical exposition.

ON THE SONG OF SONGS

235. Gordis, Robert, *The Song of Songs* (New York: Jewish Theological Seminary of America Press, 1954).
236. Meek, T. J., "Introduction and Exegesis to the Song of Solomon," in *Interpreter's Bible*, V (New York: Abingdon, 1956).
237. Rowley, H. H., "The Interpretation of the Song of Songs," in the collected essays, *The Servant* [188], pp. 195-245.

Chapter Seventeen: The Unfulfilled Drama

ON HISTORY AND LITERATURE OF THE PERIOD

238. Charles, R. H., *Apocrypha and Pseudepigrapha of the Old Testament*, 2 vols. (New York: Oxford, 1913; reprinted in 1963). The standard critical edition of these texts.
239. Foerster, Werner, *From the Exile to Christ: A Historical Introduction to Palestinian Judaism*, trans. by Gordon E. Harris (Philadelphia: Fortress, 1964).
240. Metzger, Bruce, *An Introduction to the Apocrypha* (New York: Oxford, 1957).
241. Pfeiffer, R. H., *History of New Testament Times with an Introduction to the Apocrypha* (New York: Harper & Row, 1949).
242. Strack, H. L., *Introduction to the Talmud and Midrash* (Philadelphia: Jewish Publication Society, 1931). PB: Meridian.
243. Toombs, Lawrence, *The Threshold of Christianity* (Philadelphia: Westminster, 1960). A brief but valuable guide, nontechnical in character.

ON APOCALYPTIC

244. Frost, S. B., *Old Testament Apocalyptic* (London: Epworth, 1952).
245. Jeffery, Arthur, "Introduction and Exegesis to Daniel," in *Interpreter's Bible*, VI (New York: Abingdon, 1956).
246. Klausner, Joseph, *The Messianic Idea in Israel from Its Beginning to the Completion of the Mishnah* (New York: Macmillan, 1955).
247. Porteous, Norman W., *Daniel*, Old Testament Library (Philadelphia: Westminster, 1965).

248. Rowley, H. H., *The Relevance of Apocalyptic*, 2nd ed. (London: Lutterworth, 1947).
249. Russell, D. S., *The Method and Message of Jewish Apocalyptic*, Old Testament Library (Philadelphia: Westminster, 1964). An excellent study of apocalyptic literature from 200 B.C. to 100 A.D.

See also Mowinckel, *He That Cometh* [207], part ii.

ON THE DEAD SEA SCROLLS

250. Cross, Frank M., Jr., *The Ancient Library of Qumran and Modern Biblical Studies*, rev. ed. (New York: Doubleday, 1961). A comprehensive, perceptive treatment of the scrolls and their significance.
251. Dupont-Sommer, A., *The Essene Writings from Qumran* (PB: Meridian, 1961). Introduction to and translation of Qumran literature.
252. Ringgren, Helmer, *The Faith of Qumran* (Philadelphia: Fortress, 1961).

ON THE CANON

253. Jeffery, Arthur, "The Canon of the Old Testament," in *Interpreter's Bible*, I (New York: Abingdon, 1952), pp. 32-45.
254. Robinson, H. Wheeler, ed., *The Bible in Its Ancient and English Versions* (Oxford: Clarendon, 1954).
255. Sundberg, Albert C., Jr., *The Old Testament of the Early Church*, Harvard Theological Studies, XX (Cambridge: Harvard University Press, 1964). A fresh consideration of the problem of the canon.

INDEX

AUTHOR INDEX

SUBJECT INDEX

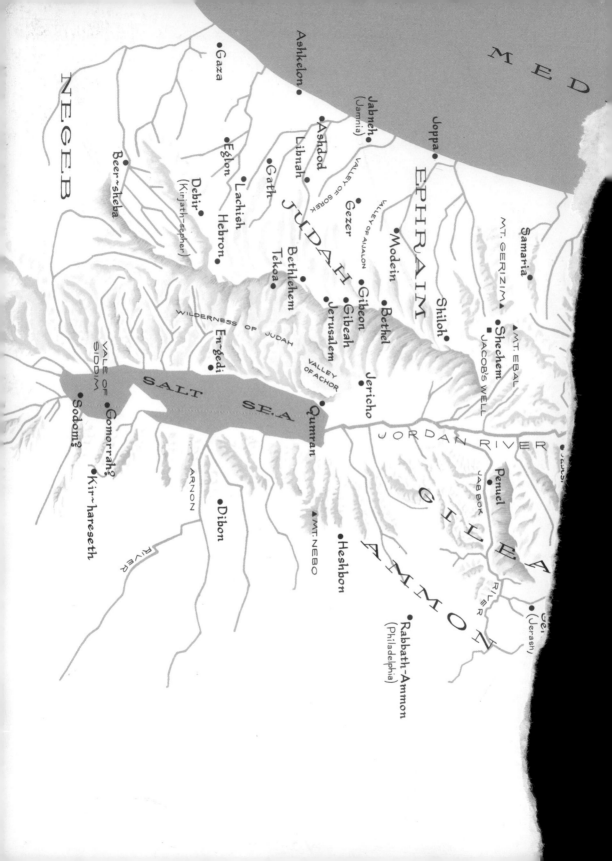